Sociology

*Exploring the Architecture
of Everyday Life*

Second Edition

READINGS

The Sociology of Work: Concepts and Cases by Carol Auster

Adventures in Social Research: Data Analysis Using SPSS® for Windows™ by Earl R. Babbie and Fred Halley

Second Thoughts: Seeing Conventional Wisdom Through the Sociological Eye by Janet Ruane and Karen Cerulo

Media/Society: Industries, Images, and Audiences by David Croteau and William Hoynes

Exploring Social Issues Using SPSS® for Windows™ by Joseph F. Healey, Earl R. Babbie, and Fred Halley

Race, Ethnicity, and Gender in the United States: Inequality, Group Conflict, and Power by Joseph F. Healey

Race, Ethnicity, Gender, and Class: The Sociology of Group Conflict and Change by Joseph F. Healey

Sociological Snapshots: Seeing Social Structure and Change in Everyday Life, 2nd ed., by Jack Levin

Sociology: Exploring the Architecture of Everyday Life (text) 2nd ed., by David M. Newman

Building Community: Social Science in Action by Philip Nyden, Anne Figert, Mark Shibley, and Darryl Burrows

The Production of Reality: Essays and Readings on Social Interaction, 2nd ed., by Jodi O'Brien and Peter Kollock

The McDonaldization of Society, Rev. ed., by George Ritzer

Shifts in the Social Contract: Understanding Change in American Society by Beth Rubin

---

The Pine Forge Press Series in Research Methods and Statistics
Edited by Kathleen S. Crittenden

- *Social Statistics for a Diverse Society* by Chava Frankfort-Nachmias
- *Investigating the Social World: The Process and Practice of Research* by Russell K. Schutt

Sociology

Exploring the Architecture
of Everyday Life
Second Edition

READINGS

David M. Newman

Department of Sociology and Anthropology
DePauw University

Pine Forge Press

Thousand Oaks, California • London • New Delhi

For information, address:

 Pine Forge Press
A Sage Publications Company
2455 Teller Road
Thousand Oaks, California 91320
(805) 499-4224
E-mail: sales@pfp.sagepub.com

Sage Publications Ltd.
6 Bonhill Street
London EC2A 4PU
United Kingdom

Sage Publications India Pvt. Ltd.
M-32 Market
Greater Kailash I
New Delhi 110 048 India

Production: Melanie Field, Strawberry Field Publishing
Interior Designer: Lisa Mirski Devenish
Typesetter: Christi Payne, Book Arts
Cover Designer: Lisa Mirski Devenish
Production Management: Scratchgravel Publishing Services
Print Buyer: Anna Chin

Printed in the United States of America
97 98 99 00 01 10 9 8 7 6 5 4 3 2

Library of Congress Cataloging-in-Publication Data
Sociology : exploring the architecture of everyday life : readings /
  [edited by] David M. Newman. — 2nd ed.
     p.   cm.
  Includes bibliographical references.
  ISBN 0-7619-8519-0 (alk. paper)
  1. Sociology. I. Newman, David M., 1958- . II. Newman, David
M., 1958- Sociology.
HM51.S6634148 1997
301—dc21
                                     96-45391
                                       CIP

About the Author

David M. Newman (Ph.D., University of Washington) is an Associate Professor of Sociology at DePauw University. In addition to the introductory course, he teaches courses in family, social psychology, deviance, research methods, and madness. He has won teaching awards at both the University of Washington and DePauw University.

About the Publisher

Pine Forge Press is a new educational publisher, dedicated to publishing innovative books and software throughout the social sciences. On this and any other of our publications, we welcome your comments.

Please call or write us at:

Pine Forge Press
A Sage Publications Company
2455 Teller Road
Thousand Oaks, CA 91320
Phone: (805) 499-4224
E-mail: sales@pfp.sagepub.com

Visit our new World Wide Web site, your direct link to a multitude of on-line resources:

http://www.sagepub.com/pineforge

CONTENTS

PART II   CONSTRUCTING SELF AND SOCIETY

One of the greatest challenges I face as a teacher of sociology is trying to get my students to see the relevance of the course material and to appreciate fully their connection to the larger society. I teach my students to see that sociology is all around us. It's in our careers, our media, our families, our goals, our interests, our desires, even our minds. Sociology can be found at the neighborhood pub or in the maintenance bay at the local gas station. Sociology can answer questions of global as well as private significance—from why poverty, discrimination, and homelessness continue to grow, to why we are attracted to some people and not others; from why people become criminals, to why we enjoy scrambled eggs rather than rice for breakfast.

With these ideas in mind I set out to compile this collection of short articles, chapters, or excerpts designed to help introduce you to sociology. Instructors and students alike responded quite positively to the readings in the first edition. It would have been easy simply to include those same readings in this second edition. But I very much wanted the book to be fresh and contemporary. Hence, over half the readings here are new additions, most of which were written within the past five years.

As in the first edition, these selections don't provide a lot of dry factual information, concept definitions, or reviews of past research. Instead, they are vivid, provocative, and eye-opening *examples* of the practice of sociology. Many of the readings are drawn from carefully conducted social research. They provide important illustrations of how sociologists support their insights and ideas with empirical evidence.

In addition to accurately representing the sociological perspective and providing rigorous coverage of the discipline, the selections are all enjoyable to read. I hope that each of them stimulates thoughtful reflection as you go about examining what society is, how it works, and, most important, your place in it.

The readings represent a variety of styles. Some use common everyday experiences and phenomena (such as credit cards, lying, elementary school playgrounds, sports, marriage, childbirth) to illustrate the relationship between the individual and society. Others focus on important social issues (sexual harassment, stalking, race relations, homelessness, multiculturalism, educational inequalities, immigration, abortion) or make use of distinct historical events (massacres during war time, racist social experiments, labor strikes). Furthermore, they are written by people from a variety of professions. You need not be a trained sociologist to see the world sociologically. So this book includes articles written by geneticists, psychologists, psychiatrists, anthropologists, social commentators, historians, and novelists as well as by sociologists.

To help you get the most out of these selections I have written brief introductions to each chapter that provide the sociological context for the readings. For those of you who are also reading the accompanying textbook, these introductions will furnish a quick intellectual link between these readings and the textbook. After each selection you will find a set of discussion questions to ponder. These items are not straight, examlike, information questions designed to determine whether you absorbed all the details in a given reading. Instead the questions make you think about the meaning and relevance of each reading. They frequently ask you to apply a specific author's conclusions to some contemporary issue in society. It is my hope that these questions will generate a lot of classroom debate and help you see the sociological merit of the readings.

Books like these are enormous projects. As with the first edition, I would like to thank Steve Rutter, Sherith Pankratz, Becky Smith, and the rest of the staff at Pine Forge Press for their useful advice and assistance in putting this reader together. I am grateful to Melanie Field at Strawberry Field Publishing for producing a high-quality book on short notice. I would also like to thank Bizz Steele for magically and promptly acquiring many of the books and articles I desperately needed.

Good Luck,

David M. Newman
Department of Sociology/Anthropology
DePauw University
Greencastle, IN 46135
E-Mail: DNEWMAN@DEPAUW. EDU

ACKNOWLEDGMENTS

We gratefully acknowledge the following for permission to reprint the selections in this anthology:

"The Mundanity of Excellence: An Ethnographic Report on Stratification and Olympic Swimmers" by Daniel F. Chambliss. *Sociological Theory,* Vol. 7, No. 1, Spring 1989, pp. 70–86. Washington, DC: American Sociological Association. Copyright © 1989 by the American Sociological Association. Reprinted by permission.

"The My Lai Massacre: A Military Crime of Obedience" in *Crimes of Obedience* (pp. 1–20), ed. Herbert Kelman and V. Lee Hamilton. Copyright 1989 by Yale University Press. Reprinted by permission.

"The Credit Card: Private Troubles and Public Issues" from *Expressing America: A Critique of the Global Credit Card Society* (pp. 1–28) by George Ritzer. Copyright © 1995 Pine Forge Press.

"Stalking Strangers and Lovers: Changing Media Typifications of a New Crime Problem" by Kathleen S. Lowney and Joel Best, from *Images of Issues: Typifying Contemporary Social Problems,* 2nd ed. (pp. 34–57), ed. Joel Best, 1995. New York: Aldine de Gruyter. Copyright © 1995 Walter de Gruyter, Inc., New York. Reprinted by permission.

"Researching Dealers and Smugglers" from *Wheeling and Dealing* (pp. 11–28) by Patricia A. Adler. Copyright © 1985 by Columbia University Press. Reprinted by permission of the publisher.

"Body Ritual Among the Nacirema" by Horace Miner. *American Anthropologist* 58:3, June 1956, pp. 503–507. Reprinted by permission of the American Anthropological Association. Not for further reproduction.

"A Pack of Lies: Towards a Sociology of Lying" from *A Pack of Lies: Towards a Sociology of Lying* (pp. 65–86) by J. A. Barnes. Copyright © Cambridge University Press 1994. Reprinted by the permission of Cambridge University Press.

"Fashions in Childbirth" from *American Way of Birth* (pp. 51–73) by Jessica Mitford. Copyright © 1992 by Jessica Mitford. Used by permission of Dutton Signet, a division of Penguin Books.

Excerpts from "The Gloried Self: The Aggrandizement and the Constriction of Self," by Patricia Adler and Peter Adler, *Social Psychology Quarterly,* 1985, 52:4, pp. 299–310. Washington, DC: American Sociological Association. Copyright © 1985 by the American Sociological Association. Reprinted by permission.

"Medical Students' Contacts with the Living and the Dead" by Allen C. Smith and Sherryl Kleinman. *Social Psychology Quarterly*, 52:1 pp. 56–69. Washington, DC: American Sociological Association. Copyright © 1989 by the American Sociological Association. Reprinted by permission.

"Boys and Girls Together . . . But Mostly Apart." Excerpts from *Gender Play: Girls and Boys in School* (pp. 29–47) by Barrie Thorne. Copyright © 1993 by Barrie Thorne. Reprinted by permission of Rutgers University Press.

"Managed Feeling" from *The Managed Heart: Commercialization of Human Feeling* (pp. 35–48) by Arlie Hochschild. Berkeley: University of California Press. Copyright © 1983 The Regents of the University of California. Reprinted by permission.

"Outsiders in the Clubhouse" from *Outsiders in the Clubhouse: The World of Women's Professional Golf* (pp. 1–2, 121–132, 175–183) by Todd Crosset. Copyright © 1995. Reprinted by permission of the State University of New York Press.

"The Saints and the Roughnecks" by William Chambliss. *Society*, 11:1, Nov/Dec, pp. 24–31. Copyright © 1973 by Transaction Publishers. Reprinted by permission.

"A Crime by Any Other Name . . ." from *The Rich Get Richer and the Poor Get Prison* (pp. 59–96) by Jeffrey Reiman. Copyright © Allyn & Bacon 1995. Reprinted by permission.

"Elvis's DNA" from *The DNA Mystique* (pp. 79–101) by Dorothy Nelkin and M. Susan Lindee. Copyright © 1995 by W. H. Freeman and Company. Used by permission.

"Exiles from Kinship" from *Families We Choose* (pp. 21–41) by Kath Weston. Copyright © 1991 by Columbia University Press. Reprinted by permission of the publisher.

"No Man's Land" from *No Man's Land* by Kathleen Gerson (pp. 41–72). Copyright © 1993 by BasicBooks, a division of HarperCollins Publishers, Inc. Reprinted by permission of BasicBooks, a division of HarperCollins Publishers, Inc.

From "The Active Worker: Compliance and Autonomy at the Workplace" by Randy Hodson. *Journal of Contemporary Ethnography*, 20:1, pp. 47–78, April 1991. © 1991 Sage Publications, Inc. Reprinted by permission of Sage Publications, Inc.

From "The Smile Factory: Work at Disneyland" by John Van Maanen, in *Reframing Organizational Culture* (pp. 58–75), ed. Peter Frost, 1991. Copyright © 1991 by Sage Publications, Inc. Reprinted by permission of Sage Publications, Inc.

From "The Routinization of Disaster," in *Beyond Caring: Hospitals, Nurses and the Social Organization of Ethics* by Daniel F. Chambliss (pp. 16–39), in the series *Morality and Society,* ed. Alan Wolfe. Copyright © 1996 University of Chicago Press. Reprinted by permission.

"Money, Morals, and Manners" from *Money, Morals & Manners: The Culture of the French and American Upper-Middle Class* (pp. 1–4, 9–12, 25–28, 33–35, 63–75, 90–98) by Michèle Lamont. Copyright © 1992 by the University of Chicago Press. Reprinted by permission.

"The Bohemian Grove." Excerpts of approximately 18 pages from *The Bohemian Grove and Other Retreats: A Study in Ruling-Class Cohesiveness* by

G. William Domhoff. Copyright © 1974 by G. William Domhoff. Reprinted by permission of HarperCollins Publishers, Inc.

"Life on the Global Assembly Line" by Barbara Ehrenreich and Annette Fuentes, 1981, *Ms. Magazine* (January), pp. 53–59. Reprinted by permission of Ms. Magazine, © 1981.

"Savage Inequalities in America's Schools" from *Savage Inequalities* (pp. 7–8, 10–14, 20–21, 23–25, 27–30, 34–35, 124–130) by Jonathan Kozol. Copyright © 1991 by Jonathan Kozol. Reprinted by permission of Crown Publishers, Inc.

"The Subculture of Street Life" from *Down on Their Luck: A Study of Homeless Street People* (pp. 77–109) by David Snow and Leon Anderson, University of California Press. Copyright © 1992 by the Regents of the University of California. Reprinted by permission.

"Invisible Man" from *Member of the Club* (pp. 1–26) by Lawrence Otis Graham. Copyright © 1995 by Lawrence Otis Graham. Reprinted by permission of HarperCollins Publishers, Inc.

From "The Moral Drama of Multicultural Education" by Shan Nelson-Rowe in *Images of Issues: Typifying Contemporary Social Problems,* 2nd ed. (pp. 81–99), ed. Joel Best. New York: Aldine de Gruyter. Copyright © 1995 Walter de Gruyter, Inc., New York. Reprinted by permission.

"Racism and Research: The Case of the Tuskegee Syphilis Study" by Allan M. Brandt, 1978, *The Hastings Center Report* (December), pp. 21–29. Copyright © 1978 by The Hastings Center. Reprinted by permission.

"Passing By: Gender and Public Harassment" from *Passing By: Gender and Public Harassment* (pp. 158–196) by Carol Brooks Gardner, 1995. Berkeley: University of California Press. Copyright © 1995 the Regents of the University of California. Reprinted by permission.

"Still a Man's World: Men Who Do 'Women's Work' " from *Still a Man's World: Men Who Do "Women's Work"* (pp. 1–5, 81–108) by Christine Williams, 1995. Berkeley: University of California Press. Copyright © 1995 by the Regents of the University of California. Reprinted by permission.

"The 21st Century Breathing Down Our Necks" from *The 13th Gen* by Neil Howe and Bill Strauss (pp. 214–228). Copyright © 1993 by Neil Howe and Bill Strauss. Reprinted by permission of Vintage Books, a Division of Random House, Inc.

"Other People's Children" from *Other People's Children* (pp. 1–47) by Julia Wrigley. Copyright © by BasicBooks, Inc. Reprinted by permission of BasicBooks, a division of HarperCollins Publishers, Inc.

"Holding the Line: Women in the Great Arizona Mine Strike of 1983" from *Holding the Line: Women in the Great Arizona Mine Strike of 1983* (pp. ix–x, 4–5, 14–15, 16–17, 24–25, 27–31, 33–36, 39–43, 46–48, 101–102, 104–107, 191–196) by Barbara Kingsolver, ILR Press, School of Industrial Relations, Cornell University, Ithaca, NY. © 1989 Barbara Kingsolver. Reprinted by permission of the author.

"World Views of Pro-Life and Pro-Choice Activists" from *Abortion and the Politics of Motherhood* (pp. 158–191) by Kristin Luker, 1984. Berkeley: University of California Press. Copyright © 1984 by the Regents of the University of California. Reprinted by permission.

Sociology

*Exploring the Architecture
of Everyday Life*

Second Edition

READINGS

I

The Individual and Society

CHAPTER 1

Taking a New Look at a Familiar World

The fundamental message of sociology is that our personal, everyday experiences are affected by, and affect, the larger society in which we live. Unlike the more "individualistic" perspectives on human behavior offered by psychology and biology, sociology emphasizes social environment rather than personal characteristics in explaining an individual's behavior.

Consider athletic performance. I'm sure you've seen televised coverage of the Olympics. If you're like me, you probably sat in awe of those remarkable athletes—the elite of their respective sports—competing at a level far beyond the reach of most "normal" people. Watching them perform, it's easy to conclude that they are a different breed, that they have some inborn, personal quality—call it "talent"—that propels them to world-class achievements. But Daniel Chambliss, in "The Mundanity of Excellence," argues that, as much as we'd like to believe otherwise, these world-class athletes are not that different from the rest of us. Their excellence comes from fundamentally ordinary activities that take place within identifiable social worlds that have their own unique values, attitudes, and behavior patterns. By explaining athletic excellence in such a way, Chambliss helps introduce us to the sociological perspective on understanding social life: Behavior commonly attributed to innate qualities can be better understood by examining the broader social context within which it takes place.

The Mundanity of Excellence
An Ethnographic Report on Stratification and Olympic Swimmers

Daniel F. Chambliss

Olympic sports and competitive swimming in particular provide an unusually clear opportunity for studying the nature of excellence. In other fields, it may be less clear who are the outstanding performers: the best painter or pianist, the best businessperson, the finest waitress or the best father. But in sport (and this is one of its attractions) success is defined more exactly, by success in competition. There are medals and ribbons and plaques for first place, second, and third; competitions are arranged for the head-to-head meeting of the best competitors in the world; in swimming and track, times are electronically recorded to the hundredth of a second; there are statistics published and rankings announced, every month or every week. By the end of the Olympic Games every four years, it is completely clear who won and who lost, who made the finals, who participated in the Games, and who never participated in the sport at all.

Within competitive swimming in particular, clear stratification exists not only between individuals but also between defined levels of the sport as well. At the lowest level, we see the country club teams, operating in the summertime as a loosely run, mildly competitive league, with volunteer, part-time coaches. Above that there are teams that represent entire cities and compete with other teams from other cities around the state or region; then a "Junior Nationals" level of competition, featuring the best younger (under 18 years old) athletes; then the Senior Nationals level (any age, the best in the nation); and finally, we could speak

of world- or Olympic-class competitors. At each such level, we find, predictably, certain people competing: one athlete swims in a summer league, never seeing swimmers from another town; one swimmer may consistently qualify for the Junior Nationals, but not for Seniors; a third may swim at the Olympics and never return to Junior Nationals. The levels of the sport are remarkably distinct from one another.

. . . Because success in swimming is so definable, . . . we can clearly see, by comparing levels and studying individuals as they move between and within levels, what exactly produces excellence. In addition, careers in swimming are relatively short; one can achieve tremendous success in a brief period of time. Rowdy Gaines, beginning in the sport when 17 years old, jumped from a country club league to a world record in the 100 meter freestyle event in only three years. This allows the researcher to conduct true longitudinal research in a few short years. . . .

. . . This report draws on extended experience with swimmers at every level of ability, over some half a dozen years. Observation has covered the span of careers, and I have had the chance to compare not just athletes within a certain level (the view that most coaches have), but between the most discrepant levels as well. Thus these findings avoid the usual . . . problem of an observer's being familiar mainly with athletes at one level. . . .

The Nature of Excellence

By "excellence" I mean "consistent superiority of performance." The excellent athlete regularly, even routinely, performs better than his or her

The author wishes to thank Randall Collins and Gary Alan Fine for their comments on an earlier draft of this paper.

competitors. Consistency of superior performances tells us that one athlete is indeed better
than another, and that the difference between
them is not merely the product of chance. This
definition can apply at any level of the sport, differentiating athletes. The superiority discussed
here may be that of one swimmer over another, or
of all athletes at one level (say, the Olympic class)
over another. By this definition, we need not
judge performance against an absolute criterion,
but only against other performances. There are
acknowledged leaders on every team, as well as
teams widely recognized as dominant.

To introduce what are sources of excellence for
Olympic athletes, I should first suggest—saving
the demonstration for later—what *does not* produce excellence.

(1) Excellence is not, I find, the product of
socially deviant personalities. These swimmers
don't appear to be "oddballs," nor are they loners
("kids who have given up the normal teenage
life").[1] If their achievements result from a personality characteristic, that characteristic is not obvious. Perhaps it is true, as the mythology of sports
has it, that the best athletes are more self-confi-
dent (although that is debatable); but such confidence could be an effect of achievement, not the
cause of it.[2]

(2) Excellence does *not* result from quantitative changes in behavior. Increased training time,
per se, does not make one swim fast; nor does
increased "psyching up," nor does moving the
arms faster. Simply doing more of the same will
not lead to moving up a level in the sport.

(3) Excellence does *not* result from some special inner quality of the athlete. "Talent" is one
common name for this quality; sometimes we talk
of a "gift," or of "natural ability." These terms are
generally used to mystify the essentially mundane
processes of achievement in sports, keeping us
away from a realistic analysis of the actual factors
creating superlative performances, and protecting
us from a sense of responsibility for our own outcomes.

So where does excellence—consistent superiority of performance—come from?

I. Excellence Requires Qualitative Differentiation

Excellence in competitive swimming is achieved
through qualitative differentiation from other
swimmers, not through quantitative increases in
activity. . . .

. . . I should clarify what is meant here by
"quantitative" and "qualitative." By quantity, we
mean the number or amount of something.
Quantitative improvement entails an increase in
the number of some one thing one does. An athlete who practices 2 hours a day and increases that
activity to 4 hours a day has made a quantitative
change in behavior. Or, one who swims 5 miles
and changes to 7 miles has made a quantitative
change. She does more of the same thing; there is
an increase in quantity. Or again, a freestyle swimmer who, while maintaining the same stroke technique, moves his arms at an increased number of
strokes per minute has made a quantitative change
in behavior. Quantitative improvements, then,
involve doing *more of the same thing*.

By quality, though, we mean the character or
nature of the thing itself. A qualitative change
involves modifying what is actually being done,
not simply doing more of it. For a swimmer doing
the breaststroke, a qualitative change might be a
change from pulling straight back with the arms to
sculling them outwards, to the sides; or from lift-
ing oneself up out of the water at the turn to staying low near the water. Other qualitative changes
might include competing in a regional meet
instead of local meets; eating vegetables and complex carbohydrates rather than fats and sugars;
entering one's weaker events instead of only one's
stronger events; learning to do a flip turn with
freestyle, instead of merely turning around and
pushing off; or training at near-competition levels
of intensity, rather than casually. Each of these
involves doing things differently than before, not
necessarily doing more. Qualitative improvements
involve doing *different kinds of things*.

Now we can consider how qualitative differentiation is manifested:

**Different levels of the sport are qualitatively dis-
tinct.** Olympic champions don't just do much
more of the same things that summer-league
country club swimmers do. They don't just swim

more hours, or move their arms faster, or attend more workouts. What makes them faster cannot be quantitatively compared with lower-level swimmers, because while there may be quantitative differences—and certainly there are, for instance in the number of hours spent in workouts—these are not, I think, the decisive factors at all.[3]

Instead, they do things differently. Their strokes are different, their attitudes are different, their groups of friends are different, their parents treat the sport differently, the swimmers prepare differently for their races, and they enter different kinds of meets and events. There are numerous discontinuities of this sort between, say, the swimmer who competes in a local City League meet and one who enters the Olympic Trials. Consider three dimensions of difference:

(1) Technique: The styles of strokes, dives and turns are dramatically different at different levels. A "C" (the lowest rank in United States Swimming's ranking system) breaststroke swimmer tends to pull her arms far back beneath her, kick the legs out very wide without bringing them together at the finish, lift herself high out of the water on the turn, fail to take a long pull underwater after the turn, and touch at the finish with one hand, on her side. By comparison, a "AAAA" (the highest rank) swimmer, sculls the arms out to the side and sweeps back in (never actually pulling backwards), kicks narrowly with the feet finishing together, stays low on the turns, takes a long underwater pull after the turn, and touches at the finish with both hands. Not only are the strokes different, they are so different that the "C" swimmer may be amazed to see how the "AAAA" swimmer looks when swimming. The appearance alone is dramatically different, as is the speed with which they swim. . . .

(2) Discipline: The best swimmers are more likely to be strict with their training, coming to workouts on time, carefully doing the competitive strokes legally (i.e., without violating the technical rules of the sport),[4] watch what they eat, sleep regular hours, do proper warmups before a meet, and the like. Their energy is carefully channeled. Diver Greg Louganis, who won two Olympic gold medals in 1984, practices only

three hours each day—not a long time—divided into two or three sessions. But during each session, he tries to do every dive perfectly. Louganis is never sloppy in practice, and so is never sloppy in meets.[5]

(3) Attitude: At the higher levels of competitive swimming, something like an inversion of attitude takes place. The very features of the sport that the "C" swimmer finds unpleasant, the top-level swimmer enjoys. What others see as boring—swimming back and forth over a black line for two hours, say—they find peaceful, even meditative,[6] often challenging, or therapeutic. They enjoy hard practices, look forward to difficult competitions, try to set difficult goals. Coming into the 5:30 A.M. practices at Mission Viejo, many of the swimmers were lively, laughing, talking, enjoying themselves, perhaps appreciating the fact that most people would positively hate doing it. It is incorrect to believe that top athletes suffer great sacrifices to achieve their goals. Often, they don't see what they do as sacrificial at all. They like it.

These qualitative differences are what distinguish levels of the sport. They are very noticeable, while the quantitative differences between levels, both in training and in competition, may be surprisingly small indeed. . . . Yet very small quantitative differences in performance may be coupled with huge qualitative differences: In the finals of the men's 100-meter freestyle swimming event at the 1984 Olympics, Rowdy Gaines, the gold medalist, finished ahead of second-place Mark Stockwell by .44 seconds, a gap of only 8/10 of 1%. Between Gaines and the 8th place finisher (a virtual unknown named Dirk Korthals, from West Germany), there was only a 2.2% difference in time. Indeed, between Rowdy Gaines, the fastest swimmer in the world that year, and a respectable 10-year-old, the quantitative difference in speed would only be about 30%.

Yet here, as in many cases, a rather small *quantitative* difference produces an enormous *qualitative difference:* Gaines was consistently a winner in major international meets, holder of the world record, and the Olympic Gold Medalist in three events.

Stratification in the sport is discrete, not continuous. There are significant, qualitative breaks—discontinuities—between levels of the sport. These include differences in attitude, discipline, and technique which in turn lead to small but consistent quantitative differences in speed. Entire teams show such differences in attitude, discipline, and technique, and consequently certain teams are easily seen to be "stuck" at certain levels.[7] Some teams always do well at the National Championships, others do well at the Regionals, others at the County Meet. And certainly swimmers typically remain within a certain level for most of their careers, maintaining throughout their careers the habits with which they began. Within levels, competitive improvements for such swimmers are typically marginal, reflecting only differential growth rates (early onset of puberty, for instance) or the jockeying for position within the relatively limited sphere of their own level. . . .

. . . Athletes move up to the top ranks through *qualitative jumps:* noticeable changes in their techniques, discipline, and attitude, accomplished usually through a change in settings, e.g., joining a new team with a new coach, new friends, etc., who work at a higher level. Without such qualitative jumps, no major improvements (movements through levels) will take place. . . .

This is really several worlds, each with its own patterns of conduct. . . . If, as I have suggested, there really are qualitative breaks between levels of the sport, and if people really don't "work their way up" in any simple additive sense, perhaps our very conception of a single swimming world is inaccurate. I have spoken of the "top" of the sport, and of "levels" within the sport. But these words suggest that all swimmers are, so to speak, climbing a single ladder, aiming towards the same goals, sharing the same values, swimming the same strokes, all looking upwards towards an Olympic gold medal. But they aren't.[8] Some want gold medals, some want to make the team, some want to exercise, or have fun with friends, or be out in the sunshine and water. Some are trying to escape their parents. The images of the "top" and the "levels" of swimming which I have used until now may simply reflect the dominance of a certain

faction of swimmers and coaches in the sport: top is what *they* regard as the top, and their definitions of success have the broadest political currency in United States Swimming. Fast swimmers take as given that faster is better—instead of, say, that more beautiful is better; or that parental involvement is better; or that "well-rounded" children (whatever that may mean) are better. . . .

So we should envision not a swimming world, but multiple worlds[9] (and changing worlds is a major step toward excellence), a horizontal rather than vertical differentiation of the sport. What I have called "levels" are better described as "worlds" or "spheres." In one such world, parents are loosely in charge, coaches are teenagers employed as lifeguards, practices are held a few times a week, competitions are scheduled perhaps a week in advance, the season lasts for a few weeks in the summertime, and athletes who are much faster than the others may be discouraged by social pressure even from competing, for they take the fun out of it.[10] The big event of the season is the City Championship, when children from the metropolitan area will spend two days racing each other in many events, and the rest of the time sitting under huge tents playing cards, reading, listening to music, and gossiping. In another world, coaches are very powerful, parents seen only occasionally (and never on the pool deck), swimmers travel thousands of miles to attend meets, they swim 6 days a week for years at a time, and the fastest among them are objects of respect and praise. The big event of the season may be the National Championships, where the athletes may spend much time—sitting under huge tents, playing cards, reading, listening to music and gossiping.[11]

Each such world has its own distinctive types of powerful people and dominant athletes, and being prominent in one world is no guarantee of being prominent in another.[12] At lower levels, the parents of swimmers are in charge; at the higher levels, the coaches; perhaps in the Masters teams which are made up only of swimmers over 25 years old, the swimmers themselves. Each world, too, has its distinctive goals: going to the Olympics, doing well at the National Junior Olympics, winning the City Meet, having a good time for a few weeks. In each world the techniques are at least somewhat distinct (as with the breaststroke, discussed above), and certain demands are made on family and friends. In all of these ways, and many more, each so-called "level" of competitive swimming is qualitatively different than others. The differences are not simply quantifiable steps along a one-dimensional path leading to the Olympic Games. Goals are varied, participants have competing commitments, and techniques are jumbled.

II. Why "Talent" Does Not Lead to Excellence

. . . "Talent" is perhaps the most pervasive lay explanation we have for athletic success. Great athletes, we seem to believe, are born with a special gift, almost a "thing" inside of them, denied to the rest of us—perhaps physical, genetic, psychological, or physiological. Some have "it," and some don't. Some are "natural athletes," and some aren't. While an athlete, we acknowledge, may require many years of training and dedication to develop and use that talent, it is always "in there," only waiting for an opportunity to come out. When children perform well, they are said to "have" talent; if performance declines, they may be said to have "wasted their talent." We believe it is that talent, conceived as a substance behind the surface reality of performance, which finally distinguishes the best among our athletes.

But talent fails as an explanation for athletic success, on conceptual grounds. It mystifies excellence, subsuming a complex set of discrete actions behind a single undifferentiated concept. To understand these actions and the excellence which they constitute, then, we should first debunk this concept of talent and see where it fails. On at least three points, I believe, "talent" is inadequate.

Factors other than talent explain athletic success more precisely. We can, with a little effort, see what these factors are in swimming: geographical location, particularly living in southern California where the sun shines year round and everybody swims; fairly high family income, which allows for the travel to meets and payments of the fees entailed in the sport, not to mention sheer access to swimming pools when one is young; one's height, weight, and proportions; the luck or choice of having a good coach, who can teach the

skills required; inherited muscle structure—it certainly helps to be both strong and flexible; parents who are interested in sports. Some swimmers, too, enjoy more the physical pleasures of swimming; some have better coordination; some even have a higher percentage of fast-twitch muscle fiber. Such factors are clearly definable, and their effects can be clearly demonstrated. To subsume all of them, willynilly, under the rubric of "talent" obscures rather than illuminates the sources of athletic excellence.

It's easy to do this, especially if one's only exposure to top athletes comes once every four years while watching the Olympics on television, or if one only sees them in performances rather than in day-to-day training. Say, for instance, that one day I turn on the television set and there witness a magnificent figure skating performance by Scott Hamilton. What I see is grace and power and skill all flowing together, seemingly without effort; a single moving picture, rapid and sure, far beyond what I could myself do. . . . "His skating," I may say, referring to his actions as a single thing, "is spectacular." With that quick shorthand, I have captured (I believe) at a stroke the wealth of tiny details that Hamilton, over years and years, has fitted together into a performance so smoothly that they become invisible to the untrained eye.[13] Perhaps, with concentration, Hamilton himself can feel the details in his movements; certainly a great coach can see them, and pick out the single fault or mistake in an otherwise flawless routine. But to me, the performance is a thing entire.

Afterwards, my friends and I sit and talk about Hamilton's life as a "career of excellence," or as showing "incredible dedication," "tremendous motivation"—again, as if his excellence, his dedication, his motivation somehow exist all-at-once. His excellence becomes a thing inside of him which he periodically reveals to us, which comes out now and then; his life and habits become reified. "Talent" is merely the word we use to label this reification.

But that is no explanation of success.

Talent is indistinguishable from its effects. One cannot see that talent exists until after its effects become obvious. Kalinowski's research on Olympic swimmers demonstrates this clearly.

One of the more startling discoveries of our study has been that it takes a while to recognize swimming talent. Indeed, it usually takes being successful at a regional level, and more often, at a national level (in AAU swimming) before the child is identified as talented. (p. 173)

"They didn't say I had talent until I started to get really good [and made Senior Nationals at sixteen]; then they started to say I had talent . . . " (p. 174)

. . . despite the physical capabilities he was born with, it took Peter several years (six by our estimate) to appear gifted. This is the predominant, though not exclusive, pattern found in our data on swimmers. Most of them are said to be "natural" or "gifted" after they had already devoted a great deal of time and hard work to the field. (p. 194)

. . .whatever superior qualities were attributed to him as he grew older and more successful, they were not apparent then [before he was thirteen]. (p. 200)

The above quotations suggest that talent is *discovered* later in one's career, the implication being that while the athlete's ability *existed* all along, we were unaware of it until late. Kalinowski, like many of us, holds to the belief that there must be this thing inside the athlete which precedes and determines success, only later to be discovered. But the recurring evidence he finds suggests a different interpretation: perhaps there is no such thing as "talent," there is only the outstanding performance itself. He sees success and immediately infers behind it a cause, a cause *for which he has no evidence other than the success itself*. Here, as elsewhere, talent (our name for this cause) cannot be measured, or seen, or felt in any form other than the success to which it supposedly gives rise. . . .

The "amount" of talent needed for athletic success seems to be strikingly low. It seems initially plausible that one must have a certain level of natural ability in order to succeed in sports (or music or academics). But upon empirical examination, it becomes very difficult to say exactly what that physical minimum is. Indeed, much of the mythology of sport is built around people who

lack natural ability who went on to succeed fabulously. An entire genre of inspirational literature is built on the theme of the person whose even normal natural abilities have been destroyed: Wilma Rudolph had polio as a child, then came back to win the Olympic 100-Meter Dash. Glenn Cunningham had his legs badly burned in a fire, then broke the world record in the mile. Such stories are grist for the sportswriter's mill.

More than merely common, these stories are almost routine. Most Olympic champions, when their history is studied, seem to have overcome sharp adversity in their pursuit of success. Automobile accidents, shin splints, twisted ankles, shoulder surgery are common in such tales. In fact, they are common in life generally. While some necessary minimum of physical strength, heart/lung capacity, or nerve density may well be required for athletic achievement (again, I am *not* denying differential advantages), that minimum seems both difficult to define and markedly low, at least in many cases. Perhaps the crucial factor is not natural ability at all, but the willingness to overcome natural or unnatural disabilities of the sort that most of us face, ranging from minor inconveniences in getting up and going to work, to accidents and injuries, to gross physical impairments.

And if the basic level of talent needed, then, seems so low as to be nearly universally available, perhaps the very concept of talent itself—no longer differentiating among performers—is better discarded altogether. It simply doesn't explain the differences in outcomes. Rather than talk about talent and ability, we do better to look at what people actually do that creates outstanding performance.

The concept of talent hinders a clear understanding of excellence. By providing a quick . . . "explanation" of athletic success, it satisfies our casual curiosity while requiring neither an empirical analysis nor a critical questioning of our tacit assumptions about top athletes. At best, it is an easy way of admitting that we don't know the answer. . . . But the attempt at explanation fails. . . . Through the notion of talent, we transform particular actions that a human being does into an object possessed, held in trust for the day when it will be revealed for all to see.

This line of thought leads to one more step. Since talent can be viewed only indirectly in the effects that it supposedly produces, its very existence is a matter of faith. The basic dogma of "talent" says that what people do in this world has a cause lying behind them, that there is a kind of backstage reality where the real things happen, and what we—you and I—see here in our lives (say, the winning of a gold medal) is really a reflection of that true reality back there. Those of us who are not admitted to the company of the elect—the talented—can never see what that other world of fabulous success is really like, and can never share those experiences. And accepting this faith in talent, I suggest, we relinquish our chance of accurately understanding excellence. . . .

III. *The Mundanity of Excellence*

"People don't know how ordinary success is," said Mary T. Meagher, winner of 3 gold medals in the Los Angeles Olympics, when asked what the public least understands about her sport. She then spoke of starting her career in a summer league country club team, of working her way to AAU meets, to faster and faster competitions, of learning new techniques, practicing new habits, meeting new challenges.[14] What Meagher said—that success is ordinary—in some sense applies, I believe, to other fields of endeavor as well: to business, to politics, to professions of all kinds, including academics. In what follows I will try to elaborate on this point, drawing some examples from the swimming research, and some from other fields, to indicate the scope of this conception.

Excellence is mundane. Superlative performance is really a confluence of dozens of small skills or activities, each one learned or stumbled upon, which have been carefully drilled into habit and then are fitted together in a synthesized whole. There is nothing extraordinary or superhuman in any one of those actions; only the fact that they are done consistently and correctly, and all together, produce excellence. When a swimmer learns a proper flip turn in the freestyle races, she will swim the race a bit faster; then a streamlined push off from the wall, with the arms squeezed together over the head, and a little faster; then how to place

the hands in the water so no air is cupped in them; then how to lift them over the water; then how to lift weights to properly build strength, and how to eat the right foods, and to wear the best suits for racing, and on and on.[15] Each of those tasks seems small in itself, but each allows the athlete to swim a bit faster. And having learned and consistently practiced all of them together, and many more besides, the swimmer may compete in the Olympic Games. The winning of a gold medal is nothing more than the synthesis of a countless number of such little things—even if some of them are done unwittingly or by others, and thus called "luck."

So the "little things" really do count. We have already seen how a very small (in quantitative terms) difference can produce a noticeable success. Even apparent flukes can lead to gold medal performances:

> In the 100-Meter Freestyle event in Los Angeles, Rowdy Gaines, knowing that the starter for the race tended to fire the gun fast, anticipated the start; while not actually jumping the gun, it seems from video replays of the race that Gaines knew exactly when to go, and others were left on the blocks as he took off. But the starter turned his back, and the protests filed afterwards by competitors were ignored. Gaines had spent years watching starters, and had talked with his coach (Richard Quick) before the race about this starter in particular. (Field notes; see Chambliss, 1988, for full description)

Gaines was not noticeably faster than several of the other swimmers in the race, but with this one extra tactic, he gained enough of an advantage to win the race. And he seemed in almost all of his races to find such an advantage; hence the gold medal. Looking at such subtleties, we can say that not only are the little things important; in some ways, the little things are the only things. . . .

In swimming, or elsewhere, these practices might at first glance seem very minimal indeed:

> When Mary T. Meagher was 13 years old and had qualified for the National Championships, she decided to try to break the world record in the 200-Meter Butterfly race. She

made two immediate qualitative changes in her routine: first, she began coming on time to all practices. She recalls now, years later, being picked up at school by her mother and driving (rather quickly) through the streets of Louisville, Kentucky, trying desperately to make it to the pool on time. That habit, that discipline, she now says, gave her the sense that every minute of practice time counted. And second, she began doing all of her turns, during those practices, correctly, in strict accordance with the competitive rules. Most swimmers don't do this; they turn rather casually, and tend to touch with one hand instead of two (in the butterfly, Meagher's stroke). This, she says, accustomed her to doing things one step better than those around her—always. Those are the two major changes she made in her training, as she remembers it.[16]

Meagher made two quite mundane changes in her habits, either one of which anyone could do, if he or she wanted. Within a year Meagher had broken the world record in the butterfly. . . .

Motivation is mundane, too. Swimmers go to practice to see their friends, to exercise, to feel strong afterwards, to impress the coach, to work towards bettering a time they swam in the last meet. Sometimes, the older ones, with a longer view of the future, will aim towards a meet that is still several months away. But even given the longer-term goals, the daily satisfactions need to be there. The mundane social rewards really are crucial (see Chambliss, 1988, Chapter 6). By comparison, the big, dramatic motivations—winning an Olympic gold medal, setting a world record—seem to be ineffective unless translated into shorter-term tasks. Viewing "Rocky" or "Chariots of Fire" may inspire one for several days, but the excitement stirred by a film wears off rather quickly when confronted with the day-to-day reality of climbing out of bed to go and jump in cold water. If, on the other hand, that day-to-day reality is itself fun, rewarding, challenging; if the water is nice and friends are supportive, the longer-term goals may well be achieved almost in spite of themselves. Again, Mary T. Meagher:

I never looked beyond the next year, and I never looked beyond the next level. I never thought about the Olympics when I was ten; at that time I was thinking about the State Championships. When I made cuts for Regionals [the next higher level of competition], I started thinking about Regionals; when I made cuts for National Junior Olympics, I started thinking about National Junior Olympics . . . I can't even think about the [1988] Olympics right now. . . . Things can overwhelm you if you think too far ahead. (Interview notes)

This statement was echoed by many of the swimmers I interviewed. While many of them were working towards the Olympic Games, they divided the work along the way into achievable steps, no one of which was too big. They found their challenges in small things: working on a better start this week, polishing up their backstroke technique next week, focusing on better sleep habits, planning how to pace their swim. . . .

. . . Many top swimmers are accustomed to winning races in practice, day after day. Steve Lundquist, who won two gold medals in Los Angeles, sees his success as resulting from an early decision that he wanted to win every swim, every day, in every practice. That was the immediate goal he faced at workouts; just try to win every swim, every lap, in every stroke, no matter what. Lundquist gained a reputation in swimming for being a ferocious workout swimmer, one who competed all the time, even in the warmup. He became so accustomed to winning that he entered meets knowing that he could beat these people— he had developed the habit, every day, of never losing. The short-term goal of winning this swim, in this workout, translated into his ability to win bigger and bigger races. Competition, when the day arrived for a meet, was not a shock to him, nothing at all out of the ordinary.[17]

This leads to a third and final point.

In the pursuit of excellence, maintaining mundanity is the key psychological challenge. In common parlance, winners don't choke. Faced with what seems to be a tremendous challenge or a strikingly unusual event, such as the Olympic

Games, the better athletes take it as a normal, manageable situation[18] ("It's just another swim meet," is a phrase sometimes used by top swimmers at a major event such as the Games) and do what is necessary to deal with it. Standard rituals (such as the warmup, the psych, the visualization of the race, the taking off of sweats, and the like) are ways of importing one's daily habits into the novel situation, to make it as normal an event as possible. Swimmers like Lundquist, who train at competition-level intensity, therefore have an advantage: arriving at a meet, they are already accustomed to doing turns correctly, taking legal starts, doing a proper warmup, and being aggressive from the outset of the competition. If each day of the season is approached with a seriousness of purpose, then the big meet will not come as a shock. The athlete will believe "I belong here, this is my world"—and not be paralyzed by fear or self-consciousness. The task then is to have training closely approximate competition conditions. . . .

The mundanity of excellence is typically unrecognized. I think the reason is fairly simple. Usually we see great athletes only after they have become great—after the years of learning the new methods, gaining the habits of competitiveness and consistency, after becoming comfortable in their world. They have long since perfected the myriad of techniques that together constitute excellence. Ignorant of all of the specific steps that have led to the performance and to the confidence, we think that somehow excellence sprang full grown from this person, and we say he or she "has talent" or "is gifted." Even when seen close up, the mundanity of excellence is often not believed:

> Every week at the Mission Viejo training pool, where the National Champion Nadadores team practiced, coaches from around the world would be on the deck visiting, watching as the team did their workouts, swimming back and forth for hours. The visiting coaches would be excited at first, just to be here; then soon—within an hour or so usually—they grew bored, walking back and forth looking at the deck, glancing around at the hills around the town, reading the bul-

letin boards, glancing down at their watches, wondering, after the long flight out to California, when something dramatic was going to happen. "They all have to come to Mecca, and see what we do," coach Mark Schubert said. "They think we have some big secret." (Field notes)

But of course there is no secret; there is only the doing of all those little things, each one done correctly, time and again, until excellence in every detail becomes a firmly ingrained habit, an ordinary part of one's everyday life.

Conclusions

The foregoing analysis suggests that we have overlooked a fundamental fact about Olympic-class athletes; and the argument may apply far more widely than swimming, or sports. I suggest that it applies to success in business, politics, and academics, in dentistry, bookkeeping, food service, speechmaking, electrical engineering, selling insurance (when the clients are upset, you climb in the car and go out there to talk with them), and perhaps even in the arts.[19] Consider again the major points:

(1) *Excellence is a qualitative phenomenon.* Doing more does not equal doing better. High performers focus on qualitative, not quantitative, improvements; it is qualitative improvements which produce significant changes in level of achievement; different levels of achievement really are distinct, and in fact reflect vastly different habits, values, and goals.

(2) *Talent is a useless concept.* Varying conceptions of natural ability ("talent," e.g.) tend to mystify excellence, treating it as the inherent possession of a few; they mask the concrete actions that create outstanding performance; they avoid the work of empirical analysis and logical explanations (clear definitions, separable independent and dependent variables, and at least an attempt at establishing the temporal priority of the cause); and finally, such conceptions perpetuate the sense of innate psychological differences between high performers and other people.

(3) *Excellence is mundane.* Excellence is accomplished through the doing of actions, ordinary in themselves, performed consistently and carefully, habitualized, compounded together, added up over time. While these actions are "qualitatively different" from those of performers at other levels, these differences are neither unmanageable nor, taken one step at a time, terribly difficult. Mary T. Meagher came to practice on time; some writers always work for three hours each morning, before beginning anything else; a businessperson may go ahead and make that tough phone call; a job applicant writes one more letter; a runner decides, against the odds, to enter the race; a county commissioner submits a petition to run for Congress; a teenager asks for a date; an actor attends one more audition. Every time a decision comes up, the qualitatively "correct" choice will be made. The action, in itself, is nothing special; the care and consistency with which it is made is.

Howard Becker has presented a similar argument about the ordinariness of apparently unusual people in his book *Outsiders* (1961). But where he speaks of deviance, I would speak of excellence. Becker says, and I concur:

> We ought not to view it as something special, as depraved or in some magical way better than other kinds of behavior. We ought to see it simply as a kind of behavior some disapprove of and others value, studying the processes by which either or both perspectives are built up and maintained. Perhaps the best surety against either extreme is close contact with the people we study (Becker, p. 176).

After three years of field work with world-class swimmers, having the kind of close contact that Becker recommends, I wrote a draft of some book chapters, full of stories about swimmers, and I showed it to a friend. "You need to jazz it up," he said. "You need to make these people more interesting. The analysis is nice, but except for the fact that these are good swimmers, there isn't much else exciting to say about them as individuals." He was right, of course. What these athletes do was rather interesting, but the people themselves were only fast swimmers, who did the particular things

one does to swim fast. It is all very mundane. When my friend said that they weren't exciting, my best answer could only be, simply put: *That's the point.*

NOTES

1. In fact, if anything they are more socially bonded and adept than their peers. The process by which this happens fits well with Durkheim's (1965) description of the sources of social cohesion.
2. These issues are addressed at length in "The Social World of Olympic Swimmers." Daniel F. Chambliss, in preparation.
3. True, the top teams work long hours, and swim very long distances, but (1) such workouts often begin after a swimmer achieves national status, not before, and (2) the positive impact of increased yardage seems to come with huge increases, e.g., the doubling of workout distances—in which case one could argue that a *qualitative* jump has been made. The whole question of "how much yardage to swim" is widely discussed within the sport itself.

Compare the (specious, I think) notion that a longer school day/term/year will produce educational improvements.
4. One day at Mission Viejo, with some sixty swimmers going back and forth the length of a 50-meter pool, coach Mark Schubert took one boy out of the water and had him do twenty pushups before continuing the workout. The boy had touched the wall with one hand at the end of a breaststroke swim. The rules require a two-handed touch.

One hundred and twenty hands *should have* touched, one hundred and nineteen *did* touch, and this made Schubert angry. He pays attention to details.
5. From an interview with his coach, Ron O'Brien.
6. Distance swimmers frequently compare swimming to meditation.
7. For example: several well-known teams consistently do well at the National Junior Olympics ("Junior Nationals," as it is called informally), and yet never place high in the team standings at the National Championships ("Senior Nationals"), the next higher meet.

These teams actually prevent their swimmers from going to the better meet, holding them in store for the easier meet so that the team will do better at that lesser event. In this way, and in many others, teams choose their own level of success.

8. March and Olsen make a similar point with regard to educational institutions and organizations in general: organizations include a variety of constituents with differing goals, plans, motivations, and values. Unity of purpose, even with organizations, cannot simply be assumed. Coherence, not diversity, is what needs explaining. March and Olsen, 1976.

9. See Shibutani in Rose, 1962, on "social worlds." Blumer, 1969.

10. These fast swimmers who come to slow meets are called hot dogs, showoffs, or even jerks. (Personal observations.)

11. Again, personal observations from a large number of cases. While there are significant differences between swimmers of the Olympic class and a country club league, the basic sociability of their worlds is not one of them.

12. "Indeed, prestige ladders in the various worlds are so different that a man who reaches the pinnacle of success in one may be completely unknown elsewhere." Shibutani in Rose, 1962.

Similarly in academia: one may be a successful professor at the national level and yet find it difficult to gain employment at a minor regional university. Professors at the regional school may suspect his/her motives, be jealous, feel that he/she "wouldn't fit in," "won't stay anyway," etc. Many top-school graduate students discover upon entering the markets that no-name colleges have no interest in them; indeed, by attending a Chicago or Harvard Ph.D. program one may limit oneself to the top ranks of employment opportunities.

13. "Now, no one can see in an artist's work how it evolved: that is its advantage, for wherever we can see the evolution, we grow somewhat cooler. The complete art of representation wards off all thought of its solution; it tyrannizes as present perfection" (Nietzsche, 1984, p. 111).

14. Meagher's entire career is described in detail in Chambliss, 1988.

15. Such techniques are thoroughly explained in Maglischo (1982) and Troup and Reese (1983).

16. Interview notes.

17. Interview notes.

18. An interesting parallel: some of the most successful generals have no trouble sleeping before and after major battles. For details on Ulysses Grant and the Duke of Wellington, see Keegan, p. 207.

19. Professor Margaret Bates, an opera enthusiast, tells me that this "mundanity of excellence" argument applies nicely to Enrico Caruso, the great singer, who carefully perfected each ordinary detail of his performance in an effort to overcome a recognized lack of "natural ability."

REFERENCES

Blumer, Herbert. 1969. *Symbolic Interactionism.* Englewood Cliffs: Prentice Hall.

Chambliss, Daniel F. 1988. *Champions: The Making of Olympic Swimmers.* New York: Morrow.

Durkheim, Emile. 1965. *The Elementary Forms of the Religious Life.* New York: Free Press.

Kalinowsky, Anthony G. "The Development of Olympic Swimmers," and "One Olympic Swimmer," in Bloom (1985), pp. 139–210.

Keegan, John. 1987. *The Mask of Command.* New York: Viking.

Maglischo, Ernest W. 1982. *Swimming Faster.* Palo Alto: Mayfield.

March, James G. and Olsen, Johan P. 1976. *Ambiguity and Choice in Organizations.* Bergen, Norway: Universitetsforlaget.

Nietzsche, Friedrich. 1984. *Human, All Too Human.* Lincoln, Neb.: University of Nebraska Press.

Shibutani, T. "Reference Groups and Social Control," in Rose, Arnold M. 1962. *Human Behavior and Social Process.* Boston: Houghton Mifflin, pp. 128–147.

Troup, John and Reese, Randy. 1983. *A Scientific Approach to the Sport of Swimming.* Gainesville, Fl.: Scientific Sports.

THINKING ABOUT THE READING

The Mundanity of Excellence

■ Why does Chambliss feel that "talent" is a useless concept in explaining success among world-class swimmers? Where, instead, does he think that athletic excellence comes from? Why do you suppose we have such a strong tendency to focus on "talent" or "natural ability" in explaining superior performances? If it's true, as Chambliss suggests, that factors such as geographical location, high family income, the luck of having a good coach, and parents who are interested in sports can all play an important role in creating world-class swimmers, then there are probably many potentially successful athletes who are prevented from excelling because of their social circumstances. Relatively few inner-city kids grow up to succeed in "wealthy" sports like swimming, tennis, and golf. On the other hand, the inner city produces many of the world's best basketball, football, and track stars. What sorts of social circumstances encourage success in these sports? Can you identify other areas of life (other than sports) where excellence is pursued that might be similarly affected by the kinds of social circumstances described in this article?

CHAPTER 2

Seeing and Thinking Sociologically

While society exists as an objective fact above and apart from us, it is also a social construction—created, reaffirmed, and altered through the day-to-day interactions of the very people it influences and controls. The interplay between personal and social forces is the defining feature of everyday life.

The effect of social structure on our personal actions is often felt when we are compelled to obey the commands of someone who has authority over us. In "The My Lai Massacre: A Military Crime of Obedience," Herbert Kelman and Lee Hamilton describe a specific example of a crime in which the individuals involved attempted to deny responsibility for their actions by claiming that they were following the orders of someone who had the legitimate right to command them. This incident occurred in the midst of wartime. Arguably, people do things under such trying conditions that they wouldn't ordinarily do, even—as in this case—kill defenseless people. Kelman and Hamilton point out that these soldiers were not necessarily psychological misfits who were especially mean or violent. Instead, the researchers argue, they were ordinary people caught up in tense circumstances that made obeying the brutal commands of an authority seem like the normatively and morally acceptable thing to do.

Over the past several decades, credit cards have become a ubiquitous feature of the American cultural and economic landscape. You'd be hard pressed to find someone who didn't "carry around some plastic." The appeal of credit cards is easy to understand: they enable us to buy things when we don't have money immediately at hand to afford them. Many financial experts predict that by the beginning of the next century cash transactions will be virtually obsolete. But, according to George Ritzer in "The Credit Card: Private Troubles and Public Issues," our growing reliance on credit cards comes with a very heavy price. His examination of the credit card as an American cultural icon and the personal and social problems it creates, offers us a sociological analysis of how and why individuals spend money.

The My Lai Massacre

A Military Crime of Obedience

Herbert Kelman and V. Lee Hamilton

March 16, 1968, was a busy day in U.S. history. Stateside, Robert F. Kennedy announced his presidential candidacy, challenging a sitting president from his own party—in part out of opposition to an undeclared and disastrous war. In Vietnam, the war continued. In many ways, March 16 may have been a typical day in that war. We will probably never know. But we do know that on that day a typical company went on a mission—which may or may not have been typical—to a village called Son (or Song) My. Most of what is remembered from that mission occurred in the subhamlet known to Americans as My Lai 4.

The My Lai massacre was investigated and charges were brought in 1969 and 1970. Trials and disciplinary actions lasted into 1971. Entire books have been written about the army's year-long cover-up of the massacre (for example, Hersh, 1972), and the cover-up was a major focus of the army's own investigation of the incident. Our central concern here is the massacre itself—a crime of obedience—and public reactions to such crimes, rather than the lengths to which many went to deny the event. Therefore this account concentrates on one day: March 16, 1968.

Many verbal testimonials to the horrors that occurred at My Lai were available. More unusual was the fact that an army photographer, Ronald Haeberle, was assigned the task of documenting the anticipated military engagement at My Lai—and documented a massacre instead. Later, as the story of the massacre emerged, his photographs were widely distributed and seared the public conscience. What might have been dismissed as unreal or exaggerated was depicted in photographs of demonstrable authenticity. The dominant image appeared on the cover of *Life:* piles of bodies jum-

bled together in a ditch along a trail—the dead all apparently unarmed. All were Oriental, and all appeared to be children, women, or old men. Clearly there had been a mass execution, one whose image would not quickly fade.

So many bodies (over twenty in the cover photo alone) are hard to imagine as the handiwork of one killer. These were not. They were the product of what we call a crime of obedience. Crimes of obedience begin with orders. But orders are often vague and rarely survive with any clarity the transition from one authority down a chain of subordinates to the ultimate actors. The operation at Son My was no exception.

"Charlie" Company, Company C, under Lt. Col. Frank Barker's command, arrived in Vietnam in December 1967. As the army's investigative unit, directed by Lt. Gen. William R. Peers, characterized the personnel, they "contained no significant deviation from the average" for the time. Seymour S. Hersh (1970) described the "average" more explicitly: "Most of the men in Charlie Company had volunteered for the draft; only a few had gone to college for even one year. Nearly half were black, with a few Mexican-Americans. Most were eighteen to twenty-two years old. The favorite reading matter of Charlie Company, like that of other line infantry units in Vietnam, was comic books" (p. 18). The action at My Lai, like that throughout Vietnam, was fought by a cross-section of those Americans who either believed in the war or lacked the social resources to avoid participating in it. Charlie Company was indeed average for that time, that place, and that war.

Two key figures in Charlie Company were more unusual. The company's commander, Capt. Ernest Medina, was an upwardly mobile Mexican-

American who wanted to make the army his career, although he feared that he might never advance beyond captain because of his lack of formal education. His eagerness had earned him a nickname among his men: "Mad Dog Medina." One of his admirers was the platoon leader Second Lt. William L. Calley, Jr., an undistinguished, five-foot-three-inch junior-college dropout who had failed four of the seven courses in which he had enrolled his first year. Many viewed him as one of those "instant officers" made possible only by the army's then-desperate need for manpower. Whatever the cause, he was an insecure leader whose frequent claim was "I'm the boss." His nickname among some of the troops was "Surfside 5 1/2," a reference to the swashbuckling heroes of a popular television show, "Surfside 6."

The Son My operation was planned by Lieutenant Colonel Barker and his staff as a search-and-destroy mission with the objective of rooting out the Forty-eighth Viet Cong Battalion from their base area of Son My village. Apparently no written orders were ever issued. Barker's superior, Col. Oran Henderson, arrived at the staging point the day before. Among the issues he reviewed with the assembled officers were some of the weaknesses of prior operations by their units, including their failure to be appropriately aggressive in pursuit of the enemy. Later briefings by Lieutenant Colonel Barker and his staff asserted that no one except Viet Cong was expected to be in the village after 7 A.M. on the following day. The "innocent" would all be at the market. Those present at the briefings gave conflicting accounts of Barker's exact orders, but he conveyed at least a strong suggestion that the Son My area was to be obliterated. As the army's inquiry reported: "While there is some conflict in the testimony as to whether LTC Barker ordered the destruction of houses, dwellings, livestock, and other foodstuffs in the Song My area, the preponderance of the evidence indicates that such destruction was implied, if not specifically directed, by his orders of 15 March" (Peers Report, in Goldstein et al., 1976, p. 94).

Evidence that Barker ordered the killing of civilians is even more murky. What does seem clear, however, is that—having asserted that civilians would be away at the market—he did not specify what was to be done with any who might

nevertheless be found on the scene. The Peers Report therefore considered it "reasonable to conclude that LTC Barker's minimal or nonexistent instructions concerning the handling of noncombatants created the potential for grave misunderstandings as to his intentions and for interpretation of his orders as authority to fire, without restriction, on all persons found in target area" (Goldstein et al., 1976, p. 95). Since Barker was killed in action in June 1968, his own formal version of the truth was never available.

Charlie Company's Captain Medina was briefed for the operation by Barker and his staff. He then transmitted the already vague orders to his own men. Charlie Company was spoiling for a fight, having been totally frustrated during its months in Vietnam—first by waiting for battles that never came, then by incompetent forays led by inexperienced commanders, and finally by mines and booby traps. In fact, the emotion-laden funeral of a sergeant killed by a booby trap was held on March 15, the day before My Lai. Captain Medina gave the orders for the next day's action at the close of that funeral. Many were in a mood for revenge.

It is again unclear what was ordered. Although all participants were alive by the time of the trials for the massacre, they were either on trial or probably felt under threat of trial. Memories are often flawed and self-serving at such times. It is apparent that Medina relayed to the men at least some of Barker's general message—to expect Viet Cong resistance, to burn, and to kill livestock. It is not clear that he ordered the slaughter of the inhabitants, but some of the men who heard him thought he had. One of those who claimed to have heard such orders was Lt. William Calley.

As March 16 dawned, much was expected of the operation by those who had set it into motion. Therefore a full complement of "brass" was present in helicopters overhead, including Barker, Colonel Henderson, and their superior, Major General Koster (who went on to become commandant of West Point before the story of My Lai broke). On the ground, the troops were to carry with them one reporter and one photographer to immortalize the anticipated battle.

The action for Company C began at 7:30 as their first wave of helicopters touched down near the subhamlet of My Lai 4. By 7:47 all of Company C was present and set to fight. But instead of the Viet Cong Forty-eighth Battalion, My Lai was filled with the old men, women, and children who were supposed to have gone to market. By this time, in their version of the war, and with whatever orders they thought they had heard, the men from Company C were nevertheless ready to find Viet Cong everywhere. By nightfall, the official tally was 128 VC killed and three weapons captured, although later, unofficial body counts ran as high as 500. The operation at Son My was over. And by nightfall, as Hersh reported: "the Viet Cong were back in My Lai 4, helping the survivors bury the dead. It took five days. Most of the funeral speeches were made by the Communist guerrillas. Nguyen Bat was not a Communist at the time of the massacre, but the incident changed his mind. 'After the shooting,' he said, 'all the villagers became Communists'" (1970, p. 74). To this day, the memory of the massacre is kept alive by markers and plaques designating the spots where groups of villagers were killed, by a large statue, and by the My Lai Museum, established in 1975 (Williams, 1985).

But what could have happened to leave American troops reporting a victory over Viet Cong when in fact they had killed hundreds of noncombatants? It is not hard to explain the report of victory; that is the essence of a cover-up. It is harder to understand how the killings came to be committed in the first place, making a cover-up necessary.

Mass Executions and the Defense of Superior Orders

Some of the atrocities on March 16, 1968, were evidently unofficial, spontaneous acts: rapes, tortures, killings. For example, Hersh (1970) describes Charlie Company's Second Platoon as entering "My Lai 4 with guns blazing" (p. 50); more graphically, Lieutenant "Brooks and his men in the second platoon to the north had begun to systematically ransack the hamlet and slaughter the people, kill the livestock, and destroy the crops. Men poured rifle and machine-gun fire into huts without knowing—or seemingly caring—who was inside" (pp. 49–50).

Some atrocities toward the end of the action were part of an almost casual "mopping-up," much of which was the responsibility of Lieutenant LaCross's Third Platoon of Charlie Company. The Peers Report states: "The entire 3rd Platoon then began moving into the western edge of My Lai (4), for the mop-up operation. . . . The squad . . . began to burn the houses in the southwestern portion of the hamlet" (Goldstein et al., 1976, p. 133). They became mingled with other platoons during a series of rapes and killings of survivors for which it was impossible to fix responsibility. Certainly to a Vietnamese all GIs would by this point look alike: "Nineteen-year-old Nguyen Thi Ngoc Tuyet watched a baby trying to open her slain mother's blouse to nurse. A soldier shot the infant while it was struggling with the blouse, and then slashed it with his bayonet." Tuyet also said she saw another baby hacked to death by GIs wielding their bayonets. "Le Tong, a twenty-eight-year-old rice farmer, reported seeing one woman raped after GIs killed her children. Nguyen Khoa, a thirty-seven-year-old peasant, told of a thirteen-year-old girl who was raped before being killed. GIs then attacked Khoa's wife, tearing off her clothes. Before they could rape her, however, Khoa said, their six-year-old son, riddled with bullets, fell and saturated her with blood. The GIs left her alone" (Hersh, 1970, p. 72). All of Company C was implicated in a pattern of death and destruction throughout the hamlet, much of which seemingly lacked rhyme or reason.

But a substantial amount of the killing was *organized* and traceable to one authority: the First Platoon's Lt. William Calley. Calley was originally charged with 109 killings, almost all of them mass executions at the trail and other locations. He stood trial for 102 of these killings, was convicted of 22 in 1971, and at first received a life sentence. Though others—both superior and subordinate to Calley—were brought to trial, he was the only one convicted for the My Lai crimes. Thus, the only actions of My Lai for which *anyone* was ever convicted were mass executions, ordered and committed. We suspect that there are commonsense reasons why this one type of killing was singled out. In the midst of rapidly moving events with people running about, an execution of stationary targets is literally a still life that stands out and whose participants are clearly visible. It can be proven that specific people committed specific deeds. An execution, in contrast to the shooting of someone on the run, is also more likely to meet the legal definition of an act resulting from intent—with malice aforethought. Moreover, American military law specifically forbids the killing of unarmed civilians or military prisoners, as does the Geneva Convention between nations. Thus common sense, legal standards, and explicit doctrine all made such actions the likeliest target for prosecution.

When Lieutenant Calley was charged under military law it was for violation of the Uniform Code of Military Justice (UCMJ) Article 118 (murder). This article is similar to civilian codes in that it provides for conviction if an accused:

> without justification or excuse, unlawfully kills a human being, when he—
>
> 1. has a premeditated design to kill;
> 2. intends to kill or inflict great bodily harm;
> 3. is engaged in an act which is inherently dangerous to others and evinces a wanton disregard of human life; or
> 4. is engaged in the perpetration or attempted perpetration of burglary, sodomy, rape, robbery, or aggravated arson. (Goldstein et al., 1976, p. 507)

For a soldier, one legal justification for killing is warfare; but warfare is subject to many legal limits and restrictions, including, of course, the inadmissibility of killing unarmed noncombatants or prisoners whom one has disarmed. The pictures of the trail victims at My Lai certainly portrayed one or the other of these. Such an action would be illegal under military law; ordering another to commit such an action would be illegal; and following such an order would be illegal.

But following an order may provide a second and pivotal justification for an act that would be murder when committed by a civilian. American military law assumes that the subordinate is inclined to follow orders, as that is the normal obligation of the role. Hence, legally, obedient subordinates are protected from unreasonable expectations regarding their capacity to evaluate those orders:

> An order requiring the performance of a military duty may be inferred to be legal. An act performed manifestly beyond the scope of authority, or pursuant to an order that a man of ordinary sense and understanding would know to be illegal, or in a wanton manner in the discharge of a lawful duty, is not excusable. (Par. 216, Subpar. *d*, Manual for Courts Martial, United States, 1969 Rev.)

Thus what *may* be excusable is the good-faith carrying out of an order, as long as that order appears to the ordinary soldier to be a legal one. In military law, invoking superior orders moves the question from one of the action's consequences—the body count—to one of evaluating the actor's motives and good sense.

In sum, if anyone is to be brought to justice for a massacre, common sense and legal codes decree that the most appropriate targets are those who make themselves executioners. This is the kind of target the government selected in prosecuting Lieutenant Calley with the greatest fervor. And in a military context, the most promising way in which one can redefine one's undeniable deeds into acceptability is to invoke superior orders. This is what Calley did in attempting to avoid conviction. Since the core legal issues involved points of mass execution—the ditches and trail where America's image of My Lai was formed—we review these events in greater detail.

The day's quiet beginning has already been noted. Troops landed and swept unopposed into the village. The three weapons eventually reported as the haul from the operation were picked up from three apparent Viet Cong who fled the village when the troops arrived and were pursued and killed by helicopter gunships. Obviously the Viet Cong did frequent the area. But it appears that by about 8:00 A.M. no one who met the troops was aggressive, and no one was armed. By the laws of war Charlie Company had no argument with such people.

As they moved into the village, the soldiers began to gather its inhabitants together. Shortly after 8:00 A.M. Lieutenant Calley told Pfc. Paul Meadlo that "you know what to do with" a group of villagers Meadlo was guarding. Estimates of the numbers in the group ranged as high as eighty women, children, and old men, and Meadlo's own estimate under oath was thirty to fifty people. As Meadlo later testified, Calley returned after ten or fifteen minutes: "He [Calley] said, 'How come they're not dead?' I said, 'I didn't know we were supposed to kill them.' He said, ''I want them dead.' He backed off twenty or thirty feet and started shooting into the people—the Viet Cong—shooting automatic. He was beside me. He burned four or five magazines. I burned off a few, about three. I helped shoot 'em" (Hammer, 1971, p. 155). Meadlo himself and others testified that Meadlo cried as he fired; others reported him later to be sobbing and "all broke up." It would appear that to Lieutenant Calley's subordinates something was unusual, and stressful, in these orders.

At the trial, the first specification in the murder charge against Calley was for this incident; he was accused of premeditated murder of "an unknown number, not less than 30, Oriental human beings, males and females of various ages, whose names are unknown, occupants of the village of My Lai 4, by means of shooting them with a rifle" (Goldstein et al., 1976, p. 497).

Among the helicopters flying reconnaissance above Son My was that of CWO Hugh Thompson. By 9:00 or soon after, Thompson had noticed some horrifying events from his perch. As he spotted wounded civilians, he sent down smoke markers so that soldiers on the ground could treat them. They killed them instead. He reported to headquarters, trying to persuade someone to stop what was going on. Barker, hearing the message, called down to Captain Medina. Medina, in turn, later claimed to have told Calley that it was "enough for today." But it was not yet enough.

At Calley's orders, his men began gathering the remaining villagers—roughly seventy-five individuals, mostly women and children—and herding them toward a drainage ditch. Accompanied by three or four enlisted men, Lieutenant Calley executed several batches of civilians who had been gathered into ditches. Some of the details of the process were entered into testimony in such accounts as Pfc. Dennis Conti's: "A lot of them, the people, were trying to get up and mostly they was just screaming and pretty bad shot up. . . . I seen a woman tried to get up. I seen Lieutenant

Calley fire. He hit the side of her head and blew it off" (Hammer, 1971, p. 125).

Testimony by other soldiers presented the shooting's aftermath. Specialist Four Charles Hall, asked by Prosecutor Aubrey Daniel how he knew the people in the ditch were dead, said: "There was blood coming from them. They were just scattered all over the ground in the ditch, some in piles and some scattered out 20, 25 meters perhaps up the ditch. . . . They were very old people, very young children, and mothers. . . . There was blood all over them" (Goldstein et al., 1976, pp. 501–502). And Pfc. Gregory Olsen corroborated the general picture of the victims: "They were—the majority were women and children, some babies. I distinctly remember one middle-aged Vietnamese male dressed in white right at my feet as I crossed. None of the bodies were mangled in any way. There was blood. Some appeared to be dead, others followed me with their eyes as I walked across the ditch" (Goldstein et al., 1976, p. 502).

The second specification in the murder charge stated that Calley did "with premeditation, murder an unknown number of Oriental human beings, not less than seventy, males and females of various ages, whose names are unknown, occupants of the village of My Lai 4, by means of shooting them with a rifle" (Goldstein et al., 1976, p. 497). Calley was also charged with and tried for shootings of individuals (an old man and a child); these charges were clearly supplemental to the main issue at trial—the mass killings and how they came about.

It is noteworthy that during these executions more than one enlisted man avoided carrying out Calley's orders, and more than one, by sworn oath, directly refused to obey them. For example, Pfc. James Joseph Dursi testified, when asked if he fired when Lieutenant Calley ordered him to: "No I just stood there. Meadlo turned to me after a couple of minutes and said 'Shoot! Why don't you shoot! Why don't you fire!' He was crying and yelling. I said, 'I can't! I won't!' And the people were screaming and crying and yelling. They kept firing for a couple of minutes, mostly automatic and semi-automatic" (Hammer, 1971, p. 143). . . .

Disobedience of Lieutenant Calley's own orders to kill represented a serious legal and moral threat to a defense *based* on superior orders, such as Calley was attempting. This defense had to assert that the orders seemed reasonable enough to carry out; that they appeared to be legal orders. Even if the orders in question were not legal, the defense had to assert that an ordinary individual could not and should not be expected to see the distinction. In short, if what happened was "business as usual," even though it might be bad business, then the defendant stood a chance of acquittal. But under direct command from "Surfside 5½," some ordinary enlisted men managed to refuse, to avoid, or at least to stop doing what they were ordered to do. As "reasonable men" of "ordinary sense and understanding," they had apparently found something awry that morning; and it would have been hard for an officer to plead successfully that he was more ordinary than his men in his capacity to evaluate the reasonableness of orders.

Even those who obeyed Calley's orders showed great stress. For example, Meadlo eventually began to argue and cry directly in front of Calley. Pfc. Herbert Carter shot himself in the foot, possibly because he could no longer take what he was doing. We were not destined to hear a sworn version of the incident, since neither side at the Calley trial called him to testify.

The most unusual instance of resistance to authority came from the skies. CWO Hugh Thompson, who had protested the apparent carnage of civilians, was Calley's inferior in rank but was not in his line of command. He was also watching the ditch from his helicopter and noticed some people moving after the first round of slaughter—chiefly children who had been shielded by their mothers' bodies. Landing to rescue the wounded, he also found some villagers hiding in a nearby bunker. Protecting the Vietnamese with his own body, Thompson ordered his men to train their guns on the Americans and to open fire if the Americans fired on the Vietnamese. He then radioed for additional rescue helicopters and stood between the Vietnamese and the Americans under Calley's command until the Vietnamese could be evacuated. He later returned to the ditch to unearth a child buried, unharmed, beneath layers of bodies. In October 1969, Thompson was awarded the Distinguished Flying Cross for heroism at My Lai, specifically

(albeit inaccurately) for the rescue of children hiding in a bunker "between Viet Cong forces and advancing friendly forces" and for the rescue of a wounded child "caught in the intense crossfire" (Hersh, 1970, p. 119). Four months earlier, at the Pentagon, Thompson had identified Calley as having been at the ditch.

By about 10:00 A.M., the massacre was winding down. The remaining actions consisted largely of isolated rapes and killings, "clean-up" shootings of the wounded, and the destruction of the village by fire. We have already seen some examples of these more indiscriminate and possibly less premeditated acts. By the 11:00 A.M. lunch break, when the exhausted men of Company C were relaxing, two young girls wandered back from a hiding place only to be invited to share lunch. This surrealist touch illustrates the extent to which the soldiers' action had become dissociated from its meaning. An hour earlier, some of these men were making sure that not even a child would escape the executioner's bullet. But now the job was done and it was time for lunch—and in this new context it seemed only natural to ask the children who had managed to escape execution to join them. The massacre had ended. It remained only for the Viet Cong to reap the political rewards among the survivors in hiding.

The army command in the area knew that something had gone wrong. Direct commanders, including Lieutenant Colonel Barker, had firsthand reports, such as Thompson's complaints. Others had such odd bits of evidence as the claim of 128 Viet Cong dead with a booty of only three weapons. But the cover-up of My Lai began at once. The operation was reported as a victory over a stronghold of the Viet Cong Forty-eighth. . . .

William Calley was not the only man tried for the event at My Lai. The actions of over thirty soldiers and civilians were scrutinized by investigators; over half of these had to face charges or disciplinary action of some sort. Targets of investigation included Captain Medina, who was tried, and various higher-ups, including General Koster. But Lieutenant Calley was the only person convicted, the only person to serve time.

The core of Lieutenant Calley's defense was superior orders. What this meant to him—in contrast to what it meant to the judge and jury—can be gleaned from his responses to a series of questions from his defense attorney, George Latimer, in which Calley sketched out his understanding of the laws of war and the actions that constitute doing one's duty within those laws:

Latimer: Did you receive any training which had to do with the obedience to orders?

Calley: Yes, sir.

Latimer: . . . what were you informed [were] the principles involved in that field?

Calley: That all orders were to be assumed legal, that the soldier's job was to carry out any order given him to the best of his ability.

Latimer: . . . what might occur if you disobeyed an order by a senior officer?

Calley: You could be court-martialed for refusing an order and refusing an order in the face of the enemy, you could be sent to death, sir.

Latimer: [I am asking] whether you were required in any way, shape or form to make a determination of the legality or illegality of an order?

Calley: No, sir. I was never told that I had the choice, sir.

Latimer: If you had a doubt about the order, what were you supposed to do?

Calley: . . . I was supposed to carry the order out and then come back and make my complaint. (Hammer, 1971, pp. 240–241)

Lieutenant Calley steadfastly maintained that his actions within My Lai had constituted, in his mind, carrying out orders from Captain Medina. Both his own actions and the orders he gave to others (such as the instruction to Meadlo to "waste 'em") were entirely in response to superior orders. He denied any intent to kill individuals and any but the most passing awareness of distinctions among the individuals: "I was ordered to go in there and destroy the enemy. That was my job on that day. That was the mission I was given. I did not sit down and think in terms of men, women, and children. They were all classified the same, and that was the classification that we dealt with, just as enemy soldiers." When Latimer asked if in his own

opinion Calley had acted "rightly and according to your understanding of your directions and orders," Calley replied, "I felt then and I still do that I acted as I was directed, and I carried out the orders that I was given, and I do not feel wrong in doing so, sir" (Hammer, 1971, p. 257).

His court-martial did not accept Calley's defense of superior orders and clearly did not share his interpretation of his duty. The jury evidently reasoned that, even if there had been orders to destroy everything in sight and to "waste the Vietnamese," any reasonable person would have realized that such orders were illegal and should have refused to carry them out. The defense of superior orders under such conditions is inadmissible under international and military law. The U.S. Army's *Law of Land Warfare* (Dept. of the Army, 1956), for example, states that "the fact that the law of war has been violated pursuant to an order of a superior authority, whether military or civil, does not deprive the act in question of its character of a war crime, nor does it constitute a defense in the trial of an accused individual, unless he did not know and could not reasonably have been expected to know that the act was unlawful" and that "members of the armed forces are bound to obey only lawful orders" (in Falk et al., 1971, pp. 71–72).

The disagreement between Calley and the court-martial seems to have revolved around the definition of the responsibilities of a subordinate to obey, on the one hand, and to evaluate, on the other. This tension . . . can best be captured via the charge to the jury in the Calley court-martial, made by the trial judge, Col. Reid Kennedy. The forty-one pages of the charge include the following:

Both combatants captured by and noncombatants detained by the opposing force . . . have the right to be treated as prisoners. . . . Summary execution of detainees or prisoners is forbidden by law. . . . I therefore instruct you . . . that if unresisting human beings were killed at My Lai (4) while within the effective custody and control of our military forces, their deaths cannot be considered justified. . . . Thus if you find that Lieutenant Calley received an order directing him to kill unresisting Vietnamese within his control or within the control of his troops, *that order would be an illegal order.*

A determination that an order is illegal does not, of itself, assign criminal responsibility to the person following the order for acts done in compliance with it. Soldiers are taught to follow orders, and special attention is given to obedience of orders on the battlefield. Military effectiveness depends on obedience to orders. On the other hand, the obedience of a soldier is not the obedience of an automaton. A soldier is a reasoning agent, obliged to respond, not as a machine, but as a person. The law takes these factors into account in assessing criminal responsibility for acts done in compliance with illegal orders.

The acts of a subordinate done in compliance with an unlawful order given him by his superior are excused and impose no criminal liability upon him unless the superior's order is one which a man of *ordinary sense and understanding* would, under the circumstances, know to be unlawful, or if the order in question is actually known to the accused to be unlawful. (Goldstein et al., 1976, pp. 525–526; emphasis added)

By this definition, subordinates take part in a balancing act, one tipped toward obedience but tempered by "ordinary sense and understanding."

A jury of combat veterans proceeded to convict William Calley of the premeditated murder of no less than twenty-two human beings. (The army, realizing some unfortunate connotations in referring to the victims as "Oriental human beings," eventually referred to them as "human beings.") Regarding the first specification in the murder charge, the bodies on the trail, [Calley] was convicted of premeditated murder of not less than one person. (Medical testimony had been able to pinpoint only one person whose wounds as revealed in Haeberle's photos were sure to be immediately fatal.) Regarding the second specification, the bodies in the ditch, Calley was convicted of the premeditated murder of not less than twenty human beings. Regarding additional specifications that he had killed an old man and a child,

Calley was convicted of premeditated murder in the first case and of assault with intent to commit murder in the second.

Lieutenant Calley was initially sentenced to life imprisonment. That sentence was reduced: first to twenty years, eventually to ten (the latter by Secretary of Defense Callaway in 1974). Calley served three years before being released on bond. The time was spent under house arrest in his apartment, where he was able to receive visits from his girlfriend. He was granted parole on September 10, 1975.

Sanctioned Massacres

The slaughter at My Lai is an instance of a class of violent acts that can be described as sanctioned massacres (Kelman, 1973): acts of indiscriminate, ruthless, and often systematic mass violence, carried out by military or paramilitary personnel while engaged in officially sanctioned campaigns, the victims of which are defenseless and unresisting civilians, including old men, women, and children. Sanctioned massacres have occurred throughout history. Within American history, My Lai had its precursors in the Philippine war around the turn of the century (Schirmer, 1971) and in the massacres of American Indians. Elsewhere in the world, one recalls the Nazis' "final solution" for European Jews, the massacres and deportations of Armenians by Turks, the liquidation of the kulaks and the great purges in the Soviet Union, and more recently the massacres in Indonesia and Bangladesh, in Biafra and Burundi, in South Africa and Mozambique, in Cambodia and Afghanistan, in Syria and Lebanon. . . .

The occurrence of sanctioned massacres cannot be adequately explained by the existence of psychological forces—whether these be characterological dispositions to engage in murderous violence or profound hostility against the target—so powerful that they must find expression in violent acts unhampered by moral restraints. Instead, the major instigators for this class of violence derive from the policy process. The question that really calls for psychological analysis is why so many people are willing to formulate, participate in, and condone policies that call for the mass killings of defenseless civilians. Thus it is more instructive to look not at the motives for violence but at the conditions under which the usual moral inhibitions against violence become weakened. Three social processes that tend to create such conditions can be identified: authorization, routinization, and dehumanization. Through authorization, the situation becomes so defined that the individual is absolved of the responsibility to make personal moral choices. Through routinization, the action becomes so organized that there is no opportunity for raising moral questions. Through dehumanization, the actors' attitudes toward the target and toward themselves become so structured that it is neither necessary nor possible for them to view the relationship in moral terms.

Authorization

Sanctioned massacres by definition occur in the context of an authority situation, a situation in which, at least for many of the participants, the moral principles that generally govern human relationships do not apply. Thus, when acts of violence are explicitly ordered, implicitly encouraged, tacitly approved, or at least permitted by legitimate authorities, people's readiness to commit or condone them is enhanced. That such acts are authorized seems to carry automatic justification for them. Behaviorally, authorization obviates the necessity of making judgments or choices. Not only do normal moral principles become inoperative, but—particularly when the actions are explicitly ordered—a different kind of morality, linked to the duty to obey superior orders, tends to take over.

In an authority situation, individuals characteristically feel obligated to obey the orders of the authorities, whether or not these correspond with their personal preferences. They see themselves as having no choice as long as they accept the legitimacy of the orders and of the authorities who give them. Individuals differ considerably in the degree to which—and the conditions under which—they are prepared to challenge the legitimacy of an order on the grounds that the order itself is illegal, or that those giving it have overstepped their authority, or that it stems from a policy that violates fundamental societal values. Regardless of

such individual differences, however, the basic structure of a situation of legitimate authority requires subordinates to respond in terms of their role obligations rather than their personal preferences; they can openly disobey only by challenging the legitimacy of the authority. Often people obey without question even though the behavior they engage in may entail great personal sacrifice or great harm to others.

An important corollary of the basic structure of the authority situation is that actors often do not see themselves as personally responsible for the consequences of their actions. Again, there are individual differences, depending on actors' capacity and readiness to evaluate the legitimacy of orders received. Insofar as they see themselves as having had no choice in their actions, however, they do not feel personally responsible for them. They were not personal agents, but merely extensions of the authority. Thus, when their actions cause harm to others, they can feel relatively free of guilt. A similar mechanism operates when a person engages in antisocial behavior that was not ordered by the authorities but was tacitly encouraged and approved by them—even if only by making it clear that such behavior will not be punished. In this situation, behavior that was formerly illegitimate is legitimized by the authorities' acquiescence.

In the My Lai massacre, it is likely that the structure of the authority situation contributed to the massive violence in both ways—that is, by conveying the message that acts of violence against Vietnamese villagers were *required,* as well as the message that such acts, even if not ordered, were *permitted* by the authorities in charge. The actions at My Lai represented, at least in some respects, responses to explicit or implicit orders. Lieutenant Calley indicated, by orders and by example, that he wanted large numbers of villagers killed. Whether Calley himself had been ordered by his superiors to "waste" the whole area, as he claimed, remains a matter of controversy. Even if we assume, however, that he was not explicitly ordered to wipe out the village, he had reason to believe that such actions were expected by his superior officers. Indeed, the very nature of the war conveyed this expectation. The principal measure of military success was the "body count"—the number of enemy soldiers killed—and any Vietnamese killed by the U.S. military was commonly defined as a "Viet Cong." Thus, it was not totally bizarre for Calley to believe that what he was doing at My Lai was to increase his body count, as any good officer was expected to do.

Even to the extent that the actions at My Lai occurred spontaneously, without reference to superior orders, those committing them had reason to assume that such actions might be tacitly approved of by the military authorities. Not only had they failed to punish such acts in most cases, but the very strategies and tactics that the authorities consistently devised were based on the proposition that the civilian population of South Vietnam—whether "hostile" or "friendly"—was expendable. Such policies as search-and-destroy missions, the establishment of free-shooting zones, the use of antipersonnel weapons, the bombing of entire villages if they were suspected of harboring guerrillas, the forced migration of masses of the rural population, and the defoliation of vast forest areas helped legitimize acts of massive violence of the kind occurring at My Lai.

Some of the actions at My Lai suggest an orientation to authority based on unquestioning obedience to superior orders, no matter how destructive the actions these orders call for. Such obedience is specifically fostered in the course of military training and reinforced by the structure of the military authority situation. It also reflects, however, an ideological orientation that may be more widespread in the general population. . . .

Routinization

Authorization processes create a situation in which people become involved in an action without considering its implications and without really making a decision. Once they have taken the initial step, they are in a new psychological and social situation in which the pressures to continue are powerful. As Lewin (1947) has pointed out, many forces that might originally have kept people out of a situation reverse direction once they have made a commitment (once they have gone through the "gate region") and now serve to keep them in the situation. For example, concern about

the criminal nature of an action, which might originally have inhibited a person from becoming involved, may now lead to deeper involvement in efforts to justify the action and to avoid negative consequences.

Despite these forces, however, given the nature of the actions involved in sanctioned massacres, one might still expect moral scruples to intervene; but the likelihood of moral resistance is greatly reduced by transforming the action into routine, mechanical, highly programmed operations. Routinization fulfills two functions. First, it reduces the necessity of making decisions, thus minimizing the occasions in which moral questions may arise. Second, it makes it easier to avoid the implications of the action, since the actor focuses on the details of the job rather than on its meaning. The latter effect is more readily achieved among those who participate in sanctioned massacres from a distance—from their desks or even from the cockpits of their bombers.

Routinization operates both at the level of the individual actor and at the organizational level. Individual job performance is broken down into a series of discrete steps, most of them carried out in automatic, regularized fashion. It becomes easy to forget the nature of the product that emerges from this process. When Lieutenant Calley said of My Lai that it was "no great deal," he probably implied that it was all in a day's work. Organizationally, the task is divided among different offices, each of which has responsibility for a small portion of it. This arrangement diffuses responsibility and limits the amount and scope of decision making that is necessary. There is no expectation that the moral implications will be considered at any of these points, nor is there any opportunity to do so. The organizational processes also help further legitimize the actions of each participant. By proceeding in routine fashion—processing papers, exchanging memos, diligently carrying out their assigned tasks—the different units mutually reinforce each other in the view that what is going on must be perfectly normal, correct, and legitimate. The shared illusion that they are engaged in a legitimate enterprise helps the participants assimilate their activities to other purposes, such as the efficiency of their performance, the productivity of their unit, or the cohesiveness of their group (see Janis, 1972).

Normalization of atrocities is more difficult to the extent that there are constant reminders of the true meaning of the enterprise. Bureaucratic inventiveness in the use of language helps to cover up such meaning. For example, the SS had a set of *Sprachregelungen,* or "language rules," to govern descriptions of their extermination program. As Arendt (1964) points out, the term *language rule* in itself was "a code name; it meant what in ordinary language would be called a lie" (p. 85). The code names for killing and liquidation were "final solution," "evacuation," and "special treatment." The war in Indochina produced its own set of euphemisms, such as "protective reaction," "pacification," and "forced-draft urbanization and modernization." The use of euphemisms allows participants in sanctioned massacres to differentiate their actions from ordinary killing and destruction and thus to avoid confronting their true meaning.

Dehumanization

Authorization processes override standard moral considerations; routinization processes reduce the likelihood that such considerations will arise. Still, the inhibitions against murdering one's fellow human beings are generally so strong that the victims must also be stripped of their human status if they are to be subjected to systematic killing. Insofar as they are dehumanized, the usual principles of morality no longer apply to them.

Sanctioned massacres become possible to the extent that the victims are deprived in the perpetrators' eyes of the two qualities essential to being perceived as fully human and included in the moral compact that governs human relationships: *identity*—standing as independent, distinctive individuals, capable of making choices and entitled to live their own lives—and *community*—fellow membership in an interconnected network of individuals who care for each other and respect each other's individuality and rights (Kelman, 1973; see also Bakan, 1966, for a related distinction between "agency" and "communion"). Thus, when a group of people is defined entirely in terms of a category to which they belong, and

when this category is excluded from the human family, moral restraints against killing them are more readily overcome.

Dehumanization of the enemy is a common phenomenon in any war situation. Sanctioned massacres, however, presuppose a more extreme degree of dehumanization, insofar as the killing is not in direct response to the target's threats or provocations. It is not what they have done that marks such victims for death but who they are—the category to which they happen to belong. They are the victims of policies that regard their systematic destruction as a desirable end or an acceptable means. Such extreme dehumanization becomes possible when the target group can readily be identified as a separate category of people who have historically been stigmatized and excluded by the victimizers; often the victims belong to a distinct racial, religious, ethnic, or political group regarded as inferior or sinister. The traditions, the habits, the images, and the vocabularies for dehumanizing such groups are already well established and can be drawn upon when the groups are selected for massacre. Labels help deprive the victims of identity and community, as in the epithet "gooks" that was commonly used to refer to Vietnamese and other Indochinese peoples.

The dynamics of the massacre process itself further increase the participants' tendency to dehumanize their victims. Those who participate as part of the bureaucratic apparatus increasingly come to see their victims as bodies to be counted and entered into their reports, as faceless figures that will determine their productivity rates and promotions. Those who participate in the massacre directly—in the field, as it were—are reinforced in their perception of the victims as less than human by observing their very victimization. The only way they can justify what is being done to these people—both by others and by themselves—and the only way they can extract some degree of meaning out of the absurd events in which they find themselves participating (see Lifton, 1971, 1973) is by coming to believe that the victims are subhuman and deserve to be rooted out. And thus the process of dehumanization feeds on itself.

REFERENCES

Arendt, H. (1964). *Eichmann in Jerusalem: A report on the banality of evil.* New York: Viking Press.

Bakan, D. (1966). *The duality of human existence.* Chicago: Rand McNally.

Department of the Army. (1956). *The law of land warfare* (Field Manual, No. 27-10). Washington, D.C.: U.S. Government Printing Office.

Falk, R. A.; Kolko, G.; & Lifton, R. J. (Eds.). (1971). *Crimes of war.* New York: Vintage Books.

French, P. (Ed.). (1972). *Individual and collective responsibility: The massacre at My Lai.* Cambridge, Mass.: Schenkman.

Goldstein, J.; Marshall, B.; & Schwartz, J. (Eds.). (1976). *The My Lai massacre and its cover-up: Beyond the reach of law?* (The Peers report with a supplement and introductory essay on the limits of law). New York: Free Press.

Hammer, R. (1971). *The court-martial of Lt. Calley.* New York: Coward, McCann, & Geoghegan.

Hersh, S. (1970). *My Lai 4: A report on the massacre and its aftermath.* New York: Vintage Books.

_____. (1972). *Cover-up.* New York: Random House.

Janis, I. L. (1972). *Victims of groupthink: A psychological study of foreign-policy decisions and fiascoes.* Boston: Houghton Mifflin.

Kelman, H. C. (1973). Violence without moral restraint: Reflections on the dehumanization of victims and victimizers. *Journal of Social Issues, 29*(4), 25–61.

Lewin, K. (1947). Group decision and social change. In T. M. Newcomb & E. L. Hartley (Eds.), *Readings in social psychology.* New York: Holt.

Lifton, R. J. (1971). Existential evil. In N. Sanford, C. Comstock, & Associates, *Sanctions for evil: Sources of social destructiveness.* San Francisco: Jossey-Bass.

_____. (1973). *Home from the war—Vietnam veterans: Neither victims nor executioners.* New York: Simon & Schuster.

Manual for courts martial, United States (rev. ed.). (1969). Washington, D.C.: U.S. Government Printing Office.

Schirmer, D. B. (1971, April 24). My Lai was not the first time. *New Republic,* pp. 18–21.

Williams, B. (1985, April 14–15). "I will never forgive," says My Lai survivor. *Jordan Times* (Amman), p. 4.

The Credit Card
Private Troubles and Public Issues

George Ritzer

The credit card has become an American icon. It is treasured, even worshipped, in the United States and, increasingly, throughout the rest of the world. . . . The credit card expresses something about the essence of modern American society and, like an express train, is speeding across the world's landscape delivering American (and more generally consumer) culture. My goal . . . is to explain what the credit card tells us, both good and (mainly) bad, about the essence of modern America as well as why and how the credit card is helping to transform much of the world.

The credit card is not the first symbol of American culture to play such a role, nor will it be the last. Other important contemporary American icons include Coca-Cola, Levi's, Marlboro, Disney, and McDonald's. What they have in common is that, like credit cards, they are products at the very heart of American society, and they are highly valued by, and have had a profound effect on, many other societies throughout the world. However, the credit card is distinctive because it is a means that can be used to obtain those other icons, as well as virtually anything else available in the world's marketplaces. It is because of this greater versatility that the credit card may prove to be the most important American icon of all. If nothing else, it is likely to continue to exist long after other icons have become footnotes in the history of American culture. When the United States has an entirely new set of icons, the credit card will remain an important means for obtaining them. . . .

The Advantages of Credit Cards

. . . The most notable advantage of credit cards, at least at the societal level, is that they permit people to spend more than they have. Credit cards thereby allow the economy to function at a much higher (and faster) level than it might if it relied solely on cash and cash-based instruments.

Credit cards also have a number of specific advantages to consumers, especially in comparison to using cash for transactions:

- Credit cards increase our spending power, thereby allowing us to enjoy a more expansive, even luxurious, lifestyle.

- Credit cards save us money by permitting us to take advantage of sales, something that might not be possible if we had to rely on cash on hand.

- Credit cards are convenient. They can be used 24 hours a day to charge expenditures by phone, mail, or home computer.* Thus, we need no longer be inconvenienced by the fact that most shops and malls close overnight. Those whose mobility is limited or who are housebound can also still shop.

- Credit cards can be used virtually anywhere in the world, whereas cash (and certainly checks) cannot so easily cross national borders. For

---

*The latter will soon become more convenient with the development of a generally available method of charging purchases in cyberspace. See John Markoff. "A Credit Card for On-Line Sprees." *New York Times,* October 15, 1994, pp. 37, 39.

example, we are able to travel from Paris to Rome on the spur of the moment in the middle of the night without worrying about whether we have, or will be able to obtain on arrival, Italian lira.

■ Credit cards smooth out consumption by allowing us to make purchases even when our incomes are low. If we happen to be laid off, we can continue to live the same lifestyle, at least for a time, with the anticipation that we will pay off our credit card balances when we are called back to work. We can make emergency purchases (of medicine, for example) even though we may have no cash on hand.

■ Credit cards allow us to do a better job of organizing our finances, because we are provided each month with a clear accounting of expenditures and of money due.

■ Credit cards may yield itemized invoices of tax-deductible expenses, giving us systematic records at tax time.

■ Credit cards allow us to refuse to pay a disputed bill while the credit card company investigates the transaction. Credit card receipts also help us in disputes with merchants.

■ Credit cards give us the option of paying our bills all at once or of stretching payments out over a length of time.

■ Credit cards are safer to carry than cash is and thus help to reduce cash-based crime.[1]

Of course, credit cards also carry advantages to merchants. Merchants who accept credit cards are, for example, likely to gain a great deal of business they would not otherwise get. And, unlike cash in the till, credit card receipts are not magnets for thieves.

Then there are the comparative disadvantages associated with cash and checks. For example, cash is far more transient than credit cards and can therefore more easily be stolen, lost, destroyed, or simply worn out. It is also not as portable as credit cards because it is bulky, especially in large amounts, and it is not easily used in other countries. Finally, to run a cash economy—to "print, mint, replace, circulate, protect" money—costs a great deal.[2] In contrast, credit cards have no direct

cost to the state. The credit card companies foot the bills out of profits derived from their credit card business.

Checks have even greater problems. They, too, can be stolen, lost, destroyed, or (less likely) worn out. Forgery is an ever-present problem with checks. Checks are also awkward to use. For example, each check must be written out individually, many places do not honor checks, and even those that do frequently require one or more forms of identification.

Credit card use has boomed because of its advantages as well as the disadvantages of its main competitors—cash and checks. However, cash and checks do have some advantages over credit cards. For example, cash and often checks can be used at no cost to the consumer, whereas credit cards often end up entailing substantial expense. More important, cash and checks avoid many of the social problems associated with credit cards.

A Key Problem with Credit Cards

In the course of the twentieth century, the United States has gone from a nation that cherished savings to one that reveres spending, even spending beyond one's means. As one European observer of America noted,

> If Americans were now to stop spending what they have not got their whole economy would falter. It is only by mortgaging their futures they avoid bankruptcy. Thrift, so highly regarded by an earlier generation of Americans, has become a dirty word. Not to live beyond your immediate means is antisocial.[3]

At one time, debt was something to be avoided at all costs, but today people seem to be rushing into debt as quickly and as deeply as possible. Instead of being measured by the amount of money we have in the bank, we are likely to be evaluated on the basis of how far we have plunged into debt. The status symbol of an ever-increasing bank balance has been replaced by efforts to impress our friends with the magnitude of our mortgage loans and home equity lines of credit, as well as the number of credit cards we possess and their upper limits.

At the level of the national government, our addiction to spending is manifest in a once-unimaginable level of national debt, the enormous growth rate of that debt, and the widespread belief that the national debt cannot be significantly reduced, let alone eliminated. As a percentage of gross national product (GNP),* the federal debt declined rather steadily after World War II, reaching 33.3% in 1981. However, it then rose dramatically, reaching almost 73% of GNP in 1992. In dollar terms, the federal debt was just under $1 trillion in 1981, but by September 1993, it had more than quadrupled, to over $4.4 trillion.[4] There is widespread fear that a huge and growing federal debt may bankrupt the nation and a near consensus that it will adversely affect future generations.

Our addiction to spending is also apparent among the aggregate of American citizens. Total personal savings was less in 1991 than in 1984, in spite of the fact that the population was much larger in 1991. Savings fell again in the early 1990s from about 5.2% of disposable income in late 1992 to approximately 4% in early 1994.[5] A far smaller percentage of families (43.5%) had savings accounts in 1989 than did in 1983 (61.7%).[6] And the citizens of many other nations have a far higher savings rate. At the same time, our indebtedness to banks, mortgage companies, credit card firms, and so on is increasing far more dramatically than similar indebtedness in other nations.

Dwindling or nonexistent savings accounts are a big problem for individual Americans. Most people have little or no financial reserves to sustain them if they should find themselves unemployed and without steady income. In other words, most people are able to survive only from paycheck to paycheck. Many of those same people owe comparatively large sums of money to banks, mortgage companies, and credit card firms ($777.3 billion altogether in 1991, as compared

to $350.3 billion in 1980).[7] With little or nothing in the way of savings, such people are likely to descend rapidly into delinquency and ultimately bankruptcy if they should lose their jobs. In fact, many have plunged so deeply into debt that they are in danger of being forced into bankruptcy even while they are employed.

Who Is to Blame?

The choking level of indebtedness that faces the federal government (as well as state and local governments), the aggregate of Americans, and many individual Americans is a significant problem. Who is to blame for this situation? The main suspects are the individual, the government, business, and banks and other financial institutions.

The Individual

In a society that is inclined to "psychologize" all problems, we are likely to blame individuals for not saving enough, for spending too much, and for not putting sufficient pressure on officials to restrain government expenditures. We also tend to "medicalize" these problems, blaming them on conditions that are thought to exist within the individual.[8] One clinical psychologist noted, "Just about everyone [I treat] who has an eating disorder—bulimia, bulimarexia or just plain overeating, or who has a drug problem—also has the spending disorder."[9] Although there are elements of truth to psychologistic and medicalistic perspectives, there is also a strong element of what sociologists term "blaming the victim." That is, although individuals bear some of the responsibility for not saving, for accumulating mounting debt, and for permitting their elected officials to spend far more than the government takes in, in the main individuals have been victimized by a social and financial system that discourages saving and encourages indebtedness.

Why are we so inclined to psychologize and medicalize problems like indebtedness? For one thing, American culture strongly emphasizes individualism. We tend to trace both success and failure to individual efforts, not larger social conditions. For another, large social and financial systems expend a great deal of time, energy, and

*While the term *GNP* is still used for historical proposes, it should be noted that the term *GDP* (gross domestic product) is now preferred. See Gary E. Clayton and Martin Gerhard Giesbrecht, *A Guide to Everyday Economic Statistics.* New York: McGraw-Hill, 1992.

money seeking, often successfully, to convince us that they are not responsible for society's problems. Individuals lack the ability and the resources to similarly "pass the buck." Of perhaps greatest importance, however, is the fact that individual, especially medical, problems appear to be amenable to treatment and even seem curable. In contrast, large-scale social problems (pollution, for example) seem far more intractable. It is for these, as well as many other reasons, that American society has a strong tendency to blame individuals for social problems.

The Government

Where does the responsibility for high levels of indebtedness lie if individuals are not the main culprits? We can begin with the federal government, which is seemingly unable and certainly unwilling to restrain its own spending. As a result, it is forced to tax at a high level and thereby to drain funds from individuals that otherwise could be used to increase personal savings and to draw down debt. Since the federal debt binge began in 1981, the government has also been responsible for creating a climate in which financial imprudence seems acceptable. After all, the public is led to feel, if it is acceptable for the government to live beyond its means, why can't individual citizens do the same? If the government can seemingly go on borrowing without facing the consequences of its debt, why can't individuals?

If the federal government truly wanted to address society's problems, it could clearly do far more both to encourage individual savings and to discourage individual debt. For example, the government could lower the taxes on income from savings accounts or even make such income tax-free. Or it could levy higher taxes on organizations and agencies that encourage individual indebtedness. The government could also do more to control and restrain the debt-creating and debt-increasing activities of the credit card industry.

Business

Although some of the blame for society's debt and savings problem must be placed on the federal government, the bulk of the responsibility belongs with those organizations and agencies associated with our consumer society that do all

they can to get people to spend not only all of their income but also to plunge into debt in as many ways, and as deeply, as possible. We can begin with American business.

Those in manufacturing, retailing, advertising, and marketing (among others) devote their working hours and a large portion of their energies to figuring out ways of getting people to buy things that they probably do not need and that many of them cannot afford. There is no need to reiterate here historic criticisms of these key elements of the capitalistic system, but it might be worth noting a few of the more recent developments. One example is the dramatic proliferation of seductive catalogs that are mailed to our homes. Another is the advent and remarkable growth in popularity of the television home shopping networks. What these two developments have in common is their ability to allow us to spend our money quickly and efficiently without ever leaving our homes. Because the credit card is the preferred way to pay for goods purchased through these outlets, catalogs and home shopping networks also help us increase our level of indebtedness.

Banks and Other Financial Institutions

The historical mission of banks was to encourage savings and discourage debt. Today, however, banks and other financial institutions lead us away from savings and in the direction of debt. Saving is discouraged by, most importantly, the low interest rates paid by banks. It seems foolish to people to put their money in the bank at an interest rate of, say, 2.5% and then to pay taxes on the interest, thereby lowering the real rate of return to 2% or even less. This practice seems especially asinine when the inflation rate is, for example, 3% or 4%. Under such conditions, the saver's money is declining in value with each passing year. It seems obvious to most people that they are better off spending the money before it has a chance to lose any more value.

While banks are discouraging savings, they are in various ways encouraging debt. One good example is the high level of competition among the banks (and other financial institutions) to offer home equity lines of credit to consumers. As the name suggests, such lines of credit allow people to borrow against the equity they have built up in their homes. If one owns a $200,000 home but owes the bank only $120,000 on the mortgage, then one has $80,000 of equity in the house. Banks eagerly lend people money against this equity. Leaving the equity in the house is a kind of savings that appreciates with the value of the real estate, but borrowing against it allows people to buy more goods and services. In the process, however, they acquire a large new debt. And the house itself could be lost if one is unable to pay either the original mortgage or the home equity loan.

The credit card is yet another invention of the banks and other financial institutions to get people to save less and spend more. In the past, only the relatively well-to-do were able to get credit, and getting credit was a very cumbersome process (involving letters of credit, for example). Credit cards democratized credit, making it possible for the masses to obtain at least a minimal amount. Credit cards are also far easier to use than predecessors like letters of credit. Credit cards may thus be seen as convenient mechanisms whereby banks and other financial institutions can lend large numbers of people what collectively amounts to an enormous amount of money.

Normally, no collateral is needed to apply for a credit card.[10] The money advanced by the credit card firms can be seen as borrowing against future earnings. However, because there is no collateral in the conventional sense, the credit card companies usually feel free to charge usurious interest rates.

Credit cards certainly allow the people who hold them to spend more than they otherwise would. Many cardholders pay their bills in full each month, but a substantial majority are in perpetual debt to the credit card companies. When a credit limit on one card is reached, another card may be obtained. Some people even make monthly payments on one credit card by taking cash advances from another card. Others, overwhelmed by credit card debt, take out home equity lines of credit to pay it off. Then, with a clean slate, at least in the eyes of the credit card companies, such people are ready to begin charging again on their credit cards. Very soon many of them find themselves deeply in debt both to the bank that holds the home equity loan and to the credit card companies.

A representative of the credit card industry might say that no one forces people to take out home equity lines of credit or to obtain credit cards; people do so of their own volition and therefore are responsible for their financial predicament. Although this is certainly true at one level, at another level it is possible to view people as the victims of a financial (and economic) system that depends on them to go deeply into debt and itself grows wealthy as a result of that indebtedness. The newspapers, magazines, and broadcast media are full of advertisements offering various inducements to apply for a particular credit card or home equity loan rather than the ones offered by competitors. Many people are bombarded with mail offering all sorts of attractive benefits to those who sign up for yet another card or loan. More generally, one is made to feel foolish, even out of step, if one refuses to be an active part of the debtor society. Furthermore, it has become increasingly difficult to function in our society without a credit card. For example, people who do not have a record of credit card debt and payment find it difficult to get other kinds of credit, like home equity loans, car loans, or even mortgage loans.

An Indictment of the Financial System

The major blame for our society's lack of savings and our increasing indebtedness must be placed on the doorstep of large institutions. . . . The financial system is responsible for making credit card debt so easy and attractive that many of us have become deeply and perpetually indebted to the credit card firms. In offering us credit cards and other financial instruments, like home equity loans, the banks and other financial institutions appear to be offering us the keys to freedom. Credit cards seem to be the means to wealth, happiness, and liberation from our otherwise humdrum lives. However, for many, credit cards become instruments of bondage locking people into a lifetime of indebtedness. More generally, credit cards play a major role in helping people become more firmly embedded in the consumer society. Finally, people are locked into a lifetime of work, frequently in unsatisfying occupations, just so they can be active consumers and perhaps so they can make more than the minimum monthly payments on their credit card bills. . . .

Case in Point: Getting Them Hooked While They're Young

Before moving on to a more specific discussion of the sociological perspective on the problems associated with credit cards, one more example of the way the credit card industry has created problems for people would be useful: the increasing effort by credit card firms to lure students into possessing their own credit cards. The over 9 million college students (of which 5.6 million are in school on a full-time basis) represent a huge and lucrative market for credit card companies. According to one estimate, about 82% of full-time college students now have credit cards.[11] The number of undergraduates with credit cards increased by 37% between 1988 and 1990.[12] The credit card companies have been aggressively targeting this population not only because of the immediate increase in business it offers but also because of the long-term income possibilities as the students move on to full-time jobs after graduation. To recruit college students, credit card firms are advertising heavily on campus, using on-campus booths to make their case and even hiring students to lure their peers into the credit card world. In addition, students have been offered a variety of inducements. I have in front of me a flyer aimed at a college-age audience. It proclaims that the cards have no annual fee, offer a comparatively low interest rate, and offer "special student benefits," including a 20% discount at retailers like MusicLand and Gold's Gym and a 5% discount on travel.

The credit card firms claim that the cards help teach students to be responsible with money (one professor calls it a "training-wheels operation"[13]). The critics claim that the cards teach students to spend, often beyond their means, instead of saving:

> I've seen kids with $50,000 to $70,000 in debt. . . . They spend money on clothes, pizza, tuition, books, fun travel, presents for girlfriends, shoes, watches, engagement presents, proms, formals. Kids just go haywire.[14]

Some students are even using credit cards to pay their tuition. Said the president of a nonprofit credit counseling firm: "They haven't been educated about credit. They think it's funny money."[15] According to an expert on credit cards, "We are taking the opportunity away from them to start on a healthy foot, to be able to take care of themselves."[16] Years after they have graduated, college students may end up paying off credit card debts run up in college. Some universities have grown uncomfortable about these problems and more generally with the incursion of credit card companies and have greatly restricted the marketing of credit cards on campus.

Some students find that they cannot pay their bills while they are still in college. Although parents are not legally liable for such bills, it is not unusual for parents to pay them. One parent who helped her daughter with a consolidation loan said, "You could say I got burned . . . but at least she learned in the process, at least I hope she did. . . . College is a time to learn, to make the transition to adulthood."[17] The credit card firms are willing to target college (and high school) students, most of whom have little or no income of their own, because they know that parents will often bail out children who get into trouble with credit card debt.

In running up credit card debt, it can be argued, college students are learning to live a lie. They are living at a level that they cannot afford at the time or perhaps even in the future. They may establish a pattern of consistently living beyond their means. However, they are merely postponing the day when they have to pay their debts.

The credit card companies have clearly been affected by the critics. Inside one brochure aimed at students is a so-called "Owner's Guide to a Chase Credit Card." Three guidelines are offered:

1. If you want to play, you've got to pay.
2. If you cannot pay your entire balance, pay at least the minimum due.
3. If you cannot pay the minimum, do not play.

The guide closes with a "bottom line": "To avoid a bad credit history, you must pay the minimum payment due each month." Thus, the credit card companies are trying to inform students of the potential dangers. However, they are doing so in the context of an extremely active advertising campaign aimed at a dramatic expansion of the use of such cards among college students.

Not satisfied with the invasion of college campuses, credit card companies have been devoting increasing attention to high schools. One survey found that as of 1993, 32% of the country's high school students had their own credit cards and others had access to an adult's card. Strong efforts are under way to greatly increase that percentage. The president of a marketing firm noted, "It used to be that college was the big free-for-all for new customers. . . . But now, the big push is to get them between 16 and 18."[18] Although adult approval is required for a person under 18 years of age to obtain a credit card, card companies have been pushing more aggressively to gain greater acceptance in this age group.

Their efforts have included annual supplements sponsored by the Discover card in magazines published by Scholastic Inc. and aimed at high school students. One supplement was titled "Extra Credit," and on the back page was an advertisement depicting a classroom, a Discover card, and this headline: "Go Ahead, We're Behind You." Similarly, Visa has developed financial education programs for the high schools that do not identify Visa as the sponsor and, at least according to the company, have the broad objective of teaching students about personal finance. To many observers, the problem with these programs is that the schools may be ceding the responsibility for teaching financial management to organizations that have a vested interest, at least to some degree, in encouraging financial mismanagement. A spokesperson for the National Association of Secondary School Principals admitted the need for such school-sponsored programs but contended that "we have to balance all needs against how many minutes there are in the day."[19] If the schools do not have time to prepare programs in financial management, the credit card companies are all too willing to fill the void. However, the credit card firms are not simply trying to help out the schools; their goal is also to increase their business. As one spokesperson for a consumer advocacy group said, "[Students] need to know that credit card companies are not doing them a favor but are in the business to make money off them."[20]

The motivation behind all these programs is the industry view that about two-thirds of all people remain loyal to their first brand of card for 15 or more years. Thus the credit card companies are trying to get high school and college students accustomed to using their card instead of a competitor's. The larger fear is that the credit card companies are getting young people accustomed to buying on credit, thereby creating a whole new generation of debtors.

A Sociology of Credit Cards

Sociology in general, and sociological theory in particular, offers a number of ways of dealing with the credit card industry and the individuals affected by it. Throughout much of the 20th century, sociological theory has been divided between macro theories (such as structural functionalism and conflict theory) that would be most useful in analyzing the credit card industry itself and micro theories (such as symbolic interactionism and phenomenological sociology) that would be most helpful in analyzing individuals within our consumer society. However, sociological theory has generally been plagued by an inability to deal in a fully adequate manner with micro-macro relationships, such as the relationships between the credit card industry and individuals. Sociologists have grown increasingly dissatisfied with having to choose between large-scale, macroscopic theories and small-scale, microscopic theories. Thus, there has been a growing interest in theories that integrate micro and macro concerns. In Europe, expanding interest in what is known there as agency-structure integration parallels the increasing American preoccupation with micro-macro integration.[21]

Mills: Personal Troubles, Public Issues
This new theoretical approach has important implications for the study of sociological issues. . . . Micro-macro integration leads the sociological study of social problems[22] back to one of its roots in the work of the American social critic and theorist C. Wright Mills (1916–1962). . . .

Of direct importance here is the now-famous distinction made by Mills in his 1959 work, *The Sociological Imagination,* between micro-level personal troubles and macro-level public issues.[23] Personal troubles tend to be problems that affect an individual and those immediately around him or her. For example, a father who commits incest with his daughter is creating personal troubles for the daughter, other members of the family, and perhaps himself. However, that single father's actions are not going to create a public issue; that is, they are not likely to lead to a public outcry that society ought to abandon the family as a social institution. Public issues, in comparison, tend to be problems that affect large numbers of people and perhaps society as a whole. The disintegration of the nuclear family would be such a public issue.

What, then, is the relationship between these two sets of distinctions—personal troubles/public issues and character/social structure—derived from the work of C. Wright Mills? The character of an individual can certainly cause personal troubles. For example, a psychotic individual can cause problems for himself and those immediately around him. When many individuals have the same character disorder (psychosis, for example), they can cause problems for the larger social structure (overtax the mental health system), thereby creating a public issue. The structure of society can also cause personal troubles for the individual. An example might be a person's depression resulting from the disjunction between the culturally instilled desire for economic success and the scarcity of well-paying jobs. And the structure of society can create public issues, as exemplified by the tendency of the capitalist economy to generate periodic recessions and depressions. All these connections and, more generally, a wide array of macro-micro relationships are possible.[24] However, the focus . . . is the credit card industry as an element of social structure and the way it generates both personal troubles and public issues.

A useful parallel can be drawn between the credit card and cigarette industries. The practices of the cigarette industry create a variety of personal troubles, especially illness and early death. Furthermore, those practices have created a

number of public issues (the cost to society of death and illness traceable to cigarette smoke), and thus many people have come to see cigarette industry practices themselves as public issues. Examples of industry practices that have become public issues are the aggressive marketing of cigarettes overseas, where restrictions on such marketing are limited or nonexistent, as well as the marketing of cigarettes to young people in this country (for example, through advertisements featuring the controversial "Joe Camel"). Similarly, the practices of the credit card industry help to create personal problems (such as indebtedness) and public issues (such as the relatively low national savings rate). Furthermore, some industry practices—such as the aggressive marketing of credit cards to teenagers—have themselves become public issues. . . .

Globalization and Americanization

A sociology of credit cards requires a look at the relationship among the credit card industry, personal troubles, and public issues on a global scale. It is not just the United States, but also much of the rest of the world, that is being affected by the credit card industry and the social problems it helps create. To some degree, this development is a result of globalization, a process that is at least partially autonomous of any single nation and that involves the reciprocal impact of many economies.[25] In the main, however, American credit card companies dominate the global market [in a process I call Americanization]. . . .

. . . In many countries around the world, Americanization is a public issue that is causing personal troubles for their citizens. . . .

Micro-Macro Relationships

. . . Although . . . the macro-level credit card industry creates a variety of public issues and personal troubles, it is important to realize that people, at the micro level, create and re-create that industry by their actions. Not only did people create the industry historically, but they help to re-create it daily by acting in accord with its demands and expectations. However, people also have the capacity to refuse to conform to the demands of the credit card industry. If they were to do so on a reasonably large scale, the industry would be forced to alter the way it operates. People can also be more pro-active in their efforts to change the credit card industry.

However, there are limits to what individuals, even when acting in concert, can do about macro-level problems. In many cases, macro-level problems require macro-level solutions. . . . The credit card industry, as well as the government, can take [action] to deal with . . . public issues and personal troubles [caused by credit cards]. . . .

Something New in the History of Money

Money in all its forms, especially . . . in its cash form, is part of a historical process.[26] It may seem hard to believe from today's vantage point, but at one time there was no money. Furthermore, some predict that there will come a time in which money, at least in the form of currency, will become less important if not disappear altogether, with the emergence of a "cashless society."[27]

Looking back, we can see a historical progression from the barter of material goods, to the use of valuable symbols like jewelry, to money made of precious metals (for example, gold coins), to money made of semiprecious metals, to paper money backed by precious metals (for example, the gold standard), to money backed solely and symbolically by the state's promise to honor it and to recognize it as having a specified value. Then there was the development of checks, which replaced currency to some extent. Checks imply that they are backed by the bank—given sufficient funds in the check writer's account. If currency is a symbol, then a check is a symbol of a symbol.

. . . Money in the form of currency is being increasingly supplanted by the credit card. Instead of plunking down cash or even writing a check, more of us are saying "Charge it!" This apparently modest act is, in fact, a truly revolutionary development in the history of money. Furthermore, it is having a revolutionary impact on the nature of consumption, the economy, and the social world more generally. In fact, rather than simply being yet another step in the development of money, I am inclined to agree with the contention that credit cards are "an entirely new idea in value exchange."[28] . . .

A Growing Industry

. . . There are now more than a billion credit cards of all types in the United States.[29] Receivables for the industry as a whole in 1993 were up by almost 16% from the preceding year and by over 400% in a decade.[30] The staggering proliferation of credit cards is also reflected in other indicators of use in the United States:

- Sixty-one percent of Americans now have at least one credit card.
- The average cardholder carries nine different cards.
- In 1992, consumers used the cards to make 5 billion transactions, with a total value of $420 billion.[31]

There has been, among other things, growth in the number of people who have credit cards, the average number of credit cards held by each person, the amount of consumer debt attributable to credit card purchases, the number of facilities accepting credit cards, and the number of organizations issuing cards. For example, the number of major credit cards in use in the United States—Visa, MasterCard, Discover, and American Express*—increased by about 174 million (from 157 million to 331 million) between 1984 and 1993.[32] The average outstanding balance owed to Visa and MasterCard increased from less than $400 in the early 1980s to $970 in 1989 and to $1,096 in 1993.[33] The amount of high-interest credit card debt owed by American consumers rose from $2.7 billion in 1969 to $50 billion in 1980 and was approaching $300 billion in 1994.[34] Because the recession of the early 1990s prompted many people to limit the increases in their credit card debt, the total of such debt will probably not grow nearly as fast in the 1990s as it did in the 1980s, although it will still expand by a substantial amount.

The growth of credit cards has not been restricted to the United States but has spread throughout the world. Although the American

*The traditional American Express card is actually a charge card, not a credit card, because no credit is extended and the bills must be paid in full each month.

market for credit cards might be approaching saturation, that is certainly not true of much of the rest of the world. According to one industry analyst, "outside of the U.S., the potential for growth is still quite phenomenal."[35] Thus, the international arena is likely to be a target for credit card companies in the coming years.

The growth in the use of credit cards has not been a function solely of consumer demand. Banks have been eager to issue more cards because their profits from those cards are far higher than the profits from other consumer loans.[36] Furthermore, the risk is spread among many small accounts, which makes credit cards less hazardous than a few large business loans would be. Also fueling growth recently has been the entrance of many "nonbanks" (AT&T, General Motors, Shell) into the credit card industry. They want to get a share of the high profits of the credit card business and, perhaps more importantly, to help sell their own products. With so much competition, all organizations involved in the credit card business have been bombarding consumers with offers for cards with no annual fees, low interest rates, and rebates. So many organizations have become involved so actively in the credit card field that an American Express official described it as resembling a "shark feeding frenzy."[37]

A Symbol of American Values
A strong case can be made that the credit card is one of the leading symbols of 20th-century America or, as mentioned earlier, that the credit card is an American icon. Indeed, one observer calls the credit card "the twentieth century's symbol par excellence."[38] Among other things, the credit card is emblematic of affluence, mobility, and the capacity to overcome obstacles in the pursuit of one's goals. Thus, those hundreds of millions of people who carry credit cards are also carrying with them these important symbols. And when they use a credit card, they are turning the symbols into material reality.

Although credit cards are American in origin, only American Express retains the name of its country of origin. The other major credit card companies have deliberately adopted names that give the sense the cards are not confined to any

nation. Although MasterCard, which was once known as Master Charge, has always sought to convey the image of "a card without a country," Visa was at one time called BankAmericard. American Express has created the Optima card with a name that disassociates it from the United States. Nevertheless, credit cards are clearly associated in the minds of most people around the world with America and its consumer culture.

Furthermore, even though they may be moving away from the use of the word *America,* the names of all of the major cards continue to reflect basic American values. The *Express* in American Express conjures up the image not only of someone or something on the move but also of great power and rapidity of movement. The name of the card conveys the sense that this thing is not going to stop anywhere or be stopped by anything; it has an inexorable quality. The holders of American Express cards are in possession of a bit of America. Therefore, such people are on the move, and everyone had better watch out.

MasterCard communicates the value Americans place on mastery, especially over others and over their environment. The possession of this credit card is supposed to allow holders to master their social and physical worlds. The name could also be interpreted in more imperialistic terms, as representing the power to handle any and all situations. There are many credit cards, but MasterCard wants us to believe that it is the master card, not only master of the world but dominant over all its competitors.

Visa gives its holders the sense that they are in possession of a pass that allows them to cross any border or of the master key that opens any lock. Again, the name of the card conveys a sense of power—the ability to go anywhere or to do anything one desires.

The names chosen for the cards are supported by the images on them. The American Express card has a picture of a helmeted warrior, whose powerful jaw and gaze fixed on the horizon support the idea of something that is moving forward and is unstoppable. The hologram on the Visa card is of a bird in flight, capable of going anywhere it pleases. And MasterCard offers a hologram of the globe, indicating that the entire world is its domain. Thus, the credit card in general has great symbolic importance, as does each specific brand of credit card. . . .

NOTES

1. Terry Galanoy. *Charge It: Inside the Credit Card Conspiracy.* New York: Putnam, 1980.

2. Terry Galanoy. *Charge It: Inside the Credit Card Conspiracy.* New York: Putnam, 1980, p. 53.

3. Francis Williams. *The American Invasion.* New York: Crown, 1962, p. 53. It is interesting to note that Williams was making this point when credit cards were of minuscule significance in comparison to their importance today.

4. Board of Governors of the Federal Reserve System. *Federal Reserve Bulletin,* vol. 80 no. 5, 1994. "Selected Measures," pp. A30, A51.

5. Fred R. Bleakley. "Consumers Loading up on Debt Again, But Many View Trend as Positive Sign." *Wall Street Journal,* March 30, 1994, pp. A2, A6.

6. U.S. Bureau of the Census. *Statistical Abstracts of the United States: 1993* (113th ed.). Washington, DC: Government Printing Office, 1993, p. 506.

7. U.S. Bureau of the Census. *Statistical Abstracts of the United States: 1992* (112th ed.). Washington, DC: Government Printing Office, 1992, p. 504.

8. Peter Conrad and Joseph Schneider. *Deviance and Medicalization: From Badness to Sickness.* St. Louis: Mosby, 1980.

9. Russell Ben-Ali. "Urge to Spend Money Can Lead to Ruin, Therapy." *Los Angeles Times,* May 6, 1991, p. B5.

10. Joseph Nocera. *A Piece of the Action: How the Middle Class Joined the Money Class.* New York: Simon & Schuster, 1994, p. 96.

11. Andree Brooks. "Lessons for Teen-Agers: Facts of Credit-Card Life." *New York Times,* November 5, 1994, p. 40.

12. "Credit Cards Become Big Part of Campus Life." *New York Times,* February 9, 1991, pp. 16, 48.

13. Albert Crenshaw. "A Crash Course in Credit." *Washington Post,* November 7, 1993, p. H3.

14. Cecilia Cassidy. "Chaarrrge!: America's Card-Carrying Teens." *Washington Post,* June 25, 1991, p. D5.

15. "Credit Card Wars on Campus." *Fortune,* April 10, 1989, p. 18.

16. Albert Crenshaw. "A Crash Course in Credit." *Washington Post,* November 7, 1993, p. H3.

17. Albert Crenshaw. "A Crash Course in Credit." *Washington Post,* November 7, 1993, p. H3.

18. Barry Meier. "Credit Cards on the Rise in High Schools." *New York Times,* September 5, 1992, p. 9; Andree Brooks. "Lessons for Teen-Agers: Facts of Credit-Card Life." *New York Times,* November 5, 1994, p. 40.

19. Barry Meier. "Credit Cards on the Rise in High Schools." *New York Times,* September 5, 1992, p. 9.

20. Barry Meier. "Credit Cards on the Rise in High Schools." *New York Times,* September 5, 1992, p. 9.

21. George Ritzer. "The 1980s: Micro-Macro (and Agency-Structure) Integration in Sociological Theory," in George Ritzer, *Metatheorizing in Sociology.* Lexington, MA: Lexington Books, 1991, pp. 207–234; George Ritzer. "The Recent History and the Emerging Reality of American Sociological Theory: A Metatheoretical Interpretation." *Sociological Forum* 6(1991): 269–287.

22. For an overview of the sociological study of social problems, see George Ritzer. "Social Problems Theory," in Craig Calhoun and George Ritzer (eds.), *Introduction to Social Problems.* New York: McGraw-Hill Primis, 1993.

23. C. Wright Mills. *The Sociological Imagination.* New York: Oxford University Press, 1959.

24. Richard Munch and Neil Smelser. "Relating the Micro and Macro," in Jeffrey C. Alexander et al. (eds.), *The Micro-Macro Link.* Berkeley: University of California Press, 1987, pp. 356–387.

25. Roland Robertson. *Globalization: Social Theory and Global Culture.* London: Sage, 1992; Mike Featherstone (ed.). *Global Culture: Nationalism, Globalization and Modernity.* London: Sage, 1990.

26. Viviana A. Zelizer. *The Social Meaning of Money.* New York: Basic Books, 1994; Kenneth O. Doyle (ed.), "The Meanings of Money." *American Behavioral Scientist,* July/August (1992):637–840.

27. Robert A. Hendrickson. *The Cashless Society.* New York: Dodd, Mead, 1972.

28. Terry Galanoy. *Charge It: Inside the Credit Card Conspiracy.* New York: Putnam, 1980, p. 212.

29. James Sterngold. "Thrift Is Under Siege in Japan as Use of Credit Cards Soars." *New York Times,* June 16, 1992, pp. A1, D9.

30. "1993—Banner Year." *Bankcard Update,* March 1994, pp. 1, 12.

31. William Dunn. "Debit It! New Breed of Cards an Alternative to Cash, Checks, Credit." *Chicago Tribune,* November 18, 1993, p. N1.

32. "Credit Card Issuer's Guide: 1995 Edition." *Credit Card News,* August 15, 1994, p. 5; "The Big Squeeze." *The Economist,* November 2, 1991, pp. 69–70; Adam Bryant. "Raising the Stakes in a War of Plastic." *New York Times,* September 13, 1992, p. F13.

33. Peter Lucas. "Buy Now, Borrow Later." *Credit Card Management,* April 1994: 74.

34. *Credit Card News,* May 15, 1994, p. 7; Jeffrey Kutler. "Uncertainty Emerges on Bank Card Industry Future." *American Banker,* September 19, 1979, p. 1; "The Big Squeeze." *The Economist,* November 2, 1991, pp. 69–70; Janice Castro. "Charge It Your Way." *Time,*

July 1, 1991, pp. 50–51; "Plastic Profits Go Pop." *The Economist,* September 12, 1992, p. 92.

35. Steve Lipin, Brian Coleman and Jeremy Mark. "Visa, American Express and MasterCard Vie in Overseas Strategies." *Wall Street Journal,* February 15, 1994, p. A1.

36. Marguerite Smith and Jordan E. Goodman. "Betting on the Value of Regional Banks' Plastic Portfolios." *Money,* January 1990, pp. 57–58.

37. Bill Saporito. "Melting Point in the Plastic War." *Forbes,* May 20, 1991, p. 72.

38. Robert A. Hendrickson. *The Cashless Society.* New York: Dodd, Mead, 1972, p. 46.

THINKING ABOUT THE READINGS

The My Lai Massacre

■ According to Kelman and Hamilton, what social processes create conditions under which restraints against violence are weakened? The incident they describe provides an uncomfortable picture of human nature. Do you think that most people would have reacted the way the soldiers at My Lai did? Are we all potential massacrers? Does this phenomenon of obedience to authority go beyond the tightly structured environment of the military? Can you think of incidents in your own life when you've done something—perhaps harmed another person—because of the powerful influence of others?

The Credit Card

■ What does Ritzer mean when he says that the credit card is "an American icon?" What are the social advantages and disadvantages of a credit card economy? Why do you suppose Americans are so willing to "rush into debt as quickly and as deeply as possible?" Given the problems that Ritzer identifies, do you think it would be possible to have a society that didn't rely so heavily on credit cards? How might such a society differ from the one we live in today? The author argues that college students are an extremely attractive market for credit card companies. Why do you think this segment of the population is targeted so aggressively?

II

Constructing Self and Society

CHAPTER 3

Building Reality

The Construction of Social Knowledge

According to the sociological perspective, reality is not something that exists "out there," waiting for someone to discover it. Reality is a social construction. How we distinguish fact from fantasy, truth from fiction, myth from reality are not merely abstract philosophical questions but are very much tied to interpersonal interaction, group membership, culture, history, power, economics, and politics.

In "Stalking Strangers and Lovers," Kathleen Lowney and Joel Best focus on the relatively new crime of stalking to show how social problems are created from media representations of news events. While the behaviors now legally defined as stalking have always existed, only recently has enough media attention been focused on the issue to create and sustain the public perception that it is a dangerous crime. In this article you will see how shifts in media coverage of these incidents coincided with shifts in the law and in public perceptions of the problem.

Unlike the casual ways we go about defining reality in our everyday lives, sociologists go about constructing truths about important aspects of social life through highly structured, systematic research. Sometimes the information needed to answer questions about important, controversial issues is difficult to obtain. Patricia Adler provides an interesting example of how sociologists do research on such topics in "Researching Dealers and Smugglers." To many people the sellers and users of illegal drugs are a dangerous scourge on American society. Adler was interested in understanding the upper echelons of the illicit drug trade—a secretive group of people condemned by most but understood by few. Given the illegal and dangerous activities involved, it is unlikely that drug smugglers would willingly answer interview or survey questions about their trade. So Adler and her husband established close friendships with dealers and smugglers and used a research technique called participant observation to collect inside information about their activities. Putting oneself in the world of one's research subjects provides rich information but can cause serious potential dangers.

Stalking Strangers and Lovers
Changing Media Typifications of a New Crime Problem

Kathleen S. Lowney and Joel Best

. . . Stalking—"men and women who are repeatedly followed, harassed, or physically threatened by other persons" (Gilligan 1992:285)—was recently and successfully constructed as a crime problem. California passed the first antistalking law in 1990. Three years later, 48 states and the District of Columbia had such laws, and several states were considering further legislation to expand or toughen their statutes. As one legislator put it:

> Michigan and its sister States are creating a new crime. We are defining it, essentially, one unknown to the common law. We are making conduct illegal which has been legal up until now, and we are using the most serious prescription our society can devise, the deprivation of liberty, through a felony penalty. This is experimental legislation. (Perry Bullard in U.S. Senate 1992:64).

Claims that stalking was a large and growing problem led to hearings before the U.S. Senate (1992, 1993); the National Institute of Justice (1993) developed a Model Anti-Stalking Code for States. By late 1993, claims about stalking had become familiar, and reports of strangers attacking women (e.g., the kidnap/murder of Polly Klaas, or the assault on figure-skater Nancy Kerrigan) often assumed that stalkers committed the crimes (Toobin 1994; Ingrassia 1994). Less than 5 years after the term "stalking" emerged, stalking had widespread recognition as a crime problem. . . .

The media play various roles in social problems construction. Studies of the construction of crime problems suggest that the press sometimes serves as the primary claimsmaker, making the initial claims (e.g., claimsmaking about urban violence [Brownstein 1991; Fishman 1978] and freeway violence [Best 1991]). Other problems emerge through secondary press reports of claimsmaking by social activists (e.g., drunk driving [Reinarman 1988], battering [Loseke 1992], and rape [Rose 1977]), professionals (e.g., child abuse [Pfohl 1977] and computer crimes [Hollinger and Lanza-Kaduce 1988]), or criminal justice officials (e.g., serial murder [Jenkins 1994]). . . . Because media attention is fleeting, crime problems constructed by the press have a short spell in the spotlight (Best 1991). For example, freeway violence received national coverage for less than a month during 1987; when no other interest group adopted the issue and continued to make claims about it, freeway violence faded from view.

Media coverage of stalking reveals a different pattern: various largely unsuccessful typifications preceded the construction that finally gained acceptance. The stalking problem came under public scrutiny after 1989, through press coverage of sensational crimes involving celebrity victims stalked by obsessed fans. However, for at least the previous decade, there had been complaints about the very behaviors that would later constitute the crime of stalking, although those claims neither evoked great public concern nor led to antistalking laws. Moreover, stalking did not vanish as a social issue because media attention shifted to other issues. Rather, social activists, particularly in the victims' and battered women's movements, assumed ownership of this new crime problem and kept the issue alive by making fresh claims about stalking. Their claims reconstructed the stalking problem, offering new characterizations of offenders, victims, and the crime. . . .

Before Stalking: Obsession and Psychological Rape, 1980–1988

Between 1980 and 1986, national magazines published seven articles describing women being followed or harassed with letters, telephone calls, or unwanted gifts. Some of the annoying behaviors continued for years; some women were physically assaulted. Any female could be a victim: although most of the victims knew their harassers as colleagues at work (Winter 1980), ex-husbands (Anonymous 1980) or ex-boyfriends (Mithers 1982), some of the men were strangers (Wilcox 1982).

The articles called these behaviors "a form of sexual harassment," "obsession," or "psychological rape" (Wilcox 1982; Mithers 1982). One psychiatrist, interviewed shortly after John Hinckley tried to assassinate President Reagan, said that psychological rape "has linked such celebrities as Jodie Foster and Caroline Kennedy to ordinary women who've found themselves pursued by men who claim to be in love with them" (Wilcox 1982:233).

The articles described the harassers, all males, as obsessive, compulsive, often passive in nature, with a limited range of sexual expression and low self-esteem (Heil 1986; Wilcox 1982). Many had "only protective feelings [toward their victim], and believe that their actions may shield their loved ones from imagined 'enemies' such as the Mafia or CIA" (Wilcox 1982:293). The term psychological rape reflected "the nonviolent nature of the harassment—letters, obscene phone calls and persistent shadowing are its most common forms" (Wilcox 1982:233). Most harassers were "lovesick" (Heil 1986:128), although a few might become violent.

The articles held the harasser responsible for his behavior. A female attorney described harassment as "plain male possessiveness" (Anonymous 1980:39). A more psychological explanation held that some men were more susceptible to rejection by women with whom they were romantically linked. The psychological rapist, however, does not acknowledge his problems; rather, he blames his victim. One harasser was quoted: *"I'll* say I have a problem, the woman I love doesn't love me. It's the worst thing that can happen to anyone" (Wilcox 1982:293). Some psychological experts held victims partially responsible for subtly encouraging their harassers:

> [T]hey can often get away with it because their ex-girlfriends unwittingly allow them to. . . . Kate [harassed for over a decade] admits that even while Will [her former boyfriend] was harassing her with phone calls and driving by her house in the middle of the night, she gave him a scarf she had knitted for him. (Heil 1986:138).

The articles portrayed victims as confused by the harassers' attention; some women acknowledged partial culpability: "He said I'd provoked him into anger last night and I had the guilty uneasy feeling that maybe that was partially true" (Anonymous 1980:34). The articles warned that common social scripts for ending relationships often do not work with psychological rapists: "It's hard to turn your back on a former lover who's obviously in pain, and it may seem cruel to avoid all contact with him. In the end, however, there's no other way" (Mithers 1982:36).

The victims in these articles complained of the criminal justice system's failure to protect them. Police often did not treat harassment as serious, even when it involved criminal behavior. But victims reported feeling terrified:

> Basically, the psychological rapist works by gradually reducing the number of places a woman feels safe or functional in her daily life. This is why relatively harmless behavior, repeated over months or years, can inspire real terror. (Wilcox 1982:233).

Victims claimed the criminal justice system did not understand their terror, and that this precluded their cases being handled properly. A Los Angeles prosecutor explained that these cases were hard to prosecute: "A jury will want to know why *emotional* harassment is damaging when the victim is never touched. . . . I see only six prose-cutable cases of emotional harassment each year" (Wilcox 1982:295—emphasis in original).

Thus, early magazine articles depicted female victims of male harassers. (In 1987, the popular movie *Fatal Attraction* [about a harassing female] inspired an article in *People* describing three men harassed by women [Kunen 1987]). Experts typ-ified the harassers' behaviors as nonviolent, and sometimes portrayed victims as coresponsible for their plight. Victims complained they felt terror, but got little help from the criminal justice system. In retrospect, these articles can be seen as early claims about what would become the stalking problem, although only one article used that word (among others) (Heil 1986). While occasional press coverage viewed the behavior as problem-atic, the issue had not yet been packaged and pre-sented so as to command public attention.

Stalking Emerges: Star-Stalkers and Celebrity Victims, 1989–1991

Stalking became a visible issue in 1989 following the sensational murder of actress Rebecca Schaef-fer, killed by fan Robert Bardo, a stranger who became obsessed with her, attempted to contact her, then shot her (Axthelm 1989). Her murder received widespread publicity as "The case that galvanized the public: the fatal attraction of a dis-turbed young man for an up-and-coming actress" (Dan Rather in *48 Hours* 1992:2). Schaeffer was not the first celebrity victim; John Hinckley stalked actress Jodie Foster before attempting to assassinate President Reagan in 1991, and a fan stalked and stabbed actress Theresa Saldana in 1982. However, claims about stalking rarely drew on these examples until Schaeffer's murder. The stalking problem did not, then, simply emerge fol-lowing a well-publicized crime against a celebrity victim. Yet Schaeffer's murder became the typify-ing example for what media now termed "star-stalking" (Cosgrove 1990; *Geraldo* 1990).

The construction of star-stalking as a crime problem typified victims as celebrities—actors and actresses, television personalities, and political fig-ures. Claimsmakers referred to such celebrity vic-

tims as talk show hosts David Letterman and Johnny Carson, author Stephen King, actor Michael J. Fox and actresses Jodie Foster, Theresa Saldana, and Sharon Gless, singers Olivia Newton-John and Sheena Easton, and musician John Lennon (Cosgrove 1990; *Geraldo* 1990). Several of these examples were not current; the harassment had occurred years earlier. During 1989 and 1990, national magazine articles and television broadcasts presented 16 typifying exam-ples of stalking; 11 (69%) involved celebrity vic-tims. In every other year, celebrity victims were a minority among the examples.

Claimsmakers depicted star-stalkers as mentally disturbed, inappropriately obsessed with their celebrity victims. Psychiatrist John Stalberg, who interviewed Robert Bardo, described him:

> On a scale of zero to 10, among schizophren-ics, he's a 10—one of the sicker people I've seen. . . . With Rebecca Schaeffer, he found a—an obsession. She was the answer to his lonely, depressed, miserable life. (*48 Hours* 1992:3–4).

. . . A primary difference between earlier claims about psychological rape and the more successful campaign against star-stalking was the redefinition of the behavior as *violent*. The stalker's behavior, which might be threatening or merely inappro-priate, needed to be seen as potentially violent (Dietz et al. 1991a, 1991b). Some claimsmakers . . . suggested that stalkers "deteriorated," becom-ing increasingly capable of violence. Unpre-dictable and possibly lethal, stalking was a form of random violence.

While earlier claimsmakers criticized the crimi-nal justice system's failure to halt psychological rape, their claims produced no legislation. How-ever, concern over star-stalking led to California passing an antistalking law; claimsmakers linked Schaeffer's murder, the 1982 stabbing of Theresa Saldana (in the news because her attacker was about to be paroled), and the deaths of four Orange County women within a 6-week period (each killed by a man against whom she had a restraining order) (Morville 1993). These cases became typifying examples, evidence of the need for an antistalking law. Supported by peace officers' associations and the Screen Actors Guild (SAG), California's law passed in 1990 (*Pacific Law Journal* 1990:500). When it took effect, the Los Angeles Police Department established a six-person Threat Management Unit (TMU) to investigate stalking cases. Both SAG's lobbying and the creation of a TMU in Los Angeles (with its many show business celebrities) reveal that concern over star-stalking fostered the initial antistalking law.

Stalking Redefined: Failed Relationships and Male Violence, 1992–1994

In 1992, other states began following California's example. Often, a highly publicized attack inspired lawmakers: "Behind almost every state stalking bill has been at least one local tragedy" (Morville 1993:929, n47). Twenty-nine states passed antistalking laws (many modeled on California's law) in 1992; 18 other states and the District of Columbia followed suit in 1993 (National Institute of Justice 1993:12). Also in 1992, Senator William Cohen (R—Maine) began calling for federal action, and the national media dramatically increased their coverage of stalking. Between 1980 and 1988, national magazines and television broadcasts averaged one story about stalking per year; during 1989–1991 (when star-stalking attracted attention) the average more than doubled to 2.3 stories per year; but there were 22.0 stories per year—another, nearly 10-fold increase—during 1992 through June 1994. Some stories achieved high visibility: *Washington Post* reporter George Lardner (1992) received a Pulitzer Prize for reporting on his daughter's murder by a stalker, and the award triggered additional press coverage; in 1993, Kathleen Krueger, wife of U.S. Senator Bob Krueger (D—Texas), used her own experiences as a stalking victim to campaign for a federal antistalking law (Ellis 1993; U.S. Senate 1993).

These new claims reframed stalking as a women's issue, a widespread precursor to serious violence, typically committed by men against former spouses or lovers. The term "stalking"—now the consensus replacement for such earlier labels as psychological rape and star-stalking . . . implied deliberate intent to harm the victim:

> The verb "stalk" is defined as: (1) "to move threateningly or menacingly;" (2)"to pursue by tracking;" and (3) to go stealthily towards an animal "for the purpose of killing or capturing it." These definitions say much about the crime of stalking, suggesting that a stalker is a hunter, is dangerous, and thus should be avoided if at all possible. (Perez 1993:265)

In this new construction, stalking was a common problem. An often-repeated estimate suggested that there were 200,000 stalkers. We do not know the origin of this statistic. It first appears in our sample of national media coverage in *U.S. News and World Report*'s February 17, 1992, issue: "researchers suggest that up to 200,000 people exhibit a stalker's traits" (Tharp 1992:28). Like other statistical estimates of social problem magnitude, this number soon took on a life of its own; it was often repeated, but never examined or explained (Best 1990). Other claimsmakers suggested that 200,000 was an underestimate:

> There are an estimated 200,000 stalkers in the United States, and those are only the ones that we have track of. (Sally Jessy Raphael in *Sally Jessy Raphael* 1994:3)
>
> Some two hundred thousand people in the U.S. pursue the famous. No one knows how many people stalk the rest of us, but the figure is probably higher. (Sherman 1994:198)
>
> Four million women that we know about—know about each year are beaten and terrorized and stalked by somebody they know. (Oprah Winfrey in *Oprah* 1994:12)

Claimsmakers variously estimated that lifetime victimization by stalkers would affect one American in 40 (Safran 1992), or 30 (Tharp 1992), or 20 (*CNN Prime News* 1993). The numbers varied, but there was agreement that stalking was increasing, "a national epidemic" (Gilligan 1992:337). . . .

Linking Stalking to Domestic Violence

This new construction connected stalking to a well-established social problem—domestic battering: "'the majority of battered women experience stalking in some form,' says Vickie Smith, head of the Illinois Coalition Against Domestic Violence" (Miller 1993:18). The battered women's movement had long complained that the criminal justice system failed to protect women trying to escape abusive partners, that restraining orders were ineffective (Loseke 1992). By reframing these women's problems as stalking, a visible issue with connotations of extreme violence, battered women's claimsmakers could move their concerns to the top of the policy agenda.

. . . Antistalking claimsmakers routinely borrowed data from research on domestic violence to characterize stalking:

Approximately 50 percent of all females who leave their husbands for reasons of physical abuse are followed, harassed, or further attacked by their former spouses. This phenomenon is known as "separation assault." . . . The broader concept is called "stalking." (Bradburn 1992:271).

Studies in Detroit and Kansas City reveal that 90 percent of those murdered by their intimate partners called police at least once. (Senator William Cohen in *Congressional Record* 1992:S9527).

Nearly one third of all women killed in America are murdered by their husbands or boyfriends, and, says Ruth Micklem, codirector of Virginians Against Domestic Violence, as many as 90 percent of them have been stalked. (Beck 992:61)

The juxtaposition of the latter two quotes reveals how evidence used in claimsmaking evolves: Senator Cohen cited a finding that 90% of women killed by husbands or lovers had previously called the police; when later claimsmakers repeated that statistic, they equated having called the police with being stalked, ignoring the likelihood that many women called to complain about abuse by partners living in the same residence (and therefore not stalkers). Presumably similar assumptions lay

behind U.S. Representative Joseph Kennedy's claim that, "Nine women a day are killed by stalkers in our country" (*Larry King Live* 1994:3). Claimsmakers described antistalking laws as "an effective deterrent to domestic abuse" (Furio 1993:90); West Virginia's original law narrowly defined victims as "those who either cohabitated or had intimate relationships with their stalkers" (Perez 1993:267).

Claims that many stalkers were former husbands or boyfriends cast virtually all women as potential victims: "We're not idiots up here that asked to be victims. This happens to anybody period" (former victim Stephanie in *Sally Jessy Raphael* 1993b:7). Here, as in earlier claims about star-stalking, victims bear no responsibility: claimsmakers emphasized that most victims did nothing to encourage their stalkers. (One exception was a talk show devoted to women harassing former boyfriends; the host repeatedly suggested that the men encouraged stalking [*Sally Jessy Raphael* 1993c]). In most ways, stalking's typification resembled that of domestic violence: "wife abuse is a label for severe, frequent, and continuing violence that escalates over time and is unstoppable. Such violence is that in which unrepentant men intentionally harm women and where women are not the authors of their own experiences which they find terrifying" (Loseke 1992:20). Once they linked stalking to battering, claimsmakers had little difficulty attributing the same characteristics to both crimes.

This link became apparent in state legislative proceedings. Illinois lawmakers, for example, justified antistalking legislation by pointing to four recent cases of victims murdered by former husbands or boyfriends in Chicago suburbs. The *Chicago Tribune*'s (1991) editorial endorsing an antistalking law shared this frame: "Hundreds of women are threatened and harassed and intimidated by ex-boyfriends or ex-husbands. . . . [An antistalking law has] the potential to be a helpful weapon against domestic violence." Supported by the Illinois Coalition Against Domestic Violence, the bill received unanimous support in both legislative houses; mothers of two of the dead victims were on hand when the bill was signed into law. Both state and national branches of the battered women's movement and the victims' rights movement supported antistalking bills. The National Victim Center lobbied in more than a dozen states, and Theresa Saldana (a former stalking victim and the founder of Victims for Victims) campaigned in behalf of the laws. In Nebraska, for instance, both the Nebraska Coalition for Victims of Crime and the Nebraska Domestic Violence-Sexual Assault Coalition supported antistalking legislation. Stalking was now a form of both violent crime and domestic violence. . . .

Retypification and the Mobilization of Cultural and Organizational Resources

. . . The case of stalking demonstrates the complexity of successfully constructing new social problems. Preceded by earlier, less successful typifications, the successful construction of stalking combined three elements: (1) typifying claims, which mobilized both (2) cultural resources and (3) organizational resources.

Typifying Claims

The raw material for the stalking problem—people who objected to being harassed, harassment sometimes ending in homicide, even well-publicized cases with celebrity victims—existed long before claimsmakers began talking about "stalking." Presumably, the stalking problem might have been constructed much earlier than it was.

A key step in social problems construction is linking a troubling event to a problematic pattern, defining a particular *incident* as an *instance* of some larger problem. In the case of stalking, this juxtaposition of event and pattern occurred at several points, producing various typifications. While some media reports described the harassment of lone individuals (e.g., Winter 1980; Safran 1992), others juxtaposed several cases, suggesting they were all instances of psychological rape (Wilcox 1982) or fatal attractions (Kunen 1987) or star-stalking (*Geraldo* 1990). Of course, the key juxtaposition occurred in Southern California after 1989, when claimsmakers linked Rebecca Schaefer's murder with the attacks on Theresa

Saldana and the four women killed in Orange County.

Table 1 summarizes this sequence of typifications, noting some of the characteristics claimsmakers associated with psychological rape (1980–1988), star-stalking (1989–1991), and stalking (1992–1994). Although our analysis links these different claims, arguing that they dealt with essentially the same phenomenon, it is interesting to note how the typifications differed in their characterizations of the gender of both victim and offender, the victim's responsibility and celebrity, the nature of the offender's psychological problem, the prior relationship between victim and offender, and the prospect of violence.

Claimsmakers rarely offer formal definitions. Rather, they illustrate a problem's nature through typifying examples. We have already noted how typifying examples presented in the media changed. By 1992, claimsmakers offered other evidence to support the current typification of stalking, including statistical claims (e.g., the number of stalking cases, the frequency of stalking-related homicides, the proportion of victims whose stalkers were former intimates). . . .

Cultural Resources

Not all claims receive ratification from press, public, and policymakers. Constructionist analysts suggest that claims attract notice when they "relate to deep mythic themes" (Hilgartner and Bosk 1988:64), have "cultural resonance" (Gamson and Modigliani 1989:5–6), or draw upon "cultural resources" (Best 1991). Claims can be packaged in ways more or less likely to elicit favorable responses, and the cultural themes that claims evoke are a key element in this packaging.

Consider a central theme in stalking claims: the victim's inability to make the harasser stop. These claims routinely emphasized the victims' emotions, e.g., their frustration and anxiety over the continuing harassment and their uncertainty and fear over what might happen next. The obsessive pursuit of another is a standard theme in American popular culture; many movies, novels, and popular songs center around obsessive love. The treatment can be comic or romantic (e.g., the would-be lover who won't give up until love is

TABLE 1 *Elements in the Construction of Stalking as a Crime Problem*

Period	Typifying Claims	Cultural Resources	Organizational Resources	Results
1980–1988	Psychological rape: males harass females; usually not violent; victim may share responsibility; obsessed offender	Vulnerability to harassment Women heading households		Occasional media coverage
1989–1991	Star-stalking: celebrity victim; offender can be either gender; offender may suffer from erotomania; offender may deteriorate; violence and homicide as outcomes; victim not responsible	Vulnerability to harassment Random violence	Screen Actors Guild lobbying Celebrity protection services	Increased media coverage California law passed
1992–1994	Stalking: males harass females; often former intimates; form of domestic violence; victim not responsible; statistical claims; homicide as outcome	Vulnerability to harassment Victimization of women Male violence Pedophilia	Crime victims' movement Battered women's movement LAPD TMU	Frequent media coverage Laws in other states Federal attention

reciprocated, as in *The Graduate*), but it is often central to horror or suspense stories (e.g., *Fatal Attraction, The Bodyguard*). This suggests widespread cultural recognition of the troubling qualities of such pursuit. Of course, the relationship between cultural resources and claimsmaking is not one-way. Claimsmakers draw upon available cultural resources, but their claims also inform and shape popular culture (Best 1990). For example, one 1994 suspense novel borrows heavily from stalking claims: the hero, a police detective in Beverly Hills' TMU, discusses the psychological and social patterns of stalkers (Woods 1994).

It is more difficult to prove a link between other, less specific cultural resources and the success of stalking claims. For instance, concern over stalking may have reflected the growing proportion of households headed by women, to the degree that women not living with a man seemed more vulnerable to a stalker's harassment. And concerns expressed in other claimsmaking campaigns seem consistent with the emergence of stalking as a social problem. These include concern over random violence (found in claims about

serial murder, freeway shootings, drive-by shootings, carjacking, and other crimes), male violence and the victimization of women (forcible rape, date and acquaintance rape, and domestic violence), and pedophilia. When claimsmakers typified stalking as random or unpredictable, violent, or gendered, they drew upon cultural resources that might encourage a favorable response to their claims. If stalking was somehow "like" other, well-established problems, then claims about stalking became more credible.

Organizational Resources

Claims also vary in the degree to which specific organizations promote them. . . .

Prior to 1989, claims about psychological rape lacked significant organizational support, and these issues never attracted prolonged attention. Mobilization of organizational resources occurred only after Rebecca Schaeffer's murder and the retypification of the problem as star-stalking. Key actors in promoting star-stalking had ties to the entertainment industry: the media's appetite for dramatic news about celebrities ensured increased coverage; individuals who specialized in providing security services for celebrities . . . discussed their work with the media (e.g., *Geraldo* 1990); and the SAG lobbied for California's antistalking law.

But antistalking laws spread only when other social movements supported the new legislation. In particular, the battered women's movement and the victims' rights movement campaigned for laws modeled on the California statute. Linking their cause with the visible problem of star-stalking gave the battered women's movement a fresh face. Coupling long-standing complaints about ineffective restraining orders to the lethal menace of stalking turned a tired topic into a hot issue. Antistalking laws put reform of the restraining order process on the public agenda, promising to give an established system of control new teeth. Media coverage of stalking increasingly cited experts from such organizations as Virginians Against Domestic Violence (Beck 1992). These statewide groups had links to the National Victim Center, Victims for Victims, and other victims' rights organizations. Like other long-term social movements, the victims' rights movement must continually reframe their claims in fresh ways. Opposition to stalking linked both the battered women's movement and the victims' rights movement to a new, dramatic, highly visible problem. By assuming ownership and using their resources to continue promoting the stalking problem, these movements kept stalking before the public and policymakers.

Mobilizing organizational resources helped pass antistalking legislation, but the absence of organized opposition may have been equally important. Violent, even murderous crimes by vengeful ex-husbands or mentally disturbed fans had few defenders; the campaign for antistalking laws met little opposition. While civil libertarians questioned the laws' constitutionality, the consensus deplored stalking. . . .

Conclusion: Stalking's Significance

. . . The current typification of stalking followed less successful claims that typified the problem in very different terms. Success required a typification that both drew upon cultural resources and attracted significant organizational support. The case of stalking suggests that this combination of typifying claims, cultural resources, and organizational resources is essential to successful claims-making. Still, the precise elements in a successful typification and the timing of the claims' success depend upon contingencies.

The construction of stalking as a new crime problem parallels the recent success of other claims about victimization. Many of these involve male violence against women. Others came to public attention through claimsmaking by victims seeking to redefine criminality and victimization. These broader shifts in public definitions of crime and victimization demand attention, but their analysis will require an analytic reconstruction of the changing typifications that led to the successful construction of specific crimes, such as stalking.

Acknowledgments
Partial support for this research came from a 1992 Faculty Research Grant from Valdosta State College and a 1993 Special Projects Grant from Southern Illinois University at Carbondale. We benefited from comments on earlier drafts by Robert A. Fein, Philip Jenkins, Donileen R. Loseke, David F. Luckenbill, and T. Memoree Thibodeau.

REFERENCES
Anonymous. 1980. "My Ex-Husband Won't Leave Me Alone." *Good Housekeeping* 190 (March):32–34, 39, 42.

Axthelm, P. 1989. "An Innocent Life, a Heartbreaking Death." *People* 32 (July 31):60–62, 64, 66.

Bacon, D. 1990. "When Fans Turn into Fanatics. . . ." *People* 33 (February 12):103, 105–106.

Beck, M. 1992. "Murderous Obsession." *Newsweek* 120 (July 13):60–62.

Best, J. 1990. *Threatened Children*. Chicago: University of Chicago Press.

———. 1991. "'Road Warriors' on 'Hair-Trigger Highways'." *Sociological Inquiry* 61:327–345.

Bradburn, Wayne E., Jr. 1992. "Stalking Statutes." *Ohio Northern University Law Review* 19:271–288.

Brownstein, H. H. 1991. "The Media and the Construction of Random Drug Violence." *Social Justice* 18(4):85–103.

Chicago Tribune. 1991. "Police Need Help to Stop Stalkers" (editorial). (November 18):1, 18.

CNN Prime News. 1993. "Michigan Legal System Takes Stalking Very Seriously." (January 1):Journal Graphics transcript 273.

Congressional Record. 1992. Senate (July 1):S9527.

Cosgrove, S. 1990. "Erotomania." *New Statesman & Society* 3(July 27):31–32.

Dietz, P. E., D. B. Matthews, D. A. Martell, T. M. Stewart, D. R. Hrouda, and J. Warren. 1991a. "Threatening and Otherwise Inappropriate Letters to Members of the United States Congress." *Journal of Forensic Sciences* 36:1445–1468.

Dietz, P. E., D. B. Matthews, C. Van Duyne, D. A. Martell, C. D. H. Parry, T. Stewart, J. Warren, and J. D. Crowder. 1991b. "Threatening and Otherwise Inappropriate Letters to Hollywood Celebrities." *Journal of Forensic Sciences* 36:185–209.

Ellis, D. 1993. "Nowhere to Hide." *People* 39 (May 17):62–66, 68, 71–72.

Fishman, M. 1978. "Crime Waves as Ideology." *Social Problems* 25:531–543.

48 Hours. 1992. "Stalker." (March 4). Transcript from Burrelle's Information Services.

Furio, J. 1993. "Can New State Laws Stop the Stalkers?" *Ms.* 3 (January):90–91.

Gamson, W., and A. Modigliani. 1989. "Media Discourse and Public Opinion on Nuclear Power." *American Journal of Sociology* 95:1–37.

Geraldo. 1990. "Tracking the Star Stalkers." (March 20):Journal Graphics transcript 654.

Gilligan, M. J. 1992. "Stalking the Stalker." *Georgia Law Review* 27:285–342.

Heil, A. 1986. "Lovesick." *Mademoiselle* 92 (December):128–130, 136–138.

Hilgartnner, S., and C. L. Bosk. 1988. "The Rise and Fall of Social Problems." *American Journal of Sociology* 94:53–78.

Hollinger, R. C., and L. Lanza-Kaduce. 1988. "The Process of Criminalization." *Criminology* 26:101–126.

Ingrassia, M. 1994. "Stalked to Death?" *Newsweek* 122 (November 1):27–28.

Jenkins, P. 1994. *Using Murder.* Hawthorne, NY: Aldine de Gruyter.

Kunen, J. S. 1987. "The Dark Side of Love." *People* 28(October 26):89–98

Lardner, G., Jr. 1992. "The Stalking of Kristen." *Washington Post* (November 22): C1–C3.

Larry King Live. 1994. "What About Nicole Simpson?" (June 22):Journal Graphics transcript 1153.

Loseke, D. R. 1992. *The Battered Woman and Shelters.* Albany: State University of New York Press.

Miller, B. 1993. "Thou Shalt Not Stalk." *Chicago Tribune Magazine* (April 18):14–16, 18, 20.

Mithers, C. L. 1982. "Can a Man Be Too Mad about You?" *Mademoiselle* 88(October):36.

Morville, D. A. 1993. "Stalking Laws." *Washington University Law Quarterly* 71:921–935.

National Institute of Justice. 1993. *Project to Develop a Model Anti-Stalking Code for States.* Washington, DC: U.S. Department of Justice.

Oprah. 1994. "Women in Fear for their Lives." (January 21). Transcript from Burrelle's Information Services.

Pacific Law Journal. 1990. "Selected 1990 Legislation." 22:500–501.

Perez, C. 1993. "Stalking." *American Journal of Criminal Law* 20:264–280.

Pfohl, S. 1977. "The 'Discovery' of Child Abuse." *Social Problems* 24:310–323.

Reinarman, C. 1988. "The Social Construction of an Alcohol Problem." *Theory and Society* 17:91–120.

Rose, V. M. 1977. "Rape as a Social Problem." *Social Problems* 25:75–89.

Safran, C. 1992. "A Stranger Was Stalking our Little Girl." *Good Housekeeping* 215(November):185, 263–266.

Sally Jessy Raphael. 1993. "I Was Stalked Like an Animal." (May 19):Journal Graphics transcript 1227.

———. 1994. "Miss America Stalked." (February 15): Journal Graphics transcript 1420.

Sherman, W. 1994. "Stalking." *Cosmopolitan* 216 (April): 198–201.

Tharp, M. 1992. "In the Mind of a Stalker." *U.S. News and World Report* 112(February 17):28–30.

Toobin, J. 1994. "The Man Who Kept Going Free." *New Yorker* 70(March 7):38–48, 53.

U.S. Senate. 1992. Antistalking legislation. Hearings held by the Committee on the Judiciary. September 29.

———. 1993. Antistalking proposals. Hearing held by the Committee on the Judiciary. March 17.

Wilcox, B. 1982. "Psychological Rape." *Glamour* 80 (October):232–233, 291–296.

Winter, P. D. 1980. "Notes on a Death Threat." *Ms.* 8 (January):60–65.

Woods, S. 1994. *Dead Eyes.* New York: HarperCollins.

Researching Dealers and Smugglers

Patricia A. Adler

I strongly believe that investigative field research (Douglas 1976), with emphasis on direct personal observation, interaction, and experience, is the only way to acquire accurate knowledge about deviant behavior. Investigative techniques are especially necessary for studying groups such as drug dealers and smugglers because the highly illegal nature of their occupation makes them secretive, deceitful, mistrustful, and paranoid. To insulate themselves from the straight world, they construct multiple false fronts, offer lies and misinformation, and withdraw into their group. In fact, detailed, scientific information about upper-level drug dealers and smugglers is lacking precisely because of the difficulty sociological researchers have had in penetrating into their midst. As a result, the only way I could possibly get close enough to these individuals to discover what they were doing and to understand their world from their perspectives (Blumer 1969) was to take a membership role in the setting. While my different values and goals precluded my becoming converted to complete membership in the subculture, and my fears prevented my ever becoming "actively" involved in their trafficking activities, I was able to assume a "peripheral" membership role. I became a member of the dealers' and smugglers' social world and participated in their daily activities on that basis. . . .

Getting In

When I moved to Southwest County [California] in the summer of 1974, I had no idea that I would soon be swept up in a subculture of vast drug trafficking and unending partying, mixed with occasional cloak-and-dagger subterfuge. I had moved to California with my husband, Peter, to attend graduate school in sociology. We rented a condominium townhouse near the beach and started taking classes in the fall. We had always felt that socializing exclusively with academicians left us nowhere to escape from our work, so we tried to meet people in the nearby community. One of the first friends we made was our closest neighbor, a fellow in his late twenties with a tall, hulking frame and gentle expression. Dave, as he introduced himself, was always dressed rather casually, if not sloppily, in T-shirts and jeans. He spent most of his time hanging out or walking on the beach with a variety of friends who visited his house, and taking care of his two young boys, who lived alternately with him and his estranged wife. He also went out of town a lot. We started spending much of our free time over at his house, talking, playing board games late into the night, and smoking marijuana together. We were glad to find someone from whom we could buy marijuana in this new place, since we did not know too many people. He also began treating us to a fairly regular supply of cocaine, which was a thrill because this was a drug we could rarely afford on our student budgets. We noticed right away, however, that there was something unusual about his use and knowledge of drugs: while he always had a plentiful supply and was fairly expert about marijuana and cocaine, when we tried to buy a small bag of marijuana from him he had little idea of the going price. This incongruity piqued our curiosity and raised suspicion. We wondered if he might be dealing in larger quantities. Keeping our suspicions to ourselves, we began observing Dave's activities a little more closely. Most of his friends were in their late twenties and early thirties and, judging by their lifestyles and automobiles, rather wealthy. They came and left his house at all hours, occasionally extending their parties through the night and the next day into the following night. Yet throughout this time we never saw Dave or any of his friends engage in any activity that resembled a legitimate job. In most places this might have evoked community suspicion, but few of the people we encountered in Southwest County seemed to hold traditionally structured jobs. Dave, in fact, had no visible means of financial support. When we asked him what he did for a living, he said something vague about being a real estate speculator, and we let it go at that. We never voiced our suspicions directly since he chose not to broach the subject with us.

We did discuss the subject with our mentor, Jack Douglas, however. He was excited by the prospect that we might be living among a group of big dealers, and urged us to follow our instincts and develop leads into the group. He knew that the local area was rife with drug trafficking, since he had begun a life history case study of two drug dealers with another graduate student several years previously. That earlier study was aborted when the graduate student quit school, but Jack still had many hours of taped interviews he had conducted with them, as well as an interview that he had done with an undergraduate student who had known the two dealers independently, to serve as a cross-check on their accounts. He therefore encouraged us to become friendlier with Dave and his friends. We decided that if anything did develop out of our observations of Dave, it might make a nice paper for a field methods class or independent study. . . .

We thus watched Dave and continued to develop our friendship with him. We also watched his friends and got to know a few of his more regular visitors. We continued to build friendly relations by doing, quite naturally, what Becker (1963), Polsky (1969), and Douglas (1972) had advocated for the early stages of field research: we gave them a chance to know us and form judgments about our trustworthiness by jointly pursuing those interests and activities which we had in common.

Then one day something happened which forced a breakthrough in the research. Dave had two guys visiting him from out of town and, after snorting quite a bit of cocaine, they turned their conversation to a trip they had just made from Mexico, where they piloted a load of marijuana back across the border in a small plane. Dave made a few efforts to shift the conversation to another subject, telling them to "button their lips," but they apparently thought that he was joking. They thought that anybody as close to Dave as we seemed to be undoubtedly knew the nature of his business. They made further allusions to his involvement in the operation and discussed the outcome of the sale. We could feel the wave of tension and awkwardness from Dave when this conversation began, as he looked toward us to see if we understood the implications of what was being said, but then he just shrugged it off as done. Later, after the two guys left, he discussed with us what happened. He admitted to us that he was a member of a smuggling crew and a major marijuana dealer on the side. He said that he knew he could trust us, but that it was his practice to say as little as possible to outsiders about his activities. This inadvertent slip, and Dave's subsequent opening up, were highly significant in forging our entry into Southwest County's drug world. From then on he was open in discussing the nature of his dealing and smuggling activities with us.

He was, it turned out, a member of a smuggling crew that was importing a ton of marijuana weekly and 40 kilos of cocaine every few months. During that first winter and spring, we observed Dave at work and also got to know the other members of his crew, including Ben, the smuggler himself. Ben was also very tall and broad shouldered, but his long black hair, now flecked with gray, bespoke his earlier membership in the hippie subculture. A large physical stature, we observed, was common to most of the male participants involved in this drug community. The women also had a unifying physical trait: they were extremely attractive and stylishly dressed. This included Dave's ex-wife, Jean, with whom he reconciled during the spring. We therefore became friendly with Jean and through her met a number of women ("dope chicks") who hung around the dealers and smugglers. As we continued to gain the friendship of Dave and Jean's associates we were progressively admitted into their inner circle and apprised of each person's dealing or smuggling role.

Once we realized the scope of Ben's and his associates' activities, we saw the enormous research potential in studying them. This scene was different from any analysis of drug trafficking that we had read in the sociological literature because of the amounts they were dealing and the fact that they were importing it themselves. We decided that, if it was at all possible, we would capitalize on this situation, to "opportunistically" (Riemer 1977) take advantage of our prior expertise and of the knowledge, entree, and rapport we had already developed with several key people in this setting. We therefore discussed the idea of doing a study of the general subculture with Dave and several of his closest friends (now becoming our friends). We assured them of the anonymity, confidentiality, and innocuousness of our work. They were happy to reciprocate our friendship by being of help to our professional careers. In fact, they basked in the subsequent attention we gave their lives.

We began by turning first Dave, then others, into key informants and collecting their life histories in detail. We conducted a series of taped, depth interviews with an unstructured, open-ended format. We questioned them about such topics as their backgrounds, their recruitment into the occupation, the stages of their dealing careers, their relations with others, their motivations, their lifestyle, and their general impressions about the community as a whole.

We continued to do taped interviews with key informants for the next six years until 1980, when we moved away from the area. After that, we occasionally did follow-up interviews when we returned for vacation visits. These later interviews focused on recording the continuing unfolding of events and included detailed probing into specific conceptual areas, such as dealing networks, types of dealers, secrecy, trust, paranoia, reputation, the law, occupational mobility, and occupational stratification. The number of taped interviews we did with each key informant varied, ranging between 10 and 30 hours of discussion.

Our relationship with Dave and the others thus took on an added dimension—the research relationship. As Douglas (1976), Henslin (1972), and Wax (1952) have noted, research relationships involve some form of mutual exchange. In our case, we offered everything that friendship could entail. We did routine favors for them in the course of our everyday lives, offered them insights

and advice about their lives from the perspective of our more respectable position, wrote letters on their behalf to the authorities when they got in trouble, testified as character witnesses at their non-drug-related trials, and loaned them money when they were down and out. When Dave was arrested and brought to trial for check-kiting, we helped Jean organize his defense and raise the money to pay his fines. We spelled her in taking care of the children so that she could work on his behalf. When he was eventually sent to the state prison we maintained close ties with her and discussed our mutual efforts to buoy Dave up and secure his release. We also visited him in jail. During Dave's incarceration, however, Jean was courted by an old boyfriend and gave up her reconciliation with Dave. This proved to be another significant turning point in our research because, desperate for money, Jean looked up Dave's old dealing connections and went into the business herself. She did not stay with these marijuana dealers and smugglers for long, but soon moved into the cocaine business. Over the next several years her experiences in the world of cocaine dealing brought us into contact with a different group of people. While these people knew Dave and his associates (this was very common in the Southwest County dealing and smuggling community), they did not deal with them directly. We were thus able to gain access to a much wider and more diverse range of subjects than we would have had she not branched out on her own.

Dave's eventual release from prison three months later brought our involvement in the research to an even deeper level. He was broke and had nowhere to go. When he showed up on our doorstep, we took him in. We offered to let him stay with us until he was back on his feet again and could afford a place of his own. He lived with us for seven months, intimately sharing his daily experiences with us. During this time we witnessed, firsthand, his transformation from a scared ex-con who would never break the law again to a hard-working legitimate employee who only dealt to get money for his children's Christmas presents, to a full-time dealer with no pretensions at legitimate work. Both his process of changing attitudes and the community's gradual reacceptance of him proved very revealing.

We socialized with Dave, Jean, and other members of Southwest County's dealing and smuggling community on a near-daily basis, especially during the first four years of the research (before we had a child). We worked in their legitimate businesses, vacationed together, attended their weddings, and cared for their children. Throughout their relationship with us, several participants became co-opted to the researcher's perspective and actively sought out instances of behavior which filled holes in the conceptualizations we were developing. Dave, for one, became so intrigued by our conceptual dilemmas that he undertook a "natural experiment" entirely on his own, offering an unlimited supply of drugs to a lower-level dealer to see if he could work up to higher levels of dealing, and what factors would enhance or impinge upon his upward mobility.

In addition to helping us directly through their own experiences, our key informants aided us in widening our circle of contacts. For instance, they let us know when someone in whom we might be interested was planning on dropping by, vouching for our trustworthiness and reliability as friends who could be included in business conversations. Several times we were even awakened in the night by phone calls informing us that someone had dropped by for a visit, should we want to "casually" drop over too. We rubbed the sleep from our eyes, dressed, and walked or drove over, feeling like sleuths out of a television series. We thus were able to snowball, through the active efforts of our key informants, into an expanded study population. This was supplemented by our own efforts to cast a research net and befriend other dealers, moving from contact to contact slowly and carefully through the domino effect.

The Covert Role

The highly illegal nature of dealing in illicit drugs and dealers' and smugglers' general level of suspicion made the adoption of an overt research role highly sensitive and problematic. In discussing this issue with our key informants, they all agreed that we shoud be extremely discreet (for both our sakes and theirs). We carefully approached new individuals before we admitted that we were studying them. With many of these people, then, we took a covert posture in the research setting. As nonparticipants in the business activities which bound members together into the group, it was difficult to become fully accepted as peers. We therefore tried to establish some sort of peripheral, social membership in the general crowd, where we could be accepted as "wise" (Goffman 1963) individuals and granted a courtesy membership. This seemed an attainable goal, since we had begun our involvement by forming such relationships with our key informants. By being introduced to others in this wise rather than overt role, we were able to interact with people who would otherwise have shied away from us. Adopting a courtesy membership caused us to bear a courtesy stigma however, and we suffered since we, at times, had to disguise the nature of our research from both lay outsiders and academicians.

In our overt posture we showed interest in dealers' and smugglers' activities, encouraged them to talk about themselves (within limits, so as to avoid acting like narcs), and ran home to write field notes. This role offered us the advantage of gaining access to unapproachable people while avoiding researcher effects, but it prevented us from asking some necessary, probing questions and from tape recording conversations. We therefore sought, at all times, to build toward a conversion to the overt role. We did this by working to develop their trust.

Developing Trust

Like achieving entree, the process of developing trust with members of unorganized deviant groups can be slow and difficult. In the absence of a formal structure separating members from outsiders, each individual must form his or her own judgment about whether new persons can be admitted to their confidence. No gatekeeper existed to smooth our path to being trusted, although our key informants acted in this role whenever they could by providing introductions and references. In addition, the unorganized nature of this group meant that we met people at different times and were constantly at different levels in our developing relationships with them. We were thus trusted more by some people than by others, in part because of their greater familiarity with us. But as Douglas (1976) has noted, just because someone knew us or even liked us did not automatically guarantee that they would trust us.

We actively tried to cultivate the trust of our respondents by tying them to us with favors. Small things, like offering the use of our phone, were followed with bigger favors, like offering the use of our car, and finally really meaningful favors, like offering the use of our home. Here we often trod a thin line, trying to ensure our personal safety while putting ourselves in enough of a risk position, along with our research subjects, so that they would trust us. While we were able to build a "web of trust" (Douglas 1976) with some members, we found that trust, in large part, was not a simple status to attain in the drug world. Johnson (1975) has pointed out that trust is not a one-time phenomenon, but an ongoing developmental process. From my experiences in this research I would add that it cannot be simply assumed to be a one-way process either, for it can be diminished, withdrawn, reinstated to varying degrees, and re-questioned at any point. Carey (1972) and Douglas (1972) have remarked on this waxing and waning process, but it was especially pronounced for us because our subjects used large amounts of cocaine over an extended period of time. This tended to make them alternately warm and cold to us. We thus lived through a series of ups and downs with the people we were trying to cultivate as research informants.

The Overt Role

After this initial covert phase, we began to feel that some new people trusted us. We tried to intuitively feel when the time was right to approach them and go overt. We used two means of approaching people to inform them that we were involved in a study of dealing and smuggling: direct and indirect. In some cases our key informants approached their friends or connections and, after vouching for our absolute trustworthiness, convinced these associates to talk to us. In other instances, we approached people directly, asking for their help with our project. We worked our way through a progression with these secondary contacts, first discussing the dealing scene overtly and later moving to taped life history interviews. Some people reacted well to us, but others responded skittishly, making appointments to do taped interviews only to break them as the day drew near, and going through fluctuating stages of being honest with us or putting up fronts about their dealing activities. This varied, for some, with their degree of active involvement in the business. During the times when they had quit dealing, they would tell us about their present and past activities, but when they became actively involved again, they would hide it from us.

This progression of covert to overt roles generated a number of tactical difficulties. The first was the problem of *coming on too fast* and blowing it. Early in the research we had a dealer's old lady (we thought) all set up for the direct approach. We knew many dealers in common and had discussed many things tangential to dealing with her without actually mentioning the subject. When we asked her to do a taped interview of her bohemian lifestyle, she agreed without hesitation. When the interview began, though, and she found out why we were interested in her, she balked, gave us a lot of incoherent jumble, and ended the session as quickly as possible. Even though she lived only three houses away we never saw her again. We tried to move more slowly after that.

A second problem involved simultaneously *juggling our overt and covert roles* with different people. This created the danger of getting our cover blown with people who did not know about our research (Henslin 1972). It was very confusing to separate the people who knew about our study from those who did not, especially in the minds of our informants. They would make occasional veiled references in front of people, especially when loosened by intoxicants, that made us extremely uncomfortable. We also frequently worried that our snooping would someday be mistaken for police tactics. Fortunately, this never happened. . . .

Problems and Issues

Reflecting on the research process, I have isolated a number of issues which I believe merit additional discussion. These are rooted in experiences which have the potential for greater generic applicability.

The first is the *effect of drugs on the data-gathering process*. Carey (1972) has elaborated on some of the problems he encountered when trying to interview respondents who used amphetamines, while Wax (1952, 1957) has mentioned the difficulty of trying to record field notes while drinking sake. I found that marijuana and cocaine had nearly opposite effects from each other. The latter helped the interview process, while the former hindered it. Our attempts to interview respondents who were stoned on marijuana were unproductive for a number of reasons. The primary obstacle was the effects of the drug. Often, people became confused, sleepy, or involved in eating to varying degrees. This distracted them from our purpose. At times, people even simulated overreactions to marijuana to hide behind the drug's supposed disorienting influence and thereby avoid divulging information. Cocaine, in contrast, proved to be a research aid. The drug's warming and sociable influence opened people up, diminished their inhibitions, and generally increased their enthusiasm for both the interview experience and us.

A second problem I encountered involved *assuming risks while doing research*. As I noted earlier, dangerous situations are often generic to research on deviant behavior. We were most afraid of the people we studied. As Carey (1972), Henslin (1972), and Whyte (1955) have stated, members of deviant groups can become hostile toward a researcher if they think that they are being treated wrongfully. This could have happened at any time from a simple occurrence, such as a misunderstanding, or from something more serious, such as our covert posture being exposed. Because of the inordinate amount of drugs they consumed, drug dealers and smugglers were particularly volatile, capable of becoming malicious toward each other or us with little warning. They were also likely to behave erratically owing to the great risks they faced from the police and other dealers. These factors made them moody, and they vacillated between trusting us and being suspicious of us.

At various times we also had to protect our research tapes. We encountered several threats to our collection of taped interviews from people who had granted us these interviews. This made us anxious, since we had taken great pains to acquire these tapes and felt strongly about maintaining confidences entrusted to us by our informants. When threatened, we became extremely frightened and shifted the tapes between different hiding places. We even ventured forth one rainy night with our tapes packed in a suitcase to meet a person who was uninvolved in the research at a secret rendezvous so that he could guard the tapes for us.

We were fearful, lastly, of the police. We often worried about local police or drug agents discovering the nature of our study and confiscating or subpoenaing our tapes and field notes. Sociologists have no privileged relationship with their subjects that would enable us legally to withhold evidence from the authorities should they subpoena it. For this reason we studiously avoided any publicity about the research, even holding back on publishing articles in scholarly journals until we were nearly ready to move out of the setting. The closest we came to being publicly exposed as drug researchers came when a former sociology graduate student (turned dealer, we had heard from inside sources) was arrested at the scene of a cocaine deal. His lawyer wanted us to testify about the dangers of doing drug-related research, since he was using his research status as his defense. Fortunately, the crisis was averted when his lawyer succeeded in suppressing evidence and had the case dismissed before the trial was to have begun. Had we been exposed, however, our respondents would have acquired guilt by association through their friendship with us.

Our fear of the police went beyond our concern for protecting our research subjects, however. We risked the danger of arrest ourselves through our own violations of the law. Many sociologists (Becker 1963; Carey 1972; Polsky 1969; Whyte 1955) have remarked that field researchers studying deviance must inevitably break the law in order to acquire valid participant observation data. This occurs in its most innocuous form from having "guilty knowledge": information about crimes that are committed. Being aware of major dealing and smuggling operations made us an accessory to their commission, since we failed to notify the police. We broke the law, secondly, through our "guilty observations," by being present at the scene of a crime and witnessing its occurrence (see also Carey 1972). We knew it was possible to get caught in a bust involving others, yet buying and selling was so pervasive that to leave every time it occurred would have been unnatural and highly suspicious. Sometimes drug transactions even occurred in our home, especially when Dave was living there, but we finally had to put a stop to that because we could not handle the anxiety. Lastly, we broke the law through our "guilty actions," by taking part in illegal behavior ourselves. Although we never dealt drugs (we were too scared to be seriously tempted), we consumed drugs and possessed them in small quantities. Quite frankly, it would have been impossible for a nonuser to have gained access to this group to gather the data presented here. This was the minimum involvement necessary to obtain even the courtesy membership we achieved. Some kind of illegal action was also found to be a necessary or helpful component of the research by Becker (1963), Carey (1972), Johnson (1975), Polsky (1969), and Whyte (1955).

Another methodological issue arose from the *cultural clash between our research subjects and ourselves*. While other sociologists have alluded to these kinds of differences (Humphreys 1970, Whyte 1955), few have discussed how the research relationships affected them. Relationships with research subjects are unique because they involve a bond of intimacy between persons who might not ordinarily associate together, or who might otherwise be no more than casual friends. When fieldworkers undertake a major project, they commit themselves to maintaining a long-term relationship with the people they study. However, as researchers try to get depth involvement, they are apt to come across fundamental differences in character, values, and attitudes between their subjects and themselves. In our case, we were most strongly confronted by differences in present versus future orientations, a desire for risk versus security, and feelings of spontaneity versus self-discipline. These differences often caused us great frustration. We repeatedly saw dealers act irrationally, setting themselves up for failure. We wrestled with our desire to point out

their patterns of foolhardy behavior and offer advice, feeling competing pulls between our detached, observer role which advised us not to influence the natural setting, and our involved, participant role which called for us to offer friendly help whenever possible. . . .

The final issue I will discuss involved the various *ethical problems* which arose during this research. Many fieldworkers have encountered ethical dilemmas or pangs of guilt during the course of their research experiences (Carey 1972; Douglas 1976; Humphreys 1970; Johnson 1975; Klockars 1977, 1979; Rochford 1985). The researchers' role in the field makes this necessary because they can never fully align themselves with their subjects while maintaining their identity and personal commitment to the scientific community. Ethical dilemmas, then, are directly related to the amount of deception researchers use in gathering the data, and the degree to which they have accepted such acts as necessary and therefore neutralized them.

Throughout the research, we suffered from the burden of intimacies and confidences. Guarding secrets which had been told to us during taped interviews was not always easy or pleasant. Dealers occasionally revealed things about themselves or others that we had to pretend not to know when interacting with their close associates. This sometimes meant that we had to lie or build elaborate stories to cover for some people. Their fronts therefore became our fronts, and we had to weave our own web of deception to guard their performances. This became especially disturbing during the writing of the research report, as I was torn by conflicts between using details to enrich the data and glossing over description to guard confidences.

Using the covert research role generated feelings of guilt, despite the fact that our key informants deemed it necessary, and thereby condoned it. Their own covert experiences were far more deeply entrenched than ours, being a part of their daily existence with non-drug world members. Despite the universal presence of covert behavior throughout the setting, we still felt a sense of betrayal every time we ran home to write research notes on observations we had made under the guise of innocent participants. . . .

Conclusions

The aggressive research strategy I employed was vital to this study. I could not just walk up to strangers and start hanging out with them as Liebow (1967) did, or be sponsored to a member of this group by a social service or reform organization as Whyte (1955) was, and expect to be accepted, let alone welcomed. Perhaps such a strategy might have worked with a group that had nothing to hide, but I doubt it. Our modern, pluralistic society is so filled with diverse subcultures whose interests compete or conflict with each other that each subculture has a set of knowledge which is reserved exclusively for insiders. In order to survive and prosper, they do not ordinarily show this side to just anyone. To obtain the kind of depth insight and information I needed, I had to become like the members in certain ways. They dealt only with people they knew and trusted, so I had to become known and trusted before I could reveal my true self and my research interests. Confronted with secrecy, danger, hidden alliances, misrepresentations, and unpredictable changes of intent, I had to use a delicate combination of overt and covert roles. Throughout, my deliberate cultivation of the norm of reciprocal exchange enabled me to trade my friendship for their knowledge, rather than waiting for the highly unlikely event that information would be delivered into my lap. I thus actively built a web of research contacts, used them to obtain highly sensitive data, and carefully checked them out to ensure validity. . . .

Finally, I feel strongly that to ensure accuracy, research on deviant groups must be conducted in the settings where it naturally occurs. As Polsky (1969:115–16) has forcefully asserted:

> This means—there is no getting away from it—the study of career criminals *au natural,* in the field, the study of such criminals as they normally go about their work and play, the study of "uncaught" criminals and the study of others who in the past have been caught but are not caught at the time you study them. . . . Obviously we can no longer afford the convenient fiction that in studying criminals in their natural habitat, we would discover nothing really important that could not be discovered from criminals behind bars.

By studying criminals in their natural habitat I was able to see them in the full variability and complexity of their surrounding subculture, rather than within the artificial environment of a prison. I was thus able to learn about otherwise inaccessible dimensions of their lives, observing and analyzing firsthand the nature of their social organization, social stratification, lifestyle, and motivation.

REFERENCES

Becker, Howard. 1963. *Outsiders.* New York: Free Press.

Blumer, Herbert. 1969. *Symbolic Interactionism.* Englewood Cliffs, N.J.:Prentice-Hall.

Carey, James T. 1972. "Problems of access and risk in observing drug scenes." In Jack D. Douglas, ed., *Research on Deviance,* pp. 71–92. New York: Random House.

Douglas, Jack D. 1972. "Observing deviance." In Jack D. Douglas, ed., *Research on Deviance,* pp. 3–34. New York: Random House.

———. 1976. *Investigative Social Research.* Beverly Hills, Calif.: Sage.

Goffman, Erving. 1963. *Stigma.* Englewood Cliffs, N.J.: Prentice-Hall.

Henslin, James M. 1972. "Studying deviance in four settings: research experiences with cabbies, suicides, drug users and abortionees." In Jack D. Douglas, ed., *Research on Deviance,* pp. 35–70. New York: Random House.

Humphreys, Laud. 1970. *Tearoom Trade.* Chicago: Aldine.

Johnson, John M. 1975. *Doing Field Research.* New York: Free Press.

Klockars, Carl B. 1977. "Field ethics for the life history." In Robert Weppner, ed., *Street Ethnography,* pp. 201–26. Beverly Hills, Calif.: Sage.

———. 1979. "Dirty hands and deviant subjects." In Carl B. Klockars and Finnbarr W. O'Connor, eds., *Deviance and Decency,* pp. 261–82. Beverly Hills, Calif.: Sage.

Liebow, Elliot. 1967. *Tally's Corner.* Boston: Little, Brown.

Polsky, Ned. 1969. *Hustlers, Beats, and Others.* New York: Doubleday.

Riemer, Jeffrey W. 1977. "Varieties of opportunistic research." *Urban Life* 5:467–77.

Rochford, E. Burke, Jr. 1985. *Hare Krishna in America*. New Brunswick, N.J.: Rutgers University Press.

Wax, Rosalie. 1952. "Reciprocity as a field technique." *Human Organization* 11:34–37.

_____. 1957. "Twelve years later: an analysis of a field experience." *American Journal of Sociology* 63: 133–42.

Whyte, William F. 1955. *Street Corner Society*. Chicago: University of Chicago Press.

THINKING ABOUT THE READINGS

Stalking Strangers and Lovers

■ How does the Lowney and Best article support the contention that reality is a social construction? Consider the broader implications of their argument: that certain crimes become serious social problems not because everyone agrees that they are objectively dangerous conditions, but because they receive the appropriate kind of media and political attention. What does this argument suggest about the way crime fears and crime waves are developed and maintained in society? Can you think of other situations in which heightened media coverage has created widespread public concern and moral outrage?

Researching Dealers and Smugglers

■ Many of the issues sociologists attempt to understand are phenomena that occur under highly secretive circumstances. Patricia Adler chose a research method which brought her and her husband extremely close to people involved in serious criminal activity. Only from this vantage point could they fully understand the forces at play. Do you think their tactic was ethically justifiable? Should social researchers be obligated to report criminal activity to the proper authorities, or is it appropriate to hide such information in the name of scientific research? Can you think of a better way to acquire trustworthy information about drug dealers and smugglers?

CHAPTER 4

Building Order
Culture and History

One of the key messages of sociology is that the social norms that mark the millions of seemingly trivial actions and social encounters of our everyday lives are what, ultimately, make social order possible. They make our lives relatively predictable by telling us what to expect from others and what others should expect from us. But these norms vary greatly across time and across cultures.

Sociology tells us that virtually every aspect of our lives is influenced by culture and history. When we examine these influences, things that were once familiar and taken for granted suddenly become unfamiliar and curious. During the course of our lives we are rarely forced to examine why we do the common things we do, we just do them. But if we take a step back and examine our common customs and behaviors, they begin to look as strange as the "mystical" rituals of some far-off, exotic land. It is for this reason that Horace Miner's article, "Body Ritual Among the Nacirema," has become a classic in sociology and anthropology.

I think if you asked a bunch of people on the street if lying is a good or bad thing, most would say it is bad. Lying threatens the cherished value of honesty, something most of us assume is essential in the formation of solid human relationships. But J. A. Barnes, in "A Pack of Lies," shows us that some cultures have very different beliefs about truthfulness and deceit than we do in the West. In some societies, lying is a common practice. Even in a culture which denounces dishonesty, lying is acceptable, even expected, under certain circumstances and within different social classes and power relations.

As Jessica Mitford shows in "Fashions in Childbirth," even our most fundamental biological experiences are touched by culture and history. Mitford points out that something so utterly natural and universal as giving birth can be affected by broader historical changes. She describes how the normal, healthy childbirth practices of one era can seem disastrous, dangerous, even barbaric, by another. Technological advances in childbirth practices are always the result of the standard practices and problems of the times. Hence what is considered an improvement for one age often turns out to be a problem for the next.

Body Ritual Among the Nacirema

Horace Miner

The anthropologist has become so familiar with the diversity of ways in which different peoples behave in similar situations that he is not apt to be surprised by even the most exotic customs. In fact, if all of the logically possible combinations of behavior have not been found somewhere in the world, he is apt to suspect that they must be present in some yet undescribed tribe. This point has, in fact, been expressed with respect to clan organization by Murdock (1949:71). In this light, the magical beliefs and practices of the Nacirema present such unusual aspects that it seems desirable to describe them as an example of the extremes to which human behavior can go.

Professor Linton first brought the ritual of the Nacirema to the attention of anthropologists twenty years ago (1936:326), but the culture of this people is still very poorly understood. They are a North American group living in the territory between the Canadian Cree, the Yaqui and Tarahumare of Mexico, and the Carib and Arawak of the Antilles. Little is known of their origin, although tradition states that they came from the east. According to Nacirema mythology, their nation was originated by a culture hero, Notgnih-saw, who is otherwise known for two great feats of strength—the throwing of a piece of wampum across the river Pa-To-Mac and the chopping down of a cherry tree in which the Spirit of Truth resided.

Nacirema culture is characterized by a highly developed market economy which has evolved in a rich natural habitat. While much of the people's time is devoted to economic pursuits, a large part of the fruits of these labors and a considerable portion of the day are spent in ritual activity. The focus of this activity is the human body, the appearance and health of which loom as a dominant concern in the ethos of the people. While such a concern is certainly not unusual, its ceremonial aspects and associated philosophy are unique.

The fundamental belief underlying the whole system appears to be that the human body is ugly and that its natural tendency is to debility and disease. Incarcerated in such a body, man's only hope is to avert these characteristics through the use of the powerful influences of ritual and ceremony. Every household has one or more shrines devoted to this purpose. The more powerful individuals in the society have several shrines in their houses and, in fact, the opulence of a house is often referred to in terms of the number of such ritual centers it possesses. Most houses are of wattle and daub construction, but the shrine rooms of the more wealthy are walled with stone. Poorer families imitate the rich by applying pottery plaques to their shrine walls.

While each family has at least one such shrine, the rituals associated with it are not family ceremonies but are private and secret. The rites are normally only discussed with children, and then only during the period when they are being initiated into these mysteries. I was able, however, to establish sufficient rapport with the natives to examine these shrines and to have the rituals described to me.

The focal point of the shrine is a box or chest which is built into the wall. In this chest are kept the many charms and magical potions without which no native believes he could live. These preparations are secured from a variety of specialized practitioners. The most powerful of these are the medicine men, whose assistance must be rewarded with substantial gifts. However, the medicine men do not provide the curative potions for their clients, but decide what the ingredients should be and then write them down in an ancient and secret language. This writing is understood only by the medicine men and by the herbalists who, for another gift, provide the required charm.

The charm is not disposed of after it has served its purpose, but is placed in the charm-box of the household shrine. As these magical materials are specific for certain ills, and the real or imagined maladies of the people are many, the charm-box is usually full to overflowing. The magical packets are so numerous that people forget what their purposes were and fear to use them again. While the natives are very vague on this point, we can only assume that the idea in retaining all the old magical materials is that their presence in the charm-box, before which the body rituals are conducted, will in some way protect the worshipper.

Beneath the charm-box is a small font. Each day every member of the family, in succession, enters the shrine room, bows his head before the charm-box, mingles different sorts of holy water in the font, and proceeds with a brief rite of ablution. The holy waters are secured from the Water Temple of the community, where the priests conduct elaborate ceremonies to make the liquid ritually pure.

In the hierarchy of magical practitioners, and below the medicine men in prestige, are specialists whose designation is best translated "holy-mouth-men." The Nacirema have an almost pathological horror of and fascination with the mouth, the condition of which is believed to have a supernatural influence on all social relationships. Were it not for the rituals of the mouth, they believe that their teeth would fall out, their gums bleed, their jaws shrink, their friends desert them, and their lovers reject them. They also believe that a strong relationship exists between oral and moral characteristics. For example, there is a ritual ablution of the mouth for children which is supposed to improve their moral fiber.

The daily body ritual performed by everyone includes a mouth-rite. Despite the fact that these people are so punctilious about care of the mouth, this rite involves a practice which strikes the uninitiated stranger as revolting. It was reported to me that the ritual consists of inserting a small bundle of hog hairs into the mouth, along with certain magical powders, and then moving the bundle in a highly formalized series of gestures.

In addition to the private mouth-rite, the people seek out a holy-mouth-man once or twice a year. These practitioners have an impressive set of paraphernalia, consisting of a variety of augers, awls, probes, and prods. The use of these objects in the exorcism of the evils of the mouth involves almost unbelievable ritual torture of the client. The holy-mouth-man opens the client's mouth and, using the above mentioned tools, enlarges any holes which decay may have created in the teeth. Magical materials are put into these holes. If there are no naturally occurring holes in the teeth, large sections of one or more teeth are gouged out so that the supernatural substance can be applied. In the client's view, the purpose of these ministrations is to arrest decay and to draw friends. The extremely sacred and traditional character of the rite is evident in the fact that the natives return to the holy-mouth-men year after year, despite the fact that their teeth continue to decay.

It is to be hoped that, when a thorough study of the Nacirema is made, there will be careful inquiry into the personality structure of these people. One has but to watch the gleam in the eye of a holy-mouth-man, as he jabs an awl into an exposed nerve, to suspect that a certain amount of sadism is involved. If this can be established, a very interesting pattern emerges, for most of the population shows definite masochistic tendencies. It was to these that Professor Linton referred in discussing a distinctive part of the daily body ritual which is performed only by men. This part of the rite involves scraping and lacerating the surface of the face with a sharp instrument. Special women's rites are performed only four times during each lunar month, but what they lack in frequency is made up in barbarity. As part of this ceremony, women bake their heads in small ovens for about an hour. The theoretically interesting point is that what seems to be a preponderantly masochistic people have developed sadistic specialists.

The medicine men have an imposing temple, or *latipso,* in every community of any size. The more elaborate ceremonies required to treat very sick patients can only be performed at this temple. These ceremonies involve not only the thaumaturge but a permanent group of vestal maidens who move sedately about the temple chambers in distinctive costume and headdress.

The *latipso* ceremonies are so harsh that it is phenomenal that a fair proportion of the really sick natives who enter the temple ever recover. Small children whose indoctrination is still incomplete have been known to resist attempts to take them to the temple because "that is where you go to die." Despite this fact, sick adults are not only willing but eager to undergo the protracted ritual purification, if they can afford to do so. No matter how ill the supplicant or how grave the emergency, the guardians of many temples will not admit a client if he cannot give a rich gift to the custodian. Even after one has gained admission and survived the ceremonies, the guardians will not permit the neophyte to leave until he makes still another gift.

The supplicant entering the temple is first stripped of all his or her clothes. In everyday life the Nacirema avoids exposure of his body and its natural functions. Bathing and excretory acts are performed only in the secrecy of the household shrine, where they are ritualized as part of the body-rites. Psychological shock results from the fact that body secrecy is suddenly lost upon entry into the *latipso*. A man, whose own wife has never seen him in an excretory act, suddenly finds himself naked and assisted by a vestal maiden while he performs his natural functions into a sacred vessel. This sort of ceremonial treatment is necessitated by the fact that the excreta are used by a diviner to ascertain the course and nature of the client's sickness. Female clients, on the other hand, find their naked bodies are subjected to the scrutiny, manipulation and prodding of the medicine men.

Few supplicants in the temple are well enough to do anything but lie on their hard beds. The daily ceremonies, like the rites of the holy-mouth-men, involve discomfort and torture. With ritual precision, the vestals awaken their miserable charges each dawn and roll them about on their beds of pain while performing ablutions, in the formal movements of which the maidens are highly trained. At other times they insert magic wands in the supplicant's mouth or force him to eat substances which are supposed to be healing. From time to time the medicine men come to their clients and jab magically treated needles into their flesh. The fact that these temple ceremonies may not cure, and may even kill the neophyte, in no way decreases the people's faith in the medicine men.

There remains one other kind of practitioner, known as a "listener." This witch-doctor has the power to exorcise the devils that lodge in the heads of people who have been bewitched. The Nacirema believe that parents bewitch their own children. Mothers are particularly suspected of putting a curse on children while teaching them the secret body rituals. The counter-magic of the witch-doctor is unusual in its lack of ritual. The patient simply tells the "listener" all his troubles and fears, beginning with the earliest difficulties he can remember. The memory displayed by the Nacirema in these exorcism sessions is truly remarkable. It is not uncommon for the patient to bemoan the rejection he felt upon being weaned as a babe, and a few individuals even see their troubles going back to the traumatic effects of their own birth.

In conclusion, mention must be made of certain practices which have their base in native esthetics but which depend upon the pervasive aversion to the natural body and its functions. There are ritual fasts to make fat people thin and ceremonial feasts to make thin people fat. Still other rites are used to make women's breasts larger if they are small, and smaller if they are large. General dissatisfaction with breast shape is symbolized in the fact that the ideal form is virtually outside the range of human variation. A few women afflicted with almost inhuman hyper-mammary development are so idolized that they make a handsome living by simply going from village to village and permitting the natives to stare at them for a fee.

Reference has already been made to the fact that excretory functions are ritualized, routinized, and relegated to secrecy. Natural reproductive functions are similarly distorted. Intercourse is taboo as a topic and scheduled as an act. Efforts are made to avoid pregnancy by the use of magical materials or by limiting intercourse to certain phases of the moon. Conception is actually very infrequent. When pregnant, women dress so as to hide their condition. Parturition takes place in secret, without friends or relatives to assist, and the majority of women do not nurse their infants.

Our review of the ritual life of the Nacirema has certainly shown them to be a magic-ridden people. It is hard to understand how they have managed to exist so long under the burdens which they have imposed upon themselves. But even such exotic customs as these take on real meaning when they are viewed with the insight provided by Malinowski when he wrote (1948:70):

> Looking from far and above, from our high places of safety in the developed civilization, it

is easy to see all the crudity and irrelevance of magic. But without its power and guidance early man could not have mastered his practical difficulties as he has done, nor could man have advanced to the higher stages of civilization.

REFERENCES

Linton, Ralph 1936 The Study of Man. New York, D. Appleton-Century Co.

Malinowski, Bronislaw 1948 Magic, Science, and Religion. Glencoe, The Free Press.

Murdock, George P. 1949 Social Structure. New York, The Macmillan Co.

A Pack of Lies

Towards a Sociology of Lying

J. A. Barnes

In 1900 the French anthropologist Topinard maintained that the various 'races' differed in their propensity to lie. He identified regions in France prone to lying, and also wrote of 'the cheating Italian, the hypocritical Englishman, the Greek without good faith, the Turk incapable of keeping his word'. Further:

> The Asiatics, the Japanese, the Chinese, the Siamese, show bad faith, and are much disposed to make deceitful promises when they struggle with the English and the Germans. It is necessary to add that they can be of good faith when they feel that they are not threatened. (Larson 1932:51)

These evaluations tell us more about contemporary French stereotypes of other national characters than about the groups labelled so dismissively. Earlier Herbert Spencer (1892: 400–409) made similar sweeping statements about the worldwide diversity in lying. There is no evidence for the causal link assumed by Topinard between propensity to lie and 'racial' type. His comments do however draw attention to the variations between one culture and another in attitudes towards lying and the incidence of telling lies. Although in the West, as well as in many non-Western cultures, deceit and lying are in general regarded as reprehensible, . . . this generalization has many exceptions; for example, the San Blas Kuna, of northeastern Panama, are said to 'enjoy deceiving each other' (Howe and Sherzer 1986:684). Likewise Basso (1987:355–356) writes of 'the preoccupation with deception' in the culture of the Kalapalo, an Amerindian group living in central Brazil, and of how Kalapalo people even welcome being tricked. . . .

. . . Societies vary not only in their recognition of the ubiquity of lying and other modes of deceit but also in the way in which they evaluate different kinds of lies. Probably there is in every culture a recognition that some lies are comparatively malevolent and others comparatively benign. But though some recognition of difference may be universal, there is no cross-cultural uniformity in the content of these contrasting categories. A speaker or writer may make a statement in one cultural code without any intention to deceive even though, taken literally, the statement is untrue; if the hearer or reader interprets the statement as if it had been made in some other code, he or she may feel deceived. Thus for instance Bailey (1991:6) notes that when he began ethnographic research in India he

> was puzzled and offended by polite young Indians who responded to a request by assuring me they would 'do the necessary', all the time (as I realized later) having no intention of doing so.

. . . Even between the industrialized societies of the West there are differences in the extent to which lying is considered justifiable. In surveys conducted in Europe and Australia in 1981 and 1983 respectively, adult respondents were asked to rate acts of lying in one's own interest on a scale ranging from 1 (never justified) to 10 (always justified). Average ratings were spread from a low of 1.95 in Italy to 3.37 in Belgium, with Australia scoring 2.7 (Harding and Phillips 1986:8–9; Jones 1989:113). An earlier study carried out on students at Harvard university in 1950 showed that the percentage of persons approving of lying in the interests of a friend varied widely according to the context; only 26 per cent approved of lying about speed in a car accident, whereas 51 per cent approved of 'shading the doubts in his favor' in a medical examination for insurance. More light is thrown on the ethical discriminations of these students in their responses to a question on what we would now call insider trading; 70 per cent approved of tipping off a close friend who would otherwise be ruined (Stouffer and Toby 1951). . . .

Cultures vary also in how entirely benign social lies are constituted. In Australia, for instance, an invitation to lunch is an invitation to lunch, particularly in rural areas. But Simpson-Herbert (1987:26) reports that in urban Iran, in the days of the Shah, invitations to a meal were extended frequently; these were almost always insincere, and were recognized as such by those who were invited. She writes 'An invitation should be extended three times in a row with an insistent tone of voice before it can be taken seriously.' In this respect, Iranians followed the example of Lewis Carroll's (1910:3) Bellman, who insisted that 'What I tell you three times is true'. Among the Navajo the fourth time a lie is repeated it becomes deceitful (Hillerman 1986:177–178). . . .

When individuals from industrial and non-industrial cultures come into contact, each will tend to judge the other in terms of his or her own cultural expectations. Generalizing about his experience as an anthropologist in Papua New Guinea, Burridge (1960:36–37) writes that

> Manam islanders, for example, feel that white men are habitual liars and hypocrites. White men say much the same of Manam islanders. And, in their own lights, both sides are right. Both white men and Manam islanders would agree that without hypocrisy, without the 'white lie' and conventional courtesy where dislike is felt, social life would become impossible. The difficulty is that the situations which call for a conventional hypocrisy among Manam islanders are not those which call for precisely the same technique in any one kind of European. What might be obnoxious to a white man might be culturally enjoined for a Manam islander and *vice versa*.

Although in industrialized societies the truth of Bacon's (1861b:253) comment that 'knowledge itself is power' is demonstrated every day, those in power find themselves more likely to be regarded as liars than are the weak and powerless. . . . Lindstrom (1990:xii, 162–163) describes a rural Melanesian society where power and truth are strongly correlated, but even in Tanna 'all alternative and resistant knowledge' is never completely silenced. . . .

Patterns of lying may reflect features of economic life in tribal societies in much the same way as they do in industrialized societies. For example, Siskind (1973:7), an American anthropologist who studied the Sharanahua people of Peru, reports that as part of her fieldwork she learnt their art of lying. The meat of wild animals is highly valued as food; people like to be generous; direct refusals are perceived as insulting. Hence people often lie about their supplies of meat. As Siskind (1973:85) says: 'Lying and secrecy solve a conflict between widespread kinship obligations and a small amount of game.' For while direct refusals are insults, it is not insulting to be called a liar. In this society, 'lying is an essential social grace'. . . .

Michael Gilsenan (1976) has made an excellent analysis of lying, based on data collected in a Muslim village in the Bekaa valley of Lebanon during 1971–72, before the civil war had become acute. In this community liars are typically young men or children. Lies are told partly for fun, to trick one's friends. Success in lying depends on skill, but the final triumph comes when the liar reveals his lie to the dupe and claims victory; 'I'm lying to you, you ate it' (Gilsenan 1976:192). There is thus an attitude of playful competition towards lying, somewhat similar to the attitude towards the tricks played on the first of April in some countries. Lying is indulged in sometimes for its own sake, without an instrumental motive, and it is not surprising that lying is a symbol of the fantastic and unbelievable. Gilsenan (1976:193) illustrates this usage with the remarks of a taxi-driver from a poor village who was describing what he had seen when he had driven some passengers to a New Year's junket in Beirut, then still a sophisticated city. The taxi driver said:

The streets were all hung in lights, decorations everywhere, . . . the girls' dresses were up to here [graphic gestures!] . . . People were kissing in the street, it was unbelievable, it would drive you mad, you can't imagine. it was—like *kizb*—absolutely—like *kizb!*

Kizb is the Arabic word Gilsenan translates as 'lying'. Yet as well as carrying the connotation of fantasy, lying is also perceived as the antithesis of truth, as revealed in the Holy Quran, and is associated with scepticism and pessimism about the world. Thus for example there is a Lebanese saying 'the world is a lie my friend, all of it's a lie' (Gilsenan 1976:194).

Gilsenan's data on lying are drawn mainly from the actions of members of what he calls the staff of the landlord of the area in which he worked. The staff belonged to a large immigrant extended family, some of whose members were socially well placed while others were little more than casual agricultural labourers. Nevertheless the so-called family had some corporate identity, at least in contrast to the true peasants on the one hand and to the landlords on the other. Gilsenan (1976:196) argues that the socially intermediate status of the family was 'riddled with contradictions' and that 'it is in this gray zone of contradiction that the lie comes into its own'. He notes that in the village men do not lie about things on which there is consensus, such as individual moral character, nor about objective evidence, such as mechanical ability, but only about matters that are essentially problematic, like social standing and prestige. Boys (Gilsenan says very little about girls) grow up in an environment in which social relations are perceived as competitive, and in which individual prestige fluctuates. Boys spar with words, and continually question one another's motives and intentions.

It is not surprising that in a cultural environment of this kind there are special devices to indicate that what is about to be said is true, and not a lie. These markers for code switching are phrases such as 'seriously,' 'will you believe me,' 'without joking,' 'by your life,' and 'by your father's life.' Gilsenan reports an incident when some young men rushed to his house to tell him that one of his friends had been shot. He refused to believe them until they said *wahyatak* (by your life); then he realized that what they said must be true. He remarks:

These cue words are particularly important among the young men, who carry on so much joking in their relations that without sign phrases it would be difficult to indicate the boundary between the authentic/real and the inauthentic/inverted-apparent. These cues establish a different domain of relevance and reference. (Gilsenan 1976:199, 215)

Social Class

. . . Cultural diversity exists not only between territorially distinct societies but also within them, particularly within large-scale industrial societies. Members of a nation-state, or of some other social unit, differ in their life chances, access to resources, and culturally determined values, expectations and attitudes. Among these differences is a diversity of attitudes to lying and the kind of lies that are told. Communities also differ in how they classify statements as lies. For instance, Heath (1983:189) notes that in a working class community she studied in the United States certain untrue tales, being perceived as 'stories', were morally acceptable; yet the same tales, if told in a nearby middle-class community, would have been classified as lies.

An early example of a perception of class differences in these attitudes is provided by Madame Necker de Saussure (1839:164), who wrote on the education of children. She stressed the importance of parents and teachers being completely honest; their example would never fail to produce similar behaviour in the children. She goes on to say:

Nurses, especially, should be most carefully instructed on this point; though this is by no means easily accomplished, for perfect truthfulness, owing perhaps to their defective education and dependent situation, is very rarely to be met with in this class of people.

. . . Class differences are demonstrated convincingly in the findings of a study of lower-class culture in a city in the eastern United States, carried out during the 1950s. One of the six focal concerns identified in this culture was 'smartness', which referred to

> the capacity to outsmart, outfox, outwit, dupe, 'take', 'con' another or others, and the concomitant capacity to avoid being outwitted, 'taken', or duped oneself. (Miller 1958:9)

This 'smartness' was highly valued by young men who grouped themselves into gangs. It was acquired through participation with peers in 'recurrent card games and other forms of gambling, mutual exchanges of insults, and "testing" for mutual "con-ability"'. Those who demonstrated their greater smartness by making dupes of fellow group members were accorded higher status. While toughness was also valued, a smart leader gained more prestige than a tough leader, reflecting, says Miller, 'a general lower class respect for "brains" in the "smartness" sense'. Miller does not explicate, but takes for granted, the divergence of these sets of norms from those of middle-class Americans; writing before the rise of labelling theories he unproblematically labels the gangs as delinquent. In retrospect, what is interesting about his findings is that competitive deception was directed at fellow gang members. Gangs did not compete with one another in deception; they fought one another over women, gambling, claims of physical prowess, and territory. There was a high level of intra-group solidarity (Miller 1958:14), manifest in inter-gang contests, but it was a solidarity based largely on reciprocal insults and competitive deception, referred to by Miller as 'aggressive repartee'. The existence of strong intra-gang hierarchies is consonant with this kind of solidarity basis. . . .

. . . Social class is yet another dimension affecting not only attitudes towards lying but also the frequency with which lies are told, the content of lies and the contexts in which they occur. Inter-class differences within any one society may not be so striking as the differences that exist between societies, including those between some pre-industrial societies and industrialized states, which are certainly of great comparative cultural interest.

But in a sense intra-societal differences are sociologically more interesting and socially more important, at least at the present time. Cultural differences between societies, including differences in patterns of lying, were certainly significant during the last two or three centuries during the process of expanding Western colonialism. In a post-colonial world marked by global cultural homogenization, many inter-societal differences still persist but they are less salient than before. Intra-societal differences have also diminished, but have not vanished; they still have to be taken into account in understanding how lying is used in intra-societal struggles. . . .

Diversity of Relations

. . . Lies are evaluated differentially not only according to domain and culture but also with reference to the status of liar and dupe, their status both relative to one another and in the wider society. For instance, studies carried out during the 1970s showed that in the United States high-status persons and those in positions of responsibility were judged more harshly when they lied than were persons of equal or low status. Lies told to a friend were considered to be more reprehensible than those told to strangers and associates (Maier and Lovrakas 1976:577). Similar American studies carried out in the 1980s showed that lies told to benefit the liar met with greater disapproval from student respondents than did lies told to benefit the dupe (Lindskold and Walters 1983). In a recent survey in the northeastern United States of physicians' attitudes to the use of deception, many more respondents said they were ready to deceive medical insurance companies and the wives of their male patients than were prepared to deceive their own patients (Novack et al. 1989).

These findings suggest that one factor affecting the evaluation of lies is the extent of trust that exists, or should exist, between liar and dupe. However, perceptions of trust and expectations of honesty in other people's relations seem to differ from those in one's own relations. In particular, lying, especially defensive and protective lying, is not necessarily perceived by the liar as a betrayal of trust, though it may be seen in that light by the dupe or by third parties. Discussing how men and women responded differently in a study of the connection between perceptions of betrayal and trust, Blum (1972:222–230) remarks

> Men are thus more concerned with lies about their activities, infidelity especially, and project that concern in the form of a belief that wives, too, are unfaithful and lie about it.

Most husbands and wives in the study, it seems, lied to one another, and realized that they were being lied to. Yet though there is some symmetry in their actions and perceptions, we cannot say that there was collaboration between them. There seems to be no evidence from Blum's study to suggest that the women accepted being lied to by their husbands; the lies they admitted telling to their husbands were not about infidelity but about protecting themselves in other contexts, or protecting their husbands and children. The men and women in Blum's sample differed significantly from . . . couples . . . where there was some mutual connivance.

These findings demonstrate that the type of relation existing between liar and dupe has a bearing on what lies are told and how they are perceived. . . .

Relations of Domination

In a hierarchical society, people tend to act in one way towards their superiors and in a different way towards those below them in the social hierarchy. Nevertheless, lies may be directed in both directions. In Albert's (1972:90) comments on the use of language in Burundi, she notes that 'No one is so high or low in the social scale, no one so secure in the affections of a superior or inferior, as to be able to afford the luxury of speaking the unedited truth'. This state of affairs has consequences for lying, particularly when someone is accused of some offence. What is needed, says Albert, is a 'rapid, graceful, and more-than-plausible falsehood'. It is considered safer to lie than to tell the truth, and men seem not to be anxious about the possible subsequent discovery of their deceit.

. . . Albert speaks of lying to both superiors and inferiors in the Rundi hierarchy. As Bailey (1991:66) says:

> Untruths provide weapons for the weak to resist the strong and for the strong to moderate the antagonism that their dominance provokes from the weak.

Many of the lies told by the powerful to deceive those who lack power have no smidgin of nobility about them but there are others that fall into the category which some translators of Plato (1935:99) have called 'noble lies' (cf. Bok 1978:165–170, 305–306). These 'lies for the public good', as Bok calls them, may emanate from a ruler, as with Plato's example, but many more issue from lower down in the hierarchy, though aimed downwards and outwards, at the public at large, rather than upwards.

The deception practiced by some experimenters on their subjects may be seen as instances of deceit in a relation of superordination, even though the experimenter's superior status is usually severely limited in content and restricted to an hour or so in time. Deception, possibly long lasting, again of those who, for the time being, are in a position of subordination, occurs whenever a physician gives a patient a placebo. The physician's aim may be to gather evidence in a scientific trial of a new medicine, with the patient forming part of a control group; alternatively the doctor may hope that even a placebo will bring relief to the patient. In either case, for the experiment to be valid or for the relief to occur, the patient must believe that the medicine has genuine curative power. It is possible to imagine that a cool-headed patient might realize that deception was taking place and yet decide to connive at the deceit; but most patients are far from being cool-headed when they seek treatment.

How are we to classify encouraging comments made to bolster the self-esteem of someone else? Friends may make such remarks to one another, but they are often made in asymmetrical relations, by a parent to a child or by a physician to a patient. Sometimes such comments are true and are made truthfully, but often they are not. A parent cheers a disconsolate child who brings home a deplorable school report by saying 'I'm sure you tried very hard'; a toddler's scrawled drawing evokes the comment 'What a pretty picture!' These remarks may be lies, but are told because the liar hopes that falsely inflated estimates of their ability will make dupes happy and encourage them to do better next time. Similar statements of doubtful accuracy made by doctors to calm or cheer their patients are usually categorized as harmless . . . even though these are statements made by a person in a relation of dominance over the dupe. In Henderson's (1970 [1935]) classic account of the physician-patient relation, he discusses the complexities of the patient's likely reaction if the physician were to make a bland pronouncement 'This is a carcinoma'. Henderson justifies his prescription of 'do no harm' rather than 'tell the truth' by referring to the probable adverse consequences of attempting to tell 'the whole truth' to the patient, and to the obligation on the physician 'to act upon the patient so as to modify his sentiments to his own advantage'. Nothing, says Henderson, is more effective to this end than the physician arousing in the patient the belief that the physician is 'concerned wholeheartedly and exclusively for his welfare'. Here, then, we have a prescription for lying by the elite not for the public good but for the benefit of an individual citizen. Evidence indicates that some harmless lies do indeed have a positive therapeutic effect (Scheibe 1980:20–21); the case for telling encouraging lies to children and sick people is much stronger than for telling lies 'for the public good' to healthy citizens. . . .

. . . I have tried to show that, as well as differences arising from social pressures specific to various domains and cultures, there are other constraints on patterns of lying that are rooted in the structural relations prevailing between liar and dupe. To some extent these constraints cut across social and cultural differences, but their manifestation is usually coloured by them. For instance, lying may everywhere be a weapon that can be used by the weak, but whether the powerful avail themselves of 'Untruths . . . to moderate the antagonism that their dominance provokes from the weak', as Bailey puts it, depends on social and cultural context. . . .

REFERENCES

Albert, Ethel M. 1972. Culture patterning of speech behavior in Burundi. In Gumperz, John Joseph, and Hymes, Dell, eds. *Directions in sociolinguistics: the ethnography of communication*. New York: Holt, Rinehart and Winston, pp. 72–105, [37, 51, 81, 83,106, 116, 138f., 158, 162]

Bacon, Francis 1861a. *The works of Francis Bacon*. Vol. 6: *Literary and professional works*, vol.1. London: Longman [158]

——— 1861b. *The works of Francis Bacon*. Vol. 7: *Literary and professional works*, vol. 2. London: Longman [69]

Bailey, Frederick George 1988. *Humbuggery and manipulation: the art of leadership*. Ithaca, N.Y.: Cornell University Press [30, 34f.]

———. 1991. *The prevalence of deceit*. Ithaca, N.Y.: Cornell University Press [16, 66, 81, 83, 91, 109, 133]

Basso, Ellen B. 1987. *In favor of deceit: a study of tricksters in an Amazonian society*. Tucson: University of Arizona Press [65]

Blum, Richard H. 1972. *Deceivers and deceived*. Springfield, Ill.: Charles C. Thomas [80]

Bok, Sissela 1978. *Lying: moral choice in public and private life*. New York: Pantheon Books [passim]

Burridge, Kenelm Oswald Lancelot 1960. *Mambu: a Melanesian millennium*. London: Methuen [69]

Carroll, Lewis 1910. *The hunting of the snark: an agony in eight fits*. London: Macmillan [67]

Gilsenan, Michael 1976. Lying, honor and contradiction. In Kapferer, Bruce, ed. *Transaction and meaning: directions in the anthropology of exchange and symbolic behavior*. (ASA essays in social anthropology 1). Philadelphia: Institute for the Study of Human Issues, pp. 191–219 [2,18, 70ff., 82f., 145]

Harding, Stephen, and Phillips, David 1986. *Contrasting values in western Europe: unity, diversity and change* (Studies in the contemporary values of modern society). London: Macmillan [1, 66, 163]

Heath, Shirley Brice 1983. *Ways with words: language, life and work in communities and classrooms*. Cambridge: Cambridge University Press [75]

Henderson, Lawrence Joseph 1970 [1935]. Physician and patient as a social system. In his *On the social system: selected writings*. Chicago: University of Chicago Press, pp. 202–213 [84]

Hillerman, Tony 1986. *Skinwalkers*. New York: Harper Paperbacks [67]

Howe, James, and Sherzer, Joel 1986. Friend Hairyfish and friend Rattlesnake or keeping anthropologists in their place. *Man* n.s. 21:680–696 [65]

Jones, Frank Lancaster 1989. Changing attitudes and values in post-war Australia. In Hancock, Keith Jackson, ed. *Australian society.* Cambridge: Cambridge University Press, pp. 94–118 [66]

Larson, John Augustus 1932. *Lying and its detection: a study of deception and deception tests.* Chicago: University of Chicago Press [5]

Lindskold, Svenn, and Walters, Pamela S. 1983. Categories for acceptability of lies. *Journal of Social Psychology* [79, 138]

Lindstrom, Lamont Carl 1990. *Knowledge and power in a South Pacific society.* Washington: Smithsonian Institution Press [69]

Maier, Richard A., and Lovrakas, Paul J. 1976. Lying behavior and evaluation of lies. *Perceptual and Motor Skills* 42:575–581 [79]

Miller, Walter B. 1958. Lower class culture as a generating milieu of gang delinquency. *Journal of Social Issues* 14(3):5–19 [76f.]

Necker de Saussure, Albertine Adrienne 1839. *Progressive education, or considerations on the course of life.* Vol. 1. London: Longman, Orme, Brown [76]

Novack, Dennis H., Detering, Barbara J., Arnold, Robert, Farrow, Lachlan, Ladinsky, Morissa, and Pezzullo, John C. 1989. Physicians' attitudes toward using deception to resolve difficult ethical problems. *Journal of the American Medical Association* 261:2980–2985 [79, 138]

Plato 1935. *Plato's Republic* (Lindsay, A. D., trans.). London: Dent [83]

———. 1966. *Plato's Republic* (Richards, I. A., trans.). Cambridge: Cambridge University Press [106, 136, 156]

Scheibe, Karl E. 1979. Mirrors masks likes and secrets: the limits of human predictability. New York: Praeger [2]

Simpson-Herbert, Mayling 1987. Women, food and hospitality in Iranian society. *Canberra Anthropology* 10(1):24–34 [67]

Siskind, Janet 1973. *To hunt in the morning.* New York: Oxford University Press [69f.]

Spencer, Herbert 1892. *The principles of ethics.* Vol. 1. London: Williams and Norgate [65, 141]

Stouffer, Samuel Andrew, and Toby, Jackson 1951. Role conflict and personality. *American Journal of Sociology* 56:395–406 [67]

Fashions in Childbirth

Jessica Mitford

In childbirth, as in other human endeavors, fashions start with the rich, are then adopted by the aspirant middle class with an assist from the ever-watchful media, and may or may not eventually filter down to the poor.

Beginning in the early years of the twentieth century, more and more well-to-do American women chose hospitals as the site of their lying-in. This was much encouraged by the medical profession, for several reasons: it relieved the family doctor of long hours at the patient's bedside waiting for the birth to happen; it gave impetus to the development of obstetrics as a medical specialty; it allowed for bringing into play the ever-proliferating technological improvements that were only available in a hospital setting; and it mandated complete control of parturition by doctors to the exclusion of midwives, marking another step in the passing of power over the birth process from traditional female to professional male. (There has been something of a parallel development in England, except that there, the really rich never have adjusted to the idea of turning out of their commodious, well-staffed houses into the sterile and regimented atmosphere of a hospital. In the 1980s it was still a matter of surprise and comment when Princess Diana decided to have her firstborn in a hospital.)

For the expectant mother, an overriding consideration in choice of hospital over home birth was the promise held out by the former of alleviation of pain, via ever more up-to-date anesthetics for those who could afford them.

Looking over the literature on pain in childbirth, beginning with the Bible (as God said to Eve in one of His bad moods, "In sorrow shalt thou bring forth children"), one can readily appreciate the terror that assailed women at the prospect. Actually God's injunction to Eve was mild compared to the horrendous description in the Church of England's *Book of Common Prayer* for "The Thanksgiving of Women After Child-Birth": "The snares of death compassed me round about; and the pains of hell gat hold upon me." As a small child, wishing—like most children—to know precisely what was in store for me when I grew up, I remember reading and rereading this awful warning each Sunday morning in church, while the clergyman droned on with his dull sermon. My mother, asked what it felt like to have a baby, was hardly reassuring: "Like an orange being stuffed up your nostril," she said.

In view of these dire predictions, it's little wonder that a principal factor determining fashions in childbirth involved the whole matter of avoidance of pain, initially centered on the quest for the best available anesthetic.

Shortly before World War I, numerous rich American women made pilgrimages to Germany for their accouchements, there to savor the delights of a new discovery, "Twilight Sleep." Having partaken of this miracle, they couldn't praise it enough; not only was delivery completely painless, they said, but their babies turned out amazingly healthy, beautiful, and intelligent. Arbiters of fashion, society leaders like Mrs. John Jacob Astor, joined forces with feminists in a campaign to end once and for all the scourge of suffering in childbirth. Newspapers and magazines took up the cause. In 1915, the Twilight Sleep Maternity Hospital was established in Boston under the leadership of Dr. Eliza Taylor Ransom, founder of the New England Twilight Sleep Association.

Confronted by this deluge of influential female demand, doctors and hospitals soon fell into line, and by the late 1930s Twilight Sleep had become the anesthetic of choice, routinely administered in the more go-ahead hospitals along the Eastern seaboard. Obstetricians welcomed it because it gave them more control over the laboring woman than the chloroform/ether routine. Furthermore, the procedure resulted in an influx of paying patients, for whom the hospitals provided luxurious, tastefully decorated private wards, far from the cluttered institutional quarters of the charity patients.

The ingredients that produced the miracle of Twilight Sleep are akin to those used in the "truth serum" we read about in sensational accounts of interrogations of prisoners of war and other captives at the mercy of their jailers. In 1940, Dr. Joseph B. De Lee described the procedure as applied to the captive patient at the mercy of her obstetrician. "Naturally," he wrote, "the profession eagerly grasped this opportunity to relieve women of the pain of childbirth, and these drugs soon were extensively employed here and abroad."

In Twilight Sleep, hypodermic injections of morphine combined with scopalomine (a powerful hallucinogenic and amnesiac) and pentobarbitol sodium were given every hour:

> The object is to maintain the patient in a state of amnesia, and this is determined by testing her memory. . . . Shortly after the second injection, the patient is asked if she remembers what has gone before, has she seen the nurse or intern? If she remembers, another dose is given. If not, nothing is done for an hour, when, if the mind seems to be clearer, $\frac{1}{300}$ grain of scopalomine is given. Care must be exercised that the woman does not attain full consciousness. . . .
>
> During the pains she moves about restlessly, or turns from one side to the other, or grunts a little, and occasionally opens her eyes. She will respond to questions, but incoherently. As the second stage [movement of baby out of the cervix into the birth canal] draws near its end she bears down and

becomes very restless. Occasionally this becomes extreme, and several nurses are required to hold her. . . . A few whiffs of ether are often needed as the head passes through the vulva.

A graphic description of Twilight Sleep as witnessed by a father appeared in *They All Hold Swords,* a memoir of pre-World War II days by Cedric Belfrage. Cedric and his wife, Molly Castle, both young, adventurous British journalists, somehow ended up in Southern California for the birth of their baby in 1936. Thinking it would surely be a boy, they named the unborn child Fred. They chose a small bungalow hospital, a unique feature of which was that Cedric was allowed to be present throughout the entire procedure—unheard of in those days.

The doctor explained that he would be giving Molly the first of several dopes which would blot out her memory. "Soon, she began to moan. . . . Between two pains she said, 'I hope you don't mind me crying out a bit now, darling. I could control my will before but now after the drugs I can't control it anymore.'" As hours went by the doctor called the nurse to administer more injections. "'She will continue to show apparent signs of consciousness during the pains,' he said. 'But tomorrow she won't remember anything about it.'"

Later, Molly was wheeled into the delivery room, where the doctor strapped her onto a table.

> The nurse put the nose-cap over Molly's face and began sprinkling ether on it from a perforated can. . . . Suddenly Molly seemed to come alive; she fought out wildly. Three of us were holding her, but she managed to wrench a hand free to claw frantically at the cap over her nose. She opened her eyes wide and gave a shrill, terrified scream. It was nearly a quarter of an hour before she was completely quiet again. The doctor remained calm, washing his hands over and over again in the corner. He said it was the dope she had had before that made her react this way to ether. She would remember nothing about it afterwards.
>
> She was snoring now, her body limp, her face almost covered by the ether cap. The

doctor began probing with his great forceps. A lot of blood came. . . .

He grasped something between the long, invisible arms of the forceps. He pulled hard. . . . He took a pair of scissors in one hand and in a careful, matter-of-fact way cut a slit to make the opening wider. A minute later the round object was almost out. . . . Everything was a mass of blood and I thought Fred must be dead already.

To Cedric Belfrage's untrained eye the newborn "was exactly, in color and texture and size, like a large rabbit freshly skinned. . . . I could see that Fred was a girl." The doctor slapped her; she yelped. Some hours later, when Molly woke up, "I told her she had had a fine rabbit. She remembered nothing since the second shot in the arm, she said, except a vague nightmare memory of seeing people in gas-masks leaning over her, which made her think the war had started."

So much for a father's viewpoint. Some observations by health professionals, beginning with Sheila Kitzinger, author of *The Complete Book of Pregnancy and Childbirth:*

Many women have described it as "twilight nightmare" because of its side effects. The usual amnesiac scopalomine (also known as "scope" or "the bomb") can cause total disorientation which may not end when the labor ends, thus its nightmarish quality. It is supposed to make women forget their labor but, in fact, most women report hazy memories of having felt like an animal howling in pain.

It was my impression from my own birth experiences in California, and those of various friends whose babies were born after 1940, that Twilight Sleep had vanished from the scene around the outbreak of World War II—presumably because of the potential dangers to mother and child of the massive amounts of anesthetic required.

I was surprised to learn that this was not so. For decades after it was forsaken by the cognoscenti, Twilight Sleep was still used in out-of-the-way places, mainly for clinic patients, indigents or the uninsured.

In 1989 Dr. Arlan Cohn, an internist in Berkeley, California, told me about "a form of outrageous anesthesia used at times during labor in the mid-fifties when I took my internship in St. Louis. The mixture of scopalomine and Demerol or morphine injected into the mother resulted in an acute psychotic reaction during which the mother would scream out the darkest secrets of her life in a stream-of-consciousness babble that would have made James Joyce blush. The mother would then awake from this nightmare with total amnesia for her wild behavior. God only knows what this crazy injection did to the fetal brain."

Mary Welcome, a certified nurse-midwife practicing in Atlanta, saw Twilight Sleep administered as late as 1974, when she was doing her nurse's training. In 1989 she told me, "I can recall we would have hordes of laboring women—the doctors would knock them out, you know, with scopalomine, an amnesia drug, heavy-duty narcotics and sedatives. The women would be thrashing about in bed and yelling—but totally unaware of any of this. You had to put the rails up to keep them safe. Our nursing instructors told us you should be listening to the heartbeat every fifteen minutes, but the nurses would do this maybe twice in an eight-hour shift. And you'd look at their nursing records and realize that those women were left alone in there for hours. They were drugged up and knocked out. And the babies were often born unconscious themselves. You'd have to give them drugs to reverse the narcotics the mother had, and they'd stay sleepy for days."

In 1990, in a belated effort to discover the precise nature of the anesthetic I had endured in 1941 (hot air pumped up the rectum), I consulted numerous local physicians, but none of them had ever heard of such a thing. They tactfully suggested that I might have been hallucinating after the inhalation of gas. One wrote, "I'll bet my career that it was inhaled gas and not an enema that put you under. Gas anesthesia tends to scramble the mind of mother (and newborn) temporarily." He added that the use of inhaled gas is now "uniformly recognized as potentially very dangerous to mother and newborn."

Eventually the mystery was solved, again by a passage from Joseph De Lee's *The Principles and*

Practice of Obstetrics. He set forth the formula for "rectal ether instillation" followed by a soothingly sophomoric lullaby presumably meant to be memorized by the attending obstetrician:

> Early in the labor the patient is addressed as follows: "Mrs. _____, we are desirous of making your labor as painless as possible, and are prepared to do so without danger to you or your baby. Our success in relieving you will depend somewhat upon your cooperation. Therefore, when your pains become uncomfortable let the nurse know and she will give you two, or perhaps three, capsules (pentobarbital sodium, each $1\frac{1}{2}$ grains) to relieve you.
>
> "When your pains again become uncomfortable notify her as before and she will give you another capsule or two (pentobarbital sodium), or maybe a hypodermic (morphine sulfate, $\frac{1}{6}$ or $\frac{1}{4}$ grain).
>
> "Later, when this medicine begins to lose its effect, let her know and she will inject a solution into your rectum (ether-oil or ether-paraldehyde oil)."

Dr. De Lee was an articulate and extremely influential early proponent of the notion that *all* births, including those designated "low-risk," are inherently pathogenic and should be treated as such. "It always strikes physicians as well as laymen as bizarre," he wrote, "to call labor an abnormal function, a disease, and yet it is a decidedly pathological process."

His theories were sprung upon a waiting world—of obstetricians, that is—in his exhaustive *Principles and Practice,* a 1,200-page tome first published in 1913 and thereafter reprinted many times until 1940. A sampling of the De Lee philosophy, following his description of scientific advances in obstetrics:

> This knowledge will raise the level and the dignity of our profession. Why is this process so slow? I believe, because, up to within a few years, the profession, and the public, considered childbirth to be a normal function, one requiring little medical supervision and hardly worth the attention of an expert surgeon. . . .

> It must be evident to anyone who will give the matter unbiased thought that, if we can invest obstetrics with the dignity of a great science, which it deserves, if we will acknowledge the pathogenic nature of this function, improvement will follow in every field of practice, and that anachronism, the midwife, will spontaneously disappear.

These concepts, incorporating as they did the twin aspirations of enhanced professional prestige and assured monopoly of their chosen field, were quickly embraced by De Lee's fellow practitioners. The fourfold remedy for the disease of childbirth, adapted from De Lee's teachings, continued to be standard practice in obstetrical wards for at least two generations. These were to be uniformly applied to all births, without distinction—forget about high risk/low risk. To summarize:

1. The patient should be placed in the "lithotomy position." (Incidentally, this expression was one I had not heard until I started consorting with childbirth professionals, who told me it means lying supine with legs in air, bent and wide apart, supported by stirrups. However, the *Oxford English Dictionary* gives but one definition: "Lithotomy: The operation or art of cutting for stone in the bladder.")

2. She should be sedated from the first stage of labor.

3. The physician should perform an episiotomy, a cut of several inches through the skin and muscles between the vagina and anus to enlarge the space through which the baby must pass.

4. The physician should use forceps to effectuate delivery.

These measures, De Lee emphasized, could offset the dangers of unaided birth, in which "only a small minority of women escape damage by the direct action of the natural process itself. So frequent are these bad effects, that I have often wondered whether Nature did not deliberately intend women to be used up in the process of reproduction, in a manner analogous to that of the salmon, which dies after spawning."

The opening shot in defense of the spawning salmon, heretofore voiceless sufferers caught in a net of obstetrical procedures, came from a most unlikely quarter: *The Ladies' Home Journal,* which in 1957 and 1958 ran a series of hair-raising letters on the subject.

To put this in context: The *LHJ* was then, is now, and ever shall be one of those multimillion-circulation women's mags whose essential loyalty is to their advertisers, their contents generally consisting of short, exhortative text pieces on how to be a better wife/mother, how to dress better for less, how to cook for a crowd of teenagers, etc., surrounded by lovely huge color ads bearing approximately the same message. In *The Feminine Mystique,* published in 1963, Betty Friedan plunged into a devastating analysis and critique of the insipid outpourings of these magazines, one of her examples being the *LHJ.* Combing through issue after issue of the late 1950s, she turned up some marvelous plums for her chapter titled "The Happy Housewife Heroine." Yet buried somewhere in those issues was a remarkable correspondence starkly headlined "Cruelty in the Maternity Wards."

Why—and how—the ultrarespectable, superbland *LHJ* got involved in a head-on confrontation with the American medical establishment remains a mystery. In 1990, I wrote to the present editor asking for enlightenment; she did not answer my letter. I can only conclude that it was one of those unpredictable moments in the life of a nation, an individual, or in this case a magazine, when a steamroller of pent-up anger may have overridden normal editorial caution.

In any event, in November 1957 *The Ladies' Home Journal* published a brief letter in its reader-mail column from a registered nurse (name withheld at her request, as she feared reprisals from the medical community) asking for an investigation of "the tortures that go on in modern delivery rooms":

I have seen doctors who have charming examination-room manners show traces of sadism in the delivery room. One I know does cutting and suturing without anesthetic. He has nurses use a mask to stifle the patient's outcry.

Great strides have been made in maternal care, but some doctors still say, "Tie them down so they won't give us any trouble."

Six months later, the *LHJ* editor reported a flood of letters' relating childbirth experiences "so shocking that they deserve national attention." The May 1958 issue devoted many pages to excerpts from this outpouring of complaints, adding the requisite sententious disclaimer that "the *Journal* does not question that the overwhelming majority of obstetricians and maternity hospitals resent such practices."

A few quotations from the *LHJ*'s letters to the editor of May 1958 convey the general feeling. A mother of three, all born in different hospitals with different doctors, seemed dismayed at the yawning chasm between promise and reality:

The practice of obstetrics is the most modern and medieval, the kindest to mothers and the cruelest. I know of many instances of cruelty, stupidity and harm done to mothers by obstetricians who are callous or completely indifferent. . . . Women are herded like sheep through an obstetrical assembly line, are drugged and strapped on tables while their babies are forceps-delivered. Obstetricians today are businessmen who run baby factories.

Another wrote:

I was immediately rushed into the labor room. A nurse prepared me. Then, with leather cuffs strapped around my wrists and legs, I was left alone for nearly eight hours, until the actual delivery.

Recurrent complaints concerned the strapping down of the laboring mother; the prohibition of the father's presence during labor and delivery; and the general assembly-line atmosphere.

The May issue gave rise to yet another avalanche of letters, many of which were printed in the issue of December 1958:

Far too many doctors, nurses and hospitals seem to assume that just because a woman is about to give birth she becomes a nitwit, an incompetent, reduced to the status of a cow (and not too valuable a cow, at that). . . .

I was strapped to the delivery table on Saturday morning and lay there until I was delivered on Sunday afternoon. When I slipped my hand from the strap to wipe sweat from my face I was severely reprimanded by the nurse. . . . For thirty-six hours my husband didn't know whether I was living or dead. I would have given anything if I could just have held his hand.

Some reported babies born dead, or hopelessly brain-damaged, victims (the writers suspected) of obstetrician-mandated delayed delivery and too much anesthetic.

With few exceptions, the doctors who responded to these allegations against the profession issued blanket denials; nothing of the kind ever happened in *their* hospitals. An obstetrician's wife wrote indignantly of the many sacrifices she had made: "I have broken many an engagement, kept many dinners warm, and cut vacations short because of my husband's concern for his patients." Well, really! Aren't these minor inconveniences supposed to be a normal part of any conscientious doctor's way of life?

Nurses, also, had their say. Like the registered nurse whose letter originally stirred up the hornet's nest, these asked for protective anonymity. Most came down squarely on the side of the complaining mothers, and deplored the mentality of the profession:

> Because of what is politely termed "medical ethics," the truth of much bad practice is kept from the public. Personally I feel it is comparable to the "ethics" which keeps criminals from telling on their accomplices. . . . What makes me angry is that the incompetent and unscrupulous people get away with so much.

Whether or not these *cris de coeur* had any direct effect on the development of a feminist birth philosophy as a feature of the women's liberation movement, then some years in the future, is at this late stage a matter of conjecture.*

The Ladies' Home Journal series is, however, mentioned in several of the books I consulted, including Wertz and Wertz's *Lying-In* and Margot Edwards and Mary Waldorf's *Reclaiming Birth*.

In any event, predating the women's movement of the sixties and seventies there arose a new phenomenon: "natural childbirth," originating with the 1933 publication of *Natural Childbirth* (later called *Childbirth Without Fear*) by an English obstetrician, Dr. Grantly Dick-Read. This was superseded in the 1950s by the work of Dr. Fernand Lamaze, a French physician whose methods derived from Pavlovian theories he had studied in the Soviet Union. Thus, as in the case of Twilight Sleep, the innovators were foreign male physicians, and the first Americans to explore the possibilities offered by the new techniques were well-to-do women who traveled to Europe for the purpose.

On the face of it, the two systems seem similar. Dr. Dick-Read's view was that the pains of childbirth are largely caused by fear-induced tension, which could be greatly ameliorated by instruction ahead of time about the childbearing process combined with classes in relaxation, exercises to keep the body supple, and training in deep breathing. Lamaze's method, which he called *"accouchement sans douleur"* (labor without pain), also required prenatal instruction in the physiology of pregnancy and labor, limbering-up exercises and breathing techniques—he favored rapid, shallow panting over Dr. Dick-Read's deep breathing.

Be that as it may—whether one is a deep breather or a shallow panter—the medical establishment after some initial resistance adopted (and modified for its convenience) the concept of natural childbirth and its concomitant, prenatal classes in which a lecturer trained in the method explains how it's done. Beginning in the 1970s as a response to the women's movement, these classes are now routinely offered in the posher U.S. hospitals under the umbrella term "prepared childbirth." Fathers, married or unmarried (discreetly termed "partners" in the promotional lit) are cordially invited to come and breathe along in class, and if inclined are welcome to stay in the hospital throughout the labor and delivery.

(Incidentally, the "prepared childbirth" sessions are not to be confused with prenatal care, in which from the earliest stages of pregnancy the expectant mother goes for regularly scheduled visits to her midwife or to her obstetrician for physical examination, advice on nutrition, and the ubiquitous tests of urine, blood, etc. Prenatal care is universally thought to be an essential preamble to a successful outcome: midwives, obstetricians, experts here and abroad, are united in its advocacy.)

Also-rans in the natural-birth sweeps—but nevertheless influential voices—were Robert Bradley of Denver and a French physician, Frédérick Leboyer. While each had his share of enthusiastic supporters, both to some extent eventually fell afoul of the feminist movement.

Dr. Bradley, a pioneer of "husband-coached childbirth" (the title of his book published in 1965 by Harper & Row), was implacably opposed to the use of drugs in childbirth, and himself presided over some thirteen thousand drug-free births in which the husband-coach was a full participant. But he used unfortunate terminology, referring to the uterus as the "baby box" and the clitoris as the "passion button." It seemed to some women that Bradley was enlisting husbands in a male power alliance in which husband and obstetrician became the benign custodians of the little woman's physiology and behavior. Bradley's reputation was not enhanced when he remarked to a father, "Let's face a fact: they [pregnant women] are nuttier than a fruitcake."

Unlike others of his contemporaries—Lamaze, Dick-Read, Bradley, *et al.*—who had embraced the cause of natural childbirth, Leboyer had scant sympathy for the laboring mother. On the contrary, his pity was all for the struggling fetus trying desperately to make its way through the rigid birth canal into an alien environment.

To help it recover from this horrible experience, he advocated "gentle birth," described in his book *Birth Without Violence* (New York: Knopf, 1975). The delivery room should be dimly lighted and all present very quiet—Leboyer didn't much like having fathers around, as they are apt to exclaim loudly at the first sight of the newborn. As soon as the babe emerged, Leboyer lowered it into a lukewarm bath, simulating its former watery home. For a soft and kindly introduction to its fellow human beings, Leboyer—*not* the mother—would give the baby a gentle, reassuring massage; only then would the mother be given it to hold.

As for the mother, Leboyer surmised that for the baby she must appear to be a monster incarnate. At the onset of labor it finds itself being crushed, stifled, assaulted:

> With its heart bursting, the infant sinks into hell . . . the mother is driving it out. At the same time she is holding it in, preventing its passage. It is she who is the enemy. She who stands between the child and life. Only one of them can prevail. It is mortal combat . . . not satisfied with crushing, the monster twists it in a refinement of cruelty.

Women who welcome Leboyer's advocacy of softly lit, quiet labor rooms in contrast to the bright lights and constant banging about encountered in many hospitals—and may also favor a nice warm bath for the newborn—can hardly be expected to choke down the rest of his strangely misogynistic views of motherhood.

The dramatic transformation of the father's role from the 1960s to the late 1980s is described by Warren Hinckle III, who sampled both. "Hink Three," as I call him for short, was one of the trio of *Ramparts* editors, all under thirty, who in the 1960s tweaked the noses of President Johnson, the CIA, and the military with stunning exposés that contributed in no small measure to LBJ's downfall and the eventual ending of the Vietnam War. "Never trust anybody over thirty!" was the slogan of Hink III and his editorial colleagues, Robert Scheer and Dugald Stermer.

Hinckle's account of fatherhood in the sixties:

> In Irish San Francisco, birthing was a simple division of labor: The woman went to the hospital, and the man went to the bar. The intimate details of birth were left to the mother and the mother-in-law on the reasonable ground that they had experience in such matters.
>
> I waited for the birth of my first two children in the yellow half-light of Cookie Picetti's Star Cafe on Kearny Street. They were born three years apart but the theater of nativity remained the same: The phone rang in the bar. Cookie picked up the receiver and listened intently. A smile as broad as a barge

crossed his face. "Ya godda goil," said Cookie. He hung up the phone. I bought drinks for the house. The house bought drinks back.

Onward to 1989. The goils are grown up and Warren Hinckle is remarried, his wife, Susan Cheever, expecting some time in November. They are living in New York; although Hink III is now in his fifties, his description of the Blessed Event seems perfectly trustworthy:

On the night of the earthquake [October 17, 1989] I was dragooned in a Lamaze class on the fifth floor of a grotty office building on New York's upper East Side, seated next to a Dentyne-popping yuppie.

"Now, everyone take off their shoes and get on the floor and the men can practice being human labor tables," said the instructor. She had a computer voice with a programmed smile.

When the men had been human labor tables long enough, there was a lot of huff-and-puff practice pain control breathing— "Let's take a deep, cleansing breath," said the computer voice. I excused myself to go to the bathroom and raced downstairs to a bar across the street and watched San Francisco burn on the television.

Back upstairs at the pain factory the ladies had finished breathing and the men were putting their penny loafers back on and there was the smell of socks in the air.

"Now you guys just remember that you're glued in the labor room with your partner— you can't move an inch, you can wait to pee until after the baby is born," the instructor said, giggling girlishly.

A couple of weeks later, the scene shifts to Mount Sinai hospital, where Dr. Herbert Jaffin decides to try for vaginal delivery, although Susan, age forty-six, had had a previous cesarean. Jaffin recommends the posture of *"Sitzfleisch,* loosely translated as sitting on your butt." Later, he proceeds "to violate the scripture of the more puritanical 'natural birth' advocates" by administering Pitocin and an epidural.

At the moment of birth, Dr. Jaffin "waved his tools [forceps] like a matador and proceeded to his art.

"Suddenly the baby was there all red, white and blue—blue of skin and red with blood and the goop of birth, with the whites of his eyes flashing, arms waving and flapping in the air."

Thus the triumphal entry of Warren Hinckle IV, also known by me as Hink Four but called Quad by his proud parents and their friends; clearly an occasion of exhilaration for his doting papa.

Autre temps, autres moeurs. John Kenneth Galbraith in June 1989, answering a letter in which I had mentioned that I was writing this book, observed:

Alas, it is a subject to which I had not previously given more than three minutes' thought. Kitty and I had, over the years, discussed the circumstances which caused her, while in perfect health, to be confined to the hospital for a full 10 days when Alan was born, now close on to 50 years ago. Our offspring handled the whole situation in approximately two days. Anyhow, quite clearly this is something to be explored.

Yes, but also worth exploring is Professor Galbraith's not previously having given more than three minutes' thought to the subject. This conjures up the picture of his wife, Kitty, struggling bravely, solo, with the pangs of labor while JKG, busy man that he always was (and is), occupies himself with vital problems of national and international import.

If the scene could be reenacted today, we might visualize Galbraith being dragged by a giant hook, like those used in French theaters to remove unpopular performers, off the world stage and into his wife's delivery chamber. There his attention would be concentrated for a lot more than three minutes, as he breathes and strains, à la Dick-Read or Lamaze, in unison with Kitty until the great moment when he is called upon to himself cut the umbilical cord.

In the wake of these developments, new inventions mushroomed, some eminently sensible, others wild enough to qualify for Ripley's *Believe It Or Not.*

Item: Birthing stool, advertised in Ina May Gaskin's quarterly publication *The Birth Gazette.* The stool is adapted from that used by centuries of midwives, whose kit included a wooden contraption that looks something like a toilet seat (minus, obviously, a watery flush), for squatting on during labor. The modern version is (according to the ad) "finely handcrafted of pine, leather and 4″ foam," and looks quite comfy for the purpose.

Item: Another *sitzfleisch* gadget, the birth cushion, invented by Jason Gardosi of St. Mary's Hospital in London. Like the birthing stool, it is designed to support the thighs and allow for squatting deliveries. According to the London *Independent,* this method had "almost halved forceps deliveries of first babies, shortened second stage labor and resulted in less injury to the mother." At least sixty National Health Service hospitals were offering British maternity patients the option of using the cushion.

Item: Underwater birth. I went to see a documentary film on this called *Water Baby,* produced and introduced by Karil Daniels of Point of View Productions. The movie shows practitioners delivering babies underwater in three countries: in the Soviet Union, Igor Charkovsky, who first promulgated the idea in the 1960s ("He's not a doctor, he's a boat builder," I was told by Sheila Kitzinger, who is something less than a fan); in France, Dr. Michel Odent of the Centre Hospitalier Général de Pithiviers, who in *The Lancet* of December 24, 1983, reported the 100th birth underwater in his hospital, almost all without subsequent complications; and in the United States, Dr. Michael Rosenthal, obstetrician of the Family Birthing Center in Upland, California.

Underwater labor, viz., lying in a warm bath to ease the discomfort of contractions in the early stages, allowing as it does for freedom of movement absent the pull of gravity, has long been an option offered by midwives and other home-birth advocates. But in *Water Baby* we see the infant's head, body, and legs slowly emerging in a small birthing pool, sometimes with the enthusiastic "partner" alongside the mom. Having been accustomed to a watery environment for nine months, the commentator explains, the babe rather likes

this. It doesn't need to breathe until the cord is cut, as it still gets oxygen from that source.

"Do many babies drown?" I asked nervously. Hardly any, Karil Daniels said; she had only heard of one case, rumored but never authenticated, in which the parents did it all by themselves in the family bathtub without a trained birth attendant.

Rather to my surprise—and relief—Ina May Gaskin, that birth innovator *par excellence . . . ,* voiced the same misgivings. She didn't know how many documented cases of fetal deaths had been attributable to underwater births; but she did feel that two of the births shown in Karil Daniels's film "came dangerously near the edge." She also questioned the hygienic precautions, especially when other people—birth assistants and those ever-present "partners"—plunge full of enthusiasm into the tub along with mom and the unborn babe.

Ms. Gaskin's main, eminently commonsensical observation is that since our ancestors from time immemorial were born into air, along with all other mammals—puppies, kittens, giraffes, elephants, etc.—why disturb the natural order?

Item: Heading into the Twilight Zone, we learn of the Empathy Belly, designed by Linda Ware, a "prenatal educator" in Redmond, Washington. The belly, consisting of a huge womb-like structure with large breasts, priced at $595, is designed to be worn by the male partner so that he can appreciate the discomfort of the later stages of pregnancy. It weighs thirty-five pounds, is guaranteed to cause backache, shortness of breath, and fatigue, and comes with a special pouch that presses on the wearer's bladder, creating an uncomfortable desire to urinate at inappropriate moments. According to its inventor, "a half hour in the Empathy Belly teaches a man more about what goes on during pregnancy. He ends up being more understanding and supportive about what a woman goes through. For most men, it opens up a new world of feelings. It's something they think about and enjoy." In short, the perfect Father's Day gift for the likes of Hink III or J. K. Galbraith.

Item: The Uterine University. In a development of the notion that one is never too young to learn, prenatal educators from Florida to Washington state are promoting devices for the in utero education of the fetus.

Offerings include Fetal Teaching Systems, cassettes to be worn by the mother-to-be on a body-belt, available from Mr. Shannon Thomas of Orlando, Florida; the "Listen Baby" fabric belt with two speakers and a little microphone, from Roger Hurst of Infant Technology in Denver; and the Pregaphone, invented by Dr. Rene Van de Carr of Santa Barbara, California.

Whether the fetus, swimming about in its amniotic fluid, enjoys the lessons—or whether it is bored by the whole idea—has not yet been fully researched, although Dr. Brent Logan of the Washington Institute of Prenatal Education in Snohomish does record a baby saying "Gogo" three times shortly after delivery. "The nurses were amazed," he said. (The newborn's utterance is, it seems to me, subject to at least two interpretations: was it saying "Go! Go!" meaning "Leave me alone!" or simply burping like any illiterate?)

Item: In what must be one of the most imaginative lawsuits of recent years, attorney Michael Box filed suit in Jefferson City, Missouri, contending that the state is illegally imprisoning an inmate's fetus. Box cited Missouri's antiabortion law, which says life begins at conception. If that is so, he said, "then fetuses are supposed to be like anyone else—they're a person, and they have constitutional rights."

He contends that key provisions of the Missouri law, upheld by the U.S. Supreme Court in its July 1989 ruling on the abortion issue, extend to the unborn "all the rights, privileges and immunities available to other persons." Hence the fetus (whose mother-to-be is serving a three-year sentence for forgery and stealing) has been illegally imprisoned—having itself never been charged with a crime, allowed to consult an attorney, convicted, or sentenced.

If this legal theory should prevail, will the courts be bombarded with Writs of Habeas Fetus?

Aside from some of the zanier products of the ever-fertile American entrepreneurial imagination, there seems to be no doubt that for the affluent, and those with large, inclusive health insurance policies, hospital birth today can be a highly enjoyable experience.

Vying to capture the carriage trade, hospitals outdo each other in advertising birth à la mode, which, they assure us, offers all the cozy benefits of home birth in a safe hospital setting. Latching on to the popularity and publicity surrounding the home-birth movement of the 1970s, a typical ad like one from Eden Hospital in Castro Valley, California, shows a couple and baby with the headline "Having My Baby at Eden Was So Comforting, Almost Like Delivering at Home." At HCA West Paces Ferry Hospital in Atlanta, "Birthing suites feature early American furniture complete with a four-poster bed and a charming cradle." (Cost: $7,000 minimum.) Most offer rooming-in with the mother for the baby and the father, who—perhaps in deference to the shade of Dr. Semmelweis—is asked to wash his hands. Not only fathers, but siblings and anyone else the mother wants to invite are welcome to attend the birth. A champagne dinner for two served in the mother's room concludes this magnificent birthday treat.

In Alexandria, Virginia, in April 1990, I went to see the Alexandria Hospital, which, I was told, is the preferred place for yuppie births. This offers all the above-described advantages plus a pink dining room called "Le Bébé" with fresh flowers on each table for two, where the new parents can choose among filet mignon, "catch of the day," and chicken Kiev.

I can visualize a TV miniseries segment showing the delighted parents as they depart from these charming surroundings, clasping their pink bébé (there would be few of darker hue) and its brand-new Vuitton diaper carrier. In the final scene, they enter their comfortable dwelling, a bower of flowers sent by well-wishers, all to the background music of the Brahms Lullaby.

NOTES

74: "Twilight Sleep Association"
  Again I am indebted to Wertz and Wertz, pp. 150–52.
  "extensively employed here and abroad"
  Joseph B. DeLee, *The Principles and Practice of Obstetrics* (Philadelphia: W. B. Saunders, 1940).
76: "an animal howling in pain"

Sheila Kitzinger, *The Complete Book of Pregnancy and Childbirth* (New York: Alfred A. Knopf, 1985) p. 241.

77: "ether-paraldehyde oil"
DeLee, op. cit.
"will spontaneously disappear"
DeLee, op. cit.

79: "labor without pain"
Fernand Lamaze, Painless Childbirth (Chicago: Henry Regnery, 1970).

80: "a refinement of cruelty"
Leboyer quotations are from *The New Our Bodies, Ourselves* (Boston Women's Health Book Collective, 1984). Other books consulted for accounts of Bradley and Leboyer are Margot Edwards and Mary Waldorf, *Reclaiming Birth;*

Kitzinger, *The Complete Book of Pregnancy and Childbirth,* and Wertz and Wertz, *Lying-In.*

81: "The house bought drinks back"
Warren Hinckle, "Fifty-something," *San Francisco Examiner*, December 3, 1989.

81: "giggling girlishly"
Hinkle, op. cit.

81: "waving and flapping in the air"
Hinckle, op. cit.

82: *"The Birth Gazette"*
Quarterly publication, The Farm, Summertown, Tennessee, 38483.
"the option of using the cushion" *The Independent,* London, July 7, 1989.

83: "Writs of Habeas Fetus"
San Francisco Chronicle, August 4, 1989.

THINKING ABOUT THE READINGS

Body Ritual Among the Nacirema

■ How long did it take you to realize that Miner was describing American culture? This article was written almost forty years ago and, of course, much has changed since then. How might you update this description of the "Nacirema" to account for current values and rituals? Imagine you are an anthropologist from a culture completely unfamiliar with our Western traditions. Using your own life as a starting point, think of common patterns of work, leisure, learning, intimacy, eating, sleeping, etc. Are there some customs that distinguish your group (religious, racial, ethnic, friendship, etc.) from others? See if you can find the reasons why these customs exist. Which customs serve an obvious purpose (e.g., health)? Which might seem arbitrary and silly to an outside observer?

A Pack of Lies

■ Barnes' article forces us to see lying not as an undesirable, perhaps sinful aberration from society's norms, but as a common, even universal feature of human life. Describe how lying might serve useful purposes for society. In what sense has lying become institutionalized? At one point Barnes states that most husbands and wives lie to one another and realize they're being lied to. If lying in such close relationships is so common, why do we continue to believe that "honesty is the best policy?" What would married life— and more generally, social life—look like if no one ever lied? In other words, could society exist without deceit?

Fashions in Childbirth

■ Describe how contemporary methods of childbirth compare to those used in the early part of the twentieth century. How does the history of childbirth conform to our conceptions of "progress"? At one point Mitford writes, ". . . for the affluent and those with large, inclusive health insurance policies, hospital birth today can be a highly enjoyable experience." But what about those who are less affluent? Describe how popular childbirth practices reflect dominant class values and maintain class differences. Also, how do these practices reflect the status of women at a given point in time?

CHAPTER 5

Building Identity
The Social Construction of Self

Sociology reminds us that humans don't develop in a social vacuum. Other people and events can determine not only what we do and say but what we value and who we become. Our self-concept, identity, and sense of self-worth are derived from the reactions, real or imagined, of other people.

In "The Gloried Self," Patricia and Peter Adler show how entry into a world of celebrity and glory can dramatically alter people's self-concepts. The authors focus on the experiences of varsity basketball players at a medium-sized university that has a tradition of basketball excellence. While very few of us will ever become famous, idolized celebrities, this article nicely shows how self-concepts are derived from the reflected appraisals of others.

Who we become is also tied to the historical events, social circumstances, and social institutions that surround us. Through socialization we learn what's expected of us in our families, our communities, and our culture, and we learn how to behave in accordance with those expectations. Perhaps the most important socializing institution in society today is education. Most of us would assume that the role of a school is to teach its students particular, explicit subject matter. Some schools, like elementary schools, high schools, and universities, provide lessons covering a variety of subjects; others, like law schools and medical schools, train students in more narrowly defined areas of study.

But schools do more than teach information. Sometimes the most important lessons students learn occur outside of the formal curriculum. Take medical school, for example. Allen Smith and Sherryl Kleinman argue in "Medical Students' Contacts with the Living and Dead" that although such subjects as doctors being disgusted by or sexually attracted to patients are not formally discussed by professors, there is nevertheless a "hidden curriculum of unspoken rules and resources for dealing with unwanted emotions."

Informal socialization within an educational setting also provides the backdrop for Barrie Thorne's article on gender role socialization in elementary school, "Boys and Girls Together...But Mostly Apart." Teaching girls to be girls and boys to be boys is not part of the formal lesson plans of elementary schools. Nevertheless, through school rules and routines and informal gender separation on the playground and in the lunchroom, children learn powerful gender lessons that they carry with them throughout their lives.

The Gloried Self

The Aggrandizement and the Constriction of Self

Patricia A. Adler and Peter Adler

. . . In this paper we describe and analyze a previously unarticulated form of self-identity: the "gloried" self, which arises when individuals become the focus of intense interpersonal and media attention, leading to their achieving celebrity. The articulation of the gloried self not only adds a new concept to our self repertoire but also furthers our insight into self-concept formation in two ways: it illustrates one process whereby dynamic contradictions between internal and external pressures become resolved, and it highlights the ascendance of an unintended self-identity in the face of considerable resistance.

The development of the gloried self is an outgrowth of individuals' becoming imbued with celebrity. It does not matter whether that celebrity is positive or negative; in our society we accord status and recognition for both fame and notoriety (Goldsmith 1983). Development of a gloried self is caused in part by the treatment of individuals' selves as objects by others. A "public persona" is created, usually by the media, which differs from individuals' private personas. These public images are rarely as intricate or as complex as individuals' real selves; often they draw on stereotypes or portray individuals in extreme fashion to accentuate their point. Yet the power of these media portrayals, reinforced by face-to-face encounters with

people who hold these images, often causes individuals to objectify their selves to themselves. Individuals thus become initially alienated from themselves through the separation of their self-concept from the conception of their selves held by others. Ultimately they resolve this disparity and reduce their alienation by changing their self-images to bridge the gap created by others' perceptions of them, even though they may fight this development as it occurs.

Characteristically, the gloried self is a greedy self, seeking to ascend in importance and to cast aside other self-dimensions as it grows. It is an intoxicating and riveting self, which overpowers other aspects of the individual and seeks increasing reinforcement to fuel its growth. Yet at the same time, its surge and display violate societal mores of modesty in both self-conception and self-presentation. Individuals thus become embroiled in inner conflict between their desire for recognition, flattery, and importance and the inclination to keep feeding this self-affirming element, and the socialization that urges them to fight such feelings and behavioral impulses. That the gloried self succeeds in flourishing, in spite of individuals' struggle against it, testifies to its inherent power and its drive to eclipse other self-dimensions. . . .

Setting and Methods

Over a five-year period (1980–1985) we conducted a participant-observation study of a major college basketball program. . . .

The research was conducted at a medium-sized (6,000 students) private university (hereafter

We would like to thank Paul Colomy, Stanford Lyman, and Ralph Turner for comments on earlier versions of this manuscript, which is a modified version of a paper presented at the 1988 annual meeting of the American Sociological Association in Atlanta. Please address all correspondence to Dr. Peter Adler, Department of Sociology, University of Denver, Denver, CO 80208.

referred to as "the University") in the mid-south central portion of the United States, with a predominantly white, suburban, middle-class student body. The basketball program was ranked in the top 40 of Division I NCAA schools throughout our research, and in the top 20 for most of two seasons. The team played in post-season tournaments every year, and in four complete seasons won approximately four times as many games as it lost. Players generally were recruited from the surrounding area; they were predominantly black (70%) and ranged from lower to middle class. In general, the basketball program was fairly representative of what Coakley (1986) and Frey (1982) term "big-time" college athletics. Although it could not compare to programs at the largest athletic universities, its recent success compensated for its size and lack of tradition. The basketball program's national ranking and its success (along with that of other athletic teams) in sending graduating members into the professional leagues further imbued the entire athletic milieu with a sense of seriousness and purpose.

The Experience of Glory

Experiencing glory was exciting, intoxicating, and riveting. Two self-dimensions were either created or expanded in the athletes we studied: the reflected self and the media self.

The Reflected Self

As a result of the face-to-face interactions between team members and people they encountered through their role as college athletes, the athletes' impressions of themselves were modified and changed. As Cooley (1902) and Mead (1934) were the first to propose, individuals engage in role-taking; their self-conceptions are products of social interaction, affected by the reflected impressions of others. According to Cooley (1902), these "looking glass" selves are formed through a combination of cognitive and affective forces; although individuals react intellectually to the impressions they perceive others forming about them, they also develop emotional reactions about these judgments. Together these reactions are instrumental in shaping their self-images. Thus individuals use what Rosenberg (1979) and

Sullivan (1953) call "reflected appraisals" in forging a new sense of self.

The forging and modification of reflected selves began as team members perceived how people *treated* them; subsequently they formed *reactions* to that treatment. One of the first things they all noticed was that they were sought intensely by strangers. Large numbers of people, individually and in groups, wanted to be near them, to get their autographs, to touch them, and to talk to them. People treated them with awe and respect. One day, for example, the head coach walked out of his office and found a woman waiting for him. As he turned towards her she threw herself in front of him and began to kiss his feet, all the while telling him what a great man he was. More commonly, fans who were curious about team matters approached players, trying to engage them in conversation. These conversations sometimes made the players feel awkward because although they wanted to be polite to their fans, they had little to say to them. Carrying on an interaction was often difficult. As one player said:

> People come walking up to you, and whether they're timid or pushy, they still want to talk. It's like, here's their hero walking face-to-face with them and they want to say anything just so they can have a conversation with them. It's *hero worshipping*. But what do you actually say to your hero when you see him?

These interactions, then, often took the form of ritualized pseudo-conversations, in which players and their fans offered each other stylized but empty words.

Many fans accorded players "cognitive recognition" (Goffman 1963), identifying them socially and expecting them to respond in kind. Players found themselves thrust into a "pseudo-intimacy" (Bensman and Lilienfeld 1979) with these fans, who had seen them so often at games and on television. Yet although their relationship with players was one-sided, fans often expected players to reciprocate their feelings of intimacy. As a result of their celebrity, team members found themselves in "exposed positions" (Goffman 1963), where they were open to engagement in personal interaction with individuals whom they did not know at all.

Players also found themselves highly prized in interacting with boosters (financial supporters of the team). Boosters showered all players with invitations to their houses for team meetings or dinner. They fought jealously to have players seen with them or gossiped about as having been in their houses. It soon became apparent to players that boosters derived social status from associating with them; boosters "basked in the reflected glory" (Burger 1985; Cialdini et al. 1976; Sigelman 1986) of the players. This situation caused players to recognize that they were "glory bearers," so filled with glory that they could confer it on anyone by their mere presence. They experienced a sense of the "Midas touch": they had an attribute (fame) that everybody wanted and which could be transmitted. Their ability to cast glory onto others and their desirability to others because of this ability became an important dimension of their new, reflected self-identity.

The Media Self

A second dimension of the self created from the glory experience was influenced largely by media portrayals. Altheide (1984) discusses the effect of the media as a fulcrum between self-feelings and the impressions, expectations, and behavior of others. He argues that modern life is characterized increasingly by media attention, leading to the creation of a "media self" whereby the self is raised to the level of self-consciousness, the focus of the individual's own attention. Fenigstein, Scheier, and Buss (1975) call this state "public self-consciousness," in which the self comes to be perceived as a social actor who serves as a stimulus for others' behavior. Most of the athletes who came to the University had received some media publicity in high school (68%), but the national level of the print and video coverage they received after arriving, coupled with the intensity of the constant focus, caused them to develop more compelling and more salient media selves than they had possessed previously.

Radio, television, and newspaper reporters covering the team often sought out athletes for "human interest" stories. These features presented media-framed angles that cast athletes into particular roles and tended to create new dimensions of their selves. Images were created from a combination of individuals' actual behavior and reporters' ideas of what made good copy. Thus through media coverage, athletes were cast into molds that frequently were distorted or exaggerated reflections of their behavior and self-conceptions.

Team members, for whom the media had created roles, felt as if they had to live up to these portrayals. For instance, two players were depicted as "good students"—shy, quiet, religious, and diligent. Special news features emphasized their outstanding traits, illustrating how they went regularly to class, were humanitarian, and cared about graduating. Yet one of them lamented:

> Other kids our age, they go to the fair and they walk around with a beer in their hand, or a cigarette, but if me and Dan were to do that, then people would talk about that. We can't go over to the clubs, or hang around, without it relaying back to Coach. We can't even do things around our teammates, because they expect us to be a certain way. The media has created this image of us as the "good boys," and now we have to live up to it.

Other players (about 20%) were embraced for their charismatic qualities; they had naturally outgoing personalities and the ability to excite a crowd. These players capitalized on the media coverage, exaggerating their antics to gain attention and fame. Yet the more they followed the media portrayal, the more likely it was to turn into a caricature of their selves. One player described how he felt when trapped by his braggart media self:

> I used to like getting in the paper. When reporters came around I would make those Mohammed Ali type outbursts—I'm gonna do this, I'm gonna do that. And they come around again, stick a microphone in your face, 'cause they figure somewhere Washington will have another outburst. But playing that role died out in me. I think sometimes the paper pulled out a little too much from me that wasn't me. But people seen me as what the paper said, and I had to play that role.

Particular roles notwithstanding, all the players shared the media-conferred sense of self as celebrity. Raised to the status of stars, larger than life, they regularly read their names and statements in the newspaper, saw their faces on television, or heard themselves whispered about on campus. One team member described the consequences of this celebrity:

> We didn't always necessarily agree with the way they wrote about us in the paper, but people who saw us expected us to be like what they read there. A lot of times it made us feel uncomfortable, acting like that, but we had to act like they expected us to, for the team's sake. We had to act like this was what we was really like.

Ironically, however, the more they interacted with people through their dramaturgically induced media selves, the more many of the team members felt familiar and comfortable with those selves ("We know what to do, we don't have to think about it no more"). The media presented the selves and the public believed in them, so the athletes continued to portray them. Even though they attempted to moderate these selves, part of them pressed for their legitimacy and acceptance. Over time the athletes believed these portrayals increasingly. . . . Athletes thus went through a gradual process of abandoning their "role distance" (Goffman 1961) and becoming more engrossed or more deeply involved in their media selves. The recurrent social situations of their everyday lives served as the foils against which both their public and their private selves developed. The net effect of having these selves placed upon them and of interacting through them with others was that athletes integrated them into their core selves.

Self-Aggrandizement

Athletes were affected profoundly by encounters with the self-images reflected onto them by others, both in person and through the media. It was exciting and gratifying to be cast as heroes. Being presented with these images and feeling obligated to interact with people through them, athletes added a new self to their repertoire: a glorified self. This self had a greater degree of aggrandizement than their previous identities. The athletes may have dreamed of glory, but until now they had never formed a structured set of relationships with people who accorded it to them. . . .

One result of receiving such intense personal interest and media attention was that players developed "big heads." They were admired openly by so many people and their exploits were regarded as so important that they began to feel more notable. Although they tried to remain modest, all of the players found that their celebrity caused them to lose control over their sense of self-importance. As one player observed:

> You try not to let it get away from you. You feel it coming all around you. People building you up. You say to yourself that you're the same guy you always were and that nothing has changed. But what's happening to you is so unbelievable. Even when you were sitting at home in high school imagining what college ball would be like, you could not imagine this. All the media, all the fans, all the pressure. And all so suddenly, with no time to prepare or ease into it. Doc, it got to go to your head. You try to fight it, and you think you do, but you got to be affected by it, you got to get a big head.

Although the players fought to normalize and diminish their feelings of self-aggrandizement, they were swept away in spite of themselves by the allure of glory, to varying degrees. Their sense of glory fed their egos, exciting them beyond their ability to manage or control it. They had never before been such glory-generating figures, had never felt the power that was now invested in them by the crowds or worshipful fans. They developed deep, powerful feelings affirming how important they had become and how good it felt.

All the members of the University's basketball program developed gloried selves, although the degree varied according to several factors. To some extent, their aggrandizement and glorification were affected by the level of attention they received. Individuals with more talent, who held central roles as team stars, were the focus of much media and fan attention. Others, who possessed the social and interpersonal attributes that made them good subjects for reporters, fruitful topics of conversation for boosters, and charismatic crowd pleasers, also received considerable notice. In addition, those who were more deeply invested in the athletic role were more likely to develop stronger gloried selves. They looked to this arena for their greatest rewards and were the most susceptible to its aggrandizing influence. Finally, individuals resisted or yielded to the gloried self depending on personal attributes. Those who were naturally more modest and more self-effacing tried harder to neutralize the effects and had more difficulty in forging grandiose self-conceptions than those who were boastful or pretentious.

The Price of Glory

Athletes' self-aggrandizement, as we have seen, was a clear consequence of the glory experience. Self-diminishment was a corresponding and concomitant effect. Athletes paid a price for becoming gloried in the form of self-narrowing or self-erosion. They sacrificed both the multidimensionality of their current selves and the potential breadth of their future selves; various dimensions of their identities were either diminished, detached, or somehow changed as a result of their increasing investment in their gloried selves.

Self-Immediacy

One of the first consequences of the ascent of the gloried self was a loss of future orientation. In all their lives, from the most celebrated player to the least, these individuals had never experienced such a level of excitement, adulation, intensity, and importance. These sensations were immediate and real, flooding all team members' daily lives and overwhelming them. As a result, their focus turned toward their present situation and became fixed on it.

This reaction was caused largely by the absorbing quality of the moment. During the intensity of the season (and to a lesser extent during the off-season), their basketball obligations and involvements were prominent. When they were lying exhausted in their hotel rooms, hundreds of miles from campus, or on their beds after a grueling practice, the responsibilities of school seemed remote and distant. One player described his state of preoccupation:

> I've got two finals tomorrow and one the next day. I should be up in the room studying right now. But how can I get my mind on that when I know I've got to guard Michael Jordan tomorrow night?

Their basketball affairs were so much more pressing, not only in the abstract but also because other people made specific demands on them, that it was easy to relegate all other activities to a position of lesser importance.

Many players who had entered college expecting to prepare themselves for professional or business careers were distracted from those plans and relinquished them (71%). The demands of the basketball schedule became the central focus of their lives; the associated physical, social, and professional dimensions took precedence over all other concerns. Despite their knowledge that only two percent of major-college players eventually play in the NBA (Coakley 1986; Leonard and Reyman 1988), they all clung to the hope that they would be the ones to succeed. . . .

Diminished Awareness

Locked into a focus on the present and stuck with a vision of themselves that grew from their celebrity status, all team members, to varying degrees, became desensitized to the concerns of their old selves. They experienced a heightened sensitivity and reflectivity toward the gloried self and a loss of awareness of the self-dimensions unrelated to glory. Nearly everyone they encountered interacted with them, at least in part, through their gloried selves. As this self-identity was fed and expanded, their other selves tended to atrophy. At times the athletes seemed to be so blinded by their glory that they would not look beyond it. As Goffman (1967, p. 43) observed, "Whatever his position in society, the person insulates himself by blindnesses, half-truths, illusions, and rationalizations." . . .

Discussion

As we have shown, high school graduates entered the world of college athletics and underwent a fundamental transformation. Thrust into a whirlwind of adulation and celebrity, they reacted to the situation through a process of simultaneous self-aggrandizement and self-diminishment. The gloried self expanded, overpowering all of their other statuses and self-dimensions; it became the aspect of self in which they lived and invested. They immersed themselves single-mindedly in this portion of their selves, and the feedback and grat-ification they derived from this identity dwarfed their other identities. They had not anticipated this situation, but gradually, as they were drawn into the arena of glory, they were swept away by star-dom and fame. Their commitment to the athletic self grew beyond anything they had ever imagined or intended. Once they had experienced the asso-ciated power and centrality, they were reluctant to give them up. They discarded their other aspira-tions, lost touch with other dimensions of their selves (even to the point of detachment), and plunged themselves into the gloried self.

Athletes' gloried selves arose originally as dra-maturgical constructions. Other people, through the media or face to face, conferred these identi-ties on athletes through their expectations of them. Athletes responded by playing the corre-sponding roles because of organizational loyalty, interactional obligations, and enjoyment. Yet in contrast to other roles, which can be played casu-ally and without consequence, athletes' actions in these roles increased their commitment and their self-involvement in them and made the athletes "more or less unavailable for alternative lines of action" (Kornhauser 1962, p. 321). The gloried self not only influenced athletes' future behavior but also transformed their self-conceptions and identities. . . .

. . . Athletes' engulfment by the glorified self was fueled both internally and externally. They developed gloried selves as new, more powerful, and more alluring identities were set before them. Then they chose to diminish the salience of other self-dimensions (see Adler and Adler 1987) in order to seek fulfillment from the new, intoxicat-ing identity. In doing so they shunted aside sig-nificant others associated with their former identities and sought the company of those who would reinforce the gloried self. . . .

REFERENCES

Adler, Patricia and Peter Adler. 1987. "The Recon-struction of Role Identity Salience: College Athletes and the Academic Role." *Social Science Journal* 24:443–55.

Altheide, David L. 1984. "The Media Self." Pp. 177–95 in *The Existential Self in Society,* edited by J. A. Kotarba and A. Fontana. Chicago: University of Chicago Press.

Bensman, Joseph and Robert Lilienfeld. 1979. *Between Public and Private.* New York: Free Press.

Burger, Jerry M. 1985. "Temporal Effects on Attribu-tions for Academic Performances and Reflected-Glory Basking." *Social Psychology Quarterly* 48:330–36.

Cialdini, Robert B., Richard J. Borden, Avril Thorne, Marcus Randall Walker, Stephen Freeman, and Lloyd Reynolds Sloan. 1976. "Basking in Reflected Glory: Three (Football) Field Studies." *Journal of Personality and Social Psychology* 34:366–75.

Coakley, Jay J. 1986. *Sport in Society.* 3d. ed. St. Louis: Mosby.

Cooley, Charles H. 1902. *Human Nature and Social Order.* New York: Scribners.

Fenigstein, Allan, Michael F. Scheier, and Arnold H. Buss. 1975. "Public and Private Self-Consciousness: Assessment and Theory." *Journal of Consulting and Clinical Psychology* 43:522–27.

Frey, James H. 1982. "Boosterism, Scarce Resources and Institutional Control: The Future of American Intercollegiate Athletics." *International Review of Sport Sociology* 17:53–70.

Goffman, Erving. 1961. *Encounters.* Indianapolis: Bobbs-Merrill.

———. 1963. *Behavior in Public Places.* New York: Free Press.

———. 1967. *Interaction Ritual.* New York: Anchor Doubleday.

Goldsmith, Barbara. 1983. "The Meaning of Celeb-rity." *New York Times Magazine,* December 4, pp. 75–82, 120.

Kornhauser, William. 1962. "Social Bases of Political Commitment: A Study of Liberals and Radicals." Pp. 321–39 in *Human Behavior and Social Processes,* edited by A. M. Rose. Boston: Houghton Mifflin.

Leonard, Wilbert M. and Jonathon E. Reyman. 1988. "The Odds of Attaining Professional Athlete Status: Refining the Computations." *Sociology of Sport Journal* 5:162–69.

Mead, George Herbert. 1934. *Mind, Self and Society.* Chicago: University of Chicago Press.

Rosenberg, Morris. 1979. *Conceiving the Self.* New York: Basic.

Sigelman, Lee. 1986. "Basking in Reflected Glory: An Attempt at Replication." *Social Psychology Quarterly* 49:90–92.

Sullivan, Harry S. 1953. *The Interpersonal Theory of Psy-chiatry.* New York: Norton.

Medical Students' Contacts with the Living and the Dead

Allen C. Smith III and Sherryl Kleinman

How do I set aside 25 years of living? Experience which made close contact with someone's body a sensual event? Maybe it's attraction, maybe disgust. But it isn't supposed to be part of what I feel when I touch a patient. I feel some of those things, and I want to learn not to (Third-year, male medical student). . . .

Medicine is the archetypal profession, and norms guiding the physician's feelings are strong. Physicians ideally are encouraged to feel moderate sympathy toward patients, but excessive concern and all feelings based on the patient's or the physician's individuality are proscribed (Daniels 1960). Presumably, caring too much for the patient can interfere with delivering good service. Other feelings such as disgust or sexual attraction, considered natural in the personal sphere, violate fundamental medical ideals. Doctors are supposed to treat all patients alike (that is, well) regardless of personal attributes, and without emotions that might disrupt the clinical process or the doctor-patient relationship. As several sociologists have shown, both doctor and patient use strategies to act "as if" the situation were neutral (Emerson 1970; Goffman 1974, p. 35). Such detachment presumably helps doctors to deal with death and dying (Sudnow 1967), with the pressure of making mistakes (Bosk 1979), and with the uncertainty of medical knowledge (Fox 1980b).

In this paper we examine another provocative issue—the physical intimacy inherent in medicine—and ask how medical students manage their inappropriate feelings as they make contact with the human body with all of their senses. We look closely at the situations that make them most uncomfortable: disassembling the dead human body (i.e., autopsy and dissection) and making "intimate" contact with living bodies (i.e., pelvic, rectal, and breast examinations). From the beginning of medical training, well before students take on clinical responsibility, dealing with the human body poses a problem for them (Mudd and Siegel 1969). Clothed in multiple meanings and connected to important rituals and norms, the body demands a culturally defined respect and provokes deep feelings. Even a seemingly routine physical exam calls for a physical intimacy that would evoke strong feelings in a personal context, feelings which are unacceptable in medicine.

The ideology of affective neutrality is strong in medicine; yet no courses in the medical curriculum deal directly with emotion management, specifically learning to change or eliminate inappropriate feelings (Hochschild 1979). Rather, two years of participant observation in a medical school revealed that discussion of the students' feelings is taboo; their development toward emotional neutrality remains part of the hidden curriculum. Under great pressure to prove themselves worthy of entering the profession, students are afraid to admit that they have uncomfortable feelings about patients or procedures, and hide those feelings behind a "cloak of competence" (Haas and Shaffir 1977, 1982). Beneath their surface presentations, how do students deal with the "unprofessional" feelings they bring over from the personal realm? Because faculty members do not address the problem, students are left with an individualistic outlook: they expect to get control of themselves through sheer willpower.

Despite the silence surrounding this topic, the faculty, the curriculum, and the organization of medical school do provide students with resources for dealing with their problem. The culture of medicine that informs teaching and provides the feeling rules also offers unspoken supports for dealing with unwanted emotions. Students draw on aspects of their experience in medical school to manage their emotions. Their strategies include transforming the patient or the procedure into an analytic object or event, accentuating the comfortable feelings that come from learning and practicing "real medicine," blaming patients, empathizing with patients, joking, and avoiding sensitive contact.

In this case study of the professionalization of emotions, we examine how students learn to handle unsettling reactions to patients and procedures in a context in which faculty members expect students to socialize themselves. We argue that the students' emotion management strategies affect the medicine they learn and threaten their individual well-being. By relying on the strategies provided by the school, the students reproduce the professional culture of medicine. . . .

The Students' Problem

As they encounter the human body, students experience a variety of uncomfortable feelings including embarrassment, disgust, and arousal. Medical school, however, offers a barrier against these feelings by providing the anesthetic effect of long hours and academic pressure.

> You know the story. On call every third night, and stay in the hospital late most other evenings. I don't know how you're supposed to think when you're that tired, but you do, plod through the day insensitive to everything (Third-year male).

Well before entering medical school, students learn that their training will involve constant pressure and continuing fatigue. Popular stories prepare them for social isolation, the impossibility of learning everything, long hours, test anxiety, and the fact that medical school will permeate their lives (Becker, Geer, Hughes, and Strauss 1961). These difficulties and the sacrifices that they entail

legitimate the special status of the profession the students are entering. They also blunt the students' emotional responses.

Yet uncomfortable feelings break through. Throughout the program, students face provocative situations—some predictable, others surprising. They find parts of their training, particularly dissection and the autopsy, bizarre or immoral when seen from the perspective they had "for 25 years" before entering medical school.

> Doing the pelvis, we cut it across the waist. . . . Big saws! The mad scientist! People wouldn't believe what we did in there. The cracking sound! That day was more than anxiety. We were really violating that person. . . . Drawn and quartered (First-year male).
>
> I did my autopsy 10 days ago. That shook me off my feet. Nothing could have prepared me for it. The person was my age. . . . She just looked (pause) asleep. Not like the cadaver. Fluid, blood, smell. It smelled like a butcher shop.
>
> And they handled it like a butcher shop. The technicians. Slice, move, pull, cut . . . all the organs, insides, pulled out in 10 minutes. I know it's absurd, but what if she's not really dead? She doesn't look like it (Second-year female).

The "mad scientist" and the "butcher" violate the students' images of medicine. Even in more routine kinds of contact, the students sometimes feel that they are ignoring the sanctity of the body and breaking social taboos.

Much of the students' discomfort is based on the fact that the bodies they have contact with are or were *people*. Suddenly students feel uncertain about the relationship of the person to the body, a relationship they had previously taken for granted.

> It felt tough when we had to turn the whole body over from time to time (during dissection). It felt like real people (First-year female).
>
> OK. Maybe he was a father. But the father part is gone. This is just the body. That sounds religious. Maybe it is. How else can I think about it? (First-year male).

When the person is somehow reconnected to the body, such as when data about the living patient who died is brought into the autopsy room, students feel less confident and more uneasy.

Students find contact with the sexual body particularly stressful. In the anatomy lab, in practice sessions with other students, and in examining patients, students find it difficult to feel neutral as contact approaches the sexual parts of the body.

> When you listen to the heart you have to work around the breast, and move it to listen to one spot. I tried to do it with minimum contact, without staring at her tit. . . . breast. . . . The different words (pause) shows I was feeling both things at once (Second-year male).

Though they are rarely aroused, students worry that they will be. They feel guilty, knowing that sexuality is proscribed in medicine, and they feel embarrassed. Most contact involves some feelings, but contact with the sexual body presents a bigger problem.

On occasion students feel unsure about differences between the personal and the professional perspectives. Recalling the first day of "surface anatomy," when they are expected to remove their shirts in order to examine each other's backs before beginning dissection of the back, students remember an unspoken tension. The lab manual suggests that women wear bathing suit tops, but few students read it in advance. Some of the few women who comply wear bras.

> I remember surface anatomy. That first day when they asked us to take our shirts off, including the girls. That was real uncomfortable. You know (pause) seeing some of the girls in bras. Some of them were wearing swimsuit tops. But (pause) and drawing on their chests. So I got a guy for a partner (First-year male).
>
> What's the difference between a bra and a bathing suit top? Don't know. But there is one! (First-year female).

When students are standing in the anatomy lab beside the cadavers, the difference between a bra and a bathing suit is surprisingly hard to describe. The differences are clear from a personal perspec-

tive, but in the technical objectivity of the laboratory, the details and meanings of the personal perspective seem elusive and irrational.

Students also feel disgust. They see feces, smell vomit, touch wounds, and hear bone saws, encountering many repulsive details with all of their senses.

> One patient was really gross! He had something that kept him standing, and coughing all the time. Coughing phlegm, and that really bothers me. Gross! Just something I don't like. Some smelled real bad. I didn't want to examine their axillae. Stinking armpits! It was just not something I wanted to do (Second-year female).

When the ugliness is tied to living patients, the aesthetic problem is especially difficult. On opening the bowels of the cadaver, for example, students permit themselves some silent expressions of discomfort, but even a wince is unacceptable with repugnant living patients.

To make matters worse, students learn early on that they are not supposed to talk about their feelings with faculty members or other students. Feelings remain private. The silence encourages students to think about their problem as an individual matter, extraneous to the "real work" of medical school. They speak of "screwing up your courage," "getting control of yourself," "being tough enough," and "putting feelings aside." They worry that the faculty would consider them incompetent and unprofessional if they admitted their problem.

> I would be embarrassed to talk about it. You're supposed to be professional here. Like there's an unwritten rule about how to talk (First-year female).
>
> It wouldn't be a problem if I weren't in medicine. But doctors just aren't supposed to feel that way. (Interviewer) How do you know? (Student) I don't know how, just sense it. It's macho, the control thing. Like, "Med student, get a grip on yourself." It's just part of medicine. It's a norm, expected (First-year male).

The "unwritten rule" is relaxed enough sometimes to permit discussion, but the privacy that surrounds these rare occasions suggests the degree to which the taboo exists. At times, students signal their uncomfortable feelings—rolling their eyes, turning away, and sweating—but such confirmation is limited. Exemplifying pluralistic ignorance, each student feels unrealistically inadequate in comparison with peers (yet another uncomfortable feeling). Believing that other students are handling the problem better than they are, each student manages his or her feelings privately, only vaguely aware that all students face the same problem.

The silence continues in the curriculum; discomfort with medical intimacy is not mentioned officially. The issue is broached once or twice in class with comments such as "You can expect to be aroused sometimes, examining an attractive woman." Yet there is no discussion, and such rare exceptions occur only according to individual faculty members' initiative. In welcoming new classes to the school, a senior orientation speaker states that although humanitarian values are critical in the competent physician, the proper purpose of the school is to address the other foundation of medicine, namely scientific knowledge.

Emotion Management Strategies

How do students manage their uncomfortable and "inappropriate" feelings? The deafening silence surrounding the issue keeps them from defining the problem as shared, or from working out common solutions. They cannot develop strategies collectively, but their solutions are not individual. Rather, students use the *same* basic emotion management strategies because social norms, faculty models, curricular priorities, and official and unofficial expectations provide them with uniform guidelines and resources for managing their feelings.

Transforming the Contact

Students feel uncomfortable because they are making physical contact with people in ways they would usually define as appropriate only in a personal context, or as inappropriate in any context. Their most common solution to this problem is cognitive (Hochschild 1979; Thoits 1985).

Mentally they transform the body and their contact with it into something entirely different from the contacts they have in their personal lives. Students transform the person into a set of esoteric body parts and change their intimate contact with the body into a mechanical or analytic problem.

> I just told myself, "OK, doc, you're here to find out what's wrong, and that includes the axillae (armpits)." And I detach a little, reduce the person for a moment. . . . Focus real hard on the detail at hand, the fact, or the procedure or the question. Like with the cadaver. Focus on a vessel. Isolate down to whatever you're doing (Second-year female).
>
> Well, with the pelvic training (pause) I concentrated on the procedure, the sequence, and the motions. . . . With the 22-year-old, I concentrated on the order, sequence (pause) and on the details to check (Second-year male). . . .

Students also transform the moment of contact into a complex intellectual puzzle, the kind of challenge they faced successfully during previous years of schooling. They interpret details according to logical patterns and algorithms, and find answers as they master the rules.

> It helped to know that we were there for a training experience. My anxiety became the anxiety of learning enough. We saw a movie on traumas, like gunshots, burns, explosions. If I had just come off the street, I would have felt sick. But I focused on learning. Occupying my mind with learning and science (Second-year male).
>
> The patient is really like a math word problem. You break it down into little pieces and put them together. The facts you get from a history and physical, from the labs and chart. They fit together, once you begin to see how to do it. . . . It's an intellectual challenge (Third-year female).

Defining contact as a part of scientific medicine makes the students feel safe. They are familiar with and confident about science, they feel supported by its cultural and curricular legitimacy, and they enjoy rewards for demonstrating their scientific know-how. In effect, science itself is an emotion management strategy. By competing for years for the highest grades, these students have learned to separate their feelings from the substance of their classes and to concentrate on the impersonal facts of the subject matter. In medical school they use these "educational skills" not only for academic success but also for emotion management.

The curriculum supports the students' efforts to focus on subpersonal facts and details. In 20 courses over the first two years, texts and teachers disassemble the body into systems and subsystems. Students are presented with an impossibly large number of anatomical and pathophysiological details which define the body as a collection of innumerable smaller objects in a complex system. Furthermore, faculty members reward students for recognizing and reciting the relevant facts and details and for reporting them in a succinct and unemotional fashion. Intellectualization is not merely acceptable; it is celebrated as evidence of superior performance in modern medicine. The curriculum equips the students with the substantive basis for their intellectual transformations of the body, and rewards them for using it.

The scientific, clinical language that the students learn also supports intellectualization. It is complex, esoteric, and devoid of personal meanings. "Palpating the abdomen" is less personal than "feeling the belly."

> When we were dissecting the pelvis, the wrong words kept coming to mind, and it was uncomfortable. I tried to be sure to use the right words, penis and testicles (pause) not cock and balls. Even just thinking. Would have been embarrassing to make that mistake that day. School language, it made it into a science project (First-year female).

Further, the structure of the language, as in the standard format for the presentation of a case, helps the students to think and speak impersonally. Second-year students learn that there is a routine, acceptable way to summarize a patient: chief complaint, history of present illness, past medical history, family history, social history, review of systems, physical findings, list of problems, medical plan. In many situations they must reduce the sequence to a two- or three-minute summary. Faculty members praise the students for their ability to present the details quickly. Medical language labels and conveys clinical information, and it leads the students away from their emotions.

Transformation sometimes involves changing the body into a nonhuman object. Students think of the body as a machine or as an animal specimen, and recall earlier, comfortable experiences in working on that kind of object. The body is no longer provocative because it is no longer a body.

> After we had the skin off (the cadaver), it was pretty much like a cat or something. It wasn't pleasant, but it wasn't human either (First-year female).
>
> (The pelvic exam) is pretty much like checking a broken toaster. It isn't a problem. I'm good at that kind of thing (Second-year male).
>
> You can't tell what's wrong without looking under the hood. It's different when I'm talking with a patient. But when I'm examining them it's like an automobile engine . There's a bad connotation with that, but it's literally what I mean (Third-year male). . . .

The curriculum supports these dehumanizing transformations by eliminating the person in most of the students' contact with the body. Contact is usually indirect, based on photographs, X-rays (and several newer technologies), clinical records, diagrams, and written words. Students would have to make an effort to reconnect these images to the people they remotely represent. It is harder to disregard the person in direct contact, but such contact constitutes a very small part of the students' school time in the first three years. In addition, a large part of the students' direct contact occurs with a cadaver in the anatomy lab. Contact with living persons represents less than three percent of their school time over the first three years. Students must take the final step in transforming the body into a specific nonhuman thing, but the curriculum provides the first step by separating the body from the person.

Accentuating the Positive

As we hinted in the previous section, transforming body contact into an analytic event does not merely rid students of their uncomfortable feelings, producing neutrality. It often gives them opportunities to have *good* feelings about what they are doing. Their comfortable feelings include the excitement of practicing "real medicine," the satisfaction of learning, and the pride of living up to medical ideals.

Students identify much of their contact with the body as "real medicine," asserting that such contact separates medicine from other professions. As contact begins in dissection and continues through the third-year clinical clerkships, students feel excited about their progress.

> I can't remember what it was like before coming. It's enveloping. When I wake up I start thinking about being in med school. It's like a honeymoon, knowing I'll be an MD some day. It's just a real good feeling. I don't know how long it will last. And the work is demanding, almost all my time. But it is real, and it does make gross (lab) easier. Lab makes it real, even if it is gross (First-year male).
>
> This (dissection) is the part that is really medical school. Not like any other school. It feels like an initiation rite, something like when I joined a fraternity. We were really going to work on people (First-year male).

After years of anticipation, they are actually entering the profession; occasions of body contact mark their arrival and their progress. The students also feel a sense of privilege and power.

> This is another part that is unique to med school. The professor told us we are the only ones who can do this legally. It is special (pause) and uneasy (First-year female).
>
> I remember my second patient. An older guy. . . . There I was, a second-year student who didn't know much of anything, and I could have done anything I wanted. He would have done whatever I told him (Second-year male).

Eventually students see contact as their responsibility and their right, and forget the sense of privilege they felt at the beginning. Still, some excite-ment returns as they take on clinical responsibility in the third year. All of these feelings can displace the discomfort which also attends most contact.

Contact also provides a compelling basis for several kinds of learning, all of which the students value. They sense that they learn something important in contact, something richer than the "dry facts" of textbooks and lectures. Physicians, they believe, rely on touch, not on text.

> I guess I learned the intuitive part in the practice sessions (on physical examination skills). After all that training in science, this was different. . . . Like feeling someone's side. Feeling (pause) it begins to mean something. . . . All the courses don't mean anything 'til I have them in my fingertips, my ears (First-year male). . . .

There are two ways in which students accentuate their pride and excitement. First, they can "go with" the good feelings that arise spontaneously. Second, they can create good feelings when they do not arise naturally. By transforming an uncomfortable contact into an analytic event, students can produce the feelings of excitement and satisfaction that they have learned to associate with problem solving. Transformation and accentuating the positive are mutually reinforcing strategies. . . .

Laughing About It

Students can find or create humor in the situations that provoke their discomfort. Humor is an acceptable way for people to acknowledge a problem and to relieve tension without having to confess weaknesses. In this case, joking also lets other students know that they are not alone with the problem. . . .

By redefining the situation as at least partially humorous, students reassure themselves that they can handle the challenge. They believe that the problem can't be so serious if there is a funny side to it. Joking also allows them to relax a little and to set ideals aside for a time.

Where do students learn to joke in this way? The faculty, including the residents (who are the real teachers on the clinical teams), participate freely, teaching the students that humor is an acceptable way to talk about uncomfortable encounters in medicine.

> We get all our grandmotherly types around the first day of (gross anatomy) lab, in case some of (the students) wimp out. Wonder why it's such a problem (Faculty member).
>
> If I had to examine her I'd toss my cookies. I mean she is enormous. That's it! Put it in the chart! Breasts too large for examination! (Resident). (The team had just commented on a variety of disturbing behaviors that they observed with the patient.)

None of these comments is particularly funny out of context and without the gestures and tone of voice that faculty members use to embellish their words. Yet the humor is evident in person, akin to gallows humor, and thick with references to sexuality and aesthetic extremes (Fox 1980a). Eager to please the faculty and to manage their emotions, students quickly adopt the faculty's humor. Joking about patients and procedures means sharing something special with the faculty, becoming a colleague. The idea implicit in the humor, that feelings are real despite the rule against discussing them, is combined with an important sense of "we-ness" that the students value.

Unlike the students' other strategies, joking occurs primarily when they are alone with other medical professionals. Jokes are acceptable in the hallways, over coffee, or in physicians' workrooms, but usually are unacceptable when outsiders might overhear. Joking is backstage behavior. Early in their training, students sometimes make jokes in public, perhaps to strengthen their identity as "medical student," but most humor is in-house, reserved for those who share the problem and have a sense of humor about it.

Avoiding the Contact
Students sometimes avoid the kinds of contact that give rise to unwanted emotions. They control the visual field during contact, and eliminate or abbreviate particular kinds of contact.

> We did make sure that it was covered. The parts we weren't working on. The head, the genitals. All of it really. It is important to keep them wrapped and moist, so they wouldn't

get moldy. That made sense. But when the cloth slipped, someone made sure to cover it back up, even if just a little (pubic) hair showed (First-year female).

Keeping personal body parts covered in the lab and in examinations prevents mold, maintains a sterile field, and protects the patient's modesty. Covers also eliminate disturbing sites and protect students from their feelings. Such nonprofessional purposes are sometimes most important. Some students, for example, examine the breasts by reaching under the patient's gown, bypassing the visual examination emphasized in training. . . .

Conveniently, the faculty do not supervise students' contact with patients in the second and third years. When the faculty members are present they do the work themselves, leaving the students to observe. This lack of supervision gives students the freedom to learn without the pressure of criticism. It also gives them opportunities to avoid the kinds of contact that make them uncomfortable. . . .

Conclusion
Medical students sometimes feel attracted to or disgusted by the human body. They want to do something about these feelings, but they find that the topic is taboo. Even among themselves, students generally refrain from talking about their problem. Yet despite the silence, the culture and the organization of medical school provide students with supports and guidelines for managing their emotions. Affective socialization proceeds with no deliberate control, but with profound effect. . . .

The emotion management strategies used by the students illustrate the culture of modern Western medicine. In relying on these strategies, the students reproduce that culture (Foucault 1973), creating a new generation of physicians who will support the biomedical model of medicine and the kind of doctor-patient relationship in which the patient is too frequently dehumanized. Students sometimes criticize their teachers for an apparent insensitivity to their patients, but they turn to desensitizing strategies themselves in their effort to control the emotions that medical situations provoke. These strategies exclude the patient's feelings, values, and social context, the important psychosocial aspects of medicine (Engel 1977; Gorlin and Zucker 1983). Contradicting their previous values, students reinforce biomedicine as they rely on its emotion management effects.

Analytic transformation is the students' primary strategy, and it does tend to produce affective neutrality. As we stated, however, the medical culture provides other strategies that involve strong feelings instead of the neutrality of medical ideals. The particular feelings allowed by faculty members and by the culture fit with the basis of all occupations that have achieved the honorific title of "profession": acquiring hierarchical distance from clients (if not always emotional indifference). Much of the humor that students learn puts down patients who are aesthetically, psychologically, or socially undesirable (Papper 1978). Blaming patients and avoiding uncomfortable contact lend power to the physician's role. Even the effort to accentuate the comfortable feelings which come with learning contributes to the distance. In concentrating on the medical problem, students distance themselves from their patients. As Becker et al. (1961) observed years ago, uninteresting patients who have nothing to teach are "crocks." All of these strategies maintain the kind of professional distance that characterizes modern medical culture, a distance which provides for comfortable objectivity as well as scientific medical care.

One of the students' strategies, however, operates differently. Empathizing with patients diminishes the students' discomfort and directs attention to the patient's feelings and circumstances. Students are taught that excessive concern for patients can cloud their clinical judgment, but moderate concern allows them to manage their own feelings *and* to pay close attention to the patient.

Depending on how easily they can switch their strategies on and off, students and physicians may influence the character of their personal relationships as well as their medical practice. For some the effects can be healthy, enhancing personal intimacy by diminishing its mystique. Yet for others

the results, particularly the long-term results, may be disruptive (Hochschild 1979). We speculate that the professionalization of private emotions may help to explain some of the health problems associated with the practice of medicine.

It would be unfair to conclude that medical training is uniquely responsible for the specific character of the students' emotion management problem and for its unspoken solution. The basic features of the culture of medicine are consistent with the wider cultural context in which medicine exists. Biomedicine fits with the emphasis in Western culture on rationality and scientific "objectivity." In Western societies the mind is defined as superior to the body, and thoughts are defined as superior to feelings (Mills and Kleinman 1988; Tuan 1982; Turner 1984). Not surprisingly, students know the feeling rules of professional life before they arrive at medical school. Childhood socialization and formal education teach them to set aside their feelings in public, to master "the facts," and to present themselves in intellectually defensible ways (Bowers 1984). Medical situations provide vivid challenges, but students come equipped with emotion management skills that they need only to strengthen.

Our study suggests that the emotional socialization of professional training will influence the character of performance in the workplace and will have consequences for life outside the workplace. Medical students accept that they must change their perspective on the body in order to practice medicine, but they worry about the consequences. Often using the word "desensitization," they are concerned that medical training will dull their emotional responses too generally.

> Those feelings just get in the way. They don't fit, and I'm going to learn to get rid of them. Don't know how yet, and some of the possibilities are scary. What's left when you succeed? But what choice is there? (Second-year female).
>
> It's kind of dehumanizing. We just block off the feelings, and I don't know what happens to them. This is pretty important to me. I'm working to keep a sense of myself through all this (Third-year male).

Quietly, because their concern is private and therefore uncertain, students ask questions we might all ask. Will we lose our sensitivity to those we serve? To others in our lives? To ourselves? Will we even know it is happening?

REFERENCES

Becker, H., B. Geer, E. Hughes and A. Strauss. 1961. *Boys in White*. New Brunswick, NJ: Transaction.

Bosk, C. 1979. *Forgive and Remember*. Chicago: University of Chicago Press.

Bowers, C. 1984. *The Promise of Theory: Education and the Politics of Cultural Change*. New York: Longmans.

Daniels, M. 1960. "Affect and Its Control in the Medical Intern." *American Journal of Sociology* 55:259–67.

Emerson, J. 1970. "Behavior in Private Places: Sustaining Definitions of Reality in Gynecological Examinations." Pp. 74–97 in *Recent Sociology* Number 2, edited by H. P. Dreitzel, London: Macmillan.

Engel, G. 1977. "The Need for a New Medical Model: A Challenge for Biomedicine." *Science* 196(4286): 129–36.

Foucault, M. 1973. *The Birth of the Clinic: An Archaeology of Medical Perception*. New York: Pantheon.

Fox, R. 1979. "The Autopsy: Its Place in the Attitude-Learning of Second-Year Medical Students." Pp. 51–77 in *Essays in Medical Sociology*, edited by R. Fox., New York: Wiley.

_____. 1980a. "The Human Condition of Health Professionals." Lecture delivered at the University of New Hampshire, November 19, 1979.

_____. 1980b. "The Evolution of Medical Uncertainty." *Millbank Memorial Fund Quarterly: Health and Society* 58(1):1–49.

Goffman, E. 1974. *Frame Analysis*. New York: Harper.

Gorlin, R. and H. Zucker. 1983. "Physicians' Reactions to Patients: A Key to Teaching Humanistic Medicine." *New England Journal of Medicine* 308(18):1059–63.

Haas, J. and W. Shaffir. 1977. "The Professionalization of Medical Students: Developing Competence and a Cloak of Competence." *Symbolic Interaction* 1:71–88.

_____. 1982. "Taking on the Role of Doctor: A Dramaturgical Analysis of Professionalization." *Symbolic Interaction* 5:187–203.

Hochschild, A. 1979. "Emotion Work, Feeling Rules, and Social Structure." *American Journal of Sociology* 85(3):551–75.

Lipsitt, D. 1970. "Medical and Psychological Characteristics of 'Crocks.'" *Psychiatry in Medicine* 1:15–25.

Mills, T. and S. Kleinman, 1988. "Emotions, Reflexivity, and Action: An Interactionist Analysis." *Social Forces* 66(4):1009–27.

Mudd, J. and R. Siegel, 1969. "Sexuality—The Experiences and Anxieties of Medical Students." *New England Journal of Medicine* 281:1397–403.

Papper, S. 1978. "The Undesirable Patient." Pp. 166–68 in *Dominant Issues in Medical Sociology*, edited by H. Schwartz and C. Kart, Reading, MA: Addison-Wesley.

Sudnow, D. 1967. *Passing On*. Englewood Cliffs, NJ: Prentice-Hall.

Thoits, P. 1985. "Self-Labeling Processes in Mental Illness: The Role of Emotional Deviance." *American Journal of Sociology* 91:221–49.

Tuan, Y.-F. 1982. *Segmented Worlds and Self: Group Life and Individual Consciousness*. Minneapolis: University of Minnesota Press.

Turner, B. 1984. *The Body and Society*. New York: Basil Blackwell.

Boys and Girls Together . . . But Mostly Apart

Barrie Thorne

The landscape of contemporary childhood includes three major sites—families, neighborhoods, and schools. Each of these worlds contains different people, patterns of time and space, and arrangements of gender. Families and neighborhoods tend to be small, with a relatively even ratio of adults and children. In contrast, schools are crowded and bureaucratic settings in which a few adults organize and continually evaluate the activities of a large number of children.[1] Within schools, the sheer press of numbers in a relatively small space gives a public, witnessed quality to everyday life and makes keeping down noise and maintaining order a constant adult preoccupation. In their quest for order, teachers and aides continually sort students into smaller, more manageable groups (classes, reading groups, hallway lines, shifts in the lunchroom), and they structure the day around routines like lining up and taking turns. In this article I trace the basic organizational features of schools as they bear upon, and get worked out through, the daily gender relations of kids. As individuals, we always display or "do" gender, but this dichotomous difference (no one escapes being declared female or male) may be more or less relevant, and relevant in different ways, from one social context to another.

School Routines, Rules, and Groups

On the first day of the Ashton school year I went early so that I could be part of the opening moments in Mrs. Smith's kindergarten. The kids began to arrive, their faces etched with wariness and expectation, each held the hand of a parent (one a father, the rest mothers) and patiently stood in line waiting to meet the teacher. As each pair came up, Mrs. Smith, an energetic teacher in her late twenties, introduced herself to the parent and then kneeled down and warmly greeted the new student, pinning a name tag on the front of each dress or shirt. The teacher then said goodbye to the parent and directed the child, after comforting a few who were tearful, to a predesignated place at one of the five long tables that filled the center of the room.

Above each table, dangling by string from the ceiling, was a piece of cardboard whose color and shape matched its printed name: "Blue Circle," "Brown Triangle," "Red Diamond." Standing above the seated kids and using a loud and deliberate voice that drew the new arrivals together as a group, Mrs. Smith introduced herself and told about her pets. The kids began to talk all at once: "We're gettin' a kitty, a baby kitty"; "My mom won't let me get a kitty"; "I wonder if you're going to give me a book or a pencil to do something." Mrs. Smith broke into the verbal chaos to instruct in a kind but firm voice, "We talk one-at-a-time; you should hold up your hand if you want to talk." Hands flew up, while the chorus of spontaneous comments continued.

Raising her voice to regain their attention, Mrs. Smith asked, "Is there a big boy or girl who would volunteer to be a leader and carry the thermometer outside so we can see how hot it is?" "Me!" Me!" urgent voices called from around the room of waving hands. "I don't call on me-me's. I'm going to pick one that doesn't say 'me.' Me-me's don't come to school," Mrs. Smith admonished. She chose Jason and asked him to go to the door and lead the line they were going to form. Tina jumped up at the same time as Jason, and Mrs. Smith told her to sit down. Raising her voice to again instruct the group, Mrs. Smith said, "When we go down the hallway, we have to stop talking.

That's a rule: Be quiet in the hallway." She asked the students to repeat the rule, and they chanted together in high sing-song voices, "Be quiet in the hallway." "Now," Mrs. Smith said, "I will choose the quietest table to line up first. She paused, looked around, and then pronounced, "Blue Circle Table," moving over to prod the two boys and three girls at that table to form a single line behind Jason.

After looking around, the teacher made a second pronouncement: "The Red Diamond Table looks ready to push in their chairs." When a short brown-haired boy jumped up and ran helter-skelter ahead of the others, Mrs. Smith admonished, "Todd, you have to walk and push in your chair." He went back to redo his actions in proper form. Mrs. Smith continued to call on tables until all thirty students, with bits of nudging and rearranging, had arrayed themselves in a single line. Admonishing them to be quiet, the teacher motioned the line to move into the hallway. Susie talked noisily, and Mrs. Smith sent her to the back of the line. "Stay in your line," Mrs. Smith called as the students moved along, "this is what you call a line; one at a time." When they passed a water fountain, several kids leaned over to drink until Mrs. Smith stated another rule: "We don't take drinks in the hall; we have a fountain in our room."

Over the next few weeks, Mrs. Smith continued to add to the young students' repertoire of school routines. They learned the named segments that divided each day: "reading time," "center time" (when they went into specialized classroom areas like "house" and "large toys"), "clean-up time," "recess." After instances of "bad behavior," the teacher sometimes threatened to take center time away, which strengthened its allure. During center time and recess the kids were relatively free to structure their own activities within bounded spaces. Mrs. Smith frequently reminded her students to take turns doing everything from sharing toys to going to the bathroom, for which she gave elaborate instructions: "You can go in when the door is open; leave the door open when you're through, but close it when you use it. Big boys and girls have doors shut in the bathroom; that's the grown-up thing to do at school."

Sorting Students into Groups

In managing almost thirty lively children within relatively small spaces, Mrs. Smith, like other teachers and aides, drew on the general power of being an adult, as well as on the more institutionalized authority of her official position. She claimed the right to regulate the students' activities, movement, posture, talking, possessions, access to water, and time and manner of eating. Such collective regulation—or "batch processing"—has a leveling effect; teachers and aides cope with the large number of students by treating them as members of groups.[2] School staff often sort students by characteristics like age, reading or math performance, or by spatial locations like "the Red Diamond Table or "boys in the large toy area." And, when given the opportunity within classrooms, hallways, lunchrooms, and on the playground, kids also form their own groups. In the process the unique qualities of individuals (the focus of much family interaction) become subordinated to ways in which they are alike.[3]

In any mass of students there are many potential strands of "alikeness" and difference that may be used as a basis for constituting groups. Age is the most institutionalized principle of grouping; before the school year even begins, the staff assign students to first grade or fourth grade, and this sorting has a continuous effect on their activities and the company they keep. All the students in Mrs. Smith's kindergarten class were alike in being five or six years old. They differed by gender, race, ethnicity, social class, and religion, but these differences were to some degree submerged by the fact that the students, placed together because they were similar in age, confronted the same teacher, received the same work assignments, and were governed by the same rules. In [the] schools [I studied] age-grading extended from classrooms into the cafeteria and auditorium, where each class was assigned its own space. Ashton School also had age-divided playgrounds: one for the kindergarten, first, and second grades; another for the third and fourth grades; and "the older kids' playground" for fifth- and sixth-graders. The Oceanside playground was not formally segmented by age, but younger and older students went out for recess at different times.

Within their age-homogeneous classrooms, teachers continually establish further divisions, some more or less arbitrary, like "the Red Diamond Table," and others based on differences in perceived talent or performance, like "the Bluebird Reading Group." The social categories and identities of the students—religion, social class, race and ethnicity, and gender—provide additional lines of difference that teachers and students evoke verbally and in their sorting practices, but to strikingly varied degrees. . . .

Apart from age, of all the social categories of the students, gender was the most formally, and informally, highlighted in the course of each school day. Gender is a highly visible source of individual and social identity, clearly marked by dress and by language; everyone is either a female or a male. In contrast, categories of race, ethnicity, religion, and social class tend to be more ambiguous and complex. Furthermore, recent public policy has set more proscriptions against officially marking race and religion (in the law, both are regarded as "suspect categories"), compared with gender (where, in a tangle of inconsistency, the law both does and does not mark difference).[4]

"Boys and Girls": The Verbal Marking of Gender

In both schools when the public address system crackled an announcement into a classroom or the cafeteria, the voice always opened with, "Boys and girls . . ." (the word "boys" invariably came first). Teachers and aides often used gender to mark out groups of students, usually for purposes of social control. For example, while the second-graders at Ashton School worked at their desks, the teacher, Mrs. Johnson, often walked around the room, verbally reining in the disruptive and inattentive: "There's three girls need to get busy. . . .You two boys ought to be busy." Other teachers also peppered their classroom language with gendered terms of address ("You boys be quiet"; "Girls, sit down"; "Ladies, this isn't a tea party"), implying that gender defined both behavior and social ties.

Why are gender terms so appealing as terms of address? Occasionally, the staffs of both schools used words like "people" or "students" to call for general attention. But they much more often used

"boys and girls," perhaps because, as one of the principals reflected, "it feels more specific." Indeed, gender categories provide a striking blend of the specific and the all-encompassing. Since everyone is assigned to either one or the other gender category, the paired terms, "boys and girls," drop an inclusive net over a group of any size. (Note that "boys and girls" is used as the generic; "boy," unlike the word "man," has never been claimed as a generic, perhaps because children of both genders are subordinated to adults, and boys have less power over girls compared with men over women.[5]) "Boys and girls" may also be an appealing term of address because the words are marked for age, making it clear that children, not adults, are the focus of a comment. The language comes in handy since the structural separation of adults and children is so fundamental to schools.[6] Finally, terms like "the Blue Circle Table" and "fourth-graders" have fleeting connections with individual identities; the words "girls" and "boys" sink more deeply into a person's sense of self.

Spencer Cahill has also noted the centrality of gender categories in the "languages of social identification" used by and toward children. Observing in a preschool, he found that the adult staff used "baby" as a sanctioning term, contrasted with "big girl" and "big boy," which they employed as more positive forms of address. Cahill argues that children pick up the association of gender labels with the praiseworthy state of maturity and begin to claim "big girl" and "big boy" identities to distinguish themselves from "babies."[7]

Use of "big boy" and "big girl" as terms of praise continues in the early years of elementary school. On the first day of kindergarten Mrs. Smith asked for a "big boy or girl" to volunteer to carry the thermometer outside, and she later described the proper bathroom comportment of "big boys and girls." By fourth grade the terms "big girl" and "big boy" have largely disappeared, but teachers continue to equate mature behavior with grown-up gendered identities by using more formal and ironic terms of address, like "ladies and gentlemen." By frequently using gender labels when they interact with kids, adults make being a girl or a boy central to self-definition, and to the ongoing life of schools.

Gender dichotomies ("girl/boy" as basic social categories and as individual identities) provide a continuously available line of difference that can be drawn on at any time in the ongoing life of schools. The manner of drawing, however, varies a great deal. In some situations, gender is highlighted; at other times, it is downplayed. As Gregory Bateson once commented, in the ongoing complexity of social life, a given difference does not always *make* a difference.[8] Individuals enter situations as girls or boys, displaying gender through details like names, dress, and adornment. But gender may or may not be central to the organization and symbolism of an encounter. In some situations . . . participants mark and ritualize gender boundaries. In other situations, gender may be far less relevant. Note that this line of analysis separates aspects of gender that are always present (individuals never leave aside their membership in the category "girl" or "boy") from those that are more fluctuating (the marking or muting of gender in the organization and symbolism of different social situations). . . .

The Choreography of Gender Separation and Integration

A series of snapshots taken in varied school settings would reveal extensive spatial separation between girls and boys. This phenomenon, which has been widely observed by researchers in schools, is often called "sex segregation among children," a term evoking images of legally enforced separation, like purdah in some Islamic societies. But school authorities separate boys and girls only occasionally. Furthermore, girls and boys sometimes interact with one another in relaxed and extended ways, not only in schools but also in families, neighborhoods, churches, and other settings. Gender separation—the word "segregation" suggests too total a pattern—is a variable and complicated process, an intricate choreography aptly summarized by Erving Goffman's phrase "with-then-apart."[9]

Boys and girls separate (or are separated) periodically, with their own spaces, rituals, and groups, but they also come together to become, in crucial ways, part of the same world. In the following verbal snapshots of classrooms, hallways, cafeterias,

and school playgrounds, it is crucial to note that although the occasions of gender separation may seem more dramatic, the mixed-gender encounters are also theoretically and practically important. Note also that groups may be formed by teachers, aides, or by kids themselves, and that criteria of group formation may or may not be explicitly mentioned or even in conscious awareness.

The "With-Then-Apart" of Classrooms

In organizing classroom seating, teachers use a variety of plans, some downplaying and others emphasizing the significance of gender. When Mrs. Smith, the kindergarten teacher at Ashton School, assigned seats, she deliberately placed girls and boys at each table, and they interacted a great deal in the formal and informal life of the classroom. Mrs. Johnson, the second-grade teacher at the same school, also assigned seats, but she organized her classroom into pairs of desks aligned in rows. With the layout came a language—"William's row". . ."Monica's row". . ."Amy's row"—for the five desks lined up behind William, Monica, Amy, and the other three students seated at the front. The overall pattern mixed girls and boys, and they participated together in much of the classroom whispering and byplay.

I asked Mrs. Johnson, who was nearing retirement after many years of teaching, what she had in mind when she assigned classroom seats. She responded with weary familiarity: "Everybody is sitting somewhere for a reason—hearing, sight, height. No two in the same reading group sit together, so I make sure they do their own work in their workbook. Or they sit in a particular place because they don't get along, or get along too well, with someone else." Differences of hearing, sight, height, and reading performance cut across the dichotomous division between boys and girls; sorting the students according to these criteria led to largely gender-integrated seating. However, the last of Mrs. Johnson's criteria, the degree to which two children get along, embeds a gender skew. Since friends are usually of the same gender, splitting up close friends tends to mix girls and boys.

Instead of assigning seats, Miss Bailey, the teacher of the combined fourth-fifth grade in Oceanside School, let the students choose their own desks in a U-shaped arrangement open at the front of the room. Over the course of the school year there were three occasions of general choosing. Each time, the students' choices resulted in an almost total cleavage: boys on the left and girls on the right, with the exception of one girl, Jessie, who frequently crossed gender boundaries and who twice chose a desk with the boys and once with the girls. . . .The teacher and students routinely spoke of "a boys' side" and "a girls' side" in the classroom.[10]

Miss Bailey made clear that she saw the arrangement as an indulgence, and when the class was unusually noisy, she threatened to change the seating and "not have a boys' side and a girls' side." "You have chosen that," she said on one such occasion, "you're sitting this way because you chose to do it at the first of the year. I may have to sit you in another way." The class groaned as she spoke, expressing ritualized preference for gender-separated seating. Miss Bailey didn't carry out her threat, and when she reseated individual students in the name of classroom order, she did so within each side. Miss Bailey framed the overall gender separation as a matter of student choice and as a privilege she had granted them, but she also built on and ratified the gender divide by pitting the girls against the boys in classroom spelling and math contests. . . .

Physical separation of girls and boys in regular classroom seating affects formal and informal give-and-take among students. One day Miss Bailey wrote sentences on the board and said she would go around the room and give each student a chance to find an error in spelling, grammar, or pronunciation. "We'll start with Beth," she said, gesturing to the right front of the U-shaped layout of the desks. Recognizing that to go around the room meant she would call on all the girls first, Miss Bailey added, "that leaves the hard part for the boys." Picking up the theme of gender opposition, several boys called out, "We're smart!" The divided seating pattern also channeled informal byplay, such as whispering, casual visiting, and collusive exchanges, among boys and among girls, whereas in classrooms with mixed-gender seating, those kinds of interaction more often took place between girls and boys.

When Miss Bailey divided the class into smaller work groups, gender receded in formal organizational importance. On these occasions, the teacher relied on sorting principles like skill at reading or spelling, whether or not someone had finished an earlier task, counting off ("one-two-one-two"), or letting students choose from alternative activities such as practicing for a play or collectively making a map out of papier-mâché. Sometimes Miss Bailey asked the fourth- and fifth-graders to meet separately and work on math or spelling. These varied organizational principles drew girls and boys out of separate halves of the classroom and into groups of varied gender composition standing at the blackboard or sitting on the floor in front or at round tables at the side of the room. When they found places in these smaller groups, girls often scrambled to sit next to girls, and boys to sit next to boys. But if the interaction had a central focus such as taking turns reading aloud or working together to build a contour map, boys and girls participated together in the verbal give-and-take.

Although I did not do systematic counting, I noticed that during formal classroom instruction, for example, when Miss Bailey invited discussion during social studies lessons, boys, taken as a whole, talked more than girls. This pattern fits with an extensive body of research finding that in classroom interaction from the elementary through college levels, male students tend to talk more than female students.[11] It should be emphasized that these are statistical and not absolute differences, and that researchers have found much variation from classroom to classroom in the degree to which boys are more visible than girls, and the degree to which individual teachers treat boys and girls differently. We need further research (my data are too sparse for these purposes) exploring possible relationships between seating practices, and patterns of talk and interaction in classrooms.

Life on the Line

When Mrs. Smith announced to her kindergarten class, "This is what you call a line . . .one at a time," she introduced a social form basic to the handling of congestion and delay in schools. In Ashton School, where classrooms opened onto an indoor hallway, kids rarely moved from the classroom unless they were in carefully regulated lines.

The separate lines meandering through the hallways reminded me of caterpillars, or of planes on a runway slowly moving along in readiness to take off. In the layout of the Oceanside School each of the classrooms opened to the outside, an arrangement facilitated by the warm California climate. Although this lessened the problem of noise and thereby relaxed the amount of adult control, the Oceanside teachers still organized students into loose lines when they headed to and from the library and the playground and when they went to the lunchroom.

Gender threaded through the routines of lining up, waiting and moving in a queue, and dispersing in a new place. In Oceanside School it was customary for girls and boys to line up separately, a pattern whose roots in the history of elementary schooling are still evident on old school buildings with separate entrances engraved with the words "Girls" and "Boys."[12] Several adults who have told me their memories of elementary school recall boys and girls lining up separately to go to different bathrooms. One woman remembered waiting in the girls' line several feet away from a row of boys and feeling an urgent need to urinate; she held her legs tightly together and hoped no one—especially the boys—would notice. This experience of bodily shame gave an emotional charge to gender-divided lines.

Like the schools of these adult memories, Oceanside had separate girls' and boys' bathrooms shared by many classrooms. But unlike the remembered schools, Oceanside had no collective expeditions to the bathrooms. Instead individual students asked permission to leave the classrooms and go to either the boys' or girls' bathroom, both of which, like the classrooms, opened to the outside. In Ashton School, as in many contemporary school buildings, each classroom had its own bathroom, used one-at-a-time by both girls and boys. This architectural shift has eliminated separate and centralized boys' and girls' facilities and hence the need to walk down the hall to take turns going to the toilet.

In Oceanside School the custom of separate girls' and boys' lines was taken for granted and rarely commented on. One of the fourth graders told me that they learned to form separate boys' and girls' lines in kindergarten and had done it ever since. A first-grade teacher said that on the first day of school she came out to find the boys and the girls already standing in two different lines. When I asked why girls and boys formed separate lines, the teachers said it was the children's doing. With the ironic detachment that adults often adopt toward children's customs, Miss Bailey told me that she thought the gender-separated lines were "funny." A student teacher who joined the classroom for part of the year rhetorically asked the kids why they had a girls' line and a boys' line. "How come? Will a federal marshal come and get you if you don't?" There was no reply.

Miss Bailey didn't deliberately establish separate lines for boys and girls; she just told the students to line up. It took both attention and effort for the kids to continually create and recreate gender-separated queues. In organizing expeditions out of the classroom, Miss Bailey usually called on students by stages, designating individuals or smaller groups ("everyone at that side table"; "those practicing spelling over in the corner") to move into line as a reward for being quiet. Once they got to the classroom door—unless it was lunchtime, when boys and girls mixed in two lines designated "hot lunch" and "cold lunch"—the students routinely separated by gender. The first boy to reach the door always stood to the left; the first girl stood to the right, and the rest moved into the appropriate queue.

The kids maintained separate boys' and girls' lines through gestures and speech. One day when the class was in the library, Miss Bailey announced, "Line up to go to assembly." Judy and Rosie hurried near the door, marking the start of one line on the right; Freddy and Tony moved to the left of the door. Other girls lined up behind Rosie, who became a sort of traffic director, gesturing a boy who was moving in behind her that he should shift to the other line. Once when the recess bell had rung and they began to line up for the return to class, a boy came over and stood at the end of a row of girls. This evoked widespread teasing—"John's in the girls' line"; "Look at that girl over there"—that quickly sent him to the row of boys. Off-bounds to those of the other gender, the separate lines sometimes became places of sanctuary, as during the close of one recess when Dennis grabbed a ball from Tracy, and she chased after him. He squeezed into line between two boys, chanting "Boys' line, boys' line," an incantation that indeed kept her away and secured his possession of the ball.

Several years before I arrived at Ashton School, the staff had moved from dual to single lines. This may have been partly a result of Title IX, the 1972 federal legislation mandating that girls and boys should have equal access to all school activities. One teacher told me she used to organize separate boys' and girls' lines, but someone told her that "wasn't the thing to do these days," so she followed her colleagues in shifting to single lines. Although individual girls and boys often stood in front of and behind one another in the single lines, they also had strategies for maneuvering within formal constraints and separating into same-gender clusters.

The front of the line is a desired and contested zone. As a reward, the teachers often let a specific child—the "line leader" or "goodest one," as a kindergartner explained—go first. After that initial selection there is often pushing and shoving for a place near the front. Because of the press to be near the front, kids usually protest attempted cuts in that zone. Farther back, individuals or smaller groups can sometimes tuck in a friend or two; it takes protest to make a cut a cut, and the deed is less likely to be challenged in back than in front. The back of the line is sometimes defined as the least desired space, even a place of punishment as suggested by the much-repeated rule: "If you cut, you have to go to the back of the line."

Although generally a devalued space, the back of the line has its uses. During the process of lining up, socially marginal kids often wait to join the line near the end, thereby avoiding the pushing and maneuvering at the front. Since the end is less tightly surveyed by teachers, aides, and other students, groups of friends may go to the back of the line so they can stand and talk together without having to be vigilant about holding their places. Occasionally when a student leaves a place in line and moves to the end, it appears to be out of a sense of being in the wrong gender territory. For example, in Ashton School after they finished eating lunch, students routinely lined up in the cafeteria waiting for a lunchtime aide to escort them to the playground. In one sequence of actions a girl moved into line behind three boys, then a boy got in line behind her. When she noticed this, a look of discomfort crossed her face, and she shifted farther back in the emerging line, joining three other girls.

Life on the line is time spent waiting. (Educational researchers have found that the time students spend waiting takes up as much as a third of each school day.[13]) The process of waiting in line was especially protracted in the Ashton School lunchroom, where lines formed slowly, the time drawn out by the varied speed of the eaters and by waiting for a lunchtime aide to finish wiping tables before she could lead the lines through the hallways and out to the playground. Bored by the delay, the waiting kids created their own forms of entertainment. They often clustered into same-gender groups, sometimes marking their solidarity with shared motions: girls sat on the floor facing one another and played clapping games (I never saw boys do this); a boy jogged shoulders with the next boy in line, starting a chain reaction that stopped when a girl was next. Separate clusters of kids, usually of different genders, marked boundaries between them by leaving a gap of space and/or through physical hassling. In one emerging lunchroom lineup of Ashton third-graders, there was a row of seven boys at the front, then several feet of empty space, then three girls, a few feet of space, then three boys. A girl reached around and leaned across the space to poke the boy behind her; he then pinned down her arms from behind, letting her go after she protested. When everyone had finally finished eating and joined the line, the aide signaled that they could go. There was a lot of pushing as smaller groups eased into the shared motion of one moving line.

The Gender Geography of Lunchroom Tables

Seating in school lunchrooms falls between the more fixed spaces of classroom desks and the arrangements kids improvise each time they sit on the floor of the classroom or the auditorium; an Oceanside teacher once referred to "their strange conglomeration way of sitting," describing the clusters, primarily of either girls or boys, arrayed on the floor. Eating together is a prime emblem of solidarity, and each day at lunchtime there is a fresh scramble as kids deliberately choose where, and with whom, to eat. The scrambling takes place within limits set by adults and defined by age-grading. In both schools, each classroom, in effect an age-grade, had two designated cafeteria tables, placed end to end from the wall.

Table seating takes shape through a predictable process: the first arrivals (who have cold lunches, a reason some children say they prefer to bring lunch from home) stake out territory by sitting and spreading out their possessions, usually at the far ends of each table. The tables fill through invitations, squeezing in, or individuals or groups going to an empty space. The groups who maneuver to eat together are usually friends and mostly of the same gender. The result is a pattern of separated clusters; many of the tables have a mix of girls and boys, but they are divided into smaller same-gender groupings. On the other hand, late-arriving individuals, who have less choice of where to sit, move into leftover spaces and tend to integrate the seating.

The collective table talk often includes both boys and girls, as do some daily rituals, like one that accompanied the opening of plastic bags of cutlery in both schools. As kids pulled out their plastic forks, they looked for and announced the small numbers stamped on the bottom: "I'm twenty-four, how old are you?" "I must have flunked; I'm in the fourth grade and I'm forty-five." "Ninety-three." "You're stupid; you were really held back in school."

Even when boys and girls are seated at the same table, their same-gender clustering may be accompanied by a sense of being on separate turfs. This became apparent when there were temporary changes in the physical ecology at Oceanside School. The combined fourth-fifth-grade class usually had two tables, but one day when the kids arrived for lunch, one of the tables was temporarily designated for another class. The kids began to crowd around the remaining table. Sherry, who had a cold lunch and arrived first, chose her usual seat by the wall; girls usually filled up that end. Scott and Jeremy sat down across from her, while three girls with hot lunches chose seats at the other end of the table. Scott looked around and asked, "Where are all the boys? Where are all the

boys?" Four boys arrived and sat across from Scott and Jeremy and next to Sherry, who began to crouch in her corner. In a small anxious voice she asked them, "What are you doing on the girls' side?" "There isn't room," one of the newly arrived boys explained.

Occasionally those who are already seated look around, take the lay of the developing table, and change places, sometimes with a gender-marking pronouncement. In the Ashton School lunchroom when the two second-grade tables were filling, a high-status boy walked by the inside table, which had a scattering of both boys and girls. He said loudly, "Oooo, too many girls," and headed for a seat at the other, nearly empty table. The boys at the inside table picked up their trays and moved to join him. After they left, no other boy sat at that table, which the pronouncement had made effectively taboo. So in the end, girls and boys ate at separate tables that day, although this was not usually the case.

I recorded many inventories of seating in the two lunchroom shifts in Ashton School. There was a great deal of variation from classroom to classroom and day to day, but completely separate boys' and girls' tables were much more frequent in fifth and sixth than in the younger grades. The sixth-graders talked matter-of-factly about "the girls' table" and "the boys' table," spaces so ritualized that they could be deliberately disrupted. A group of sixth-grade girls told me about a day when they plotted ahead, hurried into the lunchroom, and grabbed the boys' table, which was always the one next to the wall. When the boys arrived, they protested, but the girls held out, and on that day, which the girls remembered with humor, the girls and the boys switched territories.

Playground Divisions of Space and Activity

In classrooms, hallways, and lunchrooms boys and girls do the same core activities: working on math or spelling, moving from one area to another, or eating a meal. Same-gender groups might add their own, sometimes collusive agendas, such as a group of girls passing around a tube of lip gloss during a grammar lesson or a group of boys discussing sports or setting up arm wrestling during lunch. But there is no pronounced division of activity by gender.[14] In contrast, on the playground, an area where adults exert minimal control and kids are relatively free to choose their own activities and companions, there is extensive separation by gender. Activities, spaces, and equipment are heavily gender-typed; playgrounds, in short, have a more fixed geography of gender.

My inventories of activities and groups on the playground showed similar patterns in both schools. Boys controlled the large fixed spaces designated for team sports: baseball diamonds, grassy fields used for football or soccer, and basketball courts. In Oceanside School there was also a skateboard area where boys played, with an occasional girl joining in. The fixed spaces where girls predominated—bars and jungle gyms and painted cement areas for playing foursquare, jump rope, and hopscotch—were closer to the building and much smaller, taking up perhaps a tenth of the territory that boys controlled.[15] In addition, more movable activities—episodes of chasing, groups of younger children playing various kinds of "pretend," and groups milling around and talking—often, although by no means always, divided by gender. Girls and boys most often played together in games of kickball, foursquare, dodgeball, handball, and chasing or tag.

Kids and playground aides pretty much take these gender-divided patterns for granted; indeed, there is a long history in the United States of girls and boys engaging in different types of play, although the favored activities have changed with time.[16] The Ashton School aides openly regarded the space close to the building as girls' territory and the playing fields "out there" as boys' territory. They sometimes shooed away children of the other gender from what they saw as inappropriate turf, especially boys who ventured near the girls' area and seemed to have teasing in mind.

In both schools the transition from the classroom or the lunchroom to the playground began when a teacher or aide allocated equipment. Girls rarely made a bid for footballs, softballs, or basketballs, and boys rarely asked for jump ropes (an Ashton aide once refused a boy's request for a jump rope, saying with a tone of accusation, "You only want it to give rope burns"). Both boys and girls asked for the rubber balls used for kickball, handball, and foursquare. An individual with equipment could gain relatively easy access to designated play space such as a basketball or foursquare court. To indicate that they wanted to join a given activity, kids without equipment went to the routinized space, for example, getting in line to play handball or milling around the court with other would-be basketball players. Then, in games where numbers were limited or sides were essential, negotiations began. Boys rarely sought access to a game of jump rope or hopscotch, or girls to a game of softball, football, soccer, or basketball, although there were important exceptions. . . .

Kids sometimes excluded others by claiming they already had too many players, or simply by saying "you can't play." Sometimes they used gender as an excuse, drawing on beliefs connecting boys to some activities and girls to others.[17] Day after day on the Ashton playground I noticed that Evan, a first-grade boy, sat on the stairs and avidly watched girls play jump rope, his head and eyes turning around in synchrony with the rope. Once when a group of girls were deciding who would jump and who would "twirl" (the less desirable position), Evan recognized a means of access to the game and offered, "I'll swing it." Julie responded, "No way, you don't know how to do it, to swing it. You gotta be a girl." He left without protest. Although kids sometimes ignored pronouncements about what boys or girls could or could not do, I never heard them directly challenge such claims. . . .

In short, although girls and boys *are* together and often interact in classrooms, lunchrooms, and on the playground, these contacts less often deepen into friendship or stable alliances, while same-gender interactions are more likely to solidify into more lasting or acknowledged bonds. Much of the daily contact between girls and boys, as Janet Schofield comments, resembles that of "familiar strangers" who are in repeated physical proximity and recognize one another but have little real knowledge of what one another are like.[18] Some of the students in the middle school where Schofield observed felt that the gulf between boys and girls was so deep that it was fruitless to try to form cross-gender friendships, which they saw as different from romantic liaisons. . . .

NOTES

1. Philip W. Jackson (*Life in Classrooms*) highlights the centrality of *crowds, praise,* and *power* in the organization of schools.

Children who have previously attended day-care centers or preschools have already made the transition from household and neighborhood to a more bureaucratic set of experiences, as ethnographically detailed by Suransky in *The Erosion of Childhood*. During the opening weeks of Ashton School, the kindergarten teacher told me that she could tell which children had come from "group" care; they made an easier transition to school than did children coming from home-based care.

2. Cusick, *Inside High School.*

3. An observation from Robert Dreeban, *On What Is Learned in School.*

4. In an informative history of gender practices in U.S. public schools, David Tyack and Elizabeth Hansot (*Learning Together: A History of Co-education in American Schools*) trace complex relationships between official policies and the practices of school staff. Formal practices, which have changed over time, range from the gender-neutral to separating girls and boys into different classes and activities.

5. According to the *Oxford English Dictionary,* in the thirteenth and fourteenth centuries the word "girl" was used as a generic to refer to a child of either gender. Females were called "gay girls," and males were called "knave girls." "Girl" later lost the generic connotation and came to refer specifically to young females. The word "boy" appeared slightly later. "Child," a word never marked for gender, goes back to ancient times.

6. Margaret A. Eisenhart and Dorothy C. Holland, who observed in fifth- and sixth-grade classrooms in a school in the South, also found that teachers continually referred to "boys and girls," especially when directing them to start routines like reciting the Pledge of Allegiance or lining up. The authors observe that this generic usage (teachers were instructing boys and girls to do the same thing) emphasized student more than gender-differentiated identities. See Eisenhart and Holland, "Learning Gender from Peers: The Role of Peer Groups in the Cultural Transmission of Gender."

7. Spencer E. Cahill, "Language Practices and Self-Definition: The Case of Gender Identity Acquisition." Patricia M. Passuth ("Age Hierarchies within Children's Groups"), who observed in a summer day camp, also found the children were keenly aware of age differences and believed it was better to be older than younger.

8. Gregory Bateson, *Steps to an Ecology of Mind,* p. 453. Others have also called attention to social processes by which a given category may be rendered more or less salient. For example, Marilynn B. Brewer argues that "which differences are emphasized under what circumstances appears to be flexible and context dependent; this flexibility permits individuals to mobilize different group identities for different purposes" ("Ethnocentrism and Its Role in Interpersonal Trust," p. 350). In the same vein, Sandra Wallman observes that "a cultural or phenotypical difference which counts in one situation does not count in another" ("The Boundaries of 'Race': Processes of Ethnicity in England," p. 201). Also see Kay Deaux and Brenda Major, "Putting Gender into Context: An Interactive Model of Gender-related Behavior."

9. Erving Goffman, "The Arrangement between the Sexes," p. 316.

10. Cynthia A. Cone and Berta E. Perez ("Peer Groups and the Organization of Classroom Space") observed a similar pattern, including children perceiving a girls' side and a boys' side, in elementary classrooms where teachers allowed students to choose their own seating. Steven T. Bossert (*Tasks and Social Relationships in Classrooms*) compared the organization of four different classrooms; in those where the teacher let students choose their own seats, friendship groups, usually of the same-gender, sat together.

11. See reviews of research in Barrie Thorne et al., eds., *Language, Gender, and Society;* Jere E. Brophy and Thomas L. Good, *Teacher-Student Relations;* and in the American Association of University Women Educational Foundation and the Wellesley College Center for Research on Women, *How Schools Short-change Girls.* Educational researchers have also found that boys tend to receive more teacher attention, both positive and negative, than do girls, and that some teachers praise and reprimand boys and girls for different things. Several studies have found that boys are more often scolded for misbehavior and praised for their academic work, while girls are more often chastized for poor academic performance and praised for appearance, neatness, and being polite. For reviews of this research, see Marlaine S. Lockheed with Susan S. Klein, "Sex Equity in Classroom Organization and Climate," and Louise Cherry Wilkinson and Cora B. Marrett, eds., *Gender Influences in Classroom Interaction.*

12. See Tyack and Hansot, *Learning Together,* for photographs and floor plans of schools built in the early decades of this century with separate entrances and spaces designated for girls and boys.

13. Robert B. Everhart, *Reading, Writing, and Resistance,* p. 51.

14. Goffman observes that this "parallel organization," in which similar activities are organized in a segregated manner, provides a "ready base for elaborating differential treatment," such as having a row of girls file in before a row of boys ("The Arrangement between the Sexes," p. 306).

15. My observations resemble those of Janet Lever, who recorded differences in the playground activities of fifth-graders in Connecticut. She found that boys most often engaged in team sports, whereas girls focused on turn-taking play. (See Lever, "Sex Differences in the Games Children Play" and "Sex Differences in the Complexity of Children's Play and Games.") John Evans ("Gender Differences in Children's Games: A Look at the Team Selection Process") observed during recess in an Illinois public school and found that of 238 team games, 78 percent were played by boys as a group; on only 52 occasions (22 percent) did team membership include both boys and girls. Of all team games, 193 (81 percent) were played by fifth- and sixth-graders.

16. While sex differences in children's game preferences are less extreme than in earlier times, Brian Sutton-Smith and B. G. Rosenberg found that between the late 1920s and the late 1950s there were some convergences in the game choices of girls and boys in fourth, fifth, and sixth grades. The change was due mostly to girls adopting interests (swimming, tag, kites) previously limited to boys. On the other hand, boys drew away from some games (hopscotch, jacks, jump rope) that then became more typed as girls' play. The enhanced interest in organized sports for girls that emerged in the 1970s and 1980s has probably further increased the convergence of girls' and boys' game preferences, but the overall separation remains substantial. See Sutton-Smith and Rosenberg, "Sixty Years of Historical Change in the Game Preferences of American Children."

17. An early article by Carole Joffe ("As the Twig Is Bent") first alerted me to children's invocation of gender as an "ideology of control." For a detailed analysis of processes of access and exclusion among children at play in a day-care center, see William Corsaro, "We're Friends, Right? Children's Use of Access Rituals in a Nursery School."

18. Schofield, *Black and White in School.* Schofield found that race, as well as gender, was a barrier to the development of friendship; in the racially balanced middle school where she observed, close friendships between students of different genders *or* races were quite rare.

REFERENCES

American Association of University Women Educational Foundation and the Wellesley College Center for Research on Women, *How Schools Short-change Girls.* Washington, D.C.: AAUW Educational Foundation, 1992.

Bossert, Steven T. *Tasks and Social Relationships in Classrooms.* New York: Cambridge University Press, 1979.

Brophy, Jere E., and Thomas L. Good. *Teacher-Student Relations.* New York: Holt, 1974.

Cahill, Spencer E. "Language Practices and Self-Definition: The Case of Gender Identity Acquisition." *Sociological Quarterly* 27 (1987): 295–311.

Cone, Cynthia A., and Berta E. Perez. "Peer Groups and the Organization of Classroom Space." *Human Organization* 45 (1986): 80–88.

Corsaro, William A. " 'We're Friends, Right?' Children's Use of Access Rituals in a Nursery School." *Language in Society* 8 (1979): 315–336.

Cusick, Philip A. *Inside High School.* New York: Holt, Rinehart and Winston, 1973.

Deaux, Kay, and Brenda Major. "Putting Gender into Context: An Interactive Model of Gender-related Behavior." *Psychological Review* 94 (1987): 369–389.

Eisenhart, Margaret A., and Dorothy C. Holland. "Learning Gender from Peers: The Role of Peer Groups in the Cultural Transmission of Gender." *Human Organization* 42 (1983): 321–332.

Evans, John. "Gender Differences in Children's Games: A Look at the Team Selection Process." *Canadian Association for Health, Physical Education, and Recreation Journal* 52 (1986): 4–9.

Everhart, Robert B. *Reading, Writing, and Resistance.* Boston: Routledge & Kegan Paul, 1983.

Goffman, Erving. "The Arrangement between the Sexes." *Theory and Society* 4 (1977): 301–336.

Jackson, Philip W. *Life in Classrooms.* New York: Holt, Rinehart and Winston, 1968.

Joffe, Carole. "As the Twig is Bent." In *And Jill Came Tumbling After,* ed. Judith Stacey, Susan Bereaud, and Joan Daniels, 79–90. New York: Dell, 1974.

Lever, Janet. "Sex Differences in the Complexity of Children's Play and Games." *American Sociological Review* 43 (1978): 471–483.

_____. "Sex Differences in the Games Children Play." *Social Problems* 23 (1976): 478–487.

Lockheed, Marlaine S., with Susan S. Klein. "Sex Equity in Classroom Organization and Climate." In

Handbook for Achieving Sex Equity through Education, 189–217. Baltimore: Johns Hopkins University Press, 1985.

Passuth, Patricia M. "Age Hierarchies within Children's Groups." In *Sociological Studies of Child Development,* vol. 2, ed. Peter Adler and Patricia Adler, 185–203. Greenwich, Conn.: JAI Press, 1987.

Schofield, Janet W. *Black and White in School.* New York: Praeger, 1982.

Suransky, Valerie Polakow. *The Erosion of Childhood.* Chicago: University of Chicago Press.

Sutton-Smith, Brian, and B. G. Rosenberg. "Sixty Years of Historical Change in the Game Preferences of American Children." *Journal of American Folklore* 74 (1961): 17–46.

Thorne, Barrie, Cheris Kramarae, and Nancy Henley, eds. *Language, Gender, and Society.* New York: Newbury House, 1983.

Tyack, David, and Elizabeth Hansot. *Learning Together: A History of Coeducation in American Schools.* New Haven: Yale University Press, 1990.

Wilkinson, Louise Cherry, and Cora B. Marrett, eds. *Gender Influences in Classroom Interaction.* New York: Academic Press, 1985.

THINKING ABOUT THE READINGS

The Gloried Self

■ According to Adler and Adler, how do fame and celebrity alter people's self-concepts? What do they mean when they say that self-concepts are formed from the "reflected appraisals" of others? Have you ever known someone who suddenly became famous? How did this person change? Did he or she become a "completely different" person, or were some elements of his or her past self retained? What do such changes tell us about the social nature of the self? What are the personal and social costs of the gloried self?

Medical Students' Contact with the Living and the Dead

■ What are some of the techniques medical students use to manage their feelings when contacts with patients are uncomfortable? How do they learn these techniques? How might such interactional norms sustain social order in medical school? Have you ever been in a work or educational setting where colleagues had to informally socialize you into the strategies and tactics necessary to survive in that setting? What was it like? How similar or different was this experience to that of the medical school students in this article?

Boys and Girls Together . . . But Mostly Apart

■ How do school rules and routines contribute to gender socialization in elementary school? How do Thorne's observations of gender segregation compare to your own elementary school experiences? What are the long-term consequences of childhood gender segregation? That is, how do these early "lessons" carry over to adult cross-sex relationships? Given Thorne's argument and your responses to it, what do you think are the advantages and disadvantages of gender-specific elementary schools (i.e., boys' schools and girls' schools)? Explain.

CHAPTER 6

Building Image
Individual and Institutional Identities

Impression management—those tactics we use to present favorable images of ourselves to others—is an important and universal aspect of social life. It provides the link between the way we perceive ourselves and the way we want others to perceive us. We've all been in situations—a first date, a job interview, meeting a girl- or boyfriend's family for the first time—in which we've felt compelled to "make a good impression." What we often fail to realize, however, is that personal impression management is often influenced by larger organizational and institutional forces.

Arlie Hochschild combines the notion of emotional display norms with an emphasis on impression management in "Managing Feeling" to provide us with a glimpse of how feelings are molded and/or hidden to construct and sustain a particular public image. Consistent with the dramaturgical perspective on social interaction, she invokes the language of the theater to describe how we manage and control our emotions for others as well as for ourselves.

In "Outsiders in the Clubhouse," Todd Crosset shows us how impression management can be motivated by larger organizational and/or institutional needs. He describes the experiences of professional women golfers as they work in conjunction with or in conflict with the media to convey an "appropriate" corporate image of the Ladies' Professional Golf Association (LPGA) Tour. This task is made more complicated by what the golfers refer to as the "image problem"—the public's tendency to see them as masculine and sexually ambiguous. Overcoming such an image has enormous financial implications since corporate sponsorships are crucial to the survival of the tour.

Managing Feeling

Arlie Hochschild

He who always wears the mask of a friendly man must at last gain a power over friendliness of disposition, without which the expression itself of friendliness is not to be gained—and finally friendliness of disposition gains the ascendancy over him—he is benevolent. —NIETZSCHE

"Sincerity" is detrimental to one's job, until the rules of salesmanship and business become a "genuine" aspect of oneself. —C. WRIGHT MILLS

We all do a certain amount of acting. But we may act in two ways. In the first way, we try to change how we outwardly appear. As it is for the people observed by Erving Goffman, the action is in the body language, the put-on sneer, the posed shrug, the controlled sigh. This is surface acting.[1] The other way is deep acting. Here, display is a natural result of working on feeling; the actor does not try to seem happy or sad but rather expresses spontaneously, as the Russian director Constantin Stanislavski urged, a real feeling that has been self-induced. Stanislavski offers this illustration from his own experience:

> At a party one evening, in the house of friends, we were doing various stunts and they decided, for a joke, to operate on me. Tables were carried in, one for operating, the other supposedly containing surgical instruments. Sheets were draped around; bandages, basins, various vessels were brought.
>
> The "surgeons" put on white coats and I was dressed in a hospital gown. They laid me on the operating table and bandaged my eyes. What disturbed me was the extremely solicitous manner of the doctors. They treated me as if I were in a desperate condition and did everything with utmost seriousness. Suddenly

the thought flashed through my mind, "What if they really should cut me open?!"

> Now and then a large basin made a booming noise like the toll of a funeral bell.
>
> "Let us begin!" someone whispered.
>
> Someone took a firm hold on my right wrist. I felt a dull pain and then three sharp stabs. I couldn't help trembling. Something that was harsh and smarted was rubbed on my wrist. Then it was bandaged, people rustled around handing things to the surgeon.
>
> Finally, after a long pause, they began to speak out loud, they laughed, congratulated me. My eyes were unbandaged and on my left arm lay a new-born baby made out of my right hand, all swaddled in gauze. On the back of my hand they had painted a silly, infantile face.[2]

The "patient" above is not pretending to be frightened at his "operation." He is not trying to fool others. He is really scared. Through deep acting he has managed to scare himself. Feelings do not erupt spontaneously or automatically in either deep acting or surface acting. In both cases the actor has learned to intervene—either in creating the inner shape of a feeling or in shaping the outward appearance of one.

In surface acting, the expression on my face or the posture of my body feels "put on." It is not "part of me." In deep acting, my conscious mental work—the effort to imagine a tall surgeon looming over me, for example—keeps the feeling that I conjure up from being part of "myself." Thus in either method, an actor may separate what it takes to act from the idea of a central self.

But whether the separation between "me" and my face or between "me" and my feeling counts as estrangement depends on something else—the outer context. In the world of the theater, it is an honorable art to make maximum use of the resources of memory and feeling in stage performance. In private life, the same resources can be used to advantage, though to a lesser extent. But when we enter the world of profit-and-loss statements, when the psychological costs of emotional labor are not acknowledged by the company, it is then that we look at these otherwise helpful separations of "me" from my face and my feeling as potentially estranging.

Surface Acting

To show through surface acting the feelings of a Hamlet or an Ophelia, the actor operates countless muscles that make up an outward gesture. The body, not the soul, is the main tool of the trade. The actor's body evokes passion in the *audience's* soul, but the actor is only *acting* as if he had feeling. Stanislavski, the originator of a different type of acting—called Method acting—illustrates surface acting in the course of disparaging it:

> [The actor portrayed] an important general [who] accidentally found himself alone at home with nothing to do. Out of boredom he lined up all the chairs in the place so that they looked like soldiers on parade. Then he made neat piles of everything on all the tables. Next he thought of something rather spicy; after that he looked aghast over a pile of business correspondence. He signed several letters without reading them, yawned, stretched himself, and then began his silly activities all over again.
>
> All the while [the actor] was giving the text of the soliloquy with extraordinary clar-

ity; about the nobility of highly placed persons and the dense ignorance of everyone else. He did it in a cold, impersonal way, indicating the outer form of the scene without any attempt to put life or depth into it. In some places he rendered the text with technical crispness, in others he underscored his pose, gesture, play, or emphasized some special detail of his characterization. Meantime he was watching his public out of the corner of his eye to see whether what he was doing carried across.[3]

This is surface acting—the art of an eyebrow raised here, an upper lip tightened there. The actor does not really experience the world from an imperial viewpoint, but he works at seeming to. What is on the actor's mind? Not the chairs that he has commanded to line up at attention, but the audience, which is the nearest mirror to his own surface.

Stanislavski described the limitations of surface acting as follows:

> This type of art (of the Coquelin school) is less profound than beautiful. It is more immediately effective than truly powerful; [its] form is more interesting than its content. It acts more on your sense of sound and sight than on your soul. Consequently it is more likely to delight than to move you. You can receive great impressions through this art. But they will neither warm your soul nor penetrate deeply into it. Their effect is sharp but not lasting. Your astonishment rather than your faith is aroused. Only what can be accomplished through surprising theatrical beauty or picturesque pathos lies within the bounds of this art. But delicate and deep human feelings are not subject to such technique. They call for natural emotions at the very moment in which they appear before you in the flesh. They call for the direct cooperation of nature itself.[4]

Deep Acting

There are two ways of doing deep acting. One is by directly exhorting feeling, the other by making indirect use of a trained imagination.[5] Only the second is true Method acting. But in either case,

Stanislavski argued, the acting of passions grows out of living in them.

People sometimes talk as much about their *efforts* to feel (even if these efforts fail) as they do about having feelings.[6] When I asked students simply to describe an event in which they experienced a deep emotion, the responses were sprinkled with such phrases as "I psyched myself up, I squashed my anger down, I tried hard not to feel disappointed, I forced myself to have a good time, I mustered up some gratitude, I put a damper on my love for her, I snapped myself out of the depression."* In the flow of experience, there were occasional common but curious shades of will—will to evoke, will to suppress, and will to somehow allow a feeling, as in "I finally let myself feel sad about it."[7]

Sometimes there was only a social custom in mind—as when a person wished to feel sad at a funeral. But other times there was a desperate inner desire to avoid pain. Herbert Gold describes a man's effort to prevent himself from feeling love for a wife he no longer has:

> He fought against love, he fought against grief, he fought against anger. They were all linked. He reminded himself when touched, moved, overwhelmed by the sights and smell of her, or a sight and smell which recalled her, or passing their old house or eating their foods, or walking on their streets; don't do this, don't feel. First he succeeded in removing her from the struggle. . . . He lost his love. He lost his anger. She became a limited idea, like a newspaper death notice. He did not lose her entirely, but chipped away at it: don't, don't, don't, he would remind himself in the middle of the night; don't feel; and then dream what he could.[8]

These are almost like orders to a contrary horse (whoa, giddyup, steady now), attempts to exhort feeling as if feeling can listen when it is talked to.† And sometimes it does. But such coaching only addresses the capacity to duck a signal, to turn away from what evokes feeling.[9] It does not move to the home of the imagery, to that which gives power to a sight, a sound, or a smell. It does not involve the deeper work of retraining the imagination.

Ultimately, direct prods to feeling are not based on a deep look into how feeling works, and for this reason Stanislavski advised his actors against them: "On the stage there cannot be, under any circumstances, action which is directed immediately at the arousing of a feeling for its own sake. . . . Never seek to be jealous, or to make love, or to suffer for its own sake. All such feelings are the result of something that has gone before. Of the thing that goes before you should think as you can. As for the result, it will produce itself."[10]

Stanislavski's alternative to the direct prodding of feeling is Method acting. Not simply the body, or immediately accessible feeling, but the entire world of fantasy, of subconscious and semiconscious memory, is conceived as a precious resource.

If he were in the hands of Stanislavski, the man who wanted to fight off love for his former wife would approach his task differently. First, he would use "emotion memory": he would remember all the times he had felt furious at his wife's thoughtlessness or cruelty. He would focus on one most exasperating instance of this, reevoking all the circumstances. Perhaps she had forgotten his birthday, had made no effort to remember, and failed to feel badly about it afterwards. Then he would use the "if" supposition and say to himself: "How would I feel about her if this is what she really was like?" He would not prompt himself not to feel love; rather he would keep alive the cruel episode of the forgotten birthday and sustain the "if." He would not, then, fall naturally out

---

*In each instance the individual indicates awareness of acting on a feeling. A passive stance toward feeling was reflected in other examples: "I found myself filled with pride." "My stomach did a trapeze act all by itself."

†It also presupposes an *aspiration* to feel. The man who fought against love wanted to feel the same about his former wife as he thought she felt about him; if he was a limited idea to her, he wanted her to be that for him. A courtly lover in twelfth-century France or a fourteen-year-old American female rock fan might have been more disposed to aspire to one-sided love, to want it that way. Deep acting comes with its social stories about what we aspire to feel.

of love. He would actively conduct himself out of love through deep acting.

The professional actor simply carries this process further for an artistic purpose. His goal should be to accumulate a rich deposit of "emotion memories"—memories that recall feelings. Thus, Stanislavski explains, the actor must relearn how to remember:

> Two travelers were marooned on some rocks by high tide. After their rescue they narrated their impressions. One remembered every little thing he did; how, why, and where he went, where he climbed up and where he climbed down; where he jumped up or jumped down. The other man had no recollection of the place at all. He remembered only the emotions he felt. In succession came delight, apprehension, fear, hope, doubt, and finally panic.[11]

To store a wealth of emotion memories, the actor must remember experiences emotively. But to remember experiences emotively, he or she must first experience them in that way too, perhaps with an eye to using the feelings later. So the conceiving of emotion memory as a noun, as something one *has,* brings with it a conceiving of memory and of spontaneous experience itself as also having the qualities of a usable, nounlike thing. Feeling—whether at the time, or as it is recalled, or as it is later evoked in acting—is an object. It may be a valuable object in a worthy pursuit, but it is an object nonetheless.

Some feelings are more valuable objects than others, for they are more richly associated with other memorable events; a terrifying train ride may recall a childhood fall or a nightmare. Stanislavski recalled, for example, seeing an old beggar killed by a trolley car but said that the memory of this event was less valuable to him as an actor than another one:

> It was long ago—I came upon an Italian, leaning over a dead monkey on the sidewalk. He was weeping and trying to push a bit of orange rind into the animal's mouth. It would seem that this scene had affected my feelings more than the death of the beggar. It was buried more deeply into my memory. I

think that if I had to stage the street accident I would search for emotional material for my part in my memory of the scene of the Italian with the dead monkey rather than in the tragedy itself.[12]

But emotion memory is not enough. The memory, like any image drawn to mind, must *seem real now*. The actor must *believe* that an imagined happening *really is happening now*. To do this, the actor makes up an "as if," a supposition. He actively suspends the usual reality testing, as a child does at play, and allows a make-believe situation to seem real. Often the actor can manage only a precarious belief in *all* of an illusion, and so he breaks it up into sturdier small details, which taken one by one are easier to believe: "*if* I were in a terrible storm" is chopped up into "*if* my eyebrows were wet and *if* my shoes were soaked." The big *if* is broken into many little ones.[13]

The furnishings of the physical stage—a straight horse-hair chair; a pointer leaning against the wall—are used to support the actor's *if*. Their purpose is not to influence the audience, as in surface acting, but to help convince the person doing deep acting that the *if* events are really happening.

Everyday Deep Acting

In our daily lives, offstage as it were, we also develop feeling for the parts we play; and along with the workaday props of the kitchen table or office restroom mirror we also use deep acting, emotion memory, and the sense of "as if this were true" in the course of trying to feel what we sense we ought to feel or want to feel. Usually we give this little thought, and we don't name the momentary acts involved. Only when our feeling does not fit the situation, and when we sense this as a problem, do we turn our attention to the inward, imagined mirror, and ask whether we are or should be acting.

Consider, for example, the reaction of this young man to the unexpected news that a close friend had suffered a mental breakdown:

> I was shocked, yet for some reason I didn't think my emotions accurately reflected the bad news. My roommate appeared much

more shaken than I did. *I thought that I should be more upset by the news than I was.* Thinking about this conflict I realized that one reason for my emotional state might have been the spatial distance separating me from my friend, who was in the hospital hundreds of miles away. I then tried to focus on his state . . . and began to picture my friend as I thought he then existed.

Sensing himself to be less affected than he should be, he tried to visualize his friend—perhaps in gray pajamas, being led by impassive attendants to the electric-shock room. After bringing such a vivid picture to mind, he might have gone on to recall smaller private breakdowns in his own life and thereby evoked feelings of sorrow and empathy. Without at all thinking of this as acting, in complete privacy, without audience or stage, the young man can pay, in the currency of deep acting, his emotional respects to a friend.

Sometimes we try to stir up a feeling we wish we had, and at other times we try to block or weaken a feeling we wish we did not have. Consider this young woman's report of her attempt to keep feelings of love in check.

Last summer I was going with a guy often, and I began to feel very strongly about him. I knew, though, that he had broken up with a girl a year ago because she had gotten too serious about him, so I was afraid to show any emotion. I also was afraid of being hurt, so I attempted to change my feelings. *I talked myself into not caring about him* . . . but I must admit it didn't work for long. To sustain this feeling I had to *invent bad things about him and concentrate on them* or continue to tell myself he didn't care. It was a hardening of emotions, I'd say. It took a lot of work and was unpleasant because I had to concentrate on anything I could find that was irritating about him.

In this struggle she hit upon some techniques of deep acting. "To invent bad things about him and concentrate on them" is to make up a world she could honestly respond to. She could tell herself, "If he is self-absorbed, then he is unlovable, and *if* he is unlovable, which at the moment I believe, then I don't love him." Like Stanislavski during his make-believe "operation," she wavers between belief and doubt, but she nevertheless reaches for the inner token of feeling that it is her part to offer. She wavers between belief and doubt in her beloved's "flaws." But her temporary effort to prevent herself from falling in love may serve the grander purpose of waiting for him to reciprocate. So in a way, her act of momentary restraint, as she might see it, was an offering to the future of their love.

We also set a personal stage with personal props, not so much for its effect on our audience as for the help it gives us in believing in what we imagine. Serving almost as stage props, often, are fellow members of the cast—friends or acquaintances who prod our feelings in a desired direction. Thus, a young woman who was trying not to love a man used her supporting cast of friends like a Greek chorus: "I could only say horrible things about him. My friends thought he was horrible because of this and reinforced my feelings of dislike for him."

Sometimes the stage setting can be a dismayingly powerful determinant of feeling. Consider this young woman's description of her ambivalent feelings about a priest forty years her senior: "I started trying to make myself like him and fit the whole situation. When I was with him I did like him, but then I'd go home and write in my journal how much I couldn't stand him. I kept changing my feelings." What she felt while facing the priest amid the props of a living room and two cups of afternoon tea collapsed when she left that setting. At home with her diary, she felt free of her obligation to please her suitor by trying to like him. There, she felt another obligation—to be honest to her diary. What changed between the tea party and the diary session was her sense of which feeling was real. Her sense of realness seemed to shift disconcertingly with the stage setting, as if her feeling of liking the priest gained or lost its status as "real" depending on its context.

Sometimes the realness of a feeling wavers more through time. Once a love story is subject to doubt, the story is rewritten; falling in love comes to seem like the work of convincing each other that this had been true love. A nineteen-year-old Catholic college student recalled:

Since we both were somewhat in need of a close man-woman relationship and since we were thrown together so often (we lived next door to each other and it was summertime), I think that we convinced ourselves that we loved each other. I had to try to convince myself that I loved him in order to justify or somehow make "right" sleeping with him, which I never really wanted to do. We ended up living together supposedly because we "loved" each other. But I would say instead that we did it for other reasons which neither of us wanted to admit. What pretending that I loved him meant to me was having a secret nervous breakdown.

This double pretending—pretending to him and pretending to herself that she loved him—created two barriers to reflection and spontaneous feeling. First, she tried to feel herself in love—intimate, deeply enhanced, and exquisitely vulnerable—in the face of contrary evidence. Second, she tried not to feel irritation, boredom, and a desire to leave. By this effort to orchestrate feeling—to keep some feelings above consciousness and some below, and to counter inner resistances on a daily basis—she tried to suppress reality testing. She both nurtured an illusion about her lover and doubted the truth of it. It was the strain of this effort that led to her "secret nervous breakdown."

In the theater, the illusion that the actor creates is recognized beforehand as an illusion by actor and audience alike. But in real life we more often participate in the illusion. We take it into ourselves, where it struggles against the sense we ordinarily make of things. In life, illusions are subtle, changeable, and hard to define with certainty, and they matter far more to our sanity.

The other side of the matter is to live with a dropped illusion and yet want to sustain it. Once an illusion is clearly defined as an illusion, it becomes a lie. The work of sustaining it then becomes redefined as lying to oneself so that one becomes self-stigmatized as a liar. This dilemma was described by a desperate wife and mother of two:

I am desperately trying to change my feelings of being trapped [in marriage] into feelings of wanting to remain with my husband voluntarily. Sometimes I think I'm succeeding—sometimes I know I haven't. *It means I have to lie to myself and know I am lying.* It means I don't like myself very much. It also makes me wonder whether or not I'm a bit of a masochist. I feel responsible for the children's future and for my husband's, and there's the old self-sacrificer syndrome. I know what I'm doing. I just don't know how long I can hold out.

On stage, the actress doing Method acting tries to delude herself; the more voluntary, the more richly detailed the lie, the better. No one thinks she actually is Ophelia or even pretending to be. She is borrowing Ophelia's reality or something from her own personal life that resembles it. She is trying to delude herself and create an illusion for the audience, who accept it as a gift. In everyday life there is also illusion, but how to define it is chronically unclear; the matter needs constant attention, continual questioning and testing. In acting, the illusion starts out as an illusion. In everyday life, that definition is always a possibility and never quite a certainty. On stage, the illusion leaves as it came, with the curtain. Off stage, the curtains close, too, but not at our bidding, not when we expect, and often to our dismay. On stage, illusion is a virtue. But in real life, the lie to oneself is a sign of human weakness, of bad faith. It is far more unsettling to discover that we have fooled ourselves than to discover that we have been fooling others.

This is because for the professional actor the illusion takes on meaning only in relation to a professional role whereas in real life the illusion takes on meaning with reference to living persons. When in private life we recognize an illusion we have held, we form a different relation to what we have thought of as our self. We come to distrust our sense of what is true, as we know it through feeling. And if our feelings have lied to us, they cannot be part of our good, trustworthy, "true" self. To put it another way, we may recognize that we distort reality, that we deny or suppress truths, but we rely on an observing ego to comment on these unconscious processes in us and to try to find out what is going on despite them.

At the same time, everyday life clearly requires us to do deep acting. We must dwell on what it is that we want to feel and on what we must do to induce the feeling. Consider, for example, this young man's efforts to counter an apathy he dreaded:

> I was a star halfback in high school. [But in my senior year] before games I didn't feel the surge of adrenaline—in a word, I wasn't "psyched-up." This was due to emotional difficulties I was experiencing at the time, and still experience. Also, I had been an A student but my grades were dropping. Because in the past I had been a fanatical, emotional, intense player—a "hitter," recognized by coaches as a hard worker and a player with "desire"—this was very upsetting. I did everything I could to get myself "up." I tried to be outwardly rah-rah, I tried to get myself scared of my opponents—anything to get the adrenaline flowing. I tried to look nervous and intense before games, so at least the coaches wouldn't catch on . . . when actually I was mostly bored, or in any event, not "up." Before one game I remember wishing I was in the stands watching my cousin play for his school.

This young man felt a slipping sense of realness; he was clear that he felt "basically" bored, not "really" up. What also seemed real to him was the sense that he should feel driven to win and that he wanted to feel that way. What also felt real to him in hindsight was his effort to seem to the coaches like a "hitter" (surface acting) and his effort to make himself fearful of his opponents (deep acting).

As we look back at the past, we may alternate between two understandings of "what really happened." According to one, our feeling was genuine and spontaneous. According to the other, it seemed genuine and spontaneous, but in fact it was covertly managed. In doubt about which understanding will ultimately make sense, we are led to ask about our present feelings: "Am I acting now? How do I know?" One basic appeal of the theater is that the stage decides that question for us: we know for sure who is acting.

In sum, what distinguishes theater from life is not illusion, which both have, need, and use. What distinguishes them is the honor accorded to illusion, the ease in knowing when an illusion is an illusion, and the consequences of its use in making feeling. In the theater, the illusion dies when the curtain falls, as the audience knew it would. In private life, its consequences are unpredictable and possibly fateful: a love is killed, a suitor rejected, another hospital bed filled.

NOTES

EPIGRAPHS: F. W. Nietzsche (1874), cited in Gellhorn (1964); C. Wright Mills, *White Collar*, p. 183.

1. As suggested by Goffman's description of "Preedy" on the beach, in *The Presentation of Self in Everyday Life* (1959), surface acting is alive and well in Goffman's work. But the second method of acting, deep acting, is less apparent in his illustrations, and the theoretical statement about it is correspondingly weak. Goffman posits a self capable of surface acting, but not one capable of deep acting.

2. Stanislavski (1965), p. 268.

3. Ibid., p. 196.

4. Ibid., p. 22.

5. There is actually another distinguishable way of doing deep acting—by actively altering the body so as to change conscious feeling. This surface-to-center approach differs from surface acting. Surface acting uses the body to *show* feeling. This type of deep acting uses the body to *inspire* feeling. In relaxing a grimace or unclenching a fist, we may actually make ourselves feel less angry (ibid., p. 93). This insight is sometimes used in bio-feedback therapy (see Brown 1974, p. 50).

6. The direct method of cognitive emotion work is known not by the result (see Peto 1968) but by the effort made to achieve the result. The result of any given act is hard enough to discern. But if we were to identify emotion work by its results, we would be in a peculiar bind. We might say that a "cooled-down anger" is the result of an effort to reduce anger. But then we would have to assume that we have some basis for knowing what the anger "would have been like" had the individual not been managing his anger. We are on theoretically safer ground if we define emotion management as a set of acts *addressed* to feeling. (On the nature of an act of will, as separate from its effect, see Jean Piaget in Campbell 1976, p. 87.)

7. By definition, each method of emotion work is active, but just how active, varies. At the active end of the continuum we contort reality and grip our bodily

processes as though gripping the steering wheel of a car. At the passive extreme we may simply perform an act upon an act—as in deliberately relaxing already existing controls or issuing permission to "let" ourselves feel sad. (For a discussion of active versus passive concentration in autogenic training, see Wolfgang Luthe, quoted in Pelletier 1977, p. 237.) In addition we may "ride over" a feeling (such as a nagging sense of depression) in the attempt to feel cheerful. When we meet an inward resistance, we "put on" the cheer. When we meet no inward resistance, we amplify a feeling: we "put it out."

8. Gold (1979), p. 129.

9. Stanislavski (1965), p. 38. Indeed, an extra effort is required *not to focus* on the intent, the effort of trying to feel. The point, rather, is to focus on seeing the situation. Koriat et al. (1972) illustrated this second approach in a laboratory experiment in which university students were shown films of simulated wood-chopping accidents. In one film a man lacerates the tips of his fingers; in another, a woodworker cuts off his middle finger; in a third, a worker dies after a plank of wood is thrust through his midsection by a circular saw. Subjects were instructed to detach themselves when first viewing the films and then, on another viewing, to involve themselves. To deintensify the effect of the films, the viewers tried to remind themselves that they were just films and often focused on technical aspects of production to reinforce this sense of unreality. Others tried to think of the workers in the films as being responsible for their own injuries through negligence. Such detachment techniques may be common in cases when people victimize others (see Latané and Darby 1970). To intensify the films' effect, the viewers reported trying to imagine that the accidents were happening to them, or to someone they knew, or were similar to experiences they had had or had witnessed; some tried to think about and exaggerate the consequences of accidents. Koriat et al. conceive of these deintensifying or intensifying devices as aspects of appraisal that precede a "coping response." Such devices may also be seen as mental acts that adjust the "if supposition" and draw on the "emotional memory" described in Stanislavski (1965).

10. Stanislavski (1965), p. 57.

11. Ibid., p. 163.

12. Ibid., p. 127.

13. Stanislavski once admonished his actors: "You do not get hold of this exercise because . . . you are anxious to believe all of the terrible things I put into the plot. But do not try to do it all at once; proceed bit by bit, helping yourselves along by small truths. If every little auxiliary act is executed truthfully, then the whole action will unfold rightly" (Ibid., p. 126).

REFERENCES

Brown, Barbara. 1974 *New Mind, New Body*. New York: Harper & Row.

Campbell, Sarah F. (ed.). 1976 *Piaget Sampler*. New York: Wiley.

Gellhorn, E. 1964 "Motion and emotion: the role of proprioception in the physiology and pathology of the emotions." *Psychological Review* 71:457–472.

Goffman, Erving. 1959 *The Presentation of Self in Everyday Life*. New York: Doubleday Anchor.

Gold, Herbert. 1979 "The smallest part." Pp. 203–212. In William Abrahams (ed.), *Prize Stories, 1979*. The O'Henry Award. Garden City, NY: Doubleday.

Koriat, A., R. Melkman, J. R. Averill, and Richard Lazarus. 1972 "The self-control of emotional reactions to a stressful film." *Journal of Personality* 40:601–619.

Latané, Bibb, and John Darby. 1970 *The Unresponsive Bystander*. New York: Appleton-Century-Crofts.

Mills, C. Wright. 1956 *White Collar*. New York: Oxford University Press.

Nietzsche, F. W. 1876 *Menschliches alzumenschliches*, Vol. 1. Leipzig: Kroner.

Pelletier, Kenneth. 1977 *Mind as Healer, Mind as Slayer? A Holistic Approach to Preventing Stress Disorders*. New York: Dell.

Peto, Andrew. 1968 "On affect control." *International Journal of Psychoanalysis* 49(parts 2-3): 471–473.

Stanislavski, Constantin. 1965 *An Actor Prepares*. Tr. Elizabeth Reynolds Hapgood. New York: Theatre Arts Books. First published 1948.

Outsiders in the Clubhouse

Todd W. Crosset

This is a study of a world within our world; an insulated subworld on the fringe of American society. This world revolves around an elite occupation. The shared experience of the work yields a group of people linked not just by a common purpose, but by shared understandings, values, and ideals. Like other subworlds on the fringe of our society, this group's uniqueness strikes some as unusual.

One of the most distinctive aspects of this world is its focus on women within an enterprise historically monopolized by men. This organization, originally created by women, continues to be shaped by its women members. In this organization, women occupy a position of independence. Here women members don't work for anybody, don't punch a time clock, and aren't forced to sign contracts with corporations. They work for themselves. They take vacations when they want. They do the hiring and the firing. There is no network, good old boy or otherwise, which determines their place in the organization or their pay. These women are paid according to how well they perform—strictly merit raises.

Women lucky enough to join this group work in warm, comfortable climes, migrating with the summer sun. Someone else handles domestic chores like cooking and cleaning. Wealthy people give over their most prized leisure facilities and lush parks to this organization every week. Every working day they can take time out to notice the blue sky and the green grass or listen to the birds.

Typically their income is higher than the national average. Exceptional members can become very wealthy through their active participation, making between $200,000 and $400,000 a year. If they fall upon unusually hard times, there always seems to be a benevolent outsider to help defray costs.

In this organization, women are the center of attention. In each town they visit newspaper reporters and television crews report on them and even follow them, seeking interviews. But unlike most admiration for women, these women are not admired for their looks. They are admired by men and women alike for what they do. The admiration is so great that some well-established businessmen envy these women's employees. Although few well-established men actually do "drop out" and hit the road to work for these women, in every city they visit, hundreds of wealthy men pay thousands of dollars for the privilege of sharing a day with one of these women, to watch her do what she does so well, to talk to her, and to be a part of what she does. These women, you see, do what most men can only dream of doing. Nonetheless, because they are women in a male world, they remain outsiders.

The distinctiveness of this world is reflected in the way its members refer to their place in society. They are, they say, "Out Here"—as if it were other-worldly, defying time and space. "Out Here," as if any comparison to the "real world" would be inappropriate. "Out Here," they say, "it is like a fantasy world."

Admirers refer to their organization as "The Ladies Tour." Its formal name is the "Ladies Professional Golf Association," or the LPGA. This is a study of the subworld of professional women's golf. Its primary goal is to capture in words the experience of life on the tour, its tensions and conflicts with the broader culture, and the subsequent resolution of those conflicts through the players' ways of living. . . .

The Image Makers

If there is an image problem on the LPGA tour, it is manufactured by those who cover, watch, and organize the tour. At face value, there is nothing about the LPGA's presentation of competitive golf that overtly suggests that women golfers are masculine, lesbian, or sexually available. Indeed, the players and staff spend considerable time and energy trying to present a "wholesome" image. Players are instructed by LPGA staff to be as helpful to the press as possible, to respond kindly to even the rudest fans, and to dress in a professional fashion. Rookies go through an orientation to help them deal with the press and fans in order to present a "positive image."

The tour's "image" is mediated by elements outside of the players' control. At its root, the "image problem" is the tension between traditional notions of appropriate gender behavior and golf. While most players acknowledge this tension with the broader social order, most players argue that it is blown out of proportion by the press. Indeed, the players blamed the press as the catalyst and primary promoter of the "image problem."

The Press

Any press coverage (even hurtful) is better than no press, but getting good press seems to be a concern of most LPGA members. The players' suspicion of the press is complicated by the necessary relationship between the press and the tour. For the tour to be successful, the LPGA must receive media coverage. However, players view the promotion of the "image problem" as detrimental to the tour. In particular, it affects their ability to gain and maintain corporate sponsorship of tournaments.

The LPGA membership is wary of the press for a number of reasons. A commonly expressed reason is the media's astounding lack of contact with the game of golf and the golfers. Most reporters cover one or two tournaments a year. The majority of the press arrives at the course between midmorning and early afternoon. Once at the course, they rarely venture out of the press area. One sportswriter told me in hushed tones that golf was an easy sport to cover because you don't have to watch it. All the information he needed to write a story was efficiently obtained in the press tent. . . .

This lack of contact with the people that cover their sport does not go unnoticed by the players.

> It is kind of strange that we never see them. Tournament people, staff, caddies, you're always running into them somewhere. But the press you never see. They don't even come out to watch the tournament. They are in the press room watching the leader boards and getting reports via walkie talkies and such. (Cara)

. . . The players recognize rather quickly that freedom of the press means that their own voice will not be heard in the reports. From the players' perspective, the newspaper stories are not made on the golf course. They are created in the press tent.

> I think reporters do this: they already have it in their mind the story they want to write. They have their questions and they keep asking it until they get the answer they want to hear. Instead of reporting the facts of what is happening, they are going in there and formulating a story, and putting it down just the way they want to write it. (Jane)

> Sometimes I read an article about someone, and I know the truth and then I read what someone else wrote. It is like this person you know isn't like the person in the paper, or doesn't do what he says she does. (Nat)

> [The press] makes you or breaks you. They make you the person you are or they make you the person you're not. One bad swing with the press can cost you an awful lot. I don't think that the press tells the truth all the time. I know in my case I've been misquoted numerous times. (Gerri)

> The press is just looking for a story, creating a little of this here and a little of this there. (Pam)

. . . The lack of contact, the suspect reporting, and their lack of control of the institution most responsible for creating and sustaining the tour's image make most players wary of the press. But what most disturbs the players is the press' continual fascination with the sexual preference of the players on tour.

> When people get into an interview situation, you get some guys that are just going to dig and stir it up because we are women. If they did that with men, they would get flattened. I am talking about the gay lifestyle. Out here it seems to be that is all we hear about. . . . And the press loves it. Boy, do they love it. They ask about it and you say to yourself, "What do I do now?"
>
> *Q: The press asks you questions like that?*
>
> All over the place. Yeah, we were told in rookie orientation to be prepared for it. I am glad I was. I don't know what I would have said if it had not been up front and told "We know you are going to get this sort of question."
>
> *Q: And when they ask you, do they say it is "off the record?"*
>
> (*Nods an affirmation*) But you get some that must have had a bad day and they just ask you point blank. But most of the time it is more of a one-on-one situation. They say "Doris, how is it . . . " It is kind of sad, and the girls are fed up with it. But we can't escape it, unfortunately. (Doris)

The propensity of the press to push for information about the private lives of the players can be explained on two levels. The first has to do with how the press gains status among their colleagues. Peer status is measured by a press corps member's ability to gain intimate knowledge about the players. Casual conversations in the press tent revolved around trading stories about the off-course behavior of athletes or what the top-ranking players are "really" like. Comments like "and Sheehan was up there dancing," or . . . "I saw Lopez last night . . . at the mall" are common among the press corps. There is a "Can you top this" atmosphere in the press tent. Indeed, the vast majority of the comments made by press corps members about players on the tour had nothing to do with their golfing abilities. Rather than discussing fine points like swing speed, tempo, or stance, the press concerned themselves with personality, attractiveness, and off-course behavior. The more bold or intimate

the details a member of the press could share with his colleagues, the longer he held the attention of others and thus the higher his status.

The gossip swapping of the press tent stands in sharp contrast to most player/press interactions. Players are cordial but guarded with the press. Few have any contact with the press outside the official context of the press tent or an interview. Indeed, seeing Lopez at the mall was hot gossip, a rare peek into the private life of a professional athlete. In contrast to the mundane tidbits that get tossed around the press tent, most reporters retain, but rarely print, titillating stories about players on tour. These stories are rarely confirmable and almost always secondhand. The few that I listened to had all the credibility of fish-that-got-away stories.

A second explanation for the press' constant fascination with the players' private lives can be understood best as a combined desire to discredit the tour and at the same time to sell stories about it. The idea that gossip sells is fairly easy to fathom. Even harsh criticism of athletes in sports can be understood as an attempt to attract readers or viewers. But among the LPGA membership, there is an added sentiment that the media industry attempts to undermine the tour.

> I think that [the image] is created by a lot of jealousy and envy. I think men, well, I don't know if this is really the case, but you know, I think men have a little problem with seeing women that make a couple hundred thousand more than they do a year. So maybe they want to blow things out of proportion and make it more than what it is. (Fran)

Questioning the sex or sexuality of women athletes is a way of discrediting their performance. It is as if to say, "you're a good woman athlete only because you are not a real woman."

It is easy to see that the curiosity about the players' sexuality stems from assumptions about the essence of athletic prowess, independence, and ambition. Since these are taken to be essentially male traits, an explanation is sought for why some women display these attributes.

The questioning of the legitimacy of the players' claim to the female sex category may in fact not be intended to discredit the players' talents but to explain them. However, the result is the same. The questioning of one's membership in a sex category has often been used to discredit people's accomplishments in many fields in order to defend the dominant social order from a perceived threat of deviance. Thus when a female athlete's actions cannot be ignored, trivialized, or sexualized, subtle suggestions of lesbianism, and the highlighting of masculine traits or ambiguous gender behavior are often used to discredit the player's prowess. All things being equal, a more logical line of questioning would be to question the essential maleness of excellence in sport. However, that could undercut sport as a resource for doing gender, and therefore status of all men involved, whether participants, reporters, or spectators.

On the surface, the desire of the press to discredit the tour is hard to understand, given the relationship of the media industry and the sports industry. As is often pointed out, the two industries have a mutually beneficial relationship. Sports news sells papers and attracts viewers; in turn, the coverage of sports increases the public's interest in sports. Increased interest attracts readers or viewership to the news industry that covers the sport event best. The sports entertainment industry and the media industry feed each other. If undermining the tour is indeed the strategy of the press, it seems very much like shooting oneself in the foot. However, if we add to the equation the notion of "doing gender," the undermining of the tour becomes understandable. The pursuit of stories about lesbians on the tour serves to preserve golf as a "naturally" manly pursuit. This sort of coverage ensures the comfort of the sports media's primary market—men. The media industry has a stake in maintaining the image of sport as a resource for doing masculinity. It sells.

> Part of [the image problem] has been media induced. . . . It makes good copy. It seems to happen once a year or so. Somebody will rehash it, just dig it up. (Cara)

Compensatory Acts and the Company Line

. . . The demands of the sport, the conventional meanings of sport and gender, the actions of the press and the male-centered golfing community

. . . all work together to heighten tensions surrounding the presentation of gender on the tour. In an attempt to make the tour palatable to the mass market (which tends to be both homophobic and heterosexual), the LPGA and the players actively engage in actions to neutralize the gender ambiguity (or as Lynn puts it, "neutrality") that women's professional golf presents to the public.

The tour attempts to present its members as professionals and positive role models. Women's golf, the LPGA media and promotion staff insist, is wholesome family fun. As part of the effort to be unobjectionable, the LPGA actively works to counter the "image problem." Compensatory actions on the part of the LPGA staff take two forms: emphasized heterosexuality and promotion of good works.

The tour's promotion of itself is very similar to that of the annual Miss America contest—a simultaneous promotion of wholesomeness and sexuality, of Puritan sensibilities and the legitimation of men's entitlement to use women's bodies for their sexual gratification. The tour promotes the golfers as being squeaky clean (players may, for instance, be fined $100 for cursing while on the course). The LPGA media staff also promote the work players do for local charities and junior golf programs. Simultaneously, it produces swimsuit pictorials, encourages titillating interactions with pro-am partners, and consistently promotes the tour's most attractive players to the media and the general public. Married players and mothers on the tour are listed in the media guides. The LPGA staff frequently produce articles that discuss the dilemmas faced by the mothers/wives on tour. The combination of these two approaches gives the tour an overtly wholesome theme with a sexual subtext.

By subtly supporting and promoting the (hetero)sexualization of the players, the tour plays to their male patrons' sexual fantasies. The following quote by a male amateur speaks to the appeal this approach carries.

> Some of them, when you make a birdie, the pro just runs up and hugs and kisses the guys. I want to know what they do with an eagle (*laughs*). I haven't played with them yet, but I am waiting.

There are just enough examples of caddies or pro-am partners meeting, dating, and/or marrying professional golfers to maintain a colorful folklore about the women on tour.

Pro-am parties, where players are matched with amateur teams, are a further indication of the male sexual interest in the golfers that lies just below the surface. The evening is more often than not peppered with comments about the attractiveness and reputation of players. The lottery system of matching players with teams has all the trappings of computer-matched dating. The amateurs, having paid a high price to spend the afternoon with this woman, feel sexually entitled.

Although players are invited to these functions, they rarely attend. The contradictory message of being nice and sexy are irreconcilable for the players at these private, mostly male events.

> Like when I try [to act feminine], there is the flip side. I used to have really long hair. I used to get really dressed up for the pro-am parties, trying to look nice and sexy. Then the men start coming on to you. But that gets sickening. That is why a lot of girls get turned off [and don't go to those parties]. Here I am trying to be nice and promote the LPGA (*laughs*) and guys are being assholes—and they are all married. (Roslynn)

The undercurrent of male sexual entitlement (fermented within the security of the male-centered country club) is so strong that fending off advances by pro-am partners is a weekly event for some players.

> I am twenty-five, and I am not exactly physically attracted to a bunch of sixty-five-year-old men. I mean, they are nice guys, and I respect them for what they have done business-wise and just as people. But you know, I don't appreciate all the time, week after week, that they think I would be interested in joining them for dinner or going out.
>
> I am not saying it is bad. I think it is normal. Guys like to be guys, and they like to hit on women, or just try. I just kind of nicely tell them I have plans or something like that. It's kind of funny, it happens week after week. (June)

While it is impossible to know why all these men try to pick up women golfers, it is clear that the players understand the come-ons as being within the sphere of doing gender. Picking up women is a resource for men to do gender ("guys like to be guys").

In golf, driving the ball a long distance is also a resource for doing gender. For many pro-am participants, outdriving the women professionals is a symbol of their manhood. This phenomenon is not lost on the players.

> The male ego is interesting. They get up there and they try to bust it by you. They can't stand it when a 125-pound woman hits it by them. It is fun to watch them struggle with their egos for a little bit. (Hattie)
>
> Occasionally you get . . . well, I would say a lot of the times you have problems with the long hitters. When we outdrive these guys, they can't handle it. Sometimes they are trying so hard they come out of their shoes [a golfing expression for trying too hard] or they make excuses. (Ann)

The discomfort and tension the men feel, and the women sense, each week in the tee box at pro-am tournaments is a consistent reminder that sport is a proving ground for men. While the experience of outdriving men has the potential to challenge the association between sport and masculinity, some golfers choose to defuse the situation by playing up the masculine displays of the amateurs.

> Sometimes you play with guys whose big thing is to hit it good and outdrive you. Then I try to make them feel good. "God, that was a great drive. Boy, you really ripped that one." I go up and squeeze their muscle or something like that. Then, hopefully they will break out of that macho type feeling and understand I am not like that. (Nora)

What Nora means to say through her actions is that she is not going to threaten their masculinity even if she does outdrive them. Through her overt admiration of masculine gender displays, she hopes to evoke a sense of security in the male amateurs. She is "not like that"—not a threat to masculine hegemony of the country club. Once this is established, she hopes the amateurs will be able to settle down and play golf and have an enjoyable afternoon.

The overtly heterosexualized atmosphere of the tour, and particularly at the pro-am, enables the women to display their athletic prowess in a minimally threatening fashion. Players engage in compensatory actions in order that their golfing skills be palatable to golf fans and patrons. In the context of the pro-am, the "come-ons" the players face from their pro-am partners can also be seen as compensatory acts. Men whose masculinity has been threatened or damaged on the course by the play of women professionals may feel compelled to conquer a player in the bedroom or steal a kiss at the end of the round in an attempt to reclaim a sense of masculinity. . . .

The Corporate Image

Since the [1970s] LPGA has increasingly marketed itself to corporate sponsors. The tour events, once a promoter of civic pride for the benefit of local charities, are increasingly organized according to the interests of corporations and corporate leadership. In 1978, corporate funding reached 40% of total donated dollars, up from 10% a decade earlier. By 1988 corporate sponsorship, as a percentage of revenue, dropped back to [1960s] levels. The PGA, in contrast, is funded completely by corporate dollars.

The change in focus to the corporation has meant a change in the management of events from local golf enthusiasts to national business leaders. Since the mid-seventies, the guardians of the LPGA (the commissioner, the board members, and the tournament sponsors) have been recruited from the corporate elite. Most hold or have held positions on the boards of foundations, on corporate boards, as CEO's of corporations, or presidents of banks or large businesses. In a phrase, they are members of the power elite. . . .

The Tournament as Celebration of Corporate Life

The presentation of golf at a tournament reflects corporate life. There are no signs of poverty, war,

or race issues. Indeed, on the tour, the world seems to have few problems except illness (medical-related charities are preferred to those that might support social change) and inclement weather (one apparently wealthy fan actually discussed with me the difficulty he had in finding sunny weather in New England one weekend, and how he had traveled 200 miles to play golf in the sun). These tournaments celebrate a particular lifestyle.

Even the fans are a homogeneous group. Despite the variety of brightly colored golf clothing, fans look shockingly similar. At tournaments, there is a noticeable lack of diversity. In other sports, the stands hold diverse groups, although they may be segregated by section due to a variety of ticket prices. No one in the gallery comes close to resembling a "bleacher bum," or a drunken, rowdy football fan. Even the expressive behavior from fans that is common at other sporting events is absent from the LPGA tour. Fans do not take off their shirts (considered inappropriate on a golf course) or paint their faces. It is as one LPGA official explained: one of the only sporting events to which you can bring your children and not worry about being offended by other fans.

Players and tour officials are quick to point out that despite the unrealistic and self-serving atmosphere of tournaments, they are ultimately events which help the needy. Charitable monies raised through LPGA events are promoted by organizers at each tournament. In 1993, the LPGA helped raise $6.8 million for various charities.

Hidden, however, is the fact that tournament sponsors contribute at least $1.5 million to put on each tournament—far more than actually goes to charity. Most tournaments give less than $25,000 to charity, a return of less than two cents on the dollar. There are notable exceptions; the McDonald's tournament raises $2 to $3 million annually for its charity (The Ronald McDonald House). Nonetheless, in total, LPGA events donate less than 10% of what they raise each year.

If we view an LPGA event as a celebration of corporate community, an LPGA tournament is a typical charity. Most philanthropic giving (70% in 1991) is to the religious, social or educational, or adult recreational organizations to which the donors belong. The corporate elite, guardians of upper-class culture, are in effect giving themselves a gift—a corporate outing for management and their families. From this perspective, the tournament's charity is not much more than an excuse—a cover—to put on a tax-free celebration for themselves.

At the same time, event organizers increasingly present tournaments as sales and marketing opportunities to potential sponsors. The packaging of sponsorships is specifically designed to sell exposure. Corporations donate funds in exchange for ads in programs, on pairing sheets, on signs at each tee or green, on the uniforms of the officials. Indeed, almost any flat surface or printable space is for sale at a tournament. Golf attracts an audience with expendable income and, increasingly, marketers find it advantageous to associate their products with the sport so many of their prospective customers play or watch.

The golf tournament offers the perfect background for a live commercial. The players are well-groomed, polite, and professional. They work hard to ensure that pro-am partners have a good time, that sponsors are not offended, and that sufficient deference is paid to organizers. Absent from the tour are players identifiable with marginalized groups or social issues: the poor, people of color, gays and lesbians, or any other groups that might detract from the products being sold or the lifestyle being celebrated.

In contrast to the players' prowess ethic, a view which assumes worth is continually achieved, the life blood of the tournament is its ability to affirm and celebrate class, gender, and political hierarchies. For the tour to continue, it must sell itself as a viable advertising vehicle to corporations and as an entertainment value to fans with disposable income. Put slightly differently, the unstated product the LPGA sells is the affirmation of those who have gained the most in the current system. The majority of those in this group have enjoyed numerous economic advantages, yet believe they have earned their position in the world by overcoming obstacles.

Indeed, the corporate tournament celebrates class stratification. Through status boosting, the pro-am tournament, and parties, it affirms the social position of the sponsors. Similarly, preferred parking, seating around the eighteenth green, and special parties and tents feed the notion that the sponsor is deserving of special treatment. The vast differential in earnings between the top players and the rest of the field mirrors the growing disparity between corporate executives and workers. In addition, the charitable contributions associated with the event further supports current class stratification, as philanthropy confirms for the upper classes their right to wealth and the logic of class hierarchy.

The Corporate Definition of Gender

When the tour is sold as a marketing tool, image becomes an increasingly important element for maintaining the tour's viability. The market encourages the presentation of the female athlete in a fashion that supports conventional notions of gender behavior and appeals to a primarily male market. The membership of the LPGA is aware, on some level, of the discomfort women athletes seem to inspire in the public at large. To lessen this discomfort, the players actively engage in actions which uphold conventional gender norms. Within the professional women's golf community, considerable energy is directed toward maintaining the dominant social order in spite of the inherently subversive quality of professional women's golf. The LPGA staff and media services relentlessly promote the image of femininity, motherhood, and heterosexuality in an attempt to counter the "image problem." While in the field, I noted that the normally unbiased LPGA media staff tends to privately cheer for the players upholding a "feminine image" and/or who have a history of positive press relations.

Not surprisingly, players exhibiting a traditional femininity and heterosexuality are often the centerpiece of LPGA promotions, television coverage, and print media. In turn, comments by television commentators that sexualize women athletes or trivialize their accomplishments are common. In the print media, articles often focus on players who choose a traditional parenting role and femininity. While collecting data for this study, *Fairway Magazine,* an annual publication dedicated to the promotion of the LPGA, contained a photo spread of LPGA members posing in bathing suits.

Most LPGA members engage in activities that appeal to the ideological dispositions of their mostly male benefactors. Most players support the measures taken to promote a "feminine image" to the media. When asked about the photo spread, for example, Tara expressed a pragmatic need to use sexuality and femininity to sell the tour.

> It is just the way things are today. That is what they are selling. That is not all they are selling on this tour. They are also selling golf—the girls can hit the ball. Not all of us have the looks, but we all have great golf swings. Some of us have both and they do with that what they can. It is the public that buys it. If the public didn't buy it we couldn't sell it. So I suppose it is supply and demand.
>
> I can't say that I feel that it tarnishes the tour. I would hope that we would be appreciated for our skill rather than our good looks and the cheesecake role that goes with it. I think it is a viable tool to use to promote the tour. I would have trouble with it if it were the only tool that we were using. (Tara)

Because the tour is so tied to corporate marketing, the players actively work not to offend anybody. Players police themselves as does the LPGA media staff. Players who make seemingly benign but critical comments about the condition of the course, or the management of a tournament, are often reprimanded by fellow players.

In particular, the players are discouraged from associating with anything controversial or political. Overt political acts, such as taking a public stance on the abortion debate, can be damaging to a player's career.

> I was going to put on a [private] pro-am for Planned Parenthood. My major corporate sponsor didn't want to touch it with a ten-foot pole. I got the impression from the managing director that if I went real public on this issue that I was looking at not being renewed next year. At the time I thought I will find another sponsor. A month went by and I did not play well, and then another month went by and I really played crappy and

I thought the last thing I need is to start all over. (Denise)

In the end, Denise felt the risk to her career was too great, and decided against organizing a private pro-am for Planned Parenthood.

The players may privately accept lifestyles and political beliefs that are in conflict with those widely held in the broader society. But the demands of the tour and the pressure to be non-controversial is stronger than the players' willingness to spend emotional energy on political action or risk financial loss. Because the social world of the corporate elite remains essentially a heterosexual male domain, lesbian-identified players might feel the pressure to conform most acutely. Denise's comments are illustrative:

> If sexuality could become a non-issue it would be wonderful. I don't know how to do that. I am sick and fucking tired of being in the closet out here.
>
> One of the things I'd like to do before I retire is come out in a public way—really come out. But if I came out, nine out of ten players would say "Hey that's going to hurt me if you do that." No, probably ten out of ten would say that it would hurt women's golf. It would hurt our image. (Denise)

There is something of an ironic twist to the pressure women feel to remain non-controversial. The members of the recreational male golfing community often define the women professional golfers as "dykes" or "holy rollers." In either case, the display of prowess by the women professional golfers is dismissed as deviant, an attribute of odd women. The irony is that when men define women athletes as lesbians, it diminishes the golfer's threat to masculinity; but if a woman defines herself and claims a lesbian identity, she is perceived as a threat to heterosexual masculinity. Proving once again that the power of a stigma resides not so much in the name but in the naming.

Corporate Image, Reciprocity and Diversity

In some ways, it is the LPGA's success with corporations which may subvert one of the most attractive features of the tour, the reciprocal relationship between fans and athletes. As corporations find it in their interest to promote the tour, and by association their products, players increasingly see the value of the LPGA and themselves as their ability to sell products.

As the tour becomes a media event for corporate advertisers to exploit, the connection between fan support and player worth will become increasingly tenuous. The loss of openly pleasant relations between players and fans would be tragic on one level. But the financial survival of the tour may soon depend on the ability of the LPGA and the players to play to the camera to sell products.

Status, in this context, does not entail a moral obligation to reciprocate to the public but is merely a resource to be marketed and sold. This sort of status is not acquired so much through talent as by one's ability to remain in the public eye, and to establish a recognizable name, face, or voice—in other words, celebrity status. In this context, to borrow a phrase, image is everything.

Although corporate funding represents less than half of the LPGA's support, the impact on players' lives is evident, particularly among the younger players. Pam, a rookie, approached her entry to the tour in this fashion:

> I also solicited myself (*laughs*)—that's how I put it—to a couple businesses in Cherry Blossom City as soon as I turned pro. I did up a brochure—a pamphlet—of myself and I just sold myself to a couple businesses. The logo for the golf club I represent, Austin Creek, is on my bag. I also sold myself to Mr. Blackstone and put his logo on my golf bag and I went to the development company of Cherry Blossom City. I had those two endorsements. (Pam)

Pam's comment may be a sign of things to come. If the LPGA continues to develop in accord with its current path, relations on the tour will increasingly fall outside the gift exchange. In this context, young players needing financial support to cover the cost of playing on tour will increasingly turn to corporations. They will sell themselves as a vehicle to promote products. Those garnering corporate support will be obligated to reflect the sentiments of the corporation. As image becomes increasingly important, players are less likely to find support for their distinctiveness. This corporate financing of professional golf may discourage diversity and lead the tour down the path to homogeneity.

Conclusion

The homespun local chamber of commerce events of the fifties, sixties, and seventies are almost history. Today's tour competes for corporate money, and sells itself as a marketing opportunity. There is pressure on the tour players to affirm the status quo and to avoid political action. It would seem the professional women's tour poses little threat to the ideologies that support the dominant gender order and class structure. The players allow their public image to be shaped by the market. The image of the tour is quite easily molded into a "corporate outing" for corporate management and their families and into a promotion for corporate products. . . .

THINKING ABOUT THE READINGS

Managing Feeling

- What is the difference between surface acting and deep acting? How do their implications for impression management differ? Describe a situation in which you felt compelled to hide or alter what you were really feeling. Why did you do it? What do you think are the long-term consequences of a life characterized by constant emotional acting?

Outsiders in the Clubhouse

- What is the "image problem" on the LPGA tour? How is it related to impression management? Describe the difficulties female golfers have in balancing the need to overcome preconceptions about their sexual identity with the need to be competitive and win tournaments. How do they overcome, or at least deal with, these difficulties? How does concern with public image among golfers compare to that of female athletes in other sports (e.g., basketball, tennis, gymnastics, etc.)? Why are the presented images of female golfers so important to the LPGA organization and its corporate sponsors? What does Crosset mean when he says that an LPGA tournament is a celebration of corporate life?

CHAPTER 7

Constructing Difference
Social Deviance

Deviance is not an inherent feature of certain behaviors. Instead, it is a consequence of a definitional process. Since cultures create norms of acceptable behavior, they, by extension, create deviance—that is, the violation of these norms. We usually assume that there is some agreement regarding what and who are labeled as deviant. But the level of agreement within a given society over what is deviant and how it should be addressed is subject to much variation, disagreement, even overt conflict.

William Chambliss, in "The Saints and the Roughnecks," shows that deviant labels can have serious negative consequences and can determine future opportunities, especially for young people. What makes this idea important, sociologically, is that the application of these labels is not just a function of lawbreaking behavior but is affected by the social characteristics of the people engaging in such behavior. Most of us participate in some form of deviant activity when we are young: minor shoplifting, underage drinking, illegal drug use, driving over the speed limit, wearing bizarre clothes, skipping school, and so on. For most of us, these acts don't have any lasting impact on our identities. But for some they do.

Jeffrey Reiman, a conflict sociologist, is interested in how definitions of deviance reflect the interests of the powerful in society. In his article, "A Crime by Any Other Name. . . ," the focus is on crime—more specifically, why certain acts are considered crimes while others, equally dangerous or costly, are not. He argues that "we have a greater chance . . . of being killed or disabled . . . by an occupational injury or disease, by unnecessary surgery, by shoddy emergency medical services than by aggravated assault or even homicide." In other words, those actions that are the most costly or pose the greatest harm are not necessarily labeled as crimes.

In recent years, the field of biomedical research has been particularly influential in creating and applying definitions and explanations of deviance. In "Elvis's DNA," Dorothy Nelkin and Susan Lindee explore our culture's fondness for genetic explanations of deviant behavior. By attributing "evil" to some inherent genetic flaw, we, as a society, are spared the threatening task of questioning the role our long-standing social arrangements play in creating criminals or deviants. Instead, deviance is simply a result of defective individuals who, with the appropriate technology, can—and perhaps should—be identified, isolated, and treated.

The Saints and the Roughnecks

William J. Chambliss

Eight promising young men—children of good, stable, white upper-middle-class families, active in school affairs, good pre-college students—were some of the most delinquent boys at Hanibal High School. While community residents and parents knew that these boys occasionally sowed a few wild oats, they were totally unaware that sowing wild oats completely occupied the daily routine of these young men. The Saints were constantly occupied with truancy, drinking, wild driving, petty theft and vandalism. Yet not one was officially arrested for any misdeed during the two years I observed them.

This record was particularly surprising in light of my observations during the same two years of another gang of Hanibal High School students, six lower-class white boys known as the Roughnecks. The Roughnecks were constantly in trouble with police and community even though their rate of delinquency was about equal with that of the Saints. What was the cause of this disparity? the result? The following consideration of the activities, social class and community perceptions of both gangs may provide some answers.

The Saints from Monday to Friday

The Saints' principal daily concern was with getting out of school as early as possible. The boys managed to get out of school with minimum danger that they would be accused of playing hookey through an elaborate procedure for obtaining "legitimate" release from class. The most common procedure was for one boy to obtain the release of another by fabricating a meeting of some committee, program or recognized club. Charles might raise his hand in his 9:00 chemistry class and ask to be excused—a euphemism—for going to the bathroom. Charles would go to Ed's math class and inform the teacher that Ed was needed for a 9:30 rehearsal of the drama club play. The math teacher would recognize Ed and Charles as "good students" involved in numerous school activities and would permit Ed to leave at 9:30. Charles would return to his class, and Ed would go to Tom's English class to obtain his release. Tom would engineer Charles' escape. The strategy would continue until as many of the Saints as possible were freed. After a stealthy trip to the car (which had been parked in a strategic spot), the boys were off for a day of fun.

Over the two years I observed the Saints, this pattern was repeated nearly every day. There were variations on the theme, but in one form or another, the boys used this procedure for getting out of class and then off the school grounds. Rarely did all eight of the Saints manage to leave school at the same time. The average number avoiding school on the days I observed them was five.

Having escaped from the concrete corridors the boys usually went either to a pool hall on the other (lower-class) side of town or to a cafe in the suburbs. Both places were out of the way of people the boys were likely to know (family or school officials), and both provided a source of entertainment. The pool hall entertainment was the generally rough atmosphere, the occasional hustler, the sometimes drunk proprietor and, of course, the game of pool. The cafe's entertainment was provided by the owner. The boys would "accidentally" knock a glass on the floor or spill cola on the counter—not all the time, but enough to be sporting. They would also bend spoons, put salt in sugar bowls and generally tease whoever was working in the cafe. The owner had opened the cafe recently and was dependent on the boys' business which was, in fact, substantial since between the horsing around and the teasing they bought food and drinks.

The Saints on Weekends

On weekends the automobile was even more critical than during the week, for on weekends the Saints went to Big Town—a large city with a population of over a million 25 miles from Hanibal. Every Friday and Saturday night most of the Saints would meet between 8:00 and 8:30 and would go into Big Town. Big Town activities included drinking heavily in taverns or nightclubs, driving drunkenly through the streets, and committing acts of vandalism and playing pranks.

By midnight on Fridays and Saturdays the Saints were usually thoroughly high, and one or two of them were often so drunk they had to be carried to the cars. Then the boys drove around town, calling obscenities to women and girls; occasionally trying (unsuccessfully so far as I could tell) to pick girls up; and driving recklessly through red lights and at high speeds with their lights out. Occasionally they played "chicken." One boy would climb out the back window of the car and across the roof to the driver's side of the car while the car was moving at high speed (between 40 and 50 miles an hour); then the driver would move over and the boy who had just crawled across the car roof would take the driver's seat.

Searching for "fair game" for a prank was the boys' principal activity after they left the tavern. The boys would drive alongside a foot patrolman and ask directions to some street. If the policeman leaned on the car in the course of answering the question, the driver would speed away, causing him to lose his balance. The Saints were careful to play this prank only in an area where they were not going to spend much time and where they could quickly disappear around a corner to avoid having their license plate number taken.

Construction sites and road repair areas were the special province of the Saints' mischief. A soon-to-be-repaired hole in the road inevitably invited the Saints to remove lanterns and wooden barricades and put them in the car, leaving the hole unprotected. The boys would find a safe van-

tage point and wait for an unsuspecting motorist to drive into the hole. Often, though not always, the boys would go up to the motorist and commiserate with him about the dreadful way the city protected its citizenry.

Leaving the scene of the open hole and the motorist, the boys would then go searching for an appropriate place to erect the stolen barricade. An "appropriate place" was often a spot on a highway near a curve in the road where the barricade would not be seen by an oncoming motorist. The boys would wait to watch an unsuspecting motorist attempt to stop and (usually) crash into the wooden barricade. With saintly bearing, the boys might offer help and understanding.

A stolen lantern might well find its way onto the back of a police car or hang from a street lamp. Once a lantern served as a prop for a reenactment of the "midnight ride of Paul Revere" until the "play," which was taking place at 2:00 A.M. in the center of a main street of Big Town, was interrupted by a police car several blocks away. The boys ran, leaving the lanterns on the street, and managed to avoid being apprehended.

Abandoned houses, especially if they were located in out-of-the-way places, were fair game for destruction and spontaneous vandalism. The boys would break windows, remove furniture to the yard and tear it apart, urinate on the walls and scrawl obscenities inside.

Through all the pranks, drinking and reckless driving the boys managed miraculously to avoid being stopped by police. Only twice in two years was I aware that they had been stopped by a Big Town policeman. Once was for speeding (which they did every time they drove whether they were drunk or sober), and the driver managed to convince the policeman that it was simply an error. The second time they were stopped they had just left a nightclub and were walking through an alley. Aaron stopped to urinate and the boys began making obscene remarks. A foot patrolman came into the alley, lectured the boys and sent them home. Before the boys got to the car one began talking in a loud voice again. The policeman, who had followed them down the alley, arrested this boy for disturbing the peace and took him to the police station where the other Saints gathered. After paying a $5.00 fine and with the assurance that there would be no permanent record of the arrest, the boy was released.

The boys had a spirit of frivolity and fun about their escapades. They did not view what they were engaged in as "delinquency," though it surely was, by any reasonable definition of that word. They simply viewed themselves as having a little fun and who, they would ask, was really hurt by it? The answer had to be no one, although this fact remains one of the most difficult things to explain about the gang's behavior. Unlikely though it seems, in two years of drinking, driving, carousing and vandalism no one was seriously injured as a result of the Saints' activities.

The Saints in School

The Saints were highly successful in school. The average grade for the group was "B," with two of the boys having close to a straight "A" average. Almost all of the boys were popular and many of them held offices in the school. One of the boys was vice-president of the student body one year. Six of the boys played on athletic teams.

At the end of their senior year, the student body selected ten seniors for special recognition as the "school wheels"; four of the ten were Saints. Teachers and school officials saw no problem with any of these boys and anticipated that they would all "make something of themselves."

How the boys managed to maintain this impression is surprising in view of their actual behavior while in school. Their technique for covering truancy was so successful that teachers did not even realize that the boys were absent from school much of the time. Occasionally, of course, the system would backfire and then the boy was on his own. A boy who was caught would be most contrite, would plead guilty and ask for mercy. He inevitably got the mercy he sought.

Cheating on examinations was rampant, even to the point of orally communicating answers to exams as well as looking at one another's papers. Since none of the group studied, and since they were primarily dependent on one another for help, it is surprising that grades were so high. Teachers contributed to the deception in their admitted inclination to give these boys (and presumably others like them) the benefit of the

doubt. When asked how the boys did in school, and when pressed on specific examinations, teachers might admit that they were disappointed in John's performance, but would quickly add that they "knew that he was capable of doing better," so John was given a higher grade than he had actually earned. How often this happened is impossible to know. During the time that I observed the group, I never saw any of the boys take homework home. Teachers may have been "understanding" very regularly.

One exception to the gang's generally good performance was Jerry, who had a "C" average in his junior year, experienced disaster the next year and failed to graduate. Jerry had always been a little more nonchalant than the others about the liberties he took in school. Rather than wait for someone to come get him from class, he would offer his own excuse and leave. Although he probably did not miss any more classes than most of the others in the group, he did not take the requisite pains to cover his absences. Jerry was the only Saint whom I ever heard talk back to a teacher. Although teachers often called him a "cut up" or a "smart kid," they never referred to him as a troublemaker or as a kid headed for trouble. It seems likely, then, that Jerry's failure his senior year and his mediocre performance his junior year were consequences of his not playing the game the proper way (possibly because he was disturbed by his parents' divorce). His teachers regarded him as "immature" and not quite ready to get out of high school.

The Police and the Saints

The local police saw the Saints as good boys who were among the leaders of the youth in the community. Rarely, the boys might be stopped in town for speeding or for running a stop sign. When this happened the boys were always polite, contrite and pled for mercy. As in school, they received the mercy they asked for. None ever received a ticket or was taken into the precinct by the local police.

The situation in Big Town, where the boys engaged in most of their delinquency, was only slightly different. The police there did not know the boys at all, although occasionally the boys were stopped by a patrolman. Once they were caught taking a lantern from a construction site.

Another time they were stopped for running a stop sign, and on several occasions they were stopped for speeding. Their behavior was as before: contrite, polite and penitent. The urban police, like the local police, accepted their demeanor as sincere. More important, the urban police were convinced that these were good boys just out for a lark.

The Roughnecks

Hanibal townspeople never perceived the Saints' high level of delinquency. The Saints were good boys who just went in for an occasional prank. After all, they were well dressed, well mannered and had nice cars. The Roughnecks were a different story. Although the two gangs of boys were the same age, and both groups engaged in an equal amount of wild-oat sowing, everyone agreed that the not-so-well-dressed, not-so-well-mannered, not-so-rich boys were heading for trouble. Townspeople would say, "You can see the gang members at the drugstore, night after night, leaning against the storefront (sometimes drunk) or slouching around inside buying cokes, reading magazines, and probably stealing old Mr. Wall blind. When they are outside and girls walk by, even respectable girls, these boys make suggestive remarks. Sometimes their remarks are downright lewd."

From the community's viewpoint, the real indication that these kids were in for trouble was that they were constantly involved with the police. Some of them had been picked up for stealing, mostly small stuff, of course, "but still it's stealing small stuff that leads to big time crimes." "Too bad," people said. "Too bad that these boys couldn't behave like the other kids in town; stay out of trouble, be polite to adults, and look to their future."

The community's impression of the degree to which this group of six boys (ranging in age from 16 to 19) engaged in delinquency was somewhat distorted. In some ways the gang was more delinquent than the community thought; in other ways they were less.

The fighting activities of the group were fairly readily and accurately perceived by almost everyone. At least once a month, the boys would get into some sort of fight, although most fights were scraps between members of the group or involved only one member of the group and some peripheral hanger-on. Only three times in the period of observation did the group fight together: once against a gang from across town, once against two blacks and once against a group of boys from another school. For the first two fights the group went out "looking for trouble"—and they found it both times. The third fight followed a football game and began spontaneously with an argument on the football field between one of the Roughnecks and a member of the opposition's football team.

Jack had a particular propensity for fighting and was involved in most of the brawls. He was a prime mover of the escalation of arguments into fights.

More serious than fighting, had the community been aware of it, was theft. Although almost everyone was aware that the boys occasionally stole things, they did not realize the extent of the activity. Petty stealing was a frequent event for the Roughnecks. Sometimes they stole as a group and coordinated their efforts; other times they stole in pairs. Rarely did they steal alone.

The thefts ranged from very small things like paperback books, comics and ballpoint pens to expensive items like watches. The nature of the thefts varied from time to time. The gang would go through a period of systematically shoplifting items from automobiles or school lockers. Types of thievery varied with the whim of the gang. Some forms of thievery were more profitable than others, but all thefts were for profit, not just thrills.

Roughnecks siphoned gasoline from cars as often as they had access to an automobile, which was not very often. Unlike the Saints, who owned their own cars, the Roughnecks would have to borrow their parents' cars, an event which occurred only eight or nine times a year. The boys claimed to have stolen cars for joy rides from time to time.

Ron committed the most serious of the group's offenses. With an unidentified associate the boy attempted to burglarize a gasoline station. Although this station had been robbed twice previously in the same month, Ron denied any involvement in either of the other thefts. When Ron and his accomplice approached the station, the owner was hiding in the bushes beside the station. He fired both barrels of a double-barreled shotgun at the boys. Ron was severely injured; the other boy ran away and was never caught. Though he remained in critical condition for several months, Ron finally recovered and served six months of the following year in reform school. Upon release from reform school, Ron was put back a grade in school, and began running around with a different gang of boys. The Roughnecks considered the new gang less delinquent than themselves, and during the following year Ron had no more trouble with the police.

The Roughnecks, then, engaged mainly in three types of delinquency: theft, drinking and fighting. Although community members perceived that this gang of kids was delinquent, they mistakenly believed that their illegal activities were primarily drinking, fighting and being a nuisance to passersby. Drinking was limited among the gang members, although it did occur, and theft was much more prevalent than anyone realized.

Drinking would doubtless have been more prevalent had the boys had ready access to liquor. Since they rarely had automobiles at their disposal, they could not travel very far, and the bars in town would not serve them. Most of the boys had little money, and this, too, inhibited their purchase of alcohol. Their major source of liquor was a local drunk who would buy them a fifth if they would give him enough extra to buy himself a pint of whiskey or a bottle of wine.

The community's perception of drinking as prevalent stemmed from the fact that it was the most obvious delinquency the boys engaged in. When one of the boys had been drinking, even a casual observer seeing him on the corner would suspect that he was high.

There was a high level of mutual distrust and dislike between the Roughnecks and the police. The boys felt very strongly that the police were unfair and corrupt. Some evidence existed that the boys were correct in their perception.

The main source of the boys' dislike for the police undoubtedly stemmed from the fact that the police would sporadically harass the group. From the standpoint of the boys, these acts of occasional enforcement of the law were whimsical and uncalled for. It made no sense to them, for

example, that the police would come to the corner occasionally and threaten them with arrest for loitering when the night before the boys had been out siphoning gasoline from cars and the police had been nowhere in sight. To the boys, the police were stupid on the one hand, for not being where they should have been and catching the boys in a serious offense, and unfair on the other hand, for trumping up "loitering" charges against them.

From the viewpoint of the police, the situation was quite different. They knew, with all the confidence necessary to be a policeman, that these boys were engaged in criminal activities. They knew this partly from occasionally catching them, mostly from circumstantial evidence ("the boys were around when those tires were slashed"), and partly because the police shared the view of the community in general that this was a bad bunch of boys. The best the police could hope to do was to be sensitive to the fact that these boys were engaged in illegal acts and arrest them whenever there was some evidence that they had been involved. Whether or not the boys had in fact committed a particular act in a particular way was not especially important. The police had a broader view: their job was to stamp out these kids' crimes; the tactics were not as important as the end result.

Over the period that the group was under observation, each member was arrested at least once. Several of the boys were arrested a number of times and spent at least one night in jail. While most were never taken to court, two of the boys were sentenced to six months' incarceration in boys' schools.

The Roughnecks in School

The Roughnecks' behavior in school was not particularly disruptive. During school hours they did not all hang around together, but tended instead to spend most of their time with one or two other members of the gang who were their special buddies. Although every member of the gang attempted to avoid school as much as possible, they were not particularly successful and most of them attended school with surprising regularity. They considered school a burden—something to be gotten through with a minimum of conflict. If they were "bugged" by a particular teacher, it could lead to trouble. One of the boys, Al, once threatened to beat up a teacher and, according to the other boys, the teacher hid under a desk to escape him.

Teachers saw the boys the way the general community did, as heading for trouble, as being uninterested in making something of themselves. Some were also seen as being incapable of meeting the academic standards of the school. Most of the teachers expressed concern for this group of boys and were willing to pass them despite poor performance, in the belief that failing them would only aggravate the problem.

The group of boys had a grade point average just slightly above "C." No one in the group failed either grade, and no one had better than a "C" average. They were very consistent in their achievement or, at least, the teachers were consistent in their perception of the boys' achievement.

Two of the boys were good football players. Herb was acknowledged to be the best player in the school and Jack was almost as good. Both boys were criticized for their failure to abide by training rules, for refusing to come to practice as often as they should, and for not playing their best during practice. What they lacked in sportsmanship they made up for in skill, apparently, and played every game no matter how poorly they had performed in practice or how many practice sessions they had missed.

Two Questions

Why did the community, the school and the police react to the Saints as though they were good, upstanding, nondelinquent youths with bright futures but to the Roughnecks as though they were tough, young criminals who were headed for trouble? Why did the Roughnecks and the Saints in fact have quite different careers after high school—careers which, by and large, lived up to the expectations of the community?

The most obvious explanation for the differences in the community's and law enforcement agencies' reactions to the two gangs is that one group of boys was "more delinquent" than the other. Which group was more delinquent? The answer to this question will determine in part how we explain the differential responses to these groups by the members of the community and, particularly, by law enforcement and school officials.

In sheer number of illegal acts, the Saints were the more delinquent. They were truant from school for at least part of the day almost every day of the week. In addition, their drinking and vandalism occurred with surprising regularity. The Roughnecks, in contrast, engaged sporadically in delinquent episodes. While these episodes were frequent, they certainly did not occur on a daily or even a weekly basis.

The difference in frequency of offenses was probably caused by the Roughnecks' inability to obtain liquor and to manipulate legitimate excuses from school. Since the Roughnecks had less money than the Saints, and teachers carefully supervised their school activities, the Roughnecks' hearts may have been as black as the Saints', but their misdeeds were not nearly as frequent.

There are really no clear-cut criteria by which to measure qualitative differences in antisocial behavior. The most important dimension of the difference is generally referred to as the "seriousness" of the offenses.

If seriousness encompasses the relative economic costs of delinquent acts, then some assessment can be made. The Roughnecks probably stole an average of about $5.00 worth of goods a week. Some weeks the figure was considerably higher, but these times must be balanced against long periods when almost nothing was stolen.

The Saints were more continuously engaged in delinquency but their acts were not for the most part costly to property. Only their vandalism and occasional theft of gasoline would so qualify. Perhaps once or twice a month they would siphon a tankful of gas. The other costly items were street signs, construction lanterns and the like. All of these acts combined probably did not quite average $5.00 a week, partly because much of the stolen equipment was abandoned and presumably could be recovered. The difference in cost of stolen property between the two groups was trivial, but the Roughnecks probably had a slightly more expensive set of activities than did the Saints.

Another meaning of seriousness is the potential threat of physical harm to members of the community and to the boys themselves. The Roughnecks were more prone to physical violence: they not only welcomed an opportunity to fight, they went seeking it. In addition, they fought among themselves frequently. Although the fighting never included deadly weapons, it was still a menace, however minor, to the physical safety of those involved.

The Saints never fought. They avoided physical conflict both inside and outside the group. At the same time, though, the Saints frequently endangered their own and other people's lives. They did so almost every time they drove a car, especially if they had been drinking. Sober, their driving was risky; under the influence of alcohol it was horrendous. In addition, the Saints endangered the lives of others with their pranks. Street excavations left unmarked were a very serious hazard.

Evaluating the relative seriousness of the two gangs' activities is difficult. The community reacted as though the behavior of the Roughnecks was a problem, and they reacted as though the behavior of the Saints was not. But the members of the community were ignorant of the array of delinquent acts that characterized the Saints' behavior. Although concerned citizens were unaware of much of the Roughnecks' behavior as well, they were much better informed about the Roughnecks' involvement in delinquency than they were about the Saints'.

Visibility

Differential treatment of the two gangs resulted in part because one gang was infinitely more visible than the other. This differential visibility was a direct function of the economic standing of the families. The Saints had access to automobiles and were able to remove themselves from the sight of the community. In as routine a decision as to where to go to have a milkshake after school, the Saints stayed away from the mainstream of community life. Lacking transportation, the Roughnecks could not make it to the edge of town. The center of town was the only practical place for them to meet, since their homes were scattered throughout the town and any noncentral meeting place put an undue hardship on some members. Through necessity the Roughnecks congregated

in a crowded area where everyone in the community passed frequently, including teachers and law enforcement officers. They could easily see the Roughnecks hanging around the drugstore.

The Roughnecks, of course, made themselves even more visible by making remarks to passersby and by occasionally getting into fights on the corner. Meanwhile, just as regularly, the Saints were either at the cafe on one edge of town or in the pool hall at the other edge of town. Without any particular realization that they were making themselves inconspicuous, the Saints were able to hide their time-wasting. Not only were they removed from the mainstream of traffic, but they were almost always inside a building.

On their escapades the Saints were also relatively invisible, since they left Hanibal and travelled to Big Town. Here, too, they were mobile, roaming the city, rarely going to the same area twice.

Demeanor

To the notion of visibility must be added the difference in the responses of group members to outside intervention with their activities. If one of the Saints was confronted with an accusing policeman, even if he felt he was truly innocent of a wrongdoing, his demeanor was apologetic and penitent. A Roughneck's attitude was almost the polar opposite. When confronted with a threatening adult authority, even one who tried to be pleasant, the Roughneck's hostility and disdain were clearly observable. Sometimes he might attempt to put up a veneer of respect, but it was thin and was not accepted as sincere by the authority.

School was no different from the community at large. The Saints could manipulate the system by feigning compliance with the school norms. The availability of cars at school meant that once free from the immediate sight of the teacher, the boys could disappear rapidly. And this escape was well enough planned that no administrator or teacher was nearby when the boys left. A Roughneck who wished to escape for a few hours was in a bind. If it were possible to get free from class, downtown was still a mile away, and even if he arrived there, he was still very visible. Truancy for the Roughnecks meant almost certain detection, while the Saints enjoyed almost complete immunity from sanctions.

Bias

Community members were not aware of the transgressions of the Saints. Even if the Saints had been less discreet, their favorite delinquencies would have been perceived as less serious than those of the Roughnecks.

In the eyes of the police and school officials, a boy who drinks in an alley and stands intoxicated on the street corner is committing a more serious offense than is a boy who drinks to inebriation in a nightclub or a tavern and drives around afterwards in a car. Similarly, a boy who steals a wallet from a store will be viewed as having committed a more serious offense than a boy who steals a lantern from a construction site.

Perceptual bias also operates with respect to the demeanor of the boys in the two groups when they are confronted by adults. It is not simply that adults dislike the posture affected by boys of the Roughneck ilk; more important is the conviction that the posture adopted by the Roughnecks is an indication of their devotion and commitment to deviance as a way of life. The posture becomes a cue, just as the type of the offense is a cue, to the degree to which the known transgressions are indicators of the youths' potential for other problems.

Visibility, demeanor and bias are surface variables which explain the day-to-day operations of the police. Why do these surface variables operate as they do? Why did the police choose to disregard the Saints' delinquencies while breathing down the backs of the Roughnecks?

The answer lies in the class structure of American society and the control of legal institutions by those at the top of the class structure. Obviously, no representative of the upper class drew up the operational chart for the police which led them to look in the ghettoes and on street corners—which led them to see the demeanor of lower-class youth as troublesome and that of upper-middle-class youth as tolerable. Rather, the procedures simply developed from experience—experience with irate and influential upper-middle-class parents insisting that their son's vandalism was simply a prank

and his drunkenness only a momentary "sowing of wild oats"—experience with cooperative or indifferent, powerless, lower-class parents who acquiesced to the law's definition of their son's behavior.

Adult Careers of the Saints and the Roughnecks

The community's confidence in the potential of the Saints and the Roughnecks apparently was justified. If anything, the community members underestimated the degree to which these youngsters would turn out "good" or "bad."

Seven of the eight members of the Saints went on to college immediately after high school. Five of the boys graduated from college in four years. The sixth one finished college after two years in the army, and the seventh spent four years in the Air Force before returning to college and receiving a B.A. Of these seven college graduates, three went on for advanced degrees. One finished law school and is now active in state politics, one finished medical school and is practicing near Hanibal, and one boy is now working for a Ph.D. The other four college graduates entered submanagerial, managerial or executive training positions with larger firms.

The only Saint who did not complete college was Jerry. Jerry had failed to graduate from high school with the other Saints. During his second senior year, after the other Saints had gone on to college, Jerry began to hang around with what several teachers described as a "rough crowd"— the gang that was heir apparent to the Roughnecks. At the end of his second senior year, when he did graduate from high school, Jerry took a job as a used-car salesman, got married and quickly had a child. Although he made several abortive attempts to go to college by attending night school, when I last saw him (ten years after high school) Jerry was unemployed and had been living on unemployment for almost a year. His wife worked as a waitress.

Some of the Roughnecks have lived up to community expectations. A number of them were headed for trouble. A few were not.

Jack and Herb were the athletes among the Roughnecks, and their athletic prowess paid off handsomely. Both boys received unsolicited athletic scholarships to college. After Herb received his scholarship (near the end of his senior year), he apparently did an about-face. His demeanor became very similar to that of the Saints. Although he remained a member in good standing of the Roughnecks, he stopped participating in most activities and did not hang on the corner as often.

Jack did not change. If anything, he became more prone to fighting. He even made excuses for accepting the scholarship. He told the other gang members that the school had guaranteed him a "C" average if he would come to play football—an idea that seems far-fetched, even in this day of highly competitive recruiting.

During the summer after graduation from high school, Jack attempted suicide by jumping from a tall building. The jump would certainly have killed most people trying it, but Jack survived. He entered college in the fall and played four years of football. He and Herb graduated in four years, and both are teaching and coaching in high schools. They are married and have stable families. If anything, Jack appears to have a more prestigious position in the community than does Herb, though both are well respected and secure in their positions.

Two of the boys never finished high school. Tommy left at the end of his junior year and went to another state. That summer he was arrested and placed on probation on a manslaughter charge. Three years later he was arrested for murder; he pleaded guilty to second-degree murder and is serving a 30-year sentence in the state penitentiary.

Al, the other boy who did not finish high school, also left the state in his senior year. He is serving a life sentence in a state penitentiary for first-degree murder.

Wes is a small-time gambler. He finished high school and "bummed around." After several years he made contact with a bookmaker who employed him as a runner. Later he acquired his own area and has been working it ever since. His position among the bookmakers is almost identical to the position he had in the gang; he is always around but no one is really aware of him. He makes no trouble and he does not get into any. Steady, reliable, capable of keeping his mouth closed, he plays the game by the rules, even though the game is an illegal one.

That leaves only Ron. Some of his former friends reported that they had heard he was "driving a truck up north," but no one could provide any concrete information.

Reinforcement

The community responded to the Roughnecks as boys in trouble, and the boys agreed with that perception. Their pattern of deviancy was reinforced, and breaking away from it became increasingly unlikely. Once the boys acquired an image of themselves as deviants, they selected new friends who affirmed that self-image. As that self-conception became more firmly entrenched, they also became willing to try new and more extreme deviances. With their growing alienation came freer expression of disrespect and hostility for representatives of the legitimate society. This disrespect increased the community's negativism, perpetuating the entire process of commitment to deviance. Lack of a commitment to deviance works the same way. In either case, the process will perpetuate itself unless some event (like a scholarship to college or a sudden failure) external to the established relationship intervenes. For two of the Roughnecks (Herb and Jack), receiving college athletic scholarships created new relations and culminated in a break with the established pattern of deviance. In the case of one of the Saints (Jerry), his parents' divorce and his failing to graduate from high school changed some of his other relations. Being held back in school for a year and losing his place among the Saints had sufficient impact on Jerry to alter his self-image and to virtually assure that he would not go on to college as his peers did. Although the experiments of life can rarely be reversed, it seems likely in view of the behavior of the other boys who did not enjoy this special treatment by the school that Jerry, too, would have "become something" had he graduated as anticipated. For Herb and Jack outside intervention worked to their advantage; for Jerry it was his undoing.

Selective perception and labeling—finding, processing and punishing some kinds of criminality and not others—means that visible, poor, nonmobile, outspoken, undiplomatic "tough" kids will be noticed, whether their actions are seriously delinquent or not. Other kids, who have established a reputation for being bright (even though underachieving), disciplined and involved in respectable activities, who are mobile and monied, will be invisible when they deviate from sanctioned activities. They'll sow their wild oats— perhaps even wider and thicker than their lower-class cohorts—but they won't be noticed. When it's time to leave adolescence most will follow the expected path, settling into the ways of the middle class, remembering fondly the delinquent but unnoticed fling of their youth. The Roughnecks and others like them may turn around, too. It is more likely that their noticeable deviance will have been so reinforced by police and community that their lives will be effectively channelled into careers consistent with their adolescent background.

A Crime by Any Other Name . . .

Jeffrey Reiman

Think of a crime, any crime. Picture the first "crime" that comes into your mind. What do you see? The odds are you are not imagining a mining company executive sitting at his desk, calculating the costs of proper safety precautions and deciding not to invest in them. Probably what you do see with your mind's eye is one person physically attacking another or robbing something from another via the threat of physical attack. Look more closely. What does the attacker look like? It's a safe bet he (and it is a *he,* of course) is not wearing a suit and tie. In fact, my hunch is that you—like me, like almost anyone else in America—picture a young, tough, lower-class male when the thought of crime first pops into your head. You (we) picture someone like the Typical Criminal described above. The crime itself is one in which the Typical Criminal sets out to attack or rob some specific person.

This last point is important. It indicates that we have a mental image not only of the Typical Criminal but also of the Typical Crime. If the Typical Criminal is a young, lower-class male, the Typical Crime is *one-on-one harm*—where harm means either physical injury or loss of something valuable or both. If you have any doubts that this is the Typical Crime, look at any random sample of police or private eye shows on television. How often do you see the cops on "NYPD Blue" investigate consumer fraud or failure to remove occupational hazards? And when Jessica Fletcher (on "Murder She Wrote") tracks down well-heeled criminals, it is almost always for garden-variety violent crimes like murder. A study of TV crime shows by The Media Institute in Washington, D.C., indicates that, while the fictional criminals portrayed on television are on the average both older and wealthier than the real criminals who

figure in the FBI *Uniform Crime Reports,* "TV crimes are almost 12 times as likely to be violent as crimes committed in the real world."[1] TV crime shows broadcast the double-edged message that the one-on-one crimes of the poor are the typical crimes of all and thus not uniquely caused by the pressures of poverty; and that the criminal justice system pursues rich and poor alike—thus, when the criminal justice system happens mainly to pounce on the poor in real life, it is not out of any class bias.[2]

In addition to the steady diet of fictionalized TV violence and crime, there has been an increase in the graphic display of crime on many TV news programs. Crimes reported on TV news are also far more frequently violent than real crimes are.[3] An article in the *Washingtonian* says that the word around two prominent local TV news programs is, "If it bleeds, it leads."[4] What's more, a new breed of nonfictional "tabloid" TV show has appeared in which viewers are shown films of actual violent crimes—blood, screams, and all—or reenactments of actual violent crimes, sometimes using the actual victims playing themselves! Among these are "COPS," "Real Stories of the Highway Patrol," "America's Most Wanted," and "Unsolved Mysteries." Here, too, the focus is on crimes of one-on-one violence, rather than, say, corporate pollution. The *Wall Street Journal,* reporting on the phenomenon of tabloid TV, informs us that "Television has gone tabloid. The seamy underside of life is being bared in a new rash of true-crime series and contrived-confrontation talk shows."[5] Is there any surprise that a survey by *McCall's* indicates that its readers have grown more afraid of crime in the mid-1980s—even though victimization studies show a stable level of crime for most of this period?[6]

It is important to identify this model of the Typical Crime because it functions like a set of blinders. It keeps us from calling a mine disaster a mass murder even if ten men are killed, even if someone is responsible for the unsafe conditions in which they worked and died. I contend that this particular piece of mental furniture so blocks our view that it keeps us from using the criminal justice system to protect ourselves from the greatest threats to our persons and possessions.

What keeps a mine disaster from being a mass murder in our eyes is that it is not a one-on-one harm. What is important in one-on-one harm is not the numbers but the *desire of someone (or ones) to harm someone (or ones) else.* An attack by a gang on one or more persons or an attack by one individual on several fits the model of one-on-one harm; that is, for each person harmed there is at least one individual who wanted to harm that person. Once he selects his victim, the rapist, the mugger, the murderer all want this person they have selected to suffer. A mine executive, on the other hand, does not want his employees to be harmed. He would truly prefer that there be no accident, no injured or dead miners. What he does want is something legitimate. It is what he has been hired to get: maximum profits at minimum costs. If he cuts corners to save a buck, he is just doing his job. If ten men die because he cut corners on safety, we may think him crude or callous but not a murderer. He is, at most, responsible for an *indirect harm,* not a one-on-one harm. For this, he may even be criminally indictable for violating safety regulations—but not for murder. The ten men are dead as an unwanted consequence of his (perhaps overzealous or undercautious) pursuit of a legitimate goal. So, unlike the Typical Criminal, he has not committed the Typical Crime—or so we generally believe. As a result, ten men are dead who might be alive now if cutting corners of the kind that leads to loss of life, whether suffering is specifically aimed at or not, were treated as murder.

This is my point. Because we accept the belief—encouraged by our politicians' statements about crime and by the media's portrayal of crime—that the model for crime is one person specifically trying to harm another, we accept a legal system that leaves us unprotected against much greater dangers to our lives and well-being than those threatened by the Typical Criminal. Before developing this point further, let us anticipate and deal with some likely objections. Defenders of the present legal order are likely to respond to my argument at this point with irritation. Because this will surely turn to outrage in a few pages, let's talk to them now while the possibility of rational communication still exists.

The Defenders of the Present Legal Order (I'll call them "the Defenders" for short) are neither foolish nor evil people. They are not racists, nor are they oblivious to the need for reform in the criminal justice system to make it more even-handed, and for reform in the larger society to make equal opportunity a reality for all Americans. In general, their view is that—given our limited resources, particularly the resource of human altruism—the political and legal institutions we have are the best that can be. What is necessary is to make them work better and to weed out those who are intent on making them work shoddily. Their response to my argument at this point is that the criminal justice system *should* occupy itself primarily with one-on-one harm. Harms of the sort exemplified in the "mine tragedy" are really *not* murders and are better dealt with through stricter government enforcement of safety regulations. The Defenders admit that this enforcement has been rather lax and recommend that it be improved. Basically, though, they think this division of labor is right because it fits our ordinary moral sensibilities.

The Defenders maintain that, according to our common moral notions, someone who tries to do another harm and does is really more evil than someone who jeopardizes others while pursuing legitimate goals but doesn't aim to harm anyone. The one who jeopardizes others in this way at least doesn't try to hurt them. He or she doesn't have the goal of hurting someone in the way that a mugger or a rapist does. Moreover, being directly and purposely harmed by another person, the Defenders believe, is terrifying in a way that being harmed indirectly and impersonally, say, by a safety hazard, is not—even if the resultant injury is the same in both cases. And we should be tolerant of the one responsible for lax safety measures because he or she is pursuing a legitimate goal; that is, his or her dangerous action occurs as part of a productive activity, something that ultimately adds to social wealth and thus benefits everyone— whereas doers of direct harm benefit no one but themselves. Thus, the latter are rightfully in the province of the criminal justice system with its drastic weapons, and the former appropriately dealt with by the milder forms of regulation.

Further, the Defenders insist, the crimes identified as such by the criminal justice system are imposed on their victims totally against their will, whereas the victims of occupational hazards chose to accept their risky jobs and thus have in some degree consented to subject themselves to the dangers. Where dangers are consented to, the appropriate response is not blame but requiring improved safety, and this is most efficiently done by regulation rather than with the guilt-seeking methods of criminal justice.

In sum, the Defenders make four objections: 1. That someone who purposely tries to harm another is really more evil than someone who harms another without aiming to, even if the degree of harm is the same. 2. That being harmed directly by another person is more terrifying than being harmed indirectly and impersonally, as by a safety hazard, even if the degree of harm is the same. 3. That someone who harms another in the course of an illegitimate and purely self-interested action is more evil than someone who harms another as a consequence of a legitimate and socially productive endeavor. 4. That the harms of typical crimes are imposed on their victims against their wills, while harms like those due to occupational hazards are consented to by workers when they agree to a job. This too is thought to make the harms of typical crimes evil in a way that occupational harms are not.

All four of these objections are said to reflect our common moral beliefs, which are a fair standard for a legal system to match. Together they are said to show that the typical criminal does something worse than the one responsible for an occupational hazard, and thus deserves the special treatment provided by the criminal justice system. Some or all of these objections may have already

occurred to the reader. Thus, it is important to respond to the Defenders. For the sake of clarity I shall number the paragraphs in which I start to take up each objection in turn.

1. The Defenders' first objection confuses intention with specific aim or purpose, and it is intention that brings us properly within the reach of the criminal law. It is true that a mugger aims to harm his victim in the way that a corporate executive who maintains an unsafe workplace does not. But the corporate executive acts intentionally nonetheless, and that's what makes his actions appropriately subject to criminal law. What we intend is not just what we try to make happen but what we know is likely to happen as the normal causal product of our chosen actions. As criminal law theorist Hyman Gross points out: "What really matters here is whether conduct of a particular degree of dangerousness was done intentionally."[7] Whether we want or aim for that conduct to harm someone is a different matter, which is relevant to the actor's *degree* of culpability (not to whether he or she is culpable at all). Gross describes the degrees of culpability for intentional action by means of an example in which a sailor dies when his ship is fumigated while he is asleep in the hold. Fumigation is a dangerous activity; it involves spraying the ship with poison that is normally fatal to humans. If the fumigation was done in order to kill the sailor, we can say that his death is caused *purposely*. But suppose that the fumigation was done knowing that a sailor was in the hold but not in order to kill him. Then, according to Gross, we say that his death was brought about *knowingly*. If the fumigation was done without knowledge that someone was in the hold but without making sure that no one was, then the sailor's death is brought about *recklessly*. Finally, if the fumigation was done without knowledge that the sailor was there and some, but inadequate, precautions were taken to make sure no one was there, then the sailor's death is brought about *negligently*.

How does this apply to the executive who imposes dangerous conditions on his workers, conditions that, as in the mine explosion, do finally lead to death? The first thing to note is that, the difference between purposely, knowingly, recklessly, or negligently causing death is a difference within the range of intentional (and thus to some extent culpable) action. What is done recklessly or negligently is still done intentionally. Second, culpability decreases as we go from purposely to knowingly to recklessly to negligently killing because, according to Gross, the outcome is increasingly due to chance and not to the actor; that is, the one who kills on purpose leaves less room to chance that the killing will occur than the one who kills knowingly (the one who kills on purpose will take precautions against the failure of his killing, while the one who kills knowingly won't), and likewise the one who kills recklessly leaves wholly to chance whether there is a victim at all. And the one who kills negligently reduces this chance, but insufficiently.

Now, we may say that the kernel of truth in the Defenders' objection is that the common street mugger harms on purpose, while the executive harms only knowingly or recklessly or negligently. This does not justify refusing to treat the executive killer as a criminal, however, because we have criminal laws against reckless or even negligent harming—thus the kid-glove treatment meted out to those responsible for occupational hazards and the like is no simple reflection of our ordinary moral sensibilities, as the Defenders claim. Moreover, don't be confused into thinking that, because all workplaces have some safety measures, all workplace deaths are at most due to negligence. To the extent that precautions are not taken against particular dangers (like leaking methane), deaths due to those dangers are—by Gross's standard—caused recklessly or even knowingly (because the executive knows that potential victims are in harm's way from the danger he fails to reduce). And Nancy Frank concludes from a review of state homicide statutes that "a large number of states recognize unintended deaths caused by extreme recklessness as murder."[8]

But there is more to be said. Remember that Gross attributes the difference in degrees of culpability to the greater role left to chance as we descend from purposely to recklessly to negligently harming. In this light it is important to note that the executive (say, the mine owner) imposes danger on a larger number of individuals than the typical criminal typically does. So while the typical criminal purposely harms a particular individual, the executive knowingly subjects a large number of workers to a risk of harm. But as the risk gets greater and the number of workers gets greater, it becomes increasingly likely that one or more workers will get harmed. This means that the gap between the executive and the typical criminal shrinks. By not harming workers purposely, the executive leaves more to chance; but by subjecting large numbers to risk, he leaves it less and less to chance that someone will be harmed, and thus he rolls back his advantage over the typical criminal. If you keep your workers in mines or factories with high levels of toxic gases or chemicals, you start to approach 100 percent likelihood that at least one of them will be harmed as a result. And that means that the culpability of the executive approaches that of the typical criminal.

A different way to make the Defenders' argument is to say that the executive has failed to protect his workers, while the typical criminal has positively acted to harm his victim. In general, we think it is worse to harm someone than to fail to prevent their being harmed (perhaps you should feed starving people on the other side of town or of the world, but few people will think you are a murderer if you don't and the starving die). But at least in some cases we are responsible for the harm that results from our failure to act (for example, parents are responsible for failing to provide for their children). Some philosophers go further and hold that we are responsible for all the foreseeable effects of what we do, including the foreseeable effects of failing to act certain ways.[9] While this view supports the position for which I am arguing here, I think it goes too far. It entails that we are murderers every time we are doing anything other than saving lives, which surely goes way beyond our ordinary moral beliefs. My view is that in most cases, we are responsible only for the foreseeable effects likely to be caused by our action—and not responsible for those caused by our inaction. We are, however, responsible for the effects of our inaction in at least one special type of case: where we have a special obligation to aid people. This covers the parent who causes his child's death by failing to feed him, the doctor who causes her patient's death by failing to care for her, and the coal mine owner who causes his employees' death by failing to take legally mandated safety precautions. It may also cover the society that fails to rectify harm-producing injustices in its midst. This is another way in which the moral difference between the safety-cutting executive and the typical criminal shrinks away.

Further on this first objection, I think the Defenders overestimate the importance of specifically trying to do evil in our moral estimate of people. The mugger who aims to hurt someone is no doubt an ugly character. But so too is the well-heeled executive who calmly and callously chooses to put others at risk. Compare the mine executive who cuts corners with the typical murderer. Most murders, we know, are committed in the heat of some passion like rage or jealousy. Two lovers or neighbors or relatives find themselves in a heated argument. One (often it is a matter of chance *which* one) picks up a weapon and strikes the other a fatal blow. Such a person is clearly a murderer and rightly subject to punishment by the criminal justice system. Is this person more evil than the executive who, knowing the risks, calmly chooses not to pay for safety equipment?

The one who kills in a heated argument kills from passion. What she does she probably would not do in a cooler moment. She is likely to feel "she was not herself." The one she killed was someone she knew, a specific person who at the time seemed to her to be the embodiment of all that frustrates her, someone whose very existence makes life unbearable. I do not mean to suggest that this is true of all killers, although there is reason to believe it is true of many. Nor do I mean to suggest that such a state of mind justifies murder. What it does do, however, is suggest that the killer's action, arising out of anger at a particular individual, does not show general disdain for the lives of her fellows. Here is where she is different from our mine executive. Our mine executive wanted to harm no one in particular, but he *knew his acts were likely to harm someone*—and once someone is harmed, the victim is someone in particular. Nor can our executive claim that "he was not himself." His act is done not out of passion but out of cool reckoning. Precisely here his evil shows. In his willingness to jeopardize the lives of unspecified others who pose him no real

or imaginary threat in order to make a few dollars, he shows his general disdain for all his fellow human beings. Can it really be said that he is less evil than one who kills from passion? The Model Penal Code includes within the definition of murder any death caused by "extreme indifference to human life."[10] Is our executive not a murderer by this definition?

It's worth noting that in answering the Defenders here, I have portrayed harms from occupational hazards in their best light. They are not, however, all just matters of well-intentioned but excessive risk taking. Consider, for example, the Manville (formerly Johns Manville) asbestos case. It is predicted that 240,000 Americans working now or who previously worked with asbestos will die from asbestos-related cancer in the next 30 years. But documents made public during congressional hearings in 1979 show "that Manville and other companies within the asbestos industry covered up and failed to warn millions of Americans of the dangers associated with the fireproof, indestructible insulating fiber."[11] An article in the *American Journal of Public Health* attributes thousands of deaths to the cover-up.[12] Later . . . I document similar intentional cover-ups, such as the falsification of reports on coal dust levels in mines, which leads to crippling and often fatal black lung disease. Surely someone who knowingly subjects others to risks and tries to hide those risks from them is culpable in a high degree.

2. I think the Defenders are right in believing that direct personal assault is terrifying in a way that indirect impersonal harm is not. This difference is no stranger to the criminal justice system. Prosecutors, judges, and juries constantly have to consider how terrifying an attack is in determining what to charge and what to convict offenders for. This is why we allow gradations in charges of homicide or assault and allow particularly grave sentences for particularly grave attacks. In short, the difference the Defenders are pointing to here might justify treating a one-on-one murder as graver than murder due to lax safety measures, but it doesn't justify treating one as a grave crime and the other as a mere regulatory (or very minor criminal) matter. After all, although it is worse to be injured with terror than without, it is still the injury that constitutes the worst part of violent crime. Given the choice, seriously injured victims of crime would surely rather have been terrorized and not injured than injured and not terrorized. If that is so, then the worst part of violent crime is still shared by the indirect harms that the Defenders would relegate to regulation.

Furthermore, if direct personal assault is more frightening than impersonal harm, impersonal harm often takes its toll on trust. Impersonal harms from occupational hazards, dangerous consumer products, pollution, and lax government enforcement of rules against these things weaken people's trust in their employers, in their producers and merchants, and in their government. And this is likely to spread to undermine trust generally in one's fellow citizens. Both a sense of personal security and a sense of trust in one's fellows are essential aspects of civility. Where direct harm undermines the first, indirect harm undermines the second.

3. There is also something to the Defenders' claim that indirect harms, such as ones that result from lax safety measures, are part of legitimate productive activities, whereas one-on-one crimes are not. No doubt we must tolerate the risks that are necessary ingredients of productive activity (unless those risks are so great as to outweigh the gains of the productive activity). But this doesn't imply we shouldn't identify the risks, or levels of danger, that are unnecessary and excessive, and use the law to protect innocent people from them. And if those risks are great enough, the fact that they may further a productive or otherwise legitimate activity is no reason against making them crimes—if that's what's necessary to protect workers. A person can commit a crime to further an otherwise legitimate endeavor and it is still a crime. If, say, I threaten to assault my workers if they don't work faster, this doesn't make my act any less criminal. And, in general, if I do something that by itself ought to be a crime, the fact that I do it as a means to a legitimate aim doesn't change the fact that it ought to be a crime. If acts that intentionally endanger others ought to be crimes, then the fact that the acts are means to legitimate aims doesn't change the fact that they ought to be crimes.

4. . . . The Defenders overestimate the reality of the "free consent" with which workers take on the risks of their jobs. You can consent to a risk only if you know about it, and often the risks are concealed. Moreover, the Defenders overestimate generally the degree to which workers freely consent to the conditions of their jobs. Although no one is forced at gunpoint to accept a particular job, virtually everyone is forced by the requirements of necessity to take some job. At best, workers can choose among the dangers present at various work sites, but they cannot choose to face no danger at all. Moreover, workers can choose jobs only where there are openings, which means they cannot simply pick their place of employment at will. For nonwhites and women, the choices are even more narrowed by discriminatory hiring, long-standing occupational segregation (funnelling women into secretarial, nursing, or teaching jobs and blacks into janitorial and other menial occupations), not to mention subtle and not so subtle practices that keep nonwhites and women from advancing within their occupations. Consequently, for all intents and purposes, most workers *must* face the dangers of the jobs that are available to them. What's more, remember that while here we have been focusing on harms due to occupational hazards, much of the indirect harm that I shall document in what follows is done not to workers but to consumers (of food with dangerous chemicals) and citizens (breathing dangerous concentrations of pollutants).

Finally, recall that the basis of all the Defenders' objections is that the idea that one-on-one harms are more evil than indirect harms is part of our common moral beliefs, and that this makes it appropriate to treat the former with the criminal justice system and the latter with milder regulatory measures. Here I think the Defenders err by overlooking the role of legal institutions in shaping our ordinary moral beliefs. Many who defend the criminal justice system do so precisely because of its function in educating the public about the difference between right and wrong. The great historian of English law, Sir James Fitzjames Stephen, held that a

> great part of the general detestation of crime which happily prevails amongst the decent

part of the community in all civilized countries arises from the fact that the commission of offences is associated in all such communities with the solemn and deliberate infliction of punishment wherever crime is proved.[13]

One cannot simply appeal to ordinary moral beliefs to defend the criminal law because the criminal law has already had a hand in shaping ordinary moral beliefs. At least one observer has argued that making narcotics use a crime in the beginning of this century *caused* a change in the public's ordinary moral notions about drug addiction, which prior to that time had been viewed as a medical problem.[14] It is probably safe to say that in our own time, civil rights legislation has sharpened the public's moral condemnation of racial discrimination. Hence, we might speculate that if the criminal justice system began to prosecute—and if the media began to portray—those who inflict *indirect harm* as serious criminals, our ordinary moral notions would change on this point as well.

I think this disposes of the Defenders for the time being. We are left with the conclusion that there is no moral basis for treating one-on-one harm as criminal and *indirect harm* as merely a regulatory affair. What matters, then, is whether the purpose of the criminal justice system will be served by including, in the category of serious crime, actions that are predictably likely to produce serious harm, yet that are done in pursuit of otherwise legitimate goals and without the aim of harming anyone. . . .

In the remainder of this section I identify some acts that are *crimes by any other name*—acts that cause harm and suffering comparable to that caused by acts called crimes. My purpose is to confirm the first hypothesis: that the definitions of crime in the criminal law do not reflect the only or the most dangerous behaviors in our society. To do this, we will need some measure of the harm and suffering caused by crimes with which we can compare the harm and suffering caused by noncrimes. Our measure need not be too refined because my point can be made if I can show that there are some acts that we do not treat as crime but that cause harm *roughly comparable* to that caused by acts that we do treat as crimes. For that, it is not necessary to compare the harm caused by

noncriminal acts with the harm caused by *all* crimes. I need only show that the harm produced by some type of noncriminal act is comparable to the harm produced by *any* serious crime. Because the harms caused by noncriminal acts fall into the categories of death, bodily injury (including the disabling effects of disease), and property loss, I will compare the harms done by noncriminal acts with the injuries caused by the crimes of murder, aggravated assault, and theft.

According to the FBI's *Uniform Crime Reports,* in 1991, there were 24,703 murders and nonnegligent manslaughters, and 1,092,739 aggravated assaults. In 1992, there were 23,760 murders and nonnegligent manslaughters, and 1,126,970 aggravated assaults. "Murder and nonnegligent manslaughter" includes all "willful (nonnegligent) killing of one human being by another." "Aggravated assault" is defined as an "attack by one person on another for the purpose of inflicting severe or aggravated bodily injury."[15] Thus, as a measure of the physical harm done by crime in the beginning of the 1990s, we can say that reported crimes lead to roughly 24,000 deaths and 1,000,000 instances of serious bodily injury short of death a year. As a measure of monetary loss due to property crime, we can use $15.1 billion—the total estimated dollar losses due to property crime in 1992 according to the UCR.[16] Whatever the shortcomings of these reported crime statistics, they are the statistics upon which public policy has traditionally been based. Thus, I will consider any actions that lead to loss of life, physical harm, and property loss comparable to the figures in the UCR as actions that pose grave dangers to the community comparable to the threats posed by crimes. They are surely precisely the kind of harmful actions from which a criminal justice system whose purpose is to protect our persons and property ought to protect us. *They are crimes by other names.*

Work May Be Dangerous to Your Health

Since the publication of *The President's Report on Occupational Safety and Health* [17] in 1972, numerous studies have documented the astounding incidence of disease, injury, and death due to hazards in the workplace *and* the fact that much or most of this carnage is the consequence of the refusal of management to pay for safety measures and of government to enforce safety standards—and sometimes of willful defiance of existing law.[18]

In that 1972 report, the government estimated the number of job-related illnesses at 390,000 per year and the number of annual deaths from industrial disease at 100,000. For 1990, the Bureau of Labor Statistics (BLS) of the U.S. Department of Labor estimates 330,800 job-related illnesses and 2,900 work-related deaths.[19] Note that the latter figure applies only to private-sector work environments with 11 or more employees. And it is not limited to death from occupational disease but includes all work-related deaths including those resulting from accidents on the job.

Before we celebrate what appears to be a dramatic drop in work-related mortality, we should point out that the BLS itself "believes that the annual survey significantly understates the number of work-related fatalities."[20] And there is wide agreement that occupational diseases are seriously underreported. *The Report of the President to the Congress on Occupational Safety and Health* for 1980 stated that

> recording and reporting of illnesses continue to present measurement problems, since employers (and doctors) are often unable to recognize some illnesses as work-related. The annual survey includes data only on the visible illnesses of workers. To the extent that occupational illnesses are unrecognized and, therefore, not recorded or reported, the illness survey estimates may understate their occurrence.[21]

Part of the difficulty is that there may be a substantial delay between contracting a fatal disease on the job and the appearance of symptoms, and from these to death. Moreover, the Occupational Safety and Health Administration (OSHA) relies on employer reporting for its figures, and there are many incentives for underreporting. Writing in the journal *Occupational Hazards,* Robert Reid states that

OSHA concedes that many factors—including insurance rates and supervisor evaluations based on safety performance—are incentives to underreport. And the agency acknowledges that recordkeeping violations have increased more than 27 percent since 1984, with most of the violations recorded for not maintaining the injuries and illnesses log examined by compliance officers and used for BLS' annual survey.[22]

A study by the National Institute for Occupational Safety and Health (NIOSH) concludes that "there may be several thousand more workplace deaths each year than employers report."[23]

For these reasons, plus the fact that BLS's figures on work-related deaths are only for private workplaces with 11 or more employees, we must supplement the BLS figures with other estimates. In 1982, then U.S. Secretary of Health and Human Services Richard Schweiker stated that "current estimates for overall workplace-associated cancer mortality vary within a range of five to fifteen percent."[24] With annual cancer deaths currently running at about 500,000, that translates into about 25,000 to 75,000 job-related cancer deaths per year. More recently, Edward Sondik, of the National Cancer Institute, states that the best estimate of cancer deaths attributable to occupational exposure is 4 percent of the total, with the range of acceptable estimates running between 2 and 5 percent. That translates into a best estimate of 20,000 job-related cancer deaths a year, within a range of acceptable estimates between 10,000 and 40,000.[25]

Death from cancer is only part of the picture of death-dealing occupational disease. In testimony before the Senate Committee on Labor and Human Resources, Dr. Philip Landrigan, director of the Division of Environmental and Occupational Medicine at the Mount Sinai School of Medicine in New York City, stated that

> Recent data indicate that occupationally related exposures are responsible, each year in New York State for 5,000 to 7,000 deaths and for 35,000 new cases of illness (not including work-related injuries). These deaths due to occupational disease include 3,700 deaths from cancer. . . .

Crude national estimates of the burden of occupational disease in the United States may be developed by multiplying the New York State data by a factor of 10. New York State contains slightly less than 10 percent of the nation's workforce, and it includes a broad mix of employment in the manufacturing, service and agricultural sectors. Thus, it may be calculated that occupational disease is responsible each year in the United States for 50,000 to 70,000 deaths, and for approximately 350,000 new cases of illness.[26]

It is some confirmation of Dr. Landrigan's estimates that they imply work-related cancer deaths of approximately 37,000 a year—a figure that is toward the low end of the range in Secretary Schweiker's statement on this issue, and toward the top end of the range of acceptable estimates according to Sondik. Landrigan's estimates of deaths from occupational disease are also corroborated by a study reported by the National Safe Workplace Institute, which estimates that the number of occupational disease deaths is between 47,377 and 95,479. Mark Cullen, director of the occupational medicine program at the Yale University School of Medicine, praised this study as "a very balanced, very comprehensive overview of occupational health." The study's figures are low compared with a 1985 report of the Office of Technology Assessment (OTA) that estimated 100,000 Americans die annually from work-related illness.[27] Even if we discount OSHA's 1972 estimate of 100,000 deaths a year due to occupational disease or OTA's 1985 estimate of the same number, we would surely be erring in the other direction to accept the BLS figure of 2,900. We can hardly be overestimating the actual toll if we take the conservative route and set it at 25,000 deaths a year resulting from occupational disease.

The BLS estimate of 330,000 job-related illnesses for 1990 roughly matches Dr. Landrigan's estimates. For 1991, BLS estimates 368,000 job-related illnesses. These illnesses are of varying severity (the majority are so-called "repeated trauma" diseases, such as carpal tunnel syndrome). Because I want to compare these occupational harms with those resulting from

aggravated assault, I shall stay on the conservative side here too, as with deaths from occupational diseases, and say that there are annually in the United States approximately 150,000 job-related serious illnesses. Taken together with 25,000 deaths from occupational diseases, how does this compare with the threat posed by crime?

Before jumping to any conclusions, note that the risk of occupational disease and death falls only on members of the labor force, whereas the risk of crime falls on the whole population, from infants to the elderly. Because the labor force is about half the total population (124,810,000 in 1990, out of a total population of 249,900,000), to get a true picture of the relative threat posed by occupational diseases compared with that posed by crimes, we should halve the crime statistics when comparing them with the figures for industrial disease and death. Using the crime figures for the first years of the 1990s . . . we note that the *comparable* figures would be

	Occupational Disease	Crime (halved)
Death	25,000	12,000
Other physical harm	150,000	500,000

If it is argued that this paints an inaccurate picture because so many crimes go unreported, my answer is this: First of all, homicides are by far the most completely reported of crimes. For obvious reasons, the general underreporting of crimes is not equal among crimes. It is easier to avoid reporting a rape or a mugging than a corpse. Second, although not the best, aggravated assaults are among the better-reported crimes. From victimization studies, it is estimated that 59 percent of aggravated assaults were reported to the police in 1980, compared with 29 percent of thefts.[28] On the other hand, we should expect more—not less—underreporting of industrial than criminal victims because diseases and deaths are likely to cost firms money in the form of workdays lost and insurance premiums raised, occupational diseases are frequently first seen by company physicians who have every reason to diagnose complaints as either malingering or not job-related, and many occupationally caused diseases do not show symptoms or lead to death until after the employee has left the job.

> A survey conducted last year by the University of Washington reported that one in four Americans currently suffers an occupational disease. The report also disclosed that only one of the 10 workers with an occupational disease had been included in either OSHA statistics or in the state's workmen's compensation records.[29]

In sum, both occupational and criminal harms are underreported, though there is reason to believe that the underreporting is worse with occupational than criminal harms. Finally, note that I have been extremely conservative in estimating occupational deaths and other harms. However one may quibble with figures presented here, I think it is fair to say that, if anything, they understate the extent of occupational harm compared with criminal harm.

Note further that the estimates in the last chart are *only* for occupational *diseases* and deaths from those diseases. They do not include death and disability from work-related injuries. Here, too, the statistics are gruesome. The National Safety Council reported that in 1991, work-related accidents caused 9,600 deaths and 1.7 million disabling work injuries, at a total cost to the economy of $63.3 billion.[30] This brings the number of occupation-related deaths to 34,600 a year and other physical harms to 1,850,000. If, on the basis of these additional figures, we recalculated our chart comparing occupational harms from both disease and accident with criminal harms, it would look like this:

	Occupational Hazard	Crime (halved)
Death	34,600	12,000
Other physical harm	1,850,000	500,000

Can there be any doubt that workers are more likely to stay alive and healthy in the face of the danger from the underworld than in the workworld? If any doubt lingers, consider this: Lest we falter in the struggle against crime, the FBI includes in its annual *Uniform Crime Reports* a table of "crime clocks," which graphically illustrates the extent of the criminal menace. For 1992, the crime clock shows a murder occurring every 22 minutes. If a similar clock were constructed for occupational deaths—using the conservative estimate of 34,600 cited above and remembering that this clock ticks only for that half of the population that is in the labor force—this clock would show an occupational death about every 15 minutes! In other words, in the time it takes for three murders on the crime clock, four workers have died *just from trying to make a living.*

To say that some of these workers died from accidents due to their own carelessness is about as helpful as saying that some of those who died at the hands of murderers asked for it. It overlooks the fact that where workers are careless, it is not because they love to live dangerously. They have production quotas to meet, quotas that they themselves do not set. If quotas were set with an eye to keeping work at a safe pace rather than to keeping the production-to-wages ratio as high as possible, it might be more reasonable to expect workers to take the time to be careful. Beyond this, we should bear in mind that the vast majority of occupational deaths result from disease, not accident, and disease is generally a function of conditions outside a worker's control. Examples of such conditions are the level of coal dust in the air ("260,000 miners receive benefits for [black lung] disease, and perhaps as many as 4,000 retired miners die from the illness or its complications each year"; about 10,000 currently working miners "have X-ray evidence of the beginnings of the crippling and often fatal disease")[31] or textile dust (some 100,000 American cotton textile workers presently suffer breathing impairments caused by acute byssinosis, or brown lung, and another 35,000 former mill workers are totally disabled with chronic brown lung)[32] or asbestos fibers (it has been estimated that, under the lenient asbestos standard promulgated by OSHA in 1972, anywhere from 18,400 and 598,000 deaths from lung cancer would result from exposure to asbestos),[33] or coal tars ("workers who had been employed five or more years in the coke ovens died of lung cancer at a rate three and a half times that for all steelworkers"; coke oven workers develop cancer of the scrotum at a rate five times that of the general population).[34] Also, some 800,000 people suffer from occupationally related skin disease each year (according to a 1968 estimate by the U.S. surgeon general),[35] and "the number of American workers experiencing noise conditions that may damage their hearing is estimated [in a 1969 Public Health Service publication of the Department of Health, Education and Welfare] to be in excess of 6 million, and may even reach 16 million."[36]

To blame the workers for occupational disease and deaths is to ignore the history of governmental attempts to compel industrial firms to meet safety standards that would keep dangers (such as chemicals or fibers or dust particles in the air) that are outside the worker's control down to a safe level. This has been a continual struggle, with firms using everything from their own "independent" research institutes to more direct and often questionable forms of political pressure to influence government in the direction of loose standards and lax enforcement. So far, industry has been winning because OSHA has been given neither the personnel nor the mandate to fulfill its purpose. It is so understaffed that, in 1973, when 1,500 federal sky marshals guarded the nation's airplanes from hijackers, only 500 OSHA inspectors toured the nation's workplaces. By 1980, OSHA employed 1,581 compliance safety and health officers, but this still enabled inspection of only roughly 2 percent of the 2.5 million establishments covered by OSHA. The *New York Times* reports that in 1987 the number of OSHA inspectors was down to 1,044. As might be expected, the agency performs fewer inspections than it did a dozen years ago.[37] Don Lofgren, a former OSHA inspector, writes that

> because of understaffing, OSHA attorneys are sometimes forced to enter into penalty-slashing settlements just to keep a burgeoning backlog of cases at bay. Perhaps more influential, OSHA managers and attorneys know that appeal judges often discount penalties regardless of the formal procedures OSHA used in calculating the fine.[38]

According to a report issued by the AFL-CIO in 1992, 'The median penalty paid by an employer during the years 1972–1990 following an incident resulting in death or serious injury of a worker was just $480."[39] The same report claims that the federal government spends $1.1 billion a year to protect fish and wildlife and only $300 million a year to protect workers from health and safety hazards on the job.

An editorial in the January 1983 issue of the *American Journal of Public Health,* titled "Can Reagan Be Indicted for Betraying Public Health?" answers the question in its title affirmatively by listing the Reagan administration's attempts to cut back government support for public health programs. On the issue of occupational safety and health, the editorial states:

> The Occupational Safety and Health Administration (OSHA) has delayed the cotton and lead [safe exposure level] standards. It proposes to weaken the generic carcinogen policy, the labeling standard, the access to medical and exposure records standard. Mine fatalities are rising again, but the Mine Safety and Health Administration and OSHA enforcement have been cut back. Research on occupational safety and health has been slashed more than any other research program in the Department of Health and Human Services. The National Institute for Occupational Safety and Health funding in real dollars is lower in 1983 than at any time in the 12-year history of the Institute. Reporting and data requirements have been devastated.[40]

The editorial ends by asking rhetorically, "How can anyone believe that the Reagan Administration wishes to prevent disease or promote health or preserve public health in America?"

And so it goes on.

Is a person who kills another in a bar brawl a greater threat to society than a business executive who refuses to cut into his profits to make his plant a safe place to work? By any measure of death and suffering the latter is by far a greater danger than the former. Because he wishes his workers no harm, because he is only indirectly responsible for death and disability while pursuing legitimate economic goals, his acts are not called "crimes." Once we free our imagination from the blinders of the one-on-one model of crime, can there be any doubt that the criminal justice system does not protect us from the gravest threats to life and limb? It seeks to protect us when danger comes from a young, lower-class male in the inner city. When a threat comes from an upper-class business executive in an office, the criminal justice system looks the other way. This is in the face of growing evidence that for every three American citizens murdered by thugs, at least four American workers are killed by the recklessness of their bosses and the indifference of their government.

Health Care May Be Dangerous to Your Health

More than 25 years ago, when the annual number of willful homicides in the nation was about 10,000, the President's Commission on Law Enforcement and Administration of Justice reported that

> A recent study of emergency medical care found the quality, numbers, and distribution of ambulances and other emergency services severely deficient, and estimated that as many as *20,000 Americans die unnecessarily each year* as a result of improper emergency care. The means necessary for correcting this situation are very clear and would probably yield greater immediate return in reducing death than would expenditures for reducing the incidence of crimes of violence.[41]

On July 15, 1975, Dr. Sidney Wolfe of Ralph Nader's Public Interest Health Research Group testified before the House Commerce Oversight and Investigations Subcommittee that there "were 3.2 million cases of unnecessary surgery performed each year in the United States." These unneeded operations, Wolfe added, "cost close to $5 billion a year and kill as many as 16,000 Americans."[42] Wolfe's estimates of unnecessary surgery were based on studies comparing the operations performed and surgery recommended by doctors who are paid for the operations they do with those performed and recommended by salaried doctors who receive no extra income from surgery.

The figure accepted by Dr. George A. Silver, professor of public health at the Yale University School of Medicine, is 15,000 deaths a year "attributable to unnecessary surgery."[43] Silver places the annual cost of excess surgery at $4.8 billion.[44] In an article on an experimental program by Blue Cross and Blue Shield aimed at curbing unnecessary surgery, Newsweek reports that

> a Congressional committee earlier this year [1976] estimated that more than 2 million of the elective operations performed in 1974 were not only unnecessary—but also killed about 12,000 patients and cost nearly $4 billion.[45]

Because the number of surgical operations performed in the United States rose from 16.7 million in 1975 to 22.4 million in 1991,[46] there is reason to believe that at least somewhere between (the congressional committee's estimate of) 12,000 and (and Dr. Wolfe's estimate of) 16,000 people a year still die from unnecessary surgery. In 1991, the FBI reported that 3,405 murders were committed by a "cutting or stabbing instrument."[47] Obviously, the FBI does not include the scalpel as a cutting or stabbing instrument. If they did, they would have had to report that between 15,405 and 19,405 persons were killed by "cutting or stabbing" in 1991—depending on whether you take Congress's figure or Wolfe's. No matter how you slice it, the scalpel may be more dangerous than the switchblade.

And this is only a fraction of the problem: Data from the Harvard Medical Practice Study (based on over 30,000 records from New York State Hospitals in 1984 and extrapolated to the American population as a whole) indicate that more than 1.3 million Americans are injured by medical treatment, and that "each year 150,000 people die from, rather than in spite of, their medical treatment."[48] One of the authors of the study, Dr. Lucian Leape, a surgeon and lecturer at the Harvard School of Public Health, suggests that one-quarter of these deaths are due to negligence, and two-thirds are preventable.

While they are at it, the FBI should probably add the hypodermic needle and the prescription to their list of potential murder weapons. Silver points out that these are also death-dealing instruments.

Of the 6 billion doses of antibiotic medicines administered each year by injection or prescription, it is estimated that 22 percent are unnecessary. Of the doses given, 10,000 result in fatal or near-fatal reactions. Somewhere between 2,000 and 10,000 deaths probably would not have occurred if the drugs, meant for the patient's benefit, had not been given.[49]

These estimates are supported by the Harvard Medical Practice Study. Its authors write that, of the 1.3 million medical injuries, 19 percent (247,000) were related to medications, and 14 percent of these (34,580) resulted in permanent injury or death.[50]

The danger continues. The Public Citizen Health Research Group reports in its *Health Letter* of October 1988 that

> two major U.S. drug companies—Lilly and SmithKline—have pleaded guilty to criminal charges for having withheld information from the Food and Drug Administration (FDA) about deaths and life-threatening adverse drug reactions.

The response of the Justice Department has been predictably merciful:

> SmithKline, the actions of whose executives resulted in at least . . . 36 deaths, pleaded guilty to 14 criminal misdemeanor counts and was fined $34,000. Lilly and its executives, whose criminal negligence was responsible for deaths to at least 49 Americans . . . , were slapped on the wrist with a total of $45,000 in fines.[51]

In fact, if someone had the temerity to publish a *Uniform Crime Reports* that really portrayed the way Americans are murdered, the FBI's statistics on the *type of weapon* used in murder would have to be changed for 1991 from those shown in Table 1A to something like those shown in Table 1B.

The figures shown in Table 1B would give American citizens a much more honest picture of what threatens them—though remember how conservative the estimates of noncriminal harm are. Nonetheless, we are not likely to see such a

chart broadcast by the criminal justice system, perhaps because it would also give American citizens a more honest picture of *who* threatens them.

We should not leave this topic without noting that, aside from the other losses it imposes, unnecessary surgery was estimated to have cost between $4 billion and $5 billion in 1974. The price of medical care has roughly quadrupled between 1974 and 1991. Thus, assuming that the same number of unneeded operations were performed in 1991, the cost of unnecessary surgery would be between $16 and $20 billion. To this we should add the unnecessary 22 percent of the 6 billion administered doses of medication. Even at the extremely conservative estimate of $3 a dose, this adds about $4 billion. In short, assuming that earlier trends have continued, there is reason to believe that unnecessary surgery and medication cost the public between $20 and $24 billion annually—far outstripping the $15.1 billion taken by thieves that concern the FBI.[52] This gives us yet another way in which we are robbed of more money by practices that are not treated as criminal than by practices that are. . . .

Summary

Once again, our investigations lead to the same result. The criminal justice system does not protect us against the gravest threats to life, limb, or possessions. Its definitions of crime are not simply a reflection of the objective dangers that threaten us. The workplace [and] the medical profession . . . lead to far more human suffering, far more death and disability, and take far more dollars from our pockets than the murders, aggravated assaults, and thefts reported annually by the FBI. What is more, this human suffering is preventable. A government really intent on protecting our well-being could enforce work safety regulations [or] police the medical profession . . . but it does not. Instead we hear a lot of cant about law and order and a lot of rant about crime in the streets. It is as if our leaders were not only refusing to protect us from the major threats to our well-being but trying to cover up this refusal by diverting our attention to crime—as if this were the only real threat.

TABLE 1A *How Americans Are Murdered*

Total	Firearms	Knife or Other Cutting Instrument	Other Weapon: Club, Arson, Poison, Strangulation, etc.	Personal Weapon: Hands, Fists, etc.
21,505*	14,265	3,405	2,642	1,193

*Note that this figure diverges somewhat from the figure of murders and nonnegligent manslaughters used elsewhere in the FBI *Uniform Crime Reports,* 1991, since the FBI has data on the weapons used in only 21,505 of the reported murders.

Source: FBI *Uniform Crime Reports,* 1991 "Murder Victims: Weapons Used, 1987–1991."

TABLE 1B *How Americans Are (Really) Murdered*

Total	Occupational Hazard & Disease	Inadequate Emergency Medical Care	Knife or Other Cutting Instrument Including Scalpel	Firearms	Other Weapon: Club, Poison, Hypodermic, Prescription Drug,	Personal Weapon: Hands, Fists, etc.
90,105	34,600	20,000	15,405*	14,265	4,642*	1,193

*These figures represent the relevant figures in Table 1A plus the most conservative figures for the relevant categories discussed in the text.

As we have seen, the criminal justice system is a carnival mirror that presents a distorted image of what threatens us. The distortions do not end with the definitions of crime. . . . New distortions enter at every level of the system, so that in the end, when we look in our prisons to see who really threatens us, all we see are poor people. By that time, virtually all the well-to-do people who endanger us have been discreetly weeded out of the system. . . . All the mechanisms by which the criminal justice system comes down more frequently and more harshly on the poor criminal than on the well-off criminal take place after most of the dangerous acts of the well-to-do have been excluded from the definition of crime itself. The bias against the poor within the criminal justice system is all the more striking when we recognize that the door to that system is shaped in a way that excludes in advance the most dangerous acts of the well-to-do. . . .

NOTES

1. *Washington Post,* January 11, 1983. p. C10.
2. This answers Graeme Newman, who observes that most criminals on TV are white, and wonders what the "ruling class" or conservatives have to gain by deny-ing the criminality of Blacks." Graeme R. Newman, "Popular Culture and Criminal Justice: A Preliminary Analysis," *Journal of Criminal Justice* 18 (1990), pp. 261–74.
3. Newman, "Popular Culture and Criminal Justice: A Preliminary Analysis," pp. 263–64.
4. Barbara Matusow, "If It Bleeds, It Leads," *Washingtonian,* January 1988, p. 102.
5. "Titillating Channels: TV Is Going Tabloid As Shows Seek Sleaze and Find Profits, Too," *Wall Street Journal,* May 18, 1988, p. 1.
6. "Crime in America: The Shocking Truth," *McCall's,* March 1987, p. 144.
7. Hyman Gross. *A Theory of Criminal Justice* (New York: Oxford University Press, 1979), p. 78. See generally Chapter 3, "Culpability, Intention, Motive," which I have drawn upon in making the argument of this and the following two paragraphs.
8. Nancy Frank, "Unintended Murder and Corporate Risk-Taking: Defining the Concept of Justifiability," *Journal of Criminal Justice* 16 (1988), p. 18.
9. For example, see John Harris, "The Marxist Conception of Violence," *Philosophy & Public Affairs* 3, no. 2 (Winter 1974), pp. 192–220; Jonathan Glover, *Causing Death and Saving Lives* (Hammondsworth, England: Penguin, 1977), pp. 92–112; and James Rachels, *The End of Life* (Oxford: Oxford University Press, 1986), pp. 106–50.

10. *Model Penal Code,* Final Draft (Philadelphia: American Law Institute, 1962).

11. Russell Mokhiber, *Corporate Crime and Violence: Big Business Power and the Abuse of Public Trust* (San Francisco: Sierra Club, 1988), pp. 278, 285.

12. David E. Lilienfeld, "The Silence: The Asbestos Industry and Early Occupational Cancer Research—A Case Study," *American Journal of Public Health* 81, no. 6 (June 1991), p. 791. This article shows how early the asbestos industry knew of the link between asbestos and cancer and how hard they tried to suppress this information. See also Paul Brodeur, *Outrageous Misconduct: The Asbestos Industry on Trial* (New York: Pantheon, 1985).

13. Sir James Fitzjames Stephen, from his *History of the Criminal Law of England* 2 (1883), excerpted in *Crime, Law and Society,* eds., Abraham S. Goldstein and Joseph Goldstein (New York: Free Press, 1971), p. 21.

14. Troy Duster, *The Legislation of Morality: Law, Drugs and Moral Judgment* (New York: Free Press, 1970), pp. 3–76.

15. *UCR-1991,* pp. 13, 31; *UCR-1992,* pp. 58, 381.

16. *UCR-1992,* p. 36.

17. *The President's Report on Occupational Safety and Health* (Washington, D.C.: U.S. Government Printing Office, 1972).

18. "James Messerschmidt, in a comprehensive review of research studies on job related accidents, determined that somewhere between 35 and 57 percent of those accidents occurred because of direct safety violations by the employer. Laura Shill Schraeger and James Short, Jr. found 30 percent of industrial accidents resulted from safety violations and another 20 percent resulted from unsafe working conditions." Kappeler et al., *Mythology of Crime and Criminal Justice,* p. 104. See James Messerschmidt, *Capitalism, Patriarchy, and Crime: Toward a Socialist Feminist Criminology* (New Jersey: Rowman and Littlefield, 1986); and Laura Shill Schraeger and James Short, "Toward a Sociology of Organizational Crime," *Social Problems* 25 (April 1978), pp. 407–419. See also Joseph A. Page and Mary-Win O'Brien, *Bitter Wages: Ralph Nader's Study Group Report on Disease and Injury on the Job* (New York: Grossman, 1973); Rachel Scott, *Muscle and Blood* (New York: Dutton, 1974); Jeanne M. Stellman and Susan M. Daum, *Work Is Dangerous to Your Health* (New York: Vintage, 1973); Fran Lynn "The Dust in Willie's Lungs," *Nation* 222, no. 7 (February 21, 1976), pp. 209–12; and Joel Swartz, "Silent Killers at Work," *Crime and Social Justice* 3 (Summer 1975), pp. 15–20.

19. *President's Report on Occupational Safety and Health,* p. 111; National Safety Council, *Accident Facts* 1992, pp. 39, 50.

20. National Safety Council, *Accident Facts* 1992, pp. 39.

21. *Report of the President to the Congress on Occupational Safety and Health,* 1980 (August 4, 1981), p. 86, reporting on deaths and illnesses for 1979. Robert Johnson, who has conducted extensive interviews with present and former textile workers suffering from brown lung, indicates that another reason for the underreporting of occupational disease is that workers are often hesitant to admit symptoms for fear of being seen as "defective" or "worn out" and therefore losing their jobs (personal communication).

22. Robert Reid, "How Accurate Are Safety and Health Statistics?" *Occupational Hazards,* March 1987, p. 49.

23. "Is OSHA Falling Down on the Job?" *New York Times,* August 2, 1987, pp. A1, A6.

24. Letter from Schweiker to B. J. Pigg, Executive Director of the Asbestos Information Association, dated April 29, 1982.

25. Edward Sondik, "Progress in Cancer Prevention and Control," in Russell Maulitz, ed., *Unnatural Causes: Three Leading Killer Diseases in America* (New Brunswick: Rutgers University Press, 1989), p. 117.

26. Philip Landrigan, Testimony before the Senate Committee on Labor and Human Resources, April 18, 1988, p. 2. For cancer deaths, see StatAbst-1988, p. 77, Table no. 117, and p. 80, Table no. 120.

27. "Safety Group Cites Fatalities Linked to Work," *Wall Street Journal,* August 31, 1990, p. B8; and Sally Squires, "Study Traces More Deaths to Working than Driving," *Washington Post,* August 31, 1990, p. A7.

28. BJS, *Criminal Victimization,* 1991, p. 5.

29. Susan Q. Stranahan, "Why 115,000 Workers Will Die This Year," *Boston Sunday Globe,* March 21, 1976, p. A4.

30. National Safety Council, *Accident Facts* 1992, pp. 34–35.

31. Philip J. Hilts, "U.S. Fines Mine Companies for False Air Tests," *New York Times,* April 5, 1991, p. A12. The fines, by the way, amounted to a total of $5 million distributed among 500 mining companies found to have tampered with the coal dust samples used to test for the risk of black lung disease.

32. Joan Claybrook and the Staff of Public Citizen, *Retreat from Safety: Reagan's Attack on America's Health* (New York: Pantheon, 1984), p. 83. Chronic brown lung is a severely disabling occupational

respiratory disease. For a description of its impact on its victims, see Robert Johnson, "Labored Breathing: Living with Brown Lung," paper presented at the Annual Meeting of the American Society of Criminology, Fall 1982, Toronto, Canada. See also Page and O'Brien, *Bitter Wages,* p. 18.

33. Claybrook, *Retreat from Safety,* p. 97. See also Page and O'Brien, *Bitter Wages,* p. 23; and Scott, *Muscle and Blood,* p. 196.

34. Scott, *Muscle and Blood,* pp. 45–46; cf. Page and O'Brien, *Bitter Wages,* p. 25.

35. Page and O'Brien, *Bitter Wages,* p. 37.

36. Ibid., p. 45.

37. "Is OSHA Falling Down on the Job?" pp. A1, A6.

38. Don J. Lofgren, *Dangerous Premises: An Insider's View of OSHA Enforcement* (Ithaca, N.Y.: ILR Press/Cornell University, 1989), p. 223.

39. Frank Swoboda, "More for Wildlife Than for Workers." *Washington Post,* April 28, 1992, p. Al3.

40. Anthony Robbins, "Can Reagan Be Indicted for Betraying Public Health?" *American Journal of Public Health,* 73, no. 1 (January 1983), p 13.

41. *Challenge,* p. 52 (emphasis added). See also p. 3 for then-prevailing homicide rates.

42. *Washington Post,* July 16, 1975, p. A3.

43. George A. Silver, "The Medical Insurance Disease," *Nation,* 222, no. 12 (March 27, 1976), p. 369.

44. Ibid., p. 371.

45. *Newsweek,* March 29, 1976, p. 67. Lest anyone think this is a new problem, compare this passage written in a popular magazine over 40 years ago:

In an editorial on medical abuse, the *Journal of the Medical Association of Georgia* referred to "surgeons who paradoxically are often cast in the role of the supreme hero by the patient and family and at the same time may be doing the greatest amount of harm to the individual."

Unnecessary operations on women, stemming from the combination of a trusting patient and a split fee, have been so deplored by honest doctors that the phrase "rape of the pelvis" has been used to describe them. The American College of Surgeons, impassioned foe of fee-splitting, has denounced unnecessary hysterectomies, uterine suspensions, Caesarian

sections. [Howard Whitman, "Why Some Doctors Should Be in Jail," *Colliers,* October 30, 1953, p. 24.]

46. *StatAbst-1988,* p. 97, Table no. 153; and American Hospital Association, *Hospital Statistics 1992–93,* p. xlv.

47. *UCR-1991,* p. 17.

48. Paul Weiler, Howard Hiatt, Joseph Newhouse, William Johnson, Troyen Brennan, and Lucian Leape, *A Measure of Malpractice: Medical Injury, Malpractice Litigation and Patient Compensation* (Cambridge, Mass.: Harvard University Press, 1993), p. 137. The data given here come from the Harvard Medical Practice Study. See also Christine Russell, "Human Error: Avoidable Mistakes Kill 100,000 Patients a Year," *Washington Post Health,* February 18, 1992, p. 7.

49. Silver, "The Medical Insurance Disease," p. 369. Silver's estimates are extremely conservative. Some studies suggest that between 30,000 and 160,000 individuals die as a result of drugs prescribed by their doctors. See Boyce Rensberger, "Thousands a Year Killed by Faulty Prescriptions," *New York Times,* January 28, 1976, p. A1, Al 7. If we assume with Silver that at least 20 percent are unnecessary, this puts the annual death toll from unnecessary prescriptions at between 6,000 and 32,000 persons. For an in-depth look at the recklessness with which prescription drugs are put on the market and the laxness with which the Food and Drug Administration exercises its mandate to protect the public, see the series of eight articles by Morton Mintz, "The Medicine Business," *Washington Post,* June 27–30, July 14, 1976.

50. Weiler et al., *A Measure of Malpractice: Medical Injury, Malpractice Litigation and Patient Compensation,* p. 54.

51. "More Crime in the Drug and Device Industry," *Health Letter,* October 1988, p. 12.

52. Rate of increase of medical costs is calculated from StatAbst-1992, p. 104, Table no. 151. Note that the assumption that the *number* of unnecessary operations and prescriptions has remained the same between 1974 and 1991 is a conservative assumption in that it effectively assumes that the rate of these practices relative to the population has declined because population has increased in the period.

Elvis's DNA

Dorothy Nelkin and M. Susan Lindee

In popular culture, Elvis Presley has become a genetic construct, driven by his genes to his unlikely destiny. In a 1985 biography, for example, Elaine Dundy attributed Presley's success to the genetic characteristics of his mother's multi-ethnic family: "Genetically speaking," she wrote, "what produced Elvis was quite a mixture." To his "French Norman blood was added Scots-Irish blood," as well as "the Indian strain supplying the mystery and the Jewish strain supplying spectacular showmanship." All this, combined with his "circumstances, social conditioning, and religious upbringing . . . [produced] the enigma that was Elvis."[1] Dundy traced Elvis's musical talents to his father (who "had a very good voice") and his mother (who had "the instincts of a performer"). His parents did provide a musical environment, Dundy noted, but "even without it, one wonders if Elvis, with his biological musical equipment would not still have become a virtuoso."[2]

Another Elvis biographer, Albert Goldman, focused on his subject's "bad" genes, describing him as "the victim of a fatal hereditary disposition."[3] . . . Goldman attributed Elvis's character to ancestors who constituted "a distinctive breed of southern yeomanry" commonly known as hillbillies. A genealogy research organization, Goldman said, had traced Presley's lineage back nine generations to a nineteenth-century "coward, deserter and bigamist." In Goldman's narrative, this genetic heritage explained Elvis's downfall: his addiction to drugs and alcohol, his emotional disorders, and his premature death were all in his genes. His fate was a readout of his DNA.

The idea that "good" and "bad" character traits (and destinies) are the consequence of "good" and "bad" genes appears in a wide range of popular sources. In these works the gene is described in moral terms, and it seems to dictate the actions of criminals, celebrities, political leaders, and literary and scientific figures. Films present stories of "tainted blood," and "born achievers," of success and failure, of kindness and cruelty, all written in the genes. The most complicated human traits are also blamed on DNA. Media sources feature jokes about Republican genes, MBA genes, lawyer genes, and public interest genes.[4] Human behaviors linked to DNA in these accounts range from the trivial—a preference for flashy belt buckles—to the tragic—a desire to murder children.

Such popular constructions of behavior draw on the increasing public legitimacy of the scientific field of behavioral genetics. Behavioral geneticists have been able to demonstrate that some relatively complicated behaviors— certainly in experimental animals and possibly in human beings—are genetically determined.[5] Studies of animals reveal the genetic bases of survival instincts, mating rituals, and certain aspects of learning and memory. Border collies herd sheep in a unique, characteristic way whether they have been trained or not, even if they have never seen sheep before. Some behaviors associated with particular hormones have been indirectly linked to genes: Both aggressive and nurturing behaviors—in mice—can be manipulated with adjustments of hormone levels. Though such research highlights the biological events involved in some behaviors, it does not support the popular idea that genes determine human personality traits or such complex phenomena as success, failure, political leanings, or criminality. . . .

Evil in the Genes

The existence of evil has posed problems for philosophers and theologians for much of human history. Religious systems have personified evil as a supernatural being; folklore has located it in natural disaster, mythical beasts, or the "evil eye."[6] Evil can be seen as the cosmic consequence of fate (the [bad] "luck of the draw") or the result of voluntary human action or moral failure. The agents invoked to explain the presence of evil are commonly powerful, abstract, and invisible—demons, gods, witches, a marked soul, and, today, the biochemistry of the brain. Environmental contingencies, similarly powerful and abstract—such as patterns of authority (Stanley Milgram) or social reinforcement (B. F. Skinner)[7]—have also been seen as the sources of evil. But the belief that the "devil made me do it" does not significantly differ in its consequences from the belief that "my genes made me do it." Both seek to explain behavior that threatens the social contract; both locate control over human fate in powerful abstract entities capable of dictating human action in ways that mitigate moral responsibility and alleviate personal blame.

The response to research on the so-called criminal chromosome suggests the appeal of this view. In 1965 the British cytogeneticist Patricia Jacobs found that a disproportionate number of men in an Edinburgh correctional institution, instead of being XY (normal) males, were XYY males. Jacobs suggested that the extra Y chromosome "predisposes its carriers to unusually aggressive behavior."[8] Other researchers later questioned whether XYY males were more aggressive, suggesting instead that they suffered from diminished intellectual functioning that made it more likely that they would be incarcerated. And the original estimate of the rate of XYY males occurring in the population in general was later revised upward, so that the difference in the prison population and the general population appeared to be less great than it had once seemed.

But the "criminal chromosome" had a remarkable popular life, first attracting the attention of the press in April 1968 when it was invoked to explain one of the most gruesome crimes of the decade. A *New York Times* reporter wrote that Richard Speck, then awaiting sentencing in the murder, one night, of nine student nurses,

planned to appeal his case on the grounds that he was XYY. This story—which was incorrect (Speck was an XY male)—provoked a public debate about the causes of criminal behavior. *Newsweek* asked if criminals were "Born bad?" ("Can a man be born a criminal?") *Time* headlined a story "Chromosomes and crime."[9] By the early 1970s, at least two films had featured an XYY male criminal, and a series of crime novels had made their focus an XYY hero who struggled with his compulsion to commit crimes.[10]

References to the criminal chromosome continued to shape popular views of violence. In 1986, the *New York Times* asked "Should such persons [XYY males] be held responsible for their crimes, or treated as victims of conditions for which they are not responsible, on a par with the criminally insane?"[11] And in 1992, a PBS series on "The Mind" introduced a segment on violence: "Recent research suggests that even the acts of a serial killer may have a biological or genetic basis."[12] Similarly, Donahue advised his listeners on "how to tell if your child is a serial killer." His guest, a psychiatrist, described a patient who had been raised in a "Norman Rockwell" setting but then, driven by his extra Y chromosome, killed 11 women.[13]

News reporters and talk show hosts refer to "bad seeds,"[14] "criminal genes,"[15] and "alcohol genes"[16]; CBS talk show host Oprah Winfrey found it meaningful to ask a twin on her show whether her sister's "being bad" was "in her blood?"[17] In the movie *JFK* one character tells another, "You're as crazy as your mama—Goes to show it's in the genes."[18] To a *New York Times* writer, evil is "embedded in the coils of chromosomes that our parents pass to us at conception."[19] . . .

Genetic or biological explanations of "bad" behavior are sufficiently prevalent to serve as a common source of irony. A segment of the comic strip "Calvin and Hobbes" featured Calvin's perplexed father asking his son: "You've been hitting rocks in the house? What on earth would make you do something like that?" Calvin replied: "Poor genetic material."[20] In another strip, Calvin described a vicious "snow snake": "I suppose if I had two Y chromosomes I'd feel hostile too!"[21] And a barroom cartoon by Nick Downes portrayed "Dead-Eye Dan, known far and wide for his fast gun, mean temper and extra Y chromosome."[22] . . .

Some individuals, so the media imply, are "born to kill" and will do so despite environmental advantages. In December 1991 a fourteen-year-old high school boy was arrested for the murder of a schoolmate. The *New York Times* account of this event interpreted it as a key piece of evidence in "the debate over whether children misbehave because they had bad childhoods or because they are just bad seeds." The boy's parents had provided a good home environment, the reporter asserted; they had "taken the children to church almost every Sunday, and sacrificed to send them to a Catholic grammar school." Yet their son had been arrested for murder. This troubling inconsistency between the child's apparently decent background and his violent behavior called for explanation. The reporter resolved the mystery through the explanatory power of inheritance: The moral of the story was clearly stated in its headline: "Raising Children Right Isn't Always Enough." The implications? There are, indeed "bad seeds."[23] . . .

This same theme appeared in the news reports of a debate over the body and blood of Westley Allan Dodd, a serial killer of children who was hanged in January 1993. Dodd insisted that he could not be cured and that if he had the opportunity he would kill again and "enjoy it." His ordinary childhood offered no convincing explanation for his monstrous behavior. He had not been an abused child. After Dodd's execution, scientists attempted to obtain pieces of his brain and vials of his blood to determine whether his behavior could be attributed to neurological abnormalities or "gene oddities."[24] Such stories arise from a conflict between childhood experience and adult behavior; when the two seem to conflict, biological predisposition seems to provide a plausible and appealing resolution.

Research that links criminal behavior to biological forces fuels the hope that genetic information will make possible the prediction, and therefore the control, of deviant behavior.[25] Certain scientists encourage such expectations. In a 1992 *Science* editorial the journal's editor, biologist Daniel Koshland, told stories about acts of violence: "An elephant goes berserk at the circus, an elderly pillar of the community is discovered to be a child molester, a man admits to killing many young boys . . . a disgruntled employee shoots seven co-workers." Each crime, wrote Koshland, had a common origin—an abnormality of the brain.[26]

Some researchers who study aggression pique media interest by bringing their work directly to the public. In a *Psychology Today* article called "Crime in the Family Tree," behavioral psychologist Sarnoff Mednick reported that studies of adopted twins demonstrate the importance of heredity as a cause of crime: Among those boys with a biological parent who had a criminal record, 20 percent were themselves convicted. Where an adoptive parent had a criminal record, only 14.7 percent had been convicted.[27] In a *New York Times* essay called "The Aggressors," anthropologist Melvin Konner stated that the tendency for people to do harm to others is "intrinsic, fundamental, natural."[28] Such reports from scientific authorities imply there is definitive evidence for the importance of genetic predisposition as a cause of criminal behavior. . . .

Even when scientists emphasize the complexity of biological and environmental conditions that could lead to violence, media accounts highlight the importance of genetics. The press coverage of the National Research Council's 1992 report on the state of research on violence is a case in point.[29] The report said that violence arises from the "interactions among individuals' psychosocial development, neurological and hormonal differences, and social processes." It stressed the uncertain implications of research when it came to genetic influence on antisocial behavior: "These studies suggest at most a weak role for genetic processes in influencing potentials for violent behavior. The correlations and concordances of behavior in two of the three studies are consistent with a positive genetic effect, but are statistically insignificant." While not ruling out genetic processes, the NRC suggested: "If genetic predispositions to violence are discovered, they are likely to involve many genes and substantial environmental interaction rather than any simple genetic marker."

Only 14 of the 464 pages of the NRC report actually dealt with biological perspectives on violence, and less than 2 pages were about genetics. Nevertheless, the *New York Times* headlined its article about the report "Study Cites Role of Biological and Genetic Factors in Violence."[30] Genes appear far more newsworthy than social or economic circumstances as a source of antisocial behavior. While genetic theories of violence have been controversial, denounced as politically and racially motivated . . . some journalists have dismissed critiques as "politically correct." In April 1993 *Time,* looking for the causes of "the savagery that is sweeping America," suggested that society's ills cannot fully be responsible, that violence may be caused by "errant genes." "Science could help shed light on the roots of violence and offer new solutions for society. But not if the research is suppressed."[31]

Biological theories also appeal as explanations of group violence and war. A 1991 social psychology textbook uses "genetic similarity theory" to explain "the tendency to dislike members of groups other than our own." Discrimination against those who are different, say the authors, is part of inherited human tendencies to defend those possessing similar genes.[32] Extending this idea to explain war, a *Discover* journalist described a study of chimps and speculated whether "war runs in our genes like baldness or diabetes?"[33] . . .

Some biologists and social scientists have criticized research on the genetic predisposition to organized aggression for concealing inadequate methodologies behind quantitative data and for minimizing the influence of social, political, and economic factors on aggressive behavior. In May 1986, Goldstein helped assemble a group of these critics to discuss biological theories about the origin of warfare. Meeting in Spain, they produced the Seville Statement on Violence, which strongly repudiated the idea that war is biologically necessary or genetically controlled. "It is scientifically incorrect to say that war is caused by 'instinct' or any single motivation . . . scientifically incorrect to say that humans have a 'violent brain' . . . scientifically incorrect to say that in the course of human evolution there has been a selection for aggressive behavior more than for other kinds of behavior." The statement concluded that "biology does not condemn humanity to war. The

same species who invented war is capable of inventing peace."[34] . . .

The interest in "bad genes"—the genes for deviance—reflects a tendency to medicalize social problems.[35] This is especially evident in scientific and social speculation about the nature and etiology of addiction. Definitions of alcoholism have shifted over time from sin to sickness, from moral transgression to medical disease, depending on prevailing social, political and moral agendas.[36] Debates over the etiology of alcoholism go back to ancient Rome, but the modern conception of alcoholism as a disease is usually attributed to the nineteenth-century theories of Benjamin Rush (1745–1813). Early leaders of the American temperance movement, likewise, defined alcoholism as a disease, but when the movement began to advocate outright prohibition, alcoholism was redefined, along with syphilis and opiate addiction, as a "vice"—a manifestation of immoral behavior. A moral concept of voluntary addiction replaced the model of disease, and the politics of prohibition in the 1920s turned alcoholism into a problem more legal than medical. At the same time, eugenicists were compiling family studies supposedly demonstrating its inherited nature.

In 1935 E. M. Jellinek, reviewing the biological literature on alcoholism for a major Carnegie Foundation report, formulated a medical model that explained alcoholism in terms of the interaction of alcohol with an individual's physical and psychological characteristics and his or her social circumstances.[37] This analysis focused attention on what made people susceptible. The same year, Alcoholics Anonymous was founded on the doctrine that alcoholism was a compelling biological drive that could be cured only by total abstinence and moral rectitude. AA's position contributed to the revival of the medical model, promoting the idea that alcoholics had "predisposing characteristics" that distinguished them from others.[38] This view has persisted, in its contemporary form focusing on the genetic basis of alcoholism.

Common observation shows that alcoholism runs in families. As in the case of violence, however, this in itself does not reveal the cause. Many traits run in families—poverty, for example, or poor manners—without being a consequence of heredity. The prevalence of alcoholism in certain families could reflect role models, the availability of alcohol, or the reaction to abuse. Nevertheless, a common perception was expressed in a 1989 article in *Omni:* "Addicted to the bottle? It may be in your genes."[39] The gene for alcoholism became a theme on the Oprah Winfrey and Phil Donahue shows. . . .

Assumptions about the genetic basis of alcoholism have extended to other addictions: smoking, overeating, shopping, and gambling. Some news reports on diet control begin from the assumption that genetics is the underlying reality that determines obesity; "Where Fat is a Problem, Heredity is the Answer," read a 1990 headline in the *New York Times.*[40] In another *Times* story, this one on smoking, a journalist wrote: "Smoking has to do with genetics, and the degree to which we are all prisoners of our genes. . . . You're destined to be trapped by certain aspects of your personality. The best you can do is put a leash on them."[41] And in a "Dear Abby" column, a lifelong smoker announced that he had no intention of stopping. His reasoning? "Heredity plays a major role in how long we live—not diet and exercise, jogging and aerobics, or any of the other foolishness that health freaks advocate." His father was 86 and in perfect health, so he felt free to smoke, "eat ham and eggs fried in butter," and "steak and baked potatoes with plenty of sour cream."[42] . . .

To explain addictive behavior in absolute genetic or biological terms is to extract it from the social setting that defines and interprets behavior. There are no criminal genes or alcohol genes, only genes for the proteins that influence hormonal and physiological processes. And only the most general outline of social behavior can be genetically coded.[43] Even behaviors known to be genetically inscribed, such as the human ability to learn spoken language, do not appear if the environment does not promote them. Children do not learn to speak unless they hear spoken language, even though the ability to speak is genetic, a biological trait of the human species. In the case of alcoholism, for example, any biological or genetic predisposition that may exist can only become a full-blown pattern of behavior in an environment in which alcohol is readily available and socially approved. As this suggests, there are many interests at stake in the etiology of addiction, for causal explanations for addiction imply moral judgments about responsibility and blame.

If defined as a sin, alcoholism represents an individual's flaunting of social norms; if defined as a social problem, it represents a failure of the community environment; if defined as intrinsic to the product consumed, it represents the need for alcohol regulation. But if defined as a genetically determined trait, neither society nor the alcohol industry appears responsible. And if behavior is completely determined either by genetics or environment, even the addicted individual cannot really be blamed. . . .

The appropriation of DNA . . . to explain individual differences recasts common beliefs about the importance of heredity in powerful scientific terms. Science becomes a way to empower prevailing beliefs, justifying existing social categories and expectations as based on natural forces. The great, the famous, the rich and successful, are what they are because of their genes. So too, the deviant and the dysfunctional are genetically fated. Opportunity is less important than predisposition. Some are destined for success, others for problems or, at least, a lesser fate. The star—or the criminal—is not made but born.

This is a particularly striking theme in American society, where the very foundation of the democratic experiment was the belief in the improvability, indeed, the perfectibility of all human beings. Belief in genetic destiny implies there are natural limits constraining the possibilities for both individuals and for social groups. Humankind is not perfectible, because the species' flaws and failings are inscribed in an unchangeable text—the DNA—that will persist in creating murderers, addicts, the insane, and the incompetent, even under the most ideal social circumstances. In popular stories, children raised in ideal homes become murderers and children raised in difficult home situations become well-adjusted high achievers. The moral? No possible social system, no ideal nurturing plan can prevent the violent acts that seem to threaten the social fabric of contemporary American life. Only biological controls, it seems, can solve such problems. . . .

NOTES

1. Elaine Dundy, *Elvis and Gladys* (New York: St. Martin's Press, 1985), 26. See discussion in Greil Marcus, *Dead Elvis: A Chronicle of a Cultural Obsession* (New York: Doubleday, 1991).

2. Dundy, *Elvis and Gladys,* 74.

3. Albert Goldman, *Elvis* (New York: McGraw-Hill, 1981), 57. See discussion in Greil Marcus, *Dead Elvis.*

4. See, for example, Alan Wexler, "Everything into the Pool," *Newsday,* 13 August 1993.

5. See special issue of *Science* 264 (17 June 1994), 1685–1739.

6. See, for example, the anthropological literature on witchcraft, e.g. Mary Douglas, *Purity and Danger* (London: Routledge, 1966).

7. Stanley Milgram, "Behavioral Studies of Obedience," *Journal of Abnormal and Social Psychology* 67 (1963), 371–378; and B. F. Skinner, *Beyond Freedom and Dignity* (New York: Knopf, 1971).

8. P. A. Jacobs, M. Bruton, M. M. Melville, R. P. Brittan, and W. F. McClement, "Aggressive Behavior, Mental Subnormality and the XYY Male," *Nature* 208 (1965), 1351–1352.

9. Cited in Jeremy Green, "Media Sensationalism and Science: The Case of the Criminal Chromosome," in Terry Shinn and Richard Whitley, eds., *Expository Science, Sociology of the Sciences Yearbook IX* (1985), 139–161. Green provides many examples of the generalizations conveyed in both scientific and popular accounts.

10. Ibid., 144.

11. *New York Times,* 23 April 1986.

12. Richard Hutton and George Page, "The Mind/The Brain Classroom Series," PBS video, 1992.

13. "The Donahue Show," 25 February 1993. The program is described in John Horgan, "Eugenics Revisited," *Scientific American,* June 1993, 123.

14. Maria Newman, "Raising Children Right Isn't Always Enough," *New York Times,* 22 December 1991.

15. James Fallows, "Born to Rob? Why Criminals Do It," *The Washington Monthly,* December 1985, 37.

16. George Nobbe, "Alcoholic Genes," *Omni,* May 1989, 37.

17. "The Oprah Winfrey Show," 24 August 1992.

18. JFK, Warner Bros., 1991.

19. Deborah Franklin, "What a Child Is Given," *New York Times Magazine,* 3 September 1989, 36.

20. *The Atlanta Journal and Constitution,* 17 April 1991.

21. Ibid., 6 February 1991.

22. Nick Downes, cartoon in *Science* 256 (24 April 1992), 547.

23. Maria Newman, "Raising Children Right."

24. Deann Glamser, "Killer's Brain Causes Clash," *USA Today,* 6 January 1993.

25. Fox Butterfield, "Studies Find a Family Link to Criminality," *New York Times,* 31 January 1992.

26. Daniel Koshland, "Elephants, Monstrosities, and the Law," *Science* 255:5046, 14 February 1992, 777.

27. Sarnoff Mednick, "Crime in the Family Tree," *Psychology Today,* March 1985, 17.

28. Melvin Konner, "The Aggressors," *New York Times Magazine,* 14 August 1988, 33–34.

29. National Academy of Sciences, National Research Council, *Understanding and Preventing Violence* (Washington, DC: National Academy Press, November 1992).

30. Fox Butterfield, "Study Cites Role of Biological and Genetic Factors in Violence," *New York Times,* 13 November 1992.

31. Anastasia Toufexis, "Seeking the Roots of Crime," *Time,* 19 April 1993, 52–53.

32. R. A. Baron and D. Byrne, *Social Psychology* (Boston: Allyn and Bacon, 1991), 202.

33. Michael Ghiglieri, "War Among the Chimps," *Discover,* November 1987, 66.

34. The Seville Statement and list of signatories is included in Anne E. Hunter, ed., *Genes and Gender VI: On Peace, War and Gender* (New York: Feminist Press, 1991), 168–171.

35. Peter Conrad and Joseph Schneider, eds., *Deviance and Medicalization* (St. Louis: C. V. Mosby, 1980).

36. Sheila B. Blume, M.D., "The Disease Concept of Alcoholism," *Journal of Psychiatric Treatment and Evaluation* 5 (1983), 417–478; David Musto, *The American Disease* (New Haven, CT: Yale University Press, 1973), and Joseph Gusfield, *The Culture of Public Problems* (Chicago: University of Chicago Press, 1981).

37. Republished in 1960 as E. M. Jellinek, *The Disease Concept of Alcoholism* (Highland Park, NJ: Hillhouse Press). See also Sheila B. Blume, M.D., "The Disease Concept of Alcoholism."

38. Conrad and Schneider, *Deviance.*

39. George Nobbe, "Alcoholic Genes."

40. See, for example, Irish Hall, "Diet Pills Return as Long-Term Medication Not Just Diet Aids," *New York Times,* 14 October 1992, and Gina Kolata, "Where Fat

Is a Problem Heredity Is the Answer," *New York Times,* 24 May 1990.

41. Laura Mansnerus, "Smoking: Is It a Habit or Is It Genetic?" *New York Times Magazine,* 4 October 1992.

42. "Dear Abby" column, "Smoker Has No Plans to Kick Lifelong Habit," *Delaware County Times,* 7 April 1993, 49.

43. Richard C. Lewontin, *Biology as Ideology* (New York: Harper and Row, 1992), 51.

THINKING ABOUT THE READINGS

The Saints and the Roughnecks

- Have you ever known someone who had a "bad reputation?" How did it affect people's perceptions of that person? Compare your own "deviant" activities during high school with those of the "Saints" and "Roughnecks." How were you able to overcome the potential negative effects of labeling? If you were labeled as a bad kid, how were you able to shed the label?

A Crime by Any Other Name . . .

- Why aren't the dangerous activities Reiman describes defined as serious crimes by our criminal justice system? Should they be? In other words, do you think a business executive who fails to pay for safety precautions, indirectly causing the deaths of several workers, should be considered a criminal in the same way as a mugger who kills a victim after a robbery? Why or why not? How should we as a society deal with dangerous practices that aren't considered crimes?

Elvis's DNA

- Why is there such a strong tendency in this society to look to biological causes of "bad" behavior? Who, in society, benefits from such explanations of deviance? What are their potential dangers? Suppose that criminal or addictive behavior (overeating, gambling, alcoholism, etc.) could, in fact, be traced to a single "deviant gene." What then would be the most effective way to control deviance? How would the existence of this gene affect the public perception of criminals and addicts? Would deviant identities be more or less stigmatized? Explain.

CHAPTER 8

Building Social Relationships
Family and Groups

Close relationships with other people form the foundations of our social lives. Whether we're talking about small voluntary groups, neighbors, friends, lovers, or blood relatives, the need for intimacy and belonging is the driving force behind much of human behavior. Like every other aspect of our lives, these relationships can only be understood within the broader social context. Laws, customs, and social institutions often regulate the way we form these relationships, how we act inside of them, and how we dispose of them when they are no longer working.

Consider, for instance, what we as a society allow to be called a "family." In "Exiles from Kinship," Kath Weston describes the dilemmas faced by people in homosexual unions who want to be considered legitimate families. In most societies, biology (in the form of blood ties or reproduction) is the key determinant of family status. Weston, however, thinks that things are changing in American society and that "chosen families"—those tied together simply by the bonds of affection—are gaining more legitimacy. Indeed, the growing number of cities with "domestic partnership" ordinances attests to this fact. Nevertheless, there is still a profound reluctance on the part of the public to grant homosexuals complete family status.

We read a lot these days about how the expectations and requirements of men's and women's roles in the family are changing. Most of the time the topic is framed in terms of the changing roles of women—their increasing participation in the working world, their greater economic power, and so on. These shifts have indeed created new challenges within the family. What has received less attention, however, has been the response of men to the changing landscape of family economics. In "No Man's Land," Kathleen Gerson looks at the confusion and discomfort many men experience due to the decline of the traditional male breadwinner role. She focuses specifically on what happens to men when they can no longer claim the rights, privileges, and duties of the "family provider," a role many simply assumed they'd occupy.

Exiles from Kinship

Kath Weston

*Indeed, it is not so much identical conclusions that prove minds
to be related as the contradictions that are common to them.*
—ALBERT CAMUS

Lesbian and gay San Francisco during the 1980s offered a fascinating opportunity to learn something about how ideologies arise and change as people lock in conflict, work toward reconciliation, reorganize relationships, establish or break ties, and agree to disagree. In an apartment on Valencia Street, a young lesbian reassured her gay friend that his parents would get over their initially negative reaction if he told them he was gay. On Polk Street, a 16-year-old searched for a place to spend the night because he had already come out to his parents and now he had nowhere to go. While two lovers were busy organizing an anniversary party that would bring blood relations together with their gay families, a woman on the other side of the city reported to work as usual because she feared losing her job if her employer should discover that she was mourning the passing of her partner, who had died the night before. For every lesbian considering parenthood, several friends worried about the changes children would introduce into peer relationships. For every eight or nine people who spoke with excitement about building families of friends, one or two rejected gay families as an oppressive accommodation to a heterosexual society.

Although not always codified or clear, the discourse on gay families that emerged during the 1980s challenged many cultural representations and common practices that have effectively denied lesbians and gay men access to kinship. In earlier decades gay people had also fought custody battles, brought partners home to meet their parents, filed suit against discriminatory insurance policies, and struggled to maintain ties with adoptive or blood relations. What set this new discourse apart was its emphasis on the kinship character of the ties gay people had forged to close friends and lovers, its demand that those ties receive social and legal recognition, and its separation of parenting and family formation from heterosexual relations. For the first time, gay men and lesbians systematically laid claim to families of their own. . . .

Is "Straight" to "Gay" as "Family" Is to "No Family"?

For years, and in an amazing variety of contexts, claiming a lesbian or gay identity has been portrayed as a rejection of "the family" and a departure from kinship. In media portrayals of AIDS, Simon Watney (1987:103) observes that "we are invited to imagine some absolute divide between the two domains of 'gay life' and 'the family,' as if gay men grew up, were educated, worked and lived our lives in total isolation from the rest of society." Two presuppositions lend a dubious credence to such imagery: the belief that gay men and lesbians do not have children or establish lasting relationships, and the belief that they invariably alienate adoptive and blood kin once their sexual identities become known. By presenting "the family" as a unitary object, these depictions also imply that everyone participates in identical sorts of kinship relations and subscribes to one universally agreed-upon definition of family.

Representations that exclude lesbians and gay men from "the family" invoke what Blanche Wiesen Cook (1977:48) has called "the assumption that gay people do not love and do not work," the reduction of lesbians and gay men to sexual identity, and sexual identity to sex alone. In the United States, sex apart from heterosexual marriage tends to introduce a wild card into social relations, signifying unbridled lust and the limits of individualism. If heterosexual intercourse can bring people into enduring association via the creation of kinship ties, lesbian and gay sexuality in these depictions isolates individuals from one another rather than weaving them into a social fabric. To assert that straight people "naturally" have access to family, while gay people are destined to move toward a future of solitude and loneliness, is not only to tie kinship closely to procreation, but also to treat gay men and lesbians as members of a nonprocreative species set apart from the rest of humanity (cf. Foucault 1978).

It is but a short step from positioning lesbians and gay men somewhere beyond "the family"—unencumbered by relations of kinship, responsibility, or affection—to portraying them as a menace to family and society. A person or group must first be outside another in order to invade, endanger, and threaten. My own impression from fieldwork corroborates Frances FitzGerald's (1986) observation that many heterosexuals believe not only that gay people have gained considerable political power, but also that the absolute number of lesbians and gay men (rather than their visibility) has increased in recent years. Inflammatory rhetoric that plays on fears about the "spread" of gay identity and of AIDS finds a disturbing parallel in the imagery used by fascists to describe syphilis at mid-century, when "the healthy" confronted "the degenerate" while the fate of civilization hung in the balance (Hocquenghem 1978).

A long sociological tradition in the United States of studying "the family" under siege or in various states of dissolution lent credibility to charges that this institution required protection

from "the homosexual threat." Proposition 6 (the Briggs initiative), which appeared on the ballot in California in 1978, was defeated only after a massive organizing campaign that mobilized lesbians and gay men in record numbers. The text of the initiative, which would have barred gay and lesbian teachers (along with heterosexual teachers who advocated homosexuality) from the public schools, was phrased as a defense of "the family" (in Hollibaugh 1979:55):

> One of the most fundamental interests of the State is the establishment and preservation of the family unit. Consistent with this interest is the State's duty to protect its impressionable youth from influences which are antithetical to this vital interest.

Other anti-gay legislative initiative campaigns adopted the slogans "save the family" and "save the children" as their rallying cries. In 1983 the *Moral Majority Report* referred obliquely to AIDS with the headline, "Homosexual Diseases Threaten American Families" (Godwin 1983). When the *Boston Herald* opposed a gay rights bill introduced into the Massachusetts legislature, it was with an eye to "the preservation of family values" (Allen 1987).

Discourse that opposes gay identity to family membership is not confined to the political arena. A gay doctor was advised during his residency to discourage other gay people from becoming his patients, lest his waiting room become filled with homosexuals. "It'll scare away the families," warned his supervisor (Lazere 1986). Discussions of dual-career families and the implications of a family wage system usually render invisible the financial obligations of gay people who support dependents or who pool material resources with lovers and others they define as kin. Just as women have been accused of taking jobs away from "men with families to support," some lesbians and gay men in the Bay Area recalled coworkers who had condemned them for competing against "people with families" for scarce employment. Or consider the choice of words by a guard at that "all-American" institution, Disneyland, commenting on a legal suit brought by two gay men who had been prohibited from dancing with one another at a dance floor on the grounds: "This is a family park.

There is no room for alternative lifestyles here" (Mendenhall 1985).

Scholarly treatments are hardly exempt from this tendency to locate gay men and lesbians beyond the bounds of kinship. Even when researchers are sympathetic to gay concerns, they may equate kinship with genealogically calculated relations. Manuel Castells' and Karen Murphy's (1982) study of the "spatial organization of San Francisco's gay community," for instance, frames its analysis using "gay territory" and "family land" as mutually exclusive categories.

From New Right polemics to the rhetoric of high school hallways, "recruitment" joins "reproduction" in allusions to homosexuality. Alleging that gay men and lesbians must seduce young people in order to perpetuate (or expand) the gay population because they cannot have children of their own, heterosexist critics have conjured up visions of an end to society, the inevitable fate of a society that fails to "reproduce." Of course, the contradictory inferences that sexual identity is "caught" rather than claimed, and that parents pass their sexual identities on to their children, are unsubstantiated. The power of this chain of associations lies in a play on words that blurs the multiple senses of the term "reproduction."

Reproduction's status as a mixed metaphor may detract from its analytic utility, but its very ambiguities make it ideally suited to argument and innuendo. By shifting without signal between reproduction's meaning of physical procreation and its sense as the perpetuation of society as a whole, the characterization of lesbians and gay men as nonreproductive beings links their supposed attacks on "the family" to attacks on society in the broadest sense. Speaking of parents who had refused to accept her lesbian identity, a Jewish woman explained, "They feel like I'm finishing off Hitler's job." The plausibility of the contention that gay people pose a threat to "the family" (and, through the family, to ethnicity) depends upon a view of family grounded in heterosexual relations, combined with the conviction that gay men and lesbians are incapable of procreation, parenting, and establishing kinship ties.

Some lesbians and gay men in the Bay Area had embraced the popular equation of their sexual identities with the renunciation of access to kinship, particularly when first coming out. "My image of gay life was very lonely, very weird, no family," Rafael Ortiz recollected. "I assumed that my family was gone now—that's it." After Bob Korkowski began to call himself gay, he wrote a series of poems in which an orphan was the central character. Bob said the poetry expressed his fear of "having to give up my family because I was queer." When I spoke with Rona Bren after she had been home with the flu, she told me that whenever she was sick, she relived old fears. That day she had remembered her mother's grim prediction: "You'll be a lesbian and you'll be alone the rest of your life. Even a dog shouldn't be alone."

Looking backward and forward across the life cycle, people who equated their adoption of a lesbian or gay identity with a renunciation of family did so in the double-sided sense of fearing rejection by the families in which they had grown up, and not expecting to marry or have children as adults. Although few in numbers, there were still those who had considered "going straight" or getting married specifically in order to "have a family."

Bernie Margolis had been sexually involved with men since he was in his teens, but for years had been married to a woman with whom he had several children. At age 67 he regretted having grown to adulthood before the current discussion of gay families, with its focus on redefining kinship and constructing new sorts of parenting arrangements.

> I didn't want to give up the possibility of becoming a family person. Of having kids of my own to carry on whatever I built up. . . . My mother was always talking about she's looking forward to the day when she would bring her children under the canopy to get married. It never occurred to her that I wouldn't be married. It probably never occurred to me either.

The very categories "good family person" and "good family man" had seemed to Bernie intrinsically opposed to a gay identity. In his fifties at the time I interviewed him, Stephen Richter attributed never having become a father to "not having the relationship with the woman." Because he had envisioned parenting and procreation only in the context of a heterosexual relationship, regarding the two as completely bound up with one another, Stephen had never considered children an option.

Older gay men and lesbians were not the only ones whose adult lives had been shaped by ideologies that banish gay people from the domain of kinship. Explaining why he felt uncomfortable participating in "family occasions," a young man who had no particular interest in raising a child commented, "When families get together, what do they talk about? Who's getting married, who's having children. And who's not, okay? Well, look who's not." Very few of the lesbians and gay men I met believed that claiming a gay identity automatically requires leaving kinship behind. In some cases people described this equation as an outmoded view that contrasted sharply with revised notions of what constitutes a family.

Well-meaning defenders of lesbian and gay identity sometimes assert that gays are not inherently "anti-family," in ways that perpetuate the association of heterosexual identity with exclusive access to kinship. Charles Silverstein (1977), for instance, contends that lesbians and gay men may place more importance on maintaining family ties than heterosexuals do because gay people do not marry and raise children. Here the affirmation that gays and lesbians are capable of fostering enduring kinship ties ends up reinforcing the implication that they cannot establish "families of their own," presumably because the author regards kinship as unshakably rooted in heterosexual alliance and procreation. In contrast, discourse on gay families cuts across the politically loaded couplet of "pro-family" and "anti-family" that places gay men and lesbians in an inherently antagonistic relation to kinship solely on the basis of their nonprocreative sexualities. "Homosexuality is not what is breaking up the Black family," declared Barbara Smith (1987), a black lesbian writer, activist, and speaker at the 1987 Gay and Lesbian March on Washington. "Homophobia is. My Black gay brothers and my Black lesbian sisters are members of Black families, both the ones we were born into and the ones we create."

At the height of gay liberation, activists had attempted to develop alternatives to "the family,"

whereas by the 1980s many lesbians and gay men were struggling to legitimate gay families as a form of kinship. When Armistead Maupin spoke at a gathering on Castro Street to welcome home two gay men who had been held hostage in the Middle East, partners who had stood with arms around one another upon their release, he congratulated them not only for their safe return, but also as representatives of a new kind of family. Gay or chosen families might incorporate friends, lovers, or children, in any combination. Organized through ideologies of love, choice, and creation, gay families have been defined through a contrast with what many gay men and lesbians in the Bay Area called "straight," "biological," or "blood" family. If families we choose were the families lesbians and gay men created for themselves, straight family represented the families in which most had grown to adulthood.

What does it mean to say that these two categories of family have been defined through contrast? One thing it emphatically does not mean is that heterosexuals share a single coherent form of family (although some of the lesbians and gay men doing the defining believed this to be the case). I am not arguing here for the existence of some central, unified kinship system vis-à-vis which gay people have distinguished their own practice and understanding of family. In the United States, race, class, gender, ethnicity, regional origin, and context all inform differences in household organization, as well as differences in notions of family and what it means to call someone kin. . . .

Deck the Halls

Holidays, family reunions, and other celebrations culturally categorized as family occasions represent everyday arenas in which people in the Bay Area elaborated discourse on kinship. To attend was to catch a glimpse of history in the making that brought ideological oppositions to life. During the season when Hanukkah, Christmas, New Year's, and Winter Solstice converge, opportunities abounded to observe the way double-sided contrasts like the one between straight and gay families take shape. Meanings and transformations appeared far less abstract as people applied and reinterpreted them in the course of concrete activities and discussion. Their emotional power suddenly became obvious and inescapable, clearly central to ideological relations that have been approached far too cognitively in the past.

In San Francisco, gay community organizations set up special telephone hotlines during the holidays to serve as resources for lesbians and gay men battling feelings of loneliness or depression. At this time of year similar feelings were common in the population at large, given the tiring, labor-intensive character of holiday preparations and the pressure of cultural prescriptions to gather with relatives in a state of undisturbed happiness and harmony. Yet many gay people considered the "holiday blues" a more acute problem for themselves than for heterosexuals because disclosure of a lesbian or gay identity so often disrupted relations with straight relatives. The large number of gay immigrants to the Bay Area ensured that decisions about where to spend the holidays would make spatial declarations about family ties and family loyalties. . . .

For those whose sexual identity was known to biological or adoptive relatives, conflicts over gaining acknowledgment and legitimacy for relationships with lovers and others they considered gay family was never so evident as on holidays. When Chris Davidson planned to return to her childhood home in the Bay Area for the holidays, she worried about being caught in the "same old pull" between spending time with her parents and time with her close lesbian friends. That year she had written her parents a letter in advance asking that they confront their "possessiveness" and recognize the importance of these other relationships in her life. Another woman regarded her parents' decision to allow her lover in their house to celebrate New Year's Day together with "the family" as a sign of growing acceptance. Some people had decided to celebrate holidays with their chosen families, occasionally inviting relatives by blood or adoption to join the festivities. One man voiced pride in "creating our environment, our *intimate* environment. I have an extended [gay] family. I have a lot of friends who we have shared Christmas and Thanksgiving with. Birthdays. Just as you would any other extended family.". . .

When a celebration brought chosen relatives into contact with biological or adoptive kin, family occasions sometimes became a bridge to greater integration of straight and gay families. Those who felt rejected for their sexual identities, however, could experience holidays as events that forced them to ally with one or the other of these opposed categories. The feeling was widespread that, in Diane Kunin's words, "[gay] people have to make some really excruciating choices that other people are not faced with." Because contexts such as holidays evoked the more inclusive level of the opposition *between* two types of family, they seldom elicited the positive sense of choice and creativity associated with gay families. Instead, individuals too often found themselves faced with the unwelcome dilemma of making an either/or decision when they would have preferred to choose both.

Kinship and Procreation

In the United States the notion of biology as an indelible, precultural substratum is so ingrained that people often find it difficult to take an anthropological step backward in order to examine biology as symbol rather than substance. For many in this society, biology is a defining feature of kinship: they believe that blood ties make certain people kin, regardless of whether those individuals display the love and enduring solidarity expected to characterize familial relations. Physical procreation, in turn, produces biological links. Collectively, biogenetic attributes are supposed to demarcate kinship as a cultural domain, offering a yardstick for determining who counts as a "real" relative. Like their heterosexual counterparts, lesbians and gay men tended to naturalize biology in this manner.

Not all cultures grant biology this significance for describing and evaluating relationships. To read biology as symbol is to approach it as a cultural construct and linguistic category, rather than a self-evident matter of "natural fact." At issue here is the cultural valuation given to ties traced through procreation, and the meaning that biological connection confers upon a relationship in a given cultural context. In this sense biology is no less a symbol than choice or creation. Neither is inherently more "real" or valid than the other, culturally speaking.

In the United States, Schneider (1968) argues, "sexual intercourse" is the symbol that brings together relations of marriage and blood, supplying the distinctive features in terms of which kinship relations are defined and differentiated. A relationship mediated by procreation binds a mother to a daughter, a brother to a sister, and so on, in the categories of genitor or genetrix, offspring, or members of a sibling set. Immediately apparent to a gay man or lesbian is that what passes here for sex per se is actually the *heterosexual* union of two differently gendered persons. While all sexual activity among heterosexuals certainly does not lead to the birth of children, the isolation of heterosexual intercourse as a core symbol orients kinship studies toward a dominantly procreative reading of sexualities. For a society like the United States, Sylvia Yanagisako's and Jane Collier's (1987) call to analyze gender and kinship as mutually implicated constructs must be extended to embrace sexual identity.

The very notion of gay families asserts that people who claim nonprocreative sexual identities and pursue nonprocreative relationships can lay claim to family ties of their own without necessary recourse to marriage, childbearing, or childrearing. By defining these chosen families in opposition to the biological ties believed to constitute a straight family, lesbians and gay men began to renegotiate the meaning and practice of kinship from within the very societies that had nurtured the concept. Theirs has not been a proposal to number gay families among variations in "American kinship," but a more comprehensive attack on the privilege accorded to a biogenetically grounded mode of determining what relationships will *count* as kinship.

It is important to note that some gay men and lesbians in the Bay Area agreed with the view that blood ties represent the only authentic, legitimate form of kinship. Often those who disputed the validity of chosen families were people whose notions of kinship were bound up with their own sense of racial or ethnic identity. "You've got one family, one biological family," insisted Paul

Jaramillo, a Mexican-American man who did not consider his lover or friends to be kin.

> They're very good friends and I love them, but I would not call them family. Family to me is blood. . . . I feel that Western Caucasian culture, that it's much more broken down, and that they can deal with their good friends and neighbors as family. But it's not that way, at least in my background.

Because most individuals who expressed this view were well aware of the juxtaposition of blood family with families we choose, they tended to address gay kinship ideologies directly. As Lourdes Alcantara explained,

> I know a lot of lesbians think that you choose your own family. I don't think so. Because, as a Latin woman, the bonds that I got with my family are irreplaceable. They can't be replaced. They cannot. So my family is my family, my friends are my friends. My friends can be *more important* than my family, but that doesn't mean they are my family. . . . 'Cause no matter what, they are just friends—they don't have your blood. They don't have your same connection. They didn't go through what you did. For example, I starved with my family a lot of times. They know what it is like. If I talk to my friends, they will understand me, but they will never feel the same.

What Lourdes so movingly described was a sense of enduring solidarity arising from shared experience and symbolized by blood connection. Others followed a similar line of reasoning (minus the biological signifier) when they contended that a shared history testifies to enduring solidarity, which can provide the basis for creating familial relationships of a chosen, or nonbiological, sort.

In an essay on disclosing a lesbian or gay identity to relatives, Betty Berzon (1979:89) maintains that "from early on, being gay is associated with going against the family." Many people in the Bay Area viewed families as the principal mediator of race and ethnicity, drawing on folk theories of cultural transmission in which parents hand down "traditions" and identity (as well as genes) to their children. If having a family was part of what it meant to be Chicana or Cherokee or Japanese-American, then claiming a lesbian or gay identity could easily be interpreted as losing or betraying that cultural heritage, so long as individuals conceived kinship in biogenetic terms (cf. Clunis and Green 1988:105; Tremble et al. 1989). . . .

Condemnations of homosexuality might picture race or ethnicity and gay identity as antagonists in response to a history of racist attributions of "weak" family ties to certain groups (e.g., blacks), or in response to anything that appeared to menace the legacy of "strong" kinship bonds sometimes attributed to other categories of people (e.g., Latinos, Jews). In either case, depicting lesbian or gay identity as a threat to ethnic or racial identity depended upon the cultural positioning of gay people outside familial relations. The degree to which individuals construct racial identity *through* their notions of family remains a relatively unexplored aspect of why some heterosexuals of color reject gay or lesbian identity as a sign of assimilation, a "white thing."

Not all lesbians and gays of color or whites with a developed ethnic identity took issue with the concept of chosen families. Many African-Americans, for instance, felt that black communities had never held to a strictly biogenetic interpretation of kinship. "Blacks have never said to a child, 'Unless you have a mother, father, sister, brother, you don't have a family' " (Height 1989:137). Discourse and ideology are far from being uniformly determined by identities, experiences, or historical developments. Divergent perceptions of the relation between family ties and race or ethnicity are indicative of a situation of ideological flux, in which procreative and nonprocreative interpretations vie with one another for the privilege of defining kinship. As the United States entered the final decade of the twentieth century, lesbians and gay men from a broad spectrum of racial and ethnic identities had come to embrace the legitimacy of gay families.

From Biology to Choice

Upon first learning the categories that framed gay kinship ideologies, heterosexuals sometimes mentioned adoption as a kind of limiting case that appeared to occupy the borderland between biology and choice. In the United States, adopted children are chosen, in a sense, although biological offspring can be planned or selected as well, given the widespread availability of birth control. Yet adoption in this society "is only understandable as a way of creating the social fiction that an actual link of kinship exists. Without biological kinship as a model, adoption would be meaningless" (Schneider 1984:55). Adoption does not render the attribution of biological descent culturally irrelevant (witness the many adopted children who, later in life, decide to search for their "real" parents). But adoptive relations—unlike gay families—pose no fundamental challenge to either procreative interpretations of kinship or the culturally standardized image of a family assembled around a core of parent(s) plus children.

Mapping biological family and families we choose onto contrasting sexual identities (straight and gay, respectively) places these two types of family in a relation of opposition, but *within* that relation, determinism implicitly differentiates biology from choice and blood from creation. Informed by contrasting notions of free will and the fixedness often attributed to biology in this culture, the opposition between straight and gay families echoes old dichotomies such as nature versus nurture and real versus ideal. In families we choose, the agency conveyed by "we" emphasizes each person's part in constructing gay families, just as the absence of agency in the term "biological family" reinforces the sense of blood as an immutable fact over which individuals exert little control. Likewise, the collective subject of families we choose invokes a collective identity—who are "we" if not gay men and lesbians? In order to identify the "we" associated with the speaker's "I," a listener must first recognize the correspondence between the opposition of blood to choice and the relation of straight to gay.

Significantly, families we choose have not built directly upon beliefs that gay or lesbian identity can be chosen. Among lesbians and gay men themselves, opinions differ as to whether individuals select or inherit their sexual identities. In the aftermath of the gay movement, the trend has been to move away from the obsession of earlier decades with the etiological question of what "causes" homosexuality. After noting that no one subjects heterosexuality to similar scrutiny, many people dropped the question. Some lesbian-feminists presented lesbianism as a political choice that made a statement about sharing their best with other women and refusing to participate in patriarchal relations. In everyday conversations, however, the majority of both men and women portrayed their sexual identities as either inborn or a predisposition developed very early in life. Whether or not to act on feelings already present then became the only matter left to individual discretion. "The choice for me wasn't being with men or being a lesbian," Richie Kaplan explained. "The choice was being asexual or being with women."

In contrast, parents who disapproved of homosexuality could convey a critical attitude by treating gay identity as something elective, especially since people in the United States customarily hold individuals responsible for any negative consequences attendant upon a "free choice." One man described with dismay his father's reaction upon learning of his sexual identity: "I said, 'I'm gay.' And he said, 'Oh. Well, I guess you made your choice.' " According to another, "My father kept saying, 'Well, you're gonna have to live by your choices that you make. It's your responsibility.' What's there to be responsible [about]? I was who I *am*." When Andy Wentworth disclosed his gay identity to his sister,

> She asked me, how could I choose to do this and to ignore the health risks . . . implying that this was a conscious, 'Oh, I'd like to go to the movies today' type of choice. And I told her, I said, 'Nobody in their right mind would go through this hell of being gay just to satisfy a whim.' And I explained to her what it was like growing up. Knowing this other side of yourself that you can't tell anybody about, and if anybody in your family knows they will be upset and mortified.

Another man insisted he would never forget the period after coming out when he realized that he felt good about himself, and that he was not on his way to becoming "the kind of person that they're portraying gay people to be." What kind

of person is that, I asked. "Well, you know, wicked, evil people who *decide* that they're going to be evil."

Rather than claiming an elective gay identity as its antecedent, the category "families we choose" incorporates the meaningful *difference* that is the product of choice and biology as two relationally defined terms. If many gay men and lesbians interpreted blood ties as a type of social connectedness organized through procreation, they tended to associate choice and creativity with a total absence of guidelines for ordering relationships within gay families. Although heterosexuals in the Bay Area also had the sense of creating something when they established families of their own, that creativity was often firmly linked to childbearing and childrearing, the "pro-" in procreation. In the absence of a procreative referent, individual discretion regulated who would be counted as kin. For those who had constructed them, gay families could evoke utopian visions of self-determination in the absence of social constraint. Of course, the contextualization of choice and creativity within the symbolic relation that opposes them to blood and biology itself lends a high degree of structure to the notion of gay families. The elaboration of gay kinship ideologies in contrast to the biogenetic symbolism of straight family illustrates the type of structured relation Roman Jakobson (1962) has called "the unexpected arising from expectedness, both of them unthinkable without the opposite."

Certainly lesbians and gay men, with their range of backgrounds and experiences, did not always mean the same thing or advance identical cultural critiques when they spoke of blood and chosen families. Ideological contrasts utilized and recognized by all need not have the same significance for all. Neither can an examination of ideology alone explain why choice should have been highlighted as an organizing principle of gay families. Only history, material conditions, and context can account for the specific content of gay kinship ideologies, their emergence at a particular point in time, and the variety of ways people have implemented those ideologies in their daily lives. In themselves, gay families comprise only a segment of the historical transformation sequence that mapped the contrast between straight and gay first onto "family/no family," and then onto "biological family/families we choose." Gone are the days when embracing a lesbian or gay identity seemed to require a renunciation of kinship. The symbolic groundwork for gay families, laid during a period when coming out to relatives witnessed a kind of institutionalization, has made it possible to claim a sexual identity that is not linked to procreation, face the possibility of rejection by blood or adoptive relations, yet still conceive of establishing a family of one's own.

REFERENCES

Allen, Ronnie. 1987. "Times Have Changed at the Herald." *Gay Community News* (June 28–July 4).

Berzon, Betty. 1979. "Telling the Family You're Gay." In Betty Berzon and Robert Leighton, eds., *Positively Gay*, pp. 88–100. Los Angeles: Mediamix Associates.

Castells, Manuel and Karen Murphy. 1982. "Cultural Identity and Urban Structure: The Spatial Organization of San Francisco's Gay Community." In Norman I. Fainstein and Susan S. Fainstein, eds., *Urban Policy Under Capitalism*, pp. 237–259. Beverly Hills, Calif.: Sage.

Clunis, D. Merilee and G. Dorsey Green. 1988. *Lesbian Couples*. Seattle: Seal Press.

Cook, Blanche Wiesen. 1977. "Female Support Networks and Political Activism: Lillian Wald, Crystal Eastman, Emma Goldman." *Chrysalis* 3:44–61.

FitzGerald, Frances. 1986. *Cities on a Hill: A Journey Through Contemporary American Cultures*. New York: Simon & Schuster.

Foucault, Michel. 1978. *The History of Sexuality*. Vol 1. New York: Vintage.

Godwin, Ronald S. 1983. "AIDS: A Moral and Political Time Bomb." *Moral Majority Report* (July).

Height, Dorothy. 1989. "Self-Help—A Black Tradition." *The Nation* (July 24–31):136–138.

Hocquenghem, Guy. 1978. *Homosexual Desire*. London: Alison & Busby.

Hollibaugh, Amber. 1979. "Sexuality and the State: The Defeat of the Briggs Initiative and Beyond." *Socialist Review* 9(3):55–72.

Jakobson, Roman. 1962. *Selected Writings*. The Hague: Mouton.

Lazere, Arthur. 1986. "On the Job." *Coming Up!* (June).

Mendenhall, George. 1985. "Mickey Mouse Lawsuit Remains Despite Disney Dancing Decree." *Bay Area Reporter* (Aug. 22).

Schneider, David M. 1968. *American Kinship: A Cultural Account*. Englewood Cliffs, N.J.: Prentice-Hall.

_____. 1984. *A Critique of the Study of Kinship*. Ann Arbor: University of Michigan Press.

Silverstein, Charles. 1977. *A Family Matter: A Parents' Guide to Homosexuality*. New York: McGraw-Hill.

Smith, B. 1987. "From the Stage." *Gay Community News* (Nov. 8–14).

Tremble, Bob, Margaret Schneider, and Carol Appathurai. 1989. "Growing Up Gay or Lesbian in a Multicultural Context." In Gilbert Herdt, ed., *Gay and Lesbian Youth*, pp. 253–264. New York: Haworth Press.

Watney, Simon. 1987. *Policing Desire: Pornography, AIDS, and the Media*. Minneapolis: University of Minnesota Press.

Yanagisako, Sylvia Junko and Jane Fishburne Collier. 1987. "Toward a Unified Analysis of Gender and Kinship." In Jane Fishburne Collier and Sylvia Junko Yanagisako, eds., *Gender and Kinship: Essays Toward a Unified Analysis*, pp. 14–50. Stanford: Stanford University Press.

No Man's Land

Kathleen Gerson

. . . Men who have reached adulthood in recent decades have confronted confusing circumstances. The stagnation of wages has undermined their capacity to support a family alone. Women's entry into the workplace has challenged their pre-eminence as breadwinners and workers. The sexual revolution has eroded the double standard, and the revolution in cohabitation and divorce has loosened the bonds of marriage. These trends have undermined the foundations of men's modern privileges, but they have also given men opportunities to pursue new paths, claim new freedoms, and develop new identities.

Born into the post-World War II period of economic growth and a resurgent breadwinner-homemaker household, these men had few clues that they would ultimately encounter a revolution in family patterns and gender relations. Even before these changes became apparent, however, many of these men had experienced ambiguities, contradictions, and doubts about what the future would and should hold. Such childhood concerns set the stage for the unforeseen twists and turns that occurred later in their lives. Childhood experiences provide only limited clues for explaining men's adult commitments and choices, but they provide a point of departure for men's life trajectories.

To construct a picture of these starting points, we must rely on men's own retrospective accounts. Whether they represent a form of selective remembering or a way of interpreting the past, these accounts show how men actively use and make sense of early experiences rather than simply being molded by them. Indeed, the experiences these men recount cast doubt on a number of widely held beliefs about the determining influence of childhood experiences on later life choices and outlooks.

Sons and Fathers

Among the men we will meet in the following pages, only a minority became a sole or primary breadwinner. But this was not the case for their fathers, almost three-fourths of whom had been the primary or sole family breadwinners—although fathers with blue-collar and lower white-collar jobs were more likely to have shared breadwinning with a wife who worked full-time. . . . Taken together, these fathers showed a strong attachment to the workplace and not much participation in child rearing. Only 4 percent of the men recalled significant periods when their fathers were out of work. Of the remaining 96 percent, across classes and occupations, none reported fathers who averaged fewer than forty hours at work per week and many reported longer work weeks (ranging from a low of 13 percent among fathers with lower white-collar jobs to a high of 81 percent among the self-employed).

Most sons concluded that their fathers were "generally satisfied" with their jobs, and many felt that their fathers were "very satisfied" (ranging from a low of 25 percent for fathers in lower white-collar jobs to a high of 63 percent in professional occupations). Overall, only 34 percent reported that their fathers spent some time with them every day, but 50 percent of those whose fathers held lower white-collar jobs did. While there are some exceptions worth noting, most fathers embodied the prevailing masculine norm of distant parenting and good providing.

While fathers' level of job satisfaction may bear some relation to sons' outlooks as children, this relationship weakened with the passage of time. In adulthood, sons' orientations toward breadwinning are only loosely and ambiguously connected to perceptions of how much satisfaction fathers derived from a job or career. Among those whose fathers appeared moderately satisfied or dissatisfied, there was little change over time in the percentage who rejected breadwinning. Among those who perceived their fathers were very satisfied, however, 59 percent held a breadwinning orientation in childhood, but only 30 percent sustained that outlook through adulthood. As time passed, those men whose fathers were very satisfied came to resemble those whose fathers were not.

Fathers' degree of participation in child rearing had a similarly weak and ambiguous relationship to sons' adult orientations. . . . Of sons who perceived their fathers to be involved in child rearing on a daily basis, fewer than 40 percent ultimately developed an orientation of parental involvement. A similar percentage of sons who perceived their fathers to be uninvolved or only sporadically involved also developed an involved outlook. Why do fathers' employment and parental patterns bear so little relation to the ultimate choices and outlooks of their sons?

Fathers as Workers and Breadwinners

. . . Most of the respondents had fathers who worked steadily when they were growing up, and 45 percent concluded that their fathers were satisfied with their work—that is, that they found their work sufficiently fulfilling that they would not have chosen a different occupation. Another 33 percent concluded that their fathers were moderately satisfied, but found little fulfillment in their work. An additional 14 percent concluded that their fathers would have preferred a different line of work or not to have worked at all.[1] Many sons thus perceived a gap between a father's stress on hard work and his feelings about working. This discrepancy, which for some appeared to resemble hypocrisy, planted early seeds of doubt in some sons. Edward, an unmarried physician, recalled how his father's obvious distaste for his job undermined the admonition to work hard and achieve success:

> It's quite clear my father hated his job. Certainly his goal was that we have careers that we be happy with, that we could even get a certain amount of control and get more out of it. But at the same time, even though

instilling that attitude, there was the image that work is not a positive thing.

. . . Discrepancies between what fathers did and how they felt about it sent children mixed messages about the value of work commitment and economic security, but their feelings spoke louder than their actions or words. When a father appeared more frustrated than fulfilled, he conveyed the message to avoid the same fate, to take chances, and to think twice about sacrificing personal happiness at the altar of financial security. Edward explained:

> My father obviously didn't find his job satisfying. He was very much a martyr, whose whole focus was supporting and sacrificing for his family. I don't see that ability to martyr myself. I look at the grief and anxiety my father had by being the sole provider, and I would like to change that definition of being a man. So if being a man is being the rock and support of your family, that doesn't look very good to me. . . .

. . . Most fathers did not convey strong dissatisfaction with work or provide an ambiguous message about the value of breadwinning. Clearly, sons can react in a variety of ways to the images and messages their fathers provide. Over time, as sons age and establish greater personal independence, the meaning of their fathers' choices is also increasingly open to reassessment and change. And even when sons perceive little or no dissatisfaction on the part of their fathers, they may still choose a different path. . . .

Whatever its sources, a divergence between the outlooks of fathers and sons is likely to produce a painful struggle. The outcome of this struggle is indeterminate even in the short run. Chuck, a thirty-five-year-old systems analyst, learned at an early age that he did not share his father's skills or his definition of manhood:

> My dad worked in a factory. He wanted me to be interested in sports and be the All-American boy based on sort of a John Wayne model. But I realized very early that I wasn't particularly adept at sports. I used to read a lot, write, draw, go to museums. I was interested in things like cooking and art that were

not what a young boy should be doing. It took me a very long time to know that he was really proud of me, because he had a different framework about being a man or being successful.

. . . Those who rejected their fathers' breadwinning model endeavored to account for the differences between their fathers and themselves. Aware of differences in generational opportunities, they felt fortunate to have escaped the constraints to which their fathers appeared to succumb. Most rejected the preoccupation with security that seemed to prevail among this older generation, which grew to manhood during the Great Depression and World War II. They defined themselves in opposition to this ethic of security, glad to be able to take more risks. . . .

Others blamed their fathers for failing to rise above the social constraints of their era. As they strove for independence and meaning in and outside work, they came to judge their fathers harshly for refusing to be masters of their fate, for not living up to the masculine ideal of being in control. Yet they also held a grudging respect for them. Neil concluded that he was fortunate to have avoided a trap his father had not been able or willing to transcend:

> My father survived a job that he hated for thirty years. I couldn't do it. I think a lot of his choices were self-imposed. He could have been one of those few guys who found another job he would have been happy at, but he didn't do it. I'm from a different generation, who assumed that we were gonna be able to get a great job no matter what we do. I just feel I'll be a success no matter what I do. But my dad's generation didn't feel that way; they were just happy to get a damn job.

Whether they attributed the causes to social or psychological differences, men who veered away from their fathers' breadwinning models developed an identity and self-image different from— indeed, in opposition to—their fathers. The process of distancing took these sons in many disparate directions. For some, it meant becoming more ambitious and successful, with some attendant ambivalence. Michael, a psychotherapist and custodial father of two, felt some guilt and "fear of success"[2] for exceeding his father's accomplishments, but he succeeded in any case:

> My father felt threatened by my ambition and was always quick to tell me that no matter how good I got, he would always be better. He would become very angry and envious of my success, especially at school. So I'm very proud of my accomplishments, but I experience it as a problem at the same time.

. . . When sons turned away from a model of manhood based on work dedication and self-sacrifice, it held implications for how they judged their fathers' family commitments as well. When work responsibilities seemed like a trap, family responsibilities could assume a similar appearance. Arthur, a sanitation worker who was single and childless at thirty-six, concluded that his father's "sacrifices" were anchored in breadwinning obligations that might be best to avoid:

> I could see what my father went through, and I realized I'd have to make a lot of sacrifices to be married. I'm selfish. You're willing to give up your freedom when you date somebody, but with a family comes responsibilities, and you begin to resent it.

A father's work pattern thus does not account for a son's relationship to work and family life. Fathers present ambiguous, contradictory models to which sons respond in a variety of ways. Over time, they gain new perspectives on their fathers' lives. Their long-run reactions grow out of a series of personal experiences and lessons that make fathers' teachings increasingly less determinate.

Fathers and Parental Involvement

If most fathers were strongly committed to working, they showed a correspondingly low participation in child rearing. Hank, a paramedic who hoped to become an involved father, forgave his father's distance because he knew his need to earn a living precluded the kind of participation Hank would have liked. His father, a security guard and elevator operator, was locked out of fatherly involvement because he was locked into caring for his family through economic support:

I can't remember playing sports. It wasn't a father-son relationship that you see in the movies. He couldn't. He worked double time. You never knew when he was coming home. His work ethic was that you did what you had to do to put a roof over your head and feed the children. He was trapped, too.

. . . The processes that led some men away from their fathers' work model also set the stage for different approaches to parenthood. Ernie, a physical therapist who became closely involved in rearing his daughter, recalled his father's absence with bitterness and disappointment. This memory spurred him to reject his father's choices and develop a different definition of fathering:

There was no support, no one I could talk to, no male role model at all. I got the sense that he thought he was the provider, but I wasn't looking for a roof and clothing; I was looking for a father. I think he felt he was serving his role well, but there's more to it than just that.

When asked what he would have liked his father to be like, Ernie explained it this way:

A lot of the opposite. More like how I try myself to be expressing a lot more what you feel, more honesty, spending lots of time, participating in the growing-up stages. My father's negative influence has turned positive for me. He taught me how *not* to be a father.

Some of the men recalled that one of their first memories involved yearning for a more involved father. Their disappointment provoked an early determination to give their children what they had not received. Dean, a driver for the park service, realized early in life that his father didn't have time to spend time with him. He vowed "to go out of my way to try to change that." . . .

Since most fathers did not participate in caretaking, those who did stood out. But involved fathers could send a message as ambiguous as the one sent by distant fathers. And a father's involvement, like a lack of involvement, can be judged in diverse ways. A son might be thrilled to spend time with his father, but he might also notice the sacrifices and trade-offs. Gus, a planner, observed his father's dedication to child rearing and concluded that involved parenting was too time-consuming:

I would say my father was overly involved. If he didn't like the outcome of a situation, it was Mother's fault, but otherwise *he* brought us up. He was always home by a certain hour. The first thing was the family. So I feel that you can't just have children and show up at your own convenience.

Most fathers, of course, were not "overly involved." And most sons did not pay much attention to or feel much concern about their fathers' absence. As time passed, however, many sons changed their outlook. They concluded that having a distant father—and being a distant father—could have a range of unappealing consequences. When they faced their own choices, they reconsidered the meaning of their fathers' lack of participation.

Some discovered that their fathers paid an unanticipated long-run cost for their lack of involvement. Neil, the aspiring academic, observed his father's descent into unhappiness after decades in a dissatisfying job. He decided that his father had little to show for a life so detached from caretaking and so focused on unrewarding work:

I think he's unhappy looking at his life. He can't have a good self-image of himself without a good career. And since he can't fall back on his relationships with his kids, it makes him a very unhappy person at sixty.

. . . Those who became more nurturing than their own fathers tried to account for the discrepancy between the parenting they received and the parenting they were giving or planning to give. Some blamed social constraints and were grateful for a different set of opportunities. Neil realized that his father faced obstacles he did not:

I missed him, but I don't hold it against him. Things have changed so much since he was a father. I spend so much more time with my daughter, but my job is completely different from his job—it has allowed that.

. . . A son might choose to become more involved than his father, as we have just seen, but he might also reject his father's model by choosing not to have children at all. Afraid that he might repeat his father's mistakes or re-create the disappointment he experienced as a child, a man, as Chuck explained, might "try to spare somebody the type of childhood and life I had.". . .

The lesson of these reactions is not that distant fathers produce nurturing any more than non-nurturing sons. The dynamics between fathers and sons are more complicated and less determined than can be captured by theories that focus on processes that reproduce psychological capacities and proclivities across generations. Fathers provide an example, a set of experiences, and one side of a relationship to which sons are exposed. Sons can respond, however, in a variety of ways. Their responses can also change as they age and face adult conflicts over parenting and other life choices. Sons can and will appropriate the "meaning" of their fathers' lives and their own relationships with them in ways that take time to emerge. Neither the father's behavior nor the more general childhood context determines the son's early reactions, interpretations, desires, or capacities. More important, neither foretells how a son will make sense of these experiences as he grows up, faces a range of new options, and struggles to make his own choices. . . .

The Breadwinning Ethos

Those men who, as children, adopted a bread-winning outlook saw in it an ineffable but alluring image of the good life. In this dream, material affluence formed the foundation on which other goals were built. Robert, the teacher with joint custody of his two children, "always kind of blandly assumed that, no problem, I'll be rich." And Reid, a businessman with one child who hoped to re-create the suburban affluence that had surrounded him as a child, did not expect to find that economic times had made the American dream elusive: "I never dreamed I'd be stuck in a one-bedroom apartment with a wife and a child."

Of course, the breadwinner outlook means aiming for sustained and successful participation in the labor force. Even to someone like Carlos, whose parents were divorced and whose father never contributed to his support, the need to earn a good livelihood came first: "The emphasis in my family was get a good education, get a good job, and you have enough finances to meet your needs."

Those who expected to become breadwinners assumed that they would work and, more significantly, that success at work would make it easy to accomplish any other goal. Henry, a construction foreman and primary breadwinner, explained that he "always worked, even as a kid, and figured everything else would take care of itself."

For men from the middle class, success meant more than securing a steady job. It meant finding a professional career that would furnish ample social, personal, and financial rewards. Julian relinquished hopes of becoming a teacher because it could not offer sufficient compensation to support his anticipated family responsibilities. He became a lawyer instead:

> In college, I admired a lot of historians, but unanimously they dissuaded me from pursuing an academic career. When you think in terms of a good career—a career that will allow you to fulfill that role of breadwinner—everything sort of gravitated toward this one.

Hard work and a successful, well-remunerated career formed the foundation on which these men could pile other goals, such as getting married, having children, and supporting a family in comfort. Marriage, by most accounts, could simply be assumed. As Robin, a stockbroker contemplating divorce, put it, it was "the natural state." In Reid's description: "I thought, 'Fine, sure, I'll get married someday. It will happen when it does, just like crossing the street.'"

Marriage was seen as a crucial step on the road to maturity, which for these men meant stability. Ernie, the physical therapist, hoped marriage would give him the security his parents had failed to provide: "I looked at marriage as a way to stabilize me, because I always felt I was scattered. I was floating all the time.". . .

For those who aspired to breadwinning, the wish to get married involved a set of assumptions about themselves as men and about the women they would choose as mates. Like Dennis, they defined women in opposition to themselves: "I never envisioned getting into a relationship with a woman who was working full-time. I think it was just the stereotype."

Those aspiring breadwinners either did not notice the flow of women into the labor force or did not let it change their expectations. They often belittled the importance of women's employment and continued to assume that they, not their wives, would become their household's economic head. Julian's point of view was that, "even if you marry a professional woman, she's got to take some time off and start a family."

These men also assumed they would become fathers, seeing parenthood as the inevitable outcome of a smooth process of building a career and finding a mate. Like the idealized image of living happily ever after often attributed to women, such men envisioned a contented future in which children would be their reward for success at work. Since they expected their wives to care for the children, parenthood provided a way to confirm a masculine identity, but it did not appear to be a time-consuming job. Carlos initially saw children as a way of demonstrating his manliness, but later changed his view:

> I went through a phase where I was caught up in the idea of creating someone in my image. As I got older, I said, "That is not a reason to have children." I got concerned that I would not like someone seeing me as an extension of themselves and imposing their values on me to complete the dreams they didn't complete for themselves.

. . . Aware of the dangers, these men nevertheless focused on the rewards and minimized the potential difficulties of becoming a breadwinner. Contemplating the unanticipated problems adult life had wrought, Gus, the planner who ultimately decided to remain childless, compared his childhood dreams to his adult realities:

> I always had grand fantasies of how things should be, and it was difficult because nothing could ever meet them. . . . I thought I would have a family, and I had no idea life would be so difficult. We were very sheltered. I never thought it would be hard to make money or find an apartment.

. . . Regardless of their class origins, these men took it for granted that they could not only survive but prevail. They believed that the world was theirs for the taking, that all they needed was the confidence and the energy to pursue their goals. Jeremy, a forty-year-old manager, for example, claimed that "because of my upbringing, I never worried about the future. I always assumed I am one of those people who will land on their feet no matter what the circumstances." Alan, a property assessor with no college degree, concurred: "My attitude was, 'If you have confidence in yourself, no matter what comes up, I can take care of it.'"

Men who embraced the breadwinning ethos saw it as a commitment to a set of interconnected responsibilities and privileges involving work, money, marriage, and parenthood. Most recognized that it could and probably would entail difficulties, but all expected the attendant privileges to offset the potential problems. More important, whether they viewed the road to manhood as smooth or strewn with obstacles, they could envision no other path.

Alternatives to Breadwinning

Slightly more than half of the men did see other paths, ranging from a vague attraction to adventure and lifelong freedom to a strong distrust of the work ethic or family life. Fourteen percent of this group (8 percent of the total sample) planned to share economic responsibilities with a woman; 46 percent (24 percent of the total sample) hoped to remain childless and often single as well; 32 percent (17 percent of the total sample) did not form any future plans about family and work; and, sadly, 9 percent (4 percent of the total sample) succumbed to an especially acute form of pessimism: they did not expect to live to adulthood. These outlooks are united more by what they oppose than by what they affirm. Highly skeptical about the desirability of breadwinning, these men were unclear about what to put in its place.

Expecting to Share Economic Burdens

Those who expected to share economic responsibilities with a spouse believed that a working wife would make a more fulfilling and fulfilled companion than would a homemaker. Even at an early age, these men were not attracted to women who wanted or expected to be supported by a man.

Neil, the single graduate student, recalled how his earliest visions of the ideal mate involved a woman as dedicated to work as he expected to be: "I just could not see myself being attracted to somebody who was not gonna have their own career, and have the same kind of interest and passion about what they want to do as I had about my career." Joseph, a blue-collar worker who married his childhood sweetheart, had much the same thought: "I never expected my wife to sit around and bake pies. She's very intelligent, and she's got a mind of her own."

In addition to finding employed women more attractive, these men hoped their prospective spouses would lessen their own economic burdens. They looked forward to marrying and having a family, but they did not equate family commitment with becoming the sole, or even primary, support of their households. They wanted the freedom to seek personal fulfillment and not just economic security at work. This would help them avoid the greatest danger of male breadwinning: being trapped in a stifling marriage and saddled with the need to earn a big paycheck. Unlike the vast majority of their peers, this small group developed an egalitarian outlook, at least in terms of employment. They did not, however, consider the implications that sharing economic responsibilities would hold for their participation in child rearing. Eager to avoid the burdens of breadwinning, even these men did not anticipate taking on new burdens in the home.

Expecting to Remain Autonomous

By far the most popular alternative to breadwinning was to evade the dangers of domesticity rather than to minimize them. For some, early experiences made marriage look more like a trap than a reward. Hank, the paramedic, recalled that marriage was the furthest thing from his mind and claimed never to have seen a happy marriage. Others watched people they loved go through painful divorces. Gil, although his parents seemed happily married, focused instead on the unhappy ones:

> My older sister was divorced several times, so that broke the mold for the family. She had two children, and it was difficult for the chil-

dren to go through. Maybe I was selfish. I was more interested in my fulfillment. Why get married?

Some found plenty of evidence that marriage was either an extremely fragile state or a kind of perpetual purgatory—risky in either case. Doug, a sanitation worker who eventually married and had two children, originally saw much to lose and little to gain by marrying:

> When I was a teenager, everybody was like, "Get married? What for? Leave all this?" We thought we were pretty cool. And as I got older, in the marines and after, I knew I would never get married. I was having a great time, and no way I was going to get married. . . . I didn't think it was such a good deal.

. . . Negative experiences with children left some men wondering whether they wanted to have a family of their own. After taking care of his younger siblings in adolescence, Harry, a social worker, began to ask himself whether having children was worth the trouble:

> When I was very young, I thought I would get married and have a family, because everyone was married and had children. But in my teens, I carried a lot of responsibility with my brothers, and I really felt that I had done my time. So after college, I determined I was not going to get married. I was not going to have a family. I was really going to try to put some things together for myself.

. . . Most men viewed children as a threat to their freedom not to succeed at work. Fearing that becoming responsible for economic dependents would rob them of the option to pursue unpredictable careers or less demanding jobs, these men rebelled against a whole package of domestic and work commitments that embodied the established definitions of masculine success. So Rick, a junior high school teacher (and now the father of two daughters), kept "postponing with no end in sight"; Tom, the editor (and divorced father), "didn't see my life following any kind of pattern—in fact, I was probably doing whatever I could to prevent it falling into the pattern"; and Steve, an ex-addict (and now a computer programmer), embraced the 1960s counterculture and dropped out of college: "Being a breadwinner? No, thank you. Out the door."

If for some, remaining autonomous meant not having to find a challenging job, for others it meant the freedom not to take a tedious, ordinary one. Drawn to an alluring cultural symbol—the lone, often rebellious man who strikes out on his own against the system and against the odds—they hoped to seek their fortunes and lodge their identities in work that promised freedom, adventure, or risk. These men were attracted to occupations that hold a glamorous, almost mythological cultural aura. Some involved physical danger and violence. After fighting in Vietnam, for example, Doug

> ran around like a wild man. First I was contemplating being a mercenary, then some jobs on the oil pipeline in Arabia. They all included the possibility of violence. That's what I was trained for. Those were the only jobs I contemplated.

> . . . Potentially unstable and even dangerous careers were linked to a wish for freedom from having to support a family. Ron, a surveyor and father of two, preferred physical risk to the risk of domestic boredom:

> I wanted to just have fun. I wanted to be a smoke jumper for the forest service, those sickos who jump out of planes and get into the fire lines. Then I was going to join the merchant marines, but I got my draft notice, so I joined the navy. . . . Marriage was for those other guys. I'd stay single, have my fun, and continue on until the day I die. . . .

In rejecting the breadwinning ethic, some hoped other types of commitments could take the place of family life. Stuart expected to find his family among a community of men, having decided at an early age to become a Franciscan brother: "The Church was teaching that this was a worthy sacrifice, but I didn't understand, really, what it meant. . . . I had a very romantic concept of the monastery and this community life."

More common was a vague hope of remaining free and independent indefinitely—like Scott, a paramedic who sought safety in solitude after serving in Vietnam:

> Vietnam makes you want to be away from everybody. When things are starting to fall apart all around you and the world is hanging by someone else's decision, you want to hide. I saw a lot of guys breaking down, so I decided to play little mind games. I could sit in a crowd of people and just tune myself off completely from them. So the loneliness, it was kind of preferable. I thought I'd never get married.

Refusing to Think About the Future

Another group did not consciously oppose marriage, parenthood, or steady work. They simply did not formulate any well-defined goals or expectations. As Theodore, who ironically became a planner, put it, "I always had a reluctance to think about the future. I was never a person who said, 'I want to be this when I grow up.'"

Such passivity stemmed from two opposite and apparently contradictory assumptions about the future. One was that men enjoyed the luxury of not having to plan. Men who made this assumption believed that everything would work out fine with or without forethought. This unexamined optimism was most pronounced among those whose middle-class affluence guaranteed them a good start in life. When Paul, the social service administrator and a father of two, was asked whether he had any expectations about what he'd be doing at this age, he replied:

> Goodness, no. I was very bad at that. I am fortunate that things ended up as well as they have for me. I was not good at planning, foresight, determination, or any of those traits. I started off very bad scholastically. . . . My career planning was nix, horrible.

The second, more pessimistic orientation was espoused mostly by working-class men, who were more likely to feel that constricted opportunities would take any future "choices" away from them. Dean, the driver for the parks department, graduated from high school while the Vietnam War raged:

One brother was in the marines; the other in the army. I figured my destiny was controlled, so I wasn't really thinking ahead. If I was drafted, I was drafted. Otherwise, if you learned how to do roofing or how to fix a car or something like that, it seemed you could always get by.

Expecting an Early Death

. . . None exemplify this fatalistic approach more vividly than those who expected to die young. This small but notable group expected to succumb to the dangers of growing up long before the chance to face adult challenges arrived. For these men, all from the working class, future planning seemed irrational since they did not expect to have a future. Gary, a separated custodian with sole custody of his young daughter, told me: "I thought I'd be dead by now. I got involved with gang fights. I did drugs. I sniffed glue. I sniffed carbon. It's a wonder I have a brain left."

The chilling truth is that exposure to gangs, drugs, and street violence made these expectations seem reasonable to some working-class boys. For others, the Vietnam War posed even greater dangers. Those who could not afford college were vulnerable to the draft. Lacking the necessary credentials to obtain a good job, they were also more likely to see the armed forces as a palatable alternative to the civilian labor market.[3] Patrick had served in Vietnam and seen close friends die:

I never thought I'd make it to this age. I was into motorcycles, parachuting. I went into the army at twenty-one, and I really didn't think I was going to come home. I never thought about the future.

Diversity and Change

. . . Despite the modern emphasis on breadwinning as a man's proper adult status, boys and young men form their aspirations in an ambiguous cultural and social context that stresses both breadwinning and its discontents. The contradictory quality of these cultural values allows and encourages men to form diverse, vague, and conflicting expectations in childhood. Whatever goals and hopes a child forms, moreover, there is no

guarantee of their being reached. They may become firmer as later experiences confirm early expectations, or they may change as adult experiences undermine their foundation.

Becoming an adult involves a process of relinquishing past attachments and dependencies while assuming new responsibilities and commitments. In modern societies, the process can be steady or abrupt, but even under ideal circumstances it is demanding.[4] When the structures that constrain and regulate adult development contain contradictory and rapidly changing guidelines, it becomes more difficult to navigate the process of growing up and to predict the outcome. Among the whole group of men, change in adulthood was as prevalent as diversity in childhood. Regardless of the point of departure, the majority changed their orientation over time.[5]

Only 38 percent of those who developed a breadwinning orientation in childhood sustained it as adults. . . . Thirty-two percent preferred to affirm personal freedom and independence instead. The remaining 29 percent became, or hoped to become, involved in caring for their children. These men developed greater parental involvement than they could have imagined as children.

A similar pattern of change can be seen among those who developed nonbreadwinning expectations in childhood, which in most cases meant remaining autonomous. In adulthood, 29 percent still hoped not to forge parental ties. But slightly more than a third became oriented toward breadwinning despite their earlier aversion to it. More surprising, 37 percent of this group became, or expected to become, involved fathers.

This pattern of diversity and change applies to both professional and working-class groups. While more college-educated men expected as children to become primary breadwinners (55 percent compared with 43 percent for the working-class group), this disparity declined over time. Indeed, the percentage of working-class men who held a breadwinning outlook in adulthood exceeds that of men with college degrees. Only a few percentage points separate the middle-class and working-class men who moved toward involved fatherhood. The variation that exists within each class is more noteworthy than the small differences between them. A diverse and complex set of parental and family patterns emerged among men across the class spectrum, as experiences of personal change were a dominant motif among the more and less educated alike. . . .

NOTES

1. Nine percent reported either that they had no father or that they could not tell how their father felt about his work.

2. Although the concept of "fear of success" was developed to explain women's ambivalence toward careers, subsequent research has demonstrated that men are as likely to fear success as are women. For a critique of this much-publicized but never demonstrated thesis, see Kaufman and Richardson, 1982.

3. All of the men who served in the armed forces were from a working-class background. For an excellent analysis of how working-class boys went to war and middle-class boys went to training for professional careers during the Vietnam War, see Baskir and Strauss, 1978.

4. See Eisenstadt, 1956, and Elder, 1978, for classic theoretical considerations of the transition to adulthood in modern societies. Among the many who have traced historical changes in the structuring of the life course and found choice points to be increasingly less predictable, see Buchman, 1989; Demos, 1986; Modell, Furstenberg, and Hershberg, 1976; Hareven, 1977; Kett, 1977.

5. The finding of change in adulthood is a common one in contemporary research. My earlier study of women's work and family choices found a similar dynamic to be typical of contemporary women. Others who have focused on the change process in adulthood include Brim, 1992; Furstenberg, Brooks-Gunn, and Morgan, 1987; and Jacobs, Karen, and McClelland, 1991. Jacobs, et al., found that young men's occupational aspirations are highly unstable. In general, they tend to decline with age and become more stable later on, when inequality in educational attainments forces men from the lower classes to settle for less.

REFERENCES

Baskir, Lawrence M., and William A. Strauss. 1978. *Chance and Circumstance: The Draft, the War, and the Vietnam Generation.* New York: Knopf.

Brim, Gilbert G., Jr. 1992. *Ambition: How We Manage Success and Failure Throughout Our Lives.* New York: Basic Books.

Buchman, Marlis, 1989. *The Script of Life in Modern Society: Entry into Adulthood in a Changing World.* Chicago: University of Chicago Press.

Demos, John. 1986. "The Changing Faces of Fatherhood." In *Past, Present, and Personal: The Family and the Life Course in American History,* pp. 41–66. Edited by John Demos, New York: Oxford University Press.

Eisenstadt, S. N. 1956. *From Generation to Generation: Age Groups and Social Structure.* New York: Free Press.

Elder, Glen H., Jr. 1978. "Approaches to Social Change and the Family." In *Turning Points: Historical and Sociological Essays on the Family,* pp. S1–S38. Edited by John Demos and Sarane S. Boocock. Chicago: University of Chicago Press.

Furstenberg, Frank F., Jr., Jeanne Brooks-Gunn, and S. Phillip Morgan. 1987. *Adolescent Mothers in Later Life.* New York: Cambridge University Press.

Hareven, Tamara. 1977. "Family Time and Historical Time." *Daedalus* 106 (Spring): 57–70.

Jacobs, Jerry A., David Karen, and Katherine McClelland. 1991. "The Dynamics of Young Men's Career Aspirations." *Sociological Forum* 6(4) (December): 609–40.

Kaufman, Debra R., and Barbara L. Richardson. 1982. *Achievement and Women: Challenging the Assumptions.* New York: Free Press.

Kett, Joseph F. 1977. *Rites of Passage: Adolescence in America, 1790 to the Present.* New York: Basic Books.

Modell, John, Frank F. Furstenberg, Jr., and Theodore Hershberg. 1976. "Social Change and Transitions to Adulthood in Historical Perspective." *Journal of Family History* 1(Autumn): 7–32.

THINKING ABOUT THE READINGS

Exiles from Kinship

- Why do you suppose there is so much reluctance in this society to acknowledge the family status of gay couples? Why are gay families considered by many to be a threat to the institution of family? The larger sociological issue here is: Should individuals have the freedom to define their living arrangements as a family? Should we be able to call anything we want a family? What is society's interest in controlling who can and can't be considered a family? Can you envision a society based on "families of choice" rather than procreation or blood?

No Man's Land

- Describe the various ways men have adapted to the decline of the breadwinner role. As the financial status of women continues to improve, chances are that the breadwinner role will become decreasingly "male." What do you think will be the cumulative effect of this change on men's roles in families and their place in the larger society? Most of the men described in the article grew up in families where their fathers were the sole breadwinners. Today's male children are likely to grow up in dual-earner families or perhaps households headed by a single mother. How might these experiences shape perceptions of the husband/father role in the next several decades when these boys become men and start their own families?

III

Social Structure, Institutions, and Everyday Life

CHAPTER 9

The Structure of Society
Organizations and Social Institutions

One of the great sociological paradoxes of our existence is that in a society that so fiercely extols the virtues of rugged individualism and personal accomplishment, we spend most of our lives responding to the influence of larger organizations and social institutions. From the nurturing environments of our churches and schools to the cold depersonalizations of massive bureaucracies, organizations and institutions are a fundamental part of our everyday lives. But no matter how strict and unyielding a particular organization may appear to be, individuals within them are usually able to exert some control over their lives. Rarely is an organization what it appears to be, on the surface.

For most Americans, the most important organization to which they belong is their place of employment. For better or worse, our jobs are what define us. Some jobs, like factory work, appear to outside observers as monotonous, regimented places where workers can exert little, if any, autonomy. However, in "The Active Worker," Randy Hodson shows us that workers in even the most repetitive jobs can be quite active on their own terms and follow their own agendas. This behind-the-scenes look at several different workplaces reveals an intricate world of creative activity on the part of lower-level employees who find ways of adapting to the alienating environment of their jobs.

In larger organizations distinct cultures develop where similar meanings and perspectives are cultivated. As in society as a whole, however, distinct subcultures can develop. In "The Smile Factory," John Van Maanen examines the organizational culture of one of American society's most enduring icons: Disney theme parks. Disneyland and Disneyworld have a highly codified and strict set of conduct standards. Variations from tightly defined employee norms are not tolerated. You'd expect in such a place that employees would be a rather homogeneous group. However, Van Maanen discovers that beneath the surface of this self-proclaimed "Happiest Place on Earth" lies a mosaic of distinct groups that have created their own status system and that work hard to maintain the status boundaries between one another.

One type of organization that most of us are familiar with, at some level, are hospitals. We usually see them for what they are fundamentally designed to be:

places where sick people go to get better. Likewise we are inclined to see the professionals who work in them—particularly doctors and nurses—as people who are dedicated to helping people who are ailing. In "The Routinization of Disaster," Dan Chambliss shows us that the enormous pressures of such a pursuit can create in hospital employees a unique and surprising approach to their jobs. Chambliss focuses on the process by which nurses routinize and render "matter-of-fact" the experiences that to the rest of us are among the most traumatic and disastrous of our lives: sickness and death. Far from being cold and unfeeling, such an approach is a necessary adaptation to the tragedy that nurses see on a daily basis.

The Active Worker

Compliance and Autonomy at the Workplace

Randy Hodson

Workers do not leave creative activity behind when they enter the workplace. A . . . behind-the-scenes look at any workplace reveals an intricate world of creative, purposive activity, some of it related to the ongoing tasks of the organization and some of it not (Homans 1950; Mars and Nicod 1984; Van Maanen 1977). Indeed, workers' autonomous creative abilities are being called on today to rescue American productivity from its pattern of secular decline (Parker 1985; Rothschild and Russell 1986). Workers' creativity is being solicited under such banners as Quality of Work Life Programs, Group Centered Responsibility, and Participative Management.

. . . Most theories of the workplace anesthetize workers, considering them merely as objects of manipulation. . . . (Braverman 1974; Edwards 1979; Poulantzas 1975). Those theories that do include a role for workers' autonomous actions typically place workers' behaviors in theoretical straitjackets. From the management side, workers are seen as engaged in output restriction and foot-dragging (Crozier 1964; Etzioni 1971; Organ 1988). . . . From a radical perspective, workers' behaviors are forced into a theoretical straitjacket of acquiescence ("false consciousness") or resistance to capitalist control of the workplace (Edwards and Scullion 1982; Shaiken 1984; Wood 1982). . . .

Author's Note: I would like to thank Patricia and Peter Adler, Bob Althauser, Bill Corsaro, Frank Dobbin, Donna Eder, Greg Hooks, Michele Lamont, David Snow, Suzanne Staggenborg, John Van Maanen, and several anonymous reviewers for useful comments on earlier versions of this article.

Some contemporary researchers argue for a more active view of the worker. . . . For example, Burawoy (1979) argued that workers are centrally concerned with "making out"—devising a way to meet production goals without completely exhausting themselves. . . . [But] workers' creative efforts [often] make little or no difference. Thus even the small range of creative activity allowed workers . . . is rendered . . . inconsequential.

. . . I anticipated that I would find that workers were neither passive objects of manipulation nor intransigent resisters of every management and organizational goal. . . . What sorts of resistance do workers engage in, under what conditions, and toward what ends? . . .

Method

. . . I started by interviewing clerical workers and then moved to the paraprofessions and semiprofessions and finally to service and manual workers. . . . My initial contacts for securing interviews were mainly through students who had been in continuing studies classes that I have taught on the sociology of work. Although none of these students were themselves included in the study, they provided access to networks that enabled me to select respondents from a wide range of occupations. . . .

My goal throughout the research was to understand the nature of effort at the workplace and the ways it is elicited and stymied. The interviews were largely unstructured and took place in a variety of settings chosen by respondents. These settings included respondents' workplaces, restaurants, parks, and homes. I established a basis for conversation by asking about what motivated them to work hard and what caused them to feel unmotivated. The interviews typically lasted from 1.5 to 2.5 hours. Besides talking with workers, in most cases, I also visited their workplaces, some repeatedly. I thus had the opportunity to observe most of the workplaces directly and to talk further with the workers and sometimes with their co-workers. The respondents ranged in age from 19 to 54 years. They were employed in jobs arrayed across the major occupational categories and made salaries ranging from poverty-level earnings to earnings about two times the national average. . . .

I called this process to a halt when I felt that additional interviews were yielding little new information. Because of my relatively focused topic, only 17 workers were interviewed. However, these interviews yielded 178 single-spaced pages of transcribed material. When put in paragraph form and cross-filed, this material yielded approximately 2,094 paragraph-length statements by workers. . . .

Enthusiastic Compliance

. . . Workers often evaluated the quality of their jobs in terms of the degree of flexibility allowed. Jobs that were flexible enough so that workers could exercise creativity in their work provided the structural preconditions for the emergence of pride, enthusiasm, and extra effort. The worker I interviewed who had the least job flexibility was a long-distance telephone operator. The work involved was too repetitive and too closely supervised, both electronically and by direct supervision, to have a significant sphere of autonomy and flexibility; hence this was one of the most alienated and cynical workers I interviewed. Other jobs had greater spheres of flexibility, and gradations in the autonomy that this allowed provided one of the most important determinants of differential enthusiasm and extra effort. For example, a metal fabrications worker reported that

> free rein implies responsibility and people excel if they think they have responsibility. I know I do. My boss said at the beginning that "I'm not going to stand over you and there are no set breaks, but as long as you get the job done, you'll find time to rest or talk

to somebody." So he put the responsibility of knowing what to do and when to do it to me, and I thought it was good.

. . . Worker control over pace and work rules is increased where workers are expected to devise the details of their own procedures as a matter of standard practice. Having responsibility for devising their own work procedures gives workers immense power (see Lipsky 1981). Often, workers have to figure out how to do required tasks with little or no instruction from management. Workers' most frequent source of information is other workers who are currently doing the job or who have done similar work in the past. Hughes (1958) noted that the right to make judgments about the details of work practices is "most jealously guarded" by workers (p. 94).

Having a job that enables one to construct a positive personal identity is also important in motivating extra effort. An administrative secretary reported: "I like to solve problems and in this job you can do a lot of that. And I like working with people. I like meeting people. I wouldn't ever like to work by myself. If I opened my own business, I would want something where the public was involved. I'm just that kind of person." Some work settings facilitate the development of a positive personal identity. Other settings make the development of a viable identity extremely difficult. For example, Snow and Anderson (1987) discussed the problems of establishing viable personal identities among the homeless whose occupational roles are largely restricted to jobs contracted on a day-labor basis. . . .

Making Out

. . . Workers are immensely creative in devising strategies that preserve their autonomy and dignity in the face of excessive or inappropriate demands. Probably the most common behavioral strategy is to withhold enthusiasm and become detached from work. Depending on the nature of the work and the degree of the perceived managerial offenses, this detachment may mean that workers take an extra 10 minutes on breaks or that they avoid work 80% of the time. Along with giving only partial effort comes the creation of smoke screens to obscure this strategy. A worker at a sewage treatment plant reported that many workers neglect to take readings in the tanks at regular intervals and have learned to predict these readings reasonably well by taking recent rainfall amounts into account: "There is no way anyone can tell definitely whether or not we have actually taken the readings." Sometimes managers are fooled by such stratagems. More often, they are not, but the cost of challenging the scam is prohibitively large or the rewards for overturning it are too low. Thus many situations in which workers limit their efforts involve some degree of complicity or at least acquiescence by supervisors and management.

Appearances are key to successfully making out. A teacher reported the following practices at his school:

> The principal can in some schools ask to see the lesson plans every week. What you do is make lesson plans but just don't do them. So if they ask you what you did that week, you show them lesson plans that you never used. And have a whole bunch of grades. It looks like you did all that grading, but these can be based on attendance or on oral quizzes. Come up with some flashy thing once a month so everybody thinks something is going on. Open your curtains and then the principal walks by and sees this wonderful thing going on this 1 week out of the month that you do it and then the rest of the time actually close your curtains. Really advertise when you're doing something good and when you're not, close up shop.

Brownnosing

. . . Brownnosing is being ingratiating toward one's supervisors and receiving favors or privileges in return. Brownnosing is something other people do: Reports of brownnosing are always in the third person. When a worker had engaged in a behavior that someone else might call brownnosing, they will tend to interpret their behavior as "making out" or as successfully manipulating management. Brownnosing *is* akin to making out in that it rests on an overlap between managerial and worker interests. However, brownnosing is a tainted behavior because it violates the workplace norm of

solidarity with other workers and opposition to management.

The attribution of brownnosing to others is not an everyday occurrence. Only about a third of the respondents made any mention of such issues, and none dwelt on this as a major concern. More complaints are made against co-workers for slackness than for brownnosing. While brownnosing itself was not frequently noted, what was commonly condemned was managers treating workers differently. Thus the blame was placed on management for treating workers differently rather than on workers for seeking to brownnose management. A kitchen worker in a nursing home reported that

> if the boss catches someone slacking off, he gets really upset, really. He expects you to have a rag in your hand and be wiping some grease up or he will bite your ear off. You have to look busy. Unless you are one of his favorites—he has a couple of those. If he likes an individual employee, they get better treatment. It's perfectly obvious. They get more free rein. They don't have to look so busy all the time. You will see them in the break room smoking a cigarette a little bit more often.

Favoritism may simply be the way in which what I have called brownnosing is socially constructed by workers. The social construction of such behaviors as favoritism maintains the image of solidarity against an unjust and manipulative management. The implicit consensus seems to be that everyone tries to get ahead; some just have different strategies than others. The crime seems to be more in management inappropriately rewarding ingratiating behavior than in workers attempting it as a strategy.

Conditional Effort

Infringements on autonomy and flexibility were the most common basis for workers saying that they were not enthusiastic about their work. These infringements could take the form of bureaucratic rules or overly strict supervision. Workers seemed much less concerned with machine pacing and instead took it as part of the invisible background against which their roles at the workplace were played out. Human infringements on autonomy were experienced with considerably less tolerance. A waitress whose boss started holding time cards until the waitresses rolled the mandatory two trays of silverware and napkins before checking out at night identified this experience as a pivotal one in coming to dislike her job: "I felt like Larry was trying to babysit or something. A lot of people don't think it should even be our job. That's another reason we're really reluctant to do it. It's like holding our time cards to make us do something we shouldn't have to do in the first place." The reason this episode so irritated the waitress was that it undermined the dignity and honor of her position. . . . Where opportunities for the attainment of honor in work are perceived as absent, withdrawal of effort is likely to follow (Becker, Geer, and Hughes 1968, 102).

A significant share of behaviors at the workplace entail an element of deviation from some aspect of the formal organizational agenda. Relevant behaviors include the pursuit of alternative tasks, the avoidance of unpleasant tasks through delay, and physical withdrawal from work through absenteeism, tardiness, or hiding from work while on the job. Delay is a particularly common strategy. The . . . theory behind delay is that work delayed is work avoided. Someone else may do the work or the work may not get done, and the consequences may be within the range of management tolerance. A clerical worker reported the following responses to work she dislikes:

> Find something else to do. Some other kind of work that you like better. Goof off. Do my checkbook, play computer games, take a walk with somebody else in the building. I'd rather goof off and do it right later at the last minute if it still has to be done than do a poor job on it now.

Doing poor-quality work appears to be distasteful in most circumstances; it violates the principle of taking pride in one's own work. Delaying unnecessary or undesirable work, however, not only avoids such work but simultaneously realizes the principle of autonomy and creativity in arranging

one's schedule, even if one must do so through subterfuge (Fine 1984; Roy 1960).

There are often some things about work that directly anger workers. Frequently, these relate to management. Management provides a good target for discontents no matter what the complex causality of the issues involved. After all, they are in charge. . . .

Managers are condemned for such faults as inability to provide needed materials, laziness, stupidity, lack of leadership in crisis situations ("management by drift"), and destructive infighting with other managers. A waitress reported the following evaluation of her supervisor: "I'm not even sure what he does but give you a bad time. Sometimes, we sit around and wonder how this restaurant ever goes anywhere. I think the managers have no idea what is really going on.". . . A telephone worker complained about the continuing disruptions and deteriorating conditions caused by divestiture in the telephone industry:

> We don't take as much pride in our work in that we don't ever know what is going on. It is chaotic since 1983. Nobody knows what is going on. If you have any experience getting your phone fixed since divestiture, you call, and nobody knows what's going on. Sometimes you can talk to as many as 20 people. The right hand doesn't know what the left is doing. If they can't get their own act together and give decent service, why should *you* try?

. . . A female operator at a chemical plant condemned managers for laziness:

> The lower managers tend to drive around the plant—they'll spend the whole day driving around the plant, listening to the radio or park somewhere. They'll say they're doing an inspection of the plant and walk around the plant for 2 hours and not do anything. The higher management tends to disappear into their offices all day. They essentially do nothing, or they say they're going to lunch and to a meeting and then they are gone for 6 hours and don't come back. They pretty much do what they want because there's no one to see what they're doing.

... Fears associated with job insecurity also figured heavily into complaints against management. A retail store worker employed in a company in the midst of a union busting drive (which included the company filing Chapter 11 bankruptcy papers) said: "If you are worried about whether or not you are going to have a job next week, it's hard to keep a smile on your face for customers. . . . I have a wife and a son and for me to just be out of a job, it's going to be tough. . . . I'm scared."

Managers were also condemned for being abusive, for not valuing and respecting workers and their contributions, for favoritism, and for being paid so much when workers are paid so little. An administrative secretary in a not-for-profit organization reported painful experiences of status degradation:

> In many instances the whole tag of being a secretary is degrading. I think people don't look at you with the respect you deserve. They think that you are some kind of clerical person that can perform miracles but that you don't have any brains in your head. I think a lot of the lack of motivation here comes from being made fun of for grammar being corrected; there are a lot of cracks in this office about being [local bumpkins], and there are some of us who may be. But after a while it gets old.

Given the apparently light duties of management and the onerousness of their own duties, many workers also experienced steep pay differentials in favor of management as a direct slap in the face.

Along with learning the organizational rules about their jobs, workers simultaneously learn how to bend these rules to maintain their own autonomy and dignity (Willis 1977). Even the experience of learning rules whose main purpose is to limit the autonomy of workers thus becomes an opportunity to exercise creativity through the development of counterstrategies of productivity that create spheres of autonomous activity. . . .

Workers report that managers' responses to restricted effort vary dramatically. Some managers try to run a tighter ship. Sometimes, this eliminates a sphere of restricted activity, but it can also provoke additional restrictions on activity as a response to perceived managerial abuse. Some managers implement new rules or accounting systems, but often these are ineffective in the face of workers applying their full creative efforts to restricting their output and not getting caught or sanctioned (see Ditton 1976). Sometimes, managers are simply unaware of restricted output because they do not care enough to find out about it. They have their hands full with problems with customers, suppliers, or superiors and have simply delegated so much authority and autonomy that workers are pretty much able to write their own rules. Managers may also be limited in their ability to respond to restricted activity by the possibility that workers will retaliate if management seeks to discipline workers. A public school teacher reported that

> it's much easier for the principal to look the other way than to confront a teacher with a disciplinary issue. If they confront the teacher, they are going to be unpopular. Then, they are not going to have the support of the teachers, and their job is going to be made miserable. Teachers have a lot of power over administrators.

. . . Administrators are often limited in their ability to crack down on workers by the fact that they never had control over the details of the work process in the first place. The idea that managers are in control of the production process is a fiction in many settings (Juravich 1985). Whatever degree of input they have into work procedures is frequently contingent on interpretation and compliance by those who are actually doing the work. A laborer in a metal molding shop, who would certainly not be considered a traditionally skilled worker or autonomous professional, reported that "when they give me specific instructions, I just nod my head and say 'yea, sure.' Deep down I'm still gonna do it the way I want because I know it's better.". . .

It would be a mistake to reduce all deviations from management-specified agendas to examples of resistance. The diversity of such behaviors denies any such reduction. Non-task-related behaviors are an important way in which a livable working environment is constructed and are often a major part of the daily round of activities for workers. A night shift worker at an automated chemical plant reported a great deal of autonomy in how excess time can be used once one has figured out how to do the required chores in less than the available time:

> You can disappear in that plant and never be seen, especially if you are on night shift where there aren't many people. There are three people in the plant during the night. You could disappear and never be seen. We have intercoms, but you don't have to answer the intercom if you don't want to. Some sleep, some rest. Some of the supervisors don't mind because it's hard to stay up all night, and you might take an hour's nap here and there. They won't really bother you. People will sleep, talk on the phone; some have girlfriends or boyfriends come down and they'll disappear with them out in the plant somewhere, or sit out in the parking lot.

Foot-dragging

. . . Foot-dragging is differentiated from other types of conditional effort by its heavy reliance on delay, playing dumb, and sometimes rudeness. A waitress reported that if customers were rude or she did not anticipate a good tip, she would not bother to take their dirty plates away but would relax instead:

> If they're nasty, you leave things and don't take them away early. Also, if you're in a bad section and people aren't tipping, you tend not to do any of your other duties either. You keep saying to yourself: "I am only getting paid $2.01 an hour, that's not enough to deal with this."

Selective foot-dragging can also be used to manipulate the work environment so that it more closely matches the workers' preferences. For instance, the waitress just quoted routinely failed to bus tables that had less desirable locations so that the hostess would be forced to seat new customers in more favorable locations (typically window seats), thus increasing the likelihood of good tips. . . .

Playing dumb is one of the most frequently used strategies to avoid unpleasant tasks in preference for other tasks or for non-work-related activities. A teacher reported it as a favored strategy in the school setting:

> Certain teachers would act like they can't run the audio-visual equipment so they get somebody else to do it 'cuz they are just too lazy to do it. . . . Nobody wants to give a presentation in the faculty meetings about whatever is going on in their department or in their classroom—so they just act like they don't know about anything to get out of making a presentation.

Withdrawal

. . . Absenting oneself from work is the most drastic form of limiting work effort. It is, however, a common response, though generally in measured doses. In describing how his colleagues dealt with work they wanted to avoid, a public school teacher made the following observations: "They drink and they do drugs, including on the job. They rush home and turn on the TV at night and they play like they are not at work when they are actually here, busying themselves with gossip or sneaking magazines into the classroom and reading them." Active hiding is also a commonly used option, according to a nursing home worker who spoke somewhat "tongue in cheek": "We've got people who will actually bring their sleeping bag and camp out in the restroom, I think. Sometimes, it is hard to figure out a bathroom to go to. Some places out there they should almost charge rent." Finally, a chemical plant worker reported that workers intentionally hurt themselves to draw sick leave, including inflicting cuts on their hands and reporting back injuries that are hard to disprove. Avoidance of work appears to be most common where there is a breakdown in the normative social order. Such a breakdown is likely to occur where the "individual's anticipated future in the organization looks empty or grim" (Van Maanen 1977, 163). . . .

Absenting oneself from work is also associated with poor wages and/or limited flexibility on the job. As a production worker in a metal-fabricating plant reported: "They don't give me the money or the security or benefits or any of the things other jobs have. So I don't feel I owe them anything."....

Sabotage

... Machine wrecking is a heady experience, chiefly reserved for those who have both limited attachment to the job and a great deal of resentment against the organization or their immediate boss (Genovese 1974; Scott 1985). Other types of conditional effort are more common on a daily basis because correctly functioning equipment is necessary for the efficient performance of required tasks. Workers therefore have an interest in protecting machinery and maintaining its performance. Defective machinery may limit workers' latitude to do those parts of the job that they enjoy doing or may otherwise limit their ability to control the conditions of their work. Breaking machinery is simply too abrupt and total an interruption for most situations. Where it does occur, it generally involves tension-reducing destruction of peripheral equipment. For instance, at a chemical plant, golf carts were used to access some of the outlying buildings. The plant had four of these carts, so if one was damaged there would generally be another one available. As a result, workers drove them hard, laid skid marks, and banged the carts into each other. This is intentional destruction of equipment, but it does not interfere with other options the workers may want to pursue in negotiating the details of the level and direction of their effort. Such seemingly pointless activities can have significant social and symbolic payoffs for workers as they engage in playful collective activity at the expense of management. Sabotage is fun. Sabotage of all types, including the relatively playful type just discussed, occurs most frequently where, as a hospital orderly stated simply but eloquently, "workers disrespect the job because the job disrespects them." In such settings, being destructive is one of the few ways in which one can find genuine pleasure in work.

Petty theft is also a common response to felt grievances. Theft of small items occurs at most workplaces and is an important mechanism through which grievances are vented. Some degree of retribution and equity can be achieved through a small theft. At a nursing home, this involved stealing serving-size boxes of breakfast cereal. In white-collar settings, it involved stealing paper, pencils, and envelopes for home use. In situations involving food preparation or serving, it involved eating food on the job beyond what was allowed. These activities are not identified as theft by their practitioners (Mars 1982). Rather, they are the particular fringe benefits offered by the job or they are faint and often symbolic compensation for inadequate salary or excessive work demands (Hollinger and Clark 1983). Such activities often involve a certain degree of collaborative effort with other workers, or, at a minimum, an implicit agreement to look the other way. As a result, petty theft can be an important mechanism through which group solidarity is heightened and management is defined as the out-group. Mars and Nicod (1984) reported that maitre'ds in expensive restaurants differentiate between customers whose bills can be padded and those who cannot be so bilked and seat customers that can be cheated in a specific waiter's section as a reward for services rendered or in exchange for complimentary favors. . . . Larger thefts occur, too, but here the motivations, while building on the issue of retribution, also include illicit gain on a more substantial scale. For example, an expensive generator was taken from a chemical plant. Here, the motivation included the desire to have the generator itself as well as a desire for retribution arising from workplace grievances. . . .

Gossip and Infighting

... Group mechanisms . . . play a central role in developing norms about appropriate levels of effort. It was noted above that gossip about bosses is a key mechanism for defining the nature of the effort bargain. Such gossip operates through defining bosses as part of the out-group and, conversely, workers as members of the in-group whose definitions of the effort bargain are given greater credibility (Hughes 1974).

Gossip is also commonly used within work groups to create ongoing interpretations of appropriate levels of effort for the members of the group. One particularly common line of discussion among respondents focused on the problem of lazy co-workers and the upholding of group standards. In settings with task interdependence, workers who dragged their feet caused other workers extra effort and were ostracized for their laziness. A computer accounts clerk reported that "people who do not do their share find that they have fewer friends at break time."

In settings with less task interdependence, poor workers are condemned not because they cause others extra effort but because they are getting paid the same but are putting in less effort than other workers. . . . An interview with an operator at a waste water treatment plant involved discussions of workers who abused sick leave policies by declaring fictitious injuries or exaggerating minor ones:

> We earn 8 hours of sick leave per month. Some people use up all their sick time and you wonder about the motivation involved. You never see anyone with 100 hours of sick time on the books get hurt. You always see the people who use all their vacation time, and now they're hurt. That happens time and time again. It seems like you can predict who is going to be hurt and when. For example, tomorrow is the first day of the month and we earn 8 hours. Tomorrow, there will be a tremendous number of sick people. It will be the people who have zero now and will have 8 tomorrow. You won't have a person who has 100 hours today be sick tomorrow.

Workers indicated that management often appeared to be aware of conflict among workers and relied on pressure from co-workers as the first line of control. . . .

Gossip is pervasive at the workplace because it serves so many functions. These include providing an outlet for boredom and stress, social control and boundary maintenance, bragging and self-glorification, and disseminating information. Gossip is most pervasive in settings where there is strong competition between workers and in settings with a lack of leadership or with strong organizational ambiguities. . . .

The social control functions of gossip are evidenced in the following comments by a teacher:

> I guess some teachers who just did everything were seen as brownnosers and as goody-two-shoes and they were often the victim or the

butt of a lot of the social gossip. So, in a sense, they pay socially for being good 'cuz everybody is jealous, and so anytime there was any scuttlebutt possible to spread about them, it was out in force.

. . . The social outlet functions of gossip were also evidenced by a teacher's comments:

> People are so bored and burnt out by these kids that they have to do something to just kill the time, so they'll go to the teachers' lounge during their planning period instead of doing lessons and get caught up on the latest and who hates who. Getting embroiled in conflicts somehow makes it more bearable because you have some sort of social agenda that you are working as opposed to just your damn work.

Gossip is also an important mechanism whereby workers can learn about working conditions and wages for other workers. A waitress reports that "I heard that people at [another restaurant] can make their whole rent in one weekend." . . . Gossip is not all fun, however. For many workers, it can also be a source of stress and is something to be avoided. A night shift worker reported that being out of the gossip circuit was one of the things he appreciated most about the night shift. . . .

Gossip and character assassination are the primary weapons in interpersonal conflicts at the workplace. Character assassination is popular because it inflicts damage on the target with minimal risk to the attacker. Taking more concrete actions to antagonize co-workers or disrupt their work runs the risk of being called to task by other workers or by management for intentionally disrupting production.

Besides character assassination, the most common tactic in infighting is to intentionally shift work to another person. A food service worker at a nursing home reported chronic attempts by the nursing and food service staffs to shift responsibilities to each other:

> Nursing doesn't like dietary. Dietary doesn't like nursing. Neither one likes housekeeping. Because there is a grey area of responsibility between them. Nursing doesn't want to

bother feeding a particularly nasty resident, even though the person should be in their room because they are a distraction and a nuisance and a burden on other people in the dining room—other residents and their families. They will continually try to pawn off that person on the dining room staff. It's not good for the business to have someone who is extremely aggressive, is vulgar, has no control over their bowels or bladder in the dining room.

Outright interference with others' work is rare but not unknown. A waitress reported the following skirmish: "Sometimes other waitresses have even been known to take their tip from the table and then they'll just leave, and, when the customers leave, you're left with clearing off their tables. You don't mind helping but you don't like being taken advantage of."

Infighting may also involve snitching on coworkers to management. A telephone operator reported that "a certain group of employees think they can get ahead by reporting other employees." It is ugly, but it happens. Workers also sometimes try to make other workers appear as fools by pointing out their weaknesses in awkward situations.

Discussion and Conclusions

. . . To understand workplace behaviors, we need a theoretical model of the worker that is neither anesthetized nor limited to resisting management strategies of control. . . .

Our theories need to give greater weight to the ability of workers to create their own environments. Workers' power rests on their "practical autonomy"—the necessity that workers' creative and autonomous activity be solicited if the business of ongoing enterprises is to be achieved (Wardell forthcoming). The analysis of workers' practical autonomy, its varieties, and its antecedents and consequences is a vast, little explored, and terribly important area in the sociology of work. . . .

The typology of worker behaviors suggested here is based on an active view of the worker who is seen as constantly engaged in the social construction of the setting in which productive activity takes place. I have tried to give some suggestions about the settings that give rise to particular behaviors and to suggest avenues for further investigation. Under what conditions do different forms of worker activity emerge? What is the logic of these behavioral options? Enthusiastic compliance appears most likely to emerge where a considerable degree of flexibility is allowed in the execution of organizational tasks. Making out appears to occur where rewards are minimal and where alienation is high because of limited advancement possibilities. Foot-dragging and withdrawal appear most likely to occur where the work is boring or stressful, where it is overly constrained by technical and bureaucratic forms of control, and, again, where future possibilities look grim. Sabotage appears to occur primarily where there is active resentment against a specific boss or some specific aspect of organizational policy. Gossip and infighting appear most likely to occur where there is strong competition between workers resulting from organizational ambiguities about responsibilities and duties. Finally, brownnosing appears to occur where there is competition between workers and where there is extreme inequality in rewards or an ambiguous system for distributing these rewards. . . .

REFERENCES

Becker, H. S., B. Geer, and E. C. Hughes. 1968. *Making the grade: The academic side of college life.* New York: Wiley.

Braverman, H. 1974. *Labor and monopoly capital.* New York: Monthly Review Press.

Burawoy, M. 1979. *Manufacturing consent.* Chicago: University of Chicago Press.

Crozier, M. 1964. *The bureaucratic phenomena.* Chicago: University of Chicago Press.

Ditton, J. 1976. Moral horror versus folk terror: Output restriction, class, and the social organization of exploitation. *Sociological Review* 24:519–44.

Edwards, P. K., and H. Scullion. 1982. *The social organization of industrial conflict.* Oxford: Basil Blackwell.

Edwards, R. C. 1979. *Contested terrain.* New York: Basic Books.

Etzioni, A. 1971. *A comparative analysis of complex organizations.* New York: Free Press.

Fine, G. A. 1984. Negotiated orders and organizational cultures. In *The annual review of sociology*, vol. 10, edited by R. H. Turner and J. F. Short, Jr., 239–62. Palo Alto, CA: Annual Reviews.

Genovese, E. D. 1974. *Roll, Jordon, roll: The world the slaves made.* New York: Pantheon.

Hollinger, R. C., and J. P. Clark. 1983. *Theft by employees.* Lexington, MA: D. C. Heath.

Homans, G. 1950. *The human group.* New York: Harcourt, Brace & World.

Howard, R. 1985. *Brave new workplace.* New York: Viking.

Hughes, E. C. 1958. *Men and their work.* Glencoe, IL: Free Press.

———.1974. Comments on "Honor in dirty work." *Work and Occupations* 1:284–87.

Juravich, T. 1985. *Chaos on the shop floor.* Philadelphia: Temple University Press.

Lipsky, M. 1981. *Street-level bureaucracy.* New York: Russell Sage.

Mars, G. 1982. *Cheats at work.* London: Unwin.

Mars, G., and M. Nicod. 1984. *The world of waiters.* London: Allen & Unwin.

Organ, D. W. 1988. A restatement of the satisfaction-performance hypothesis. *Journal of Management* 14:547–57.

Parker, M. 1985. *Inside the circle: A union guide to QWL.* Boston: South End Press.

Poulantzas, N. 1975. *Classes in contemporary capitalism.* London: New Left Books.

Rothschild, J., and R. Russell. 1986. Alternatives to bureaucracy: Democratic participation in the economy. In *The annual review of sociology*, vol. 12, edited by R. H. Turner and J. F. Short, Jr., 307–28. Palo Alto, CA: Annual Reviews.

Roy, D. 1960. "Banana time": Job satisfaction and informal interaction. *Human Organization* 18:158–68.

Scott, J. C. 1985. *Weapons of the weak: Everyday forms of peasant resistance.* New Haven, CT: Yale University Press.

Shaiken, H. 1984. *Work transformed.* New York: Holt, Rinehart & Winston.

Snow, D. A., and L. Anderson. 1987. Identity work among the homeless: The verbal construction and avowal of personal identities. *American Journal of Sociology* 92:1 336–71.

Van Maanen, J. 1977. *Organizational careers.* London: Wiley.

Wardell, M. Forthcoming. Organizations: A bottom-up approach. In *Rethinking organizations,* edited by Michael L. Reed and Michael Hughes. London: Sage.

Willis, P. 1977. *Learning to labor: How working class kids get working class jobs.* New York: Columbia University Press.

Wood, S., ed. 1982. *The degradation of work?* London: Hutchinson.

The Smile Factory
Work at Disneyland

John Van Maanen

Part of Walt Disney Enterprises includes the theme park Disneyland. In its pioneering form in Anaheim, California, this amusement center has been a consistent money maker since the gates were first opened in 1955. Apart from its socio-logical charm, it has, of late, become something of an exemplar for culture vultures and has been held up for public acclaim in several best-selling publi-cations as one of America's top companies. . . . To outsiders, the cheerful demeanor of its employees, the seemingly inexhaustible repeat business it gen-erates from its customers, the immaculate condi-tion of park grounds, and, more generally, the intricate physical and social order of the business itself appear wondrous.

Disneyland as the self-proclaimed "Happiest Place on Earth" certainly occupies an enviable position in the amusement and entertainment worlds as well as the commercial world in general. Its product, it seems, is emotion—"laughter and well-being." Insiders are not bashful about pro-moting the product. Bill Ross, a Disneyland exec-utive, summarizes the corporate position nicely by

Author's Note: This paper has been cobbled together using three-penny nails of other writings. Parts come from a paper presented to the American Anthropological Association Annual Meetings in Washington D.C. on November 16, 1989 called "Whistle While You Work." Other parts come from J. Van Maanen and G. Kunda, 1989. "Real feelings: Emotional expressions and organization culture." In B. Staw & L. L. Cummings (Eds.), *Research in Organization Behav-ior* (Vol. 11, pp. 43–103). Greenwich, CT: JAI Press. In coming to this version, I've had a good deal of help from my friends Steve Barley, Nicloe Biggart, Michael Owen Jones, Rosanna Hertz, Gideon Kunda, Joanne Martin, Maria Lydia Spinelli, Bob Sutton, and Bob Thomas.

noting that "although we focus our attention on profit and loss, day-in and day-out we cannot lose sight of the fact that this is a feeling business and we make our profits from that."

The "feeling business" does not operate, how-ever, by management decree alone. Whatever ser-vices Disneyland executives believe they are providing to the 60 to 70 thousand visitors per day that flow through the park during its peak summer season, employees at the bottom of the organiza-tion are the ones who most provide them. The work-a-day practices that employees adopt to amplify or dampen customer spirits are therefore a core concern of this feeling business. The happiness trade is an interactional one. It rests partly on the symbolic resources put into place by history and park design but it also rests on an animated work-force that is more or less eager to greet the guests, pack the trams, push the buttons, deliver the food, dump the garbage, clean the streets, and, in gen-eral, marshal the will to meet and perhaps exceed customer expectations. False moves, rude words, careless disregard, detected insincerity, or a sleepy and bored presence can all undermine the enter-prise and ruin a sale. The smile factory has its rules.

It's a Small World

. . . This rendition is of course abbreviated and selective. I focus primarily on such matters as the stock appearance (vanilla), status order (rigid), and social life (full), and swiftly learned codes of conduct (formal and informal) that are associated with Disneyland ride operators. These employees comprise the largest category of hourly workers on the payroll. During the summer months, they number close to four thousand and run the 60-odd rides and attractions in the park.

They are also a well-screened bunch. There is—among insiders and outsiders alike—a rather fixed view about the social attributes carried by the standard-make Disneyland ride operator. Single, white males and females in their early twenties, without facial blemish, of above average height and below average weight, with straight teeth, conservative grooming standards, and a chin-up, shoulder-back posture radiating the sort of good health suggestive of a recent history in sports are typical of these social identifiers. There are representative minorities on the payroll but because ethnic displays are sternly discouraged by management, minority employees are rather close copies of the standard model Disneylander, albeit in different colors.

This Disneyland look is often a source of some amusement to employees who delight in pointing out that even the patron saint, Walt himself, could not be hired today without shaving off his trademark pencil-thin mustache. But, to get a job in Disneyland and keep it means conforming to a rather exacting set of appearance rules. These rules are put forth in a handbook on the Disney image in which readers learn, for example, that facial hair or long hair is banned for men as are aviator glasses and earrings and that women must not tease their hair, wear fancy jewelry, or apply more than a modest dab of makeup. Both men and women are to look neat and prim, keep their uniforms fresh, polish their shoes, and maintain an upbeat countenance and light dignity to complement their appearance—no low spirits or cornball raffishness at Disneyland.

The legendary "people skills" of park employees, so often mentioned in Disneyland publicity and training materials, do not amount to very much according to ride operators. Most tasks require little interaction with customers and are physically designed to practically insure that is the case. The contact that does occur typically is fleeting and swift, a matter usually of only a few seconds. In the rare event sustained interaction with customers might be required, employees are taught to deflect potential exchanges to area supervisors or security. A Training Manual offers

the proper procedure: "On misunderstandings, guests should be told to call City Hall. . . . In everything from damaged cameras to physical injuries, don't discuss anything with guests . . . there will always be one of us nearby." Employees learn quickly that security is hidden but everywhere. On Main Street security cops are Keystone Kops; in Frontierland, they are Town Marshalls; on Tom Sawyer's Island, they are Cavalry Officers, and so on.

Occasionally, what employees call "line talk" or "crowd control" is required of them to explain delays, answer direct questions, or provide directions that go beyond the endless stream of recorded messages coming from virtually every nook and cranny of the park. Because such tasks are so simple, consisting of little more than keeping the crowd informed and moving, it is perhaps obvious why management considers the sharp appearance and wide smile of employees so vital to park operations. There is little more they could ask of ride operators whose main interactive tasks with visitors consist of being, in their own terms, "information booths," "line signs," "pretty props," "shepherds," and "talking statues."

A few employees do go out of their way to initiate contact with Disneyland customers but, as a rule, most do not and consider those who do to be a bit odd. In general, one need do little more than exercise common courtesy while looking reasonably alert and pleasant. Interactive skills that are advanced by the job have less to do with making customers feel warm and welcome than they do with keeping each other amused and happy. This is, of course, a more complex matter.

Employees bring to the job personal badges of status that are of more than passing interest to peers. In rough order, these include: good looks, college affiliation, career aspirations, past achievements, age (directly related to status up to about age 23 or 24 and inversely related thereafter), and assorted other idiosyncratic matters. Nested closely alongside these imported status badges are organizational ones that are also of concern and value to employees.

Where one works in the park carries much social weight. Postings are consequential because the ride and area a person is assigned provide rewards and benefits beyond those of wages. In-the-park stature for ride operators turns partly on whether or not unique skills are required. Disneyland neatly complements labor market theorizing on this dimension because employees with the most differentiated skills find themselves at the top of the internal status ladder, thus making their loyalties to the organization more predictable.

Ride operators, as a large but distinctly middle-class group of hourly employees on the floor of the organization, compete for status not only with each other but also with other employee groupings whose members are hired for the season from the same applicant pool. A loose approximation of the rank ordering among these groups can be constructed as follows:

1. The upper-class prestigious Disneyland Ambassadors and Tour Guides (bilingual young women in charge of ushering—some say rushing—little bands of tourists through the park);

2. Ride operators performing coveted "skilled work" such as live narrations or tricky transportation tasks like those who symbolically control customer access to the park and drive the costly entry vehicles such as the antique trains, horse-drawn carriages, and Monorail);

3. All other ride operators;

4. The proletarian Sweepers (keepers of the concrete grounds);

5. The sub-prole or peasant status Food and Concession workers (whose park sobriquets reflect their lowly social worth—"pancake ladies," "peanut pushers," "coke blokes," "suds divers," and the seemingly irreplaceable "soda jerks").

Pay differentials are slight among these employee groups. The collective status adheres, as it does internally for ride operators, to assignment or functional distinctions. As the rank order suggests, most employee status goes to those who work jobs that require higher degrees of special skill, relative freedom from constant and direct supervision, and provide the opportunity to organize and direct customer desires and behavior rather than to merely respond to them as spontaneously expressed.

The basis for sorting individuals into these various broad bands of job categories is often unknown to employees—a sort of deep, dark secret of the casting directors in personnel. When prospective employees are interviewed, they interview for "a job at Disneyland," not a specific one. Personnel decides what particular job they will eventually occupy. Personal contacts are considered by employees as crucial in this job-assignment process as they are in the hiring decision. Some employees, especially those who wind up in the lower ranking jobs, are quite disappointed with their assignments as is the case when, for example, a would-be Adventureland guide is posted to a New Orleans Square restaurant as a pot scrubber. Although many of the outside acquaintances of our pot scrubber may know only that he works at Disneyland, rest assured, insiders will know immediately where he works and judge him accordingly.

Uniforms are crucial in this regard for they provide instant communication about the social merits or demerits of the wearer within the little world of Disneyland workers. Uniforms also correspond to a wider status ranking that casts a significant shadow on employees of all types. Male ride operators on the Autopia wear, for example, untailored jump-suits similar to pit mechanics and consequently generate about as much respect from peers as the grease-stained outfits worn by pump jockeys generate from real motorists in gas stations. The ill-fitting and homogeneous "whites" worn by Sweepers signify lowly institutional work tinged, perhaps, with a reminder of hospital orderlies rather than street cleanup crews. On the other hand, for males, the crisp, officer-like Monorail operator stands alongside the swashbuckling Pirate of the Caribbean, the casual cowpoke of Big Thunder Mountain, or the smartly vested Riverboat pilot as carriers of valued symbols in and outside the park. Employees lust for these higher status positions and the rights to small advantages such uniforms provide. A lively internal labor market exists wherein there is much scheming for the more prestigious assignments.

For women, a similar market exists although the perceived "sexiness" of uniforms, rather than social rank, seems to play a larger role. To wit, the rather heated antagonisms that developed years ago when the ride "It's a Small World" first opened and began outfitting the ride operators with what were felt to be the shortest skirts and most revealing blouses in the park. Tour Guides, who traditionally headed the fashion vanguard at Disneyland in their above-the-knee kilts, knee socks, tailored vests, black English hats, and smart riding crops were apparently appalled at being upstaged by their social inferiors and lobbied actively (and, judging by the results, successfully) to lower the skirts, raise the necklines, and generally remake their Small World rivals.

Important, also, to ride operators are the break schedules followed on the various rides. The more the better. Work teams develop inventive ways to increase the number of "time-outs" they take during the work day. Most rides are organized on a rotational basis (e.g., the operator moving from a break, to queue monitor, to turnstile overseer, to unit loader, to traffic controller, to driver, and, again, to a break). The number of break men or women on a rotation (or ride) varies by the number of employees on duty and by the number of units on line. Supervisors, foremen, and operators also vary as to what they regard as appropriate break standards (and, more importantly, as to the value of the many situational factors that can enter the calculation of break rituals—crowd size, condition of ride, accidents, breakdowns, heat, operator absences, special occasions, and so forth). Self-monitoring teams with sleepy supervisors and lax (or savvy) foremen can sometimes manage a shift comprised of 15 minutes on and 45 minutes off each hour. They are envied by others, and rides that have such a potential are eyed hungrily by others who feel trapped by their more rigid (and observed) circumstances.

Movement across jobs is not encouraged by park management, but some does occur (mostly within an area and job category). Employees claim that a sort of "once a sweeper, always a sweeper" rule obtains but all know of at least a few exceptions to prove the rule. The exceptions offer some (not much) hope for those working at the social margins of the park and perhaps keep them on the job longer than might otherwise be expected.

Dishwashers can dream of becoming Pirates, and with persistence and a little help from their friends, such dreams just might come true next season (or the next).

These examples are precious, perhaps, but they are also important. There is an intricate pecking order among very similar categories of employees. Attributes of reward and status tend to cluster, and there is intense concern about the cluster to which one belongs (or would like to belong). To a degree, form follows function in Disneyland because the jobs requiring the most abilities and offering the most interest also offer the most status and social reward. Interaction patterns reflect and sustain this order. Few Ambassadors or Tour Guides, for instance, will stoop to speak at length with Sweepers who speak mostly among themselves or to Food workers. Ride operators, between the poles, line up in ways referred to above with only ride proximity (i.e., sharing a break area) representing a potentially significant intervening variable in the interaction calculation. . . .

Paid employment at Disneyland begins with the much renowned University of Disneyland whose faculty runs a day-long orientation program (Traditions I) as part of a 40-hour apprenticeship program, most of which takes place on the rides. In the classroom, however, newly hired ride operators are given a very thorough introduction to matters of managerial concern and are tested on their absorption of famous Disneyland fact, lore, and procedure. Employee demeanor is governed, for example, by three rules:

> First, we practice the friendly smile.
> Second, we use only friendly and courteous phrases.
> Third, we are not stuffy—the only Misters in Disneyland are Mr. Toad and Mr. Smee.

Employees learn too that the Disneyland culture is officially defined. The employee handbook put it in this format:

> Dis-ney Cor-po-rate Cul-ture (diz'ne kor'pr'it kul'cher) *n* 1. Of or pertaining to the Disney organization, as a: the philosophy underlying all business decisions; b: the commitment of

top leadership and management to that philosophy; c: the actions taken by individual cast members that reinforce the image.

Language is also a central feature of university life, and new employees are schooled in its proper use. Customers at Disneyland are, for instance, never referred to as such, they are "guests." There are no rides at Disneyland, only "attractions." Disneyland itself is a "Park," not an amusement center, and it is divided into "back-stage," "on-stage," and "staging" regions. Law enforcement personnel hired by the park are not policemen, but "security hosts." Employees do not wear uniforms but check out fresh "costumes" each working day from "wardrobe." And, of course, there are no accidents at Disneyland, only "incidents."....

The university curriculum also anticipates probable questions ride operators may someday face from customers, and they are taught the approved public response. A sample:

> *Question (posed by trainer):* What do you tell a guest who requests a rain check?
> *Answer (in three parts):* We don't offer rain checks at Disneyland because (1) the main attractions are all indoors; (2) we would go broke if we offered passes; and (3) sunny days would be too crowded if we gave passes.

Shrewd trainees readily note that such an answer blissfully disregards the fact that waiting areas of Disneyland are mostly outdoors and that there are no subways in the park to carry guests from land to land. Nor do they miss the economic assumption concerning the apparent frequency of Southern California rains. They discuss such matters together, of course, but rarely raise them in the training classroom. In most respects, these are recruits who easily take the role of good student.

Classes are organized and designed by professional Disneyland trainers who also instruct a well-screened group of representative hourly employees straight from park operations on the approved newcomer training methods and materials. New-hires seldom see professional trainers in class but are brought on board by enthusiastic peers who concentrate on those aspects of park

procedure thought highly general matters to be learned by all employees. Particular skill training (and "reality shock") is reserved for the second wave of socialization occurring on the rides themselves as operators are taught, for example, how and when to send a mock bobsled caroming down the track or, more delicately, the proper ways to stuff an obese adult customer into the midst of children riding the Monkey car on the Casey Jones Circus Train or, most problematically, what exactly to tell an irate customer standing in the rain who, in no uncertain terms, wants his or her money back and wants it back now.

During orientation, considerable concern is placed on particular values the Disney organization considers central to its operations. These values range from the "customer is king" verities to the more or less unique kind, of which "everyone is a child at heart when at Disneyland" is a decent example. This latter piety is one few employees fail to recognize as also attaching to everyone's mind as well after a few months of work experience. Elaborate checklists of appearance standards are learned and gone over in the classroom and great efforts are spent trying to bring employee emotional responses in line with such standards. Employees are told repeatedly that if they are happy and cheerful at work, so, too, will the guests at play. Inspirational films, hearty pep talks, family imagery, and exemplars of corporate performance are all representative of the strong symbolic stuff of these training rites. . . .

Yet, like employees everywhere, there is a limit to which such overt company propaganda can be effective. Students and trainers both seem to agree on where the line is drawn, for there is much satirical banter, mischievous winking, and playful exaggeration in the classroom. As young seasonal employees note, it is difficult to take seriously an organization that provides its retirees "Golden Ears" instead of gold watches after 20 or more years of service. All newcomers are aware that the label "Disneyland" has both an unserious and artificial connotation and that a full embrace of the Disneyland role would be as deviant as its full rejection. It does seem, however, because of the corporate imagery, the recruiting and selection devices, the goodwill trainees hold toward the organization at entry, the peer-based employment context, and the smooth fit with real student calendars, the job is considered by most ride operators to be a good one. The University of Disneyland, it appears, graduates students with a modest amount of pride and a considerable amount of fact and faith firmly ingrained as important things to know (if not always accept).

Matters become more interesting as new hires move into the various realms of Disneyland enterprise. There are real customers "out there" and employees soon learn that these good folks do not always measure up to the typically well mannered and grateful guest of the training classroom. Moreover, ride operators may find it difficult to utter the prescribed "Welcome Voyager" (or its equivalent) when it is to be given to the 20-thousandth human being passing through the Space Mountain turnstile on a crowded day in July. Other difficulties present themselves as well, but operators learn that there are others on-stage to assist or thwart them.

Employees learn quickly that supervisors and, to a lesser degree, foremen are not only on the premises to help them, but also to catch them when they slip over or brazenly violate set procedures or park policies. Because most rides are tightly designed to eliminate human judgment and minimize operational disasters, much of the supervisory monitoring is directed at activities ride operators consider trivial: taking too long a break; not wearing parts of one's official uniform such as a hat, standard-issue belt, or correct shoes; rushing the ride (although more frequent violations seem to be detected for the provision of longer-than-usual rides for lucky customers); fraternizing with guests beyond the call of duty; talking back to quarrelsome or sometimes merely querisome customers; and so forth. All are matters covered quite explicitly in the codebooks ride operators are to be familiar with, and violations of such codes are often subject to instant and harsh discipline. The firing of what to supervisors are "malcontents," "trouble-makers," "bumblers," "attitude problems," or simply "jerks" is a frequent occasion at Disneyland, and among part-timers, who are most subject to degradation and being fired, the threat is omnipresent. There are few workers who have not witnessed firsthand the

rapid disappearance of a co-worker for offenses they would regard as "Mickey Mouse." Moreover, there are few employees who themselves have not violated a good number of operational and demeanor standards and anticipate, with just cause, the violation of more in the future.

In part, because of the punitive and what are widely held to be capricious supervisory practices in the park, foremen and ride operators are usually drawn close and shield one another from suspicious area supervisors. Throughout the year, each land is assigned a number of area supervisors who, dressed alike in short-sleeved white shirts and ties with walkie-talkies hitched to their belts, wander about their territories on the lookout for deviations from park procedures (and other signs of disorder). Occasionally, higher level supervisors pose in "plainclothes" and ghost-ride the various attractions just to be sure everything is up to snuff. Some area supervisors are well-known among park employees for the variety of surreptitious techniques they employ when going about their monitoring duties. Blind observation posts are legendary, almost sacred, sites within the park ("This is where Old Man Weston hangs out. He can see Dumbo, Storybook, the Carousel, and the Tea Cups from here"). Supervisors in Tomorrowland are, for example, famous for their penchant of hiding in the bushes above the submarine caves, timing the arrivals and departures of the supposedly fully loaded boats making the 8 1/2 minute cruise under the polar icecaps. That they might also catch a submarine captain furtively enjoying a cigarette (or worse) while inside the conning tower (his upper body out of view of the crowd on the vessel) might just make a supervisor's day—and unmake the employee's. In short, supervisors, if not foremen, are regarded by ride operators as sneaks and tricksters out to get them and representative of the dark side of park life. Their presence is, of course, an orchestrated one and does more than merely watch over the ride operators. It also draws operators together as cohesive little units who must look out for one another while they work (and shirk). . . .

Employees are also subject to what might be regarded as remote controls. These stem not from supervisors or peers but from thousands of paying guests who parade daily through the park. The public, for the most part, wants Disneyland employees to play only the roles for which they are hired and costumed. If, for instance, Judy of the Jets is feeling tired, grouchy, or bored, few customers want to know about it. Disneyland employees are expected to be sunny and helpful; and the job, with its limited opportunities for sustained interaction, is designed to support such a stance. Thus, if a ride operator's behavior drifts noticeably away from the norm, customers are sure to point it out—"Why aren't you smiling?" "What's wrong with you?" "Having a bad day?" "Did Goofy step on your foot?" Ride operators learn swiftly from the constant hints, glances, glares, and tactful (and tactless) cues sent by their audience what their role in the park is to be, and as long as they keep to it, there will be no objections from those passing by.

> I can remember being out on the river looking at the people on the Mark Twain looking down on the people in the Keel Boats who are looking up at them. I'd come by on my raft and they'd all turn and stare at me. If I gave them a little wave and a grin, they'd all wave back and smile; all ten thousand of them. I always wondered what would happen if I gave them the finger? (Ex-ride operator, 1988)

Ride operators also learn how different categories of customers respond to them and the parts they are playing on-stage. For example, infants and small children are generally timid, if not frightened, in their presence. School-age children are somewhat curious, aware that the operator is at work playing a role but sometimes in awe of the role itself. Nonetheless, these children can be quite critical of any flaw in the operator's performance. Teenagers, especially males in groups, present problems because they sometimes go to great lengths to embarrass, challenge, ridicule, or outwit an operator. Adults are generally appreciative and approving of an operator's conduct provided it meets their rather minimal standards, but they sometimes overreact to the part an operator is playing (positively) if accompanied by small children. . . .

The point here is that ride operators learn what the public (or, at least, their idealized version of

the public) expects of their role and find it easier to conform to such expectations than not. Moreover, they discover that when they are bright and lively others respond to them in like ways. This . . . balancing of the emotional exchange is such that ride operators come to expect good treatment. They assume, with good cause, that most people will react to their little waves and smiles with some affection and perhaps joy. When they do not, it can ruin a ride operator's day.

With this interaction formula in mind, it is perhaps less difficult to see why ride operators detest and scorn the ill-mannered or unruly guest. At times, these grumpy, careless, or otherwise unresponsive characters insult the very role the operators play and have come to appreciate—"You can't treat the Captain of the USS Nautilus like that!" Such out-of-line visitors offer breaks from routine, some amusement, consternation, or the occasional job challenge that occurs when remedies are deemed necessary to restore employee and role dignity.

By and large, however, the people-processing tasks of ride operators pass good naturedly and smoothly, with operators hardly noticing much more than the bodies passing in front of view (special bodies, however, merit special attention as when crew members on the subs gather to assist a young lady in a revealing outfit on board and then linger over the hatch to admire the view as she descends the steep steps to take her seat on the boat). Yet, sometimes, more than a body becomes visible, as happens when customers overstep their roles and challenge employee authority, insult an operator, or otherwise disrupt the routines of the job. In the process, guests become "dufusses," "ducks," and "assholes" (just three of many derisive terms used by ride operators to label those customers they believe to have gone beyond the pale). Normally, these characters are brought to the attention of park security officers, ride foremen, or area supervisors who, in turn, decide how they are to be disciplined (usually expulsion from the park).

Occasionally, however, the alleged slight is too personal or simply too extraordinary for a ride operator to let it pass unnoticed or merely inform others and allow them to decide what, if anything, is to be done. Restoration of one's respect is called for, and routine practices have been developed for these circumstances. For example, common remedies include: the "seatbelt squeeze," a small token of appreciation given to a deviant customer consisting of the rapid cinching-up of a required seatbelt such that the passenger is doubled-over at the point of departure and left gasping for the duration of the trip; the "break-toss," an acrobatic gesture of the Autopia trade whereby operators jump on the outside of a norm violator's car, stealthily unhitching the safety belt, then slamming on the brakes, bringing the car to an almost instant stop while the driver flies on the hood of the car (or beyond); the "seatbelt slap," an equally distinguished (if primitive) gesture by which an offending customer receives a sharp, quick snap of a hard plastic belt across the face (or other parts of the body) when entering or exiting a seat-belted ride; the "break-up-the-party" gambit, a queuing device put to use in officious fashion whereby bothersome pairs are separated at the last minute into different units, thus forcing on them the pain of strange companions for the duration of a ride through the Haunted Mansion or a ramble on Mr. Toad's Wild Ride; the "hatch-cover ploy," a much beloved practice of Submarine pilots who, in collusion with mates on the loading dock, are able to drench offensive guests with water as their units pass under a waterfall; and, lastly, the rather ignoble variants of the "Sorry-I-didn't-see-your-hand" tactic, a savage move designed to crunch a particularly irksome customer's hand (foot, finger, arm, leg, etc.) by bringing a piece of Disneyland property to bear on the appendage, such as the door of a Thunder Mountain railroad car or the starboard side of a Jungle Cruise boat. This latter remedy is, most often, a "near miss" designed to startle the little criminals of Disneyland.

All of these unofficial procedures (and many more) are learned on the job. Although they are used sparingly, they are used. Occasions of use provide a continual stream of sweet revenge talk to enliven and enrich colleague conversation at break time or after work. Too much, of course, can be made of these subversive practices and the rhetoric that surrounds their use. Ride operators are quite aware that there are limits beyond which

they dare not pass. If they are caught, they know that restoration of corporate pride will be swift and clean.

In general, Disneyland employees are remarkable for their forbearance and polite good manners even under trying conditions. They are taught, and some come to believe, for a while at least, that they are really "on-stage" at work. And, as noted, surveillance by supervisory personnel certainly fades in light of the unceasing glances an employee receives from the paying guests who tromp daily through the park in the summer. Disneyland employees know well that they are part of the product being sold and learn to check their more discriminating manners in favor of the generalized countenance of a cheerful lad or lassie whose enthusiasm and dedication is obvious to all.

At times, the emotional resources of employees appear awesome. When the going gets tough and the park is jammed, the nerves of all employees are frayed and sorely tested by the crowd, din, sweltering sun, and eyeburning smog. Customers wait in what employees call "bullpens" (and park officials call "reception areas") for up to several hours for a 3½ minute ride that operators are sometimes hell-bent on cutting to 2½ minutes. Surely a monument to the human ability to suppress feelings has been created when both users and providers alike can maintain their composure and seeming regard for one another when in such a fix.

It is in this domain where corporate culture and the order it helps to sustain must be given its due. Perhaps the depth of a culture is visible only when its members are under the gun. The orderliness—a good part of the Disney formula for financial success—is an accomplishment based not only on physical design and elaborate procedures, but also on the low-level, part-time employees who, in the final analysis, must be willing, even eager, to keep the show afloat. The ease with which employees glide into their kindly and smiling roles is, in large measure, a feat of social engineering. Disneyland does not pay well; its supervision is arbitrary and skin-close; its working conditions are chaotic; its jobs require minimal amounts of intelligence or judgment; and asks a kind of sacrifice and loyalty of its employees that is almost fanatical. Yet, it attracts a particularly able workforce whose personal backgrounds suggest abilities far exceeding those required of a Disneyland traffic cop, people stuffer, queue or line manager, and button pusher. As I have suggested, not all of Disneyland is covered by the culture put forth by management. There are numerous pockets of resistance and various degrees of autonomy maintained by employees. Nonetheless, adherence and support for the organization are remarkable. And, like swallows returning to Capistrano, many part-timers look forward to their migration back to the park for several seasons.

The Disney Way

Four features alluded to in this unofficial guide to Disneyland seem to account for a good deal of the social order that obtains within the park. First, socialization, although costly, is of a most selective, collective, intensive, serial, sequential, and closed sort. These tactics are notable for their penetration into the private spheres of individual thought and feeling. . . . Incoming identities are not so much dismantled as they are set aside as employees are schooled in the use of new identities of the situational sort. Many of these are symbolically powerful and, for some, laden with social approval. It is hardly surprising that some of the more problematic positions in terms of turnover during the summer occur in the food and concession domains where employees apparently find little to identify with on the job. Cowpokes on Big Thunder Mountain, Jet Pilots, Storybook Princesses, Tour Guides, Space Cadets, Jungle Boat Skippers, or Southern Belles of New Orleans Square have less difficulty on this score. Disneyland, by design, bestows identity through a process carefully set up to strip away the job relevance of other sources of identity and learned response and replace them with others of organizational relevance. It works.

Second, this is a work culture whose designers have left little room for individual experimentation. Supervisors, as apparent in their focused wandering and attentive looks, keep very close tabs on what is going on at any moment in all the lands. Every bush, rock, and tree in Disneyland is numbered and checked continually as to the part it is playing in the park. So too are employees. Dis-

cretion of a personal sort is quite limited while employees are "on-stage." Even "back-stage" and certain "off-stage" domains have their corporate monitors. Employees are indeed aware that their "off-stage" life beyond the picnics, parties, and softball games is subject to some scrutiny, for police checks are made on potential and current employees. Nor do all employees discount the rumors that park officials make periodic inquiries on their own as to a person's habits concerning sex and drugs. Moreover, the sheer number of rules and regulations is striking, thus making the grounds for dismissal a matter of multiple choice for supervisors who discover a target for the use of such grounds. The feeling of being watched is, unsurprisingly, a rather prevalent complaint among Disneyland people, and it is one that employees must live with if they are to remain at Disneyland.

Third, emotional management occurs in the park in a number of quite distinct ways. From the instructors at the university who beseech recruits to "wish every guest a pleasant good day," to the foremen who plead with their charges to, "say thank you when you herd them through the gate," to the impish customer who seductively licks her lips and asks, "what does Tom Sawyer want for Christmas?" appearance, demeanor, and etiquette have special meanings at Disneyland. Because these are prized personal attributes over which we normally feel in control, making them commodities can be unnerving. Much self-monitoring is involved, of course, but even here self-management has an organizational side. Consider ride operators who may complain of being "too tired to smile" but, at the same time, feel a little guilty for uttering such a confession. Ride operators who have worked an early morning shift on the Matterhorn (or other popular rides) tell of a queasy feeling they get when the park is opened for business and they suddenly feel the ground begin to shake under their feet and hear the low thunder of the hordes of customers coming at them, oblivious of civil restraint and the small children who might be among them. Consider, too, the discomforting pressures of being "on-stage" all day and the cumulative annoyance of having adults ask permission to leave a line to go to the bathroom, whether the water in the lagoon is real, where the well-marked entrances might be, where Walt Disney's cryogenic tomb is to be found, or—the real clincher—whether or not one is "really real."

The mere fact that so much operator discourse concerns the handling of bothersome guests suggests that these little emotional disturbances have costs. There are, for instance, times in all employee careers when they put themselves on "automatic pilot," "go robot," "can't feel a thing," "lapse into a dream," "go into a trance," or otherwise "check out" while still on duty. Despite a crafty supervisor's (or curious visitor's) attempt to measure the glimmer in an employee's eye, this sort of willed emotional numbness is common to many of the "on-stage" Disneyland personnel. Much of this numbness is, of course, beyond the knowledge of supervisors and guests because most employees have little trouble appearing as if they are present even when they are not. It is, in a sense, a passive form of resistance that suggests there still is a sacred preserve of individuality left among employees in the park.

Finally, taking these three points together, it seems that even when people are trained, paid, and told to be nice, it is hard for them to do so all of the time. But, when efforts to be nice have succeeded to the degree that is true of Disneyland, it appears as a rather towering (if not always admirable) achievement. It works at the collective level by virtue of elaborate direction. Employees—at all ranks—are stage-managed by higher ranking employees who, having come through themselves, hire, train, and closely supervise those who have replaced them below. Expression rules are laid out in corporate manuals. Employee time-outs intensify work experience. Social exchanges are forced into narrow bands of interacting groups. Training and retraining programs are continual. Hiding places are few. Although little sore spots and irritations remain for each individual, it is difficult to imagine work roles being more defined (and accepted) than those at Disneyland. Here, it seems, is a work culture worthy of the name.

The Routinization of Disaster

Daniel F. Chambliss

How the Hospital Is Different

. . . Much [in a hospital] is the same as in other organizations: the daily round of paper processing, answering the phone, making staffing decisions, collecting bills, ordering supplies, stocking equipment rooms; there are fights between departments, arguments with the boss, workers going home tired or satisfied. And medical sociology has made much of these similarities, using its research to create broader theories of, for instance, deviance or of the structure of professions.

But in one crucial respect the hospital remains dramatically different from other organizations: *in hospitals, as a normal part of the routine, people suffer and die.* This is unusual. "[A] good working definition of a hospital is that place where death occurs and no one notices; or, more sharply, the place where others agree to notice death as a social fact only so far as it fits their particular purposes." Only combat military forces share this feature. To be complete, theories of hospital life need to acknowledge this crucial difference, since adapting themselves to pain and death is for hospital workers the most distinctive feature of their work. It is that which most separates them from the rest of us. In building theories of organizational life, sociologists must try to see how hospitals resemble other organizations . . . but we should not make a premature leap to the commonalities before appreciating the unique features of hospitals that make a nurse's task so different from that of a teacher or a businessman or a bureaucrat.[1]

A quick survey of typical patients in one Surgical Intensive Care Unit on one Saturday evening should make the point. The words in brackets are additions to my original field notes:

Room 1. 64-year-old white woman with an aortic valve replacement: five separate IMEDs [intravenous drip-control devices] feeding in nitroglycerine, vasopressors, Versed [a pain killer which also blocks memory]. Chest tube [to drain off fluids]. On ventilator [breathing machine], Foley [catheter in the bladder], a pulse oximeter on her finger, a[rterial monitoring] line. Diabetic. In one 30-second period during the night, her blood pressure dropped from $160/72$ to $95/50$, then to $53/36$, before the nurse was able to control the drop. N[urse]s consider her "basically healthy."

Room 2. Man with pulmonary artresia, pulmonary valvotomy [heart surgery].

Room 3. Woman with CABG [coronary artery bypass graft; a "bypass operation"]. Bleeding out [i.e., hemorrhaging] badly at one point during the night, they sent her back to the OR [Operating Room]. On heavy vasopressors [to keep blood pressure up].

Room 4. Older woman with tumor from her neck up to her temple. In OR from 7 a.m. until 2 a.m. the next morning having it removed. Infarct [dead tissue] in the brain.

Room 5. 23-year old woman. MVA [motor vehicle accident]. ICP [intracranial pressure—a measure of brain swelling] measured—terrible. Maybe organ donor. [Patient died next day.]

Room 6. Don't know.

Room 7. Abdominal sepsis, possibly from surgery. DNR [Do Not Resuscitate] today.

Room 8. Big belly guy [an old man with a horribly distended abdomen, uncontrollable. Staff says it's from poor sterile technique in surgery by Doctor M., who is notoriously sloppy. This patient died within the week.] [Field Notes]

This is a typical patient load for an Intensive Care Unit. Eight beds, three patients dead in a matter of days. "Patients and their visitors often find the ICU to be a disturbing, even terrifying place. Constant artificial light, ceaseless activity, frequent emergencies, and the ever-present threat of death create an atmosphere that can unnerve even the most phlegmatic of patients. Some are so sick that they are unaware of their surroundings or simply forget the experience, but for others the ICU is a nightmare remembered all too well."[2] On floors—the larger, less critical care wards of the hospital—fatalities are less common, and patients are not so sick; even so, one-third of the patients may have AIDS, another one-third have cancer, and the rest suffer a variety of serious if not immediately lethal diseases. The ICUs just get patients whose deaths are imminent.

It is interesting that this density of disease presents one of the positive attractions of nursing. People don't become nurses to avoid seeing suffering or to have a quiet day. Every day nurses respond to and share the most intense emotions with total strangers. "People you don't know are going through the most horrible things, and you are supposed to help them. That's intense," says one nurse. And another enthuses about coming home as the sun is coming up; the rest of the world thinks things are just starting, and here you're coming off a big emergency that lasted half the night: "[T]here's a real adrenaline kick in all this stuff. If you deny that, you're denying a big part of [nursing]."

The abnormality of the hospital scene liberates the staff from some niceties of everyday life and allows them a certain freedom. . . . Two small, even silly, examples may illustrate the point. (1) Many nurses wear scrub suits—the pajama-like pants and tops worn in operating rooms and on some units. Written on the suits are phone numbers, vital statistics, or even doodles drawn during surgery. It's more convenient than finding a piece of paper. One observer, Judith André, has commented, "It's like a childhood fantasy" to scribble things on your clothes. (2) During a "code," as a patient was being resuscitated, one nurse who was having her period began to leak menstrual fluid. She ran into the patient's bathroom to change her sani-

tary pad. When she came out, another nurse, seeing the stain on her pants, yelled, "Well, J. got her period!"—a comment unthinkable in the everyday world. But this isn't the everyday world. As Everett Hughes wrote, "All occupations—most of all those considered professions and perhaps those of the underworld—include as part of their very being a licence to deviate in some measure from common modes of behavior."[3] In this sense, the hospital is like a war zone, in which common niceties and rules of decorum are discarded in the pursuit of some more immediate, desperate objective. There is an excitement, and a pressure, that frees hospital workers in the "combat zone" from an array of normal constraints on what they say and do.

And yet, for them their work has become normal, routine. On a medical floor, with perhaps two-thirds of the patients suffering eventually fatal diseases, I say to a nurse, "What's happening?" and she replies, walking on down the hall, "Same ol' same ol'." Nothing new, nothing exciting. Or in an Intensive Care Unit in the same hospital, "What's going on?" The resident replies, with a little shrug of the shoulders, "People are living, people are dying." Again, no surprises, nothing new. The routine goes on.

As other writers have noted, the professional treats routinely what for the patient is obviously not routine. For the health worker, medical procedures happen to patients every day, and the hospital setting is quite comfortable: "The staff nurse . . . belongs to a world of relative health, youth, and bustling activity. She may not yet have experienced hospitalization herself for more than the removal of tonsils or the repair of a minor injury. Although she works in an environment of continuous sickness, she has been so conditioned to its external aspects that she often expresses surprise when someone suggests that the environment must be anxiety evoking."[4] Everett Hughes's formulation of this divergence of experience is classic: "In many occupations, the workers or practitioners . . . deal routinely with what are emergencies to the people who receive their services. This is a source of chronic tension between the two." Or, more precisely, "[O]ne man's routine of work is made up of the emergencies of other people."[5]

To the patient, though, the hospital world is special, frightening, a jarring break from the everyday world. For the nurse, it's just the "same ol' same ol'." How extreme the gap is was observed in an ICU one evening:

> Three residents were attempting an LP [lumbar puncture—a "spinal tap" in which a long needle is inserted into the spinal column to draw out spinal fluid]. This is a very painful procedure and is difficult to perform. The television over the foot of the patient's bed was turned on, and "LA Law" was playing. While the resident was inserting the needle, she kept glancing up at the television, trying to simultaneously watch the show and do the LP. The patient, curled into the fetal position to separate the vertebrae, was unaware of this. The other two residents as well were glancing back and forth from procedure to television. The resident tried for several minutes drawing out blood instead of fluid. Eventually, she called the head resident, who came in and successfully finished the LP. [Field Notes].

This illustrates how casual staff can become, to the point of malfeasance.

How do staff, nurses in particular, routinize the abnormal? Or more fundamentally, what do we even mean by routinization?

What Routinization Entails: The Operating Room

The most egregious violation of commonsense morality—the profound physical violation of another person's body—is made completely routine in the hospital operating room. To help the reader understand routinization, we will consider this example in some detail.

In large teaching hospitals like Northern General or Southwest Regional, there are some twelve to twenty operating rooms in the "OR suite," with the rooms organized in a long hallway around a central equipment and supply area. The entire suite is "sterile," that is, everyone coming in and out wears scrub suits and face masks, shoe covers, and hair bonnets. Each operating room is furnished with a narrow padded table on which the patient lies during surgery, as well as with huge movable overhead lights and rolling tables for equipment of all sorts. Certain rooms are typically reserved for cardiac, neurological, orthopedic, and other special types of surgery, and the peculiar equipment for each of these is always available in those rooms. There are also one or two "crash rooms," for emergency surgery of the sort associated with the automobile wrecks or shootings frequently seen in large urban medical centers. Each room may be scheduled for one to six operations in a day; several dozen surgeries are scheduled for the hospital each weekday morning, usually starting at 6:00 and running until 2:00 or so in the afternoon.

Nurses manage these rooms between operations, supervising the flow of patients and the resupply of equipment (sponges, surgical tools, clean linens, etc.), answering the telephone or intercom and letting the physicians know when it is time to begin. There are typically at least two such nurses, the "scrub nurse" who assists the surgeon, handing tools and dealing directly with the sterile field, and the "circulating nurse" who can move in and out of the OR, touch nonsterile areas (such as the telephone), and keep the supplies flowing as needed to the surgical team. The circulating nurse is a kind of stage manager and fills in as needed, solving problems arising outside the surgery itself.

During surgery, the circulating nurse has several duties. First, she must document everything that happens: the time when surgery begins, what specific procedures are being conducted, what personnel are participating, when the procedure is done and "closing" begins, and when the patient is wheeled out of the room. Working together with the scrub nurse, she repeatedly counts and recounts the number of "sponges" (absorbent pads) used in the operation (there may be dozens). She must account for all of them both before and after the operation, to ensure that none are mistakenly left in the patient's body. She does the same for the surgical needles used, making certain that all are accounted for and disposed of properly, a serious concern since the advent of AIDS. The best circulating nurses, it would seem, are precise to the point of obsessiveness. The scrub nurse shares in these duties, counting sponges and accounting for all equipment, as well as passing to the surgeon, quickly and reliably, the specific tools needed at different stages of the operation. The scrub nurse also "preps" the patient: she drapes the patient with sterile cloths, leaving bare then shaving the area to be cut open, disinfecting the body surface with an iodine solution, and covering the skin with a clear plastic film called "Opsite" which protects the uncut area. A screen of cloth is usually set up between the patient's head and the rest of the body, so conscious patients will not see what's going on. This also means that the operating area is detached from the patient as a person, an important feature of the scene. The nurses carry out routine tasks dozens of times in a single day—for instance, the one-by-one counting of sponges, carried with tongs from a table to a waste bucket, perhaps two dozen of them counted aloud. The failure to perform these tasks conscientiously could be disastrous.

Once both room and patient are "prepped," the medical team can begin. The patient's body, fundamentally, is transformed into an object. An anesthesiologist (a physician), or a nurse anesthetist, will administer either a spinal anesthetic, which numbs the body below the injection point on the spinal cord, or a general anesthetic, which puts the patient to sleep. From then on, the operative area, screened from the patient's head and deadened of all feeling, effectively becomes to the surgeons a piece of nonhuman meat. The target area is isolated and immobilized; the patient is either asleep or, with a spinal, may be chatting away up at the head of the table with the anesthesiologist. In one case, a man's leg was being removed at one end of the table while at the other he was telling the anesthesiologist about his recent vacation trip. Looking at the operating area, the skin being cut or bone being sawed, you think, "No one I know has ever looked like this." Anesthetized flesh doesn't respond as the flesh of a living human being would. In amputations, the flesh being removed is usually dead and looks it—dark, hard, lifeless. But living flesh, too, on the table, looks more like what it "objectively" is, that is, meat. Human fat looks like the chicken fat you see on the stove; human skin peels back the way a chicken's does when peeled. An old man's tanned skin, when cut, looks like leather—which, precisely speaking, it is: old, tanned, animal skin. Surgeons working inside the body cavity remind one of cooks stuffing the Thanksgiving turkey, pulling open a section here, pushing a hand deep inside, feeling around for something there, stretching back tendons, trimming the fat, snipping pieces here and there with a small pair of scissors. The fine details of surgery are remarkably complex and refined, but its basic principles are brutally simple:

> To amputate this diabetic lady's toes, Dr. R., a small woman, used a thing like a big pair of bolt cutters to actually cut the bones, one toe at a time—with the big toe she had some difficulty, and she was almost lifted off the floor squeezing the big handles together before the "crunch" and the blades snapped through the toe. Then the last flesh was snipped away and five toes, all together, like a section of beef or chicken, came off in a single piece, and the scrub nurse laid it into a specimen tray. [Field Notes]

This primitive business is executed with simple tools: a razor-edge knife to cut open the skin (the scalpel); scissors to trim away flesh inside the body; smooth hooks to pull back the skin while the operation is under way (retractors); needle-nose pliers to shut off blood vessels (hemostats); and a small electric probe, essentially a soldering iron, used to cauterize the open ends of small blood vessels (the "Bovie"). Tools come in many sizes and specialized shapes, but this is the basic array. Orthopedic surgery adds its various saws, drills, and bits; the equipment table looks like a bench in an immaculate hobbyist's workshop, which in a sense it is.

To the senior staff, these tools and their uses become commonplace. During one routine orthopedic operation (routine for the staff, not for the patient), a group of young residents were working on a teenage patient's shoulder. The supervising attending physician, nominally in charge, popped in occasionally during the three-hour operation to see how things were going. On one visit he stopped for fifteen minutes to flip through the "swimsuit issue" of *Waterski* magazine, which one of the residents had brought. His pointed air of "no big deal" was more than casual; it seemed almost an assertion of his own power and sophistication, contrasted with the barely concealed anxiety of the residents he was monitoring. When he left, the residents visibly relaxed and resumed openly discussing how to perform the operation. One actually shuttled back and forth to a table against the wall to look at the diagrams in his textbook to see how the surgery should be done. Then the attending anesthesiologist came in to check on his resident and to sign a form ("So I'll get my cut," he said smiling) and walked out again. Music by popular musicians Phil Collins and Los Lobos was on a portable tape cassette player as the residents worked. The residents were learning to do highly skilled surgery and how to regard it as part of everyday life.

Routinization in the OR or elsewhere in the hospital seems to mean several things: that actions are repeated, that they violate normal taboos, and that routine is embedded in behavior. Consider each in turn, drawing on further examples from other settings in the hospital:

1. *Repeatability.* Each operation is not the first of its kind; most in fact are done several times each day and hundreds of times each year, even by a single team of surgeons, nurses, and technical aides. What the team sees, they have seen many times. Gallbladder removals, hernia repairs and shoulder operations on athletes—these are all very common procedures in the major medical center.[6]

And those repeated procedures take place against the even less dramatic background of the repeated daily events of the nurse's work: starting intravenous lines, taking blood pressures four times a day on every patient on the floor, drawing blood samples, charting vital signs, writing nurses' progress notes, passing food trays, helping patients on and off the bedpan. Both trivial and consequential activities are repeated over and over until each one becomes much like the next; indeed, as Hughes says, the professional's "very competence comes from having dealt with a thousand cases of what the client likes to consider his unique experience."[7] Says one nurse, "You get to the point where you don't really care for the patients anymore, and one GI [gastrointestinal] bleeder gets to be the same as the next GI bleeder."

In a Medical Intensive Care Unit, death itself becomes an often-repeated event:

Another MICU patient just coded and died; that's five in the past six days. Incredible. The docs are here one month—N[urse]s are here for good . . .

I just came in unit; first N[urse] says, "You just missed it." They said that to me a few days ago. It's not that I "just miss," I think, but rather that so much [is] going on. You'll always "just miss" something. [Field Notes]

Death becomes a routinized part of daily life, incorporated into the flow. "Mr. Smith died last night," says one nurse to another. "Oh, that's too bad. He was such a nice man"; a casual exchange. One day is like another, if not for Mr. Smith, then at least for the rest of us. For the nurses, Mr. Smith will be replaced by another man, a Mr. Jones, with similar ailments and a similar end. . . .

The repeatability of the events—the sense that the same things happen over and over—is part of what is meant by routinization.

2. *Profanation.* Normally, we experience our bodies and the bodies of others as sacred, as areas to be approached with reverence or even with awe. To the healthy person outside the hospital, the body is special, a thing distinct from other things in the world, and must be treated as different. Physical contact with other bodies is emotionally provocative, in ways good and bad. A touch, a hug, a kiss arouse some sensitivity; a slap, however light, provokes humiliation or perhaps rage. But for patients in the hospital, their bodies are dramatically profaned. The body is often exposed to strangers, older and younger, male and female, even in groups. Many times a day the patient's body is punctured by injection needles. It is the object of teachers' lectures to their students. It is touched frequently, often without special preliminaries. It is probed with fingers and hands and tools in ways that are sometimes brutal, with little respect for the body as a sacred object. Even when professionals are respectful (and many of them always are), the effect on patients is one of the secularization of their own flesh. . . .

3. *Existentiality.* Routinization of the abnormal involves not so much a mental leap as an existential action; creating a routine is not some trick of the conscious mind but rather a whole way of acting that involves physical as well as mental components. It comprises embodied habits. Routinization is not "all in the head"; it is something one does. It is carried out in the way a nurse walks and talks while in the presence of abnormal events. It entails that "matter of factness" with which she inserts a bladder catheter or cleans up feces; it is evidenced in the full range of emotions she shows, laughing with a dying man, chatting and even laughing with colleagues during a code (a resuscitation effort), glancing casually through a nursing journal filled with full-color advertisements for ileostomy appliances and crèmes for cancer lesions. After a middle-aged woman died late one night in room 5 of a medical ICU, her family, loudly crying and hugging each other, came into the room to see their dead mother. Outside the room, three nurses who had tried for thirty minutes to resuscitate the patient sat around a table eating corn chips and gossiping, as if nothing had happened. One of those nurses said to me, "We're pretty dehumanized, huh?" But it wasn't true: if she were dehumanized no such comment would even be made. She knew what was happening, and eating corn chips, even then, is in fact quite human. In a unit where three patients die each week, to get upset with every death would be humanly unacceptable.

So in the Operating Room and elsewhere events are repeated over and over, in an attitude of secularized treatment of the body, and this repeated attitude is built into and expressed in the very ordinary doings of the staff. Sometimes routinization goes beyond mere commonplace into an attitude of detachment, unconcern, or sheer boredom—one of the more common emotions of the nurse's life, to the surprise of laypersons. Indeed, one of the most frequent questions nurses asked me during my research was, "Aren't you bored?" . . .

How Routinization Is Accomplished: Creating Conditions for Ordinary Life

Thus, for the nurse, hospital life is ordinary—not extraordinary, or mystical, or even an object of thoughtful scrutiny. We saw in the last section how the nurse's ordinary daily life consists largely of repeated, secular activities. Things happen, time and time again, in essentially the same way; these happenings are for the most part devoid of any special, sacred character; and they are carried out in the working world, through concrete actions, not merely (or not even) thought about in any conscious way. "The ambience of nursing units is not tragic, but mundane and businesslike. The work of nurses and aides is largely repetitive and is carried on largely in a habitual manner . . . For the most part, nursing personnel seem to be hardly perturbed at the graphic condition of their patients . . . When they enter the presence of a sorely afflicted patient, their countenances are not likely to betray more than a flicker of emotion."[8] This is what we mean by saying the nurse has routinized the world of the hospital. Her life here has taken on a quality of mundane sameness, often to the point of sheer boredom.

> The first time I had to interview a patient in my first year of nursing school, he said he had a scar [on his chest]. I asked to see it, he just pulled up his gown [around his neck; she gestures to show how he was bare]. I was . . . [rolls her eyes, embarrassed] "Oh, my God." And now . . . [waves her hand, flutters eyes to indicate her totally blasé attitude]. [Field Notes]

No layperson would experience such exposure so casually. And nudity is simple; witnessing open heart surgery, or an endotracheal intubation, or CPR, is far more threatening to one's everyday reality. But nurses see these events every day, without becoming upset. The nurse's view—or more accurately, the nurse's very way of *living* here and dealing with such trauma—is different from ours.

How does this casual attitude develop? How does the abnormal become routine? The conventional answer is that "you just get used to it." This implies that over time, with enough exposure, one adapts, willy-nilly, to whatever is happening in the environment. This may be true, but it is insufficient. "Getting used to it" suggests that routinization is purely a matter of the passage of time, with repetition as the implied causative agent. Yes, routinization happens "over time," but time alone is insufficient to cause routinization. Some nurses never become accustomed, as we will see, to deformed newborns, or psychotic teenagers, or incontinent geriatric patients. Then, too, some people "get used to it" virtually immediately. Before my own first witnessing of surgery, I conscientiously followed all the head nurse's instructions to avoid physical or emotional upset: I rose early, ate a full breakfast, and was wide awake before going to the OR suite. After donning the scrub suit, bonnet, and shoe covers, I went into the OR and asked the circulating nurse what the first case would be, hoping for something "easy," maybe a wrist or ankle operation. She looked at the chart and said, without missing a beat, "leg amputation." I nearly panicked, but I stayed. To my own amazement, I was not in the least upset by the amputation or any of the surgeries I witnessed, including the repair of a ruptured ectopic pregnancy that drove at least two experienced nurses from the OR in dismay. For some reason, there seemed to be no period of "getting used to it" at all. So repeated exposure as a means of routinization is insufficient; more is at work.

At least four phenomenological tasks go into the routinization of the hospital world: learning one's geographical surroundings, so that the routine is physically manageable; learning the language so one can meet and work with other people; learning the technique of the work being done (if you don't know how to start an IV, it's hard to be casual about it); and learning the "types" of patients and the standard procedures for recognizing and dealing with them. . . . There is also, harder to define, a fifth task, a perceptual "leap," which I will describe after presenting these components. . . .

1. *Learning the geography.* The first step in the routinization of a world is simply to learn one's way around the physical setting. It's difficult to be casual when rooms are unfamiliar, hallways look long and forbidding, and one can't find the bathroom. Supplies are often kept in unexpected places, telephones sometime work in strange ways ("You have to dial 8 first"), even chairs may have traditional claims on them (until recently in American hospitals, nurses stood while physicians sat). Hospital beds come in various models, and working them isn't always easy.

This geography has social meanings and implications, too, which must be learned. One has to know that "this is Joanne's chair," or that the clerk always gets the phone, or that everyone cleans their own coffee cup. The physical setting, that is, must be known in its social ramifications. . . .

2. *Learning the language.* To move easily in the world of the hospital, the nurse must learn its peculiar language, the technical jargon, and the informal slang. The jargon is technically complex, even daunting. DNR: an order to Do Not Resuscitate a terminal patient when his or her breathing or heartbeat stops. CABG: pronounced "Cabbage," a coronary artery bypass graft, what the layperson calls bypass surgery. Or consider this description of the possible causes of one common symptom.

> [It is found] accompanying diaphragmatic pleurisy, pneumonia, uremia, or alcoholism . . . abdominal causes include disorders of the stomach, and esophagus, bowel diseases, pancreatitis, pregnancy, bladder irritation, hepatic metastases, or hepatitis. Thoracic and mediastinal lesions or surgery may be responsible. Posterior fossa tumors or infarcts may stimulate centers in the medulla oblongata . . . [9]

Pity the poor layperson who overhears such language to discuss his or her symptom—which in this case is hiccups.

Besides medical jargon, informal slang is highly developed, as the staff live in an experiential world far different than the layperson. Here, a dying patient is "going down the tubes," "circling the drain." The dead have "bought the farm," "straight-lined," or perhaps "Marshalled"—a reference to the name of the building that houses the morgue. An older patient who violently resists the nurses is "confused" and after drug sedation become much more "appropriate." Every emergency room has its "Gomers"—one of the most ubiquitous cases of hospital slang, derived from "Grand Old Man of the ER," or variants, and referring generically to old people with no treatable problems who are virtually permanent residents of the hospital.[10] On the acute psychiatric unit, there is the "quiet room": what once was called a padded cell, where a suicidal teenage girl huddles in a corner, crying, visible through the peephole in the door. The patient is regularly technicized in discussions of "input" and "output" (of food and waste). Learning the peculiar language is a vital part of becoming an insider. To understand what people are talking about, much less to become comfortable here, you need to learn the slang.[11] And even when no special jargon is used, the very matter-of-factness of the talk can be disarming: "Well, he had a stool; it was soft, but he said there was some diarrhea." Most of us simply don't talk in that way with fellow workers.

3. *Learning the techniques.* Routinization requires learning the techniques of one's work: the job itself must be familiar. One reason that I was immediately "used to" seeing surgery was that I was only observing it, not participating. Observing is a skill at which, as a sociologist, I have had much practice. There was no further technical learning necessary.

Nursing entails a great number of specific technical skills, and until one learns them the job can be overwhelming. "Being organized" is a prime job skill for nurses. The staff nurse dispenses hundreds of pills a day to dozens of patients, starts and maintains intravenous lines, gives bed baths, documents on paper virtually everything she does, monitors temperatures, blood pressures, and urine "outputs," delivers food trays, and responds more or less to all the miscellaneous patient and family requests that, from her point of view, often get in the way of her finishing her basic required work. Simply getting through an eight-hour shift without mistakenly giving Mrs. Jones the pills for Ms. Smith, or forgetting to check Mr. Martin's IV line, or not helping Miss Garcia eat her lunch is challenge enough. And these are the everyday, nonemergency tasks, the basics of the job. In the operating room, a circulating nurse is responsible for setting up tables with hundreds of small tools, stocking the correct combination of gauze sponges, suture kits, sterile gowns, and all the rest, knowing that surgeons are notoriously demanding; the scrub nurse sequentially passes the surgeon dozens of tools, when it matters most. Indeed, the mass of details that nurses organize can appear overwhelming. And each

detail, so apparently innocuous, can have enormous implications—as when a single sponge, one out of dozens used, is left inside the patient after surgery, or when one wrong pill goes to a heavily medicated patient. Thus, outstanding nurses often are described as "really well organized.". . .

4. *Learning the patients.* Patient types, too, become routine to the nurse. Despite an outsider's first impression of a multitude of different medical problems, most patients suffer one of a fairly small number of predictable ailments: cancer, heart disease, COPD (chronic obstructive pulmonary disease, such as emphysema or bronchitis), and now AIDS. These cover most of the severe cases. Treatments are relatively predictable as well, from the nursing staff's perspective: surgery, intravenous therapy, the usual medications. In heart disease, there are perhaps a half-dozen routinely used drugs; for cancer, there is surgery and the usual chemotherapy or radiation. So patients quickly become typed: the COPD lady in room 8, the AIDS guy in 2. . . .

An advantage of being used to seeing pain is that one can then work with suffering people. The "detached concern" that Merton writes about allows a nurse to lose the embarrassment many of us feel in front of sick people and allows her to talk with sick or dying patients. A dying woman can tell a nurse her fears; she may hesitate to burden a friend with them. A nurse, one may believe, has seen it all, so seeing one more thing perhaps won't upset her. It's probably true. One nurse told me that a friend said to her, "My dad is on oxygen!" and she, the nurse, thought to herself, "What would these people think if they saw someone in the unit with IV lines, an NG [nasogastric] tube, chest tubes, a catheter stuck in the bladder, and another tube stuck up the rectum? Ye gods, everyone I *know* is on oxygen!" She has become familiar with patients.

Having learned the geography of the hospital, the language, the techniques of work, and the types of patient, a nurse is well prepared to convert what was a chaos of disasters into a routine, well-organized round of daily activities.

5. *Routinization of the world.* But learning the specifics of the job—the geography, the jargon, the techniques, the patients—does not automatically produce an acceptance of the hospital world as normal. Some nurses learn the techniques but still never accept the daily disasters; they leave the profession, or move to less acute care settings, working in a school, a physician's office, or perhaps a home health care agency. More is demanded than simply accruing new information about work, or people, or the setting. Routinization itself demands a qualitative transformation in one's thinking, an entirely new way of relating to events and people. It can happen suddenly. Some nurses say that after six months or so on the job, having struggled through the heavy demands, often near to despair, one day they realize that the work no longer bothers them; they are "into" it.

> When I [first] walked into that unit, I had never seen any of these machines . . . there are 15,000 machines, they all have different alarms, they all have different ways to work them, different trouble-shooting things, and here you are expected to take care of this patient who's crumping every minute . . . it's just overwhelming.
>
> And then all of a sudden, one day, you say, Gee, I've survived this shift, and all of these things happened, and it was OK. . . .
>
> [So what happened that you got used to it?]
>
> You know, I have absolutely no idea . . . You go in and you do it again and again, and your patient codes for the fifth time . . . I can't even tell you when it happens, it's different for different people . . .
>
> Then the scary thing happens. You start to *like* it. [Field Notes]

What this nurse describes is not just a gradual transition over time, not a simple accumulation of experiences that finally equal "getting used to it." The accumulation of experiences is part of it, to be sure. But these only make possible the major shift, a qualitative transformation of consciousness, a *routinization of the world*. It is as if one takes the proverbial journey of a thousand single steps and discovers that the final step is in fact a fifteen-foot jump over a deep mountain gorge.

Without that final leap, the journey is incomplete, almost a waste. But even that analogy doesn't quite fit, since many nurses "jump the gorge" without every realizing what they have done. Usually, it just happens ("How did you get used to it?" "I have absolutely no idea."). Still, it is the nurse who "does" this happening, who makes the leap, even if unconsciously. . . .

NOTES

1. On the routinization of dying, see David Sudnow, *Passing On: The Social Organization of Dying.* (Englewood Cliffs, NJ: Prentice-Hall, 1967).

2. Arnold S. Relman, "Intensive Care Units: Who Needs Them?" *New England Journal of Medicine* 302 (April 1980), p. 965.

3. Hughes, E. C. *Men and Their Work* (Westport, CT: Greenwood Press, 1958), p. 79.

4. Esther Lucile Brown, "Nursing and Patient Care," in Fred Davis, *The Nursing Profession: Five Sociological Essays* (New York: John Wiley & Sons, 1966), p. 202.

5. Hughes, E. C. *Men and Their Work* (Westport, CT: Greenwood Press, 1958), pp. 54, 88.

6. Some physicians have astonishing numbers of routinized operations to their credit. For example, Dr. Denton Cooley of Houston has performed over 75,000 open heart surgeries with his team. Over two-thirds were personally performed by Dr. Cooley. *Guinness Book of World Records* (New York: Bantam Books, 1988).

7. Hughes, E. C. *Men and Their Work* (Westport, CT: Greenwood Press, 1958), p. 54.

8. Ronald Philip Preston, *The Dilemmas of Care: Social and Nursing Adaptations to the Deformed, the Disabled and the Aged* (New York: Elsevier, 1979), p. 93.

9. *The Merck Manual of Diagnosis and Therapy,* 15th ed. (Rahway, NJ: Merck Sharp & Dohme Research Laboratories, 1987). pp. 1356–1357.

10. See Samuel Shem, M.D. *The House of God* (New York: Dell Publishing Co., 1978), for many more examples.

11. "No profession can do its work without licence to talk in shocking terms about clients and their problems." Hughes, *Men and their Work*, p. 82.

THINKING ABOUT THE READINGS

The Active Worker

- The employees in Hodson's study were extremely creative in their attempts to overcome feelings of alienation in the workplace. Nevertheless, conformity and obedience were often stressed at the expense of their own individual autonomy. Does holding a job in a large company necessarily mean a loss of personal freedom for the worker? Why do you think some workers enthusiastically complied with company policies while others routinely broke the bureaucratic rules? Have you ever been in a situation in which you felt tension between conforming to the formal rules of the organization and conforming to the informal code of co-workers? How did this article change the way you view people who work in lower-level, monotonous occupations?

The Smile Factory

- What is the significance of the title, "The Smile Factory?" What, exactly, is the factory-made product that Disney sells in its theme parks? How does the Disney organizational culture shape the lives of employees? Disney is frequently criticized for its strict—some would say oppressive—employee rules and regulations. But would it be possible to run a "smile factory" with a more relaxed code of conduct where employees could regularly make their own decisions and act as they pleased? Explain. Disney theme parks abroad (in Japan and France) have not been nearly as successful as Disneyland and Disneyworld. Why has it been so difficult to export the "feeling business" to other countries? Consider also how Van Maanen describes the ways in which employees define the social rank of different positions within Disneyland. Describe an organizational situation you've been in where such a ranking of members occurred. What were the criteria upon which such rankings were made?

The Routinization of Disaster

- Describe the techniques nurses use to routinize disaster in the hospital. Why is such routinization necessary? Answer this question both in terms of personal survival and the institutional needs of the field of medicine. It is ironic that at precisely those moments when a sick patient wants the nurse to take a deep personal interest in him or her that the nurse must work hard to maintain emotional distance. What would happen to the American health care system if nurses and other medical professionals didn't do this and had ordinary emotional responses to misery and death?

CHAPTER 10

The Architecture of Stratification
Power, Class, and Privilege

Class stratification is the most important defining feature of American society today. It is tempting to see class differences as simply the result of an economic stratification system that exists at a level above the individual. But while inequality is created and maintained by larger social institutions, it is often felt most forcefully and is reinforced most effectively in the chain of interactions that take place in our day-to-day lives.

Michèle Lamont argues in "Money, Morals, and Manners" that class boundaries are not based on economics alone but are, instead, constructed and perpetuated by individual action. She goes beyond simple measures of wealth to reveal the role that people's perceptions of moral and cultural distinctions play in setting boundaries between the upper-middle class and the classes above and below.

Taking the notion of class boundaries one step further, William Domhoff argues in "The Bohemian Grove," that there is a tiny but cohesive ruling class in American society that makes decisions of national and international significance in its own narrowly defined interests. Often these decisions are made not in corporate boardrooms, the halls of Congress, or the White House, but in the comfortable, relaxing, and secluded confines of private, exclusive social clubs. Not only are business and political relationships among wealthy, powerful individuals formed here, but marriages between members of wealthy, powerful families are often arranged as well, thereby sustaining and strengthening the boundary between the ruling class and the other classes.

It is important to remember that stratification extends beyond national borders. Third World laborers have become a crucial part of the global economy and an important resource for multinational corporations. Low-skilled jobs are exported to developing countries that have cheap labor costs. On the surface, it would appear as if such an arrangement benefits all involved: the multinational corporations benefit from higher profits and the Third World countries benefit from higher rates of employment. However, Barbara Ehrenreich and Annette Fuentes point out in "Life on the Global Assembly Line" that Third World workers—who are overwhelmingly female—are often thoroughly exploited. They regularly face exhausting and hazardous conditions for subsistence wages or less. The tragic irony, the authors suggest, is that few countries seem to be concerned about such exploitation.

Money, Morals, and Manners

Michèle Lamont

How do people get access to valued professional resources such as well-paying jobs, interesting assignments, and promotions? Degrees, seniority, and experience are essential, but also important are being supported by a mentor, being included in networks of camaraderie, and receiving informal training. Getting access to these informal resources largely depends on sharing a valued cultural style. Indeed, research shows that managers favor employees who resemble them culturally, and that corporate success partly depends on making other managers "comfortable" by conforming in cultural matters and not "standing out."[1]

The present study explores the cultural categories through which the upper-middle class defines valued cultural styles. This task is a particularly important one because upper-middle-class members tend to control the allocation of many of the resources most valued in advanced industrial societies. Moreover, the mass media and the advertising industry constantly offer upper-middle-class culture as a model to members of other classes,[2] who often come to emulate it or to define their identities against it.[3] Despite the influence of upper-middle-class culture in the United States and elsewhere, and despite the fact that much has been written on resistance to dominant culture, the latter has rarely been submitted to close scrutiny.

What is primarily at issue here is the nature of the criteria that people use to define and discriminate between worthy and less worthy persons, i.e., between "their sort of folks" and "the sort they don't much like." To identify these criteria I scrutinize symbolic boundaries—the types of lines that individuals draw when they categorize people—and high-status signals—the keys to our evaluative distinctions. More specifically, different ways of believing that "we" are better than "them" are compared by analyzing both the standards that underlie status assessments and the characteristics of symbolic boundaries themselves—their degree of rigidity, for instance. This contributes to developing a more adequate and complex view of status, i.e., of the salience of various status dimensions across contexts. It also helps us to understand how societies and social classes differ culturally. By contrasting the cultures of members of the French and American upper-middle classes, we will see that the disapproval that New Yorkers often express toward Midwestern parochialism, the frequent criticisms that the French address to American puritan moralism, the scorn that businessmen voice toward intellectualism, and the charges that social and cultural specialists frequently make against materialism and business interests can be interpreted as specific instances of a pervasive phenomenon (i.e., as boundary work) rather than as incommensurable manifestations of national character, political attitudes, regionalism, etc.[4] Using the framework presented here, it will be possible to view prejudices and stereotypes as the supraindividual by-products of basic social processes that are shaped by the cultural resources that people have at their disposal and by the structural situations they live in.

[I study] upper-middle-class culture using the comparative method, on the assumption that cultural differences—the shock of otherness—will make valued cultural traits salient.[5] The analysis is based on 160 semidirected interviews conducted with a random stratified sample of male college-graduate professionals, managers, and businessmen living in and around Indianapolis, New York,

Paris, and Clermont-Ferrand, the regional metropolis of an agricultural *département* in the Massif Central that is not unlike Indianapolis. I focus on France and the United States because, being a Quebecer, I am an outsider to both cultures, and yet I know both of them from the inside, having lived in France and the United States for four and five years, respectively, at the time I conducted the interviews. Furthermore, as I will argue below, French and American cultures show somewhat different formal characteristics that illuminate important theoretical issues.

At the outset of this project I intended to study differences in the ways in which French and American upper-middle-class members draw cultural boundaries.[6] However, I rapidly discovered while conducting interviews that the signals used by individuals to assess high status often pertained to moral and socioeconomic standing as well as to cultural attainment. Furthermore, it appeared that the large majority of these signals pertained to at least one of these standards; some signals, such as self-actualization, were taken to be simultaneously a proof of high moral character, strong success orientation, and cultural sophistication. Consequently, my study focuses on these three standards or types of symbolic boundaries:

Moral boundaries are drawn on the basis of moral character; they are centered around such qualities as honesty, work ethic, personal integrity, and consideration for others.

Socioeconomic boundaries are drawn on the basis of judgments concerning people's social position as indicated by their wealth, power, or professional success.

Cultural boundaries are drawn on the basis of education, intelligence, manners, tastes, and command of high culture. Someone who describes all of his friends as refined is drawing cultural boundaries. . . .

The Importance of Being Honest: Keys to Moral Boundaries

Howard Becker and Erving Goffman have studied deviants and outsiders to sharpen our understanding of moral rules.[7] Following their lead, moral boundaries can be understood by looking at contrasted conceptions of honesty that are revealed when French and American interviewees explicate the labels they mobilize to describe "dishonest people." Americans use three rather well-circumscribed polluting labels: the "phony," the "social climber," and the "low-morals" type. On the other hand, French interviewees tend to define honest people in opposition to individuals who are "intellectually dishonest" or who are judged to be *salaud* (best translated as "bastard").

In a large modern hospital overlooking the Hudson River in Westchester County, north of Manhattan, I met John Bailey, a laid-back family man. John, who is about fifty, is the chief financial executive of the institution, with approximately seventy-five people working under him. While we were exploring his likes and dislikes in people, the category of "phony" kept popping up. So I asked John what he meant by a "phony" and how he recognizes them. He said:

> I'm thinking of an example: my old boss. I had a good relationship with him, but he was the type of guy who would always ask me, "How you doing? How's your wife doing? How's your kids doing?" and always look sincere, all right? But meanwhile, he didn't really give a darn, it was all show, all right? I'd rather a person, honestly, not ask me that question if they really didn't mean it.

When I asked John how he knew that his boss was a phony, he said:

> I know because I was around him for seven years. It would be the case when we went to meetings and that kind of thing, professional gatherings, I'd be next to him, and he would say, "Whose this guy coming up?" under his breath. I'd tell him the guy's name and he would go up and greet him like he was a long-lost brother, and he didn't even know the guy's name. I don't think it's real . . . I like people to be themselves. I don't have to put on airs, to be somebody I'm not when I'm with a friend. I'm just me.

The *phony* is a genuinely American category which has no adequate equivalent in French.[8] It was used again and again by John Bailey and others to describe people who are not sincere, who pretend to know more than they do, or to be something they are not, who have no substance and judge a book by its cover. They "do things that are totally without basis"; they try to put on a show. In contrast, nonphonies are "honest, they don't 'put on the dog,' they work hard, and they're not trying to scam the public" (informant, Indianapolis). In brief, the nonphony is a doer and not a "big mouth." He is who he is, "take it or leave it." He delivers the merchandise, judges others by their deeds, and keeps his eyes on the bottom line. Transparency is his middle name.

As often disparaged as the phony, the *social climber* is criticized because of the way he treats his subordinates and the methods by which he achieves upward mobility. He is ambitious, which is good, but he overdoes it. Like the phony, he manipulates his environment to accelerate his professional advancement. Paul Anderson, an Indianapolis senior executive, put it best: social climbers are "real aggressive, eager . . . they probably have many people against them, and not that many for. [They are in it] only for themselves and don't sort of look out for their subordinates and care for people first." They also have little consideration for their family's emotional needs as they put their own ambition above everything.

Neither the phony nor the social climber obey the Golden Rule. Because they are pushy and manipulative, strong boundaries are often drawn against them, as their unscrupulous ambition threatens others. There is a genuine feeling of moral superiority among those who condemn them. Tales of coworkers who climbed the professional ladder at great speed; only to rapidly fall back, are told gleefully. Those who achieved mobility at the price of important personal sacrifices (e.g., mental health problems, divorce, or estranged children) are offered as negative examples, particularly by Midwesterners. In fact, a few Midwesterners equate New York with social climbing, divorce, and low moral standards, clustering these lexical terms within a single, all-encompassing polluting category. In so doing, they affirm the common rules for living by which they abide as participants in a symbolic community.

For American upper-middle-class men, dishonest people also include the *low-morals type*. Don Bloom, an Indianapolis consultant near retire-ment, offers his definition of the "low-moral type" when he tells us the sort of people to whom he feels superior:

> Well, I should say first of all, I don't believe in equality. I believe the Lord made us all very different individuals. But I feel superior to people who don't work and who expect that the world owes them a living, and I feel superior to people that have unclean minds and unclean bodies, and I feel superior to people who think they've accomplished something but they've done it immorally or illegally.

Like many Americans, Don Bloom gauges moral impurity by examining work ethics and obedience to the law and to the Ten Commandments, with particular attention given to the tenth which concerns "thy neighbor's wife." In general, given that American egalitarianism might militate against admitting feelings of superiority, my interviewees were extraordinarily prompt to affirm their superiority toward those who lie, cheat, and are not law abiding, i.e., toward people who have *low morals.*[9]

How do these polluting categories contrast with the ones used by the Frenchmen I talked to? If the French share a noticeable dislike for social climbers and for people who are not sincere, rarely do they refer to sexual behavior as a standard for differentiating between "us" and "them." The contrast between American and French conceptions of honesty (and morality) is described by an intense intellectual who teaches literature at a *lycée* located in the Paris *banlieue* (suburb). I met him in a *café* catty-corner from Paris City Hall. Over his third *pastis,* amidst the hubbub of the dining room's noon rush, Denis Homier explains:

> For me, morality is not located between your thighs, but elsewhere. The Judeo-Christian education where morality is above all a sexual issue is wrong. . . . The individual is not essentially defined by his physical dimension . . . I am completely indifferent to whether or not the president of the United States has one, two, three, or ten mistresses, whether he likes little boys, or is homosexual or bisexual. I would simply ask him not to spend too

much time at it . . . At this level, the situation in the United States seems unbearable. That society is completely based on money, and when a candidate for the presidency screws his secretary, it is the end of the world.

The definition of honesty that this literature professor promotes presents a stark contrast with this so-called American approach:

> For me honesty in general, intellectual honesty, material honesty, honesty in relation to oneself, in relation to others [is essential]. In honesty, there is the idea of honor. The *honnête homme* [honest man] is a complex notion. There is certainly something more in it than the notion that you should not steal from your neighbor.

Clearly, Denis Homier himself is not very concerned with promiscuity and deviant sexual behavior. His position reflects wider trends: a cross-national survey revealed that 31 percent of the French respondents and only 5 percent of the American consider the Tenth Commandment which prohibits coveting one's neighbor's wife to be outdated (*dépassé*).[10] In this context, it is not surprising that, in the course of the interviews, three of the French interviewees offered, without probing, information concerning their extramarital relationships, while two mentioned being bisexual.[11] None of the American interviewees volunteered information concerning such relationships.[12]

The World of Success, Money, and Power: Keys to Socioeconomic Boundaries

Whereas people who draw moral boundaries take moral character as indicative of an individual's worth, individuals who draw socioeconomic boundaries define desirability on the basis of social position as read through professional prestige, race, financial standing, class background, power, and visibility in prestigious social circles. Typically, people who fall in this category feel inferior to "highly successful, highly aggressive people" (proprietor, car leasing company, New York),

which might mean "obviously people who are wealthy, in a higher position, just higher on a social level type of thing" (staff assistant, Indianapolis). They might be envious of people who "succeed very well and very strongly" (banker, Paris).[13] They judge people's worth by external status signals, such as "where you came from, where you went to school, what you're doing now, that sort of thing. Who you work for, how much money you make, where you live in town," and "whether you had the ability to achieve."[14] They don't like to associate with losers and they mostly choose their friends on the basis of "how well they have done for themselves"; they describe these friends as well-off professionals and businessmen[15]—"the other people you just put up with, but you don't want to be with" (corporate lawyer, New York). In short, people who draw socioeconomic boundaries are attracted by success. As a New York realtor, a "nouveau riche," explains: "I prefer dealing with people who are more successful than I am . . . I do work with them, I'm involved in politics; I've got lots of friends who are much bigger folks than I am and I enjoy being out there with them. . . . Naturally, success breeds success; so I'm hanging around success."[16]

People who draw strong socioeconomic boundaries are consumed by professional success, as measured by career curve and velocity. Success gives them a sense of self-worth, of psychological well-being, and of personal satisfaction; as a French entrepreneur says, "[Success] is the full realization of oneself." These men sometimes see people who are less successful as "anxious, jealous, revengeful" (accountant, Clermont-Ferrand), because they conceive worldly success as the only real way to gain peace of mind. They take money to be the crucial signal of ability and desirability, and such external attributes as place of residence and type of car to be sure indices of success. For them, money is the key to everything, including social acceptance and membership.[17]

Whereas sociologists often tend to posit the predominance of ascribed characteristics (gender, race, ethnicity) in the creation of social closure,[18] or that of material standards of evaluation (i.e., income, ownership of durable consumer goods) in determining social status,[19] one of [my] goals is to attempt to assess which standards of evaluation are in fact most salient in determining socioeconomic status, at least in the context of interviews.[20] Simultaneously, I analyze the relative salience of class in contrast to other aspects of social identity.[21] Important cross-national differences emerge with significant conceptual consequences for rational choice theory and other approaches that presume that economic resources are by definition more crucial than others.

For many interviewees, signals of high socioeconomic status are the only status signals that are really significant: our quantitative comparison of the ranking of respondents on the moral, cultural, and socioeconomic dimensions reveals that, overall, socioeconomic boundaries are slightly more important than cultural or moral boundaries.[22] Socioeconomic boundaries, however, are considerably more salient in America than they are in France.[23] Moreover, with only a few exceptions, the French, and the Parisians in particular, rarely mention feeling inferior to wealthier or more successful people. In fact, the men I talked to were often uncomfortable with probes concerning their "success." They almost never describe their friends as "being successful," this notion itself sounding uncouth in French ("*ça fait prétentieux,*" as a Paris dentist pointed out).[24] They also rarely take people who are very success-oriented as models, as illustrated by a young and dynamic Paris investment banker I talked to:

> I really am not envious of them. I find them limited, sad, even if often they have succeeded in doing impressive things. I think they are sad because they think that they're—I would not say the "masters of the world," but that nothing will stop them and they possess the truth . . . they are so small if you think in terms of the planet. For me, it is almost physical. I find them completely ridiculous, which is paradoxical because often they have succeeded very well.

In contrast, the American men I met with were considerably more prone to describe themselves as feeling inferior to rich, powerful, and successful people. For example, when asked to describe people they admire, they were more likely to point to Donald Trump and Lee Iacocca than the French are to point to Bernard Tapie. And when asked to describe qualities that leave them indifferent, only nine New Yorkers and four Hoosiers chose "successful," in contrast to seventeen Clermontois and nineteen Parisians. Previous research suggests that this stress on success is not confined to the upper-middle class alone in the United States.[25]

The French in general are clearly less money-oriented than Americans. Indeed, 93 percent of the upper-middle-class Frenchmen interviewed by the European values/CARA surveys, in contrast to 68 percent of the Americans, think that it would be good if people were to attach less importance to money. This undoubtedly affects the likelihood that people draw symbolic boundaries on the basis of income. Indeed, among the men I talked with, 68 percent of the Parisians say that, in their evaluations of others, affluence is a feature to which they are indifferent, compared to 57 percent of the Clermontois, 51 percent of the New Yorkers, and 41 percent of the Hoosiers.[26]

Viviana Zelizer and others have noted that, far from having a simply utilitarian value, money has a wide range of meanings.[27] Indeed, while Frenchmen have an ambivalent attitude toward money, Americans see it as an essential means to control and freedom. This affects the role that money is likely to play as a signal of high socioeconomic status. Consequently, it is useful to discuss these various meanings at some length.

I have identified four distinct patterns in the way French individuals think about money. A first, rather important, group of respondents think of money as impure. The second group, the established traditional bourgeoisie, views money as a means of maintaining one's social position rather than of improving it. A third, smaller group, mostly concentrated in Clermont-Ferrand, is much more materialistic in orientation despite a certain asceticism. Finally, the last group conceives of money as the symbol and the reward of their upward mobility and as a means to reach a higher social position.

For many Frenchmen I talked to, money is unworthy of pursuit, for it has the power to desacralize life, infusing it with values that are purely instrumental rather than inherently worthy. Therefore, according to these people, money should not be considered the ultimate professional goal. As a successful Clermont-Ferrand architect states: "The aesthetic, the creative aspect, helping others to live better is really what is appealing. The goal is not at all to make money, but to reach a level of personal satisfaction."

For others, money symbolizes an embarrassing and profane relationship with customers and institutions. We see this in the case of a Parisian lawyer who can't bear the thought of having to bill his clients. This man has six children and owns a very large nineteenth-century house which is in great need of repairs. He says:

> I am ashamed of asking for money. Charging a fee for preparing a case seems to me. . . . I don't know, I'd rather do it for free. . . . It makes me uncomfortable to ask. I am always afraid of asking too much, of making people feel uncomfortable. But when I analyze the situation, I know it is stupid, because I offer a service which should be paid for. I don't like money.

Such negative attitudes toward money, which might be associated with a Catholic disregard for worldly contingencies, are very rare among the Americans with whom I met. The few who partake of them do not go as far as repudiating the importance of money altogether. More typically, they emphasize the place of self-actualization and interpersonal relationships in their lives without belittling money the way the French often do.

A second group of French interviewees is more materialistic without, however, drawing socioeconomic boundaries on the basis of income. They frequently understand money as the nineteenth-century landed bourgeoisie did, that is, as a way to support a lifestyle, a way to live "not only honorably, but comfortably" (hospital controller, Clermont-Ferrand). In Paris, this means to many men being able to eat out on a very regular basis, to go to the theater and to various cultural events;[28] to offer frequent hospitality to a large number of friends and kin both at their city home and, on weekends, at the country house, and to support the country house itself. In short, money is a means of reproducing a traditional bourgeois way of life. It is a way of *maintaining* a social identity rather than of improving one's social position, of signaling one's progress on the consumption ladder. It is, therefore, not surprising that in these bourgeois circles "earned" money is deemphasized in favor of the *patrimoine* (i.e., wealth, especially inherited wealth, including real estate properties, art, and furniture, that incarnate the family history) of things which have always been there. As a Parisian human resources consultant puts it, "We had them, we always had them, and our children will have them."[29] These bourgeois rarely talk about prices and purchases ("*ça ne se fait pas parmi les gens bien*"). They play down commercial relationships as if such considerations collided with their "coté grand seigneur," i.e., their noble appreciation for the disinterested and the gratuitous. Such attitudes did not surface among the American men with whom I talked.[30]

The ambivalence of many of the French interviewees toward money is not surprising given that a number of members of the French bourgeoisie are downwardly mobile economically and maintain a high social position mostly because their family has been part of the upper-middle class for several generations, because they are culturally part of the group, and because they have access to large resourceful social networks.

A third group of Frenchmen are much more money-oriented than the majority of their compatriots. This group was mostly concentrated in Clermont-Ferrand. As is the case for many Auvergnats—the residents of the region where Clermont-Ferrand is located, who have a reputation for being hardnosed and astute businessmen—these men view the accumulation of riches as a major motivation in their lives. They talked to me about their awareness of the economic standing of their neighbors and their own interest in making their *patrimoine* grow. Like American participants, they consider making money to be the road to freedom. This is expressed by an upwardly mobile engineer whose father was a poor farmer, and who shows great pride in working for

Michelin. This man's passion is to speculate on the stock market:

> The consumer is dominated; the investor wants to dominate. The consumer is a hostage in a ghetto, even if it is a golden cage. The investor dominates because he has the initiative. The consumer is the victim. On the one side, you have someone who wants to do things. On the other side, you have the one who swallows, who endures, who is conditioned and manipulated.

In contrast, people whose values are antimaterialistic see the drive to make money as a constraint, because it requires adapting to an organization's culture and norms and thereby losing one's individuality and personal integrity.

A last, very small group of the French participants, most of them first-generation upper-middle class, value consumerism as such—i.e., the spending of money rather than the mere making of it—as the symbol and reward of upward mobility. These men talk openly about the villa, the luxury car, and the other consumption goods they are now able to afford. Even in this last group, however, not a single interviewee equates a person's worth with his or her income. Members of this fourth group are often ostracized for their materialism by the traditional bourgeoisie, whose attitude toward money they are pressured to adopt, as if, unlike their American counterparts, this "bourgeoisie de promotion" had not yet fully developed a distinct and legitimate culture and was being pushed into mimicking the norms of the old bourgeoisie.

The ambivalence of the French attitudes toward money contrast highly with the more positive attitudes that were most frequently expressed by American upper-middle-class men. For these individuals money means above all freedom, control, and security, these being clearly circumscribed by level of personal income. In this context it is not surprising that money is itself more salient as a basis for socioeconomic boundaries for Americans than for French participants.

The first American respondent to associate freedom with control was a young, high-powered New York investment portfolio manager who makes around $200,000 a year. I interviewed him on the patio of his beautiful Riverside home. He explained his perspective in the following terms:

> I like to have control . . . I want to do what makes me happy and not feel that I'm being pushed around and forced into corners. [My job] is not a self-fulfilling job. The financial incentive is really what I'm here for. It gives me the freedom to do what I want, to go places, do things. I've never been good at budgeting. I would like to have enough money to retire in five years from now if I want to. To me this means freedom. A lot of people are saying to me, "You're too money-oriented." I'm just being honest. If the money went away on this job, I wouldn't be there more than another month.

Here freedom means being able to take off regularly for a weekend of skiing in Vermont, or being able to buy a luxury home in an exclusive area. For others, it simply means being able to afford a house in a safe neighborhood where their children will have access to good schools and be somewhat less exposed to drugs and other real or imaginary social evils, and where real estate values are likely to climb. It might also mean being wealthy enough to retire or become self-employed, a dream that looms much larger in American definitions of success than in the French.

For these American men, money is also seen as providing a certain "comfort level" that becomes the symbol and the reward of professional success. "Comfort level" is measured by the value of the items one can afford, including cars, homes, trips, electronic equipment, and so forth. It is also measured by the kids' ballet classes and piano lessons, and their tennis and computer camps, as well as by the time spent at work versus the time the adults spend golfing or enjoying other leisure-time activities. And because "comfort level" reflects level of success, many are caught in an endless spiral of consumption.[31] A New York software developer who makes more than a hundred thousand dollars a year puts it best: "I find myself admiring the latest cars, the latest clothes, wanting to go to the nicest resort. . . . I want these things even though I can rationalize and intellectualize it away. Those are not the things that make me happy, yet I still want the new car, the latest stereo . . . there are a lot of things that I'd like to have that I don't have." This infinite desire is echoed in a striking way by a middle-aged Indianapolis minister who also takes money to be a measure of his "professional" success:

> I would not be honest unless I said that economic success is important. It certainly is. . . . It has been a sign value to how successful I am in the institutional church. Because that's important in determining or perceiving the level of success of a minister, i.e., by how much money he makes. I struggle almost constantly with the pressures of society, and particularly advertising and entertainment, which emphasize money and the things money buys as the most important thing in life. . . . What television portrays both in its programming and news programs and advertising . . . is that there's an awful lot more out there that you should be able to buy, and things you should be able to do. . . . It bothers me. . . . But after a while [it] can make one feel that you really haven't achieved all that much. . . . I am a child of my own culture and success has been worshipped, there is no doubt about that. Success is almost always defined in terms of either professional success or accumulation of material goods.

A valence foreign to spiritual salvation shapes in a significant way the sense of accomplishment that this minister gets from his work. His views are indicative of the fact that in America socioeconomic boundaries can be mobilized to evaluate even activities that are explicitly noneconomic in character, as conceptions of success centering on "comfort level" is diffused by the mass media to all groups.[32] It is, therefore, not surprising that overall, in the United States, socioeconomic boundaries are very frequently drawn on the basis of income. In France people more often associate a high income less with freedom than with a loss of personal integrity, and less with "success" than with a denial of the intrinsic value of work.[33]

The importance of a high-income level as a signal of socioeconomic status for American participants can be explained by the fact that money is more central to their quality of life and to that of their dependents, the welfare functions of the state being relatively underdeveloped in the United States in contrast to France. Indeed, in America, the quality of schooling is less uniform than it is in France because it is more exclusively dependent on local taxes and, indirectly, on local real estate prices.[34] Also, health care and child care have to be privately purchased by the American middle class. College education is very costly, and most American upper-middle class men spend a considerable part of their life savings for the education of their children. This factor is important particularly because higher education is at the heart of the reproduction of the upper-middle class. In contrast, in France, higher education is less expensive and the quality of schooling tends to be more consistent across neighborhoods, because elementary and secondary schools are financially supported and controlled by the central government. Health care and child care, too, are free or available at low cost.

The importance of income as a signal of socioeconomic status in the United States is also sustained by the fact that professional success is measured more by income level than by nomination to prestigious positions. In general, market principles have more influence in the allocation of professional rewards, which strengthens the role of money—rather than, say, office—as a universal media of exchange. . . .

Most of My Friends Are Refined: Keys to Cultural Boundaries

Given the importance that college education and expert knowledge play in defining the identity of members of the upper-middle class, it is not surprising that differences in level of education and intelligence are two of the most common bases on which my French and American respondents draw cultural boundaries. In fact, many people, including men who do not define themselves as culturally sophisticated, put a premium on intelligence when discussing the types of people with whom they want to interact. Time and time again, they portray their friends and favorite coworkers as bright and intellectually stimulating. They describe the types of people they are interested in as people who "have a certain intellectual level" (lawyer, New York), and who "think well, or try to think well, rigorously, logically, with continuity. They are superior to those who think in a discontinuous way or who refuse to think" (literature professor, Paris). These groups also put a premium on higher education, which is the most important barrier to upper-middle-class status both in terms of access to job and of social integration,[35] as shown by the voluminous literature on educational and status attainment.[36]

The French men I met with appear to be especially concerned with intelligence, for they repeatedly acknowledge finding it very difficult to tolerate stupidity. Again, their diatribes against *la bêtise* reach a level of violence only comparable to American diatribes against incompetence. As Louis Dupont, a Versailles business management specialist, explains, stupidity is the worst sin of all, far worse than dishonesty:

> Thinking and trying to find solutions to problems is one of the greatest pleasures that life offers. . . . There are surprising degrees of mediocrity and stupidity. I prefer to have to deal with someone who is devious and intelligent, because at least we will be able to understand each other. If they are devious, it's not my problem. Someone who is stupid leaves me powerless.

This opinion is shared by Julien Lafitte, [a] physicist. For Julien, dishonesty is not as bad as narrow-mindedness because "it is still possible to converse with someone who is dishonest. It is possible to bring him back in the right direction. Whereas there is nothing you can do against someone who is narrow-minded." Not a single American interviewee expressed so clearly a preference for cultural over moral standards of evaluation.

The fact that the French participants are particularly concerned with intelligence is also reflected in their descriptions of their heroes and role-models: great intellectuals—Raymond Aron, Jacques Attali, Jean-Paul Sartre—occupy a place of choice. One of the French individuals I talked with, Jacques Mendel, a museum curator in Clermont-Ferrand, expresses a widely shared feeling when he admits that he often evaluates himself as "inferior to people who strictly at the intellectual

level make me feel very small . . . because I think that they have succeeded at what I am trying to succeed at." Ultimately, for these men, intellectual achievement is the achievement par excellence, beyond the money and the worldly success it can bring. Several features of French society reflect this belief. To take only one example, many top French politicians have written serious political essays; they are quite interested in gaining intellectual respectability and in deriving prestige from their involvement in Parisian intellectual life.[37]

The French and American men I talked with understand intelligence (like honesty) through strongly contrasted cultural categories. The French stress having *un sens critique* (a critical approach), which they take to be a measure of one's analytical power. They also read intelligence through intellectual playfulness, capacity for abstraction, eloquence, and style. In contrast, we saw that the Americans highly value competence. Hence, they largely read intelligence through expertise, attributing great importance to "knowing the facts," and most of all to knowing "relevant," i.e., useful, facts. I discuss these cross-national differences in turn. . . .

The importance of this *sens critique* and the charismatic (and Promethean) view of the life of the mind it suggests is sustained in part by the philosophical education required for obtaining the *baccalauréat*, a selective terminal high school degree. The private Catholic *lycées*, where a sizable percentage of the upper-middle class send their children, particularly emphasize philosophical training.[38] In this context, students are implicitly encouraged to approach rhetoric as an intellectual game in which to display intellectual playfulness, suppleness, and rapidity; reasoning capabilities, including one's capacity for abstraction, are crucial, as are articulateness and breadth of reading.[39] On the other hand, mastering facts is not highly valued, for students learn to develop complex arguments on theoretical grounds only. The attitude of Didier Aucour, the architecture professor, exemplifies a reaction to factualism that one often encounters. When asked if it was important to him that he be well-informed, he replies, "I could not care less. Current events are in the order of insignificant, transient knowledge."

"What is not clear is not French," says the dictum. The French intellectual tradition puts a premium on clarity of thought and expression, which are taken to be further signals of intelligence. One of the men reached an apex of lyricism when explaining to me the importance of "the equilibrium between the sentences, the attention paid to the selection of words and to their exact meaning, and to the thoughts on which they fundamentally rest" (human resource consultant, Paris). "Bad grammar reveals vulgarity of thought," I was told on another occasion. Many displayed their participation in the cult of the French language by noting with disapproval a spelling error on a questionnaire I submitted to them.[40] Competing conceptions of what intelligence consists of were also strikingly dramatized by the tone respondents used during the interviews: while the answers of Americans were short and to the point, the answers of the French, and particularly of the Parisians, were considerably more lengthy and more convoluted, richer in details and in self-reflexive comments.

The importance of these various signals of intelligence is reflected in the standards of evaluation used by French teachers. Indeed, style of presentation, accent, and diction have a strong impact on the assessment of the performance of students at all levels. Total mastery of the language is a key to being socially constructed as brilliant, especially given that national standardized aptitude tests are not used in the French educational system.[41]

This stress on eloquence carries over to the sphere of professional interactions, where verbal duels are frequent, just as competition through performance is an everyday occurrence for Americans. Hence, the art of outwitting the opponent is cultivated up to the highest level of sophistication.[42] Such a form of competition has its drawbacks. An old-time Parisian diplomat describes to me the elite members of his administrative department who graduated from the prestigious "Ecole nationale d'administration." He does not hold them in high esteem because

[t]hey are people who don't know everything, but who are able to talk about every-

thing without knowing the problem. It is really unpleasant. You put them in front of a situation they don't know, and they'll talk about it as if they did.

. . . The categories through which the French define intelligence are still strongly contrasted with the ones Americans use, the latter being largely organized around the mastery of facts and around practical knowledge. We saw that Americans admire competence. Consequently, they read intelligence largely through one's capacity to present, organize, and analyze specific facts in a coherent and clearly workable, if not necessarily elegant, way. This factualism emerges when the Americans discuss feelings of inferiority, as exemplified by this statement made by Craig Neil, the owner of the Long Island car leasing business:

Somebody that knows an area that I am not familiar with makes me feel uncomfortable. If I sat down and had a long lengthy conversation, for example, with a stockbroker, I probably would feel uncomfortable because I don't know a thing about the stock brokerage business. If somebody sat down with me and started talking architectural design, I would feel uncomfortable because I don't know a thing about architectural design.

Expertise both opens and closes boundaries. Indeed, it can signal superiority and can thus make others "feel uncomfortable." On the other hand, the American men I talked with often define people they find interesting as having "a wealth of information"; they are "not necessarily intellectually stimulating, but stimulating, they know things about what they do, where they've been, who they've seen, how they fit into society" (environment specialist, New York). The line dividing "us" and "them" is less a *sens critique* and proper diction than the mastery of broad information about the world. As explained by an Indianapolis recruitment specialist,

It bothers me if somebody is not worldly enough to know much about history, geography, or current events. I don't even say that a person has to know a lot about sports. It helps, it helps, if they don't have any of those other things . . . I've got a good friend who's a neighbor, who doesn't know a lot about sports—he fell asleep during the I.U. [Indiana University] national championship game last year. I still like him because he knows current events and he knows history pretty well. That's two out of three, or out of four.

The appreciation of expertise characteristic of American upper-middle-class culture is revealed in the types of reading the American participants say they do. More than the French, they are interested in magazines and trade publications that help them keep up with recent developments in their specialized areas of interest and to make informed purchasing decisions. The reading tastes of this New York recreation specialist are representative of that of a number of American men: "[I] love to read . . . sports magazines, clothing catalogues, housing catalogues, you know, it's about housing, real estate, mortgaging, etc. For pleasure, I like an occasional documentary book, an autobiography." *Consumer Reports, Car and Driver, Sports Illustrated,* and sundry computer magazines are frequently mentioned publications, along with professional and current events magazines. John Craig, a New York marketing specialist . . . , described the reading habits of many as he explained when and why his wife takes on a book: "She reads when something motivates her, when she needs to find out something. Like, her mother is very ill and is under hospice care now, and she's reading a book on hospices and what it's really all about." A questionnaire on leisure-time activities which was administered after the interviews revealed that a larger percentage of the French than of the American interviewees define themselves as frequent book readers (72 percent of the Clermontois and 77 percent of the Parisians, in contrast to 44 percent of the New Yorkers and 58 percent of the Hoosiers).[43]

This appreciation for information sometimes goes hand in hand with a quantitative approach to knowledge that underscores the number of books read and facts known. The popularity of this approach is revealed, for instance, by the high circulation of magazines such as *Reader's Digest,* of television game shows like "Jeopardy," and of party games such as "Trivial Pursuit." Of course, a large number of Americans do not partake of this quantitative factualism. It does, however, remain a distinctive feature of the American cultural landscape that is absent from the French;[44] the way the French focus on abstraction and diction is of comparatively little significance for Americans.[45]

I suggested above that the American men I talked with also have a more practical view of intelligence than the French. This is revealed, for instance, when Americans are probed on their heroes and role models; those who mention "great minds" are more likely to bring up a brilliant entrepreneur (à la Dr. Wang) than a pure intellectual (à la Jean-Paul Sartre). We will see, however, that there exists important variations across professions in this respect.

The reasons Hoosiers and New Yorkers put a premium on practical intelligence might relate to the fact that, in general, they more highly value success and often interpret success as resulting from having the wherewithal to use one's brains advantageously. As a down-to-earth Indianapolis realtor said, some smart people

> may have book learning, but when it comes to what I would consider a very simple practical judgment, they come up with ridiculous conclusions. In the business world, it's common sense in the extreme. There is no secret to it, it's not esoteric, you don't have to be a trained physicist to be a businessman.

In this context, intelligence is viewed as an "ability to recognize opportunities, to seize opportunities, to capitalize on them and to make them work. While other people at the same time, the same place, under the same circumstances, miss it all" (real estate developer, Indianapolis).

This practical view of intelligence is telling of the way Americans draw cultural boundaries, in contrast to their French counterparts; while it is acceptable for a Frenchman to be incompetent in the organization of everyday life—in France, as mentioned above, men even vaunt their ineptitude concerning matters deemed prosaic—Americans are much more critical of those who are lacking in this sphere. However, again, I did of course encounter some Americans who had an appreciation of knowledge for its own sake, but even these generally valued competence and practical know-how in everyday life. . . .

The very same qualities that would allow one to be socially constructed as brilliant in the French workplace are likely to be useless in the American workplace. While eloquence, general competence, *un sens critique,* and a strong capacity of abstraction are key in one case, factualism, efficiency, expertise, and pragmatism are more central in the other.

NOTES

1. Kanter, *Men and Women of the Corporation, Jackall, Moral Mazes: The World of Corporate Manager.* On the importance of networks see Granovetter, *Getting a Job: A Study of Contacts and Careers.*

2. A recent study, which surveyed three decades of domestic sitcoms from the beginning of network television in 1946 down to 1978, found that these programs mostly depicted middle-class lifestyles: ". . . only 2.6% of series portrayed families headed by blue collar workers. Even including clerical and service workers the total percent rises to only 8.4% . . . By contrast almost two-thirds (63.5%) of television families were middle class." Similar results were found for the 1979–90 period. Butsch, "Class and Gender in Four Decades of TV Families. Plus Ça Change . . ." See also Butsch and Glennon, "Social Class: Frequency Trends in Domestic Situation Comedy, 1946/1978."

3. A recent study of television audiences showed that working-class women use entertainment programs to learn middle-class lifestyles. See Press, *Women Watching Television: Gender, Class and Generations in the American Television Experience.*

4. The concept of boundary work is borrowed from Gieryn, "Boundary-Work and the Demarcation of Science from Non-Science: Strains and Interests in Professional Ideologies of Scientists." Gieryn refers to the "symbolic work" scientists produce to create a public image of science by defining it in opposition to religion. As used here, the term "boundary work" refers to the process by which individuals define their identity in opposition to that of others by drawing symbolic boundaries.

5. On the advantages of the comparative method for studying culture see Lipset, *Continental Divide: The Values and Institutions of the United States and Canada,* xiii–xviii.

6. Here and elsewhere I introduce a distinction between "symbolic boundaries," which is used to refer to all types of boundaries regardless of their content, and "cultural boundaries," which is used to refer to symbolic boundaries that are drawn on the basis of high status signals related to intelligence, education, refinement or cultivation.

7. Becker, *Outsiders,* Goffman, *Stigma: Notes on the Management of Spoiled Identity.*

8. *Harrap's* French-English dictionary translates *phony* as "fumiste" and "imposteur." Neither term was ever used by my French respondents to describe dishonest people.

9. I interviewed a relatively small group of Christians who assess moral purity on the basis of attitudes toward alcohol, pornography, abortion, divorce, homosexuality, drugs, and atheistic humanism, but these issues did not come up often in interviews. Most interviewees put more emphasis on honesty and work ethics.

10. Source: European Values Survey/Gallup for the Center for Applied Research in the Apostolate (CARA). Information on the attitudes of French professionals and managers is based on the following occupations: the *patrons* from large, medium-size, and small businesses, the *cadres supérieurs* and *cadres moyeus,* and the *membres de professions libérales* (N = 256). The American survey includes 192 professionals, managers, and businessmen. [These surveys] are based on the same questionnaire and were both conducted in 1981. The total number of respondents is 1,729 for the United States and 1,199 for France.

11. For instance, when asked what he does during the weekend, a Parisian human resource consultant answered: "It depends whether I am in love or not. If I am very much in love, then I make love, which I think is the greatest thing in life. I am almost a mystic on this issue . . . It is not always with my wife . . . It can be with her. I can be in love with my wife, but not always. We have been married for thirty years. It can be with someone else. It has been with someone else for a while."

12. It is important to note, however, that studies of female and male adultery show that in the United States "one quarter to about one half of married women have at least one lover after they are married in any given marriage," as have "50 percent to 65 percent of men by the age of forty." Lawson, *Adultery: An Analysis of Love and Betrayal,* 75.

13. An Indianapolis civil servant talks about how his feelings of inferiority are linked to success: "There are times when I feel inferior to my brother because I think he's been successful . . . He's been personally successful

—he is a doctor. And there are times when I feel that I should've done as well. There are probably a lot of times when I feel I should've done as well."

14. In *Social Standing in America*, Coleman and Rainwater give a systematic description of the *worldly* signals that are used to read status in America, using data collected in Kansas City and Boston. They focus less on distinctions within the middle class than on differences between classes. Earlier analyses, such as *Crestwood Heights*, are also useful for identifying symbols of worldly success, and especially the role played by professional associations and social and service clubs as arenas within which to acquire and enact status. See Seeley, Sim, and Loosley, *Crestwood Heights: A Study of the Culture of Suburban Life*, 292–302. See also Huber, *The American Idea of Success*.

15. An Indianapolis informant, e.g., describes his friends as follows: "One of them is president of the Illinois Gas Company, which serves two-thirds of the state. Another one is a chap just up the street whose wife is very active, almost pushy, socially. He was president of the Good Life Insurance Company. He's one of those fat cats who put money into the Republican Party and raises money . . . My wife belongs to two or three groups like the bridge club, and there's a golf-playing group and a church group. Some of [our friends] came from business, like Jack Grey, the fellow who's president of the Green Company. Another one is Charlie Black, who was with Mobil. And also, this other fellow who was editor of the paper, friends of my wife."

16. The ideal type of the socioeconomically exclusive depicted here corresponds to the success-oriented manager described in Bellah et al., *Habits of the Heart*. He has little concern for wider political or social issues, and he understands morality as the capacity to "do your own thing" if you have the money to do it (77).

17. On money and social membership, see Rainwater, *What Money Buys*.

18. See Murphy, *Social Closure: The Theory of Monopolization and Exclusion*, Parkin, "Strategies of Closure in Class Formation."

19. Chapin, *The Measurement of Social Status by the Use of the Social Status Scale,* W. Lloyd Warner and P. S. Lunt, *Status System of a Modern Community,* Veblen, *The Theory of the Leisure Class*.

20. One exception in this tradition of predefining status signals is the work of William Faunce which shows that status is not always judged on the basis of work- or occupation-related characteristics. See esp. "On the Meaning of Occupational Status: Implications

of Increasing Complexity for How Status Is Conceived"; "Occupational Status-Assignment Systems: The Effect of Status on Self-Esteem."

21. This topic has been largely neglected by the available studies of subjective dimensions of class. See Mary R. Jackman and Robert W. Jackman, *Class Awareness in the United States,* Vanneman and Cannon, *The American Perception of Class*.

22. The average score for all interviewees on this scale is 3.6 in contrast to 3.3 for both cultural and moral boundaries.

23. The average score for the French is 3.2 compared to 4.0 for Americans. I find a weak positive relationship between the fact of residing in the United States and of drawing strong socioeconomic boundaries with a Somers' D of .26 at the .01 level of significance. The measure used here and elsewhere in this book is Somers' D, which accounts for the ranking of cases on an independent variable. In the present statement, Somers' D refers to the likelihood that American interviewees will score 3–5 on the socioeconomic scale. The level of significance is indicated by Tau C. It should be noted that 68 percent of the Hoosiers and 70 percent of the New Yorkers score high (i.e., 4 or 5) on the socioeconomic scale. Only 38 percent of the Parisians score this high on the socioeconomic scale as compared to 50 percent of the Clermontois.

24. Hofstede notes that the word *achievement* does not have a perfect equivalent in French (*Culture's Consequences,* 350). He also criticizes D K. McClelland's theory of achievement as ethnocentric and as applying mostly to American society (171). See McClelland, *The Achieving Society*.

25. Contributing to the controversy around Merton's thesis of success orientation, L. Richard Della Fave found a weak relationship between success orientation and social class in the United States, which he interprets as indicating a considerable amount of overlap in level of aspiration from class to class. His conclusions are based on a questionnaire administered to high school students in the early seventies. "Success Values: Are They Universal or Class-Differentiated?"

26. Studies provide mixed evidence of these cross-national differences between France and the United States. For instance, in *Culture Shift* (92), Inglehart showed that a roughly equal number of Americans in prestigious occupations—i.e., occupations with a prestige ranking in the top quartile—are materialistic as compared to their French counterparts (the figures are 30 percent and 33 percent, respectively).

27. Zelizer, "The Social Meaning of Money: 'Special Monies,'" 342–77.

28. On the importance of the *culture de sortie* (outings culture) in the French upper-middle class, see Donnat and Cogneau, *Les pratiques culturelles des Français 1973–1989.*

29. On this topic see Pinçon and Pinçon-Charlot, *Dans les beaux quartiers,* chap. 9.

30. More frequent disregard for money as such might have emerged from the American interviews if I had talked with upper-middle-class people residing in the Connecticut suburbs of New York City. Indeed, these suburbs are known to be the choice area for upper-middle-class families that have been part of this class for several generations. Many of my New Jersey interviews, however, were conducted in two historic summer resorts (Madison and Summit) that have traditionally attracted "old money"—a factor that helps to correct possible biases created by my limited sample.

31. On consumption goods as a sign of status see also W. Lloyd Warner et al. *Yankee City,* and Mills, *White Collar: The American Middle Class.* This last book discusses the status panic of white-collar workers who consume and follow rules out of uncertainty. See also Veblen, *The Theory of the Leisure Class.*

32. On the diffusion of an economic definition of success to the lower classes see Powers, "Second Class Finish: The Effect of a Working Class High School." Also Schwartz, *Beyond Conformity and Rebellion: Youth and Authority in America,* 193.

33. A study shows that 79 percent of Americans and 46 percent of the British surveyed use an economic criterion for class differentiation. See Wendell Bell and Robert V. Robinson, "Cognitive Maps of Class and Racial Inequality in England and the United States," 341. The American emphasis on money extends beyond the French-American comparison. Americans are nearly twice as likely as the English to specify income or wealth as a basis of class membership.

34. On the growing importance of the politics of residence in the United States, i.e., on the de facto segregation of the population on the basis of real estate prices, see Reich, "The Secession of the Successful," 16.

35. As suggested by Randall Collins in *The Credential Society,* by using educational credentials as a criterion of selection, organizations control for a number of character traits and habits that are seen as essential for adaptation in an upper-middle-class environment. For the excluded, the lack of a college degree has palpable consequences. Hence, in *America's Working Man,* David Halle argues that the non-college-educated are more conscious of their economic handicap which results in their inability to gain access to jobs than of the properly cultural handicap (e.g., not being familiar with the names of classical composers) that results from the lack of a college education.

36. On the role of French education in passing on privileges, see Girard, *La réussite sociale en France: Ses caractères, ses lois, ses effets;* Bourdieu and Passeron, *Reproduction in Education, Society and Culture;* Boudon, *L'inégalité des chances;* Thélot, *Tel père, tel fils.*

37. For a comparison of the attraction that intellectual prestige exerts on French and American politicians see Clark, *Literary France: The Making of a Culture,* 26–33.

38. As of 1982–83, 16 percent of France's schoolchildren were being educated in private Catholic schools. Data on the class background of these children, however, as for private school students generally, is not readily available. See Ambler, "Educational Pluralism in the French Fifth Republic," 10.

39. On the abstract character of the French curriculum see Crozier, *The Bureaucratic Phenomenon,* 242.

40. On the cult of the French language see again the insightful book by Clark, *Literary France,* esp chap. 5. She writes: "The cultivation of clarity and the exaltation of reason define the basic intellectuality of French literary culture. The French language, French writers and French literature appear 'intellectual' in ways that other languages, other literatures and other writers do not . . . the spirit of Cartesian logic suffuses the entire culture to this day . . . The *esprit de géométrie,* a sense of order, system and logic [are all crucial]" (99).

41. Eloquence is essential for gaining admission to many of the most prestigious grandes écoles. On this topic see the excellent analysis of Bourdieu, in "Epreuves scolaires et consécration sociale," 69. Also his *La noblesse d'état,* p 1. While this emphasis on style and eloquence is most characteristic of elite education, it also permeates the university and the upper-middle class at large because, according to Bourdieu and Passeron, elite schools define what constitutes legitimate culture for French society as a whole (see *Reproduction*). The vocational schools (*lycées d'enseignement professionel* (LEP)) do, however, put less emphasis on verbal skills and stress instead properly technical skills. On this topic, see Hamon and Rotman, *Tant qu'il y ama des profs.*

42. According to Bourdieu, apprenticeship in such skills is an intrinsic part of the preparatory courses for

the *grandes écoles,* which courses are the "archetypical form of French academic culture" ("Epreuves scolaires et consécration sociale," 21).

43. For information on the reading tastes of the upper-middle class in France see Parmentier, "Les genres et leurs lecteurs," and Donnat and Cogneau, *Les pratiques culturelles des Français 1973–1989,* chap. 4.

44. It is revealing that the distinction fiction/nonfiction that serves as an organizing principle in American bookstores is not used in France. Furthermore, the French never describe their reading interests as "facts" the way this New York computer specialist does: "[I read] facts, science, mainly. I could read a book on computers; I could read a book on relativity. I could read excerpts from medical journals, scientific journals like *Scientific American.* Those are the type of things I enjoy reading, popular science, popular mechanics, but mainly factual. I am not into fiction . . . Science by magazines, science by books, things of that nature, news, current events, uhm . . . anything factual."

45. While some American men I interviewed insist on the importance of proper grammar, this is never accompanied by a cult of language such as one finds in France. The extraordinary popularity of the televised French dictation championships reveals how widespread this cult is in France. They do not compare with American spelling bees because these dictations are a celebration of the beauty and the grammatical complexity of the French language; the "dictée" are generally taken from classical literary works.

REFERENCES

Alexander, C. N., and Mathilda G. Wiley. 1981. "Situated Activity and Identity Formation." In *Social Psychology: Sociological Perspective,* edited by Morris Rosenberg and Ralph H. Turner. New York: Basic Books, 269–89.

Ambler, John S. 1991. "Educational Pluralism in the French Fifth Republic." In *Searching for the New France,* edited by James F. Hollifield and George Ross. New York and London: Routledge, 193–221.

Becker, Howard D. 1963. *Outsiders: Studies in the Sociology of Deviance.* New York: Free Press.

Bell, Wendell, and Robert V. Robinson. 1980. "Cognitive Maps of Class and Racial Inequality in England and the United States." *American Journal of Sociology* 86, no. 2:331–49.

Bellah, Robert N., Richard Madsen, William W. Sullivan, Ann Swidler, and Steven Tipton. 1985. *Habits of the Heart: Individualism and Commitment in American Life.* Berkeley: University of California Press.

Blum, Linda, and Vicky Smith. 1988. "Women's Mobility in the Corporation: A Critique of the Politics of Optimism." *Signs* 13, no. 3:528–45.

Boudon, Raymond. 1973. *L'inégalité des chances.* Paris: Armand Collin.

Bourdieu, Pierre. 1981. "Epreuves scolaires et consécration sociale." *Actes de la Recherche en Sciences Sociales* 39:3–70.

———. 1989. *La noblesse d'Etat: Grandes écoles et esprit de corps.* Paris: Editions de Minuit.

Brint, Steven. 1985. "The Political Attitudes of Professionals." *Annual Review of Sociology* 11:389–414.

Brodsky, Jody Ellen. 1987. "Intellectual Snobbery: A Socio-Historical Perspective." Unpublished Ph.D. diss., Department of Sociology, State University of New York, Stonybrook.

Butsch, Richard. 1991. "Class and Gender in Four Decades of TV Families: Plus Ça Change—" Unpublished ms., Rider College.

Butsch, Richard, and Lynda M. Glennon. 1983. "Social Class: Frequency Trends in Domestic Situation Comedy, 1946–1978." *Journal of Broadcasting* 27, no. 1:77–81.

Chapin, J. S. 1933. *The Measurement of Social Status by the Use of the Social Status Scale.* Minneapolis: University of Minnesota Press.

Clark, Priscilla Parkhurst. 1979. "Literary Culture in France and the United States." *American Journal of Sociology* 84:1047–76.

———. 1987. *Literary France: The Making of a Culture.* Berkeley: University of California Press.

Coleman, Richard P., and Lee Rainwater, with Kent A. McClelland. 1978. *Social Standing in America: New Dimensions of Class.* New York: Basic Books.

Collins, Randall. 1979. *The Credential Society.* New York: Academic Press.

———. 1988. *Theoretical Sociology.* San Diego: Harcourt, Brace, Jovanovich.

Davis, James A. 1982. "Achievement Variables and Class Cultures: Family Schooling, Job and Forty-Nine Dependent Variables in the Cumulative GSS." *American Sociological Review* 47:569–86.

Della Fave, L. Richard. 1974. "Success Values: Are They Universal or Class-Differentiated?" *American Journal of Sociology* 80, no. 1:153–69.

Donnat, Olivier, and Denis Cogneau. 1990. *Les pratiques culturelles des Français 1973–1989.* Paris: La Découverte/La Documentation Française.

Epstein, Cynthia Fuchs. 1992. "Tinkerbells and Pinups: The Construction and Reconstruction of Gender Boundaries at Work." In *Cultivating Differences: Symbolic Boundaries and the Making of Inequality,* edited by Michèle Lamont and Marcel Fournier. Chicago: University of Chicago Press.

Faunce, William A. 1989. "On the Meaning of Occupational Status: Implications of Increasing Complexity for How Status Is Conceived." Paper presented at the annual meeting of the American Sociological Association, San Francisco, August.

_____. 1989. "Occupational Status-Assignment Systems: The Effect of Status on Self-Esteem." *American Journal of Sociology* 95, no. 2:378–400.

Giddens, Anthony. 1991. *Modernity and Self-Identity: Self and Society in the Late Modern Age.* Cambridge: Polity Press.

Gieryn, Thomas F. 1983. "Boundary-Work and the Demarcation of Science from Non-Science: Strains and Interests in Professional Ideologies of Scientists." *American Sociological Review* 48:781–95.

Girard, Alain. 1961. *La réussile sociale en France: Ses caractères, ses lois, ses effets.* Paris: Presses Universitaires de France.

Goffman, Erving. 1963. *Stigma: Notes on the Management of Spoiled Identity.* Englewood Cliffs, N.J.: Prentice Hall.

Granovetter, Mark S. 1974. *Getting a Job: A Study of Contacts and Careers.* Cambridge, Mass.: Harvard University Press.

Halle, David. 1984. *America's Working Man: Work, Home and Politics among Blue-Collar Property Owners.* Chicago: University of Chicago Press.

Hamon, Hervé, and Patrick Rotman. 1984. *Tant qu'il y aura des profs.* Paris: Editions du Seuil.

Herzfeld, Michael. 1980. "Honour and Shame: Problems in the Comparative Analysis of Moral Systems." *Man* 15:339–51.

Huber, Richard M. 1971. *The American Idea of Success.* Wanscott, N.Y.: Pushcart Press.

Hurrelmann, Klaus. 1988. *Social Structure and Personality Development: The Individual as a Productive Processor of Reality.* Cambridge: Cambridge University Press.

Inglehart, Ronald. 1990. *Culture Shift in Advanced Industrial Societies.* Princeton: Princeton University Press.

Jackman, Mary R., and Robert W. Jackman. 1983. *Class Awareness in the United States.* Berkeley: University of California Press.

Kalmijn, Matthijs. 1991. "Status Homogamy in the United States." *American Journal of Sociology* 97, no. 2:496–523.

Kanter, Rosabeth Moss. 1977. *Men and Women of the Corporation.* New York: Basic Books.

Keller, Suzanne. 1989. "Women in the 21st Century: Summing Up and Moving Forward." Paper presented at the first Radcliffe Conference on "Defining the Challenge," January.

Lamont, Michèle, and Robert Wuthnow. 1990. "Betwixt and Between: Recent Cultural Sociology in Europe and the United States." In *Frontiers of Social Theory: The New Synthesis,* edited by George Ritzer. New York: Columbia University Press, 287–315.

Lawson, Annette. 1988. *Adultery: An Analysis of Love and Betrayal.* New York: Basic Books.

Lévy-Leboyer, Maurice. 1980. "The Large Corporation in Modern France." In *Managerial Hierarchies: Comparative Perspectives on the Rise of the Industrial Enterprise,* edited by A. Chandler and H. Daems. Cambridge, Mass.: Harvard University Press, 117–70.

Lipset, Seymour Martin. 1990. *Continental Divide: The Values and Institutions of the United States and Canada.* New York and London: Routledge.

McClelland, David K. 1961. *The Achieving Society.* New York: Nostrand.

Mills, C. Wright. 1953. *White Collar: The American Middle Class.* New York: Oxford University Press.

Murphy, Raymond. 1988. *Social Closure: The Theory of Monopolization and Exclusion.* Oxford: Clarendon.

Parkin, Frank. 1974. "Strategies of Closure in Class Formation." In *The Social Analysis of Class Structure.* London: Tavistock, 1–18.

Parmentier, Patrick. 1986. "Les genres et leurs lecteurs." *Revue Française de Sociologie* 27: 397–430.

Pinçon, Michel, and Monique Pinçon-Charlot. 1989. *Dans les beaux quartiers.* Paris: Editions du Seuil.

Powers, Brian. 1987. "Second Class Finish: The Effect of a Working Class High School." Ph.D. diss., Department of Sociology, University of California, Berkeley.

Press, Andrea. 1991. *Women Watching Television: Gender, Class and Generations in the American Television Experience.* Philadelphia: University of Pennsylvania.

Rainwater, Lee. 1974. *What Money Buys: Inequality and the Social Meaning of Income.* New York: Basic Books.

Reich, Robert B. 1991. "The Secession of the Successful." *New York Times Sunday Magazine,* 20 January.

Rosenbaum, James E., and Takehiko Kariya, Rich Settersten, and Tony Maier. 1990. "Market and Networks Theory of the Transition from High School to Work: Their Application to Industrialized Societies." *Annual Review of Sociology* 16:263–99.

Rosenberg, Morris. 1981. "The Self Concept: Social Product and Social Force." In *Social Psychology: Sociological Perspectives,* edited by Morris Rosenberg and Ralph H. Turner. New York: Basic Books, 593–624.

Schutz, Alfred, and Thomas Luckman. 1989. *The Structures of the Life-World.* Vol 2. Evanston: Northwestern University Press.

Schwartz, Gary. 1987. *Beyond Conformity and Rebellion: Youth and Authority in America.* Chicago: University of Chicago Press.

Seeley, J. R., R. A. Sim, and E. W. Loosley. 1956. *Crestwood Heights: A Study of the Culture of Suburban Life.* New York: Basic Books.

Stryker, Sheldon. 1980. *Symbolic Interactionism: A Social Structural Version.* Menlo Park, Calif.: Benjamin/Cummings Pub. Co.

Thèlot, Claude. 1982. *Tel pére, tel fils.* Paris: Dunot.

Vanneman, Reeve, and Lynn Weber Cannon. 1987. *The American Perception of Class.* Philadelphia: Temple University Press.

Veblen, Thorstein. 1912. *The Theory of the Leisure Class.* New York: B. W. Huelsh.

Warner, W. Lloyd, J. O. Low, P. S. Lunt, and Leo Srole. 1963. *Yankee City.* New Haven: Yale University Press.

Warner, W. Lloyd, and P. S. Lunt. 1963. *Status System of a Modern Community.* New Haven: Yale University Press.

Waters, Mary C. 1990. *Ethnic Options: Choosing Identities in America.* Berkeley: University of California Press.

Weber, Max. 1978. *Economy and Society.* Vol 1. Berkeley: University of California Press.

Zelizer, Viviana. 1989. "The Social Meaning of Money: 'Special Monies.'" *American Journal of Sociology* 95, no. 2:342–77.

The Bohemian Grove

G. William Domhoff

Picture yourself comfortably seated in a beautiful open-air dining hall in the midst of twenty-seven hundred acres of giant California redwoods. It is early evening and the clear July air is still pleasantly warm. Dusk has descended, you have finished a sumptuous dinner, and you are sitting quietly with your drink and your cigar, listening to nostalgic welcoming speeches and enjoying the gentle light and the eerie shadows that are cast by the two-stemmed gaslights flickering softly at each of the several hundred outdoor banquet tables.

You are part of an assemblage that has been meeting in this redwood grove sixty-five miles north of San Francisco for over a hundred years. It is not just any assemblage, for you are a captain of industry, a well-known television star, a banker, a famous artist, or maybe a member of the President's Cabinet. You are one of fifteen hundred men gathered together from all over the country for the annual encampment of the rich and the famous at the Bohemian Grove.

[Recent "Bohemians" include former presidents Ronald Reagan, George Bush, Gerald Ford and Richard Nixon; former Attorney General William French Smith; former cabinet members George Shultz, Richard Cheney and James Baker III; journalist William F. Buckley; and various wealthy investment bankers, university presidents, entertainers, high level government officials and Fortune 500 CEO's. In June of 1993 White House counselor David Gergen resigned his membership in the club at the behest of the President.]

The Cremation of Care is the most spectacular event of the midsummer retreat that members and guests of San Francisco's Bohemian Club have taken every year since 1878. However, there are several other entertainments in store. Before the Bohemians return to the everyday world, they will

be treated to plays, variety shows, song fests, shooting contests, art exhibits, swimming, boating, and nature rides. . . .

A cast for a typical Grove play easily runs to seventy-five or one hundred people. Add in the orchestra, the stagehands, the carpenters who make the sets, and other supporting personnel, and over three hundred people are involved in creating the High Jinks each year. Preparations begin a year in advance, with rehearsals occurring two or three times a week in the month before the encampment, and nightly in the week before the play.

Costs are on the order of $20,000 to $30,000 per High Jinks, a large amount of money for a one-night production which does not have to pay a penny for salaries (the highest cost in any commercial production). "And the costs are talked about, too," reports my second informant. "'Hey, did you hear the High Jinks will cost $25,000 this year?' one of them will say to another. The expense of the play is one way they can relate to its worth." . . .

Entertainment is not the only activity at the Bohemian Grove. For a little change of pace, there is intellectual stimulation and political enlightenment every day at 12:30 P.M. Since 1932 the meadow from which people view the Cremation of Care also has been the setting for informal talks and briefings by people as varied as Dwight David Eisenhower (before he was President), Herman Wouk (author of *The Caine Mutiny*), Bobby Kennedy (while he was Attorney General), and Neil Armstrong (after he returned from the moon).

Cabinet officers, politicians, generals, and governmental advisers are the rule rather than the exception for Lakeside Talks, especially on weekends. Equally prominent figures from the worlds of art, literature, and science are more likely to make their appearance during the weekdays of the encampment, when Grove attendance may drop to four or five hundred (many of the members only come up for one week or for the weekends because they cannot stay away from their corporations and law firms for the full two weeks).

Members vary as to how interesting and informative they find the Lakeside Talks. Some find them useful, others do not, probably depending on their degree of familiarity with the topic being discussed. It is fairly certain that no inside or secret information is divulged, but a good feel for how a particular problem will be handled is likely to be communicated. Whatever the value of the talks, most members think there is something very nice about hearing official government policy, orthodox big-business ideology, and new scientific information from a fellow Bohemian or one of his guests in an informal atmosphere where no reporters are allowed to be present.

One person who seems to find Lakeside Talks a useful forum is President Richard M. Nixon, a Bohemian Club member since 1953. A speech he gave at the Grove in 1967 was the basis for a public speech he gave a few months later. Richard J. Whalen, one of Nixon's speech writers in the late sixties, tells the story as follows:

> He would speak at the Hoover Institution, before a conference on the fiftieth anniversary of the Bolshevik revolution. "I don't want it to be the typical anti-Communist harangue—you know, there's Nixon again. Try to *lift* it. I want to take a *sophisticated* hard line. I'd like to be very fair and objective about their achievements—in fifty years they've come from a cellar conspiracy to control of half the world. But I also want to underline the horrible costs of their methods and system." He handed me a copy of his speech the previous summer at Bohemian Grove, telling me to take it as a model for outlining the changes in the Communist world and the changing U.S. Policy toward the Soviet Union.[1]

The ease with which the Bohemian Grove is able to attract famous speakers for no remuneration other than the amenities of the encampment

attests to the high esteem in which the club is held in the higher circles. Down through the years the Lakeside podium has hosted such luminaries as Lee DuBridge (science), David Sarnoff (business), Wernher von Braun (space technology), Senator Robert Taft, Lucius Clay (military and business), Earl Warren (Supreme Court), former California Republican Governor Goodwin J. Knight, and former California Democratic Governor Pat Brown. For many years former President Herbert C. Hoover, who joined the club in 1913, was a regular feature of the Lakeside Talks, with the final Saturday afternoon being reserved for his anachronistic counsel.

Politicians apparently find the Lakeside Talks especially attractive. "Giving a Lakeside" provides them with a means for personal exposure without officially violating the injunction "Weaving spiders, come not here." After all, Bohemians rationalize, a Lakeside Talk is merely an informal chat by a friend of the family.

Some members, at least, know better. They realize that the Grove is an ideal off-the-record atmosphere for sizing up politicians. "Well, of course when a politician comes here, we all get to see him, and his stock in trade is his personality and his ideas," a prominent Bohemian told a *New York Times* reporter who was trying to cover Nelson Rockefeller's 1963 visit to the Grove for a Lakeside Talk. The journalist went on to note that the midsummer encampments "have long been a major showcase where leaders of business, industry, education, the arts, and politics can come to examine each other." . . .

For 1971, [then] President Nixon was to be the featured Lakeside speaker. However, when newspaper reporters learned that the President planned to disappear into a redwood grove for an off-the-record speech to some of the most powerful men in America, they objected loudly and vowed to make every effort to cover the event. The flap caused the club considerable embarrassment, and after much hemming and hawing back and forth, the club leaders asked the President to cancel his scheduled appearance. A White House press secretary then announced that the President had decided not to appear at the Grove rather than risk the tradition that speeches there are strictly off the public record.[2]

However, the President was not left without a final word to his fellow Bohemians. In a telegram to the president of the club, which now hangs at the entrance to the reading room in the San Francisco clubhouse, he expressed his regrets at not being able to attend. He asked the club president to continue to lead people into the woods, adding that he in turn would redouble his efforts to lead people out of the woods. He also noted that, while anyone could aspire to be President of the United States, only a few could aspire to be president of the Bohemian Club.

Not all the entertainment at the Bohemian Grove takes place under the auspices of the committee in charge of special events. The Bohemians and their guests are divided into camps which evolved slowly over the years as the number of people on the retreat grew into the hundreds and then the thousands. These camps have become a significant center of enjoyment during the encampment.

At first the camps were merely a place in the woods where a half-dozen to a dozen friends would pitch their tents. Soon they added little amenities like their own special stove or a small permanent structure. Then there developed little camp "traditions" and endearing camp names like Cliff Dwellers, Moonshiners, Silverado Squatters, Woof, Zaca, Toyland, Sundodgers, and Land of Happiness. The next steps were special emblems, a handsome little lodge or specially constructed tepees, a permanent bar, and maybe a grand piano.[3] Today there are 129 camps of varying sizes, structures, and statuses. Most have between 10 and 30 members, but there are one or two with about 125 members and several with less than 10. A majority of the camps are strewn along what is called the River Road, but some are huddled in other areas within five or ten minutes of the center of the Grove.

The entertainment at the camps is mostly informal and impromptu. Someone will decide to bring together all the jazz musicians in the Grove for a special session. Or maybe all the artists or writers will be invited to a luncheon or a dinner at a camp. Many camps have their own amateur piano players and informal musical and singing groups which perform for the rest of the members.

But the joys of the camps are not primarily in watching or listening to performances. Other pleasures are created within them. Some camps become known for their gastronomical specialties, such as a particular drink or a particular meal. The Jungle Camp features mint juleps, Halcyon has a three-foot-high martini maker constructed out of chemical glassware. At the Owl's Nest [former President Reagan's club] it's the gin-fizz breakfast—about a hundred people are invited over one morning during the encampment for eggs Benedict, gin fizzes, and all the trimmings.

Poison Oak is famous for its Bulls' Balls Lunch. Each year a cattle baron from central California brings a large supply of testicles from his newly castrated herds for the delectation of Poison Oakers and their guests. No one goes away hungry. Bulls' balls are said to be quite a treat. Meanwhile, one small camp has a somewhat different specialty, which is not necessarily known to members of every camp. It houses a passé pornographic collection which is more amusing than erotic. Connoisseurs do not consider it a great show, but it is an easy way to kill a lazy afternoon. . . .

The men of Bohemia are drawn in large measure from the corporate leadership of the United States. They include in their numbers directors from major corporations in every sector of the American economy. An indication of this fact is that one in every five resident members and one in every three nonresident members is found in Poor's *Register of Corporations, Executives, and Directors,* a huge volume which lists the leadership of tens of thousands of companies from every major business field except investment banking, real estate, and advertising.

Even better evidence for the economic prominence of the men under consideration is that at least one officer or director from 40 of the 50 largest industrial corporations in America was present, as a member or a guest, on the lists at our disposal. Only Ford Motor Company and Western Electric were missing among the top 25! Similarly, we found that officers and directors from 20 of the top 25 commercial banks (including all of the 15 largest) were on our lists. Men from 12 of the first 25 life-insurance companies were in attendance (8 of these 12 were from the top 10). Other business sectors were represented somewhat less: 10 of 25 in transportation, 8 of 25 in utilities, 7 of 25 in conglomerates, and only 5 of 25 in retailing. More generally, of the top-level businesses ranked by *Fortune* for 1969 (the top 500 industrials, the top 50 commercial banks, the top 50 life-insurance companies, the top 50 transportation companies, the top 50 utilities, the top 50 retailers, and the top 47 conglomerates), *29 percent of these 797 corporations were "represented" by at least 1 officer or director. . . .*

Do Bohemians Rule America?

The foregoing material on [Bohemian Grove], which I have presented in as breezy a manner as possible, is relevant to highly emotional questions concerning the distribution of power in modern America. In this final [section] I will switch styles somewhat and discuss these charged questions in a sober, simple, and straightforward way.

It is my hypothesis that there is a ruling social class in the United States. This class is made up of the owners and managers of large corporations, which means the members have many economic and political interests in common, and many conflicts with ordinary working people. Comprising at most 1 percent of the total population, members of this class own 25 to 30 percent of all privately held wealth in America, own 60 to 70 percent of the privately held corporate wealth, receive 20 to 25 percent of the yearly income, direct the large corporations and foundations, and dominate the federal government in Washington.

Most social scientists disagree with this view. Some dismiss it out of hand, others become quite vehement in disputing it. The overwhelming majority of them believe that the United States has a "pluralistic" power structure, in which a wide variety of "veto groups" (e.g., businessmen, farmers, unions, consumers) and "voluntary associations" (e.g., National Association of Manufacturers, Americans for Democratic Action, Common Cause) form shifting coalitions to influence decisions on different issues. These groups and associations are said to have differing amounts of interest and influence on various questions. Contrary to my view, pluralists assert that no one group, not even the owners and managers of large

corporations, has the cohesiveness and ability to determine the outcome of a wide variety of social, economic, and political issues. . . .

This means that wealthy families from all over the country, and particularly from major cities like New York, San Francisco, Chicago, and Houston, are part of interlocking social circles which perceive each other as equals, belong to the same clubs, interact frequently, and freely intermarry.

Whether we call it a "social class" or a "status group," many pluralistic social scientists would deny that such a social group exists. They assert that there is no social "cohesiveness" among the various rich in different parts of the country. For them, social registers, blue books, and club membership lists are merely collections of names which imply nothing about group interaction.

There is a wealth of journalistic evidence which suggests the existence of a national upper class. It ranges from Cleveland Amory's *The Proper Bostonians and Who Killed Society?* to Lucy Kavaler's *The Private World of High Society* and Stephen Birmingham's *The Right People.* But what is the systematic evidence which I can present for my thesis? There is first of all the evidence that has been developed from the study of attendance at private schools. It has been shown that a few dozen prep schools bring together children of the upper class from all over the country. From this evidence it can be argued that young members of the upper class develop lifetime friendship ties with like-status age-mates in every section of the country.[4]

There is second the systematic evidence which comes from studying high-status summer resorts. Two such studies show that these resorts bring together upper-class families from several different large cities.[5] Third, there is the evidence of business interconnections. Several different studies have demonstrated that interlocking directorships bring wealthy men from all over the country into face-to-face relationships at the board meetings of banks, insurance companies, and other corporations.[6]

And finally, there is the evidence developed from studying exclusive social clubs. Such studies have been made in the past, but the present investigation of the Bohemian Club is a more comprehensive effort. *In short, I believe the present [study] to be significant evidence for the existence of a cohesive American upper class.*

The Bohemian Grove, as well as other watering holes and social clubs, is relevant to the problem of class cohesiveness in two ways. First, the very fact that rich men from all over the country gather in such close circumstances as the Bohemian Grove is evidence for the existence of a socially cohesive upper class. It demonstrates that many of these men do know each other, that they have face-to-face communications, and that they are a social network. In this sense, we are looking at the Bohemian Grove and other social retreats as a *result* of social processes that lead to class cohesion. But such institutions also can be viewed as facilitators of social ties. Once formed, these groups become another avenue by which the cohesiveness of the upper class is maintained.

In claiming that clubs and retreats like the Bohemians are evidence for my thesis of a national upper class, I am assuming that cohesion develops within the settings they provide. Perhaps some readers will find that assumption questionable. So let us pause to ask: Are there reasons to believe that the Bohemian Grove and its imitators lead to greater cohesion within the upper class?

For one thing, we have the testimony of members themselves. There are several accounts by leading members of these groups, past and present, which attest to the intimacy that develops among members. John J. Mitchell, El Presidente of Los Rancheros Visitadores [a club similar to Bohemian Grove] from 1930 to 1955, wrote as follows on the twenty-fifth anniversary of the group:

> All the pledges and secret oaths in the universe cannot tie men, our kind of men, together like the mutual appreciation of a beautiful horse, the moon behind a cloud, a song around the campfire, or a ride down the Santa Ynez Valley. These are experiences common on our ride, but unknown to most of our daily lives. Our organization, to all appearances, is the most informal imaginable. Yet there are men here who see one another once a year, yet feel a bond closer than between those they have known all their lives.[7]

A second reason for stressing the importance of retreats and clubs like the Bohemian Grove is a body of research within social psychology which deals with group cohesion. "Group dynamics" suggests the following about cohesiveness: (1) *Physical proximity is likely to lead to group solidarity.* Thus, the mere fact that these men gather together in such intimate physical settings implies that cohesiveness develops. (The same point can be made, of course, about exclusive neighborhoods, private schools, and expensive summer resorts.) (2) *The more people interact, the more they will like each other.* This is hardly a profound discovery, but we can note that the Bohemian Grove and other watering holes maximize personal interactions. (3) *Groups seen as high in status are more cohesive.* The Bohemian Club fits the category of a high-status group, further, its stringent membership requirements, long waiting lists, and high dues also serve to heighten its valuation in the eyes of its members. Members are likely to think of themselves as "special" people, which would heighten their attractiveness to each other, and increase the likelihood of interaction and cohesiveness. (4) *The best atmosphere for increasing group cohesiveness is one that is relaxed and cooperative.* Again the Bohemian Grove [is an] ideal example of this kind of climate. From a group-dynamics point of view, then, we could argue that one of the reasons for upper-class cohesiveness is the fact that the class is organized into a wide variety of small groups which encourage face-to-face interaction and ensure status and security for members.[8]

In summary, if we take these several common settings together—schools, resorts, corporation directorships, and social clubs—and assume on the basis of members' testimony and the evidence of small-group research that interaction in such settings leads to group cohesiveness, then I think we are justified in saying that wealthy families from all over the United States are linked together in a variety of ways into a national upper class.

Even if the evidence and arguments for the existence of a socially cohesive national upper class are accepted, there is still the question of whether or not this class has the means by which its members can reach policy consensus on issues of importance to them.

A five-year study based upon information obtained from confidential informants, interviews, and questionnaires has shown that social clubs such as the Bohemian Club are an important consensus-forming aspect of the upper class and big-business environment. According to sociologist Reed Powell, "the clubs are a repository of the values held by the upper-level prestige groups in the community and are a means by which these values are transferred to the business environment." Moreover, the clubs are places where problems are discussed:

> On the other hand, the clubs are places in which the beliefs, problems, and values of the industrial organization are discussed and related to other elements in the larger community. Clubs, therefore, are not only effective vehicles of informal communication, but also valuable centers where views are presented, ideas are modified, and new ideas emerge. Those in the interview sample were appreciative of this asset; in addition, they considered the club as a valuable place to combine social and business contacts.[9]

The revealing interview work of Floyd Hunter, an outstanding pioneer researcher on the American power structure, also provides evidence for the importance of social clubs as informal centers of policy making. Particularly striking for our purposes is a conversation he had with one of the several hundred top leaders that he identified in the 1950s. The person in question was a conservative industrialist who was ranked as a top-level leader by his peers:

> Hall [a pseudonym] spoke very favorably of the Bohemian Grove group that met in California every year. He said that although over the entrance to the Bohemian Club there was a quotation, "Weaving spiders come not here," there was a good deal of informal policy made in this association. He said that he got to know Herbert Hoover in this connection and that he started work with Hoover in the food administration of World War I.[10]

Despite the evidence presented by Powell and Hunter that clubs are a setting for the development of policy consensus, I do not believe that

such settings are the only, or even the primary, locus for developing policy on class-related issues. For policy questions, other organizations are far more important, organizations like the Council on Foreign Relations, the Committee for Economic Development, the Business Council, and the National Municipal League. These organizations, along with many others, are the "consensus-seeking" and "policy-planning" organizations of the upper class. Directed by the same men who manage the major corporations, and financed by corporation and foundation monies, these groups sponsor meetings and discussions wherein wealthy men from all over the country gather to iron out differences and formulate policies on pressing problems.

No one discussion group is *the* leadership council within the upper class. While some of the groups tend to specialize in certain issue areas, they overlap and interact to a great extent. Consensus slowly emerges from the interplay of people and ideas within and among the groups.[11] This diversity of groups is made very clear in the following comments by Frazar B. Wilde, chairman emeritus of Connecticut General Life Insurance Company and a member of the Council on Foreign Relations and the Committee for Economic Development. Mr Wilde was responding to a question about the Bilderbergers, a big-business meeting group which includes Western European leaders as well as American corporation and foundation directors:

> Business has had over the years many different seminars and discussion meetings. They run all the way from large public gatherings like NAM [National Association of Manufacturers] to special sessions such as those held frequently at Arden House. Bilderberg is in many respects one of the most important, if not the most important, but this is not to deny that other strictly off-the-record meetings and discussion groups such as those held by the Council on Foreign Relations are not in the front rank.[12]

Generally speaking, then, it is in these organizations that leaders within the upper class discuss the means by which to deal with problems of major concern. Here, in off-the-record settings, these leaders try to reach consensus on general issues that have been talked about more casually in corporate boardrooms and social clubs. These organizations, aided by funds from corporations and foundations, also serve several other functions:

1. They are a training ground for new leadership within the class. It is in these organizations, and through the publications of these organizations, that younger lawyers, bankers, and businessmen become acquainted with general issues in the areas of foreign, domestic, and municipal policy.

2. They are the place where leaders within the upper class hear the ideas and findings of their hired experts.

3. They are the setting wherein upper-class leaders "look over" young experts for possible service as corporation or governmental advisers.

4. They provide the framework for expert studies on important issues. Thus, the Council on Foreign Relations undertook a $1 million study of the "China question" in the first half of the 1960s. The Committee for Economic Development created a major study of money and credit about the same time. Most of the money for these studies was provided by the Ford, Rockefeller, and Carnegie foundations.[13]

5. Through such avenues as books, journals, policy statements, discussion groups, press releases, and speakers, the policy-planning organizations greatly influence the "climate of opinion" within which major issues are considered. For example, *Foreign Affairs,* the journal of the Council on Foreign Relations, is considered the most influential journal in its field, and the periodic policy statements of the Committee for Economic Development are carefully attended to by major newspapers and local opinion leaders.

It is my belief, then, that the policy-planning groups are essential in developing policy positions which are satisfactory to the upper class as a whole. As such, I think they are a good part of the answer to any social scientist who denies that members of the upper class have institutions by which they deal with economic and political challenges.

However, the policy-planning groups could not function if there were not some common interests within the upper class in the first place.

The most obvious, and most important, of these common interests have to do with the shared desire of the members to maintain the present monopolized and subsidized business system which so generously overrewards them and makes their jet setting, fox hunting, art collecting, and other extravagances possible. But it is not only shared economic and political concerns which make consensus possible. The Bohemian Grove and other upper-class social institutions also contribute to this process: *Group-dynamics research suggests that members of socially cohesive groups are more open to the opinions of other members, and more likely to change their views to those of fellow members.*[14] Social cohesion is a factor in policy consensus because it creates a desire on the part of group members to reconcile differences with other members of the group. It is not enough to say that members of the upper class are bankers, businessmen, and lawyers with a common interest in profit maximization and tax avoidance who meet together at the Council on Foreign Relations, the Committee of Economic Development, and other policy-planning organizations. We must add that they are Bohemians.

NOTES

1. Richard J. Whalen, *Catch the Falling Flag: A Republican's Challenge to His Party* (Boston: Houghton Mifflin, 1972), p. 25. Earlier in this book, on page 4, Whalen reports that his own speech in 1969 at the Bohemian Grove, which concerned the U.S.-Soviet nuclear balance, was distributed by President Nixon to cabinet members and other administration officials with a presidential memorandum commending it as an "excellent analysis." I am grateful to sociologist Richard Hamilton of McGill University for bringing this material to my attention.

2. James M. Naughton, "Nixon Drops Plan for Coast Speech" (*New York Times,* July 31, 1971), p. 11.

3. There is a special moisture-proof building at the Grove to hold the dozens of expensive Steinway pianos belonging to the club and various camps.

4. Baltzell, *Philadelphia Gentlemen,* chapter 12. Domhoff, *The Higher Circles,* p. 78.

5. Baltzell, *Philadelphia Gentlemen,* pp. 248–51. Domhoff, *The Higher Circles,* pp. 79–82. For recent anecdotal evidence on this point, see Stephen

Birmingham, *The Right People* (Boston: Little, Brown, 1968), Part 3.

6. *Interlocks in Corporate Management* (Washington: U.S. Government Printing Office, 1965) summarizes much of this information and presents new evidence as well. See also Peter Dooley, "The Interlocking Directorate" (*American Economic Review,* December, 1969).

7. Neill C. Wilson, *Los Rancheros Visitadores,* p. 2.

8. Dorwin Cartwright and Alvin Zander, *Group Dynamics* (New York: Harper & Row, 1960), pp. 74–82; Albert J. Lott and Bernice E. Lott, "Group Cohesiveness as Interpersonal Attraction" (*Psychological Bulletin,* 64, 1965), pp. 259–309; Michael Argyle, *Social Interaction* (Chicago: Aldine Publishing Company, 1969), pp. 220–23. I am grateful to sociologist John Sonquist of the University of California, Santa Barbara, for making me aware of how important the small-groups literature might be for studies of the upper class. Findings on influence processes, communication patterns, and the development of informal leadership also might be applicable to problems in the area of upper-class research.

9. Reed M. Powell, *Race, Religion, and the Promotion of the American Executive* (College of Administrative Science Monograph No AA-3, Ohio State University, 1969), p. 50.

10. Floyd Hunter, *Top Leadership, U.S.A.* (Chapel Hill: University of North Carolina Press, 1959), p. 109. Hunter also reported (p. 199) that the most favored clubs of his top leaders were the Metropolitan, Links, Century, University (New York), Bohemian, and Pacific Union. He notes (p. 223 n.) that he found clubs to be less important in policy formation on the national level than they are in communities.

11. For a detailed case study of how the process works, see David Eakins, "Business Planners and America's Postwar Expansion," in David Horowitz, editor, *Corporations and the Cold War* (New York: Monthly Review Press, 1969). For other examples and references, see Domhoff, *The Higher Circles,* chapters 5 and 6.

12. Carl Gilbert, personal communication, June 30, 1972. Mr. Gilbert has done extensive research on the Bilderberg group, and I am grateful to him for sharing his detailed information with me. For an excellent discussion of this group, whose role has been greatly distorted and exaggerated by ultra-conservatives, see Eugene Pasymowski and Carl Gilbert, "Bilderberg, Rockefeller, and the CIA" (*Temple Free Press,* November 16, 1968). The article is most conveniently located in a recently revised form in the *Congressional Record,* September 15, 1971, under the title "Bilderberg: The Cold War Internationale."

13. The recent work of arch-pluralist Nelson Polsby is bringing him dangerously close to this formulation. Through studies of the initiation of a number of new policies, Polsby and his students have tentatively concluded that "innovators are typically professors or interest group experts." Where Polsby goes wrong is in failing to note that the professors are working on Ford Foundation grants and/or Council on Foreign Relations fellowships. If he would put his work in a sociological framework, people would not gain the false impression that professors are independent experts sitting in their ivory towers thinking up innovations for the greater good of humanity. See Nelson Polsby, "Policy Initiation in the American Political System," in Irving Louis Horowitz, editor, *The Use and Abuse of Social Science* (New Brunswick, N.J.: TransAction Books, 1971), p. 303.

14. Cartwright and Zander, *Group Dynamics,* p. 89; Lott and Lott, "Group Cohesiveness as Interpersonal Attraction," pp. 291–96.

Life on the Global Assembly Line

Barbara Ehrenreich and Annette Fuentes

In Ciudad Juárez, Mexico, Anna M. rises at 5 A.M. to feed her son before starting on the two-hour bus trip to the maquiladora (factory). He will spend the day along with four other children in a neighbor's one-room home. Anna's husband, frustrated by being unable to find work for himself, left for the United States six months ago. She wonders, as she carefully applies her new lip gloss, whether she ought to consider herself still married. It might be good to take a night course, become a secretary. But she seldom gets home before eight at night, and the factory, where she stitches brassieres that will be sold in the United States through J.C. Penney, pays only $48 a week.

In Penang, Malaysia, Julie K. is up before the three other young women with whom she shares a room, and starts heating the leftover rice from last night's supper. She looks good in the company's green-trimmed uniform, and she's proud to work in a modern, American-owned factory. Only not quite so proud as when she started working three years ago—she thinks as she squints out the door at a passing group of women. Her job involves peering all day through a microscope, bonding hair-thin gold wires to a silicon chip destined to end up inside a pocket calculator, and at 21, she is afraid she can no longer see very clearly.

Every morning, between four and seven, thousands of women like Anna and Julie head out for the day shift. In Ciudad Juárez, they crowd into *ruteras* (run-down vans) for the trip from the slum neighborhoods to the industrial parks on the outskirts of the city. In Penang they squeeze, 60 or more at a time, into buses for the trip from the village to the low, modern factory buildings of the Bayan Lepas free trade zone. In Taiwan, they walk from the dormitories—where the night shift is already asleep in the still-warm beds—through the checkpoints in the high fence surrounding the factory zone.

This is the world's new industrial proletariat: young, female, Third World. Viewed from the "first world," they are still faceless, genderless "cheap labor," signaling their existence only through a label or tiny imprint—"made in Hong Kong," or Taiwan, Korea, the Dominican Republic, Mexico, the Philippines. But they may be one of the most strategic blocs of womanpower in the world of the 1980s. Conservatively, there are 2 million Third-World female industrial workers employed now, millions more looking for work, and their numbers are rising every year. Anyone whose image of Third-World women features picturesque peasants with babies slung on their backs should be prepared to update it. Just in the last decade, Third-World women have become a critical element in the global economy and a key "resource" for expanding multinational corporations.

It doesn't take more than second-grade arithmetic to understand what's happening. In the United States, an assembly-line worker is likely to earn, depending on her length of employment, between $3.10 and $5 an hour. In many Third-World countries, a woman doing the same work will earn $3 to $5 a *day*. According to the magazine *Business Asia*, in 1976 the average hourly wage for unskilled work (male or female) was 55 cents in Hong Kong, 52 cents in South Korea, 32 cents in the Philippines, and 17 cents in Indonesia. The logic of the situation is compelling: why pay someone in Massachusetts $5 an hour to do what someone in Manila will do for $2.50 a day?

Or, as a corollary, why pay a male worker anywhere to do what a female worker will do for 40 to 60 percent less?

And so, almost everything that can be packed up is being moved out to the Third World; not heavy industry, but just about anything light enough to travel—garment manufacture, textiles, toys, footwear, pharmaceuticals, wigs, appliance parts, tape decks, computer components, plastic goods. In some industries, like garment and textile, American jobs are lost in the process, and the biggest losers are women, often black and Hispanic. But what's going on is much more than a matter of runaway shops. Economists are talking about a "new international division of labor," in which the process of production is broken down and the fragments are dispersed to different parts of the world. In general, the low-skilled jobs are farmed out to the Third World, where labor costs are minuscule, while control over the overall process and technology remains safely at company headquarters in "first world" countries like the United States and Japan.

The American electronics industry provides a classic example: circuits are printed on silicon wafers and tested in California; then the wafers are shipped to Asia for the labor-intensive process by which they are cut into tiny chips and bonded to circuit boards; final assembly into products such as calculators or military equipment usually takes place in the United States. Garment manufacture too is often broken into geographically separated steps, with the most repetitive, labor-intensive jobs going to the poor countries of the southern hemisphere. Most Third-World countries welcome whatever jobs come their way in the new division of labor, and the major international development agencies—like the World Bank and the United States Agency for International Development (AID)—encourage them to take what they can get.

So much any economist could tell you. What is less often noted is the *gender* breakdown of the emerging international division of labor. Eighty to 90 percent of the low-skilled assembly jobs that go to the Third World are performed by women—in a remarkable switch from earlier patterns of foreign-dominated industrialization. Until now, "development" under the aegis of foreign corporations has usually meant more jobs for men and—compared to traditional agricultural society—a diminished economic status for women. But multinational corporations and Third-World governments alike consider assembly-line work—whether the product is Barbie dolls or missile parts—to be "women's work."

One reason is that women can, in many countries, still be legally paid less than men. But the sheer tedium of the jobs adds to the multinationals' preference for women workers—a preference made clear, for example, by this ad from a Mexican newspaper: *We need female workers; older than 17, younger than 30; single and without children: minimum education primary school, maximum education one year of preparatory school [high school]: available for all shifts.*

It's an article of faith with management that only women can do, or will do, the monotonous, painstaking work that American business is exporting to the Third World. Bill Mitchell, whose job is to attract United States businesses to the Bermudez Industrial Park in Ciudad Juarez told us with a certain macho pride: "A man just won't stay in this tedious kind of work. He'd walk out in a couple of hours." The personnel manager of a light assembly plant in Taiwan told anthropologist Linda Gail Arrigo: "Young male workers are too restless and impatient to do monotonous work with no career value. If displeased, they sabotage the machines and even threaten the foreman. But girls? At most, they cry a little."

In fact, the American businessmen we talked to claimed that Third-World women genuinely enjoy doing the very things that would drive a man to assault and sabotage. "You should watch these kids going into work," Bill Mitchell told us. "You don't have any sullenness here. They smile." A top-level management consultant who specializes in advising American companies on where to relocate their factories gave us this global generalization: "The [factory] girls genuinely enjoy themselves. They're away from their families. They have spending money. They can buy motorbikes, whatever. Of course it's a regulated experience too—with dormitories to live in—so it's a healthful experience."

What is the real experience of the women in the emerging Third-World industrial work force? The conventional Western stereotypes leap to mind: You can't really compare, the standards are so different. . . . Everything's easier in warm countries. . . . They really don't have any alternatives. . . . Commenting on the low wages his company pays its women workers in Singapore, a Hewlett-Packard vice-president said, "They live much differently here than we do. . . ." But the differences are ultimately very simple. To start with, they have less money.

The great majority of the women in the new Third-World work force live at or near the subsistence level for one person, whether they work for a multinational corporation or a locally owned factory. In the Philippines, for example, starting wages in U.S.-owned electronics plants are between $34 to $46 a month, compared to a cost of living of $37 a month; in Indonesia the starting wages are actually about $7 a month less than the cost of living. "Living," in these cases, should be interpreted minimally: a diet of rice, dried fish, and water—a Coke might cost a half-day's wages—lodging in a room occupied by four or more other people. Rachael Grossman, a researcher with the Southeast Asia Resource Center, found women employees of U.S. multinational firms in Malaysia and the Philippines living four to eight in a room in boardinghouses, or squeezing into tiny extensions built onto squatter huts near the factory. Where companies do provide dormitories for their employees, they are not of the "healthful," collegiate variety implied by our corporate informant. Staff from the American Friends Service Committee report that dormitory space is "likely to be crowded, with bed rotation paralleling shift rotation—while one shift works, another sleeps, as many as twenty to a room." In one case in Thailand, they found the dormitory "filthy," with workers forced to find their own place to sleep among "splintered floorboards, rusting sheets of metal, and scraps of dirty cloth."

Wages do increase with seniority, but the money does not go to pay for studio apartments or, very likely, motorbikes. A 1970 study of young women factory workers in Hong Kong found that 88 percent of them were turning more than half their earnings over to their parents. In areas that are still largely agricultural (such as parts of the

Philippines and Malaysia), or places where male unemployment runs high (such as northern Mexico), a woman factory worker may be the sole source of cash income for an entire extended family.

But wages on a par with what an 11-year-old American could earn on a paper route, and living conditions resembling what Engels found in 19th-century Manchester are only part of the story. The rest begins at the factory gate. The work that multinational corporations export to the Third World is not only the most tedious, but often the most hazardous part of the production process. The countries they go to are, for the most part, those that will guarantee no interference from health and safety inspectors, trade unions, or even free-lance reformers. As a result, most Third-World factory women work under conditions that already have broken or will break their health—or their nerves—within a few years, and often before they've worked long enough to earn any more than a subsistence wage.

Consider first the electronics industry, which is generally thought to be the safest and cleanest of the exported industries. The factory buildings are low and modern, like those one might find in a suburban American industrial park. Inside, rows of young women, neatly dressed in the company uniform or T-shirt, work quietly at their stations. There is air conditioning (not for the women's comfort, but to protect the delicate semiconductor parts they work with), and high-volume piped-in Bee Gees hits (not so much for entertainment, as to prevent talking).

For many Third-World women, electronics is a prestige occupation, at least compared to other kinds of factory work. They are unlikely to know that in the United States the National Institute on Occupational Safety and Health (NIOSH) has placed electronics on its select list of "high health-risk industries using the greatest number of toxic substances." If electronics assembly work is risky here, it is doubly so in countries where there is no equivalent of NIOSH to even issue warnings. In many plants toxic chemicals and solvents sit in open containers, filling the work area with fumes that can literally knock you out. "We have been told of cases where ten to twelve women passed out at once," an AFSC field worker in northern

Mexico told us, "and the newspapers report this as 'mass hysteria.'"

In one stage of the electronics assembly process, the workers have to dip the circuits into open vats of acid. According to Irene Johnson and Carol Bragg, who toured the National Semiconductor plant in Penang, Malaysia, the women who do the dipping "wear rubber gloves and boots, but these sometimes leak, and burns are common." Occasionally, whole fingers are lost. More commonly, what electronics workers lose is the 20/20 vision they are required to have when they are hired. Most electronics workers spend seven to nine hours a day peering through microscopes, straining to meet their quotas.

One study in South Korea found that most electronics assembly workers developed severe eye problems after only one year of employment; 88 percent had chronic conjunctivitis; 44 percent became nearsighted; and 19 percent developed astigmatism. A manager for Hewlett-Packard's Malaysia plant, in an interview with Rachael Grossman, denied that there were any eye problems: "These girls are used to working with 'scopes.' We've found no eye problems. But it sure makes me dizzy to look through those things."

Electronics, recall, is the "cleanest" of the exported industries. Conditions in the garment and textile industry rival those of any 19th-century (or 20th—see below) sweatshop. The firms, generally local subcontractors to large American chains such as J.C. Penney and Sears, as well as smaller manufacturers, are usually even more indifferent to the health of their employees than the multinationals. Some of the worst conditions have been documented in South Korea, where the garment and textile industries have helped spark that country's "economic miracle." Workers are packed into poorly lit rooms, where summer temperatures rise above 100 degrees. Textile dust, which can cause permanent lung damage, fills the air. When there are rush orders, management may require forced overtime of as much as 48 hours at a stretch, and if that seems to go beyond the limits of human endurance, pep pills and amphetamine injections are thoughtfully provided. In her diary (originally published in a magazine now banned by the South Korean government) Min Chong

Suk, 30, a sewing-machine operator, wrote of working from 7 A.M. to 11:30 P.M. in a garment factory: "When [the apprentices] shake the waste threads from the clothes, the whole room fills with dust, and it is hard to breathe. Since we've been working in such dusty air, there have been increasing numbers of people getting tuberculosis, bronchitis, and eye diseases. Since we are women, it makes us so sad when we have pale, unhealthy, wrinkled faces like dried-up spinach. . . . It seems to me that no one knows our blood dissolves into the threads and seams, with sighs and sorrow."

In all the exported industries, the most invidious, inescapable health hazard is stress. On their home ground United States corporations are not likely to sacrifice productivity for human comfort. On someone else's home ground, however, anything goes. Lunch breaks may be barely long enough for a woman to stand in line at the canteen or hawkers' stalls. Visits to the bathroom are treated as privilege; in some cases, workers must raise their hands for permission to use the toilet, and waits up to a half hour are common. Rotating shifts—the day shift one week, the night shift the next—wreak havoc with sleep patterns. Because inaccuracies or failure to meet production quotas can mean substantial pay losses, the pressures are quickly internalized; stomach ailments and nervous problems are not unusual in the multinationals' Third-World female work force. In some situations, good work is as likely to be punished as slow or shoddy work. Correspondent Michael Flannery, writing for the AFL-CIO's *American Federationist*, tells the story of 23-year-old Basilia Altagracia, a seamstress who stitched collars onto ladies' blouses in the La Romana (Dominican Republic) free trade zone (a heavily guarded industrial zone owned by Gulf & Western Industries, Inc.):

A nimble veteran seamstress, Miss Altagracia eventually began to earn as much as $5.75 a day. . . . "I was exceeding my piecework quota by a lot." . . . But then, Altagracia said, her plant supervisor, a Cuban emigré, called her into his office. "He said I was doing a fine job, but that I and some other of the women were making too much money, and he was being forced to lower what we earned for each piece we sewed." On the best days, she now can clear barely $3, she said. "I was earning less, so I started working six and seven days a week. But I was tired and I could not work as fast as before."

Within a few months, she was too ill to work at all.

As if poor health and the stress of factory life weren't enough to drive women into early retirement, management actually encourages a high turnover in many industries. "As you know, when seniority rises, wages rise," the management consultant to U.S. multinationals told us. He explained that it's cheaper to train a fresh supply of teenagers than to pay experienced women higher wages. "Older" women, aged 23 or 24, are likely to be laid off and not rehired.

We estimate, based on fragmentary data from several sources, that the multinational corporations may already have used up (cast off) as many as 6 million Third-World workers—women who are too ill, too old (30 is over the hill in most industries), or too exhausted to be useful any more. Few "retire" with any transferable skills or savings. The lucky ones find husbands.

The unlucky ones find themselves at the margins of society—as bar girls, "hostesses," or prostitutes.

At 21, Julie's greatest fear is that she will never be able to find a husband. She knows that just being a "factory girl" is enough to give anyone a bad reputation. When she first started working at the electronics company, her father refused to speak to her for three months. Now every time she leaves Penang to go back to visit her home village she has to put up with a lecture on morality from her older brother—not to mention a barrage of lewd remarks from men outside her family. If they knew that she had actually gone out on a few dates, that she had been to a discotheque, that she had once kissed a young man who said he was a student . . . Julie's stomach tightens as she imagines her family's reaction. She tries to concentrate on the kind of man she would like to marry: an engineer or technician of some sort, someone who had been to California, where the company headquarters are located and where even the grandmothers wear tight pants and lipstick—some-

one who had a good attitude about women. But if she ends up having to wear glasses, like her cousin who worked three years at the "scopes," she might as well forget about finding anyone to marry her.

One of the most serious occupational hazards that Julie and millions of women like her may face is the lifelong stigma of having been a "factory girl." Most of the cultures favored by multinational corporations in their search for cheap labor are patriarchal in the grand old style: any young woman who is not under the wing of a father, husband, or older brother must be "loose." High levels of unemployment among men, as in Mexico, contribute to male resentment of working women. (Ironically, in some places the multinationals have increased male unemployment—for example, by paving over fishing and farming villages to make way for industrial parks.) Add to all this the fact that certain companies—American electronics firms are in the lead—actively promote Western-style sexual objectification as a means of insuring employee loyalty: there are company-sponsored cosmetics classes, "guess whose legs these are" contests, and swim-suit-style beauty contests where the prize might be a free night *for two* in a fancy hotel. Corporate-promoted Westernization only heightens the hostility many men feel toward any independent working women—having a job is bad enough, wearing jeans and mascara to work is going too far.

Anthropologist Patricia Fernandez, who has worked in a *maquiladora* herself, believes that the stigmatization of working women serves, indirectly, to keep them in line. "You have to think of the kind of socialization that girls experience in a very Catholic—or, for that matter, Muslim—society. The fear of having a 'reputation' is enough to make a lot of women bend over backward to be 'respectable' and ladylike, which is just what management wants." She points out that in northern Mexico, the tabloids delight in playing up stories of alleged vice in the *maquiladoras*—indiscriminate sex on the job, epidemics of venereal disease, fetuses found in factory rest rooms. "I worry about this because there are those who treat you differently as soon as they know you have a job at a *maquiladora*," one woman told Fernandez.

"Maybe they think that if you have to work, there is a chance you're a whore."

And there is always a chance you'll wind up as one. Probably only a small minority of Third-World factory workers turn to prostitution when their working days come to an end. But it is, as for women everywhere, the employment of last resort, the only thing to do when the factories don't need you and traditional society won't—or, for economic reasons, can't—take you back. In the Philippines, the brothel business is expanding as fast as the factory system. If they can't use you one way, they can use you another.

There has been no international protest about the exploitation of Third-World women by multinational corporations—no thundering denunciations from the floor of the United Nations' general assembly, no angry resolutions from the Conference of the Non-Aligned Countries. Sociologist Robert Snow, who has been tracing the multinationals on their way south and eastward for years, explained why: "The Third-World governments *want* the multinationals to move in. There's cutthroat competition to attract the corporations."

The governments themselves gain little revenue from this kind of investment, though—especially since most offer tax holidays and freedom from export duties in order to attract the multinationals in the first place. Nor do the people as a whole benefit, according to a highly placed Third-World woman within the UN. "The multinationals like to say they're contributing to development," she told us, "but they come into our countries for one thing—cheap labor. If the labor stops being so cheap, they can move on. So how can you call that development? It depends on the people being poor and staying poor." But there are important groups that do stand to gain when the multinationals set up shop in their countries: local entrepreneurs who subcontract to the multinationals; Harvard- or Berkeley-educated "technocrats" who become local management; and government officials who specialize in cutting red tape for an "agent's fee" or an outright bribe.

In the competition for multinational investment, local governments advertise their women shamelessly, and an investment brochure issued by the Malaysian government informs multinational executives that: "The manual dexterity of the Oriental female is famous the world over. Her hands are small, and she works fast with extreme care. . . . Who, therefore, could be better qualified by nature and inheritance, to contribute to the efficiency of a bench-assembly production line than the Oriental girl?"

The Royal Thai Embassy sends American businesses a brochure guaranteeing that in Thailand, "the relationship between the employer and employee is like that of a guardian and ward. It is easy to win and maintain the loyalty of workers as long as they are treated with kindness and courtesy." The facing page offers a highly selective photo-study of Thai womanhood: giggling shyly, bowing submissively, and working cheerfully on an assembly line.

Many "host" governments are willing to back up their advertising with whatever amount of brutality it takes to keep "their girls" just as docile as they look in the brochures. Even the most polite and orderly attempts to organize are likely to bring down overkill doses of police repression:

- In Guatemala in 1975 women workers in a North American-owned factory producing jeans and jackets drew up a list of complaints that included insults by management, piecework wages that turned out to be less than the legal minimum, no overtime pay, and "threats of death." In response, the American boss made a quick call to the local authorities to report that he was being harassed by "Communists." When the women reported for work the next day they found the factory surrounded by two fully armed contingents of military police. The "Communist" ringleaders were picked out and fired.

- In the Dominican Republic, in 1978, workers who attempted to organize at the La Romana industrial zone were first fired, then obligingly arrested by the local police. Officials from the AFL-CIO have described the zone as a "modern slave-labor camp," where workers who do not meet their production quotas during their regular shift must stay and put in unpaid overtime until they do meet them, and many women workers are routinely strip-searched at the end of the day. During the 1978 organizing attempt, the government sent in national police in full combat gear and armed with automatic weapons. Gulf & Western supplements the local law with its own company-sponsored motorcycle club, which specializes in terrorizing suspected union sympathizers.

- In Inchon, South Korea, women at the Dong-Il Textile Company (which produces fabrics and yarn for export to the United States) had succeeded in gaining leadership in their union in 1972. But in 1978 the government-controlled, male-dominated Federation of Korean Trade Unions sent special "action squads" to destroy the women's union. Armed with steel bars and buckets of human excrement, the goons broke into the union office, smashed the office equipment, and smeared the excrement over the women's bodies and in their hair, ears, eyes, and mouths.

Crudely put (and incidents like this do not inspire verbal delicacy), the relationship between many Third-World governments and the multinational corporations is not very different from the relationship between a pimp and his customers. The governments advertise their women, sell them, and keep them in line for the multinational "johns." But there are other parties to the growing international traffic in women—such as the United Nations' Industrial Development Organization (UNIDO), the World Bank, and the United States government itself.

UNIDO, for example, has been a major promoter of "free trade zones." These are enclaves within nations that offer multinational corporations a range of creature comforts, including: freedom from paying taxes and export duties; low-cost water, power, and buildings; exemption from whatever labor laws may apply in the country as a whole; and, in some cases, such security features as barbed-wire, guarded checkpoints, and government-paid police.

Then there is the World Bank, which over the past decade has lent several billion dollars to finance the roads, airports, power plants, and even the first-class hotels that multinational corporations need in order to set up business in Third-World countries. The Sri Lankan garment industry, which like other Third-World garment industries survives by subcontracting to major Western firms, was set up on the advice of the World Bank and with a $20 million World Bank loan. This particular experiment in "development" offers young women jobs at a global low of $5 for a six-day week. Gloria Scott, the head of the World Bank's Women and Development Program, sounded distinctly uncomfortable when we asked her about the bank's role in promoting the exploitation of Third-World women. "Our job is to help eliminate poverty. It is not our responsibility if the multinationals come in and offer such low wages. It's the responsibility of the governments." However, the Bank's 1979 World Development Report speaks strongly of the need for "wage restraint" in poor countries.

But the most powerful promoter of exploitative conditions for Third-World women workers is the United States government itself. For example, the notoriously repressive Korean textile industry was developed with the help of $400 million in aid from the U.S. State Department. Malaysia became a low-wage haven for the electronics industry, thanks to technical assistance financed by AID and to U.S. money (funneled through the Asian Development Bank) to set up free trade zones. Taiwan's status as a "showcase for the free world" and a comfortable berth for multinationals is the result of three decades of financial transfusions from the United States. On a less savory note, the U.S. funds an outfit called the Asian-American Free Labor Institute, whose ostensible purpose is to encourage "free" (i.e., non-Communist) trade unions in Asia, but whose actual mission is to discourage any truly militant union activity. AAFLI works closely with the Federation of Korean Trade Unions, which was responsible for the excrement-smearing incident described above.

But the most obvious form of United States involvement, according to Lenny Siegel, the director of the Pacific Studies Center, is through "our consistent record of military aid to Third-World governments that are capitalist, politically repressive, and are not striving for economic independence." Ironically, says Siegel, there are "cases where the United States made a big investment—through groups like AAFLI or other kinds of political pressure—to make sure that any unions that formed would be pretty tame. Then we put in even more money to support some dictator who doesn't allow unions at all." And if that doesn't seem like a sufficient case of duplicate spending, the U.S. government also insures (through the Overseas Private Investment Corporation) outward-bound multinationals against any lingering possibility of insurrection or expropriation.

What does our government have to say for itself? It's hard to get a straight answer—the few parts of the bureaucracy that deal with women and development seem to have little connection with those that are concerned with larger foreign policy issues. A spokesman for the Department of State told us that if multinationals offer poor working conditions (which he questioned), this was not their fault: "There are just different standards in different countries." Offering further evidence of

a sheltered life, he told us that "corporations today are generally more socially responsible than even ten years ago. . . . We can expect them to treat their employees in the best way they can." But he conceded in response to a barrage of unpleasant examples, "Of course, you're going to have problems wherever you have human beings doing things." Our next stop was the Women's Division within AID. Staffer Emmy Simmons was aware of the criticisms of the quality of employment multinationals offer, but cautioned that "we can get hung up in the idea that it's exploitation without really looking at the alternatives for women." AID's concern, she said, was with the fact that population is outgrowing the agricultural capacity of many Third-World countries, dislocating millions of people. From her point of view, multinationals at least provide some sort of alternative: "These people have to go somewhere."

THINKING ABOUT THE READINGS

Money, Morals, and Manners

- How do the French and American upper-middle-class men interviewed by Lamont differ in the information they use to make class distinctions? How does the existence of moral and cultural boundaries support the contention that class is a social construction? To put it another way, why is it important that we examine the human tendency to draw boundaries between ourselves and others? Can you think of some specific situations in your life where you found yourself marking cultural and/or moral boundaries between yourself and others? What sorts of information did you use to judge the "worthiness" of these other people?

The Bohemian Grove

- What do you think of Domhoff's argument about a cohesive upper class? Can recreational clubs provide the sort of "social cohesiveness" necessary for a self-contained ruling class to exist? How do you think places like Bohemian Grove contribute to class stratification in American society? How does the existence of such clubs change your thinking about the way important political and economic decisions are made in this country?

Life on the Global Assembly Line

- Why are women rather than men the predominant workers in this international division of labor? Why are they so easily exploited? Why do you think there has been so little international protest over these employment practices? How do the labor practices described by Ehrenreich and Fuentes support global stratification?

CHAPTER 11

The Architecture of Disadvantage
Poverty and Wealth

It is impossible to fully examine the American stratification system without addressing the plight of those at the bottom. Poverty is a social problem that is becoming larger and more deadly with each passing day. But while the problem is getting worse, public attitudes toward poverty and poor people are frequently indifferent or even hostile. Furthermore, many important organizations and institutions inadvertently contribute to the problem.

In "Savage Inequalities in America's Schools," Jonathan Kozol provides a troubling portrait of inequality in the American educational system by examining the school experiences of children in two very different cities. Although the children of East St. Louis, Illinois, and Rye, New York, are citizens of the same country, they live in two different worlds. Their vastly different educational experiences make it difficult to sustain the myth that all children are competing in a fair race for society's opportunities.

To those of us who have a home to live in, the life of a homeless person appears chaotic and unstructured. In "The Subculture of Street Life," David Snow and Leon Anderson, however, make it clear that there is a patterned set of behaviors and routines that homeless people use to adapt to their conditions. Homelessness falls under organizational and institutional constraints as much as any other societal phenomenon. When we think of the role that organizations play regarding the problem of homelessness it is usually in terms of the important resources they provide for people's survival (shelter, food, etc.). And yet, Snow and Anderson suggest, some organizations that deal with homelessness are not very interested in the welfare of homeless people and may even impede their survival.

Savage Inequalities in America's Schools
Life on the Mississippi: East St. Louis, Illinois

Jonathan Kozol

"East of anywhere," writes a reporter for the *St. Louis Post-Dispatch*, "often evokes the other side of the tracks. But, for a first-time visitor suddenly deposited on its eerily empty streets, East St. Louis might suggest another world." The city, which is 98 percent black, has no obstetric services, no regular trash collection, and few jobs. Nearly a third of its families live on less than $7,500 a year; 75 percent of its population lives on welfare of some form. The U.S. Department of Housing and Urban Development describes it as "the most distressed small city in America."

Only three of the 13 buildings on Missouri Avenue, one of the city's major thoroughfares, are occupied. A 13-story office building, tallest in the city, has been boarded up. Outside, on the sidewalk, a pile of garbage fills a ten-foot crater.

The city, which by night and day is clouded by the fumes that pour from vents and smokestacks at the Pfizer and Monsanto chemical plants, has one of the highest rates of child asthma in America.

It is, according to a teacher at the University of Southern Illinois, "a repository for a nonwhite population that is now regarded as expendable." The *Post-Dispatch* describes it as "America's Soweto."

Fiscal shortages have forced the layoff of 1,170 of the city's 1,400 employees in the past 12 years. The city, which is often unable to buy heating fuel or toilet paper for the city hall, recently announced that it might have to cashier all but 10 percent of the remaining work force of 230. In 1989 the mayor announced that he might need to sell the city hall and all six fire stations to raise needed cash. Last year the plan had to be scrapped after the city lost its city hall in a court judgment to a creditor. East St. Louis is mortgaged into the next century but has the highest property-tax rate in the state.

Since October 1987, when the city's garbage pickups ceased, the backyards of residents have been employed as dump sites. In the spring of 1988 a policeman tells a visitor that 40 plastic bags of trash are waiting for removal from the backyard of his mother's house. Public health officials are concerned the garbage will attract a plague of flies and rodents in the summer. The policeman speaks of "rats as big as puppies" in his mother's yard. They are known to the residents, he says, as "bull rats." Many people have no cars or funds to cart the trash and simply burn it in their yards. The odor of smoke from burning garbage, says the *Post-Dispatch*, "has become one of the scents of spring" in East St. Louis.

Railroad tracks still used to transport hazardous chemicals run through the city. "Always present," says the *Post-Dispatch*, "is the threat of chemical spills. . . . The wail of sirens warning residents to evacuate after a spill is common." The most recent spill, the paper says, "was at the Monsanto Company plant. . . . Nearly 300 gallons of phosphorous trichloride spilled when a railroad tank was overfilled. About 450 residents were taken to St. Mary's Hospital. . . . The frequency of the emergencies has caused Monsanto to have a 'standing account' at St. Mary's." . . .

The dangers of exposure to raw sewage, which backs up repeatedly into the homes of residents in East St. Louis, were first noticed, in the spring of 1989, at a public housing project, Villa Griffin. Raw sewage, says the *Post-Dispatch*, overflowed into a playground just behind the housing project, which is home to 187 children, "forming an oozing lake of . . . tainted water." Two schoolgirls, we are told, "experienced hair loss since raw sewage flowed into their homes."

While local physicians are not certain whether loss of hair is caused by the raw sewage, they have issued warnings that exposure to raw sewage can provoke a cholera or hepatitis outbreak. A St. Louis health official voices her dismay that children live with waste in their backyards. "The development of working sewage systems made cities livable a hundred years ago," she notes. "Sewage systems separate us from the Third World."

The sewage, which is flowing from collapsed pipes and dysfunctional pumping stations, has also flooded basements all over the city. The city's vacuum truck, which uses water and suction to unclog the city's sewers, cannot be used because it needs $5,000 in repairs. Even when it works, it sometimes can't be used because there isn't money to hire drivers. A single engineer now does the work that 14 others did before they were laid off. By April the pool of overflow behind the Villa Griffin project has expanded into a lagoon of sewage. Two million gallons of raw sewage lie outside the children's homes. . . .

The Daughters of Charity, whose works of mercy are well known in the Third World, operate a mission at the Villa Griffin homes. On an afternoon in early spring of 1990, Sister Julia Huiskamp meets me on King Boulevard and drives me to the Griffin homes.

As we ride past blocks and blocks of skeletal structures, some of which are still inhabited, she slows the car repeatedly at railroad crossings. A seemingly endless railroad train rolls past us to the right. On the left: a blackened lot where garbage has been burning. Next to the burning garbage is a row of 12 white cabins, charred by fire. Next: a lot that holds a heap of auto tires and a mountain of tin cans. More burnt houses. More trash fires. The train moves almost imperceptibly across the flatness of the land.

Fifty years old, and wearing a blue suit, white blouse, and blue head-cover, Sister Julia points to the nicest house in sight. The sign on the front reads MOTEL. "It's a whorehouse," Sister Julia says.

When she slows the car beside a group of teenage boys, one of them steps out toward the car, then backs away as she is recognized.

The 99 units of the Villa Griffin homes—two-story structures, brick on the first floor, yellow wood above—form one border of a recessed park and playground that were filled with fecal matter last year when the sewage mains exploded. The sewage is gone now and the grass is very green and looks inviting. When nine-year-old Serena and her seven-year-old brother take me for a walk, however, I discover that our shoes sink into what is still a sewage marsh. An inch-deep residue of fouled water still remains.

Serena's brother is a handsome, joyous little boy, but troublingly thin. Three other children join us as we walk along the marsh: Smokey, who is nine years old but cannot yet tell time; Mickey, who is seven; and a tiny child with a ponytail and big brown eyes who talks a constant stream of words that I can't always understand.

"Hush, Little Sister," says Serena. I ask for her name, but "Little Sister" is the only name the children seem to know.

"There go my cousins," Smokey says, pointing to two teen-age girls above us on the hill.

The day is warm, although we're only in the second week of March; several dogs and cats are playing by the edges of the marsh. "It's a lot of squirrels here," says Smokey. "There go one!"

"This here squirrel is a friend of mine," says Little Sister.

None of the children can tell me the approximate time that school begins. One says five o'clock. One says six. Another says that school begins at noon.

When I ask what song they sing after the flag pledge, one says "Jingle Bells."

Smokey cannot decide if he is in the second or third grade.

Seven-year-old Mickey sucks his thumb during the walk.

The children regale me with a chilling story as we stand beside the marsh. Smokey says his sister was raped and murdered and then dumped behind his school. Other children add more details: Smokey's sister was 11 years old. She was beaten with a brick until she died. The murder was committed by a man who knew her mother.

The narrative begins when, without warning, Smokey says, "My sister has got killed."

"She was my best friend," Serena says.

"They had beat her in the head and raped her," Smokey says.

"She was hollering out loud," says Little Sister.

I ask them when it happened. Smokey says, "Last year." Serena then corrects him and she says, "Last week."

"It scared me because I had to cry," says Little Sister.

"The police arrested one man but they didn't catch the other," Smokey says.

Serena says, "He was some kin to her."

But Smokey objects, "He weren't no kin to me. He was my momma's friend."

"Her face was busted," Little Sister says.

Serena describes this sequence of events: "They told her go behind the school. They'll give her a quarter if she do. Then they knock her down and told her not to tell what they had did."

I ask, "Why did they kill her?"

"They was scared that she would tell," Serena says.

"One is in jail," says Smokey. "They can't find the other."

"Instead of raping little bitty children, they should find themselves a wife," says Little Sister.

"I hope," Serena says, "her spirit will come back and get that man."

"And *kill* that man," says Little Sister.

"Give her another chance to live," Serena says.

"My teacher came to the funeral," says Smokey.

"When a little child dies, my momma say a star go straight to Heaven," says Serena.

"My grandma was murdered," Mickey says out of the blue. "Somebody shot two bullets in her head."

I ask him, "Is she really dead?"

"She dead all right," says Mickey. "She was layin' there, just dead."

"I love my friends," Serena says. "I don't care if they no kin to me. I care for them. I hope his mother have another baby. Name her for my friend that's dead."

"I have a cat with three legs," Smokey says.

"Snakes hate rabbits," Mickey says, again for no apparent reason.

"Cats hate fishes," Little Sister says.

"It's a lot of hate," says Smokey.

Later, at the mission, Sister Julia tells me this: "The Jefferson School, which they attend, is a decrepit hulk. Next to it is a modern school, erected two years ago, which was to have replaced the one that they attend. But the construction was not done correctly. The roof is too heavy for the walls, and the entire structure has begun to sink. It can't be occupied. Smokey's sister was raped and murdered and dumped between the old school and the new one."

As the children drift back to their homes for supper, Sister Julia stands outside with me and talks about the health concerns that trouble people in the neighborhood. In the setting sun, the voices of the children fill the evening air. Nourished by the sewage marsh, a field of wild daffodils is blooming. Standing here, you wouldn't think that anything was wrong. The street is calm. The poison in the soil can't be seen. The sewage is invisible and only makes the grass a little greener. Bikes thrown down by children lie outside their kitchen doors. It could be an ordinary twilight in a small suburban town.

Night comes on and Sister Julia goes inside to telephone a cab. In another hour, the St. Louis taxis will not come into the neighborhood. . . .

East St. Louis—which the local press refers to as "an inner city without an outer city"—has some of the sickest children in America. Of 66 cities in Illinois, East St. Louis ranks first in fetal death, first in premature birth, and third in infant death. Among the negative factors listed by the city's health director are the sewage running in the streets, air that has been fouled by the local plants, the high lead levels noted in the soil, poverty, lack of education, crime, dilapidated housing, insufficient health care, unemployment. Hospital care is deficient too. There is no place to have a baby in East St. Louis. The maternity ward at the city's Catholic hospital, a 100-year-old structure, was shut down some years ago. The only other hospital in town was forced by lack of funds to close in 1990. The closest obstetrics service open to the women here is seven miles away. The infant death rate is still rising.

As in New York City's poorest neighborhoods, dental problems also plague the children here.

Although dental problems don't command the instant fears associated with low birth weight, fetal death or cholera, they do have the consequence of wearing down the stamina of children and defeating their ambitions. Bleeding gums, impacted teeth and rotting teeth are routine matters for the children I have interviewed in the South Bronx. Children get used to feeling constant pain. They go to sleep with it. They go to school with it. Sometimes their teachers are alarmed and try to get them to a clinic. But it's all so slow and heavily encumbered with red tape and waiting lists and missing, lost or canceled welfare cards, that dental care is often long delayed. Children live for months with pain that grown-ups would find unendurable. The gradual attrition of accepted pain erodes their energy and aspiration. I have seen children in New York with teeth that look like brownish, broken sticks. I have also seen teenagers who were missing half their teeth. But, to me, most shocking is to see a child with an abscess that has been inflamed for weeks and that he has simply lived with and accepts as part of the routine of life. Many teachers in the urban schools have seen this. It is almost commonplace.

Compounding these problems is the poor nutrition of the children here—average daily food expenditure in East St. Louis is $2.40 for one child—and the underimmunization of young children. Of every 100 children recently surveyed in East St. Louis, 55 were incompletely immunized for polio, diphtheria, measles and whooping cough. In this context, health officials look with all the more uneasiness at those lagoons of sewage outside public housing.

On top of all else is the very high risk of death by homicide in East St. Louis. In a recent year in which three cities in the state of roughly the same size as East St. Louis had an average of four homicides apiece, there were 54 homicides in East St. Louis. But it is the heat of summer that officials here particularly dread. The heat that breeds the insects bearing polio or hepatitis in raw sewage also heightens asthma and frustration and reduces patience. "The heat," says a man in public housing, "can bring out the beast. . . ."

The fear of violence is very real in East St. Louis. The CEO of one of the large companies out on the edge of town has developed an "evac-uation plan" for his employees. State troopers are routinely sent to East St. Louis to put down disturbances that the police cannot control. If the misery of this community explodes someday in a real riot (it has happened in the past), residents believe that state and federal law-enforcement agencies will have no hesitation in applying massive force to keep the violence contained. . . .

The problems of the streets in urban areas, as teachers often note, frequently spill over into public schools. In the public schools of East St. Louis this is literally the case.

"Martin Luther King Junior High School," notes the *Post-Dispatch* in a story published in the early spring of 1989, "was evacuated Friday afternoon after sewage flowed into the kitchen. . . . The kitchen was closed and students were sent home." On Monday, the paper continues, "East St. Louis Senior High School was awash in sewage for the second time this year." The school had to be shut because of "fumes and backed-up toilets." Sewage flowed into the basement, through the floor, then up into the kitchen and the students' bathrooms. The backup, we read, "occurred in the food preparation areas."

School is resumed the following morning at the high school, but a few days later the overflow recurs. This time the entire system is affected, since the meals distributed to every student in the city are prepared in the two schools that have been flooded. School is called off for all 16,500 students in the district. The sewage backup, caused by the failure of two pumping stations, forces officials at the high school to shut down the furnaces.

At Martin Luther King, the parking lot and gym are also flooded. "It's a disaster," says a legislator. "The streets are underwater; gaseous fumes are being emitted from the pipes under the schools," she says, "making people ill."

In the same week, the schools announce the layoff of 280 teachers, 166 cooks and cafeteria workers, 25 teacher aides, 16 custodians and 18 painters, electricians, engineers and plumbers. The president of the teachers' union says the cuts, which will bring the size of kindergarten and primary classes up to 30 students, and the size of fourth to twelfth grade classes up to 35, will have "an unimaginable impact" on the students. "If you have a high school teacher with five classes each day and between 150 and 175 students . . . , it's going to have a devastating effect." The school system, it is also noted, has been using more than 70 "permanent substitute teachers," who are paid only $10,000 yearly, as a way of saving money.

Governor Thompson, however, tells the press that he will not pour money into East St. Louis to solve long-term problems. East St. Louis residents, he says, must help themselves. "There is money in the community," the governor insists. "It's just not being spent for what it should be spent for."

The governor, while acknowledging that East St. Louis faces economic problems, nonetheless refers dismissively to those who live in East St. Louis. "What in the community," he asks, "is being done right?" He takes the opportunity of a visit to the area to announce a fiscal grant for sewer improvement to a relatively wealthy town nearby.

In East St. Louis, meanwhile, teachers are running out of chalk and paper, and their paychecks are arriving two weeks late. The city warns its teachers to expect a cut of half their pay until the fiscal crisis has been eased.

The threatened teacher layoffs are mandated by the Illinois Board of Education, which, because of the city's fiscal crisis, has been given supervisory control of the school budget. Two weeks later the state superintendent partially relents. In a tone very different from that of the governor, he notes that East St. Louis does not have the means to solve its education problems on its own. "There is no natural way," he says, that "East St. Louis can bring itself out of this situation." Several cuts will be required in any case—one quarter of the system's teachers, 75 teacher aides, and several dozen others will be given notice—but, the state board notes, sports and music programs will not be affected.

East St. Louis, says the chairman of the state board, "is simply the worst possible place I can imagine to have a child brought up. . . . The community is in desperate circumstances." Sports and music, he observes, are, for many children here, "the only avenues of success." Sadly enough, no matter how it ratifies the stereotype, this is the truth; and there is a poignant aspect to the fact that, even with class size soaring and one quarter of the system's teachers being given their dismissal, the state board of education demonstrates

its genuine but skewed compassion by attempting to leave sports and music untouched by the overall austerity.

Even sports facilities, however, are degrading by comparison with those found and expected at most high schools in America. The football field at East St. Louis High is missing almost everything—including goalposts. There are a couple of metal pipes—no crossbar, just the pipes. Bob Shannon, the football coach, who has to use his personal funds to purchase footballs and has had to cut and rake the football field himself, has dreams of having goalposts someday. He'd also like to let his students have new uniforms. The ones they wear are nine years old and held together somehow by a patchwork of repairs. Keeping them clean is a problem, too. The school cannot afford a washing machine. The uniforms are carted to a corner laundromat with fifteen dollars' worth of quarters. . . .

In the wing of the school that holds vocational classes, a damp, unpleasant odor fills the halls. The school has a machine shop, which cannot be used for lack of staff, and a woodworking shop. The only shop that's occupied this morning is the auto-body class. A man with long blond hair and wearing a white sweat suit swings a paddle to get children in their chairs. "What we need the most is new equipment," he reports. "I have equipment for alignment, for example, but we don't have money to install it. We also need a better form of egress. We bring the cars in through two other classes." Computerized equipment used in most repair shops, he reports, is far beyond the high school's budget. It looks like a very old gas station in an isolated rural town.

The science labs at East St. Louis High are 30 to 50 years outdated. John McMillan, a soft-spoken man, teaches physics at the school. He shows me his lab. The six lab stations in the room have empty holes where pipes were once attached. "It would be great if we had water," says McMillan. . . .

Leaving the chemistry labs, I pass a double-sized classroom in which roughly 60 kids are sitting fairly still but doing nothing. "This is supervised study hall," a teacher tells me in the corridor. But when we step inside, he finds there is no teacher. "The teacher must be out today," he says.

Irl Solomon's history classes, which I visit next, have been described by journalists who cover East St. Louis as the highlight of the school. Solomon, a man of 54 whose reddish hair is turning white, has taught in urban schools for almost 30 years. A graduate of Brandeis University in 1961, he entered law school but was drawn away by a concern with civil rights. "After one semester, I decided that the law was not for me. I said, 'Go and find the toughest place there is to teach. See if you like it.' I'm still here. . . ."

Teachers like Mr. Solomon, working in low-income districts such as East St. Louis, often tell me that they feel cut off from educational developments in modern public schools. "Well, it's amazing," Solomon says. "I have done without so much so long that, if I were assigned to a suburban school, I'm not sure I'd recognize what they are doing. We are utterly cut off."

"Very little education in the school would be considered academic in the suburbs. Maybe 10 to 15 percent of students are in truly academic programs. Of the 55 percent who graduate, 20 percent may go to four-year colleges: something like 10 percent of any entering class. Another 10 to 20 percent may get some other kind of higher education. An equal number join the military. . . ."

"Sometimes I get worried that I'm starting to burn out. Still, I hate to miss a day. The department frequently can't find a substitute to come here, and my kids don't like me to be absent."

Solomon's advanced class, which soon comes into the room, includes some lively students with strong views.

"I don't go to physics class, because my lab has no equipment," says one student. "The typewriters in my typing class don't work. The women's toilets. . . ." She makes a sour face. "I'll be honest," she says. "I just don't use the toilets. If I do, I come back into class and I feel dirty."

"I wanted to study Latin," says another student. "But we don't have Latin in this school."

"We lost our only Latin teacher," Solomon says.

A girl in a white jersey with the message DO THE RIGHT THING on the front raises her hand. "You visit other schools," she says. "Do you think the children in this school are getting what we'd get in a nice section of St. Louis?"

I note that we are in a different state and city. "Are we citizens of East St. Louis or America?" she asks. . . .

Clark Junior High School is regarded as the top school in the city. I visit, in part, at the request of school officials, who would like me to see education in the city at its very best. Even here, however, there is a disturbing sense that one has entered a backwater of America.

"We spend the entire eighth grade year preparing for the state exams," a teacher tells me in a top-ranked English class. The teacher seems devoted to the children, but three students sitting near me sleep through the entire period. The teacher rouses one of them, a girl in the seat next to me, but the student promptly lays her head back on her crossed arms and is soon asleep again. Four of the 14 ceiling lights are broken. The corridor outside the room is filled with voices. Outside the window, where I see no schoolyard, is an empty lot.

In a mathematics class of 30 children packed into a space that might be adequate for 15 kids, there is one white student. The first white student I have seen in East St. Louis, she is polishing her nails with bright red polish. A tiny black girl next to her is writing with a one-inch pencil stub.

In a seventh grade social studies class, the only book that bears some relevance to black concerns—its title is *The American Negro*—bears a publication date of 1967. The teacher invites me to ask the class some questions. Uncertain where to start, I ask the students what they've learned about the civil rights campaigns of recent decades.

A 14-year-old girl with short black curly hair says this: "Every year in February we are told to read the same old speech of Martin Luther King. We read it every year. 'I have a dream. . . .' It does begin to seem—what is the word?" She hesitates and then she finds the word: "perfunctory."

I ask her what she means.

"We have a school in East St. Louis named for Dr. King," she says. "The school is full of sewer water and the doors are locked with chains. Every student in that school is black. It's like a terrible joke on history."

It startles me to hear her words, but I am startled even more to think how seldom any press reporter has observed the irony of naming segregated schools for Martin Luther King. Children reach the heart of these hypocrisies much quicker than the grown-ups and the experts do.

Public Education in New York

The train ride from Grand Central Station to suburban Rye, New York, takes 35 to 40 minutes. The high school is a short ride from the station. Built of handsome gray stone and set in a landscaped campus, it resembles a New England prep school. On a day in early June of 1990, I enter the school and am directed by a student to the office.

The principal, a relaxed, unhurried man who, unlike many urban principals, seems gratified to have me visit in his school, takes me in to see the auditorium, which, he says, was recently restored with private charitable funds ($400,000) raised by parents. The crenellated ceiling, which is white and spotless, and the polished dark-wood paneling contrast with the collapsing structure of the auditorium at Morris High. The principal strikes his fist against the balcony: "They made this place extremely solid." Through a window, one can see the spreading branches of a beech tree in the central courtyard of the school.

In a student lounge, a dozen seniors are relaxing on a carpeted floor that is constructed with a number of tiers so that, as the principal explains, "they can stretch out and be comfortable while reading."

The library is wood-paneled, like the auditorium. Students, all of whom are white, are seated at private carrels, of which there are approximately 40. Some are doing homework; others are looking through the *New York Times*. Every student that I see during my visit to the school is white or Asian, though I later learn there are a number of Hispanic students and that 1 or 2 percent of students in the school are black.

According to the principal, the school has 96 computers for 546 children. The typical student, he says, studies a foreign language for four or five years, beginning in the junior high school, and a second foreign language (Latin is available) for two years. Of 140 seniors, 92 are now enrolled in AP classes. Maximum teacher salary will soon reach $70,000. Per-pupil funding is above $12,000 at the time I visit.

The students I meet include eleventh and twelfth graders. The teacher tells me that the class is reading Robert Coles, Studs Terkel, Alice Walker. He tells me I will find them more than willing to engage me in debate, and this turns out to be correct. Primed for my visit, it appears, they arrow in directly on the dual questions of equality and race.

Three general positions soon emerge and seem to be accepted widely. The first is that the fiscal inequalities "do matter very much" in shaping what a school can offer ("That is obvious," one student says) and that any loss of funds in Rye, as a potential consequence of future equalizing, would be damaging to many things the town regards as quite essential.

The second position is that racial integration— for example, by the busing of black children from the city or a nonwhite suburb to this school— would meet with strong resistance, and the reason would not simply be the fear that certain standards might decline. The reason, several students say straightforwardly, is "racial" or, as others say it, "out-and-out racism" on the part of adults.

The third position voiced by many students, but not all, is that equity is basically a goal to be desired and should be pursued for moral reasons, but "will probably make no major difference" since poor children "still would lack the motivation" and "would probably fail in any case because of other problems."

At this point, I ask if they can truly say "it wouldn't make a difference" since it's never been attempted. Several students then seem to rethink their views and say that "it might work, but it would have to start with preschool and the elementary grades" and "it might be 20 years before we'd see a difference."

At this stage in the discussion, several students speak with some real feeling of the present inequalities, which, they say, are "obviously unfair," and one student goes a little further and proposes that "we need to change a lot more than the schools." Another says she'd favor racial integration "by whatever means—including busing —even if my parents disapprove." But a contradictory opinion also is expressed with a good deal of fervor and is stated by one student in a rather biting voice: "I don't see why we should do it. How could it be of benefit to us?"

Throughout the discussion, whatever the views the children voice, there is a degree of unreality about the whole exchange. The children are lucid and their language is well chosen and their arguments well made, but there is a sense that they are dealing with an issue that does not feel very vivid, and that nothing that we say about it to each other really matters since it's "just a theoretical discussion." To a certain degree, the skillfulness and cleverness that they display seem to derive precisely from this sense of unreality. Questions of unfairness feel more like a geometric problem than a matter of humanity or conscience. A few of the students do break through the note of unreality, but, when they do, they cease to be so agile in their use of words and speak more awkwardly. Ethical challenges seem to threaten their effectiveness. There is the sense that they were skating over ice and that the issues we addressed were safely frozen underneath. When they stop to look beneath the ice they start to stumble. The verbal competence they have acquired here may have been gained by building walls around some regions of the heart.

"I don't think that busing students from their ghetto to a different school would do much good," one student says. "You can take them out of the environment, but you can't take the environment out of *them*. If someone grows up in the South Bronx, he's not going to be prone to learn." His name is Max and he has short black hair and speaks with confidence. "Busing didn't work when it was tried," he says. I ask him how he knows this and he says he saw a television movie about Boston.

"I agree that it's unfair the way it is," another student says. "We have AP courses and they don't. Our classes are much smaller." But, she says, "putting them in schools like ours is not the answer. Why not put some AP classes into *their* school? Fix the roof and paint the halls so it will not be so depressing."

The students know the term "separate but equal," but seem unaware of its historical associations. "Keep them where they are but make it equal," says a girl in the front row.

A student named Jennifer, whose manner of speech is somewhat less refined and polished than that of the others, tells me that her parents came here from New York. "My family is originally from the Bronx. Schools are hell there. That's one reason that we moved. I don't think it's our responsibility to pay our taxes to provide for *them*. I mean, my parents used to live there and they wanted to get out. There's no point in coming to a place like this, where schools are good, and then your taxes go back to the place where you began."

I bait her a bit: "Do you mean that, now that you are not in hell, you have no feeling for the people that you left behind?"

"It has to be the people in the area who want an education. If your parents just don't care, it won't do any good to spend a lot of money. Someone else can't want a good life for you. You have got to want it for yourself." Then she adds, however, "I agree that everyone should have a chance at taking the same courses. . . ."

I ask her if she'd think it fair to pay more taxes so that this was possible.

"I don't see how that benefits me," she says.

It occurs to me how hard it would have been for anyone to make that kind of statement, even in the wealthiest suburban school, in 1968. Her classmates would have been unsettled by the voicing of such undisguised self-interest. Here in Rye, in 1990, she can say this with impunity. She's an interesting girl and I reluctantly admire her for being so straightforward.

Max raises a different point. "I'm not convinced," he says, "that AP courses would be valued in the Bronx. Not everyone is going to go to college."

Jennifer picks up on this and carries it a little further. "The point," she says, "is that you cannot give an equal chance to every single person. If you did it, you'd be changing the whole economic system. Let's be honest. If you equalize the money, someone's got to be shortchanged. I don't doubt that children in the Bronx are getting a bad deal. But do we want *everyone* to get a mediocre education?"

"The other point," says Max, "is that you need to match the money that you spend to whether children in the school can profit from it. We get twice as much as kids in the South Bronx, but our school is *more* than twice as good and that's because of who is here. Money isn't the whole story. . . ."

"In New York," says Jennifer, "rich people put their kids in private school. If we equalize between New York and Rye, you would see the same thing happen here. People would pull out their kids. Some people do it now. So it would happen a lot more."

An eleventh grader shakes her head at this. "Poor children need more money. It's as simple as that," she says. "Money comes from taxes. If we have it, we should pay it."

It is at this point that a boy named David picks up on a statement made before. "Someone said just now that this is not our obligation, our responsibility. I don't think that that's the question. I don't think you'd do it, pay more taxes or whatever, out of obligation. You would do it just because . . . it is unfair the way it is." He falters on these words and looks a bit embarrassed. Unlike many of the other students who have spoken, he is somewhat hesitant and seems to choke up on his words. "Well, it's easy for me to be sitting here and say I'd spend my parents' money. I'm not working. I don't earn the money. I don't need to be conservative until I do. I can be as open-minded and unrealistic as I want to be. You can be a liberal until you have a mortgage."

I ask him what he'd likely say if he were ten years older. "Hopefully," he says, "my values would remain the same. But I know that having money does affect you. This, at least, is what they tell me."

Spurred perhaps by David's words, another student says, "The biggest tax that people pay is to the federal government. Why not take some money from the budget that we spend on armaments and use it for the children in these urban schools?"

A well-dressed student with a healthy tan, however, says that using federal taxes for the poor "would be like giving charity," and "charitable things have never worked. . . . Charity will not instill the poor with self-respect."

Max returns to something that he said before: "The environment is everything. It's going to take something more than money." He goes on to speak of inefficiency and of alleged corruption in the New York City schools. "Some years ago the chancellor was caught in borrowing $100,000

from the schools. I am told that he did not intend to pay it back. These things happen too much in New York. Why should we pour money in, when they are wasting what they have?"

I ask him, "Have we *any* obligations to poor people?"

"I don't think the burden is on us," says Jennifer again. "Taxing the rich to help the poor—we'd be getting nothing out of it. I don't understand how it would make a better educational experience for me."

"A child's in school only six hours in a day," says Max. "You've got to deal with what is happening at home. If his father's in the streets, his mother's using crack . . . how is money going to make a difference?"

David dismisses this and tells me, "Here's what we should do. Put more money into preschool, kindergarten, elementary years. Pay college kids to tutor inner-city children. Get rid of the property tax, which is too uneven, and use income taxes to support these schools. Pay teachers more to work in places like the Bronx. It has to come from taxes. Pay them extra to go into the worst schools. You could forgive their college loans to make it worth their while."

"Give the children Head Start classes," says another student. "If they need more buildings, give them extra money so they wouldn't need to be so crowded."

"It has got to come from taxes," David says again.

"I'm against busing," Max repeats, although this subject hasn't been brought up by anybody else in a long while.

"When people talk this way," says David, "they are saying, actually—" He stops and starts again: "They're saying that black kids will never learn. Even if you spend more in New York. Even if you bring them here to Rye. So what it means is—you are writing people off. You're just dismissing them. . . ."

"I'd like it if we had black students in this school," the girl beside him says.

"It seems rather odd," says David when the hour is up, "that we were sitting in an AP class discussing whether poor kids in the Bronx deserve to get an AP class. We are in a powerful position.

The Subculture of Street Life

David Snow and Leon Anderson

Street life in Austin [Texas], just as in every other community throughout the country, is embedded in a loose network of organizations that range from social-service agencies to neighborhood associations and governmental task forces. These organizations not only affect the survival opportunities and resources available to the homeless but also contribute to the texture of street life. In attempting to understand the relative importance of the various organizations that comprise this constraining matrix we are concerned not so much with their manifest or ostensible functions as with how they actually respond to the homeless from day to day and with their underlying operating perspectives. Simply put, we focus on what the various organizations do and on the working ideologies that organize and justify their activities.

We discerned five patterns of functioning or response among the various organizations intervening in the lives and routines of the homeless in Austin. Table 1 presents these five patterns, along with their operating perspectives and organizational carriers. We discuss each of these patterns in turn.

Accommodative Response

In *The Urban Villagers,* Herbert Gans notes that a significant feature of the urban landscape, especially in low-income areas such as the Italian-American one he studied in Boston's West End, is the existence of a spate of "caretakers." They encompass the "agencies and individuals who not only give patient care, but other kinds of aid that they think will benefit the client, and who offer aid as an end in itself, rather than as a means to a more important end." Generic examples include medical and psychiatric facilities, case-work and social-welfare agencies, many employment agencies and educational programs, and various facilities for the down-and-out, such as the missions and single-room-occupancy tenements (SROs) that lined the skid rows of the past. The landscape of the urban world the homeless know is dotted with an array of such caretakers. Not all of them are of the same stripe, however. Some function primarily in an accommodative fashion; others are essentially restorative.

The accommodative response attends to the basic subsistence needs of the homeless, particularly the need for food and shelter. As a mode of response that helps the homeless manage street life, it facilitates their survival as homeless persons but does little to help them off the streets. This pattern of functioning characterizes the work of most shelters, missions, and soup kitchens, including, in Austin, the Salvation Army, Caritas, Angels House, and the day-labor operation of the Texas Employment Commission. . . .

Of the various organizations and agencies that cater to the homeless in Austin, none offers more accommodative services than the Salvation Army's downtown shelter. The Sally is the only facility that provides free shelter, free breakfast and dinner, and an opportunity to shower, and until mid-1985 it was the only shelter of any kind in town. Its liberal shelter policy also heightened homeless persons' dependence on it as a place to stay. Many shelters restrict lodgers to only two or three nights in a row, but the Sally has an open-door policy: admission is based on a first-come, first-served queue system and the willingness to abide by the Sally's few regulations. Homeless individuals can stay night after night, provided they queue up early enough to get their lodging

TABLE 1 *Organizational Responses and Perspectives*

Organizational Response	Operational Perspective	Local Organizational Carriers
Accommodative	Sustenance-oriented caretaker	Salvation Army Caritas Angels House Texas Employment Commission
Restorative	Treatment-oriented caretaker	
	Medical perspective	City hospital Mental health and mental retardation Detox units Substance treatment programs
	Salvationist perspective	Assembly of God church Detox units
Exploitative	Market-oriented	Plasma centers Labor pool Labor corner Bunkhaus
Exclusionist/Expulsionist	NIMBY* perspective	Neighborhood associations
Containment	Harassment	Police department

* "Not in my back yard"

ticket and provided they are sober at the time the door opens and do not have a history of "making trouble" on previous stays. This is not the ideal policy, of course. The social-service director told us that he tried to initiate "a program where a person is allowed to stay for only one week" and is then required to talk with the director "about his situation and come up with a cut-off date." But he conceded that the increasing number of homeless and "the pressure from the city to keep them off the streets" have made it difficult to institute such a program.

These considerations notwithstanding, the Sally actually shelters only a small proportion of the city's homeless. The reasons are threefold, having to do with space, atmosphere, and availability. The dormitory, built at a time when the need for shelter was not so pressing, has room for only twenty-two beds. These are given to the Sally's homeless employees, parolees from the Texas prison system, and occasionally, if there is room, "first nighters." All others are lodged in the recreation room, which is transformed into a sleeping area at night. The Sally can accommodate only around ninety homeless men and another

twenty homeless women and children. This dearth of shelter space becomes particularly problematic when the temperature begins to plummet. Recognizing the need for additional shelter, especially during the winter, in 1983 the city council opened a vacant warehouse for use as a makeshift shelter from December 1 to April 30. This provided shelter for around 350 homeless and was operated by the Sally. But the net gain was only 240 shelter spaces, since for lack of personnel to staff both places, the Sally closed its own shelter during this five-month period.

Except for an occasional cold, blustery day, however, the winter shelter is rarely filled to capacity. One reason for its unpopularity is its dreary, forbidding, almost ominous ambience. It is an old meat-packing warehouse with barren concrete walls, a roof that leaks, and iron rails along which sides of beef used to move still hanging from the ceiling. It makes occupants feel truly "warehoused" and reminds them of how far they have fallen. As one observer noted, "There's something ill-boding about down-and-out live men being housed in a building that in its better days was used to house dead animals."

What makes matters even worse is that many of the homeless sleep on two-by-six-foot mats that are too thin to protect them from the bone-chilling cold of the stained, cracked cement floor. The smell of chemicals used to sanitize the four Port-a-Boy johns pervades the warehouse, and a cloud of cigarette smoke hovers midway between the roof and the cement floor. The constant cacophony of coughs, hacks, and muffled talk, punctuated by an occasional scream, makes it impossible to sleep soundly. In fact, the warehouse is not regarded so much as a place to sleep as a temporary retreat from the elements, especially the rain and the cold. Because of such conditions, which a number of well-traveled homeless regarded as among the worst they had experienced, the winter shelter averaged only around 150 lodgers per night.

In Austin, as elsewhere, then, many of the homeless turn their backs on available shelter space. Most do so not because of insanity or judgmental incompetence, as some officials would have us believe, but because of the deplorable and often dehumanizing conditions in shelters. "Fuck it, man," replied one straddler when asked why he did not use the winter shelter, "the conditions at the dog pound are better than in there. I ain't no animal. Hell, I deserve better." Hidden in such comments is a more subtle but perhaps salient reason why the homeless often eschew shelters in favor of makeshift sleeping arrangements: they are exercising a bit of autonomy in a world in which their choices and options are highly constrained. . . .

Besides such social psychological considerations [another] limits the number of homeless the Sally shelters: its facilities are simply not open or available to all who seek to use them. Like Lazarus at the gate, some homeless are turned away. This is not really surprising. As do all people-processing and service organizations, the Sally must make choices about whom to assist, both because their resources are limited and because the orderly dispensation of services is contingent on client control. As the major in charge of the Sally commented:

I'll sleep and feed almost anybody, but such help requires that they be deserving. Some people would say I'm cold-hearted, but I rule with an iron hand. I have to because these guys need to respect authority. . . . The experience of working with these guys has taught us the necessity of rules in order to avoid problems.

Thus, the Sally tends to close its doors to the momentarily inebriated, the chronic drunks, and "the troublemakers," those who are deemed both undeserving and difficult to control. In actuality, only a small proportion of the homeless who knock at Sally's door fall into one or more of these categories. But some do, including a number of our key informants. Marilyn, for one, was occasionally denied access to the Sally because of drunkenness. And her friend Nona George, who is a chronic alcoholic, was banned for extended periods of time for both drunken and unruly behavior. In fact, she would boast on occasion that she had been "86'ed from the Sally for giving them a lot of shit."

For all of these reasons, then, the Sally shelters only a small proportion of the city's homeless—perhaps 10 to 20 percent on any given night. But it is the only inn in town, so to speak, so it is the place the homeless turn to when they are new to Austin, when they have been dislodged from their private sleeping arrangements by the police or construction crews, or when the weather turns bad. Even seasoned street veterans like Banjo and Gypsy Bill are driven in by the weather on occasion. One wet, snowy January day when the temperature hovered in the twenties and the Sally opened its rec room early, we found both Banjo and Gypsy, along with two hundred other homeless, bunched together in search of warmth. Banjo much preferred a weed patch or jungle to the Sally, but "the weather was just too damn nasty," he told us. And Gypsy, who customarily slept in his stranded car, "couldn't sleep all last night because of the cold." "I shivered all night," he said. "I didn't have enough blankets to keep warm."

Like bad weather, hunger drives some reluctant homeless into the Sally. As was noted previously, the Sally is the city's only provider of free breakfasts and dinners. In 1984 it served 122 breakfasts and 182 dinners per day. The meals are seldom eaten without complaint and speculation about their "actual" ingredients. One evening, for example, near-consensus was reached that what was alleged to be meat and mashed potatoes was really "Alpo and potatoes." But the meals are eaten, nonetheless, because they momentarily quiet the rumbling of empty stomachs and they are free.

Before relocation of the Sally became a political issue, the homeless would line up for dinner as early as they wanted. But pressure from neighbors of possible relocation sites prompted the Sally to improve its image by demonstrating that it could control its clients. One strategy was to restrict the times at which the homeless could line up for the evening meal. Before the restriction, often four to six men were sitting against the Sally's wall by 11:00 A.M. on Saturday (when food is not available elsewhere) or by 2:30 P.M. on a weekday. After the Sally's downtown location became an issue, the staff forbade the men to line up before 3:15 P.M. They were instructed to congregate instead in the parking lot across the street and wait until the major came out and gave them a nod. Twenty to forty men would then rush across the street to queue up.

Being at the front of the Sally dinner line means more than just getting an early dinner. It also guarantees a good spot for the night in the shelter. On a particularly busy night it may even make the difference between securing a place to stay in the shelter and not getting one. Those at the front of the dinner line also had a chance of showering at the Sally, until it changed its policy, opening the showers only to staff, families, and women staying overnight.

The Sally offers a few other services, such as free used clothes and shoes, and even some counseling for women and families, but for the most part, at least for unattached males, its services are limited to the provision of food and shelter. . . .

The homeless are keenly aware of [the] accommodative function and its insufficiency. As Tony Jones, a recently dislocated man from Chicago, observed as he was standing in the dinner line one evening, "The Sally doesn't really do anything for these people. It just gives 'em something to eat and a place to sleep, but it doesn't really help them get off the streets." Echoing Tony's sentiments, Banjo observed that "everybody's back in the same spot in the morning as they were the night before, because the Sally don't do anything here but give people food and a place to sleep." Banjo had a solution. An ardent, born-again Christian, Banjo saw salvation as the answer. "People need something to put their faith in, but most street people don't have anything," he preached. "They're like shifting sand. But God is solid rock." The problem, as Banjo saw it, was that the Sally had abandoned its mission. Instead of saving souls and giving the homeless "something to put their faith in," the Sally was merely "feeding and sleeping."

Neither the major nor the Sally's social services director would take exception to Banjo's lament. On the contrary, this disjunction between their idealized mission and what they were actually doing was a constant source of frustration. They could rationalize it by pointing to the growing imbalance between the demand for assistance and available facilities and resources, but the fact remained that they were conducting "little more than a turn-key operation" that left their clients standing in "shifting sand."

Many of the homeless, including most of the recently dislocated, would be hard-pressed to survive were it not for the food and shelter provided by these agencies. But the fact remains that these services are basically accommodative: they help the homeless endure life on the streets rather than escape it.

Restorative Response

A second set of organizations that deal with a segment of the homeless approach them primarily from a treatment-oriented rather than a sustenance-oriented perspective. Their general aim is to attend to actual or perceived physiological, psychological, or spiritual problems that are seen as impeding their clients' functioning. The response these caretaker organizations make to the homeless is more rehabilitative than accommodative. Examples of such institutions include mental hospitals, outpatient mental-health facilities, regular hospitals, drug and alcohol rehabilitation clinics, detoxification facilities, various counseling services, and some skid row-like missions that make access contingent on participation in salvationist rituals. In Austin, at least four caretaker organizations or agency complexes fall into this treatment-oriented category. They include the city's major hospital, the state's mental health and mental retardation facilities, several detoxification facilities and substance-treatment programs, and the homeless outreach program of the Central Assembly of God Church.

None of these treatment-oriented caretaker facilities is concerned with the problem of homelessness per se. Rather, their attention is focused on homeless individuals and the problems they are perceived as having, be they physiological, psychological, characterological, or spiritual in origin. Agency personnel recognize that many of the homeless are on the streets because of socioeconomic forces beyond their control. Even the head preacher of the homeless ministry at the Assembly of God church conceded that some of the homeless he knows "are on the streets because of social circumstances." But this group, often referred to as the "new poor" or "the new and temporary homeless," is seldom seen as comprising more than 20 to 30 percent of the homeless. The majority are seen as riddled with physical or mental problems, interactional incompetencies, and characterological flaws. Such a view is not surprising. Not only do these remedial caretaker organizations see some homeless who indeed suffer from such problems, but since the agencies have neither the mandate nor the wherewithal to alter socioeconomic forces, they are unlikely to focus on such issues. What they can do, however, is exactly what they do: treat individual ailments, whether actual or perceived, or arrange for such treatment.

This commonality notwithstanding, these caretaker organizations espouse a variety of treatment-oriented ideologies. At one extreme, as is noted in the middle column of Table 1, is the medical model or perspective, and at the other is the salvationist or conversionist orientation. The former see many of the problems of the homeless as symptomatic of illness or at least as treatable within a medical framework. The salvationists, by contrast, identify the issue as one of moral weakness and spiritual degeneration. The city hospital and mental-health facilities approach the homeless from a medical standpoint, whereas the Assembly

of God church is almost purely salvationist. The several detoxification facilities slide on this continuum, but tend to be skewed toward the salvationist orientation.

These remedial caretaker organizations also vary in the scope of their aims. Some seek only to repair debilitating physical ailments as quickly and cheaply as possible so that the client can be sent on his or her way, typically back to the social niche from which he or she came. This is the approach taken by the city hospital, where the vast majority of the homeless are seen on an outpatient basis, typically in the emergency room, and then sent back onto the streets. This pattern of contact is clearly reflected in our tracking data. As is indicated in Table 2, which shows the distribution of hospital contacts among the homeless in the tracking sample, 94 percent of the 174 homeless with one or more contacts received outpatient treatment in the emergency room; in other words, they were treated and released. In contrast, fewer than 25 percent received inpatient treatment; that is, less than a quarter ever stayed overnight in a hospital bed.

The kinds of contacts these homeless had are at least partially explicable by the sorts of problems that sent them to the hospital: cuts and abrasions (20 percent), followed in descending order by alcohol- and drug-related ailments (13 percent), fractures and sprains (12 percent), and skin infections (11 percent). However, although such ailments are acute rather than chronic, there is little question but that the healing process would be expedited if some homeless with these ailments were hospitalized. Marilyn's experience with a broken ankle provides a case in point. She slipped on ice one wintry January evening while on her way to a motel room she and four other homeless were renting for the night. The next day she went to the city hospital and was diagnosed as having a sprained ankle. The ankle was taped and she was sent on her way with instructions to stay off her feet. Such directions are difficult enough for the domiciled to follow; when a person is homeless and her feet are her primary mode of transportation, they are impossible. Not surprisingly, then, Marilyn returned to the hospital a few days later complaining of persistent pain. Her ankle was examined again and rediagnosed as

TABLE 2 *Nature of City Hospital Contacts Among the Homeless*

Type of Contact	Homeless Persons with Contact in Each Category		Total Contacts in Each Category	
	(N: 174) No.	%*	(N: 508) No.	%
Inpatient/nonemergency (*regular admission*)	(15)	8.6	(19)	3.7
Inpatient/emergency (*admission through emergency*)	(25)	14.4	(31)	6.1
Outpatient/emergency	(163)	93.7	(401)	78.9
Hospital clinics	(23)	13.2	(57)	11.2

* Total for this column is more than 100 percent because many of the homeless had contacts in more than one category.

broken. It was placed in a cast and she was again sent on her way, albeit with crutches this time. Clearly her ankle would have benefited more from several days of bed rest than from beating the pavement to and from the hospital. But hospitalization, even just for a bed, is quite expensive, so the homeless and other indigents are dealt with as outpatients.

Exceptions occur, of course, as when an acquaintance of Marilyn's, nicknamed Giggles, was hospitalized for several days before she died of cirrhosis of the liver. Giggles was obviously in a life-threatening situation, and it is in such situations that the homeless are most likely to be hospitalized. But we suspect that the number who are seriously ill is far greater than the number who are admitted to a hospital bed. For one thing, the homeless tend not to be very attentive to their physical condition until they are incapacitated, as Marilyn was, or gravely ill, as was Giggles. Physical complaints that prompt remedial action by the domiciled, middle-class citizen are likely to be ignored by the homeless. Not only do the needs of daily subsistence seem more pressing, but medical facilities that treat the homeless are not always within easy walking distance. Thus, Tom Fisk had deep, infected cuts on his right hand for several days before he went to the hospital. Gypsy Bill ignored an infection on one hand until it began to move up his arm. He was diagnosed as having a staph infection, given some antibiotics, and sent back onto the streets. And a young female hippie tramp failed for some time to seek medical attention for a severe leg infection. She had initially broken an ankle and had had a cast put on it at the city hospital. When she was sleeping rough shortly afterward, fire ants crawled into the cast and infected her encased foot. The end result was gangrene and several weeks in the hospital.

Such hospitalizations are rare, though, not only for the reasons indicated above but also because the hospital is disinclined to keep the homeless overnight because they are financial liabilities. According to one of the hospital's administrators, the homeless cannot pay their own way, they find it difficult to qualify for medical financial assistance because of residency requirements, and the funds provided by the city to help cover the hospital's "indigent" debt have not kept pace with the city's growing indigent population and its utilization of the hospital. Consequently, the hospital tries to avoid inpatient care for the homeless except in life-threatening situations. Still, 81 percent of the total cost of treatment for the homeless in 1984 was in the inpatient category, even though fewer than 25 percent of the homeless who received medical care from the hospital received such treatment.

In practice, then, the hospital has dealt with the homeless in a Band-Aid, revolving-door fashion, quickly dispensing remedial assistance and sending them back onto the streets. And, in time, many return for further treatment, as is indicated by the fact that 50 percent of the homeless in our sample with hospital contact had at least two contacts and 26 percent had four or more contacts.

A similar short-term, revolving-door pattern is evident in the relationship between the homeless and the state's psychiatric hospital system and local mental-health centers. This pattern is due in no small part to the outpatient orientation of the local catchment center, but it also surfaces upon inspection of the length and frequency of institutionalization of the homeless within the state hospital system. Of the eighty-four homeless in the tracking sample who were institutionalized one or more times, two-thirds were hospitalized for less than thirty days, and none stayed longer than three months. The frequency of these commitments, which were voluntary in nearly 60 percent of the cases, ranged from one to fifteen, with two-thirds having one or two commitments. The remaining third experienced a revolving-door pattern of brief, repeated voluntary stays—entering from the streets and exiting back to the streets.

Lance McCay's experience is illustrative. During the four-year period between September, 1980, and October, 1984, Lance was institutionalized on fourteen different occasions. Nine of the commitments were for seven days or less, two were for one to two weeks, and four were for between one and three months. Jorge Herrera's record is less clear, but he, too, was institutionalized within the state hospital system on numerous occasions between 1966 and 1974. What is more, both Lance and Jorge continued to be obviously mentally ill, whatever the diagnostic criteria used.

Contact between the homeless and the mental health system is not extensive, at least not in Austin. All told, 16 percent of the tracking sample had one or more contacts with this system: eighty-four with the state institutions, seventy-eight with the local outpatient center, and thirty-eight with both. Clearly, the mental health system does not figure as prominently in the subculture of street life as either the accommodative street agencies or the city hospital. But it still casts a shadow over the lives of around a sixth of the homeless. It tends to be revolving-door contact, though, like that with the city hospital, characterized by a brief encounter, often followed by a series of visits.

Moreover, any treatment is of the stop-the-bleeding rather than cure-the-wound variety. Some of the homeless in need are attended to, but they are not so much cured as restored to a level of physical or psychic functioning that allows them to limp back to the streets. . . .

[Another] set of restorative caretaker organizations that affect the lives and routines of some of the homeless are the drug and alcohol rehabilitation facilities. Of the four such facilities in the area, two deal almost exclusively with the homeless. One is an in-town facility operated by the Salvation Army; the other, a rural facility operated by a private, nonprofit corporation. Both facilities provide residential treatment for chronic inebriates, especially of the traditional tramp and bum varieties. The majority of the clients of each facility are older than the average street person, and they are long-term alcoholics. Many of them, according to the head of the Salvation Army rehabilitation facility, "come into the program in rough physical shape . . . with ulcers, parasites, and broken bones that haven't healed right and need attention." Even more damaging, she emphasized, is that "they have all sunk into moral turpitude as alcohol has taken control of their lives." Or, as the ex-alcoholic in charge of day operations at the rural facility described his constituency, "They are real down-and-outers." As a consequence, he added, "This is not a place for virgins."

The treatment programs at both facilities are AA-oriented and thus are skewed toward the salvationist perspective. This quickly appears at the Salvation Army's evening meetings, where much of the time is spent discussing the "second step" of the AA doctrine: "Believe that a power greater than ourselves can restore us to sanity." Such a step may not be easy. One of the men we came to know, a fellow in his mid-thirties named Alvin, complained that he was "just unable to take that leap of faith." He was not the only homeless person to express such reservations. Still, these detox and rehab facilities, as they are commonly called on the streets, provide a place to dry out and regain a modicum of health. Thus, when the homeless leave, they typically are better off physically than when they arrived.

Yet these rehab programs are only partially successful at best. They restore their clients' health so that they can function physically, but they seldom provide the resources or training their clients need in order "to get back into society." Consequently, clients often end up back on the streets after being discharged. . . . Moreover, once back on the streets, they quickly return to their old ways and frequently end up in another detox program. The day operator of the rural rehab facility told us that "most of the men who are here have been in and out of treatment program after program." We had sensed this anyway, especially after getting to know Shotgun, Hoyt, Nona, and Willie Hastings, all of whom have experienced that revolving door.

Like the city hospital [and] mental health facilities, the detox and rehab facilities seem more effective at dispensing palliatives than curatives. In each case, an attempt is made to restore the physical, mental, or spiritual health of the homeless sufficiently to return them to the streets in better shape than they were in when they entered the facility. But these restorative agencies, whether their treatment is medically or spiritually based, seem to do little to help their clients climb back into the domiciled world. They are, then, only restorative in part and thus complement the more accommodative caretaker agencies.

Exploitative Response

A third set of organizational actors that cater to the homeless do so from a market-oriented perspective. This perspective, unlike the caretaker perspectives, shows little authentic concern with the welfare of the homeless. Rather, the homeless are commodified as sources of cheap labor and plasma or are approached as just another set of consumers. In either case, the homeless become objects of economic exploitation.

Several commercial organizations in Austin deal with the homeless in this fashion. The two plasma centers near the university clearly fall into this category, as do the two downtown day-labor operations, one sanctioned by the city and the other run by a Houston-based corporation.

The Houston-based company also operates the Bunkhaus, a hundred-bed barracks-style boarding house in east Austin, about three miles from its downtown day-labor operation, the Labor Pool.

Although the Bunkhaus is a late addition to the institutional sector of the city's street subculture, it quickly came to be favored by some of the homeless as a place to stay at night because it has showers available and has fewer restrictions than the Salvation Army. The men can bring beer into the boarding house and drink while watching the color cable television, and they sleep on army-style bunks instead of mats. There is a catch, though. It costs $6.50 per night. This amount, insignificant for most working nonhomeless, means a good deal to the homeless, for whom work is unsteady and wages are minimal. Nonetheless, the Bunkhaus is generally full. The lights go out at 10:00 P.M. and on at 5:00 A.M. Free coffee is served from 5:00 to 5:30, and a van is available for a ride downtown to the Labor Pool, where the men can sign on for day-labor jobs.

In return, the corporation siphons off a portion of the wages earned by those lucky enough to secure a job for the day. A van awaits those who want to return to the Bunkhaus for the night. Thus, if a homeless person grosses $15.00 for four to five hours of work, his net after the Labor Pool takes out income tax, Social Security, and other deductions and the $6.50 for the Bunkhaus is a little less than $5.50, barely enough for dinner and a couple of beers or a bottle of "Thunder Chicken" or "Mad Dog 20/20." When the $6.50 extracted for the Bunkhaus is added to the money the Labor Pool received from the employers for the labor exchange services provided, it becomes clear that the company is conducting a profitable business. Indeed, it is already operating in three other Texas cities, and the manager has commented, "We're doing so well that we're planning to expand to other cities!"

The plasma centers also find the homeless to be a source of profit, as do those building contractors and other industries who hire the homeless for day labor. This exploitative response is not without some benefit to the homeless, though. A cheap place to sleep and money, albeit minimal, for giving blood or working by the day facilitate the daily survival of the homeless. But the exchange relationship is uneven and exploitative: money is being made off of the homeless at a rate that is seemingly far greater than the value they receive in return.

Exclusionist/Expulsionist Response

In whatever city the homeless find themselves, their daily routines and survival options are likely to be affected by a political climate that slides on a continuum ranging from generosity to hostility. At one end of the scale, the homeless are objects of sympathy who are seen as victims of social forces and bad luck. At the other, they are objects of fear and scorn who are thought to have chosen this way of life and who therefore should be run out of town or at least constrained ecologically so that they do not contaminate respectable citizens. Both orientations can be found in most communities, and which sentiment predominates is likely to vary over time. But at any particular moment within a given community, the political climate with respect to the homeless is likely to be skewed in one direction or the other. If it is in the direction of sympathy, the homeless are likely to feel more welcome and to have greater latitude for pursuing their survival routines. If hostility rules, then they are likely to feel less welcome and to have less elbow room for making do. Either attitude is likely to affect their survival routines.

In Austin, the dominant sentiment and corresponding political climate became increasingly hostile as the city's homeless population began to mount in the early 1980s and the pending relocation of the Salvation Army shelter became a community issue. Outcroppings of something other than sympathetic concern for the homeless first surfaced in 1982, when City Hall began to receive a steady flow of complaints from business proprietors around the Salvation Army shelter and from citizens using the nearby park system along the river. One of the more persistent complainants, a real estate broker whose office was several blocks east of the Sally, related that although he knew "the homeless have their problems," they also "create big problems," especially "when you get hundreds of them together hanging out in the same area. They shit in the bushes. They steal and sleep in our yard and on our porch, and they hassle the customers. You name it," he complained, "we've had it." To strengthen his case, he took us on a tour of his property, pointing out the sleeping "nests" the homeless made in the bamboo and weeds and even the scattered piles of feces where they had relieved themselves.

At the urging of this complainant and other concerned citizens, in the spring of 1983 the city formulated its initial Task Force on the Homeless. Its appointed members included four business proprietors and representatives from the Sally, the police department, Caritas, TEC, and three other social-service agencies. Its chair, who also headed the Greater Austin Track Club, had gotten involved because he "was sick and tired of being hassled by the homeless while running along the river." Six months later the task force issued a list of recommendations, including establishment of a controlled day-labor pick-up site; strict enforcement of city ordinances that prohibit sleeping in public places, begging, and public intoxication; construction of a minimum-security detention center for persons arrested on misdemeanors such as public intoxication; and establishment of a temporary winter shelter. Taken together, the recommendations seemed aimed at controlling and segregating the city's homeless population. The task force was not oblivious to the needs of the homeless, but, according to one of its members, it felt that "there's a real danger of doing too much." As this individual explained, "Word travels fast in the underground of street people. Austin has a problem because of a good climate and the abundance of work anyway. So if we provide good social services the word will get out, and pretty soon . . . trouble."

Trouble over the homeless was already beginning to percolate within the community, but it was hardly due to the provision of services. With only one legitimate street shelter, one soup kitchen, and a mid-morning sandwich spot, Austin's street services for the homeless were meager in comparison to those available in other cities of similar size. Instead, the rumblings of citizen unrest were over the pending relocation of the Salvation Army.

The Sally had to move not only because the building was too small but also because its weathered appearance was out of step with the glittering redevelopment of much of the downtown. Moreover, the land it sat on was coveted by developers, one of whom eventually bought the lot for $1,500,000—$750,000 cash plus title to 3.74 acres several miles south of the downtown but still within the city.

The path to a new site was thorny, engendering rancorous community opposition as it wound its way through one prospective neighborhood after another before ending up back in the downtown area within a block of the city police station. Underlying citizen opposition to the "frightening possibility" of the Sally relocating nearby was the repeatedly voiced fear that "thousands of womanless, homeless men" would inundate their neighborhoods and "rob their homes" and "rape the women." Thus, in one prospective neighborhood, signs were hung on doors asking, "Do you want your women raped and your children mauled?" In another, residents appeared before the city council carrying placards that read "Vagrance [*sic*] and kids don't mix" and gave testimony highlighting the threat to women and children posed by the homeless. One neighborhood resident emphasized "how the neighborhoods will be unfit for raising children," and another angrily asked the council whether they understood the "impact these womanless men will have on schoolchildren, on women, and on families." The local Catholic university located adjacent to one of the prospective sites joined the resistance, similarly framing its opposition in terms of the danger the homeless posed to its students. As the chairman of the university's board of trustees emphasized on three different occasions at one board meeting: "We have to be able to reassure the thousand coeds on campus, and I don't think we can."

Such beliefs and fears were succinctly rationalized by a prominent local resident in one of her occasional columns written for the city newspaper:

> What the good people of Austin and everywhere have come to fear are the unpredictable ones who have joined the vast army of the indigent and who are being dumped on Sally as the last resort. I speak of the young, strong, but stoned druggies whose next move may be robbery, assault, or murder . . . [and] the criminals dumped by the justice system from overcrowded prisons and jails and left to prey on the innocent, just as they did before incarceration. Salvation Army is not to blame because the nature of the clientele has changed from the hobo of the 1930's

to the wino of the 1950's to the unpredictable stranger of the 1980's. But neither are the upstanding citizens of Austin to be blamed for looking over their shoulders.

Thus, the dominant local perception of the homeless evolved from one that portrayed them as public nuisances whose routines interfered with those of other citizens to one that framed them as dangerous criminals who threatened the lives and property of others, particularly women and children. The result was a decline in sympathy for the homeless and the emergence of an exclusionist/expulsionist response that said, "Don't put the homeless in my backyard, and if they're already there, get rid of them." For the homeless, this meant a darkening of the cloud that already hung over their heads, a corresponding narrowing of their survival options, and increased official attentiveness to some of their daily routines. Shotgun, the traditional tramp who had traveled widely, was street-smart, and claimed to "have a sense about these things," related one morning at the outset of the Sally furor, "the police here used to be less into hassling street people than in other places I've been. But I've got this funny feeling that something's about to happen, like the police are going to start coming down on people."

Containment Response

Shotgun's premonition was grounded not only in the contentious political climate spawned by local neighborhood associations but also in the increased vigilance of the police. The police were not particularly enthused about getting involved in this political issue, however. For one thing, there was reluctance to deal with "the wider social problems." One of the officers in charge of the uniform patrol division made this clear on several occasions. He emphasized that "it stretches our responsibility and resources to have to deal with problems like homelessness." There was also a sense that whatever the police did, "it won't be enough as long as this Sally thing is an issue." But, most important, the police were keenly aware that neighborhood claims and fears had little empirical substance. Their own preliminary figures on crime among the homeless who had been arrested revealed that only 5 percent were arrested for felonies, around 62 percent for public intoxication, and the remaining 33 percent for other misdemeanors. Thus, at one of the initial meetings of the city's second Task Force on the Homeless a perceptive police officer explained, "The problem with the homeless . . . is not necessarily how criminal they are, but how the public perceives them to be criminal. What is actually true and what the public feels or is afraid of may be two different things." And indeed they were. But neighborhood assertions drowned out the actual facts, pressuring the police into greater vigilance toward the homeless.

Like most police work, the police response toward the homeless was essentially reactive, in that it was conducted in response to calls for increased vigilance. But it was conducted, not on behalf of the homeless, but for the benefit of other citizens who were the primary complainants. This distinction was not lost on the homeless. Hoyt, who worked at the Sally, often complained about the treatment he thought the homeless received relative to other groups. He told us a number of times, "We can call the cops down at the Sally, and it takes them forty-five minutes to get there." To illustrate, he related the following instance:

> Did you see the fight here a couple of weeks ago with the James Gang [the redneck tramps]? . . . About forty-five minutes after the police were called, they arrived. And there's a fight out there in the middle of Second Avenue, stopping traffic for fifteen minutes or so. In other parts of town, the police would come faster, you know. Guys on the streets see that and they don't think it's fair. They got their own problems, you know. It's no wonder a lot of them hate the cops!

Marilyn's sentiments were similar, as the following excerpt from our field notes shows:

> As we were walking in the vicinity of the Sally early this morning, we spotted Marilyn from a distance. She had on a pair of baggy, ragged jeans, and she was limping worse than the last time we saw her. When we got closer, we could see that her face was swollen. She seemed in pretty bad shape, and we thought

she might have just come off a long drunk. But she was stone sober. She greeted us, then shook her head dispiritedly and stretched out her arms for us to look at. There were two open wounds the size of dimes on her left arm, and both arms were scraped. We asked her what had happened. She said she was "jumped the other night by three men." She "was walking back from Brackenridge to find a place to sleep for the night when three men hanging out in front of Twin Liquors followed me and drug me into an alley." There "they stripped off my clothes, beat and kicked me, and robbed me of twenty-five bucks, a necklace, and my watch." They also "put cigarettes out on my arms." When we asked whether she had reported the incident to the police, she said she "never even considered it. The law wouldn't do anything anyway. They'd just say I'm a tramp and let it go. The law won't help a tramp."

Many of the homeless, then, seemed to see themselves as victims rather than beneficiaries of police work. This is not surprising, considering the other characteristic feature of the police response to the homeless. It is captured by the word *containment*. Applied to the homeless, containment is a mode of response that seeks to minimize the threat they pose to the sense of public order by curtailing their mobility or ecological range and by reducing their public visibility. Its aim, as one police officer put it in an offhand way, "is to keep the homeless out of the face of other citizens."

The police department pursued this objective through four interconnected lines of action. One entailed stricter enforcement of existing ordinances regarding begging, public intoxication, and disorderly conduct, coupled with an appeal to City Hall to pass ordinances prohibiting both the use of city land between 12:00 midnight and 5:00 A.M. and "sleeping in any public place, vehicle, or building not designated for overnight sleeping." In order to assure enforcement of these ordinances, the police asked for both additional manpower and a minimum-security detention center to avoid overcrowding the city jail with persons arrested on misdemeanor charges. This latter request seemed especially reasonable in the light of police statistics suggesting that most homeless arrests were for misdemeanors and the fact that violations of the existing and proposed ordinances are misdemeanors. The most visible outcomes of the requests, though, were an increase in the number of foot patrolmen and the addition of a mounted patrol in the downtown area, concentrated on the revitalized Sixth Street strip of bars and honky-tonk clubs that functioned as the hub of the city's night life and on the Drag, where the hippie tramps hung out. Plainclothesmen were also dispatched to the Drag.

The result was a more enthusiastic and focused vigilance that smacked of harassment. Whether the harassment was attributable to officially formulated policy or to overly zealous and unconstrained street officers is unclear. That it occurred, though, seems incontestable. Not only was it felt by the homeless, but we too observed it rather frequently. Late one afternoon at the south end of the Drag, for example, we saw a panhandler, to whom we had just given some change, shoved up against a sign by two preppily dressed young men. Thinking they were a couple of college students harassing the guy, we ran over to them to intervene. As we approached, they pulled out their police IDs and told us, "Get out of here if you don't want to be a part of it." They then proceeded to empty the man's pockets and frisk him, whereupon one of them said, "What do you think you're doing, asking me if I want to fight? Now pick up your stuff and get off my street." We followed them into a nearby convenience store to press them a bit about what had just transpired. They were obviously uninterested in talking, but they did say they were undercover police officers whose job was "to arrest transients on the Drag." They justified their aggressive action in this case by claiming the guy had "tried to pick a fight" with them—a reversal of what had actually happened.

On another occasion, when we were sitting on the ledge outside the Sally talking with Pat Manchester and some other homeless, we observed a similar instance of questionable police action:

Several police cars pulled up in response to a call from the Sally about a troublesome drunk.

Two officers got out and were greeted by a couple of guys working at the Sally. They pointed out the drunk, who was propped up against the building. The police told the man to get up and put his hands on his head. After he struggled to his feet, the police frisked him. As he was being frisked the drunk stepped on one of the officer's shoes. The officer shook his head and told the guy, who was too inebriated to understand, "Well, now you did it. . . . Now I'm going to have to get you for assault." This statement wasn't lost on the other homeless, one of whom said, "Man, that's tight. Step on a cop's shoe and he gets you for assault." The other officer, apparently wanting to get some action too, came over to the rest of us on the ledge and told us, "Get up, turn around, and put your hands on the ledge." He then proceeded to frisk us.

In this and the previous episode we see police action toward the homeless that is unprovoked and excessive, and that seemingly disregards the issue of culpability. Previous research on police work on skid row has noted that although "it is well known that policemen exercise discretionary freedom in invoking the law," the exercise of such discretion was particularly pronounced on skid row where there was little regard for questions of culpability and heightened ad hoc decision making. These observations apply equally to police work we observed among the homeless, with the addendum that it often had a flavor of harassment.

All of these police behaviors were experienced one evening when one of us was arrested with two homeless males near Sixth Street, in the downtown area. As we were sitting under a bridge on the bank of the creek with a couple of open cans of beer, two police officers approached. They demanded identification and asked about our places of residence. When the two homeless men were unable to provide IDs and admitted having stayed at the Salvation Army, they were immediately arrested and handcuffed for violation of the city's ordinance prohibiting open containers of alcohol near the Sixth Street area. The researcher, who had provided an ID and a local address, was simply told to leave the area. It was only after he protested the arrest that the researcher was arrested too. The arresting officer informed him, "I was going to let you go because you're cleaner than they are and you have a place to stay." On another occasion, riding with a downtown beat officer for a night, one of us witnessed several university students having alcohol confiscated but not being arrested for the same open-container violation.

These contrasting experiences underscore the discretionary and ad hoc nature of much police work, as well as its harassment of the homeless. Whether these measures had the effect of containing the homeless to a smaller area is difficult to determine. But they most certainly made the homeless more circumspect about where they roamed, hung out, and slept. Hoyt, who had been on the streets in several cities, including Dallas, was particularly sensitive to the furor over relocation of the Sally and to the harassments of the police. He commented one afternoon, "It looks like we're going to have to be looking over our shoulders more now than ever before. It used to be that Austin didn't have a bad reputation on the streets. But it ain't that way anymore. It's getting as bad as Dallas."

Summary

The essence of the subculture of street life, we have suggested, resides not so much in a distinctive set of cherished values as in a shared fate and the adaptive behaviors and routines the homeless fashion in order to deal with that fate. But those adaptive behaviors and routines are not fashioned willy-nilly. Rather, they are embedded in and structured by a set of organizational [and] political constraints that constitute the cornerstones of the subculture of street life. In this chapter we have identified and examined these constraining cornerstones as they materialized in Austin, and we have provided glimpses of the daily routines and experiences of the homeless as they are filtered through or affected by these constraints.

THINKING ABOUT THE READINGS

Savage Inequalities in America's Schools

- What do you suppose would happen if a student from a place like East St. Louis were to attend school in a place like Rye? Or vice versa? At one point in the reading, one of the students from Rye says, "You can take them out of the environment, but you can't take the environment out of them." Do you agree or disagree with that assessment of the problem of unequal education? Do you think this is a common attitude? Does it enhance or impede progress regarding poverty in this country?

The Subculture of Street Life

- How do you respond to the contention that some organizations that may, on the surface, be designed to help homeless people actually perpetuate the problem? Use the conflict and functionalist perspectives to describe the relationship between homeless people and the organizations described in this selection.

CHAPTER 12

The Architecture of Inequality
Race and Ethnicity

Social class isn't the only thing that influences people's opportunities and life chances. From its inception, the United States has been bitterly divided along racial and ethnic lines. Racial inequality is both a personal and structural phenomenon. It is lodged in individual prejudice and discrimination on the one hand and in our language, collective beliefs, and important social institutions on the other.

It is sometimes difficult for those of us who have never suffered the indignity of racial discrimination to appreciate the destructive power of such experiences. In "Invisible Man," Lawrence Otis Graham, a black, Harvard-educated lawyer goes undercover as a busboy in an all-white country club to provide a first-hand account of face-to-face racism. The author, in the traditional sense of the word, has "made" it in American society. He's well-educated, wealthy, and has a prestigious job; he's married to a woman with the same qualities. Yet with all those credentials he is excluded from elite institutions where, like Domhoff's "Bohemian Grove" in chapter 10, important connections and deals are made. His story is a powerful and vivid portrait of the continuing significance of race in American society.

There is no denying that the United States is becoming more racially and ethnically diverse. Such a change is having a dramatic impact on our social institutions. *Multiculturalism* is perhaps the most controversial word in the field of education today. To some it is a long-awaited correction of the omissions and distortions that typically characterized the histories and experiences of Americans of color. To others, however, it symbolizes not only an unfortunate break with tradition (usually referred to as "Western culture") but an extreme and silly bow toward political correctness that will surely weaken an already weak educational system and ultimately place Americans at a competitive disadvantage in the international marketplace. Both sides of the issue work hard to dramatize their respective beliefs. In "The Moral Drama of Multicultural Education," Shan Nelson-Rowe examines how the campaign to promote multicultural education uses melodramatic rhetorical devices to influence public perception.

In "Racism and Research" Allan Brandt describes a vivid historical example of *institutional* racism—discriminatory treatment built into the day-to-day functioning of large social institutions. Because of commonly held beliefs on the part of public health officials and medical researchers in the 1930s about the sexual proclivities of poor Southern blacks, hundreds of men were denied treatment for their syphilis as part of an experiment run by the government to better understand the health complications that result during the final phase of the disease. What makes this research particularly troublesome is that the men "participated" in it without their knowledge or consent. Treatment that could have easily cured them was purposely withheld.

Invisible Man

Why This Harvard-Trained Lawyer Went Undercover as a Busboy at an All-White Connecticut Country Club

Lawrence Otis Graham

I drive up the winding lane past a long stone wall and beneath an archway of sixty-foot maples. At one bend of the drive, a freshly clipped lawn and a trail of yellow daffodils slope gently up to the four-pillared portico of a white Georgian colonial. The building's six huge chimneys, the two wings with slate gray shutters, and the white-brick facade loom over a luxuriant golf course. Before me stands the one-hundred-year-old Greenwich Country Club—*the* country club—in the affluent, patrician, and very white town of Greenwich, Connecticut, where there are eight clubs for fifty-nine thousand people.

I'm a thirty-year-old corporate lawyer at a Midtown Manhattan firm, and I make $105,000 a year. I'm a graduate of Princeton University (1983) and Harvard Law School (1988), and I've written ten nonfiction books. Although these might seem like impressive credentials, they're not the ones that brought me here. Quite frankly, I got into this country club the only way that a black man like me could—as a $7-an-hour busboy.

After seeing dozens of news stories about Dan Quayle, Billy Graham, Ross Perot, and others who either belonged to or frequented white country clubs, I decided to find out what things were really like at a club where I heard there were no black members.

I remember stepping up to the pool at a country club when I was ten and setting off a chain reaction: Several irate parents dragged their chil-

dren out of the water and fled. When the other kids ran out of the pool, so did I—foolishly thinking that there was something in the water that was going to harm all of us. Back then, in 1972, I saw these clubs only as places where families socialized. I grew up in an affluent white neighborhood in Westchester, and all my playmates and neighbors belonged to one or more of these private institutions. Across the street, my best friend introduced me to the Westchester Country Club before he left for Groton and Yale. My teenage tennis partner from Scarsdale introduced me to the Beach Point Club on weekends before he left for Harvard. The family next door belonged to the Scarsdale Golf Club. In my crowd, the question wasn't "Do you belong?" It was "Where?"

My grandparents owned a Memphis trucking firm, and as far back as I can remember, our family was well off and we had little trouble fitting in even though I was the only black kid on the high school tennis team, the only one in the orchestra, the only one in my Roman Catholic confirmation class.

Today, I'm back where I started—on a street of five- and six-bedroom colonials with expensive cars and neighbors who all belong somewhere. Through my experiences as a young lawyer, I have come to realize that these clubs are where businesspeople network, where lawyers and investment bankers meet potential clients and arrange deals. How many clients and deals am I going to line up on the asphalt parking lot of my local public tennis courts?

This piece appeared as a cover story for *New York* magazine, August 17, 1992.

I am not ashamed to admit that I one day want to be a partner and a part of this network. When I talk to my black lawyer or investment-banker friends or my wife, a brilliant black woman who has degrees from Harvard College, Harvard Law School, and Harvard Business School, I learn that our white counterparts are being accepted by dozens of these elite institutions. So why shouldn't we—especially when we have the same credentials, salaries, social graces, and ambitions?

My black Ivy League friends and I know of black company vice presidents who have to ask white subordinates to invite them out for golf or tennis. We talk about the club in Westchester that rejected black Scarsdale resident and millionaire magazine publisher Earl Graves, who sits on *Fortune* 500 boards, owns a Pepsi distribution franchise, raised three bright Ivy League children, and holds prestigious honorary degrees. We talk about all the clubs that face a scandal and then run out to sign up one quiet, deferential black man who will accept a special "limited-status" membership, remove the taint, and deflect further scrutiny.

I wanted some answers. I knew I could never be treated as an equal at this Greenwich oasis—a place so insular that the word *Negro* is still used in conversation. But I figured I could get close enough to understand what these people were thinking and why country clubs were so set on excluding people like me.

MARCH 28 TO APRIL 7, 1992
I invented a completely new résumé for myself. I erased Harvard, Princeton, and my upper-middle-class suburban childhood from my life. So that I'd have to account for fewer years, I made myself seven years younger—an innocent twenty-three. I used my real name and made myself a graduate of the actual high school I attended. Since it would be difficult to pretend that I was from "the street," I decided to become a sophomore-year dropout from Tufts University, a midsize college in suburban Boston. My years at nearby Harvard and the fact that my brother had gone there had given me enough knowledge about the school to pull it off. I contacted some older friends who owned large companies and restaurants in the Boston and New York areas and asked them to serve as references.

I was already on a short leave of absence from my law firm to work on a book.

I pieced together a wardrobe that consisted of a blue polyester blazer, white oxford shirt, ironed blue slacks, black loafers, and a horrendous pink, black, and silver tie, and I set up interviews at clubs. Over the telephone, five of the eight said that I sounded as if I would make a great waiter. During each of my phone conversations, I made sure that I spoke to the person who would make the hiring decision. I also confirmed exactly how many waiter positions were available, and I arranged a personal interview within forty minutes to an hour of the conversation, just to be sure that they could not tell me that no such job was available.

"We don't have any job openings—and if you don't leave the building, I will have to call security," the receptionist said at the first club I visited in Greenwich.

I was astounded by the speed with which she made this remark, particularly when I saw that she had just handed an application to a young-looking Hispanic man wearing jeans, sneakers, a T-shirt, and sunglasses. "I'm here to see Donna, your maître d'," I added defensively as I forced a smile at the pasty-looking woman who sat behind a window.

"There's no Donna here."

"But I just spoke to her thirty minutes ago and she said to come by to discuss the waiter job."

"Sorry, but there are no jobs and no one here named Donna."

After convincing the woman to give me an application, I completed it and then walked back into the dining room, which was visible from the foyer.

I came upon a white male waiter and asked him, "Is there a Donna here?"

"The maître d'?" he asked. "Yeah, she's in the kitchen."

When I found Donna and explained that I was the one she had talked to on the phone forty minutes earlier, she crossed her arms and shook her head. "You're the 'Larry' I talked to on the phone?"

"Yes," I answered.

"No way."

"I beg your pardon," I said.

"No. No way," she said while refusing to take the application I waved in front of her.

"We just talked on the phone less than an hour ago. You said I sounded perfect. And I've waited in three different restaurants—I've had two years of college—You said you had five waiter jobs open—I filled out the application—I can start right away—"

She still shook her head. And held her hands behind her back—unwilling to even touch my application. "No," she said. "Can't do it."

My talking did no good. It was 1992. This was the Northeast. If I hadn't been involved, I would never have believed it. I suddenly thought about all the times I quietly disbelieved certain poor blacks who said they had tried to get jobs but no one would hire them. I wanted to say then and there, "Not even as a waiter?"

Only an hour earlier, this woman had enthusiastically urged me to come right over for an interview. Now, as two white kitchen workers looked on, she would only hold her hands tightly behind her back and shake her head emphatically. So I left.

There were three other clubs to go to. When I met them, the club managers told me I "would probably make a much better busboy."

"Busboy? Over the phone, you said you needed a waiter," I argued.

"Yes, I know I said that, but you seem very alert, and I think you'd make an excellent busboy instead."

In his heavy Irish brogue, the club manager said he needed to give me a "perception test." He explained it this way: "This ten-question test will give us an idea of your perception, intellectual strength, and conscious ability to perform the duties assigned to you as a busboy."

I had no idea how much intellectual strength and conscious ability (whatever that meant) could be required of a busboy, but here are some of the questions he asked me:

1. If there are three apples and you take two away, how many do you have?

2. How many of each species of animal did Moses put on his new ark?

3. It's 1963 and you set your digital clock to ring at 9:00 A.M. when you go to bed at 8:00 P.M. How many hours will you sleep?

4. If a house gets southern exposure on all four sides, what color is the bear that walks by the house?

And the responses . . .

1. I answered "one apple" because I thought this was a simple math question, as in "three minus two equals one," but the correct answer was "two" because, as the manager said, "You've got to think, Larry—if you take away two apples and put them in your pocket, you've got two apples, not one."

2. Fortunately, I answered this question as it was presumably designed to smoke out any applicants who hadn't been raised in a Judeo-Christian culture. It was Noah, not Moses, who built an ark.

3. I scored major credibility points here by lying and saying, "Wow, I wasn't even born yet in 1963. . . ." The "right" answer was that there were no digital clocks in 1963. I took his word for it.

4. Although I believed that a house could get southern exposure on all four sides only at the South Pole—and thus the bear had to be a white polar bear—I was told that I was "trying to act too smart" and that all bears are, of course, brown.

APRIL 8 TO 11

After interviewing for advertised waiter jobs at five clubs, I had gotten only two offers—both for non-waiter jobs. One offer was to split my time as a towel boy in the locker room and a busboy in the dining room. The second offer—which followed a callback interview—was to work as a busboy. When I told the club manager that I had only wanted a waiter job, he responded, "Well, we've discussed it here and everyone would feel more comfortable if you took a busboy job instead."

"But I've never worked as a busboy," I reminded him.

He nodded sympathetically. "People here have decided that it's busboy or nothing."

Given these choices, I made my final job selection in much the way I had decided on a college and a law school: I went for prestige. Not only was the Greenwich Country Club celebrating its hundredth anniversary but its roster boasted former president Gerald Ford, baseball star Tom Seaver, former Securities and Exchange Commission chairman and U.S. ambassador to the Netherlands John Shad, as well as former Timex spokesman John Cameron Swayze. Add to that a few dozen *Fortune* 500 executives, bankers, Wall Street lawyers, European entrepreneurs, a Presbyterian minister, and cartoonist Mort Walker, who does *Beetle Bailey*. (The Greenwich Country Club did not respond to any questions about the club and its members.)

For three days, I worked on my upper-arm muscles by walking around the house with a sterling-silver tray stacked high with heavy dictionaries. I allowed a mustache to grow in, then added a pair of arrestingly ugly Coke-bottle reading glasses.

APRIL 12 (SUNDAY)
Today was my first day at work. My shift didn't start until 10:30 A.M., so I laid out my clothes at home: a white button-down shirt, freshly ironed cotton khaki pants, white socks, and white leather sneakers. I'd get my official club uniform in two days. Looking in my wallet, I removed my American Express Gold Card, my Harvard Club membership ID, and all of my business cards.

When I arrived at the club, I entered under the large portico, stepping through the heavy doors and onto the black-and-white checkerboard tiles of the entry hall.

A distracted receptionist pointed me toward Mr. Ryan's office. (*All names of club members and personnel have been changed*.) I walked past glistening silver trophies and a guest book on a pedestal to a windowless office with three desks. My new boss waved me in and abruptly hung up the phone.

"Good morning, Larry," he said with a sufficiently warm smile. The tight knot in his green tie made him look more fastidious than I had remembered from the interview.

"Hi, Mr. Ryan. How's it going?"

Glancing at his watch to check my punctuality, he shook my hand and handed me some papers. "Oh, and by the way, where'd you park?"

"In front, near the tennis courts."

Already shaking his head, he tossed his pencil onto the desk. "That's off-limits to you. You should always park in the back, enter in the back, and leave from the back. No exceptions."

"I'll do the forms right now," I said. "And then I'll be an official busboy."

Mr. Ryan threw me an ominous nod. "And Larry, let me stop you now. We don't like that term busboy. We find it demeaning. We prefer to call you busmen."

Leading me down the center stairwell to the basement, he added, "And in the future, you will always use the back stairway by the back entrance." He continued to talk as we trotted through a maze of hallways. "I think I'll have you trail with Carlos or Hector—no, Carlos. Unless you speak Spanish?"

"No." I ran to keep up with Mr. Ryan.

"That's the dishwasher room, where Juan works. And over here is where you'll be working." I looked at the brass sign. MEN'S GRILL.

It was a dark room with a mahogany finish, and it looked like a library in a large Victorian home. Dark walls, dark wood-beamed ceilings. Deep-green wool carpeting. Along one side of the room stood a long, highly polished mahogany bar with liquor bottles, wineglasses, and a two-and-a-half-foot-high silver trophy. Fifteen heavy round wooden tables, each encircled with four to six broad wooden armchairs padded with green leather on the backs and seats, broke up the room. A big-screen TV was set into the wall along with two shelves of books.

"This is the Men's Grill," Mr. Ryan said. "Ladies are not allowed except on Friday evenings."

Next was the brightly lit connecting kitchen. "Our kitchen serves hot and cold foods. You'll work six days a week here. The club is closed on Mondays. The kitchen serves the Men's Grill and an adjoining room called the Mixed Grill. That's where the ladies and kids can eat."

"And what about men? Can they eat in there, too?"

This elicited a laugh. "Of course they can. Time and place restrictions apply only to women and kids."

He showed me the Mixed Grill, a well-lit, pastel-blue room with glass French doors and white wood trim.

"Guys, say hello to Larry. He's a new busman at the club."

I waved.

"And this is Rick, Stephen, Drew, Buddy, and Lee." Five white waiters dressed in white polo shirts with blue "1892" club insignias nodded while busily slicing lemons.

"And this is Hector, and Carlos, the other busmen." Hector, Carlos, and I were the only nonwhites on the serving staff. They greeted me in a mix of English and Spanish.

"Nice to meet all of you," I responded.

"Thank God," one of the taller waiters cried out. "Finally—somebody who can speak English."

Mr. Ryan took me and Carlos through a hall lined with old black-and-white portraits of former presidents of the club. "This is our one hundredth year, so you're joining the club at an important time," Mr. Ryan added before walking off. "Carlos, I'm going to leave Larry to trail with you—and no funny stuff."

Standing outside the ice room, Carlos and I talked about our pasts. He was twenty-five, originally from Colombia, and hadn't finished school. I said I had dropped out, too.

As I stood there talking, Carlos suddenly gestured for me to move out of the hallway. I looked behind me and noticed something staring down at us. "A video camera?"

"They're around," Carlos remarked quietly while scooping ice into large white tubs. "Now watch me scoop ice."

After we carried the heavy tubs back to the grill, I saw another video camera pointed down at us. I dropped my head.

"You gonna live in the Monkey House?" Carlos asked.

"What's that?"

We climbed the stairs to take our ten-minute lunch break before work began. "Monkey House is where workers live here," Carlos said.

I followed him through a rather filthy utility room and into a huge white kitchen. We got on line behind about twenty Hispanic men and women—all dressed in varying uniforms. At the head of the line were the white waiters I'd met earlier.

I was soon handed a hot plate with two red lumps of rice and some kind of sausage-shaped meat. There were two string beans, several pieces of zucchini, and a thin, broken slice of dried meat loaf that looked as if it had been cooked, burned, frozen, and then reheated. Lurking at the very edge of my dish was an ice-cream-scoop-sized helping of yellowish mashed potatoes.

I followed Carlos, plate in hand, out of the kitchen. To my surprise, we walked back into the dank and dingy utility room, which turned out to be the workers' dining area.

The white waiters huddled together at one end of the tables, while the Hispanic workers ate quietly at the other end. Before I could decide which end to integrate, Carlos directed me to sit with him on the Hispanic end.

I was soon back downstairs working in the grill. At my first few tables, I tried to avoid making eye contact with members as I removed dirty plates and wiped down tables and chairs. Having known so many people who belonged to these clubs, I was sure I'd be recognized by someone from childhood, college, or work.

At around 1:15, four men who looked to be in their mid- to late fifties sat down at a six-chair table. They pulled off their cotton windbreakers and golf sweaters.

"It's these damned newspeople that cause all the problems," said golfer number one, shoving his hand deep into a popcorn bowl. "These Negroes wouldn't even be thinking about golf. They can't afford to join a club, anyway."

Golfer number two squirmed out of his navy blue sweater and nodded in agreement. "My big problem with this Clinton fellow is that he apologized." As I stood watching from the corner of the bar, I realized the men were talking about then-governor Bill Clinton's recent apology for playing at an all-white golf club in Little Rock, Arkansas.

"Holt, I couldn't agree with you more," added golfer number three, a hefty man who was biting off the end of a cigar.

"You got any iced tea?" golfer number one asked as I put the silverware and menus around the table. Popcorn flew out of his mouth as he attempted to speak and chew at the same time.

"Yes, we certainly do."

Golfer number three removed a beat-up Rolex from his wrist. "It just sets a bad precedent. Instead of apologizing, he should try to discredit them—undercut them somehow. What's to apologize for?" I cleared my throat and backed away from the table.

Suddenly, golfer number one waved me back to his side. "Should we get four iced teas or just a pitcher and four glasses?"

"I'd be happy to bring whatever you'd like, sir."

Throughout the day, I carried "bus buckets" filled with dirty dishes from the grill to the dishwasher room. And each time I returned to the grill, I scanned the room for recognizable faces. Fortunately, I saw none. After almost four hours of running back and forth, clearing dishes, wiping down tables, and thanking departing members who left spilled coffee, dirty napkins, and unwanted business cards in their wake, I helped out in the coed Mixed Grill.

"Oh, busboy," a voice called out as I made the rounds with two pots of coffee. "Here, busboy. Here, busboy," the woman called out. "Busboy, my coffee is cold. Give me a refill."

"Certainly, I would be happy to." I reached over for her cup.

The fiftyish woman pushed her hand through her straw blond hair and turned to look me in the face. "Decaf, thank you."

"You are quite welcome."

Before I turned toward the kitchen, the woman leaned over to her companion. "My goodness. Did you hear that? That busboy has diction like an educated white person."

A curly-haired waiter walked up to me in the kitchen. "Larry, are you living in the Monkey House?"

"No, but why do they call it that?"

"Well, no offense against you, but it got that name since it's the house where the workers have

lived at the club. And since the workers used to be Negroes—blacks—it was nicknamed the Monkey House. And the name just stuck—even though Negroes have been replaced by Hispanics."

APRIL 13 (MONDAY)

I woke up and felt a pain shooting up my calves. As I turned to the clock, I realized I'd slept for eleven hours. I was thankful the club was closed on Mondays.

APRIL 14 (TUESDAY)

Rosa, the club seamstress, measured me for a uniform in the basement laundry room while her barking gray poodle jumped up on my feet and pants. "Down, Margarita, down," Rosa cried with pins in her mouth and marking chalk in her hand. But Margarita ignored her and continued to bark and do tiny pirouettes until I left with all of my new country-club polo shirts and pants.

Today, I worked exclusively with the "veterans," including sixty-five-year-old Sam, the Polish bartender in the Men's Grill. Hazel, an older waitress at the club, is quick, charming, and smart—the kind of waitress who makes any restaurant a success. She has worked for the club nearly twenty years and has become quite territorial with certain older male members. Whenever I was on my way to hand out menus or clear dishes at a table, Hazel would either outrun me or grab me by the arm when she saw that the table contained important male members. Inevitably, Hazel would say, "Oh, Larry, let me take care of Dr. Collingsworth. You go fill this salt shaker," or "Larry, I'll take Judge Wilson's dirty dish. You go slice some lemons in the kitchen," or "Larry, I'll clean up Reverend Gundersen's cracker crumbs. You go find some peanut oil."

During a lull, Sam, who I swear reminded me of a Norman Lear creation circa 1972, asked me to run out and get some supplies from a Mr. Chang.

"Who is Mr. Chang?" I asked.

"You know, the Chinaman. Mr. Chang."

I had recalled seeing an elderly Asian man with a gray uniform in the halls, but we had not been introduced.

"And where would I find him?"

"He's down at the other end of the hall beyond the stairs." Sam handed me a list of items on a printed form. "He's the Chinaman and it's easy to remember 'cause he's right next to the laundry room."

Hector came along and warned me not to lose the signed form because I could be accused of stealing food and supplies if the signed list wasn't given to Mr. Chang.

Down a dark, shadowy hall, we found Mr. Chang, who, in Spanish, shouted phrases at me while swinging his arms in the air.

"Do you understand him?" I asked Hector.

"He said to follow him and bring a cart."

We followed the methodical Mr. Chang from storage room to storage room, where he pulled out various items like a magician. Lemons were stored with paper goods, cans of ketchup were stored with pretzels and simultaneously served as shelves for large sacks of onions. Bottles of soda were stored with old boxes that had "Monkey House" written on them. Combustible popcorn oil and boxes of matches were stored with Styrofoam cups in the furnace room. It was all in a disorder that seemed to make complete sense to Mr. Chang.

Back in the Mixed Grill, members were talking about hotel queen and Greenwich resident Leona Helmsley, who was on the clubhouse TV because of her upcoming prison term for tax evasion.

"I'd like to see them haul her off to jail," one irate woman said to the rest of her table. "She's nothing but a garish you-know-what."

"In every sense of the word," nodded her companion as she adjusted a pink headband in her blondish white hair. "She makes the whole town look bad. The TV keeps showing those aerial shots of Greenwich and that dreadful house of hers."

A third woman shrugged her shoulders and looked into her bowl of salad. "Well, it is a beautiful piece of property."

"Yes, it is, except for those dreadful lampposts all over the lawn," said the first woman. "But why here? She should be in those other places like Beverly Hills or Scarsdale or Long Island, with the rest of them. What's she doing here?"

Woman number three looked up. "Well, you know, *he's* not Jewish."

"Really?"

"So that explains it," said the first woman with an understanding expression on her tanned forehead. "Because, you know, the name didn't sound Jewish."

The second woman agreed: "I can usually tell."

APRIL 15 (WEDNESDAY)

Today, we introduced a new, extended menu in the two grill rooms. We added shrimp quesadillas ($6) to the appetizer list—and neither the members nor Hazel could pronounce the name of the dish or fathom what it was. One man pounded on the table and demanded to know which country the dish had come from. He told Hazel how much he hated "changes like this. I like to know that some things are going to stay the same."

Another addition was the "New Dog in Town" ($3.50). It was billed as knockwurst, but one woman of German descent sent the dish back: "This is not knockwurst—this is just a big hot dog."

As I wiped down the length of the men's bar, I noticed a tall stack of postcards with color photos of nude busty women waving hello from sunny faraway beaches. I saw they had been sent from vacationing members with fond regards to Sam or Hazel. Several had come from married couples. One glossy photo boasted a detailed frontal shot of a red-haired beauty who was naked except for a shoestring around her waist. On the back, the message said, *Dear Sam, Pull string in an emergency. Love always, The Atkinson Family.*

APRIL 16 (THURSDAY)

This afternoon, I realized I was learning the routine. I was fairly comfortable with my few "serving" responsibilities and the rules that related to them:

- When a member is seated, bring out the silverware, cloth napkin, and a menu.

- Never take an order for food, but always bring water or iced tea if it is requested by a member or waiter.

- When a waiter takes a chili or salad order, bring out a basket of warm rolls and crackers along with a scoop of butter.

- When getting iced tea, fill a tall glass with ice and serve it with a long spoon, a napkin on the bottom, and a lemon on the rim.

- When a member wants his alcoholic drink refilled, politely respond, "Certainly, I will have your waiter come right over."

- Remember that the member is always right.

- Never make offensive eye contact with a member or his guest.

- When serving a member fresh popcorn, serve to the left.

- When a member is finished with a dish or glass, clear it from the right.

- Never tell a member that the kitchen is out of something.

But there were also some "informal" rules that I discovered (but did not follow) while watching the more experienced waiters and kitchen staff in action:

- If you drop a hot roll on the floor in front of a member, apologize and throw it out. If you drop a hot roll on the floor in the kitchen, pick it up and put it back in the bread warmer.

- If you have cleared a table and are 75 percent sure that the member did not use the fork, put it back in the bin with the other clean forks.

- If, after pouring one glass of Coke and one of diet Coke, you get distracted and can't remember which is which, stick your finger in one of them to taste it.

- If a member asks for decaffeinated coffee and you have no time to make it, use regular and add water to cut the flavor.

- When members complain that the chili is too hot and spicy, instead of making a new batch, take the sting out by adding some chocolate syrup.

- If you're making a tuna on toasted wheat and you accidentally burn one side of the bread, don't throw it out. Instead, put the tuna on the burned side and lather on some extra mayo.

APRIL 17 (FRIDAY)

Today, I heard the word "nigger" four times. And it came from someone on the staff.

In the grill, several members were discussing Arthur Ashe, who had recently announced that he had contracted AIDS through a blood transfusion.

"It's a shame that poor man has to be humiliated like this," one woman golfer remarked to a friend over pasta-and-vegetable salad. "He's been such a good example for his people."

"Well, quite frankly," added a woman in a white sun visor, "I always knew he was gay. There was something about him that just seemed too perfect."

"No, Anne, he's not gay. It came from a blood transfusion."

"Ohh," said the woman. "I suppose that's a good reason to stay out of all those big-city hospitals. All that bad blood moving around."

Later that afternoon, one of the waiters, who had worked in the Mixed Grill for two years, told me that Tom Seaver and Gerald Ford were members. Of his brush with greatness, he added, "You know, Tom's real first name is George."

"That's something."

"And I've seen O. J. Simpson here, too."

"O. J. belongs here, too?" I asked.

"Oh, no, there aren't any black members here. No way. I actually don't even think there are any Jews here, either."

"Really? Why is that?" I asked.

"I don't know. I guess it's just that the members probably want to have a place where they can go and not have to think about Jews, blacks, and other minorities. It's not really hurting anyone. It's really a WASP club. . . . But now that I think of it, there is a guy here who some people think is Jewish, but I can't really tell. Upstairs, there's a Jewish secretary too."

"And what about O. J.?"

"Oh, yeah, it was so funny to see him out there playing golf on the eighteenth hole." The waiter paused and pointed outside the window. "It never occurred to me before, but it seemed so odd to see a black man with a golf club here on this course."

APRIL 18 (SATURDAY)

When I arrived, Stephen, one of the waiters, was hanging a poster and sign-up sheet for a soccer league whose main purpose was to "bridge the ethnic and language gap" between white and Hispanic workers at the country clubs in the Greenwich area. I congratulated Stephen on his idea. He said he was tired of seeing the whites and Hispanics split up during meals, breaks, and evening activities. "We even go to separate bars and diners," he explained. "I think a weekly soccer game might bring us all closer together."

Later, while I was wiping down a table, I heard a member snap his fingers in my direction. I turned to see a group of young men smoking cigars. They seemed to be my age or a couple of years younger. "Hey, do I know you?" the voice asked.

As I turned slowly toward the voice, I could hear my own heartbeat. I was sure it was someone I knew.

"No," I said, approaching the blond cigar smoker. He had on light green khaki pants and a light yellow V-neck cotton sweater adorned with a tiny green alligator. As I looked at the other men seated around the table, I noticed that all but one had alligators on their sweaters or shirts. Each one of them was a stranger to me.

"I didn't think so. You must be new—what's your name?"

"My name is Larry. I just started a few days ago."

The cigar-smoking host grabbed me by the wrist while looking at his guests. "Well, Larry, welcome to the club. I'm Mr. Billings. And this is Mr. Dennis, a friend and new member."

"Hello, Mr. Dennis," I heard myself saying to a freckle-faced young man who puffed uncomfortably on his fat roll of tobacco.

The first cigar smoker gestured for me to bend over as if he were about to share some important confidence. "Now, Larry, here's what I want you to do. Go get us some of those peanuts and then give my guests and me a fresh ashtray. Can you manage that?"

My workday ended at 4:20.

EVENING OF APRIL 18 (SATURDAY)

After changing back into my street clothes at around 8:00 P.M., I drove back to the club to get together with Stephen and Lillie, two of the friendlier waiters (and the only ones willing to socialize with a busboy), in Stephen's room on the grounds. We sat, ate Hostess donuts, drank wine, watched the Saturday-night NBC-TV lineup, and talked about what it would be like to be a rich member of the club.

Squeezed into the tiny room and sitting on the bed, which was pushed against the wall, we each promised to look out for and warn the others if anyone else tried to backstab us in the grill. Stephen was talking about his plans for the intercultural soccer league and what it could do for all eight clubs in the area.

"After spending a couple semesters in Japan," Stephen explained, "I realized how afraid Americans are of other cultures." Stephen told me that he was working at the club to pay for the rest of his college education. He was taking a two-year break between his sophomore and junior years at a midwestern university, where he was majoring in Japanese.

Lillie talked about the formal dinner that she had just worked at that evening. It was then that I learned she was half South American. Her father, who was from Colombia, was an outdoor groundskeeper at the club. "I'm taking college courses now," she explained. "And maybe I'm crazy to say this, but I think I'd like to go into broadcasting." Given her nearly flawless English and her very white skin, I wondered if the members were aware of her Hispanic background. She felt very strong about her South American heritage, and she often acted as interpreter for some of the club workers who spoke only Spanish.

They were both such nice people, I felt terrible for intruding under such fraudulent circumstances.

APRIL 19 (SUNDAY)

It was Easter Sunday, and the Easter-egg hunt began with dozens of small children scampering around the tulips and daffodils while well-dressed parents watched from the rear patio of the club. A giant Easter bunny gave out little baskets filled with jelly beans to parents and then hopped over to the bushes, where he hugged the children. As we peered out from the closed blinds in the grill, we saw women in mink, husbands in gray suits, children in Ralph Lauren and Laura Ashley. Hazel let out a sigh. "Aren't they beautiful?" she said. For just a moment, I found myself agreeing.

"So, Larry." Sam laughed as I poured fresh oil into the popcorn machine's heated pan. It was my second day at the machine in the Men's Grill. "When you decide to move on from the club, you'll be able to get yourself a job at the popcorn counter in one of those big movie theaters."

I forced a smile.

"And you can tell them," he continued, "that you just about have a master's degree in popcorn popping. Tell 'em you learned everything you know from Sam at the country club."

I laughed. "Sure, Sam."

"Yeah, tell them I awarded you a master's degree."

I had already become an expert at yucking it up with Sam.

As I raced around taking out orders of coffee and baskets of hot rolls, I got a chance to see groups of families. The men seemed to be uniformly taller than six feet. Most of them were wearing blue blazers, white shirts, and incredibly out-of-style silk ties—the kind with little blue whales or little green ducks floating downward. They were bespectacled and conspicuously clean-shaven.

The "ladies," as the club prefers to call them, almost invariably had straight blond hair. Whether or not they had brown roots and whether they were twenty-five or forty-eight, they wore their hair blond, straight, and off the face. No dangling earrings, five-carat diamonds, or designer handbags. Black velvet or pastel headbands were de rigueur.

There were also groups of high-school kids who wore torn jeans, sneakers, or unlaced L.L. Bean shoes, and sweatshirts that said things like "Hotchkiss Lacrosse" or "Andover Crew." At one table, two boys sat talking to two girls.

"No way, J.C.," one of the girls cried in disbelief while playing with the straw in her diet Coke.

The strawberry blond girl next to her flashed her unpainted nails in the air. "Way. She said that if she didn't get her grades up by this spring, they were going to take her out altogether."

"And where would they send her?" one of the guys asked.

The strawberry blonde's grin disappeared as she leaned in close. "Public school."

The group, in hysterics, shook the table. The guys stomped their feet.

"Oh, my God, J.C., oh, J.C., J.C.," the diet-Coke girl cried.

Sitting in a tableless corner of the room beneath the TV set was a young, dark-skinned black woman dressed in a white uniform and a thick wool coat. On her lap was a baby with silky white blond hair. The woman sat patiently, shifting the baby in her lap while glancing over to where the baby's family ate, two tables away.

I ran to the kitchen, brought back a glass of tea, and offered it to her. The woman looked up at me, shook her head, and then turned back to the gurgling infant.

APRIL 21 (TUESDAY)

The TV in the Men's Grill was tuned to one of the all-day cable news channels and was reporting on the violent confrontations between pro-choice marchers and right-to-life protesters in Buffalo, New York.

"Look at all those women running around," a man in his late forties commented as he sat by himself at one of the larger tables in the Men's Grill.

At 11:10 A.M., the grill wasn't even officially opened yet.

As I walked around doing a final wipe of the tables, the man cried out into the empty room. "That's just a damned shame," he said while shaking his head and pulling at his yellow polo shirt in disbelief.

I nodded as he looked at me over his bowl of peanuts. "I agree with you."

He removed his sun visor and dropped it onto a table closer to the television. We both watched images of police dragging women who lay sprawled in the middle of a Buffalo city street.

"You know, it just scares me to see all these women running around like that," the middle-aged member continued as we both watched screaming crowds of placard-carrying activists and hand-cuffed protesters. "Someone's gotta keep these women reined in. A good, hard law that forces them to have those babies when they get pregnant will teach them to be responsible."

I looked at the man as he sat there hypnotized by the screen.

"All this equal rights bull," he finally added. "Running around getting pregnant and then running around doing what they want. Enough to make you sick."

Later, while Hector and I stood inside a deep walk-in freezer, we scooped balls of butter into separate butter dishes and talked about our life plans. "Will you go finish school sometime?" he asked as I dug deep into a vat of frozen butter.

"Maybe. In a couple years, when I save more money, but I'm not sure." I felt lousy about having to lie.

"Maybe? If I had money, I'd go now—and I'm twenty-three years old." He shook his head in disapproval. "In my country, I had education. But here I don't because I don't know much English. It's tough because we have no work in South America. And here, there's work, but you need English to get it and make money."

We agreed that since 75 percent of the club employees were Spanish-speaking South Americans, the club really needed a bilingual manager or someone on staff who understood their concerns.

"Well," I offered. "I'll help you with English if you teach me some Spanish."

He joked that my Spanish was a lot worse than his English. After all, I only knew the words *gracias, buenos días,* and *por favor.* So, during an illegal twelve-minute break, he ran through a quick vocabulary lesson while we walked to his minuscule room just across the sweaty congested halls of the noisy squash courts.

The room that he took me into overlooked the driving range and was the size of a walk-in closet. The single bed touched three walls of the room. The quarter-sized refrigerator served as a stand for a stereo. There were a small dresser and small desk plastered with many different pictures of a young Spanish-looking woman and a cute baby girl.

"My family" is all Hector would say in explanation while simultaneously pushing me out of the room and into the sweaty hall. "We go now—before we lose our job."

Just as we were all leaving for the day, Mr. Ryan came down to hand out the new policies for those who were going to live in the Monkey House. Amazingly, without a trace of discomfort, he and everyone else referred to the building as "the Monkey House." Many of the workers had been living temporarily in the squash building. Since it had recently been renovated, the club was requiring all new residents to sign the form. The policy

included a rule that forbade employees to have overnight guests. Rule 14 stated that the club management had the right to enter an employee's locked bedroom at any time, without permission and without giving notice.

As I was making rounds with my coffeepots, I overheard a raspy-voiced woman talking to a mother and daughter who were thumbing through a catalog of infants' clothing.

"The problem with au pairs is that they're usually only in the country for a year."

The mother and daughter nodded in agreement.

"But getting one that is a citizen has its own problems. For example, if you ever have to choose between a Negro and one of these Spanish people, always go for the Negro."

One of the women frowned, confused. "Really?"

"Yes," the raspy-voiced woman responded with cold logic, "Even though you can't trust either one, at least the Negroes can speak English and follow your directions."

Before I could refill the final cup, the raspy-voiced woman looked up at me and smiled. "Oh, thanks for the refill, Larry."

APRIL 22 (WEDNESDAY)
"This is our country, and don't you forget it. They came here and have to live by our rules!" Hazel pounded her fist into the palm of her pale white hand.

I had made the mistake of telling her I had learned a few Spanish phrases to help me communicate better with some of my coworkers. She wasn't impressed.

"I'll be damned if I'm going to learn or speak one word of Spanish. And I'd suggest you do the same," she said. She took a long drag on her cigarette while I loaded the empty shelves with clean glasses.

Today, the TV was tuned to testimony and closing arguments from the Rodney King police-beating trial in California.

"I am so sick of seeing that awful videotape," one woman said to friends at her table. "It shouldn't be on TV."

At around two, Lois, the club's official secretary, asked me to help her send out a mailing to six hundred members after my shift. It seemed that none of the waiters wanted to stay late. And since the only other choice was the non-English-speaking bus staff and dishwashers, I was it.

She took me up to her office on the main floor and introduced me to the two women who sat with her.

"Larry, this is Marge, whom you'll talk with in three months, because she's in charge of employee benefits."

I smiled at the brunette.

"And Larry, this is Sandy, whom you'll talk with after you become a member at the club, because she's in charge of members' accounts."

Both Sandy and I looked up at Lois with shocked expressions.

Lois winked, and at the same moment, the three jovial women burst out laughing.

Lois sat me down at a table in the middle of the club's cavernous ballroom and had me stamp "Annual Member Guest" on the bottom of small postcards and stuff them into envelopes.

As I sat in the empty ballroom, I looked around at the mirrors and the silver-and-crystal chandeliers that dripped from the high ceiling. I thought about all the beautiful weddings and debutante balls that must have taken place in that room. I could imagine members asking themselves, "Why would anybody who is not like us want to join a club where they're not wanted?"

I stuffed my last envelope, forgot to clock out, and drove back to the Merritt Parkway and into New York.

APRIL 23 (THURSDAY)
"Wow, that's great," I said to Mr. Ryan as he posted a memo entitled "Employee Relations Policy Statement: Employee Golf Privileges."

After quickly reading the memo, I realized this "policy" was a crock. The memo opened optimistically: "The club provides golf privileges for staff. . . . Current employees will be allowed golf privileges as outlined below." Unfortunately, the only employees the memo listed "below" were department heads, golf-management personnel, teaching assistants, the general manager, and "key staff that appear on the club's organizational chart."

At the end of the day, Mr. Ryan handed me my first paycheck. Perhaps now the backbreaking work would seem worthwhile. When I opened the envelope and saw what I'd earned—$174.04 for five days—I laughed out loud.

Back in the security of a bathroom stall, where I had periodically been taking notes since my arrival, I studied the check and thought about how many hours—and how hard—I'd worked for so little money. It was less than one-tenth of what I'd make in the same time at my law firm. I went upstairs and asked Mr. Ryan about my paycheck.

"Well, we decided to give you $7 an hour," he said in a tone overflowing with generosity. I had never actually been told my hourly rate. "But if the check looks especially big, that's because you got some extra pay in there for all of your terrific work on Good Friday. And by the way, Larry, don't tell the others what you're getting, because we're giving you a special deal and it's really nobody else's business."

I nodded and thanked him for his largesse. I stuffed some more envelopes, emptied out my locker, and left.

The next morning, I was scheduled to work a double shift. Instead, I called and explained that I had a family emergency and would have to quit immediately. Mr. Ryan was very sympathetic and said I could return when things settled down. I told him, "No, thanks," but asked that he send my last paycheck to my home. I put my uniform and the key to my locker in a brown padded envelope, and I mailed it all to Mr. Ryan.

Somehow it took two months of phone calls for me to get my final paycheck ($123.74 after taxes and a $30 deduction for my uniform).

I'm back at my law firm now, dressed in one of my dark gray Paul Stuart suits, sitting in a handsome office thirty floors above Midtown. While it's a long way from the Monkey House, we still have a long way to go.

The Moral Drama of Multicultural Education

Shan Nelson-Rowe

Multicultural education is a social movement within education that seeks to transform the organization, practice, and ideological content of schooling. More specifically, the movement calls for greater cultural diversity in matters of curriculum, pedagogy, faculty, and other educational issues. Multicultural educators view themselves as representing subordinate cultural groups within schools in a challenge to the dominance of an institutional elite.

. . . I examine how multicultural educators in particular have created identities that reflect a melodramatic view of the moral order, with victims, villains, and heroes. . . .

The melodrama is one kind of moral order typically constructed by social problems claimsmakers, including multicultural educators as I will show. In the melodramatic moral order, the principal identities are those of victim, villain, and hero. Melodramas portray power relations, interests, values, and motives in terms of good and evil, weak and strong characters (see Table 1). Victims are completely powerless to confront the villain, and need to be rescued or protected by the heroes. Villains are unremittingly evil and heroes are paragons of virtue. Villains pursue their victims

out of selfishness and malevolence. Heroes are altruistically motivated by their benevolent values. . . .

Multicultural education (MCE) means different things to different people. The root idea, however, is that the United States contains culturally diverse groups, each with its own traditions, customs, and ways of living. Rather than viewing cultural diversity as a problem to be solved by creating a unified national culture, via "Anglo-conformity" or a "melting pot," multiculturalists see a resource to be preserved and celebrated. The problem, from their perspective, is that educational leaders in the United States traditionally have suppressed minority cultures because they viewed them as deficient next to the dominant Anglo-American culture. Multiculturalists claim the suppression of diversity leads minority pupils, who find their languages and heritages denigrated, to develop negative self-images and perform poorly in school. "Monocultural" education also perpetuates racial and ethnic tensions in society. To multiculturalists, the need for MCE is growing as demographic trends, including immigration, birth, and death rates, cause a decline in the Anglo-American population relative to

TABLE 1 *The Melodramatic Moral Order*

	Victim	Villain	Hero
Power	Weak	Strong	Strong
Interest	Overcoming domination	Dominating the weak	Preventing domination
Values	Positive	Negative	Positive
Motives	Alienated	Selfish	Altruistic

TABLE 2 *The Moral Drama of Multicultural Education*

	Victim **Culturally Different Students**	Villain **Anglocentric Schools**	Hero **Multicultural Educators**
Power	Powerless in the face of school authorities	Powerful use of institutional resources	Powerful use of pedagogical knowledge and techniques
Interest	Developing ethnic pride and self-esteem	Maintenance of power and privilege in the status quo	General concern for human survival and welfare of subordinate groups
	Recognizing Anglo-centric schools as cause of problems	Narrow self-interest	Altruistic
Values	Love of learning	Antidemocratic Racist WASP cultural superiority	Democracy Individual freedom Interracial harmony
Motives	Alienated indifference to school brought on by official ignorance and denigration of cultural diversity, and lack of MCE	Able but unwilling to make changes that would afford culturally different students a positive education	Able and willing to act in a morally responsible fashion to promote cultural diversity, equality, and MCE

Hispanic-, African-, and Asian-Americans. MCE advocates claim the reforms they promote are of paramount importance. This brief definition of MCE cannot do justice to the variety of beliefs about what it is and why it is necessary, but it does capture what the various reformers have in common.

Even in this rough sketch of the multiculturalists' position, we begin to see the identities they impute to themselves and others. For example, "educational leaders" have the power to suppress minority cultures. MCE rhetoric also involves claims about the power, interests, values, and motives of multiculturalists and others engaged in multicultural reform. Multiculturalists' discourse also constructs three principal collective identities—"culturally different students" as victims, "Anglocentric schools" as villains, and "multicultural educators" as protectors (see Table 2).

Casting "Culturally Different Students" as Victims

The most salient attribute MCE reformers assign to school children, especially those from ethnic and racial minority groups, is their powerlessness within schools. In his pioneering monograph, Jack Forbes described "Negroes, Indians, and Mexican-Americans and other racial-cultural minorities" as "guinea pigs for 'experiments' in monocultural, monolingual, 'vacuum ideology,' 'compensatory education'" (Forbes 1969:16). The National Catholic Education Association (1983:3) criticized the failure of education to match "reality" and "ideals, particularly in its treatment of the poor and powerless." This criticism highlights what multiculturalists view as the schools' dominant tendency to impose Anglo-American culture on all students regardless of their own cultural backgrounds.

Cultural imposition impedes the development of positive self-images among minority children. This is a crucial problem in American education, according to proponents of MCE, who tend to view self-esteem, ethnic or racial pride, and success in school as intimately bound together. "Culturally different students," writes one MCE advocate, "need to know that they are a legitimate part of society" (Baker 1983:45). Curricula, textbooks, and other school characteristics that exclude or denigrate racial and ethnic heritages send students "a message that does little to enhance self-esteem," says another reformist (Johnson 1991:4). . . . Disputes exist among MCE activists about how to go about reforming schools, but all agree that "monocultural" approaches to education fail to give minority children the self-esteem necessary to be confident of their power to act for themselves. Children become "victims of the culture of silence . . . [who] have lost faith in their ability to transform and alter their life circumstances" (Cross, Long, and Ziajka 1978:266).

Multiculturalists see minority youths' powerlessness as closely linked to student values. MCE advocates claim all children come to school with enthusiasm. The long struggle to gain admittance to unsegregated schools is offered as evidence. Poor student values cannot account for poor performance, rather schools themselves "are often guilty of destroying the passion for learning that people of color bring to school" (Grant 1988:16). In part this is due to "bland curricular approaches" that deprive all students of "opportunities to exchange ideas and experiences" (Soto 1989:145). But minority students are doubly victimized by teaching styles and curricula that do not take into account cultural differences in how people learn. As a result, culturally different students become alienated from school, and display behaviors white, middle-class teachers incorrectly interpret as evidence of negative attitudes toward learning (Forbes 1969; Slaughter 1974). . . .

In short, the collective identity of "culturally different students" constructed by multiculturalists portrays the students as powerless, alienated victims of an educational system that either ignores or denigrates their cultural backgrounds, and crushes their enthusiasm for learning. Multicultural rhetoric also attributes to culturally different students an interest in changing how schools and other social institutions operate, and argues that MCE should empower these students to take action.

Multiculturalists use two principal rhetorical idioms to construct the collective identity of culturally different children: the rhetorics of endangerment and entitlement. The rhetoric of endangerment involves claims about threats to health and well-being (Ibarra and Kitsuse 1993:39). Multiculturalists invoke such threats metaphorically, speaking of racism as a "disease" and MCE as a cure. One writer describes racism as "one of the most crippling diseases" facing the United States (Kendall 1983:11). More literally, the notion that conventional educational practices threaten the self-esteem of culturally different students suggests that schools endanger the mental, if not physical, health and welfare of these pupils. Such rhetoric evokes a sense of moral urgency to safeguard the children's well-being.

The rhetoric of entitlement also calls forth a sense of moral urgency. This idiom "emphasizes the virtue of securing for all persons . . . equal institutional access as well as the unhampered freedom to exercise choice of self-expression" (Ibarra and Kitsuse 1993:38). MCE rhetoric features numerous appeals to democracy, individualism, freedom, and rights. The American Association of Colleges for Teacher Education's Commission on Multicultural Education, for example, supports "explorations in alternative and emerging lifestyles" (1973:264), while the Association for Supervision and Curriculum Development argues that MCE will improve the possibilities for developing individual "potential" (ASCD 1977:2). . . .

Casting "Anglocentric Schools" as Villains

The moral drama of multiculturalism casts "Anglocentric" schools as the villain. Multiculturalists' claims about schools criticize the melting pot ideology (e.g., Barnes 1979:419-423).

This ideology claims that immigrants to the United States have all of their cultural differences melted down and combined into a new and uniquely American culture. MCE advocates, by contrast, believe that minority immigrants are compelled to adopt Anglocentric cultural practices and to abandon their own cultures. In criticizing schools the multiculturalists portray the vicious nature of the melting pot ideology as something to be taken for granted and not open to debate. "There is no need here to dwell extensively on the well-known litany of wrongs perpetrated on minority students" by schools imbued with the melting pot ideology (Arciniega 1975:164). Other critics decry the "Anglo-centric curriculum" (Banks 1981:8) as "dominated by white European facts, exploits and miracles" (Sizemore 1973:49).

This characterization of American schools attributes significant power to Anglocentric, or WASP (White, Angle-Saxon, Protestant) educators, as they are often called. It does so by implication rather than by directly naming individuals or groups responsible for conditions in the schools. The quotations in the preceding paragraph, for example, focus on curriculum, as do many claims in the MCE literature (e.g., Cardenas and Fuller 1973; Garcia 1977; Leyba 1973). Other claims criticize "schools" as institutions for producing the "institutionalization of racism" through "the use of racially biased textbooks, the general lack of minority teachers and administrators . . . [and] the misuse of testing materials" (Grant 1975:185).

Attributing values to actors within biased schools is also indirect. MCE rhetoric attacks values embedded within Anglocentric schools rather than attributing values to specific individuals or groups: "What kind of democracy would utilize public schools to suppress the heritage of a minority simply because it is a minority . . . ? What kind of free society can use the schools as a means to diminish individual freedom and enforce conformity?" (Forbes 1969:43). Without naming names, this assigns to schools (and the society that produced them) values opposed to democracy and individual freedom, and committed to suppressing minority heritages and enforcing confor-

mity. The theme that American schools are anti-democratic and authoritarian recurs throughout the MCE literature. One critic claims "schools preach a lot about democracy, freedom, and equality" but actually "promote values and behaviors . . . antithetical to these ideals" (Suzuki 1984:303–04). Others suggest schools reflect the values "of a rather narrow cultural elite" (Edson 1988:24), and seek "to impose the order of ethnic and cultural definitions on minority students" (Piper 1986:27). . . .

Multiculturalists attribute inegalitarian interests and motives to educators who do not actively support MCE reforms. "Teachers . . . need to be willing to allocate opportunities to culturally diverse learners" (Soto 1989:145). Others suggest the failure to implement MCE rests not with the lack of knowledge or solutions, but instead with a lack of leadership, will, and commitment (Goodlad 1984; Kagan, Schreiber, and Zigler 1984). Taken together, these claims portray educators within Anglocentric schools as able but unwilling to promote more democratic schools committed to the freedom and individual expression MCE offers culturally different students.

In sum, the collective identity attributed to Anglocentric schools and, by implication, educators within them, is that of very powerful institutions committed to the preservation of a dominant culture and the elimination of diverse, less powerful cultures. Anglocentric schools and their leaders are hypocritical, insofar as they "preach" about democracy and individual freedom while acting to deny them to culturally different children. Although MCE claims do not explicitly attribute interests and motives to the school-villains, they rule out inability to act as an excuse and place moral responsibility on the schools to redress the injustices inflicted on culturally different students.

The construction of Anglocentric schools as villains reveals two interesting patterns. First, the idioms used to construct this identity are the same as those used to construct culturally different children as victims. Just as the idiom of endangerment portrayed minority youth as victims of psychological assault, the same idiom casts schools, and indirectly educators, as the source of the assault.

Similarly, the idiom of entitlement claims the right to a culturally diverse education for minority children, and it portrays schools as subverting that same right. . . .

Casting "Multicultural Educators" as Heroes

Multiculturalists' collective presentation of self defines their identity in opposition to that of Anglocentric schools and educators. For example, MCE advocates claim to have the power to change how schools teach children and shape children's identities, and thereby to reduce social problems outside the school. Emphasizing the power of classroom teachers, one critic claims that "sharp teachers can change the real curriculum" (Cuban 1972:273), implying that teachers who resist change are either dull or uncommitted to the goals of MCE. Education in world music has the power to help "students deepen their own cultural identities . . . and gain a better understanding of the identities of other students as well" (Gamble 1983:40). Such collective identity claims portray multicultural educators with the same level of power as Anglocentric educators. The difference is that multiculturalists can use their power to help students build positive identities and self-images.

Most of all, MCE advocates believe they have the power to reduce racial and ethnic hostility and promote harmony. The Task Force on Ethnic Studies Curriculum Guidelines of the National Council for the Social Studies (1976:4) claims that schools have "an important role to play in reducing the tensions and injustices, including the misgivings about self, that result from unexamined ethnic beliefs and attitudes." Similar rhetoric describes educators as "a powerful force," as being able to "play a part," and as "show[ing] promise for" eliminating racism and reducing tensions between ethnic, religious, and national-origin groups (Freedman 1984; Kendall 1983; Lee 1983).

Teachers of multicultural education can have these salutary effects by promoting understanding and tolerance of cultural differences. This claim depends on a fundamental belief that racial and ethnic hostilities are based on ignorance that MCE can reduce. Thus one writer suggests that MCE "should lead to a greater respect for [all] cultural groups . . . and fewer intergroup conflicts caused by ignorance and misunderstanding" (Gollnick 1980:14). Others suggest that MCE will help to "clarify moral imperatives and expand social consciousness," lead to a "greater tolerance and respect" for others, "deenergize the attitude that Western systems are the norm," and reduce the appeal of "persuasive racist propaganda" (Dodds 1983; Gamble 1983; O'Brien 1980; Perry 1975). In these claims, multicultural educators have the power to disabuse children of culturally biased beliefs, and to instill an attitude of tolerance, if not appreciation, for cultural differences. . . .

In portraying themselves as heroes, multiculturalists use the rhetoric of loss (Ibarra and Kitsuse 1993:37) to portray the eradication of diverse cultural beliefs, knowledge, and practices as a problem. They also use the rhetoric of calamity (Ibarra and Kitsuse 1993:39) by claiming the United States faces dire consequences if MCE reforms are not adopted.

The rhetoric of loss praises the protective actions of those who challenge the devaluation of "sacred" objects, characterizing them as heroes or saviors. Thus, we have seen movements to save the whales, save the planet, and save our schools. Multiculturalists attack the loss or devaluation of cultures different from the dominant WASP culture in the United States. . . .

The rhetorical presentation of cultural diversity as a threatened resource, and MCE as the means of preserving and extending that resource, casts the multiculturalists as protectors. This protector identity receives further support from claims about the changing demographic composition of the United States. In general, multiculturalists argue that the United States, while always a multicultural nation, is becoming even more so as a result of immigration, birth, and death rates. . . .

. . . Multiculturalists [also] use the rhetoric of calamity. This idiom evokes imagery of unimaginable disaster, and calls for immediate action. MCE claimsmakers describe "intergroup conflict" as a "serious threat to our nation and the ideals of American democracy" (Banks 1973:750). "If we are to survive (literally!), we must learn to respect each other's strengths and weaknesses" (Barnes 1979:424). Multiculturalists also point to a perceived resurgence of the Ku Klux Klan (Lee 1983:406), and an increasingly technological and industrialized world (ASCD 1977; Barnes 1979; Corder and Quisenberry 1987) as ominous developments. The combined threats of racial wars and technological domination make MCE necessary for the "future of our planet and our own survival" (Corder and Quisenberry 1987:158), and to avoid "being alienated, bureaucratized, and depersonalized by the rationality of the ethos of industrial technology" (ASCD 1977:2). "The challenge is herculean. The odds are against us. The hour is late" (Banks 1973:750), but "we can't afford to ignore it" (Standifer 1987).

This rhetoric of calamity establishes the interests of multicultural educators as general rather than parochial. Their rhetoric appeals to a broad audience by proclaiming that MCE serves the interests of everyone in preventing race wars, depersonalization, and social destruction. Their claims use inclusive pronouns such as us, we, and our. MCE claims imply that Anglocentric educators are self-interested, seeking to preserve WASP power and privilege; in contrast, multicultural educators are concerned with the interests of all. Where human survival itself is at stake, no one can be disinterested, and no one can be selfish in acting to assure survival. . . .

In short, multiculturalists cast themselves as protectors, not only of cherished American values such as democracy, individual freedom, justice, and liberty, but also of the rights of children to receive an education that treats their cultural heritages with dignity. Multiculturalists give themselves the power to redefine how schools operate and to instill the value of cultural diversity in the curriculum, pedagogy, and other aspects of education. The power they wield is similar to that of Anglocentrists. The difference is that multiculturalists attribute to themselves motives guided by values and interests that will benefit humanity rather than parochial groups within society. . . .

REFERENCES

Arciniega, T. A. 1975. "The Thrust Toward Pluralism: What Progress?" *Educational Leadership* 33 (December):163–167.

ASCD Multicultural Education Commission. 1977. "Encouraging Multicultural Education." Pp. 1–5 in *Multicultural Education: Commitments, Issues, and Applications,* edited by C. A. Grant. Washington, D.C.: Association for Supervision and Curriculum Development.

Baker, G. C. 1983. "Motivating the Culturally Different Student." *Momentum* 14(February):45–46.

Banks, J. A. 1973. "Teaching for Ethnic Literacy: A Comparative Approach." *Social Education* 37:738–750.

———. 1981. *Multiethnic Education: Theory and Practice.* Boston: Allyn and Bacon.

Barnes, W. J. 1979. "Developing a Culturally Pluralistic Perspective: A Community Involvement Task." *Journal of Negro Education* 48:419–430.

Cardenas, R., and L. W. Fuller. 1973. "Toward a Multicultural Society." *Today's Education* 62(Sept./Oct.):83–88.

Commission on Multicultural Education. 1973. "No One Model American." *Journal of Teacher Education* 24:264–265.

Corder, L. J., and N. L. Quisenberry. 1987. "Early Education and Afro-Americans: History, Assumptions and Implications for the Future." *Childhood Education* 63(February):154–158.

Cross, D. E., M. A. Long, and A. Ziajka. 1978. "Minority Cultures and Education in the United States." *Education and Urban Society* 10:263–276.

Cuban, L. 1972. "Ethnic Content and 'White' Instruction." *Phi Delta Kappan* 53:270–273.

Dodds, J. B. P. 1983. "Music as a Multicultural Education." *Music Educators Journal* 69(May):33–34.

Edson, C. H. 1988. "Chicago: 1893." *Educational Studies* 19:1–29.

Forbes, J. D. 1969. *Education for the Culturally Different: A Multi-Cultural Approach.* Berkeley: Far West Laboratory for Educational Research and Development.

Freedman, P. I. 1984. "Multiethnic/Multicultural Education: Establishing the Foundations." *The Social Studies* 75:202–204.

Gamble, S. 1983. "A Multicultural Curriculum," *Music Educator's Journal* 69:39–41.

Garcia, F. C. 1977. "Politics and Multicultural Education Do Mix." *Journal of Teacher Education* 28(May–June):21–25.

Gollnick, D. 1980. "Multicultural Education." *Viewpoints in Teaching and Learning* 56:1–17.

Goodlad, J. 1984. "The Uncommon Common School." *Education and Urban Society* 16:243–252.

Grant, C. A. 1975. "Racism in School and Society." *Educational Leadership* 33(December):184–188.

_____. 1988. "Race, Class, Gender and Schooling." *Education Digest* 54(December):15–18.

Ibarra, P., and J. I. Kitsuse. 1993. "Vernacular Constituents of Moral Discourse: An Interactionist Proposal for the Study of Social Problems." Pp. 25–58 in *Constructionist Controversies: Issues in Social Problems Theory*, edited by J. A. Holstein and G. Miller. Hawthorne, NY: Aldine de Gruyter.

Johnson, P. 1991. "Traditional Offerings Won't Cut It." *American Teacher* 75(March):4.

Kagan, S., E. Schreiber, and E. Zigler. 1984. "Recognizing Commonalities—Respecting Differences." *Education and Urban Society* 16:382–389.

Kendall, F. E. 1983. "Presenting Multicultural Education to Parents." *Momentum* 14(February):11–13.

Lee, M. K. 1983. "Multiculturalism: Educational Perspectives for the 1980s." *Education* 103:405–409.

Leyba, C. F. 1973. "Cultural Identity: Problems and Dilemmas." *Journal of Teacher Education* 24 (Winter):272–276.

National Catholic Education Association. 1983. "Relishing 'The Stew' of Cultural Diversity." *Momentum* 14(February):2–3.

National Council for the Social Studies. 1976. *Curriculum Guidelines for Multiethnic Education*. Arlington, VA: National Council for the Social Studies.

O'Brien, J. P. 1980. "Integrating World Music in the Music Appreciation Course." *Music Educator's Journal* 67(Sept):39–42.

Perry, J. 1975. "Notes Toward a Multicultural Curriculum." *English Journal* 64:8–9.

Piper, D. 1986. "Language Growth in the Multiethnic Classroom." *Language Arts* 63:23–36.

Sizemore, B. A. 1973. "Making the Schools a Vehicle for Cultural Pluralism." Pp. 43–54 in *Cultural Pluralism in Education: A Mandate for Change*, edited by M. D. Stent, W. R. Hazard, and H. N. Rivlin. New York: Appleton-Century-Crofts.

Slaughter, D. T. 1974. "Alienation of Afro-American Children." Pp. 144–174 in *Cultural Pluralism*, edited by E. Pipps. Chicago: University of Chicago Press.

Soto, L. D. 1989. "Enhancing the Written Medium for Culturally Diverse Learners Via Reciprocal Interaction." *The Urban Review* 21:145–149.

Standifer, J. A. 1987. "The Multicultural, Non-Sexist Principle: We Can't Afford to Ignore It." *Journal of Negro Education* 56:471–474.

Suzuki, B.H. 1984. "Curriculum Transformation for Multicultural Education." *Education and Urban Society* 16:294–322.

Racism and Research

The Case of the Tuskegee Syphilis Study

Allan M. Brandt

In 1932 the U.S. Public Health Service (USPHS) initiated an experiment in Macon County, Alabama, to determine the natural course of untreated, latent syphilis in black males. The test comprised 400 syphilitic men, as well as 200 uninfected men who served as controls. The first published report of the study appeared in 1936 with subsequent papers issued every four to six years, through the 1960s. When penicillin became widely available by the early 1950s as the preferred treatment for syphilis, the men did not receive therapy. In fact on several occasions, the USPHS actually sought to prevent treatment. Moreover, a committee at the federally operated Center for Disease Control decided in 1969 that the study should be continued. Only in 1972, when accounts of the study first appeared in the national press, did the Department of Health, Education, and Welfare halt the experiment. At that time seventy-four of the test subjects were still alive; at least twenty-eight, but perhaps more than 100, had died directly from advanced syphilitic lesions.[1] In August 1972, HEW appointed an investigatory panel which issued a report the following year. The panel found the study to have been "ethically unjustified," and argued that penicillin should have been provided to the men.[2]

This article attempts to place the Tuskegee Study in a historical context and to assess its ethical implications. Despite the media attention which the study received, the HEW *Final Report,* and the criticism expressed by several professional organizations, the experiment has been largely misunderstood. The most basic questions of *how* the study was undertaken in the first place and *why* it continued for forty years were never addressed

by the HEW investigation. Moreover, the panel misconstrued the nature of the experiment, failing to consult important documents available at the National Archives which bear significantly on its ethical assessment. Only by examining the specific ways in which values are engaged in scientific research can the study be understood.

Racism and Medical Opinion

A brief review of the prevailing scientific thought regarding race and heredity in the early twentieth century is fundamental for an understanding of the Tuskegee Study. By the turn of the century, Darwinism had provided a new rationale for American racism.[3] Essentially primitive peoples, it was argued, could not be assimilated into a complex, white civilization. Scientists speculated that in the struggle for survival the Negro in America was doomed. Particularly prone to disease, vice, and crime, black Americans could not be helped by education or philanthropy. Social Darwinists analyzed census data to predict the virtual extinction of the Negro in the twentieth century, for they believed the Negro race in America was in the throes of a degenerative evolutionary process.[4]

The medical profession supported these findings of late nineteenth- and early twentieth-century anthropologists, ethnologists, and biologists. Physicians studying the effects of emancipation on health concluded almost universally that freedom had caused the mental, moral, and physical deterioration of the black population.[5] They substantiated this argument by citing examples in the comparative anatomy of the black and white races. As Dr. W. T. English wrote: "A careful inspection reveals the body of the negro a mass of minor defects and imperfections from the crown of the head to the soles of the feet. . . ."[6] Cranial structures, wide nasal apertures, receding chins, projecting jaws, all typed the Negro as the lowest species in the Darwinian hierarchy.[7]

Interest in racial differences centered on the sexual nature of blacks. The Negro, doctors explained, possessed an excessive sexual desire, which threatened the very foundations of white society. As one physician noted in the *Journal of the American Medical Association,* "The negro springs from a southern race, and as such his sexual appetite is strong; all of his environments stimulate this appetite, and as a general rule his emotional type of religion certainly does not decrease it."[8] Doctors reported a complete lack of morality on the part of blacks:

> Virtue in the negro race is like angels' visits— few and far between. In a practice of sixteen years I have never examined a virgin negro over fourteen years of age.[9]

A particularly ominous feature of this overzealous sexuality, doctors argued, was the black males' desire for white women. "A perversion from which most races are exempt," wrote Dr. English, "prompts the negro's inclination towards white women, whereas other races incline towards females of their own."[10] Though English estimated the "gray matter of the negro brain" to be at least a thousand years behind that of the white races, his genital organs were overdeveloped. As Dr. William Lee Howard noted:

> The attacks on defenseless white women are evidences of racial instincts that are about as amenable to ethical culture as is the inherent odor of the race. . . . When education will reduce the size of the negro's penis as well as bring about the sensitiveness of the terminal fibers which exist in the Caucasian, then will it also be able to prevent the African's birthright to sexual madness and excess.[11]

One southern medical journal proposed "Castration Instead of Lynching," as retribution for black sexual crimes. "An impressive trial by a ghost-like kuklux klan [sic] and a 'ghost' physician or surgeon to perform the operation would make it an event the 'patient' would never forget," noted the editorial.[12]

According to these physicians, lust and immorality, unstable families, and reversion to barbaric tendencies made blacks especially prone to venereal diseases. One doctor estimated that over 50 percent of all Negroes over the age of twenty-five were syphilitic.[13] Virtually free of disease as slaves, they were now overwhelmed by it, according to informed medical opinion. Moreover, doctors believed that treatment for venereal disease among blacks was impossible, particularly because in its latent stage the symptoms of syphilis become quiescent. As Dr. Thomas W. Murrell wrote:

> They come for treatment at the beginning and at the end. When there are visible manifestations or when harried by pain, they readily come, for as a race they are not averse to physic; but tell them not, though they look well and feel well, that they are still diseased. Here ignorance rates science a fool. . . .[14]

Even the best educated black, according to Murrell, could not be convinced to seek treatment for syphilis.[15] Venereal disease, according to some doctors, threatened the future of the race. The medical profession attributed the low birth rate among blacks to the high prevalence of venereal disease which caused stillbirths and miscarriages. Moreover, the high rates of syphilis were thought to lead to increased insanity and crime. One doctor writing at the turn of the century estimated that the number of insane Negroes had increased thirteen-fold since the end of the Civil War.[16] Dr. Murrell's conclusion echoed the most informed anthropological and ethnological data:

> So the scourge sweeps among them. Those that are treated are only half cured, and the effort to assimilate a complex civilization driving their diseased minds until the results are criminal records. Perhaps here, in conjunction with tuberculosis, will be the end of the negro problem. Disease will accomplish what man cannot do.[17]

This particular configuration of ideas formed the core of medical opinion concerning blacks, sex, and disease in the early twentieth century. Doctors generally discounted socioeconomic explanations of the state of black health, arguing that better medical care could not alter the evolutionary scheme.[18] These assumptions provide the backdrop for examining the Tuskegee Syphilis Study.

The Origins of the Experiment

In 1929, under a grant from the Julius Rosenwald Fund, the USPHS conducted studies in the rural South to determine the prevalence of syphilis among blacks and explore possibilities for mass treatment. The USPHS found Macon County, Alabama, in which the town of Tuskegee is located to have the highest syphilis rate of the six counties surveyed. The Rosenwald Study concluded that mass treatment could be successfully implemented among rural blacks.[19] Although it is doubtful that the necessary funds would have been allocated even in the best economic conditions, after the economy collapsed in 1929, the findings were ignored. It is, however, ironic that the Tuskegee Study came to be based on findings of the Rosenwald Study that demonstrated the possibilities of mass treatment.

Three years later, in 1932, Dr. Taliaferro Clark, Chief of the USPHS Venereal Disease Division and author of the Rosenwald Study report, decided that conditions in Macon County merited renewed attention. Clark believed the high prevalence of syphilis offered an "unusual opportunity" for observation. From its inception, the USPHS regarded the Tuskegee Study as a classic "study in nature,"* rather than an experiment.[20] As long as syphilis was so prevalent in Macon and most of the blacks went untreated throughout life, it seemed

only natural to Clark that it would be valuable to observe the consequences. He described it as a "ready-made situation."[21] Surgeon General H. S. Cumming wrote to R. R. Moton, Director of the Tuskegee Institute:

> The recent syphilis control demonstration carried out in Macon County, with the financial assistance of the Julius Rosenwald Fund, revealed the presence of an unusually high rate in this county and, what is more remarkable, the fact that 99 per cent of this group was entirely without previous treatment. This combination, together with the expected cooperation of your hospital, offers an unparalleled opportunity for carrying on this piece of scientific research which probably cannot be duplicated anywhere else in the world.[22]

Although no formal protocol appears to have been written, several letters of Clark and Cumming suggest what the USPHS hoped to find. Clark indicated that it would be important to see how disease affected the daily lives of the men:

> The results of these studies of case records suggest the desirability of making a further study of the effect of untreated syphilis on the human economy among people now living and engaged in their daily pursuits.[23]

It also seems that the USPHS believed the experiment might demonstrate that antisyphilitic treatment was unnecessary. As Cumming noted: "It is expected the results of this study may have a marked bearing on the treatment, or conversely the non-necessity of treatment, of cases of latent syphilis."[24] . . .

Selecting the Subjects

Clark sent Dr. Raymond Vonderlehr to Tuskegee in September 1932 to assemble a sample of men with latent syphilis for the experiment. The basic design of the study called for the selection of syphilitic black males between the ages of twenty-five and sixty, a thorough physical examination including x-rays, and finally, a spinal tap to determine the incidence of neuro-syphilis.[25] They had no intention of providing any treatment for the infected men.[26] The USPHS originally scheduled

---

*In 1865, Claude Bernard, the famous French physiologist, outlined the distinction between a "study in nature" and experimentation. A study in nature required simple observation, an essentially passive act, while experimentation demanded intervention which altered the original condition. The Tuskegee Study was thus clearly not a study in nature. The very act of diagnosis altered the original conditions. "It is on this very possibility of acting or not acting on a body," wrote Bernard, "that the distinction will exclusively rest between sciences called sciences of observation and sciences called experimental."

the whole experiment to last six months; it seemed to be both a simple and inexpensive project.

The task of collecting the sample, however, proved to be more difficult than the USPHS had supposed. Vonderlehr canvassed the largely illiterate, poverty-stricken population of sharecroppers and tenant farmers in search of test subjects. If his circulars requested only men over twenty-five to attend his clinics, none would appear, suspecting he was conducting draft physicals. Therefore, he was forced to test large numbers of women and men who did not fit the experiment's specifications. This involved considerable expense since the USPHS had promised the Macon County Board of Health that it would treat those who were infected, but not included in the study.[27] Clark wrote to Vonderlehr about the situation: "It never once occurred to me that we would be called upon to treat a large part of the county as return for the privilege of making this study. . . . I am anxious to keep the expenditures for treatment down to the lowest possible point because it is the one item of expenditure in connection with the study most difficult to defend despite our knowledge of the need therefor."[28] Vonderlehr responded: "If we could find from 100 to 200 cases . . . we would not have to do another Wassermann on useless individuals. . . ."[29]

Significantly, the attempt to develop the sample contradicted the prediction the USPHS had made initially regarding the prevalence of the disease in Macon County. Overall rates of syphilis fell well below expectations; as opposed to the USPHS projection of 35 percent, 20 percent of those tested were actually diseased.[30] Moreover, those who had sought and received previous treatment far exceeded the expectations of the USPHS. Clark noted in a letter to Vonderlehr:

> I find your report of March 6th quite interesting but regret the necessity for Wassermanning [sic] . . . such a large number of individuals in order to uncover this relatively limited number of untreated cases.[31]

Further difficulties arose in enlisting the subjects to participate in the experiment, to be "Wassermanned," and to return for a subsequent series of examinations. Vonderlehr found that only the offer of treatment elicited the cooperation of the men. They were told they were ill and were promised free care. Offered therapy, they became willing subjects.[32] The USPHS did not tell the men that they were participants in an experiment; on the contrary, the subjects believed they were being treated for "bad blood"—the rural South's colloquialism for syphilis. They thought they were participating in a public health demonstration similar to the one that had been conducted by the Julius Rosenwald Fund in Tuskegee several years earlier. In the end, the men were so eager for medical care that the number of defaulters in the experiment proved to be insignificant.[33]

To preserve the subjects' interest, Vonderlehr gave most of the men mercurial ointment, a noneffective drug, while some of the younger men apparently received inadequate dosages of neoarsphenamine.[34] This required Vonderlehr to write frequently to Clark requesting supplies. He feared the experiment would fail if the men were not offered treatment. . . .

The readiness of the test subjects to participate of course contradicted the notion that blacks would not seek or continue therapy.

The final procedure of the experiment was to be a spinal tap to test for evidence of neurosyphilis. The USPHS presented this purely diagnostic exam, which often entails considerable pain and complications, to the men as a "special treatment." Clark explained to Moore:

> We have not yet commenced the spinal punctures. This operation will be deferred to the last in order not to unduly disturb our field work by any adverse reports by the patients subjected to spinal puncture because of some disagreeable sensations following this procedure. These negroes are very ignorant and easily influenced by things that would be of minor significance in a more intelligent group.[35]

The letter to the subjects announcing the spinal tap read:

> Some time ago you were given a thorough examination and since that time we hope you have gotten a great deal of treatment for bad blood. You will now be given your last chance

to get a second examination. This examination is a very special one and after it is finished you will be given a special treatment if it is believed you are in a condition to stand it. . . .

REMEMBER THIS IS YOUR LAST CHANCE FOR SPECIAL FREE TREATMENT. BE SURE TO MEET THE NURSE.[36]

The HEW investigation did not uncover this crucial fact: the men participated in the study under the guise of treatment.

Despite the fact that their assumption regarding prevalence and black attitudes toward treatment had proved wrong, the USPHS decided in the summer of 1933 to continue the study. Once again, it seemed only "natural" to pursue the research since the sample already existed, and with a depressed economy, the cost of treatment appeared prohibitive—although there is no indication it was ever considered. Vonderlehr first suggested extending the study in letters to Clark and Wenger:

At the end of this project we shall have a considerable number of cases presenting various complications of syphilis, who have received only mercury and may still be considered untreated in the modern sense of therapy. Should these cases be followed over a period of from five to ten years many interesting facts could be learned regarding the course and complications of untreated syphilis.[37]

"As I see it," responded Wenger, "we have no further interest in these patients *until they die*."[38] Apparently, the physicians engaged in the experiment believed that only autopsies could scientifically confirm the findings of the study.

Bringing the men to autopsy required the USPHS to devise a further series of deceptions and inducements. Wenger warned Vonderlehr that the men must not realize that they would be autopsied:

There is one danger in the latter plan and that is if the colored population become aware that accepting free hospital care means a postmortem, every darkey will leave Macon

County and it will hurt [Dr. Eugene] Dibble's hospital.[39]

The USPHS offered several inducements to maintain contact and to procure the continued cooperation of the men. Eunice Rivers, a black nurse, was hired to follow their health and to secure approval for autopsies. She gave the men non-effective medicines—"spring tonic" and aspirin—as well as transportation and hot meals on the days of their examinations.[40] More important, Nurse Rivers provided continuity to the project over the entire forty-year period. By supplying "medicinals," the USPHS was able to continue to deceive the participants, who believed that they were receiving therapy from the government doctors. Deceit was integral to the study. When the test subjects complained about spinal taps one doctor wrote:

They simply do not like spinal punctures. A few of those who were tapped are enthusiastic over the results but to most, the suggestion causes violent shaking of the head; others claim they were robbed of their procreative powers (regardless of the fact that I claim it stimulates them).[41]

Letters to the subjects announcing an impending USPHS visit to Tuskegee explained: "[The doctor] wants to make a special examination to find out how you have been feeling and whether the treatment has improved your health."[42] In fact, after the first six months of the study, the USPHS had furnished no treatment whatsoever.

Finally, because it proved difficult to persuade the men to come to the hospital when they became severely ill, the USPHS promised to cover their burial expenses. The Milbank Memorial Fund provided approximately $50 per man for this purpose beginning in 1935. This was a particularly strong inducement as funeral rites constituted an important component of the cultural life of rural blacks.[43] One report of the study concluded, "Without this suasion it would, we believe, have been impossible to secure the cooperation of the group and their families."[44]

Reports of the study's findings, which appeared regularly in the medical press beginning in 1936, consistently cited the ravages of untreated syphilis. The first paper, read at the 1936 American Medical Association annual meeting, found "that syphilis in this period [latency] tends to greatly increase the frequency of manifestations of cardiovascular disease."[45] Only 16 percent of the subjects gave no sign of morbidity as opposed to 61 percent of the controls. Ten years later, a report noted coldly, "The fact that nearly twice as large a proportion of the syphilitic individuals as of the control group has died is a very striking one." Life expectancy, concluded the doctors, is reduced by about 20 percent.[46]

A 1955 article found that slightly more than 30 percent of the test group autopsied had died *directly* from advanced syphilitic lesions of either the cardiovascular or the central nervous system.[47] Another published account stated, "Review of those still living reveals that an appreciable number have late complications of syphilis which probably will result, for some at least, in contributing materially to the ultimate cause of death."[48] In 1950, Dr. Wenger had concluded, "We now know, where we could only surmise before, that we have contributed to their ailments and shortened their lives."[49] As black physician Vernal Cave, a member of the HEW panel, later wrote, "They proved a point, then proved a point, then proved a point."[50]

During the forty years of the experiment the USPHS had sought on several occasions to ensure that the subjects did not receive treatment from other sources. To this end, Vonderlehr met with groups of local black doctors in 1934, to ask their cooperation in not treating the men. Lists of subjects were distributed to Macon County physicians along with letters requesting them to refer these men back to the USPHS if they sought care.[51] The USPHS warned the Alabama Health Department not to treat the test subjects when they took a mobile VD unit into Tuskegee in the early 1940s.[52] In 1941, the Army drafted several subjects and told them to begin antisyphilitic treatment immediately. The USPHS supplied the draft board with a list of 256 names they desired to have excluded from treatment, and the board complied.[53]

In spite of these efforts, by the early 1950s many of the men had secured some treatment on their own. By 1952, almost 30 percent of the test subjects had received some penicillin, although only 7.5 percent had received what could be considered adequate doses.[54] Vonderlehr wrote to one of the participating physicians, "I hope that the availability of antibiotics has not interfered too much with this project."[55] A report published in 1955 considered whether the treatment that some of the men had obtained had "defeated" the study. The article attempted to explain the relatively low exposure to penicillin in an age of antibiotics, suggesting as a reason: "the stoicism of these men as a group; they still regard hospitals and medicines with suspicion and prefer an occasional dose of time-honored herbs or tonics to modern drugs."[56] The authors failed to note that the men believed they already were under the care of the government doctors and thus saw no need to seek treatment elsewhere. Any treatment which the men might have received, concluded the report, had been insufficient to compromise the experiment.

When the USPHS evaluated the status of the study in the 1960s they continued to rationalize the racial aspects of the experiment. For example, the minutes of a 1965 meeting at the Center for Disease Control recorded:

> Racial issue was mentioned briefly. Will not affect the study. Any questions can be handled by saying these people were at the point that therapy would no longer help them.
> They are getting better medical care than they would under any other circumstances.[57]

A group of physicians met again at the CDC in 1969 to decide whether or not to terminate the study. Although one doctor argued that the study should be stopped and the men treated, the consensus was to continue. Dr. J. Lawton Smith remarked, "You will never have another study like this; take advantage of it."[58] A memo prepared by Dr. James B. Lucas, Assistant Chief of the Venereal Disease Branch, stated: "Nothing learned will prevent, find, or cure a single case of infectious syphilis or bring us closer to our basic mission of controlling venereal disease in the United

States."[59] He concluded, however, that the study should be continued "along its present lines." When the first accounts of the experiment appeared in the national press in July 1972, data were still being collected and autopsies performed.[60]

The HEW Final Report

HEW finally formed the Tuskegee Syphilis Study Ad Hoc Advisory Panel on August 28, 1972, in response to criticism that the press descriptions of the experiment had triggered. The panel, composed of nine members, five of them black, concentrated on two issues. First, was the study justified in 1932 and had the men given their informed consent? Second, should penicillin have been provided when it became available in the early 1950s? The panel was also charged with determining if the study should be terminated and assessing current policies regarding experimentation with human subjects.[61] The group issued their report in June 1973.

By focusing on the issues of penicillin therapy and informed consent, the *Final Report* and the investigation betrayed a basic misunderstanding of the experiment's purposes and design. The HEW report implied that the failure to provide penicillin constituted the study's major ethical misjudgment; implicit was the assumption that no adequate therapy existed prior to penicillin. Nonetheless medical authorities firmly believed in the efficacy of arsenotherapy for treating syphilis at the time of the experiment's inception in 1932. The panel further failed to recognize that the entire study had been predicated on nontreatment. Provision of effective medication would have violated the rationale of the experiment—to study the natural course of the disease until death. On several occasions, in fact, the USPHS had prevented the men from receiving proper treatment. Indeed, there is no evidence that the USPHS ever considered providing penicillin.

The other focus of the *Final Report*—informed consent—also served to obscure the historical reality the experiment. In light of the deceptions and exploitations which the experiment perpetrated, it is an understatement to declare, as the panel did, that the experiment was "ethically

unjustified," because it failed to obtain informed consent from the subjects. The *Final Report's* statement, "Submitting voluntarily is not informed consent," indicated that the panel believed that the men had volunteered *for the experiment*.[62] The records in the National Archives make clear that the men did not submit voluntarily to an experiment; they were told and they believed that they were getting free treatment from expert government doctors for a serious disease. The failure of the HEW *Final Report* to expose this critical fact—that the USPHS lied to the subjects—calls into question the thoroughness and credibility of their investigation.

Failure to place the study in a historical context also made it impossible for the investigation to deal with the essentially racist nature of the experiment. The panel treated the study as an aberration, well-intentioned but misguided.[63] Moreover, concern that the *Final Report* might be viewed as a critique of human experimentation in general seems to have severely limited the scope of the inquiry. The *Final Report* is quick to remind the reader on two occasions: "The position of the Panel must not be construed to be a general repudiation of scientific research with human subjects."[64] The *Report* assures us that a better designed experiment could have been justified:

> It is possible that a scientific study in 1932 of untreated syphilis, properly conceived with a clear protocol and conducted with suitable subjects who fully understood the implications of their involvement, might have been justified in the pre-penicillin era. This is especially true when one considers the uncertain nature of the results of treatment of late latent syphilis and the highly toxic nature of therapeutic agents then available.[65]

This statement is questionable in view of the proven dangers of untreated syphilis known in 1932.

Since the publication of the HEW *Final Report*, a defense of the Tuskegee Study has emerged. These arguments, most clearly articulated by Dr. R. H. Kampmeier in the *Southern Medical Journal*, center on the limited knowledge of effective therapy for latent syphilis when the experiment began. Kampmeier argues that by 1950, penicillin would have been of no value for these men.[66] Others have suggested that the men were fortunate to have been spared the highly toxic treatments of the earlier period.[67] Moreover, even these contemporary defenses assume that the men never would have been treated anyway. As Dr. Charles Barnett of Stanford University wrote in 1974, "The lack of treatment was not contrived by the USPHS but was an established fact of which they proposed to take advantage."[68] Several doctors who participated in the study continued to justify the experiment. Dr. J. R. Heller, who on one occasion had referred to the test subjects as the "Ethiopian population," told reporters in 1972:

> I don't see why they should be shocked or horrified. There was no racial side to this. It just happened to be in a black community. I feel this was a perfectly straightforward study, perfectly ethical, with controls. Part of our mission as physicians is to find out what happens to individuals with disease and without disease.[69]

These apologies, as well as the HEW *Final Report,* ignore many of the essential ethical issues which the study poses. The Tuskegee Study reveals the persistence of beliefs within the medical profession about the nature of blacks, sex, and disease—beliefs that had tragic repercussions long after their alleged "scientific" bases were known to be incorrect. Most strikingly, the entire health of a community was jeopardized by leaving a communicable disease untreated.[70] There can be little doubt that the Tuskegee researchers regarded their subjects as less than human.[71] As a result, the ethical canons of experimenting on human subjects were completely disregarded.

The study also raises significant questions about professional self-regulation and scientific bureaucracy. Once the USPHS decided to extend the experiment in the summer of 1933, it was unlikely that the test would be halted short of the men's deaths. The experiment was widely reported for forty years without evoking any significant protest within the medical community. Nor did any bureaucratic mechanism exist within the government for the periodic reassessment of

the Tuskegee experiment's ethics and scientific value. The USPHS sent physicians to Tuskegee every several years to check on the study's progress, but never subjected the morality or usefulness of the experiment to serious scrutiny. Only the press accounts of 1972 finally punctured the continued rationalizations of the USPHS and brought the study to an end. Even the HEW investigation was compromised by fear that it would be considered a threat to future human experimentation.

In retrospect the Tuskegee Study revealed more about the pathology of racism than it did about the pathology of syphillis; more about the nature of scientific inquiry than the nature of the disease process. The injustice committed by the experiment went well beyond the facts outlined in the press and the HEW *Final Report.* The degree of deception and damages have been seriously underestimated. As this history of the study suggests, the notion that science is a value-free discipline must be rejected. The need for greater vigilance in assessing the specific ways in which social values and attitudes affect professional behavior is clearly indicated.

NOTES

1. The best general accounts of the study are "The 40-Year Death Watch," *Medical World News* (August 18, 1972), pp. 15–17; and Dolores Katz, "Why 430 Blacks with Syphilis Went Uncured for 40 Years," *Detroit Free Press* (November 5, 1972). The mortality figure is based on a published report of the study which appeared in 1955. See Jesse J. Peters, James H. Peers, Sidney Olansky, John C. Cutler, and Geraldine Gleeson, "Untreated Syphilis in the Male Negro: Pathologic Findings in Syphilitic and Nonsyphilitic Patients," *Journal of Chronic Diseases* 1 (February 1955), 127–48. The article estimated that 30.4 percent of the untreated men would die from syphilitic lesions.

2. *Final Report* of the Tuskegee Syphilis Study Ad Hoc Advisory Panel, Department of Health, Education, and Welfare (Washington, D.C.: GPO, 1973). (Hereafter, HEW *Final Report*).

3. See George M. Frederickson, *The Black Image in the White Mind* (New York: Harper and Row, 1971), pp. 228–55. Also, John H. Haller, Outcasts From

Evolution (Urbana, Ill.: University of Illinois Press, 1971), pp. 40–68.

4. Frederickson, pp. 247–49.

5. "Deterioration of the American Negro," *Atlanta Journal-Record of Medicine* 5 (July 1903), 287–88. See also J. A. Rodgers, "The Effect of Freedom upon the Psychological Development of the Negro," Proceedings of the American Medico-Psychological Association 7 (1900), 88–99. "From the most healthy race in the country forty years ago," concluded Dr. Henry McHatton, "he is today the most diseased." "The Sexual Status of the Negro—Past and Present," *American Journal of Dermatology and Genito-Urinary Diseases* 10 (January 1906), 7–9.

6. W. T. English, "The Negro Problem from the Physician's Point of View," *Atlanta Journal-Record of Medicine* 5 (October 1903), 461. See also, "Racial Anatomical Peculiarities," *New York Medical Journal* 63 (April 1896), 500–01.

7. "Racial Anatomical Peculiarities," p. 501. Also, Charles S. Bacon, "The Race Problem," *Medicine* (Detroit) 9 (May 1903), 338–43.

8. H. H. Hazen, "Syphilis in the American Negro," *Journal of the American Medical Association* 63 (August 8, 1914), 463. For deeper background into the historical relationship of racism and sexuality see Winthrop D. Jordan, *White Over Black* (Chapel Hill: University of North Carolina Press, 1968; Pelican Books, 1969), pp. 32–40.

9. Daniel David Quillian, "Racial Peculiarities: A Cause of the Prevalence of Syphilis in Negroes." *American Journal of Dermatology and Genito-Urinary Diseases* 10 (July 1906), 277.

10. English, p. 463.

11. William Lee Howard, "The Negro as a Distinct Ethnic Factor in Civilization," *Medicine* (Detroit) 9 (June 1903), 424. See also, Thomas W. Murrell, "Syphilis in the American Negro," *Journal of the American Medical Association* 54 (March 12, 1910), 848.

12. "Castration Instead of Lynching," *Atlanta Journal-Record of Medicine* 8 (October 1906), 457. The editorial added: "The badge of disgrace and emasculation might be branded upon the face or forehead, as a warning, in the form of an 'R,' emblematic of the crime for which this punishment was and will be inflicted."

13. Searle Harris, "The Future of the Negro from the Standpoint of the Southern Physician," *Alabama Medical Journal* 14 (January 1902), 62. Other articles on the prevalence of venereal disease among blacks are:

H. L. McNeil, "Syphilis in the Southern Negro," *Journal of the American Medical Association* 67 (September 30, 1916), 1001–04; Ernest Philip Boas, "The Relative Prevalence of Syphilis Among Negroes and Whites," *Social Hygiene* 1 (September 1915), 610–16. Doctors went to considerable trouble to distinguish the morbidity and mortality of various diseases among blacks and whites. See, for example, Marion M. Torchia, "Tuberculosis Among American Negroes: Medical Research on a Racial Disease, 1830–1950," *Journal of the History of Medicine and Allied Sciences* 32 (July 1977), 252–79.

14. Thomas W. Murrell, "Syphilis in the Negro: Its Bearing on the Race Problem," *American Journal of Dermatology and Genito-Urinary Diseases* 10 (August 1906), 307.

15. "Even among the educated, only a very few will carry out the most elementary instructions as to personal hygiene. One thing you cannot do, and that is to convince the negro that he has a disease that he cannot see or feel. This is due to lack of concentration rather than lack of faith; even if he does believe, he does not care; a child of fancy, the sensations of the passing hour are his only guides to the future." Murrell, "Syphilis in the American Negro," p. 847.

16. "Deterioration of the American Negro," *Atlanta Journal-Record of Medicine* 5 (July 1903), 288.

17. Murrell, "Syphilis in the Negro; Its Bearing on the Race Problem," p. 307.

18. "The anatomical and physiological conditions of the African must be understood, his place in the anthropological scale realized, and his biological basis accepted as being unchangeable by man, before we shall be able to govern his natural uncontrollable sexual passions." See, "As Ye Sow That Shall Ye Also Reap," *Atlanta Journal-Record of Medicine* 1 (June 1899), 266.

19. Taliaferro Clark, *The Control of Syphilis in Southern Rural Areas* (Chicago: Julius Rosenwald Fund, 1932), 53–58. Approximately 35 percent of the inhabitants of Macon County who were examined were found to be syphilitic.

20. See Claude Bernard, *An Introduction to the Study of Experimental Medicine* (New York: Dover, 1865, 1957), pp. 5–26.

21. Taliaferro Clark to M. M. Davis, October 29, 1932. Records of the USPHS Venereal Disease Division, Record Group 90, Box 239, National Archives, Washington National Record Center, Suitland, Maryland. (Hereafter, NA-WNRC). Materials in this collec-

tion which relate to the early history of the study were apparently never consulted by the HEW investigation. Included are letters, reports, and memoranda written by the physicians engaged in the study.

22. H. S. Cumming to R. R. Moton, September 20, 1932, NA-WNRC.

23. Clark to Davis, October 29, 1932, NA-WNRC.

24. Cumming to Moton, September 20, 1932, NA-WNRC.

25. Clark Memorandum, September 26, 1932, NA-WNRC. See also, Clark to Davis, October 29, 1932, NA-WNRC.

26. As Clark wrote: "You will observe that our plan has nothing to do with treatment. It is purely a diagnostic procedure carried out to determine what has happened to the syphilitic Negro who has had no treatment." Clark to Paul A. O'Leary, September 27, 1932, NA-WNRC.

27. D. G. Gill to O. C. Wenger, October 10, 1932, NA-WNRC.

28. Clark to Vonderlehr, January 25, 1933, NA-WNRC.

29. Vonderlehr to Clark, February 28, 1933, NA-WNRC.

30. Vonderlehr to Clark, November 2, 1932, NA-WNRC. Also, Vonderlehr to Clark, February 6, 1933, NA-WNRC.

31. Clark to Vonderlehr, March 9, 1933, NA-WNRC.

32. Vonderlehr later explained: "The reason treatment was given to any of these men was twofold: First, when the study was started in the fall of 1932, no plans had been made for its continuation and a few of the patients were treated before we fully realized the need for continuing the project on a permanent basis. Second it was difficult to hold the interest of the group of Negroes in Macon County unless some treatment was given." Vonderlehr to Austin V. Diebert, December 5, 1938, Tuskegee Syphilis Study Ad Hoc Advisory Panel Papers, Box 1, National Library of Medicine, Bethesda, Maryland. (Hereafter, TSS-NLM.) This collection contains the materials assembled by the HEW investigation in 1972.

33. Vonderlehr to Clark, February 6, 1933, NA-WNRC.

34. H. S. Cumming to J. N. Baker, August 5, 1933, NA-WNRC.

35. Clark to Moore, March 25, 1933, NA-WNRC.

36. Macon County Health Department, "Letter to Subjects," n.d., NA-WNRC.

37. Vonderlehr to Clark, April 8, 1933, NA-WNRC. See also, Vonderlehr to Wenger, July 18, 1933, NA-WNRC.

38. Wenger to Vonderlehr, July 21, 1933, NA-WNRC. The italics are Wenger's.

39. Wenger to Vonderlehr, July 21, 1933, NA-WNRC.

40. Eunice Rivers, Stanley Schuman, Lloyd Simpson, Sidney Olansky, "Twenty-Years of Followup Experience In a Long-Range Medical Study," *Public Health Reports* 68 (April 1953), 391–95. In this article Nurse Rivers explains her role in the experiment. She wrote: "Because of the low educational status of the majority of the patients, it was impossible to appeal to them from a purely scientific approach. Therefore, various methods were used to maintain their interest. Free medicines, burial assistance or insurance (the project being referred to as 'Miss Rivers' Lodge'), free hot meals on the days of examination, transportation to and from the hospital, and an opportunity to stop in town on the return trip to shop or visit with their friends on the streets all helped. In spite of these attractions, there were some who refused their examinations because they were not sick and did not see that they were being benefitted." (p. 393).

41. Austin V. Diebert to Raymond Vonderlehr, March 20, 1939, TSS-NLM, Box 1.

42. Murray Smith to Subjects (1938), TSS-NLM, Box 1. See also, Sidney Olansky to John C. Cutler, November 6, 1951, TSS-NLM, Box 2.

43. The USPHS originally requested that the Julius Rosenwald Fund meet this expense. See Cumming to Davis, October 4, 1934, NA-WNRC. This money was usually divided between the undertaker, pathologist, and hospital. Lloyd Isaacs to Raymond Vonderlehr, April 23, 1940, TSS-NLM, Box 1.

44. Stanley H. Schuman, Sidney Olansky, Eunice Rivers, C. A. Smith, Dorothy S. Rambo, "Untreated Syphilis in the Male Negro: Background and Current Status of Patients in the Tuskegee Study," *Journal of Chronic Diseases* 2 (November 1955), 555.

45. R. A. Vonderlehr and Taliaferro Clark, "Untreated Syphilis in the Male Negro," *Venereal Disease Information* 17 (September 1936), 262.

46. J. R. Heller and P. T. Bruyere, "Untreated Syphilis in the Male Negro: II. Mortality During 12 Years of Observation," *Venereal Disease Information* 27 (February 1946), 34–38.

47. Jesse J. Peters, James H. Peers, Sidney Olansky, John C. Cutler, and Geraldine Gleeson, "Untreated

Syphilis in the Male Negro: Pathologic Findings in Syphilitic and Non-Syphilitic Patients," *Journal of Chronic Diseases* 1 (February 1955), 127–48.

48. Sidney Olansky, Stanley H. Schuman, Jesse J. Peters, C. A. Smith, and Dorothy S. Rambo, "Untreated Syphilis in the Male Negro, X. Twenty Years of Clinical Observation of Untreated Syphilitic and Presumably Nonsyphilitic Groups," *Journal of Chronic Diseases* 4 (August 1956), 184.

49. O. C. Wenger, "Untreated Syphilis in Male Negro," unpublished typescript, 1950, p. 3. Tuskegee Files, Center for Disease Control, Atlanta, Georgia. (Hereafter TF-CDC).

50. Vernal G. Cave, "Proper Uses and Abuses of the Health Care Delivery System for Minorities with Special Reference to the Tuskegee Syphilis Study," *Journal of the National Medical Association* 67 (January 1975), 83.

51. See for example, Vonderlehr to B. W. Booth, April 18, 1934; Vonderlehr to E. R. Lett, November 20, 1933, NA-WNRC.

52. "Transcript of Proceedings—Tuskegee Syphilis Ad Hoc Advisory Panel," February 23, 1973, unpublished typescript, TSS-NLM, Box 1.

53. Raymond Vonderlehr to Murray Smith, April 30, 1942; and Smith to Vonderlehr, June 8, 1942, TSS-NLM, Box 1.

54. Stanley H. Schuman, Sidney Olansky, Eunice Rivers, C. A. Smith, and Dorothy S. Rambo, "Untreated Syphilis in the Male Negro: Background and Current Status of Patients in the Tuskegee Study," *Journal of Chronic Diseases* 2 (November 1955), 550–53.

55. Raymond Vonderlehr to Stanley H. Schuman, February 5, 1952. TSS-NLM, Box 2.

56. Schuman et al., p. 550.

57. "Minutes, April 5, 1965" unpublished typescript, TSS-NLM, Box 1.

58. "Tuskegee Ad Hoc Committee Meeting—Minutes, February 6, 1969," TF-CDC.

59. James B. Lucas to William J. Brown, September 10, 1970, TF-CDC.

60. Elizabeth M. Kennebrew to Arnold C. Schroeter, February 24, 1971, TSS-NLM, Box 1.

61. See *Medical Tribune* (September 13, 1972), pp. 1, 20; and "Report on HEW's Tuskegee Report,"

Medical World News (September 14, 1973), pp. 57–58.

62. HEW *Final Report,* p. 7.

63. The notable exception is Jay Katz's eloquent "Reservations About the Panel Report on Charge 1," HEW *Final Report,* pp. 14–15.

64. HEW *Final Report,* pp. 8, 12.

65. HEW *Final Report,* pp. 8, 12.

66. See R. H. Kampmeier, "The Tuskegee Study of Untreated Syphilis," *Southern Medical Journal* 65 (October 1972), 1247–51; and "Final Report on the 'Tuskegee Syphilis Study,'" *Southern Medical Journal* 67 (November 1974), 1349–53.

67. Leonard J. Goldwater, "The Tuskegee Study in Historical Perspective," unpublished typescript, TSS-NLM; see also "Treponemes and Tuskegee," *Lancet* (June 23, 1973), 1438; and Louis Lasagna, *The VD Epidemic* (Philadelphia: Temple University Press, 1975), pp. 64–66.

68. Quoted in "Debate Revives on the PHS Study," *Medical World News* (April 19, 1974), 37.

69. Heller to Vonderlehr, November 28, 1933, NA-WNRC; quoted in *Medical Tribune* (August 23, 1972), p. 14.

70. Although it is now known that syphilis is rarely infectious after its early phase, at the time of the study's inception latent syphilis was thought to be communicable. The fact that members of the control group were placed in the test group when they became syphilitic proves that at least some infectious men were denied treatment.

71. When the subjects are drawn from minority groups, especially those with which the researcher cannot identify, basic human rights may be compromised. Hans Jonas has clearly explicated the problem in his "Philosophical Reflections on Experimentation," *Daedalus* 98 (Spring 1969), 234–37. As Jonas writes: "If the properties we adduced as the particular qualifications of the members of the scientific fraternity itself are taken as general criteria of selection, then one should look for additional subjects where a maximum of identification, understanding, and spontaneity can be expected—that is, among the most highly motivated, the most highly educated, and the least 'captive' members of the community."

THINKING ABOUT THE READINGS

Invisible Man

■ What do you think is the significance of the title of this article? How does being "invisible" compare with being the target of outright racial hatred? Why do you suppose country clubs have been so slow to allow blacks and other racial minorities to become members? Do you think that Graham's experiences are a valid indicator of the way wealthy whites, in general, think of people of color? What are some of the shortcomings of his "study?"

The Moral Drama of Multicultural Education

■ From a conflict perspective, can you explain the resistance on the part of some (who Nelson-Rowe calls "Anglocentrists") to the implementation of multicultural education programs? Do you think the use of terms like "villain," "hero," and "victim" are appropriate in this context? How does your university deal with the issue of multiculturalism in the curriculum? What sorts of ethnic studies programs are taught? How do your instructors address issues of racial and ethnic diversity in the classroom? What are the long-term consequences for society if we continue to move from a "melting pot" ideal where people are encouraged to shed their cultural differences to a "patchwork quilt" ideal where people are encouraged to maintain and celebrate their cultural differences? After reading this article, what do you think about the growing popularity of so-called "Afro-centric" schools?

Racism and Research: The Tuskegee Syphilis Study

■ What, specifically, were the racist beliefs that supported the Tuskegee syphilis study? Do you think that such an experiment could have been undertaken with white subjects instead of black subjects? Do you think the scientific gains of this research outweighed the personal costs to those who participated? Explain. In what ways do stereotypical perceptions of race and ethnicity still drive scientific and social scientific research?

CHAPTER 13

The Architecture of Inequality
Gender

Along with racial and class inequality, sexual inequality—and the struggle against it—has been a fundamental part of the historical development of our national identity. Along the way it has influenced the lives and dreams of individual people, shaped popular culture, and created or maintained social institutions. Gender is a major criterion for the distribution of important resources in most societies.

Women have made significant advances politically, economically, education-ally, and socially over the past decade. The traditional obstacles to advancement continue to fall. Yet despite such positive strides, many women still suffer in their interpersonal encounters with men. Carol Brooks Gardner, in "Passing By," looks at women's experiences with the age-old phenomenon of public sexual harassment—the abuses and annoyances characteristic of public encounters with strangers. While whistles, cat calls, pinches and pats are a common experience for most women, not all think such treatment is offensive. Gardner describes the dif-ferent ways women (and men) romanticize or politicize public harassment.

Despite women's growing presence in the paid labor force and their entry into historically male occupations, rarely do they work alongside men or perform the same tasks and functions. Jobs within an occupation still tend to be divided into "men's work" and "women's work." Such sex segregation has serious conse-quences for women in the form of blocked advancement and lower salaries. But looking at sex segregation on the job as only something that happens to women gives us an incomplete picture of the situation. It is just as important to examine what keeps men out of "female" jobs as it is to examine what keeps women out of "male" jobs. While the proportion of women in male jobs has increased over the past several decades, the proportion of men in female jobs has remained vir-tually unchanged. In "Still a Man's World," Christine Williams looks at the expe-riences of male nurses, social workers, elementary school teachers, and librarians. She finds that although these men do feel somewhat stigmatized by their non-traditional career choices they still enjoy significant gender advantages.

Passing By
Gender and Public Harassment

Carol Brooks Gardner

Imagine yourself walking down the street. Someone passes from the opposite direction, and as they pass, they hurl at you the most vile epithet for your group that you can think of. Now imagine that you are African-American, and the other person is white. Imagine you use a wheelchair, but the other person does not, or imagine that you stutter, a usually silent stigma in public that is revealed when you must ask the other person for directions. Imagine you are Asian-American, and the other person is African-American.

Imagine you are a woman, and the other person is a man.

How does your interpretation of what happened change, if it does, depending on your group membership? Most people match their interpretation of what happened to the group membership of the people involved. If you are like many people, you will be unhappy, disturbed, or outraged at every case but the last. In the last case alone, the presumption of romance intrudes to cloud what has happened—as it intrudes on all gender-based public harassment. . . .

Many of our expectations for the performance of etiquette imply a heterosexual romanticization, even eroticization, of public order. Many assume, for instance, that a man's evaluative comments on a strange woman's appearance have something to do with his estimate of her as a potential romantic or sexual partner. More accurately, he uses his evaluation of her as potential partner not only to express an opinion but to express his right to express an opinion. This romanticization and eroticization are upheld by the delicts of public harassment, as well as by the dictates of etiquette. In fact, what the individual must support is the demonstration of the public norms of identifiably heterosexual society. . . .

. . . Public harassment therefore can be an emblem of the harasser's ratification and support of the existing hierarchy of heterosexual preference and the existing romantic basis for attraction, centered on appearance-based evaluation. In public places it is not so much that "love at first sight" rules the day, as that "a reliable estimate of gender and sexual preference" does—and ought to—rule the public realm. Thus, in sustaining public order, the individual is habitually called on to sustain values that she or he does not actually support elsewhere, and the individual sometimes agrees to do so. As individuals appear to support behavior and countenance norms they do not in fact practice, they subtly undermine their own activities and perhaps their identity. . . .

. . . Some women (sometimes many women) try to explain what is happening in public harassment by using the template of a heterosexual romantic or erotic attraction: that is, they use a romanticized interpretation. Some women explain public harassment by using the template of a feminist politicization: that is, they refer to harassment that occurs in public places as being on a continuum with sexual harassment in school and workplace and violence in the home and street. Most women interviewed, including those who identified themselves as feminists, ended by using a mixed romanticized and politicized rhetoric. No matter how outspoken a woman was of public harassment, she often fell back on criticizing her own appearance or behavior as culpable—tacit admission that romantic attraction was at the root of public harassment by men. A parallel in race-based public harassment would be the African-American informant who suggested that, had she not had such dark skin or such nappy hair, the white men who screamed "Nigger!" at her from a truck would not have done so.

. . . Men also used (although rarely) a politicized rhetoric for dealing with public harassment, but it was often the verso to politicized rhetoric: Men who interpreted public harassment as politicized sometimes did so by envisioning it as a reaction to the women's movement, seeing it not as proof that they themselves were abusers in the street as well as the workplace, then, but as proof that, given women's current strident political stance, public harassment was punishment well deserved and appropriately meted out. That it might not go to those who had "earned" it escaped the attention of virtually all men politicizers. Although women and men typically placed harassment within either the romanticized framework or the politicized framework, they sometimes employed both—uncomfortably, for some women especially.

Women and men were likely to interpret incidents of public harassment differently: Even when women and men used the dominant and widely disseminated romanticized rhetoric, they—quite reasonably—did so, if nothing else, from their own points of view and with what was at stake for their own sex foremost. . . . As both genders explain and account for public harassment, they also unwittingly reveal their assumptions about the opposite sex. These revelations suggest we have far to travel merely to understand the diversity of the opposite sex, much less to make peace and live with respect. . . .

A Fine Romance: Women's Romanticized Interpretations for Public Harassment

Most women arrive eventually at strategies for accounting for public harassment. Broadly, this accounting may be divided into four types of claimsmaking activities by a romanticized vocabulary of events. First, there are those that claim that public harassment is essentially innocuous,

and buttress their claims by mentioning that women as well as men are among the offenders, that offenders can be reliably specified by categories of class, race, appearance (often a cover for concerns of class and race), and sexual orientation (often under the guise of reference to a man's "masculinity," lack of same, or the use of a specific homophobic slur). Second, there are accounts that argue that men's nature is to blame and present as proof men's ineluctable sexuality or their adoption of allegedly boyish traits such as showing off or teasing; the simplest version of this explanation held that "men just can't help it." Third is the claim that men in fact flatter women—that men only *seem* to be insulting, hitting, groping, trailing, ogling, or engaging in unwanted conversation. Fourth, women who use romanticized rhetoric often claim that the acts are basically breaches of etiquette; what happens is undeserved criticism by unappreciative observers. Unfortunately, this claimsmaking style opens the gate for critical espousers to note that women too breach traditional etiquette when they dress inappropriately, act loosely available, or in other ways denigrate the portrait of the traditional woman who keeps comfortably to her home and ventures out only when need be—and then with proper respect for the situation at large.

Public Harassment as Flattery

. . . Many nonfeminist women, and many men as well, argued that public harassment was in fact "complimentary." This account is, when examined, a particularly difficult one to sustain. There are probably few compliments between close friends that feature obscene slurs, threats, and slaps, yet it is an explanation that is customary for public harassment.

Current etiquette books and advice articles often support this rationale: They counsel women to interpret street remarks in particular in the most flattering light possible by saying, for example, that a street remark "goes a long way toward filling your need for spontaneous, frank praise" and, furthermore, that it is "merely [and this is the best 'merely' I know of] a tribute freely offered and meant to be just as freely accepted. . . . Unphony, no strings—simply one person vocalizing pleasure at seeing beauty in another" (Geng 1979:76). These works of etiquette rely on interpreting public harassment as positive, helpful, and salutary simply because it is anonymous.

Traditional folk interpretations counsel women that much public harassment is innocuously intended and flattering; it is the reward due to the woman who correctly projects beauty, femininity, and attention to appearance. Such an interpretation suggests not only that it can help the woman feel better about herself in the immediate situation but that "when a street compliment has made you feel beautiful, you can project that aura to the men who are really in your life and just passing by" (Geng 1979:75). Thus, it can be an anonymous practice or socialization session for the woman on how she can expect to be evaluated in private circumstances. In fact, flattering incidents of public harassment could, some women claimed, actually help a woman. Incidents like these could at times make them "feel better about themselves," feel like "real women," boost self-confidence, and socialize women in the skills of pleasing men. . . .

Gallantry as Proof of Flattery

In making the argument that public harassment is truly flattery, women often mentioned that men bestowed public harassment on those not truly compliment-worthy. This observation was used to bolster claims of men's charity, even chivalry, in harassing women. . . .

Some woman noted that men sometimes committed public harassment in such a way that the act neutralized or at least minimized the offense, thus making it as likely as it could be that a woman might feel commended. Women might count this as another proof that public harassment was charity or flattery rather than hostility. For instance, an African-American law student was walking by "a bunch of white boys going the same way when one bowed as I went by and said very seriously, '*Very* beautiful.'" She continued, "This elaborate and formal ritual" was proof of their sincere efforts to compliment her; moreover, "they spared me my race. It could've been nasty, if they'd said 'Nigger bitch!' for example." A white homemaker noted that she knew that the middle-aged white man who pinched her painfully as she waited in line at a public utility office was in fact trying to "pay me a compliment," because "he patted my butt afterwards, then he carefully smoothed out the fabric on my skirt. I felt it was respectful of me." . . .

The men in these examples may have defused offense partly for their own protection, which sets these situations apart from skillful street remarks or modified exploitations of presence. These men cast themselves as neither disrespectful lechers nor serious suitors, thereby bypassing the possibility that they could be seriously refused and implicitly substantiating the romantic ideal. Such ambiguous tangles of implication and definition make it all the more difficult for women to act when they resent public harassment: When women try to react assertively in circumstances where marriage or romantic companionship is invoked, they seem to criticize not just harassers but values of marriage and family as well. Of course, regardless of how they are mitigated, these occurrences of harassment nevertheless reinforce traditional gender relations, substantiating that it is a man's prerogative to evaluate women. Mitigation here implies the author's right (even duty) to calibrate the impact of an action rather than the recipient's right to avoid it. . . .

When a woman goes to what she feels is considerable trouble to maintain, alter, or modify her appearance in order to secure men's attention, she might be all the more likely to feel that a wide range of public harassment was evidence that her efforts had not been made in vain and thus all the less likely to question the character of the attention. . . .

In fact, twenty-three women informants revealed that they had had cosmetic surgery to alter the way they were treated in public (I did not routinely ask this question). Eleven of these women reported that they had had cosmetic surgery to make themselves more attractive to men and suggested that attention in public places was an expected part of that. Eleven, on the other hand, told me that they undertook cosmetic surgery at least in part to escape that same attention. If nothing else, public harassment would seem to be a great support of plastic surgery as a medical specialty. Thus, one young African-

American file clerk told me that she had had her breasts enlarged to ensure that men on the street would look at her with what she felt was admiration: "It cost me two months' salary to get these breast implants," she said, "and you best believe that I did it so guys would look at me. I don't care if they feel me up, or what they do. That's what I paid all that money for." These are quite serious modifications—face or breast surgery, liposuction, and leg recontouring are the most common surgical measures—to endure for the sake of peace in public places. . . .

Public Harassment as the Result of Men's Natures: Men as Rampant Beasts

Women who romanticized public harassment were likely to support the idea that acts of public harassment stemmed from the allegedly unalterable character of the strange man who was offender, thus in fact accepting the intransigence of men as a social category. To these women, men are equipped with a certain nature comprising character, constitution, genes, brain, and hormones, and really have no choice but to be constantly sexually appetent; women, then, are left with no recourse but to endure or to strategize in minor ways when public harassment occurs. One woman who identified herself as "firmly traditional" said that changing men's behavior toward women in public was as likely as "changing a leopard's spots, and a lot more dangerous." African-American women were especially likely to allude to some vaguely biologically based rationale for men's public harassment of women: in fact, nearly 75 percent of the African-American women interviewed did so. (In contrast, white women of the middle and working classes were especially likely to espouse and elaborate on women's responsibility to categorize correctly the membership of potential offenders.) . . .

Other women were more inclined to use quasi-sociological analyses of men's public harassment, suggesting that public harassment was comparable to pulling on a girl's pigtails or dipping them in the inkwell, male-initiation rites of primitive cultures, or simply demonstrating "machismo," a term women used to cover a great variety of acts that could be thought of as rude but might be judged to be battery or sexual battery should our lawmakers choose to consider them. When women cited machismo as a spur for public harassment, they often sympathized with the harasser, implying that is was, on the whole, too bad that men were bound to constantly strive, approach, and be sadly disappointed. A twenty-year-old white receptionist noted:

> All men are insecure with their masculinity. This is our culture that does this to them. If they were headhunters, there'd be no problem. But now it's very hard to be a man. You have to keep it up, keep proving it. They *have* to tease women constantly, touch them, try to talk to them, do anything they can. Otherwise, they'd be wimps. You've got to feel sorry for them when you think about it, don't you?

This woman had been hooted at by construction workers on her way to work for weeks, so that she eventually took to creeping around the back of the building to take a service elevator. . . .

Women who were inclined to theorize more about society said that "men's nature" leads to a truly awe-inspiring sex drive, which made them look at every woman, even strangers in public, as potential sex partners. However, many women who mentioned men's "strong sex drive" also noted the characteristics that accompanied it, such as "a sense of superiority," "dominance," and "bossing women around." To suggest, sometimes pityingly as these women did, that men who publicly harass women do so out of insubstantial masculinity or attempted bravery is, in some measure, to justify their offenses. It also presents public incursions as marks of men's failure when they are, quite clearly, marks of men's domination and effective power over women—an effective power that can depend on women's acquiescence, even though it can be a prudent acquiescence. . . .

Just Deserts: Harassment as Women's Fault

Some women and men felt that women provoked public harassment not only by the clothing that they wore but with a smile or eye contact (acts that might be taken as suggestive behavior) or simply by their attractiveness. Several women suggested that they were catcalled, pinched, or followed because they were prettier, sexier, more cheerful, or simply "nicer" than most other women. Some women said that women were to blame for their harassment, although the women criticized were customarily not of the same class or did not adhere to the informant's belief systems, and the informant seldom criticized herself. A typical remark condemned women who dress "to show off their bodies." Another typical remark suggested that men quite reasonably assumed from their experience that these women were "loose" or "sluts," and that such women appreciated public harassment of any type. Moreover, these women poisoned the well of public order for decent women like the speakers: Men could not be blamed for treating those they assumed to be sluts like sluts.

A few women, however, argued that the responsibility was their own and that harassment could be controlled by controlling women's appearance. This was also an argument of some politicized feminists who believe that if women moderate their attractiveness they will escape notice in public and hence the harassment that is the traditional woman's lot. Moreover, many women who otherwise resented exploitation, and roundly criticized the men who authored it, suggested that an element of their own attractiveness was the cause. Indeed, they suggested it was women's responsibility to dress and act "modestly" or to expect consequences. In fact, these women said that the consequences were a compliment, the result of the man looking for the most attractive target he could find.

Other women were less certain of how to interpret public harassment, but they still found cause in their own behavior, saying they may have looked too vulnerable or shy (it is difficult not to when you are in an environment that exacerbates your vulnerability and which is not crafted for you), seemed too polite (although part of what you learn is to be polite to strange men, in part because the dangerous ones may not attend to you if you are), dressed inappropriately (of course, you are not always dressing to please the diverse tastes of diverse strangers, nor is the street or shop always your final destination). . . .

The Politicization of the Public Order: A Different Way of Accounting for Harassment

. . . When women politicized public harassment, they sometimes gave it a noble cause, ratified the existence of other claims about the situation of women (or men, or African-Americans, or people with disabilities), and stimulated a sense of justice undermined or, when the target of the harassment took action, justice upheld. Women offered the following similes and metaphors for incidents of public harassment like ogling, following, pinching and grabbing, street remarks, and vitiations of expected public aid: women compared public harassment to, prominently, rape, prostitution, socialization to the "nice girl" model, women as entertaining visual objects, wife-beating, sexual and racial discrimination, sexual and racial harassment in workplace and school. Mentioned less frequently were pornography, child abuse, the revictimization of victims, the Holocaust, Balkan genocide, crimes against women and girls, and the Rodney King and Reginald Denny beatings in the Los Angeles riots of 1992. Many women considered street remarks and exploitive touch on a continuum with rape, a possible "preamble to rape," "verbal rape," "a little rape," or connected to "sexual terrorism" in general.

When women implicitly or explicitly claim that their situation is comparable to situations that form a larger political issue, however modestly the claim is made, these women acquire the benefits of sympathetic popular opinion, and they also acquire the right to claim that they understand something of the point of view, experience, or trauma of those who have suffered in similar situations. (And so, of course, does anyone who invokes such metaphors for her or his own troubles.) For the moment, then, being pinched on a bus or being run through the gauntlet by a group of construction workers has the high gloss of a political cause. At the same time, indignation over the plight of others who are more obviously injured can fuel a woman's fear, anger, and resentment. A young white graduate student told of her experience of being painfully hit on the breast by a stranger, who then conveniently ran off into a crowd:

[M]y feminist consciousness dates from that incident. It was so wrong. It made me furious, and then I knew that there was absolutely nothing I could do about it. It did something else: It made me understand how a rape survivor feels. I don't mean that I'm as bad off as a woman that's been raped, but the mechanics of the thing are the same. Now I find I really watch men carefully. Now I think, "You never know that they'll do." I feel I understand more what Blacks suffer in the society, too.

Not all women who cast public harassment in politicized terms went much beyond that label in suggesting it was offensive. A few spoke of public or sexual harassment, but only to trivialize offenses, either saying that they were something a women should learn to manage or ignore or identifying only a few of the mildest sort of offenses as harassment and then concluding that these minor, verbal offenses were unremarkable. One college student said:

Sure, women get sexually harassed in the street. Sure, they get terrified. But so what? Women just get yelled at, or they get goosed or grab-assed. Maybe sometimes hit, like I was. But nothing worse. Nobody gets killed. Women can handle it. So just forget about it. It's not a big deal. It's not important.

[Are you aware that some of the offenses we've been talking about are against the law?]

Well, they shouldn't be. All the guys do it. Get real.

Needless to say, to invoke a cause with a well-worked-out pattern of claimsmaking typically emphasized a woman's lack of responsibility for what happened to her (although the previous example neatly puts the responsibility back on the woman's shoulders). By and large, women who politicized public harassment said that they "accept no responsibility for being the victim of someone's vulgar remarks or actions," in the words of a lab technician in her forties from Indianapolis. Yet even women who were deeply offended were also often at a loss to know what to do when public harassment occurred. . . .

Men: The Situationally Advantaged Interpretation of Public Harassment

Most men's interpretations made clear that they, without shame, took for granted their right to evaluate women. In the words of one of a group of young white men I observed shouting at a passing woman, men have the right to "put a price tag" on women they do not know. Such metaphors ran through men's accounts in abundance, especially in the accounts of white working- and middle-class men. These similes and metaphors were rarely present in women's accounts of men's action and, if present, they were criticized or laboriously rationalized. . . .

The Situationally Advantaged in Public Places

There are certain common features of the viewpoints of groups situationally advantaged in public places that deserve mentioning. My current research on public harassment across race, health status, sexual preference, and social class suggests in part that these are elements of a viewpoint that any situationally advantaged group member can adopt with relation to . . . situationally disadvantaged group members. Thus, heterosexual women and men have these views toward homosexuals; able-bodied women and men have them in regard to women and men who are disabled; whites of both sexes have them with regard to people of color; younger people have them with regard to older people. Although membership in one group that is situationally disadvantaged in public places will certainly tend to increase the chances that an individual will gain insight into the experience of other situationally disadvantaged groups—as gay and bisexual men tend to be more sensitive to women's plight—this identification depends somewhat on how revered or how despised the other group is.

Neatly demonstrating these gradations of sensitivity was a fifty-five-year-old gay white man, who spoke sympathetically about a white waitress he had seen harassed the previous week: "Finally, I just feel so bad for her. I knew what it was like, because that's what happens to queens [as he counts himself] especially. It's everything from sneering and mocking, to being raped and being beat up, or kicked. It's a power thing from men, straight men, for both of us." A hallmark of most situationally advantaged groups is the tendency of their members to define the troubles of the disadvantaged as being a flight of fancy of a whining minority. . . .

Public Places as Romantic Frontiers

. . . The tradition of "girl-watching" is considered by many to be a pleasant feature of some public spaces such as plazas. Thus, some analysts have suggested that girl-watching should be encouraged with other "delights" and marks of "sociability" such as lunching in the outdoors and the presence of buskers, mimes, musicians, and other street entertainers. . . .

A man who sees a public place as a romantic frontier will probably choose an active role while in that place, either that of critical watcher (of women) and kin (of men), or that of competitor. A young white man, a college student, said that in general he preferred to "watch people instead of having people watch me." A white salesman in his late thirties noted he was effectively "glued to women" and fascinated by judging them, to the exclusion of attending to his own sex entirely. If, for instance, he "saw a man and a woman together and you asked me the next day if I remembered them or something on that order, I couldn't tell you anything about the man, [but] I could tell you everything about the woman, as far as physical characteristics."

Action—public harassment—on the romantic frontier was interpreted as playful or sportive competition. One man, when asked how he judged incidents of public harassment, noted that they made public places lively and enjoyable: "Are those incidents acceptable? Let me just put it this way: If they weren't the world would be a very dull place." This frontier ethos sometimes resulted in showdowns with seeming competitors who passed in cars, while jogging, or while walking. A young white student noted that he would "get mildly offended when somebody passes me [in a car]," and another said that he "had at least one drag race a day with someone who thinks he can pass me—I don't *let* that happen." Some men simply noted that this frontier was, for them,

home. Said one African-American engineer: "I'm at home anywhere in public, unafraid and unsure why anyone else would be afraid either." An Asian-American health-care professional said that "in public places I have a real feeling of well-being." And a white sales manager said that in public "I feel like I belong."

The Advantaged Are in Fact Disadvantaged

Men often argue that they, not women, were disadvantaged in public places. This disadvantage was sometimes described as a result of distrust: "Women don't trust us, and because of that they treat us badly," a young white manager said. An appliance service technician in his forties specified that women

> get waited on before men, by men. In some ways they are treated well, because men buy their drinks for them when they are out. Woman bully other drivers—men and women—by being pushy, getting on each other's tails, and forcing their way into wherever they want to go.

Often women's ostensible status as a group deserving special etiquette and consideration from strangers was offered as proof of favored treatment in actuality.

Some men offered incidents of their own humiliation as a justification for public harassment that they or other men had committed. One man related that a group of women had laughed at him when his fly was open, causing him to feel "angry and pissed off, embarrassed." Other men recounted stories of women dealing competently with their public harassment, as when a pair of young women responded to a man who had "patted both their heinies" while he walked down the middle of a crowded mall. One woman stuck out her tongue, and the other kicked him. This man said he was "angry and deeply, thoroughly hurt" by the incident.

Romance, Flattery, and Heterosexual Masculinity

. . . Men frequently suggested that public harassment often was honest and frank evaluation, an attempt to meet a woman or, failing that, to communicate admiration, or just a response to the calculated provocation of a woman's appearance. Thus both attempts at acquaintance and evaluation were foremost in men's accounts. A medical student "on a tight schedule" said tartly: "Of course I pass comments—at the malls, at the Laundromat, at the grocery store, on my lunchbreak. With my schedule, how else am I going to meet women?" Such artless attempts to establish acquaintance with a woman can rarely be successful, since responding to a street remark with a bid for friendship or a date currently makes a woman seem too available. In any event, most of her responses will be used as fodder for further comment.

The argument that public harassment is in fact a sincere attempt at courtship is bolstered by men who note that they would commit these intrusions anytime, anywhere, to anyone *except* a woman escorted by a man. One man said that both nonselectivity in targets and using an escorted woman as a target constituted harassment: "If you constantly do it to everyone who walks down the street, then it ought to be considered as harassment or whatever. But as far as she's with her husband or boyfriend or male boyfriend, you know, you should have respect for him and her." A white salesman in his forties suggested that there was "nothing wrong with going up to a woman and complimenting her on her hair, unless she's sitting with her husband. That's just rude." In cases of women escorted by men, other men said, acts were "criminal," "bad man-ners," "disrespecting," or "crazy—why would you do it?" And harassers were also, it should be noted, likely to get retaliation from the escort.

Most men informants reported public harassment by women as flattering, a compliment, a proof of manhood, or a seal of approval on sexual attractiveness. One man said to be spoken to by a strange woman (he could not name an instance where it had happened) was "applause" for him, signifying that women appreciated him "as is." Such interpretations and feelings are in strong contrast to most women's reactions, which were to question self, appearance, and behavior. No man reported that he had reacted in this way; of course, men experienced far fewer of these incidents than did women, and then only in relatively narrow circumstances and range. Some perceived women harassers—those who pinched, prodded, spoke, or gazed, since women reported little else more daring—as offering compliments of the same sort. Yet others perceived women harassers as "odd," since the behavior itself was "not something you'd expect from a decent woman"—although something, apparently, that one would expect from any decent man. . . .

REFERENCES

Geng, Veronica. 1979. "Scorn Not the Street Compliment!" In Helen Gurley Brown, ed., *Cosmopolitan's New Etiquette Guide*. North Hollywood, Calif.: Wilshire.

Still a Man's World

Men Who Do "Women's Work"

Christine L. Williams

Gendered Jobs
and Gendered Workers

A 1959 article in *Library Journal* entitled "The Male Librarian—An Anomaly?" begins this way:

> My friends keep trying to get me out of the library. . . . Library work is fine, they agree, but they smile and shake their heads benevolently and charitably, as if it were unnecessary to add that it is one of the dullest, most poorly paid, unrewarding, off-beat activities any man could be consigned to. If you have a heart condition, if you're physically handicapped in other ways, well, such a job is a blessing. And for women there's no question library work is fine; there are some wonderful women in libraries and we all ought to be thankful to them. But let's face it, no healthy man of normal intelligence should go into it.[1]

Male librarians still face this treatment today, as do other men who work in predominantly female occupations. In 1990, my local newspaper featured a story entitled "Men Still Avoiding Women's Work" that described my research on men in nursing, librarianship, teaching, and social work. Soon afterwards, a humor columnist for the same paper wrote a spoof on the story that he titled, "Most Men Avoid Women's Work Because It Is Usually So Boring."[2] The columnist poked fun at hairdressing, librarianship, nursing, and babysitting—in his view, all "lousy" jobs requiring low intelligence and a high tolerance for bore-

dom. Evidently people still wonder why any "healthy man of normal intelligence" would willingly work in a "woman's occupation."

In fact, not very many men do work in these fields, although their numbers are growing. In 1990, over 500,000 men were employed in these four occupations, constituting approximately 6 percent of all registered nurses, 15 percent of all elementary school teachers, 17 percent of all librarians, and 32 percent of all social workers. These percentages have fluctuated in recent years: As Table 1 indicates, librarianship and social work have undergone slight declines in the proportions of men since 1975; teaching has remained somewhat stable; while nursing has experienced noticeable gains. The number of men in nursing actually doubled between 1980 and 1990; however, their overall proportional representation remains very low.

Very little is known about these men who "cross over" into these nontraditional occupations. While numerous books have been written about women entering male-dominated occupations, few have asked why men are underrepresented in traditionally female jobs.[3] The underlying assumption in most research on gender and work is that, given a free choice, both men and women would work in predominantly male occupations, as they are generally better paying and more prestigious than predominantly female occupations. The few men who willingly "cross over" must be, as the 1959 article suggests, "anomalies."

TABLE 1 *Men in the "Women's Professions":
Number (in thousands) and Distribution of Men
Employed in the Occupations, Selected Years*

Profession	1975	1980	1990
Registered Nurses			
Number of men	28	46	92
% men	3.0	3.5	5.5
Elementary Teachers[a]			
Number of men	194	225	223
% men	14.6	16.3	14.8
Librarians			
Number of men	34	27	32
% men	18.9	14.8	16.7
Social Workers			
Number of men	116	134	179
% men	39.2	35.0	31.8

Sources: U.S. Department of Labor, Bureau of Labor Statistics, *Employment and Earnings* 38, no. 1 (January 1991), table 22 (employed civilians by detailed occupation), p. 185; vol. 28, no. 1 (January 1981), table 23 (employed persons by detailed occupation), p. 180; vol. 22, no. 7 (January 1976), table 2 (employed persons by detailed occupation), p. 11.

[a]Excludes kindergarten teachers.

Popular culture reinforces the belief that these men are "anomalies." Men are rarely portrayed working in these occupations, and when they are, they are represented in extremely stereotypical ways. For example, in the 1990 movie *Kindergarten Cop*, muscle-man Arnold Schwarzenegger played a detective forced to work undercover as a kindergarten teacher; the otherwise competent Schwarzenegger was completely overwhelmed by the five-year-old children in his class. . . .

[I] challenge these stereotypes about men who do "women's work" through case studies of men in four predominantly female occupations: nursing, elementary school teaching, librarianship, and social work. I show that men maintain their masculinity in these occupations, despite the popular stereotypes. Moreover, male power and privilege is preserved and reproduced in these occupations through a complex interplay between gendered expectations embedded in organizations, and the gendered interests workers bring with them to their jobs. Each of these occupations is "still a man's world" even though mostly women work in them.

I selected these four professions as case studies of men who do "women's work" for a variety of reasons. First, because they are so strongly associated with women and femininity in our popular culture, these professions highlight and perhaps even exaggerate the barriers and advantages men face when entering predominantly female environments. Second, they each require extended periods of educational training and apprenticeship, requiring individuals in these occupations to be at least somewhat committed to their work (unlike those employed in, say, clerical or domestic work). Therefore I thought they would be reflective about their decisions to join these "nontraditional" occupations, making them "acute observers" and, hence, ideal informants about the sort of social and psychological processes I am interested in describing.[4] Third, these occupations vary a great deal in the proportion of men working in them. Although my aim was not to engage in between-group comparisons, I believed that the proportions of men in a work setting would strongly influence the degree to which they felt accepted and satisfied with their jobs.[5]

I traveled across the United States conducting in-depth interviews with seventy-six men and twenty-three women who work in nursing, teaching, librarianship, and social work. Like the people employed in these professions generally, those in my sample were predominantly white (90 percent). Their ages ranged from twenty to sixty-six, and the average age was thirty-eight. I interviewed women as well as men to gauge their feelings and reactions to men's entry into "their" professions. Respondents were intentionally selected to represent a wide range of specialties and levels of education and experience. I interviewed students in professional schools, "front line" practitioners, administrators, and retirees, asking them about their motivations to enter these professions, their on-the-job experiences, and their opinions about men's status and prospects in these fields. . . .

Riding the Glass Escalator

Men earn more money than women in every occupation—even in predominantly female jobs (with the possible exceptions of fashion modeling and prostitution).[6] Table 2 shows that men out-earn women in teaching, librarianship, and social work; their salaries in nursing are virtually identical. The ratios between women's and men's earnings in these occupations are higher than those found in the "male" professions, where women earn 74 to 90 percent of men's salaries. That there is a wage gap at all in predominantly female professions, however, attests to asymmetries in the workplace experiences of male and female tokens. These salary figures indicate that the men who do "women's work" fare as well as, and often better than, the women who work in these fields. . . .

Hiring Decisions

Contrary to the experience of many women in the male-dominated professions, many of the men and women I spoke to indicated that there is a *preference* for hiring men in these four occupations. A Texas librarian at a junior high school said that his school district "would hire a male over a female":

[CW: Why do you think that is?]

Because there are so few, and the . . . ones that they do have, the library directors seem to really . . . think they're doing great jobs. I don't know, maybe they just feel they're being progressive or something, [but] I have had a real sense that they really appreciate having a male, particularly at the junior high. . . . As I said, when seven of us lost our jobs from the high schools and were redistributed, there were only four positions at junior high, and I got one of them. Three of the librarians, some who had been here longer than I had with the school district, were put down in elementary school as librarians. And I definitely think that being male made a difference in my being moved to the junior high rather than an elementary school.

Many of the men perceived their token status as males in predominantly female occupations as an *advantage* in hiring and promotions. When I asked an Arizona teacher whether his specialty (elementary special education) was an unusual area for men compared to other areas within education, he said,

TABLE 2 *Median Weekly Earnings of Full-Time Professional Workers, by Sex, and Ratio of Female:Male Earnings, 1990*

Occupation	Both	Men	Women	Ratio
Registered Nurses	608	616	608	.99
Elementary Teachers	519	575	513	.89
Librarians	489	—*	479	—
Social Workers	445	483	427	.88
Engineers	814	822	736	.90
Physicians	892	978	802	.82
College Teachers	747	808	620	.77
Lawyers	1,045	1,178	875	.74

Source: U.S. Department of Labor, Bureau of Labor Statistics, *Employment and Earnings* 38, no. 1 (January 1991), table 56, p. 223.

*The Labor Department does not report income averages for base sample sizes consisting of fewer than 50,000 individuals.

Much more so. I am extremely marketable in special education. That's not why I got into the field. But I am extremely marketable because I am a man.

. . . Sometimes the preference for men in these occupations is institutionalized. One man landed his first job in teaching before he earned the appropriate credential "because I was a wrestler and they wanted a wrestling coach." A female math teacher similarly told of her inability to find a full-time teaching position because the schools she applied to reserved the math jobs for people (presumably men) who could double as coaches. . . .

. . . Some men described being "tracked" into practice areas within their professions which were considered more legitimate for men. For example, one Texas man described how he was pushed into administration and planning in social work, even though "I'm not interested in writing policy; I'm much more interested in research and clinical stuff." A nurse who is interested in pursuing graduate study in family and child health in Boston said he was dissuaded from entering the program specialty in favor of a concentration in "adult nursing." And a kindergarten teacher described his difficulty finding a job in his specialty after graduation: "I was recruited immediately to start getting into a track to become an administrator. And it was men who recruited me. It was men that ran the system at that time, especially in Los Angeles."

This tracking may bar men from the most female-identified specialties within these professions. But men are effectively being "kicked upstairs" in the process. Those specialties considered more legitimate practice areas for men also tend to be the most prestigious, and better-paying specialties as well. For example, men in nursing are overrepresented in critical care and psychiatric specialties, which tend to be higher paying than the others.[7] The highest paying and most prestigious library types are the academic libraries (where men are 35 percent of librarians) and the special libraries which are typically associated with businesses or other private organizations (where men constitute 20 percent of librarians).[8]

A distinguished kindergarten teacher, who had been voted citywide "Teacher of the Year," described the informal pressures he faced to advance in his field. He told me that even though people were pleased to see him in the classroom, "there's been some encouragement to think about administration, and there's been some encouragement to think about teaching at the university level or something like that, or supervisory-type position."

The effect of this "tracking" is the opposite of that experienced by women in male-dominated occupations. Researchers have reported that many women encounter "glass ceilings" in their efforts to scale organizational and professional hierarchies. That is, they reach invisible barriers to promotion in their careers, caused mainly by the sexist attitudes of men in the highest positions.[9] In contrast to this "glass ceiling," many of the men I interviewed seem to encounter a "glass escalator." Often, despite their intentions, they face invisible pressures to move up in their professions. Like being on a moving escalator, they have to work to stay in place. . . .

Supervisors and Colleagues:
The Working Environment
. . . Respondents in this study were asked about their relationships with supervisors and female colleagues to ascertain whether men also experienced "poisoned" work environments when entering nontraditional occupations.

A major difference in the experience of men and women in nontraditional occupations is that men are far more likely to be supervised by a member of their own sex. In each of the four professions I studied, men are overrepresented in administrative and managerial capacities, or, as in the case of nursing, the organizational hierarchy is governed by men. For example, 15 percent of all elementary school teachers are men, but men make up over 80 percent of all elementary school principals and 96 percent of all public school superintendents and assistant superintendents.[10] Likewise, over 40 percent of all male social workers hold administrative or managerial positions, compared to 30 percent of all female social workers.[11] And 50 percent of male librarians hold administrative positions, compared to 30 percent of female librarians, and the majority of deans and directors of major university and public libraries are men.[12] Thus, unlike women who enter "male fields," the men in these professions often work under the direct supervision of other men.

Many of the men interviewed reported that they had good rapport with their male supervisors. It was not uncommon in education, for example, for the male principal to informally socialize with the male staff, as a Texas special education teacher describes:

> Occasionally I've had a principal who would regard me as "the other man on the campus" and "it's us against them," you know? I mean, nothing really that extreme, except that some male principals feel like there's nobody there to talk to except the other man. So I've been in that position.

These personal ties can have important consequences for men's careers. For example, one California nurse, whose performance was judged marginal by his nursing superiors, was transferred to the emergency room staff (a prestigious promotion) due to his personal friendship with the physician in charge. And a Massachusetts teacher acknowledged that his principal's personal interest in him landed him his current job:

> [CW: You had mentioned that your principal had sort of spotted you at your previous job and had wanted to bring you here [to this school]. Do you think that has anything to do with the fact that you're a man, aside from your skills as a teacher?]
>
> Yes, I would say in that particular case, that was part of it. . . . We have certain things in common, certain interests that really lined up.
>
> [CW: Vis-à-vis teaching?]
>
> Well, more extraneous things—running specifically, and music. And we just seemed to get along real well right off the bat. It is just kind of a guy thing; we just liked each other. . . .

Interviewees did not report many instances of male supervisors discriminating against them, or refusing to accept them because they were male. Indeed, these men were much more likely to report that their male bosses discriminated against the *females* in their professions. . . .

Of course, not all the men who work in these occupations are supervised by men. Many of the men interviewed who had female bosses also reported high levels of acceptance—although the level of intimacy they achieved with women did not seem as great as with other men. But in some cases, men reported feeling shut-out from decision making when the higher administration was constituted entirely by women. I asked this Arizona librarian whether men in the library profession were discriminated against hiring because of their sex:

> Professionally speaking, people go to considerable lengths to keep that kind of thing out of their [hiring] deliberations. Personally, is another matter. It's pretty common around here to talk about the "old girl network." This is one of the few libraries that I've had any intimate knowledge of which is actually controlled by women. . . . Most of the department heads and upper level administrators are women. And there's an "old girl network" that works just like the "old boy network," except that the important conferences take place in the women's room rather than on the golf course. But the political mechanism is the same, the exclusion of the other sex from decision making is the same. The reasons are the same. It's somewhat discouraging. . . .

Although I did not interview many supervisors, I did include twenty-three women in my sample to ascertain their perspectives about the presence of men in their professions. All of the women I interviewed claimed to be supportive of their male colleagues, but some conveyed ambivalence. For example, a social work professor said she would like to see more men enter the social work profession, particularly in the clinical specialty (where they are underrepresented). She said she would favor affirmative action hiring guidelines for men in the profession, and yet, she resented the fact that her department hired "another white male" during a recent search. I confronted her about this apparent ambivalence:

> [CW: I find it very interesting that, on the one hand, you sort of perceive this preference and perhaps even sexism with regard to how men are evaluated and how they achieve higher positions within the profession, yet, on the other hand, you would be encouraging of more men to enter the field. Is that contradictory to you, or . . . ?]
>
> Yeah, it's contradictory. . . .

Men's reception by their female colleagues is thus somewhat mixed. It appears that women are generally eager to see men enter "their" occupations, and the women I interviewed claimed they were supportive of their male peers. Indeed, several men agreed with this social worker that their female colleagues had facilitated their careers in various ways (including college mentorship). At the same time, however, women often resent the apparent ease with which men seem to advance within these professions, sensing that men at the higher levels receive preferential treatment, and thus close off advancement opportunities for women.

But this ambivalence does not seem to translate into the "poisoned" work environment described by many women who work in male-dominated occupations. Among the male interviewees, there were no accounts of sexual harassment (indeed, one man claimed this was a disappointment to him!) However, women do treat their male colleagues differently on occasion. It is not uncommon in nursing, for example, for men to be called upon to help catheterize male patients, or to lift especially heavy patients. Some librarians also said that women asked them to lift and move heavy boxes of books because they were men. . . .

Another stereotype confronting men, in nursing and social work in particular, is the expectation that they are better able than women to handle aggressive individuals and diffuse violent situations. An Arizona social worker who was the first male caseworker in a rural district, described this preference for men:

> They welcomed a man, particularly in child welfare. Sometimes you have to go into some tough parts of towns and cities, and they felt

it was nice to have a man around to accompany them or be present when they were dealing with a difficult client. Or just doing things that males can do. I always felt very welcomed.

But this special treatment bothered some respondents: Getting assigned all the violent patients or discipline problems can make for difficult and unpleasant working conditions. Nurses, for example, described how they were called upon to subdue violent patients. A traveling psychiatric nurse I interviewed in Texas told how his female colleagues gave him "plenty of opportunities" to use his wrestling skills. . . .

But many men claimed that this differential treatment did not distress them. In fact, several said they liked being appreciated for the special traits and abilities (such as strength) they could contribute to their professions.

Furthermore, women's special treatment of men sometimes enhanced—rather than detracted from—the men's work environments. One Texas librarian said he felt "more comfortable working with women than men" because "I think it has something to do with control. Maybe it's that women will let me take control more than men will." Several men reported that their female colleagues often cast them into leadership roles. . . .

The interviews suggest that the working environment encountered by "nontraditional" male workers is quite unlike that faced by women who work in traditionally male fields. Because it is not uncommon for men in predominantly female professions to be supervised by other men, they tend to have closer rapport and more intimate social relationships with people in management. These ties can facilitate men's careers by smoothing the way for future promotions. Relationships with female supervisors were also described for the most part in positive terms, although in some cases, men perceived an "old girls'" network in place that excluded them from decision making. But in sharp contrast to the reports of women in nontraditional occupations, men in these fields did not complain of feeling discriminated against because they were men. If anything, they felt that being male was an asset that enhanced their career prospects.

Those men interviewed for this study also described congenial workplaces, and a very high level of acceptance from their female colleagues. The sentiment was echoed by women I spoke to who said that they were pleased to see more men enter "their" professions. Some women, however, did express resentment over the "fast-tracking" that their male colleagues seem to experience. But this ambivalence did not translate into a hostile work environment for men: Women generally included men in their informal social events and, in some ways, even facilitated men's careers. By casting men into leadership roles, presuming they were more knowledgeable and qualified, or relying on them to perform certain critical tasks, women unwittingly contributed to the "glass escalator effect" facing men who do "women's work."

Relationships with Clients

Workers in these service-oriented occupations come into frequent contact with the public during the course of their work day. Nurses treat patients; social workers usually have client case loads; librarians serve patrons; and teachers are in constant contact with children, and often with parents as well. Many of those interviewed claimed that the clients they served had different expectations of men and women in these occupations, and often treated them differently.

People react with surprise and often disbelief when they encounter a man in nursing, elementary school teaching, and, to a lesser extent, librarianship. (Usually people have no clear expectations about the sex of social workers.) The stereotypes men face are often negative. For example, according to this Massachusetts nurse, it is frequently assumed that male nurses are gay:

Fortunately, I carry one thing with me that protects me from [the stereotype that male nurses are gay], and the one thing I carry with me is a wedding ring, and it makes a big difference. The perfect example was conversations before I was married. . . . [People would ask], "Oh, do you have a girlfriend?" Or you'd hear patients asking questions along that idea, and they were simply implying,

"Why is this guy in nursing? Is it because he's gay and he's a pervert?" And I'm not associating the two by any means, but this is the thought process.

. . . It is not uncommon for both gay and straight men in these occupations to encounter people who believe that they are "gay 'til proven otherwise," as one nurse put it. In fact, there are many gay men employed in these occupations. But gender stereotypes are at least as responsible for this general belief as any "empirical" assessment of men's sexual lifestyles. To the degree that men in these professions are perceived as not "measuring up" to the supposedly more challenging occupational roles and standards demanded of "real" men, they are immediately suspected of being effeminate—"like women"—and thus, homosexual.

An equally prevalent sexual stereotype about men in these occupations is that they are potentially dangerous and abusive. Several men described special rules they followed to guard against the widespread presumption of sexual abuse. For example, nurses were sometimes required to have a female "chaperone" present when performing certain procedures or working with specific populations. This psychiatric nurse described a former workplace:

I worked on a floor for the criminally insane. Pretty threatening work. So you have to have a certain number of females on the floor just to balance out. Because there were female patients on the floor too. And you didn't want to be accused of rape or any sex crimes.

Teachers and librarians described the steps they took to protect themselves from suspicions of sexual impropriety. A kindergarten teacher said:

I know that I'm careful about how I respond to students. I'm careful in a number of ways—in my physical interaction with students. It's mainly to reassure parents. . . . For example, a little girl was very affectionate, very anxious to give me a hug. She'll just throw herself at me. I need to tell her very carefully: "Sonia, you need to tell me when you want to hug me." That way I can come down, crouch down. Because you don't want a child giving you a hug on your hip. You just don't want to do that. So I'm very careful about body position.

. . . Although negative stereotypes about men who do "women's work" can push men out of specific jobs, their effects can actually benefit men. Instead of being a source of negative discrimination, these prejudices can add to the "glass escalator effect" by pressuring men to move *out* of the most feminine-identified areas and *up* to those regarded as more legitimate for men.

The public's reactions to men working in these occupations, however, are by no means always negative. Several men and women reported that people often assume that men in these occupations are more competent than women, or that they bring special skills and expertise to their professional practice. For example, a female academic librarian told me that patrons usually address their questions to the male reference librarian when there is a choice between asking a male or a female. A male clinical social worker in private practice claimed that both men and women generally preferred male psychotherapists. And several male nurses told me that people often assume that they are physicians and direct their medical inquiries to them instead of to the female nurses.[13]

The presumption that men are more competent than women is another difference in the experience of token men and women. Women who work in nontraditional occupations are often suspected of being incompetent, unable to survive the pressures of "men's work." As a consequence, these women often report feeling compelled to prove themselves and, as the saying goes, "work twice as hard as men to be considered half as good." To the degree that men are assumed to be competent and in control, they may have to be twice as incompetent to be considered half as bad. One man claimed that "if you're a mediocre male teacher, you're considered a better teacher than if you're a female and a mediocre teacher. I think there's that prejudice there." . . .

There are different standards and assumptions about men's competence that follow them into nontraditional occupations. In contrast, women in both traditional and nontraditional occupations must contend with the presumption that they are neither competent nor qualified. . . .

The reasons that clients give for preferring or rejecting men reflect the complexity of our society's stereotypes about masculinity and femininity. Masculinity is often associated with competence and mastery, in contrast to femininity, which is often associated with instrumental incompetence. Because of these stereotypes, men are perceived as being stricter disciplinarians and stronger than women, and thus better able to handle violent or potentially violent situations. . . .

Conclusion

Both men and women who work in nontraditional occupations encounter discrimination, but the forms and the consequences of this discrimination are very different for the two groups. Unlike "nontraditional" women workers, most of the discrimination and prejudice facing men in the "female" professions comes from clients. For the most part, the men and women I interviewed believed that men are given fair—if not preferential—treatment in hiring and promotion decisions, are accepted by their supervisors and colleagues, and are well-integrated into the workplace subculture. Indeed, there seem to be subtle mechanisms in place that enhance men's positions in these professions—a phenomenon I refer to as a "glass escalator effect."

Men encounter their most "mixed" reception in their dealings with clients, who often react negatively to male nurses, teachers, and to a lesser extent, librarians. Many people assume that the men are sexually suspect if they are employed in these "feminine" occupations either because they do or they do not conform to stereotypical masculine characteristics.

Dealing with the stress of these negative stereotypes can be overwhelming, and it probably pushes some men out of these occupations.[14] The challenge facing the men who stay in these fields is to accentuate their positive contribution to what our society defines as essentially "women's work." . . .

NOTES

1. Allan Angoff, "The Male Librarian—An Anomaly?" *Library Journal,* February 15, 1959, p. 553.

2. *Austin-American Statesman,* January 16, 1990; response by John Kelso, January 18, 1990.

3. Some of the most important studies of women in male-dominated occupations are: Rosabeth Moss Kanter, *Men and Women of the Corporation* (New York: Basic Books, 1977); Susan Martin, *Breaking and Entering: Policewomen on Patrol* (Berkeley: University of California Press, 1980); Cynthia Fuchs Epstein, *Women in Law* (New York: Basic Books, 1981); Kay Deaux and Joseph Ullman, *Women of Steel* (New York: Praeger, 1983); Judith Hicks Stiehm, *Arms and the Enlisted Woman* (Philadelphia: Temple University Press, 1989); Jerry Jacobs, *Revolving Doors: Sex Segregation and Women's Careers* (Stanford: Stanford University Press, 1989); Barbara Reskin and Patricia Roos, *Job Queues, Gender Queues: Explaining Women's Inroads into Male Occupations* (Philadelphia: Temple University Press, 1990).

Among the few books that do examine men's status in predominantly female occupations are Carol Tropp Schreiber, *Changing Places: Men and Women in Transitional Occupations* (Cambridge: MIT Press, 1979); Christine L. Williams, *Gender Differences at Work: Women and Men in Nontraditional Occupations* (Berkeley: University of California Press, 1989); and Christine L. Williams, ed., *Doing "Women's Work": Men in Nontraditional Occupations* (Newbury Park, CA: Sage Publications, 1993).

4. In an influential essay on methodological principles, Herbert Blumer counseled sociologists to "sedulously seek participants in the sphere of life who are acute observers and who are well informed. One such person is worth a hundred others who are merely unobservant participants." See "The Methodological Position of Symbolic Interactionism," in *Symbolic Interactionism: Perspective and Method* (Berkeley: University of California Press, 1969), p. 41.

5. The overall proportions in the population do not necessarily represent the experiences of individuals in my sample. Some nurses, for example, worked in groups that were composed almost entirely of men, while some social workers had the experience of being the only man in their group. The overall statistics provide a general guide, but relying on them exclusively can distort the actual experiences of individuals in the workplace. The statistics available for research on occupational sex segregation are not specific enough to measure internal divisions among workers. Research that uses firm-level data finds a far greater degree of segregation than research that uses national data. See William T. Bielby and James N. Baron, "A Woman's Place Is with Other Women: Sex Segregation within Organizations," in *Sex Segregation in the Workplace: Trends, Explanations, Remedies,* ed. Barbara Reskin (Washington, D.C.: National Academy Press, 1984), pp. 27–55.

6. Catharine MacKinnon, *Feminism Unmodified* (Cambridge: Harvard University Press, 1987), pp. 24–25.

7. Howard S. Rowland, *The Nurse's Almanac,* 2d ed. (Rockville, MD: Aspen Systems Corp., 1984), p. 153; Johw W. Wright, *The American Almanac of Jobs and Salaries,* 2d ed. (New York: Avon, 1984), p. 639.

8. King Research, Inc., *Library Human Resources: A Study of Supply and Demand* (Chicago: American Library Association, 1983), p. 41.

9. See, for example, Sue J. M. Freeman, *Managing Lives: Corporate Women and Social Change* (Amherst: University of Massachusetts Press, 1990).

10. Patricia A. Schmuck, "Women School Employees in the United States," in *Women Educators: Employees of Schools in Western Countries* (Albany: State University of New York Press, 1987), p. 85; James W. Grimm and Robert N. Stern, "Sex Roles and Internal Labor Market Structures: The Female Semi-Professions," *Social Problems* 21(1974): 690–705.

11. David A. Hardcastle and Arthur J. Katz, *Employment and Unemployment in Social Work: A Study of NASW Members* (Washington, D.C.: NASW, 1979), p. 41; Reginold O. York, H. Carl Henley and Dorothy N. Gamble, "Sexual Discrimination in Social Work: Is It Salary or Advancement?" *Social Work* 32 (1987): 336–40; Grimm and Stern, "Sex Roles and Internal Labor Market Structures."

12. Leigh Estabrook, "Women's Work in the Library/Information Sector," in *My Troubles Are Going to Have Trouble with Me,* ed. Karen Brodkin Sacks and Dorothy Remy (New Brunswick, NJ: Rutgers University Press, 1984), p. 165.

13. Liliane Floge and D. M. Merrill found a similar phenomenon in their study of male nurses. See "Tokenism Reconsidered: Male Nurses and Female Physicians in a Hospital Setting," *Social Forces* 64 (1986): 931–32.

14. Jim Allan makes this argument in "Male Elementary Teachers: Experiences and Perspectives," in *Doing "Women's Work": Men in Nontraditional Occupations,* ed. Christine L. Williams (Newbury Park, CA: Sage Publications, 1993), pp. 113–27.

THINKING ABOUT THE READINGS

Passing By

■ Sexual harassment has received a great deal of public attention recently. While some people argue that it is a dangerous, demeaning act that perpetuates men's power over women, others depict it as an ordinary, harmless or even beneficial activity. Assess the relative merits of a "romanticized" versus a "politicized" interpretation of public harassment. After reading this article, do you feel that public harassment is a serious form of exploitation or a benign form of communication that's been blown out of proportion? How do we, as a society, balance comments men make about women's physical appearance with the constitutional right of "free speech?" Is it desirable or even possible to legislate against "sexual remarks?"

Still a Man's World

■ Compare the discrimination men experience in traditionally female occupations to that experienced by women in traditionally male occupations. What is the "glass escalator effect?" In what ways can the glass escalator actually be harmful to men? What do you suppose might happen to the structure of the American labor force if men did, in fact, begin to enter predominantly female occupations in the same proportion as women entering predominantly female occupations?

CHAPTER 14

The Dynamics of Population
Demographic and Global Trends

In the past several chapters we have examined the various interrelated sources of social stratification. Race, class, and gender continue to determine access to cultural, economic, and political opportunities. Yet another source of inequality that we don't think much about but which has enormous local, national, and global stratification is the changing size and shape of the human population. Globally, population imbalances between richer and poorer societies underlie most if not all of the other important forces for change that are taking place today. Nationally, population imbalance—and therefore unequal economic opportunities—among different age groups will be one of our most important demographic phenomena in the decades to come.

We hear a lot of criticism these days about the youthful generation of Americans in their teens and twenties. The news media depicts them as a directionless wasteland of academic underachievement, political apathy, disease-ridden sex, and reckless self-absorption. Older generations often see them as "hard-to-like kids who deserve not a break but a kick . . . " Making predictions about the future of a large group of people is always risky business, but in their article, "The 21st Century Breathing Down Our Necks," Neil Howe and Bill Strauss offer some provocative thoughts about what is going to become of America's "13th Generation" (people born between 1961 and 1981) over the next 40 years. In doing so, they provide a vivid illustration of the importance of age groupings (what demographers call birth cohorts) on our everyday experiences.

One of the most important and controversial demographic processes in the United States today is immigration. While politicians continue to argue over proposed immigration restrictions, people from all corners of the globe enter this country legally or illegally looking for a better life. In her article, "Other People's Children," Julia Wrigley examines the lives and experiences of one segment of the immigrant population: foreign women who work as nannies. In many ways newly arrived immigrants make attractive employees since they are willing to work for low wages. In addition, they benefit from the opportunity of working in a relatively healthy and comfortable home environment (compared, let's say, to a sweatshop garment factory). However, Wrigley points out that for these immigrants, raising other people's children can be alienating and dreary. Furthermore, despite the fact that they sometimes become "part of the family," they are easily exploited and disposed of when their services are no longer needed.

The 21st Century Breathing Down Our Necks

Neil Howe and Bill Strauss

. . . To figure out where any generation is heading, you have to know two things: its current location and its future direction.

Location is the easy part. You can find out where a generation is today by identifying its collective personality, its cultural center of gravity, and its attitudes, habits, and skills. To answer any number of trivial questions about the future, current location may be all you need to know. Take music, for example. Even in old age, a generation retains a special fondness for the songs it first hears in its mid-teens to early 20s. Thus, we could have predicted many years ago that today's senior citizens would still be listening to Glenn Miller and Benny Goodman. And we can safely predict that, sometime around 2040, America's 70-year-olds will feel a special nostalgia for (believe it or not) the staccato rhythm of a vintage urban rapper.

Yet even if a generation can't alter many of the specific traits it acquires young, it is equally true that such traits get applied to new purposes and are shaped by new attitudes over the course of its life cycle. Along the way, a generation typically finds that its personality in old age is very different from its personality in youth. . . .

To make more important predictions, therefore, you need some understanding of a generation's sense of *direction*—what Ortega y Gasset called its "preestablished vital trajectory" and Karl Mannheim its "essential destiny." It's not easy to identify this direction. It's like unwrapping some hidden sociogenetic code. You have to read motives and questions and dreams that are hidden inside a generation like an oak within an acorn and that don't become fully apparent until they are expressed in history.

But one thing is certain: If you don't know the direction, you'll be clueless about the future,

because no generation ever starts and ends its collective journey in the same location. Consider a generation (like the G.I.s [today's senior citizens]) that comes of age saving, working, and building big things. Who would guess that this same group of people, entering retirement, would create the biggest consumption and leisure lobby in world history? Or consider a generation (like the Silent [the 40 million Americans now in their 50s]) that spends the first half of its life doing everything by the rules—and ever since midlife yearns to break all the taboos. Or consider a generation (like the Baby Boomers) that celebrates the libido at age 18—and then three decades later begins to engage in what marketers call "non-ism," the ascetic art of celebrating whatever it is you're *not* enjoying.

To understand how generations acquire a sense of direction, you have to ask how they interpret their world early in life. Coming of age, what is their agenda? What's their greatest challenge—the biggest problem they want to solve or the obstacle they need to overcome? For G.I.s in the early 1930s, the challenge was national poverty and pessimism—which helps explain the affluent, upbeat image of today's senior citizen. For the Silent in the early '50s, it was "yes sir" determination and conformism—hence the ambivalent, open-minded image of today's midlifer. For the Boomers in the early '70s, soulless abundance and complacency—hence the (still evolving) values-fixated image of today's 40-year-old.

This brings us to the future of the 13th Generation [Americans born between 1961 and 1981]. What is it about America's current social mood that is likely to leave the most lasting impression on Americans now coming of age? We don't know for sure, but we can make some fair guesses:

chaotic individualism; social fragmentation; cultural openness; institutions grown over-complex and irrelevant; a consumption-based economy that devours its own future; a political system that debates everything but chooses nothing. Were you to extrapolate the future strictly on the basis of how 13ers are now coping with this world, you could indeed draw a very dismal scenario. Imagine a place in which civilization has crumbled into dust, leaving only a bunch of aging Road Warriors and Blade Runners. But this scenario is likely to be as wildly inaccurate as the totalitarian 1984 projections made for the compliant young Silent Generation in the wake of Hitler and Stalin. It's wrong because it looks at where a generation is without paying attention to what's happening *inside* that generation—where it's going, what it's on the way to becoming.

So what *is* the 13er direction? Here's where history helps. . . . If 13ers follow the trajectory of prior generations . . . we can make a good number of informed predictions about how their collective personality will evolve as they grow older; which attitudes and habits will stay constant, and which will reverse; what lifelong lessons they will carry with them from the circa-'80s and '90s world in which they are coming of age; how they will behave toward other generations, and how other generations will behave toward them; what kind of leadership they will someday provide; and how history will someday remember them.

The most important lesson of history is this: Once previous 13er-like generations reached midlife, they underwent a profound personality transformation. Their risk-taking gave way to caution, their wildness and alienation turned into exhaustion and conservatism, and their nomadic individualism matured into a preference for strong community life. The same unruly rebels and adventurers who alarmed older colonists during the 1760s later became the crusty old Patrick Henrys and George Washingtons who warned younger statesmen against gambling with the future. The same gold-chasing '49ers and Civil War brigands whom Oliver Wendell Holmes, Jr., called "a generation touched with fire" later became the stodgy "Old Guard" Victorians of the Gilded Era. The same gin-fizz "Flaming Youth" who electrified America during the 1920s later became the Norman Rockwells and Dwight Eisenhowers who calmed America during the 1950s.

With history as a guide, we offer 13 predictions for the 13th Generation:

1. *Over the next fifteen years, the festering quarrel between 13ers and Boomers will grow into America's next great "generation gap."* As their stamp on American culture increasingly looks, tastes, smells, and sounds anti-Boom, everything 13ers do that Boomers already consider frenetic, shallow, or shocking will grow even more so, confirming public opinion that this truly is a "wasted" generation. Like the Lost Generation of the 1920s, 13ers will have their greatest cultural impact on the marketplace (entertainment, products, styles, advertising), yet over time their what-you-see-is-what-you-get brassiness will spill over into religion and politics. Thirteeners will vent their social alienation by stressing bucks and deals where their next-elders once talked about ideas and values. In response, midlife Boomers will try to insulate their families from a mainstream culture gone rotten and will project heavy-handed value judgments into public life. Interpreting these judgments as pitiless and Scroogelike, 13ers will blast away at Boomer hypocrisy and pomposity—and get blasted back for their own cynicism and wildness. Only during the first decade of the next century, when Atari-wave 13ers reach midlife, will this age war subside.

2. *Thirteeners will never outgrow their "bad" image.* The children allowed to grow up unskilled, unschooled, and unwanted in the 1970s and '80s will carry those pathologies with them. They will be just as unemployable and socially undesirable at age forty as they are today at age twenty. Remedial adult education will lose funding, young-adult welfare will be cut further, and expanded health-care benefits will help young parents only to the extent that it targets their kids. Many of today's youth gangsters will ripen into their adult facsimile, waging Capone-like wars with police. Already the most incarcerated generation in American history, 13ers will in time be (thanks to Boomer legislators, judges, and juries) the most executed generation as well. Efforts to prevent antisocial behavior and to encourage cooperation and teamwork will be focused exclusively on the young. By the year 2020—roughly thirty years from now—Americans in their fifties will be generally regarded as worse-behaved (and worse-educated) than Americans in their twenties—exactly the opposite of today.

3. *The 13th will become one of the most important immigrant generations in U.S. history.* Ultimately, its membership will include the highest percentage of naturalized U.S. citizens of any generation born in the twentieth century. The politics of ethnic group rivalry and the cultural impact of racial diversity will play a far more serious role in the lives of 13ers than they ever did in the lives of the Boom and Silent. As immigrants and non-whites flaunt their unique identities, many white 13ers will see themselves as endangered, sparking social movements that others will regard as know-nothing nativism. Over time, the perception that large numbers of 13er immigrants threaten to fragment society beyond repair will persuade Americans of all ages to clamp down on immigration—ensuring that the foreign-born share of the next generation will be smaller. Meanwhile, foreign-born high-achievers will catapult new ethnic groups, especially Asians and Hispanics, into national prominence much as [earlier] generations did for the Italians, Eastern Europeans . . . Irish, and Germans.

4. *Early in life, the most successful 13ers will be risk takers who exploit opportunities overlooked by established businesses.* The leading 13er frontier will be overseas, where this generation can most fully apply its entrepreneurial instincts and take advantage of its linguistic, computer, and marketing skills. At home, 13ers will revitalize the unskilled service sector, turn small manufacturers into exporters, mount gray-market challenges to credentialed monopolies (law, medicine, finance), and set up profitable alternatives to rule-encrusted state enterprises (mail, schools, waste disposal, security). As contract work employees, many will dart from job to job, while others mix steady wages during the day with get-rich-quick deals at night—discouraging companies from offering job training, career ladders, or pension programs. As managers, 13ers will seek market niches where quick deals matter more than long memos. Pro-

fessional and union loyalties will continue to decline. The bottom line is that 13ers will leave public and private bureaucracies leaner, more personalized, and more oriented toward doing the job than staffing the process.

5. *Reaching midlife, the 13ers' economic fears will be confirmed: They will become the only generation born this century . . . to suffer a one-generation backstep in living standards.* Compared to their own parents at the same age, the 13ers' poverty rate will be higher, their rate of home ownership lower, their pension and health-care benefits skimpier. They will not match the Boomers' inflation-adjusted levels of disposable income or wealth, at the same age. Thirteeners will also experience a much wider distribution of income and wealth than today's older generations, with startling proportions either falling into destitution or shooting from rags to riches. They will change the focus of class politics—away from raising low-income families to the median toward preventing the rootless poor from sinking into a total abyss. Finding their youthful dreams broken on the shoals of marketplace reality, 13ers will internalize their disappointment. Around the year 2020, accumulated "hard knocks" will give midlife 13ers much of the same gritty determination about life that the Great Depression gave the midlife Lost [Generation]. . . .

6. *Thirteeners will restrengthen the American family.* Dedicated spouses, they will work hard to shield their marriages from the risk and stress of their work lives. Around the year 2000, these efforts will be reflected in a marked downturn in the national divorce rate. First as parents and later as community leaders, 13ers will practice and advocate a heavily protective, even smothering style of nurture. They will revive the innocence of childhood by deliberately shielding their own kids from the harsher realities of life, and by prohibiting those kids from taking the same liberties they themselves once took at the same age. Having no illusions about sex themselves, they will appreciate the advantages of creating illusions (and resurrecting modesty) for their children. . . .

7. *Reaching their fifties in a mood of collective exhaustion, 13ers will settle into the midlife role of* national anchor, calming the social mood and slowing the pace of social change. As senior educators, political leaders, and media executives, 13ers will reverse the frenzied and centrifugal cultural directions of their younger years. In alliance with old Boomers, they will clean up entertainment, de-diversify the culture, reinvent core symbols of national unity, reaffirm rituals of family and neighborhood bonding, and re-erect barriers to cushion communities from unwanted social upheaval. As architects and civic officials, they will oversee the rebuilding of urban America and pioneer the next great era of (high-tech) infrastructure. Cities will define and energize them—but Boomer-run exurbs will surround them and constantly preach to them. . . . As elder role models, 13ers will make near-perfect 50-year-olds: irascible, full of mischief, with that Twainlike twinkle in the eye, but also worldly wise and experienced in the stark realities of pleasure and pain. . . .

8. *Throughout their lives, 13ers will be America's most politically conservative generation [since the turn of the century].* Until their mid-40s, the dominant brand of 13er conservatism will have a strong libertarian and free-market leave-me-alone flavor; later in life, it will lean toward cautious, pragmatic stewardship. Their attachment to the "conservative" banner will be sealed if aging Boomers rely on liberal standards to rekindle a spirit of national community and to rally younger generations to their cause—say, through some new . . . mandatory youth service. Ever the social contrarians, 13ers will be tempted to take the other side and try to keep their elders (and juniors) from going off the deep end. Regardless of party or ideology, 13ers will be drawn to candidates who avoid hype, spell out the bottom line, do what it takes to get the job done, and shed no tears. In politics as in other spheres of social life, they will be most effective where the issues are local and personal. They will press to simplify the complex, narrow the bloated, and eliminate the unworkable. They will gain their first Senate seats and governorships before the year 2000. Their weak political profile in national affairs, however, will prevent them from winning a generational plurality in Congress until relatively late in life, perhaps not until around 2020. . . .

9. *As they reach their turn for national leadership, 13ers will produce no-nonsense winners who will excel at cunning, flexibility, and deft timing.* If 13ers turn out like every earlier generation of their type . . . they will ultimately become a stellar generation of get-it-done warriors, able to take charge of whatever raging conflicts are initiated by their elders and bring them to successful conclusions. In the tradition of George Washington, Ulysses Grant, and Dwight Eisenhower, the most memorable 13er Presidents may themselves be ex-generals. Military or not—and regardless of sex—13er leaders will be cagey, jockish, unpretentious, inelegant with words, more inclined to deal than to argue, and more admired for their personality than for their vision or learning. As they come to power around the year 2020, younger voters will view them as a welcome change from the ponderous, principles-first Boomer style. In public, they'll come across a bit shallow. But, as any 13er already knows, low expectations can be a game you can use to your advantage—in a poker game or in the White House.

10. *Before the year 2030, events will call on pock-marked 13ers to make aging Boomers get real—and, perhaps, to stop some righteous old Aquarian from doing something truly catastrophic.* Gazing down the road, some 13ers already wonder how they're going to cope with their next elders when those crusading Boomers finally go gaga. It's not an idle worry. Just think about it: Of all of today's living generations, which one is someday most likely to risk blowing up the world just to prove a point? When that nightmare possibility appears, it may compel a grown-up cadre of shouted-at Breakfast Clubbers to insist on having the last word after all—and to demand that principle defer to survival. . . .

11. *Throughout their lives, 13ers will neither ask for nor receive much assistance from government.* In their thirties, they will vote to cut young-adult welfare benefits. In their fifties, they will vote to raise income taxes. In their seventies, they will vote to cut Social Security. A generation of low collective self-esteem, 13ers will never voice much objection to their own "bad" reputation in the eyes of others (today their elders, forty years from now their juniors). Nor will 13ers ever effectively organize or vote in their own self-interest. Instead, they will take pride in the handouts they don't receive, in their lifelong talent for getting by on their own, and in their ability to divert government resources to help those younger than themselves. Policy experts who today worry about the cost of Social Security and Medicare past the year 2025 seldom reflect on the political self-image of those who will then be entering their late sixties. Will they become entitled "senior citizens"? Hardly. Like Lost Generation elders in 1964—who voted more for Barry Goldwater than any younger generation even after he promised to slash their retirement benefits—old 13ers will feel less deserving of public attention than richer and smarter young people who lack their fatalism about life.

12. *As mature leaders and voters, 13ers will favor investment over consumption, endowments over enticements, the needs of the very young over the needs of the very old.* Whether by raising taxes, by freezing the money supply, by discouraging debt, or by shifting public budgets toward education, public works, and child welfare, elder 13ers will tilt the economy back toward the future. They will use any available policy lever to raise national savings far above what private households would otherwise choose on their own—exactly the opposite of the national choice they will remember from their own youth. . . . 13ers will leave behind a smaller federal debt than they inherited; . . . they will prefer recession to an out-of-kilter national balance sheet. . . . 13ers will be national survivalists, determined to store up capital for future contingencies and opposed to doing anything too risky, too wasteful, or too ambitious. Exiting power, they will—like the elder Washington, Twain, and Eisenhower—warn against the danger of pushing too fast in a world rigged with pitfalls.

13. *Thirteeners will make caustic, independent, yet self-effacing elders. When old, 13ers will watch America (once again) lose interest in people their own age and rediscover a fascination with the energy and promise of youth.* They will watch younger generations ignore their "old fogey" warnings and unleash new dreams of national ambition. They will watch younger people zoom past them eco-

nomically. But 13er oldsters won't mind. They'll have reason to take pride in what they see happening down the age ladder. Pride in having pulled America back together and in having restored ballast to the ship of state. Pride in having rebuilt the social foundations that will by then be supporting a renaissance in public confidence and cultural optimism. Pride in having produced more than they consumed, in having made simple things work again, *in having done more for others than others ever did for them.*

Life is a sneaky fortune wheel for the 13th Generation. It spins, it turns—and just when you think you've lost, it tantalizes. Just when you think you've won, it clicks again, and you lose. But, by losing, 13ers help others gain. That could well be the story of their future.

History is not invariant, with predetermined outcomes. Any generation can bring forward good or bad leaders, or just run into good or bad luck. But each generation gets only one script. And how history turns out often depends on how well each generation plays its script.

To date, 13ers are a generation without a self-perceived mission. They know full well that they can't do or be what the G.I.s or Silent or Boomers did or were. Unite in the face of global crisis? Add nuance to a conformist society? Scream out against spirit-dead affluence? It makes no sense for them to attempt even a pale imitation of their elders—nor for those elders to condemn them for not following the paths others blazed in youth. Instead, 13ers have to find their own path, to develop their own sense of mission, to follow their own script.

Over a half-century ago, historian James Truslow Adams first defined the "American Dream" as giving every young person "the chance to grow into something bigger and finer, as bigger and finer appeared to him." This Dream is each generation's unique vision of progress, each generation's unique sense of how to improve on the legacy that has been handed down by its ancestors. The G.I.s defined their Dream through economics. The Silent defined it through social justice. Boomers defined it through inner consciousness.

So where do 13ers fit in? Have all the dreams been defined? Is anything left for them?

Yes, 13ers *do* have a mission. Theirs is the American generation that history has charged with the task of cleaning up after everybody else's mess. (Somebody had better—before it's too late.) So too is theirs the generation charged with showing others how, in this millennial era, Americans can still enjoy "life, liberty, and the pursuit of happiness" without letting the world fly to pieces, without bankrupting the nation, and without squandering scarce global resources. History is calling on the 13th Generation to provide the youthful entrepreneurship, midlife investments, and elder generosity that will enable future generations once again to define the American Dream in economic terms, if that is what they wish to do.

Do the dirty work, have a little fun, help the kids behind them. Not bad. Let others call 13ers "underachievers." They can take it. We, their elders, will never live to see how their story turns out. They will. The rest of us can only imagine how, when their job's done, they'll look history straight in the eye, give a little smile, and move on.

Other People's Children

Julia Wrigley

The Parents' Dilemma

As more mothers go out to work, more couples are seeking child care. Many of those with the money to hire nannies consider this the ideal choice. They believe a nanny will give their children personal attention. They also think they can control the care their children get, as the nanny is their own employee. For parents of more than one child, a nanny can be cheaper than other forms of care. Working parents, who may be on the job long hours, value the flexibility of private caregivers who will stay late if need be and who will clean the house as well as look after the children. Nannies can ease parents' lives in a way that day care centers cannot. Seemingly, they offer a superior option for both parents and children. . . .[1]

These caregivers work in the privacy of their employers' homes and little is known about them. Most of the jobs are semi-underground, found through informal networks; many nannies do not pay taxes or have Social Security taxes paid for them. Immigrants represent a large part of the labor pool. Those in the country illegally face less risk of detection in private homes than they do in factories or hotels, and they are not barred by educational requirements. . . .

In open-plan houses built for family togetherness rather than social exclusion, these parents share the care of their children and, sometimes, their living space with women very different from themselves. Race differences between parents and caregivers are immediately obvious, with dark-skinned women pushing blond babies in strollers a common sight in wealthy neighborhoods. Less visible, but just as pervasive, are class differences: middle-class employers hire working-class nannies.

People from very different backgrounds seldom have intimate encounters. Caregiving relationships, though, bring parents and caregivers together in the emotionally and culturally charged sphere of child rearing. Their conflicts, power struggles, and attachments illuminate tacit cultural assumptions. Only when people are faced with "the shock of the other" do they realize what their own values are. Many caregivers and parents have this experience daily. Based on 155 interviews with caregivers and parents in Los Angeles and New York, this [study] explores how parents and caregivers manage their differences. It examines middle-class parents' strategies for having their children socialized as they wish while being cared for by women who come from economic and social backgrounds vastly different from theirs.

The interviews show caregiving relationships to be enormously varied. Some employers and employees become personal friends. Others barely exchange a word. The most oppressed immigrant caregivers depict a world closer to Dickens than to Mary Poppins. One Salvadoran woman was slapped in the face by an enraged employer; another routinely had her purse searched the one day a week she left her employer's house. A Mexican caregiver did not know the name of the baby in her charge, after three weeks of working for her Los Angeles employers. Other parents and caregivers get along so well they partially fuse their lives. A Guatemalan caregiver, and eventually her husband and daughter, shared the home of a Los Angeles professor and her lawyer husband for seven years. Relationships differ as much in longevity as in closeness. One New York mother has employed the same caregiver for seventeen years. Another went through so many caregivers, she snapped their pictures so her young son could remember them. . . .

Those parents who hire immigrants from Third World countries maximize class differences between themselves and their caregivers, but they also maximize the control they have. They can secure more housework from immigrant women than from caregivers who are more culturally similar to them. Experienced employers sometimes instruct new ones on the benefits of control. In one interview, a mother who is a computer consultant said she had complained to a friend that her Kenyan caregiver did not seem intelligent. The friend, an experienced employer, told her that sometimes it was better to accept "dumb" employees who were under the parents' control rather than deal with cocky ones. . . .

Choosing Difference

Parents can create class and cultural chasms in their homes when they hire immigrant caregivers from developing countries. Parents and caregivers do not always share a language. Many parents turn these workers into low-skill laborers. They keep sensitive child-rearing tasks for themselves and delegate to employees the most routinized aspects of child care, including, particularly, the physical maintenance of young children.

Parents who routinize child care are minimizing expense and maximizing their control. Socially subordinate workers, many of them trying to support children or elderly parents, rarely reject tasks as beneath them. Employers can assign them housework and child care in whatever proportions they wish. The parents retain full control of child-rearing decisions. Not surprisingly, they pay an emotional price for these advantages. While some caregivers invest in their employers' children, no matter what their working conditions, many low-wage, revolving-door workers do not become close to the children in their charge.

Domestic work, despite being near the bottom of the occupational ladder, has its own limited career structure.[2] Workers can move from low-wage, confining, and demanding jobs to ones where they earn more and have some autonomy. The career structure is an uncertain one and no formal steps mark workers' progress along it.

Workers cannot count on ground once gained being held; they can fall back in pay and working conditions. But overall, there are differences between the jobs obtained by newly arrived, inexperienced immigrants and those who are more acculturated. Immigrant women's employment traces an arc; employers can intersect this arc at many points, with some hiring workers who are at its lowest point and others hiring those from its highest. . . .

Employers' Strategies

Some employers focus on hiring cheap workers. This can lead to high turnover, but most accept this as a cost of their employment strategy. Parents have a variety of reasons for hiring workers who are at the bottom of the employment arc. In families where the mother does not work outside the home, she can supervise a caregiver; parents may not see a reason to pay high wages to an experienced or acculturated worker. Some parents of babies believe that infants do not require specialized care. And, finally, some parents would prefer an experienced, highly skilled caregiver, but do not think they can afford such a person, so they reluctantly "settle" for a new immigrant with fewer marketable skills. . . .

Why Caregivers Take the Jobs

Recently arrived immigrant women are . . . willing to take even jobs that strike the experienced as very undesirable. These women often must find work quickly. They do not have the financial reserves to adjust to their new environment before getting a job. They have to start earning and, in many cases, sending money back to their relatives in their home countries. Knowing little about the local labor market, and comparing their wages with what they would have earned at home, they can feel content with wages that later strike them as painfully low.

Immigrant women seeking first jobs usually look for live-in work. Most have divested themselves of dependents they must personally tend, though not those they must support: "Paradoxically, to be good mothers, women leave their children and migrate."[3] They recognize that if they move to the United States, they will not be able to get their own apartments for some time.

They cannot afford rent and utilities. If they live with employers, they can save much of their pay. They also do not have to deal with transportation, a major problem in cities such as Los Angeles, where those without private cars can spend hours on buses every day.

Most of the immigrant women in our study reported that they came to the United States because they could not support themselves and other family members at home. Some suffered actual hunger in their home countries. Others came to escape violence in El Salvador or Guatemala. A few of the young single women said they came to the United States for "adventure," but most of those interviewed had dependents to support, either children or parents.

For those who left children, their sacrifice has meaning only if they can send money back. They are proud of supporting their children, although anguished by their separation from them.[4] A thirty-six-year-old Guatemalan woman, Carmen, who left three daughters, ages six, four, and two, said that she sends $300 a month home (out of monthly earnings of about $850) and that her daughters are "sad but happy because they now have some things." Mothers said that when they first separated from their children they felt intense grief; too busy during the day to dwell on it, they found nights the hardest. They reported crying themselves to sleep for months or even years after they first left their children. A woman from Guyana who left her son, now eleven, when he was six, occasionally talks to him on the telephone, but says it takes her two weeks to recover emotionally from each call.

New workers often take the first job offered. The luckiest ones receive assistance from friends or relatives already in the country, who orient them to the local job market and help them find good employers. A woman from Trinidad was able to live out from the beginning because a sister, also a caregiver in New York, helped her get a high-paying job. Those who find good employers are grateful. One woman from Guyana, who left children of two, three, and eight, said she could not have borne her pain except for her New Jersey employers' kindness.

Other caregivers, operating without assistance, or having aid only from workers who themselves are stuck in the low-wage part of the market, can end up earning almost nothing for long hours of work. A twenty-three-year-old Salvadoran woman who arrived in Los Angeles in 1987 looked after two preschool girls and was paid $85 a week at her first job, where she stayed for a year and a half; she worked from the time she got up at 6:00 A.M. until 11:00 at night. Another Salvadoran woman earned less than $100 a week for looking after five children. A Guatemalan woman worked six days a week, from 7:00 A.M. until 9:00 P.M., for $150 in 1988; it took her a year, she said, to realize that she had worse-than-average conditions: "I found out how the situation was over here in the United States. I found out that I had a job that was not paying enough and that I was being treated badly." Already unhappy, the woman left her job after being accused of theft, rejecting her employer's apology.

One Caregiver's Experience

Newly arrived immigrants do often take low-wage jobs, but they can be dismayed by what those jobs entail. This was the experience of Beverly, an immigrant from Trinidad.

Beverly, a slender, pretty woman who projects dignity and friendliness, had moved to New York to earn money for herself and her eleven-year-old daughter, whom she left in her mother's care. One of eleven children, Beverly had little schooling. Within a week after arriving, she had landed her first job, obtained through an agency.

Beverly's employers had three boys, an eight-year-old and four-year-old twins, with a baby boy born shortly after she arrived. The mother worked part-time in an office, and the father had regular hours as an accountant. Beverly cleaned, cooked under the mother's direction, looked after the three older boys when they got home from school and preschool, and had primary responsibility for the baby.

The family lived in a large house, but Beverly did not have a room of her own. She slept on a fold-out couch in the den. The mother explained to Beverly that she did not like getting up in the night with the baby, because it left her too tired the next day. The baby slept in a crib in the parents' room, but when he woke up, the mother rang a bell to rouse Beverly, sleeping a floor below.

As Beverly came up the stairs, the parents would pull down a screen in their room. Beverly would enter their room and try to comfort the baby. If she could do so in a few minutes, she would put the baby back in his crib. If she couldn't, she took him downstairs with her and put him in a crib next to her couch in the den. At 6 A.M., she would start getting the three older children ready for school. Beverly also looked after the baby in the early morning. The parents ate their own breakfast separately from the boys.

While the baby took his morning nap, Beverly cleaned. The mother often interrupted her work by peremptory commands to come and do something else. If the baby woke, the mother would cry "Beverly!" On the days when the mother was home, she often left the baby in Beverly's care while she read, talked on the phone, or wrote. Sometimes she played with the baby, but if he began to cry, she would immediately call for Beverly. This mother had divided baby care into desirable and undesirable parts. She played with a just-fed and happy baby, while Beverly dealt with the night wakings and the soothing of a cranky baby. In the common division of labor observed between mothers and fathers, this mother had managed to create something akin to the father's role for herself.[5]

The mother also assigned Beverly the routine care of her older children. Beverly ate dinner with the children, while the parents ate by themselves. After dinner, though, while Beverly cleaned up, the parents would spend time with their three older children and read to them.

Beverly liked the boys, particularly the eight-year-old, but never felt close to them. With no space of her own, with a day that stretched from early in the morning through the evening, she struggled just to keep going.[6] Beverly never saw friends in the evenings, but fell into bed as soon as she finished her tasks. She lost weight and felt exhausted and depressed.

After Beverly had worked there for some months, the father abruptly fired her, telling her that, although they found her pleasant, she was not strong enough to handle the three older boys. He told her to leave that day. The parents did not allow her to say good-bye to the boys, keeping them in an upstairs room while she left.

Beverly's employers had treated her as someone who could lift tasks from the mother, but not as someone who could apply intelligence or insight to her job. They were not interested in acknowledging or developing her skills, and clearly saw their sons as receiving their socialization not from Beverly, but from the parents (in the evening time they spent together) and from their (private) schools. A neighbor told Beverly they had had many caregivers before her.

After losing her job, Beverly considered going back to Trinidad. She did not think she could endure another such experience. Her cousin persuaded her to try again, and Beverly soon found another job, this time in Manhattan rather than a suburb. Her new employer, who had interviewed eighty candidates, decided on Beverly when she walked in the door, impressed by her capable and pleasant air. Beverly looked after two preschool children in a more responsible position and developed a close relationship with the mother, who describes Beverly as a talented caregiver. Rather than confining her to drudge work, the mother organized her household so Beverly had the time and energy to actively engage with the children.

In Beverly's case, she advanced in the labor market not because of her own skill development, but because she happened to move from an employer who pursued a low-wage, low-skill strategy (where skills were not recognized even if present) to one who pursued a strategy of finding and paying for a worker able to take on the emotional and intellectual side of child care, as well as its routine aspects.

Work Overload

Most employers expect socially subordinate caregivers to do housework as well as child care. For many, this can lead to heavy workloads. This is especially the case for new immigrants.

Elena exemplifies a caregiver who found her employers' demand that she simultaneously do housework and child care intolerable. Elena had finished high school in Guatemala and then had held a variety of jobs there, including office and factory positions, but not speaking English, and with no working papers, she found herself at the bottom of the caregiver market when she came to Los Angeles. She went to a domestic employment agency where she was placed in a room with other applicants. "We would have to sit there and wait for someone to arrive and check us all out as if we were Ms. Universe candidates. 'I like this one; I'll take her with me.'" Elena found this treatment painful, but insisted she was not embarrassed to be doing domestic work.[7]

Elena got a job working for a family with three children: two preschoolers and one seven-year-old. She found it difficult to vacuum and scrub while trying to keep an eye on her charges. Her divided attention helped precipitate a crisis in the home. The children had acquired a dog, which, in Elena's view, they tormented nonstop and turned savage. The family then installed a fence to keep the dog from the children, but one day the little girl let the dog out. The dog scratched the girl's hand and bit the leg of the middle boy, whom Elena described as "the terror." Elena was taking clothes out of the dryer when she heard screams. She ran outside, where an angry scene between the mother, the children, and Elena ensued. "In the mother's moment of hysteria she asked me why I wasn't watching them, why I wasn't checking up on them. So I asked her, 'Should I finish cleaning the house or should I attend to them?'"

In Elena's view, the mother was not really concerned about her children. "She was neither interested nor grateful about good care. All she wanted was to not have to deal with her children. It was that simple. She neither wanted to have to deal with them nor to know about them." For her part, Elena disliked the children, seeing them as rude. The mother, she said indignantly, would do nothing when her children insulted Elena.

Elena concluded that the only good thing about the job was that the mother paid her in cash. "If this is the way of all Americans, what a horror. What a horror." In Guatemala, she said, children did not express themselves so freely and were far more obedient. . . .

The Language Barrier

Many newly arrived Latina immigrants face a particular difficulty in dealing with the children in their charge, an inability to speak English. In this, they are typical of other undocumented immigrants; one study of undocumented women immigrants from Mexico, carried out in Los Angeles in the early 1980s, found that nearly 80 percent spoke little or no English.[8] Some employers refuse to consider non-English-speaking workers, screening them on the phone for language ability. Almost 40 percent of the employers interviewed, though, had hired caregivers who spoke little or no English.

Some employers overcame initial doubts when they hired non-English-speaking caregivers, captivated by the appeal of particular candidates. A lawyer in Los Angeles, with a six-year-old son and a baby daughter, said: "I didn't want to hire a Spanish-speaking housekeeper. I'm not fluent in Spanish. I thought that it would be no fun for my son. Then I thought, Well, I'll try it, because Rosario was so loving and nurturing and warm with the baby."

From employers' interviews, it is clear that many parents worry more about their ability to speak with caregivers than about their children's ability to do so. Parents who speak fluent Spanish (there were six such employers interviewed) are often happy to have Spanish-speaking caregivers. Other employers brushed up on high school Spanish, studied phrase books, or took Spanish classes. Some relied on Spanish-speaking colleagues at work to interpret for them if anything complex needed to be explained. There were, however, employers who spoke no Spanish at all, who had caregivers who spoke no English. They communicated through sign language.

Some employers prefer workers who do not speak English because they are cheaper than those who do. But many parents value their children's exposure to another language. They want their children to learn Spanish and see this as a positive aspect of having hired an immigrant caregiver. Unfortunately, in practice the children do not seem to learn much Spanish, unless the parents themselves also speak Spanish to them. Parents reported that few children became fluent in Spanish, no matter how much time they spent with Spanish-speaking caregivers. Even those children who came to understand Spanish often refused to speak it.

From the caregivers' side, not knowing the language of their employers can be frustrating. They worry that they will misunderstand employers' instructions or not be able to explain their own concerns. Afraid their employers will be irritated if they have to repeat things, they sometimes just nod when employers ask if they have understood. More seriously, not speaking English restricts the kinds of conversations caregivers can have with their charges. Researchers report that caregivers who speak often with children enhance their language development. Those who examine and talk about objects with children, or who describe activities, do the most to help foster children's language learning.[9] It is hard for caregivers who do not speak the child's language to play this kind of role; they do speak with their charges in Spanish, but the conversations tend to be fairly simple.

Perhaps because of the language barrier, many low-wage Latina caregivers approach their jobs anxiously. They describe themselves as oppressed by worry, finding the responsibility of keeping children safe to be overwhelming. A Salvadoran said the toddler she looked after was very active.

> He gets into everything. I have to be after him because in a moment of not paying attention he could fall, and Oh my God. When a child falls I feel very bad, because when their parents come and see a bruise I feel bad, bad, bad, bad, and I try at all costs to avoid such a thing.

Some are reluctant to take children out, fearing accidents. They also can worry about breaking things in their employers' homes or otherwise bringing their employers' wrath down upon them. With limited ability to communicate with their employers, they cannot easily explain any accidents or mishaps.[10] No Caribbean caregivers (or class peers) we interviewed expressed the same type of anxiety over possible accidents.

The most socially subordinate Latina caregivers describe their main task as "watching" the children in their charge. This "watching" does not necessarily entail any active engagement with the children. They speak less about the children's personalities than about any risks their behavior might present. Many describe their duties in very limited terms. When asked what her responsibilities were for the toddler in her charge, one Sal-

vadoran caregiver replied: "Feed him. And change his diaper when it is dirty." Santos, a thirty-year-old Guatemalan caregiver with a sixth-grade education, saw her duties to her charges in much the same way: "Take care of them. Just make sure that nothing happens to them. That they don't go into the street. If I bring them to the park, to make sure they don't hurt themselves. When they're eating, make sure that they don't choke." The caregivers feel a commitment to the well-being of the children in their charge, worrying about them getting hurt, but some define that well-being narrowly.[11]

Apprehensive about employer displeasure, often unable to communicate anything very complicated to the children because of language differences, with limited educations, minimal autonomy, and heavy responsibilities, socially subordinate caregivers can find that their days pass slowly and their lives pass sadly. As Tila put it, too young to accept her fate, "the fun is over." It is not surprising that women who work sixty-hour weeks for sub-minimum-wage pay might not always bring a playful or inspired attitude to their caregiving duties, even though nearly all bring a strong sense of personal responsibility.

A Temporary Job

In general, immigrant caregivers' hold on their jobs starts to weaken as soon as children become verbal. Many employers see immigrant women with little education as being suitable caregivers for young children, but not for older ones. Cultural differences loom larger for them when children are asking questions or learning language skills.[12]

No matter how attentive they have been, or how deeply attached to the children in their charge, the caregivers' utility to middle-class families diminishes as children get older. Many make a conscious effort to hold on to their jobs; they suppress their own values and they try to avoid challenging the children in their charge. One Guatemalan caregiver said that she took pains to always agree with her employer: "If she told me white was black, I would agree with her and say it was black." Despite these efforts, few class subordinates can overcome the profound disadvantages of their social position. Middle-class parents increasingly move their children into their own cultural orbit as they get older. . . .

Parents' changing attitudes as their children get older are reflected in their views on language issues. Some who thought Spanish-speaking caregivers were fine for their babies rethought the matter once their children became verbal. Seven of the thirty-one parents who hired non-English-speaking caregivers switched to English speakers. In some cases, this occurred because the children themselves became frustrated and said they wanted caregivers who spoke English. A Santa Monica mother described how her sons, ages four and two, became increasingly resistant to their Guatemalan caregiver's speaking Spanish to them:

> There was a point where they just decided they weren't going to speak Spanish. Maybe when [the older boy] went to preschool. And now they're incredibly anxious when we have somebody here who only speaks Spanish. They just get so frustrated and anxious that their needs aren't going to be understood and met.

. . . One Los Angeles mother employed a Salvadoran woman, Adela, for about six years; despite occasional crises in their relationship, both women described it as close. Adela became so attached to the two girls in her charge that her own daughter felt bitterly jealous. Even Adela herself said that she had taken better care of her employers' children than she had of her daughter. Adela had no formal schooling at all (her father had required her to work in the fields), but she had been able to assume much responsibility for her employers' household. The mother thought that Adela was outstanding when her daughters were infants and toddlers, but she became more dubious once they reached five or six. For babies, "any loving, kind, nurturing, intelligent, responsible" person would do; for older children, more was required.

> I love Adela with all my heart, but her idea of art is very different from mine; Adela would not enjoy taking the kids to the art museum. I believe that what you put into their little

heads in these formative years, five, six, seven, and eight, is crucial. Expose them to ten thousand different things, you know, art museums, talk about nuclear power, explain the eclipse.

Skill Development

Not all employers opt for low-wage workers. Some look for caregivers who can assume highly responsible positions in their households; rather than accepting turnover, they try to structure jobs so as to minimize it. They create responsible positions of authority. These positions may go to class peers, women who are culturally similar to the parents. This arrangement does not appeal to all employers, though, partly because many class peers refuse to do all the desired tasks. Some employers who want full housework done as well as child care, and want both done by a self-starting woman, create jobs that they fill with acculturated immigrant women. With time, skill development, and English proficiency, immigrant women from Central America or the Caribbean can escape from the low-wage ghetto into these better "housekeeper" jobs.

Immigrants without legal working papers, and with little formal schooling, find many occupations are closed to them. These immigrants have better prospects for moving up in the hierarchy of domestic work, however limited that occupation might be, than of switching occupations entirely.[13] Domestic work does offer some limited upward mobility, with some workers able to secure increasingly responsible and better-rewarded jobs over time. They cannot easily upgrade their general level of education, but they can try to acquire those specific skills that win them higher wages or better working conditions in the caregiving market.

In part, achieving a housekeeper-type position depends on workers' skills. In Los Angeles and in suburban areas, caregivers move up several notches if they can drive. To caregivers, the best employers are those who allow them to develop their skills, by giving them time in the evenings to take English classes or by helping them get a driver's license and letting them use their cars. Some employers tie pay raises to skill acquisition.

Not all employers, though, want to help their employees gain skills. They may have created such routinized jobs that they prefer to stick with low-skill workers. Others might ideally prefer an English-speaking worker but might not want to give an employee regular time off to attend classes. Ironically, caregivers can be particularly unlucky if their employers speak even a fractured version of Spanish. This can make it harder for live-in workers to learn English and can reduce their employers' incentive to help them do so.

Some caregivers are bitter when long-term employers do not help them develop the skills that the employers demand. Melba, a thirty-six-year-old Salvadoran, has worked for her present employer for six years, but the employer has told Melba that she is thinking of replacing her. In an interview, the mother said she found it tiring getting her children to their activities. "You need to take them to art classes, soccer classes, piano classes, this, that, and the other thing. They require a chauffeur, so it's very hard." Melba was dismayed by the mother's plans:

> She told me that she would hire someone who spoke English and had a car. So I told her that if I didn't know how to speak English, it was because she had not given me the opportunity to learn it. If I don't have a car, it's because I can't afford it. "So what are you complaining about? If I don't know English, it's because of you," I told her.

While it is possible this is what Melba *wanted* to tell her employer rather than what she *did* tell her, the sentiment is the same in either case.

In general, Caribbean women seem to have an easier time rising to high-level housekeeping jobs than do Latina women. They have some advantages. Most come from English-speaking countries, so language is not an issue; in northeastern cities, where they are concentrated, driving is less important than in southwestern cities, such as Los Angeles, where Latina workers predominate. Usually older than Latina women when they come to the United States, they tend to be more established and confident. They are somewhat better educated (an average of eight years of schooling compared to six). And finally, as their children are usually older than the Latina workers' children, they have fewer outside demands on them as they build their careers. . . .[14]

Conclusions

Employers can see advantages in hiring workers very different from themselves. They minimize their costs, and they can assign these workers almost any housecleaning or child-rearing task. Except for those with high-level housekeepers, seldom do they see their caregivers as superior workers, but they do see them as meeting their needs. The employers do not expect the caregivers to read to their children or to help develop their language skills. They foster the middle-class acculturation of their children through other means, including their own involvement and their children's attendance at preschools.

Immigrant caregivers work in the home, but do not take on parents' roles. They also, however, differ from trained caregivers who adopt what could be called a "nursery school style" of interaction with children. Researchers who study child care have concluded that "children are more likely to learn social and intellectual skills when caregivers are stimulating and educational, responsive and respectful, moderately affectionate and appropriately demanding."[15] The most socially subordinate caregivers have little capacity to be "appropriately demanding," given that they themselves are not in a position to make many demands. They also cannot necessarily be "stimulating and educational," as many of them do not speak the children's language and many are distracted by heavy housework duties. They are always vulnerable to parents' sudden critiques on these matters, yet the parents themselves create the job structure that prevents caregivers from enhancing their own skills or, indirectly, those of the children in their charge.

For the workers themselves, low-skill child-rearing jobs can be alienating and dreary. The most dissatisfied caregivers can be young immigrant women who see themselves as being "locked up" in their employers' houses. More grim and resigned are the older immigrant women stuck in the low-wage ghetto, who have worked all their adult lives as deeply subordinate employees in other people's homes. Immigrant caregivers fare best when employers decide they do value skills and that the women they hire have more than a custodial role to play. This can require actively helping workers to develop skills, but not all employers make this commitment. . . .

NOTES

1. Rosanna Hertz, *More Equal Than Others: Women and Men in Dual-Career Marriages* (Berkeley: University of California Press, 1986), pp. 147–95, discusses dual career couples and their preference for hiring nannies.

2. Most people with a choice leave the occupation. This fact emerged in a study of three types of workers in Los Angeles in the early 1980s: undocumented Mexican immigrants; legal Mexican immigrants; and native-born workers of Mexican parentage. Only undocumented immigrant women did domestic service in any numbers. Even those workers just one step above them—the legal Mexican immigrants—were rarely in the occupation. David M. Heer, *Undocumented Mexicans in the United States,* American Sociological Association Rose Monograph Series (Cambridge: Cambridge University Press, 1990), p. 147. Not all workers are able to leave, though, confined partly by undocumented status or lack of English skills. The jobs open to such workers are limited, so they improve their position more by rising within occupations than by switching from one type of work to another. Kevin F. McCarthy and R. Burciaga Valdez, *Current and Future Effects of Mexican Immigration in California* (Santa Monica, Calif.: Rand, May 1986), p. 34.

3. Shellee Colen, "'Just a Little Respect': West Indian Domestic Workers in New York City," in *Muchachas No More: Household Workers in Latin America and the Caribbean,* ed. Elsa M. Chaney and Mary Garcia Castro (Philadelphia: Temple University Press, 1989), pp. 172–73.

4. It often takes many years before the women are in a position to retrieve their children. They have to save enough money to switch to live-out status, which requires renting an apartment. They must then pay to return to their home countries; coming back to the United States, those who enter the country illegally must pay coyotes (guides) to help them and their children across the border. This can run into many hun-

dreds of dollars. The women reported paying coyotes very different amounts (ranging from $300 for a Mexican to $3,000 for a Salvadoran). For comparison, see the discussion of coyotes and their costs in Heer, *Undocumented Mexicans in the United States,* pp. 20–21.

5. Arlie Hochschild with Anne Machung, *The Second Shift: Working Parents and the Revolution at Home* (New York: Viking, 1989).

6. Mary Romero, *Maid in the U.S.A.* (New York: Routledge, 1992), p. 117, discusses the negative effects of domestic workers' not having private space: "Although domestics are expected to create and to respect the private space of employers and their families, they themselves are denied privacy. . . . The combination of not having a bedroom and not having access to the rest of the house for resting or leisure activity continually affirms the worker's inferior status in the employer's home."

7. A New York mother described going to an employment agency where women were lined up waiting to be selected by prospective employers. The job candidates had suitcases with them so they could immediately go to the employers' houses.

8. Heer, *Undocumented Mexicans in the United States,* p. 124.

9. Cheryl D. Hayes, John L. Palmer, and Martha J. Zaslow, eds., *Who Cares for America's Children? Child Care Policy for the 1990s* (Washington, D.C.: National Academy Press, 1990), p. 123.

10. Evelyn Nakano Glenn describes similar anxiety among Japanese American domestic workers about accidentally breaking employers' possessions in *Issei, Nisei, War Bride: Three Generations of Japanese American Women in Domestic Service* (Philadelphia: Temple University Press, 1986), p. 173.

11. See Caroline Zinsser, *Raised in East Urban: Child Care Changes in a Working-Class Community* (New York: Teachers College Press, 1991), pp. 65–66, for an account of how white working-class babysitters in a Northeastern city also focused on the physical care of the children in their charge.

12. On class-related language differences, see Shirley Brice Heath, *Ways with Words: Language, Life, and Work in Communities and Classrooms* (Cambridge: Cambridge University Press, 1983).

13. Kevin F. McCarthy and R. Burciaga Valdez, *Current and Future Effects of Mexican Immigration in California* (Santa Monica, Calif.: Rand, May 1986), p. 34.

14. Domestic workers whose children are with them in the United States face very difficult circumstances.

They usually work such long hours that it is very hard for them to look after their own children. These women managed in different ways. Several who had babies born in the United States had the children live with them at their employers' houses, an arrangement that became strained as the children got older. Caregivers said they became disturbed by the contrast between the employers' lifestyle and that which their children would experience. They also did not want their children to feel inferior to the wealthy children around them.

Four caregivers with children kept live-in jobs but had their children live separately from them in the United States. One child stayed with a friend for a year; in two families the fathers looked after the children; and in the fourth, two teenage children stayed in an apartment by themselves during the week and were joined by their mother on weekends. Caregivers understandably expressed pain and anxiety about these arrangements, finding it very difficult to have their children live near them and yet be inaccessible most of the week. Even young children could be on their own a great deal; a live-in Guatemalan caregiver, who felt "sad and lonely" that she could see her children only on weekends, knew her six- and eight-year-old boys were untended after school until her husband got home. The younger boy became critically ill with a burst appendix while on his own. He had called his mother to tell her he had a stomach ache, but she did not think she could leave work. After this crisis, she switched to a live-out job.

Caregivers who lived out enjoyed much better circumstances, but they still had to find child care, a tough challenge on their meager incomes. They left children with friends and neighbors, but often did not feel they could pay them adequately. A Guatemalan caregiver in Los Angeles, for example, left her one-year-old daughter with a friend while she worked. She herself earned $200 a week; she paid her friend $40 a week to look after her baby from 7:30 in the morning until 6:00 at night. Another Guatemalan left her baby with an elderly neighbor, but was distressed that the child was not allowed to move around, as the apartment was very crowded. Even worse, when she picked him up one day she had to brush cockroaches off his clothes. Not surprisingly, it creates emotional conflicts in women to spend their days attending to other people's children while they know their own are receiving marginal care. And, of course, live-out caregivers with children face a true "second shift," with child care and housecleaning awaiting them when they get home.

15. Alison Clarke-Stewart, *Daycare*, rev. ed. (Cambridge, Mass.: Harvard University Press, 1993), p. 97.

THINKING ABOUT THE READINGS

The 21st Century Breathing Down Our Necks

- Summarize the predictions Howe and Strauss offer about the future of today's youth. Do you think they are overly optimistic or pessimistic? Given all you've heard about the 13th Generation (or as they're sometimes called, "Generation X," or the "Twentysomething Generation"), do you think these predictions are warranted? If you are a member of the generation the authors describe, how would you characterize those older and younger than you? If you are a member of an older generation (like the Baby Boom or the Silent Generation), what is your assessment of "13ers?" How do you personally feel the effects of conflict with other generations? Is generational conflict inevitable? Explain.

Other People's Children

- According to Wrigley, why do so many middle- and upper-middle-class parents hire legal (and sometimes illegal) immigrants from Third World countries to care for their children? What do you think are the effects on children of being raised by someone from a different culture who speaks a different language? These immigrant women obviously play a vital economic role in the lives of many wealthy and powerful Americans. But the vast majority of people want to see their numbers limited and their access to governmental services severely restricted if not abolished altogether. Why do you suppose there aren't more people demonstrating and lobbying for not against immigrants' rights?

CHAPTER 15

Architects of Change

Reconstructing Society

Throughout this book you have seen examples of how society is socially constructed and how these social constructions, in turn, affect the lives of individuals. It's hard not to feel a little helpless when discussing the control that culture, massive bureaucracies, institutions, systems of social stratification, and population trends have over our individual lives. However, social change is as much a part of society as social order. Individuals, acting collectively, can shape institutions and alter the course of society.

One of the striking features of social movements is that they are often organized and supported by people who might be considered relatively powerless as individuals yet who collectively represent a driving force for social change. Barbara Kingsolver's description of the role of women in the Arizona copper mine strike in "Holding the Line" reveals just such a situation. When the miners (mostly men) were barred by court injunction from assembling outside the gates of the mines, the women began holding mass pickets of their own. In addition, they formed the Women's Auxiliary to boost morale, raise money, and generate public support. For 18 months—often in the face of jail sentences and threats of violence against them and their families—they sustained the strike, driven by their enduring commitment to the union and the solidarity they felt with one another. In the end there were no outright winners: the unions were decertified, the mining company closed several mines, and some of the small communities became ghost towns. Nevertheless, the actions of these women permanently altered the social order in southwestern mining towns, making the mines safer places for the workers and ultimately changing the way large mining companies deal with their employees.

Similarly, Kristin Luker, in "World Views of Pro-Life and Pro-Choice Activists," vividly portrays the "real people" within large-scale social movements. Luker takes a peek into the ideals and beliefs of the people involved in both sides of one of the most controversial social issues today: abortion. We find that the ideologies that underlie movements to either ensure or prohibit legal access to abortion are significantly more complex than we think, drawing not only on ideas about when life begins but on ideas about sexuality and parenthood. The labels "pro-life" and "pro-choice" simply don't tell us much about the depth of abortion activists' belief systems or about the areas of agreement in their ideologies.

Holding the Line
Women in the Great Arizona Mine Strike of 1983

Barbara Kingsolver

This is an account of eighteen months, between June 1983 and December 1985, during which a strike against the Phelps Dodge Copper Corporation permanently altered the social order in several southwestern mining towns. The strike proved to be an important moment in U.S. labor history, but more than that, it was one of those rare events that forces a turning point in many lives at once.

When it began, anyone who was paying attention believed this was going to be a brief and conventional strike. But within a month, things were happening that I'd never seen before, or heard of happening in my lifetime. People were being jailed for simply calling a neighbor "scab." Helicopters and squads of men with hefty-looking automatic weapons were coming in to break the strike, and strike supporters were answering back with extraordinary resistance. A fair number of the faces and hands on the strike's front lines belonged to women. All of this looked interesting to me, and terrifying, and it looked like history.

For the next year and a half I did my best to watch it happen. Some half-dozen mining towns were involved, but the focal point of the strike, over the long haul, was at the Morenci mine, and to a lesser extent the Ajo mine. The former is a four-hour drive, and the latter, three hours, from my home in Tucson. I put a lot of miles on my pickup, spending as much time as possible in Morenci and nearby Clifton and making briefer trips to the other striking towns in Arizona. (The strike also affected a few towns in New Mexico and Texas, which I was never able to visit.) I taped extensive interviews with about seventy-five people, mostly women, who were in some way involved with the strike; I talked with several of

them again many times over the course of two years, tracking their changes of heart and mind. From my own observations and accumulation of taped interviews—which came to fill half a dozen shoeboxes and spill onto the floor of my bedroom/office—I've made this account of the strike. . . .

The Devil's Domain

The history of mining is a story of inevitable disaster. Between 1961 and 1973, more than half a million disabling injuries occurred in mines in the United States—nearly twice as many as incurred by all U.S. soldiers in Vietnam. The mean death rate for miners during those years was approximately 1,080 per million, and for active-duty military personnel, about 1,270 per million (figures from the National Safety Council and Department of Defense Information). If war is hell, so is mining: underground shafts collapse, smelter furnaces explode, lung disease is endemic. In few other professions are the odds so stacked against living long enough to retire.

These odds aren't so much laws of nature as of economics. Many cave-ins could have been prevented had there been enough supporting timbers; extra drying time will keep damp ore from exploding inside a furnace. But every penny spent on such precautions is a penny robbed from the business of mining ore. Safety costs money; speedy production costs lives. The familiar formula has never yet been solved by cool algebra. Obviously, the miners have a strong interest in their side of the equation and have forever sought to organize for better working conditions, longer lives, and better-fed children. And this, too, is a history punctuated by disaster. Every country that has tapped its mineral wealth has also accumulated grisly stories of strikes, repression, and massacres. This part of mining tradition has been far less exclusive of women.

History tends to polish the marble surface of a wall and ignore the mortar that holds the slabs in place; likewise, the contributions of women to mining history are mostly invisible, but they are a good part of the reason the wall still stands. For the most part their participation must simply be taken for granted, but in a few cases it is well documented. The film *Norma Rae,* loosely based on an actual strike in a textile mill, popularized the image of a modern working woman devoted to her union. But at least three earlier U.S. strikes in which women played leading roles have been recorded or reenacted on film. *With Babies and Banners* documents the 1937 strike against General Motors in Flint, Michigan, in which women auto workers and workers' wives—dubbed the "Red Berets"—held the battle lines out front while male workers occupied the Fisher I and II automotive plants for more than a month. (Women workers were sent out before the sit-down, to avoid suggestions of licentiousness.) Similarly, in 1973, women sustained the ultimately disastrous coal strike at the Brookside mine in Kentucky on a steady diet of soup-kitchen stamina and political zeal; the strike was the subject of the documentary *Harlan County USA.* And at a point in time almost exactly halfway between the Flint and Brookside strikes, while McCarthyism burned white-hot, a militant strike led by women against Empire Zinc in Hanover, New Mexico, was immortalized at some peril both to actors (many of whom were strike supporters themselves) and filmmakers in the now-famous film *Salt of the Earth.*

It's tempting to wonder, after watching these films, if many other strikes would now be remembered as largely or partly led by women if a movie camera had been on hand. All three documentaries portray events very much like those of the 1983 strike against Phelps Dodge Copper in Arizona, in which the same forces again called women to the line: loyalty to the union, desperation over their families' living conditions, and the fact that men were legally or physically barred from action. The 1951 Empire Zinc strike, in particular, strongly foreshadowed the complexities of the Phelps Dodge strike, mainly because of geography. Like the strike in Arizona three decades later, it was shaped by the special conflicts of economics, ethnicity, and gender that are woven into the social fabric of these isolated, predominantly Mexican-American mining towns, where a woman's place is in the home, or on the line—depending. . . .

Long before their contract expired at midnight on June 30, 1983, a consortium of more than twenty miners' unions attempted to reach a settlement on basic contract issues with all the major copper-producing companies. The practice of arriving at a standard set of terms for workers throughout an industry (known as pattern bargaining) has been used in mining for years. The miners knew times weren't good for the company, and they offered what they felt they could give: frozen wages for the duration of the next three-year contract, provided that they would continue to receive cost-of-living protection tied to the consumer price index. Four of the companies—Kennecott, Asarco, Magma Copper, and Inspiration Consolidated Copper—settled with little delay. The fifth, Phelps Dodge, refused the offer, asking the miners to accept further cuts in wage scales, benefits, holiday and vacation time, and an end to cost-of-living protection. Deciding that it was less than they could live with, Phelps Dodge miners at Morenci, Ajo, Bisbee, and Douglas walked off their jobs one minute after midnight on July 1. The normal cacophony of mining and smelting noises went dead still. Outside in the hot desert night, supporters waited along the road to clap and cheer as the strikers trailed away from the mine gates in a long caravan of cars and pickup trucks.

But Phelps Dodge didn't intend to let its operations be closed down. When the company began bringing in workers to replace them, striking miners lined up at the mine gates in protest. A few days later, when Phelps Dodge won a court injunction barring the miners from assembling at the gates, women strike supporters began holding mass pickets of their own. When the National Guard and riot troops from Arizona's Department of Public Safety (DPS) were summoned to occupy Clifton and Morenci, no one expected the strike to last much longer. The women organized rallies, pickets, and more rallies. They were tear-gassed and arrested. They swore and screamed and sometimes threw rocks, and always they showed up for the picket. Thirteen months later, when they were still on the line, a DPS officer remarked, in what was to become the most famous summation of the strike, "If we could just get rid of these broads, we'd have it made."

Fina Roman, president of the Morenci Miners Women's Auxiliary, responded to this statement before a gathering of supporters and the press. "They'll never be rid of us," she declared with controlled anger. "Do they ask us to forget the elderly being tear-gassed? Do they ask us to forget the beatings and arrests? To forget the past generations who handed down a sacred trust to preserve a dignified way of life won through tremendous sacrifices? Many did not live long enough to benefit from those sacrifices, yet because of them we enjoy those benefits today. Do they ask us to give them up without a fight?"...

Spokespeople for the other copper companies continued to express contentment with the unions' proposed compromise, but Phelps Dodge officials pointed to the company's $75 million losses in 1982 and maintained that they could afford to offer nothing but cuts. Tom McWilliams, assistant director of labor relations for Phelps Dodge, told the *Arizona Republic,* "We are a separate company and have no connections with those [other copper-producing] firms. We feel we can't continue on the same road we've been on for the last 15 years, making settlements not consistent with the economic condition of the industry." Vice-President Pat Scanlon knew a strike was coming, because the unions were committed to the pattern-bargaining precedent. He admitted later, "If you'd asked me, at that point, what would be the likely outcome, I'd say, 'Well, the unions will see that we'll be able to operate in the face of a strike, and they'll find some way to come to an agreement that gives us what we need, and will be face-saving for them. We'll work it out, once they see that the alternative is that we're going to keep the place running.' "

On their side of the fence, the miners saw the erosion of their standard of living as not only personally dangerous but as an insult to their ancestors. In their tiny, isolated towns they had been steeped for half a century in their own labor traditions and had extracted a sense of pride that preserved them through hard times. When asked about their reasons for striking, most mentioned before anything else the community's self-respect and the parents who struggled all their years for a decent living. The miners also had a sophisticated awareness of pattern bargaining and the connections between themselves and other workers: if they gave in, the miners in other towns and other states, the railroad workers, and the auto workers would suffer.

The women who carried their own flag into this battle were miners' wives and daughters, and a few were miners themselves. Their grandfathers had walked out of the Morenci mine in 1915 or left Bisbee by cattle car in 1917. They had grown up with the union, a tool as familiar to them as a can opener or a stove. They knew exactly where they would be without it. . . .

On the Line

While people in distant cities clamp iron grills over the windows and warn their children about talking to strangers, Clifton [Arizona's] front doors have gone for generations without being locked. Four men comprise the police force—about one per thousand residents. The telephone directory could be torn in half by a small child. When people here try to describe what happened in 1983, they quickly become exasperated. "It's hard to explain this to somebody who doesn't live here," one woman told me. "You just can't understand what we felt."

How *does* it feel to someone who's at home in a neighborhood of unlocked doors—who calls every police officer in town by his first name—when the governor marches in four hundred armed state troopers, armored personnel carriers, Huey helicopters, and seven units of the National Guard?

Clifton was stunned. Diane McCormick shook her head, remembering the day they came in. "All

I could think was, this isn't Russia. We're supposed to be a free country here. I couldn't believe what was happening to us, and I still can't. We were under martial law. I just couldn't understand *why*."

Diane and her sisters—Berta, Lolly, and Cindy—are an energetic quartet, dark-eyed, direct, quick to laugh and slow to get mad. Their parents raised them to be good Catholic girls, but also to act on their beliefs, and this they do. During the strike and after, mention of the "Delgado sisters" was likely to provoke a woolly reminiscence from anyone in town.

None of the sisters is a miner, but Phelps Dodge could no more be separated from their lives than could honey from a bee's. Their father is a retired miner; Cindy and Berta married miners; Berta and Diane have worked in the company store. They were all active in the strike, they say, "even before day one."

Berta is a born organizer. Diane says that for weeks before the strike started, Berta talked constantly about reviving the Morenci Miners Women's Auxiliary, which had existed since the 1940s but always died down between strikes. After meeting with union officials, they and three other friends convened the auxiliary. According to Berta, no one paid much attention at that point. Once, several weeks into the strike, during a meeting attended by nearly the whole town at Clifton's American Legion Hall, someone asked if the auxiliary was around. "I stood up—I was way in the back—and I yelled, 'Yes, it's still around!' I gave them my phone number, which got a big laugh, because I told them, 'It's unlisted, so here it is.'" After that, Berta's phone began to ring.

But revival was slow. "The women didn't want to be involved in anything," Diane said. "Their husbands would say, 'No, you can't go to the union hall.' It was always a place for just men, see? They didn't want the women going in there. All the time we were trying to recruit women into coming, they would say, 'Go into the union hall? With all those men?' We told them, 'Get off it. Jeez, wake up. It's a new generation!'"

"It wasn't like later in the strike, where all you saw was women on the line," Berta agreed. One of the women's first and most enduring tasks

would be to get people out on the line for the shift changes.

Holding a picket line is a simple act with many levels of consequence. It's the strike's public face, meant to elicit support, discourage would-be strikebreakers, and serve as a constant reminder to the company that the union is alive. But it is far more than a symbolic protest: if it's respected by outside unions, the picket can be as functional as a tourniquet. Until the strike is settled, the Teamster driver is honor-bound not to bring in smelter parts from Detroit or to haul out ore. No matter what the railroad boss wants, if a picket is on the tracks, a union engineer can't take the train across.

Picketers who hold up their signs at the gate know their strike is as fragile or as strong as their interlocked arms. For as long as it lasts, holding this line is the striker's job. Sometimes it doesn't amount to much more than passing the time with co-workers and friends in the long, uncharted days of waiting to work again. And sometimes it is a harder, more dangerous job than mining ore. . . .

Phelps Dodge stepped up recruitment on all fronts. In Arizona, one of twenty right-to-work states, employees in a unionized industry aren't required to join a union, and, conversely, employers need not honor picket lines, union jurisdiction, or the sanctity of a striker's job. A letter mailed on July 7 stated: "If you are a present employee and want to be sure of having your old job back when the strike is over, you should return to work immediately, before your job is given to someone else."

Patience turned to panic: a striker's labor is his or her only bargaining chip. Skeleton crews of foremen and secretaries weren't a threat, but if Phelps Dodge planned on massive recruitment, the strikers couldn't stand by and watch.

Early on the morning of August 8, busloads of workers were spotted going into the Morenci mine. Word ran through town like a grass fire. Carmina Garcia, a retired school bus driver married to a retired miner, was at home in Clifton. To her mind the danger was clear: "We knew if P.D. got all those people in there, they weren't going to give us a contract," she explained. "It was 11:30 in the morning when Beaver came and told us, 'Hey, we wanna close down the mine—we *have* to close down the mine. Something's going to happen. They're taking in mattresses and taking in food, so we'd better have some people up there.' "

Carmina went. Her husband, Willie, was away for the morning, so she called her friends Jessie and Velia, the mayor's wife. "We went around the side to check the Columbine gate and saw that the trucks were coming in and out through the back, bringing in food, cots, and whatnot. Then they told us there were more people going through the main gate, so we went to the main road and there we saw the people were coming in *buses*. They were scared to come to work. Don't you see, they shouldn't have been working—there was a strike! So P.D. hired those buses to bring in the scabs from Safford, and even a few from Clifton. They would stop and pick them up and drive them around back.

"We had to put a stop to it. People from Duncan, Safford, *everywhere*, were coming in to help us close it down. They said in the papers there were one or two thousand, but it was more than that, I know. As time went on you started seeing a little bit more and a little bit more." . . .

Berta Chavez and her sisters were there, of course. Berta was up above the mine. "We could look down into the mine where the scabs were. They had their hats over their faces; I guess they were afraid, because we had control. And they'd come in disguises. One guy came in with a paper sack over his head, with holes cut for the eyes. They were ashamed because they knew they shouldn't be in there scabbing for P.D.

"Outside, there were people from the mine gate all the way to the general office. It was full of people. A couple of thousand, I'd say. We had our trucks there—we backed them up—and we had our beer and our ice chests—it was just like a picnic. We were just waiting. We gave them till 12:00 to get the scabs out. We said after 12:00, nobody comes in or out."

Diane was on the opposite side of the crowd, closer to the road. "P.D. did send people home," she said, "and we were happy. Our union leaders said 'Okay, let them through.' We let them through, yelling 'hurray!' and laughing and screaming. That's exactly what we wanted, all the

scabs out. But I started looking around and said, 'Hey, wait a minute. Not everyone is out of there, not even half.' We were there in the morning and saw all those cars going in, and not that many, really, were coming out. Tom Aguilar, the mayor, had been sitting and counting the cars, going and coming. So what they did is they kept some in. They said they needed a 'skeleton crew,' that they couldn't just shut it down, they had to do it gradually. I said, 'Uh-uh.' "

The crowd, a whole town threatened with the loss of livelihood, was as volatile as kerosene-soaked tinder. This last news was enough to strike the spark. Plans of action sprang up spontaneously and began to roar: the crowd was ready to march into the mine and take it over. Berta asked her friend Liza, who worked in the mill, "What should we do, once we get in?" Liza said, "Just follow me and push all kinds of buttons."

At noon, P.D. officials appeared at the gate, conferred briefly, and agreed not to bring in the next shift. Diane said, "Our union leaders told us, 'They've given us their word, they're going to shut down. We have to be peaceful, we have to maintain.' But I heard Berta up on top, saying, 'No, don't believe them.' I was yelling, 'No! They've lied to us before! Don't trust them.' "

Berta said, "Sure, I knew better. They've messed us up so many times. But our union president said, 'Brothers, let's wait and see what happens.' In my mind I kept thinking something was going on. See, we could have had full control of the mine, taken it over. We could have made them close down until we settled, the way a strike is supposed to go. But the guys were saying, 'Let's show them our word is good, that we're good people standing behind our company.' That's what they decided, so we obeyed. We had our hopes high so many times. That was one of the times." . . .

Carmina, who is something like the force of a typhoon packed into a polyester pants suit, never fails to get excited as she relates the events of that day. She produces photos from her scrapbook to confirm her estimates of crowd sizes, numbers of cars, weapons carried by DPS officers. Frequently, she leans forward and yells to emphasize a point.

"So then a WHOLE BUNCH of officers marched down the highway, like an army. They marched DOWN with their riot sticks and guns and told us to move OUT of the road. They kept marching back and forth, back and forth; they made us so mad. But we couldn't move because there were people and cars EVERYWHERE, and it was getting dark. We were stuck. My husband was down here, and we were up there, and there was no way to get out.

"By around six o'clock it was raining and pouring but we STAYED there. The DPS parked their cars and closed the highway. It was 9:30 that night when I got back home. My husband knew I was up there; he had gone to see the horses that day, and when he came back he kept waiting and waiting. He tried going up, but a deputy told him, 'No need to go up there, you can't get through.' A lot of people were going through anyway. They would say, 'We live up there,' whether they did or not. Everybody I knew that wasn't working was up there—kids, husbands, wives, everybody.

"When I finally got home my husband said, 'What's happened, what's happened? I tried to get up there but I couldn't; they wouldn't let me.' 'You should have gone up there!' I said. But he said, 'Oh, they told me . . . He's the type, you know, that wouldn't dare. Whatever they told him, well, that's it. Now I'm the type that I don't care what they tell me, I'm STILL going to go through, one way or another. I'll tell them *something!*

"That night Bert Drucher called from Governor Babbitt's office. They couldn't get hold of Tom Aguilar, the mayor, or Eddie Marquez, or none of the Democratic party—they were all over there at the courthouse. The only name they could find, after those guys, was me. I belong to the Precinct Committee Women.

"So he said to me, 'Carmina, can you please get hold of Lalo [Eduardo] Marquez and tell him to tell the union that Governor Babbitt is on his way; he just had trouble on account of it's been raining. He says everybody has to have a ten-day cooling-off period—the unions, P.D., everybody.' I says, 'NO WAY! I just came from up there. Tell Babbitt to get here, and we're NOT COOLING OFF. He has to close it down until the unions sign a contract.'"

Laughing, Carmina remembered that Drucher was not amused. "He said, *'Carmina!* You just pay attention to what I'm telling you!' Oh, he

hollered at me. He was wanting to set up the ten-day cooling. I told him to FORGET it.

"But I guess P.D. had already called them, and they had already planned it that very night. We all went home, and in those ten days the union officials tried to talk to [Vice-President] Bolles, trying to meet together, and waiting and waiting. The unions wanted everybody out of the plant. They met at the conference room down here at the Clifton courthouse, and there was Governor going back and forth." . . .

Because the company couldn't legally fire strikers without cause, Phelps Dodge kept a file of films documenting activities for which they were being terminated. When Gloria viewed the films, she realized she wasn't in the cast; on the day for which her warrant had been issued, she wasn't even on the line. She had witnesses and decided to fight the termination.

Seventy-four other strikers in Ajo were fired and ordered to vacate their company-owned homes during the next weeks. Eleven Ajo strikers were arrested on charges of rioting, obstructing traffic, or "interfering with the judicial process."

Pat Scanlon felt that on balance the firings were good for the company. "We discharged throughout Arizona 188 of the strikers for strike-related misconduct," he commented later. "Our perception of that group is that in general it included a lot of the less desirable employees that were working, either because they were general troublemakers, or unreliable, or drunks, or whatever. So it had the effect of purging the work force of a lot of people who were not really on the company's side . . . so in that respect, we upgraded the work force."

Soila Bom, in the very first arrest of the strike, was jailed for using her telephone to tell a former friend that she now considered him a scab. Those arrested were booked into the Ajo annex of the Pima County Jail, but most were later moved to a jail in Tucson. For the three-hour drive they sat handcuffed in the back of a van without water or air-conditioning. The arrests were a shock, and the extremely high bonds set—up to $20,000—bankrupted union coffers overnight. Union attorney Duane Ice reported that the unions planned to fight back and would seek jury trials. Years later, Soila and the others would be vindicated by appalled juries. But at the time, and in the months to come, being legally in the right did them no more good than if they had been pedestrians run down in a crosswalk.

In Clifton, the mood of the day was wildly upbeat. The Morenci mine was closed for ten days: long enough, surely, to negotiate a contract and settle the strike. A celebratory racket rang from the Wagon Wheel bar, the Social Club, and the union halls, echoing up and down the high brick facades of Chase Creek.

"That was the start of the ten-day cooling-off period," Diane McCormick explained. "Phelps Dodge told us no one was in there, so we didn't go back up to the mine. There was nothing for those ten days. We were just down in Chase Creek, hanging out at the union hall and that kind of thing. We really felt good that first day. But now, looking back, we can see that it was just to give them time to bring in the National Guard, to get protection for the scabs. That's what they were doing with those ten days, not cooling off! All this time they knew that, but still we were so trustful. Never again. God, I wish we'd done something when we had the chance."

Berta said that at first they just heard rumors. "There are a lot of guys around who are in the National Guard [reserves], and they were hearing things, but we didn't believe it. We said, they're not going to waste money on that!"

The following day Diane was sitting on her front porch overlooking Highway 666. This memory still makes her stomach hurt. "All of a sudden we saw these caravans passing. I said, 'Oh, God, they've betrayed us.'"

Carmina heard the bad news from her brother-in-law Clyde, who lives in Safford, half an hour to the south of Clifton. "He lives right by the road," Carmina said, "and he saw all of the trucks, and trucks, and *trucks* coming through town. Then the tankers. He called and said, 'Are they going to fight another world war?' He's older than my husband—they've been in the service—and you know what he said? That it reminded him of when they were overseas. He said he feared for us.

"It *was* like they were going to start a war—with the TANKERS. A whole ARMY coming in to this little community, can you imagine? And there were helicopters coming in, dropping men off, and then the trucks, with water, the machine guns, and everything. We thought they were going to have a machine gun at every home. They started gathering down by the drive-in that's closed. People passing by kept saying, 'There's a lot of National Guards coming in.' We were just waiting.

"At the beginning, we didn't know what it would come to. I thought probably somebody would get killed. I was born and raised here, and I've never seen anything like that day. Just on TV. If somebody gets run over, that's a big thing here in this town, you know. It's a small community. When some kids got killed in the Marines, that was the saddest day. That was the worst we could think of."

Diane and her children watched from the porch. "I thought, we've had it. This is it. What were we going to do, throw rocks? Against their machine guns? It took a couple of days to get them all in here. We felt like we were being invaded. You couldn't do anything. You'd wake up in the middle of the night and hear the helicopters."

Berta drove down into town to watch them come in. "We couldn't figure out where they were going. My friend and I went all the way to the freeway, because we thought they were going to be posted there, but they weren't. They were putting them up on top, on P.D. property! Way up on top of the mound, where nobody could see them."

Soon, though, the troops were too numerous to hide. They swarmed over the little town like hornets, with about the same effect on its inhabitants. Cleo Robledo says she was less frightened than furious. "It was just the fact that they had done such a thing, you know? You'd go in a store to get your milk and your eggs and look around and it was National Guard and DPS all over the place. It was unbelievable. You'd have to walk right by them in the stores." . . .

When the mine gates reopened on August 19, National Guardsmen were lined up on Phelps Dodge property, guns pointing out. Patrolling activity was stepped up for the shift changes when, after the ten-day "cooling-off" period, Phelps Dodge again began bringing busloads of nonstrikers in and out of the mine. When Phelps Dodge reopened the employment office, armed National Guardsmen were standing on the roof. The sensation of being stared at through a rifle-scope is unsettling, to say the least. When strikers and their families walked the picket lines, uniformed sharpshooters followed their movements with automatic weapons. Strike sympathy still ran high in the town, and the memory of the shutdown—the astonishing power of their numbers—was fresh in the strikers' minds. But they reluctantly came to understand, as many have learned before them, that a majority opinion means nothing against guns. . . .

The occupation of Clifton and Morenci left indelible marks. The character of the strike, and the tactics of its supporting organizations, were forced to change. The Women's Auxiliary in particular hardened its core.

According to Jean Lopez, the auxiliary used to be "a group where the ladies would get together and air their complaints." She says it made them feel better to see that other families were in the same boat. "You'd come feeling depressed and leave feeling great. And it was kind of a support group for the men—the women would get together and make tortillas to take to the picketers up at the mine. And parties for the children at Christmas, that kind of thing. This is basically what it was. But it changed. The women were forced to take a stand. We were always behind the lines, and the men were up in front. But in this strike, the women had to move to the front."

Fina Roman explained how this had come about. "Everybody was on the line at first, including the women. But the women are the ones who have never stayed away from it. Partly this is because there was an injunction against the men, but also because it was very important to us to keep that picket line active. The men, after the injunction, were in danger of being arrested for just being there. The women took over."

The injunction against the unions said that no more than five miners could be at the picket shacks, and not more than a hundred on the line at the main gate. "We argued with the unions that that meant there could be ninety-nine," Fina said, "but the men were hard-pressed to come up with

those ninety-nine, so the auxiliary took it upon themselves to be on that picket line."

And this they did. As Trudy Morgan put it, "We went up there to hold the line, and we *held* the line."

"The Women's Auxiliary would say they were going to meet up there," Diane McCormick recalled, "and we would just go and do it. A *lot* of us would show up, just us women. P.D. was threatening the men, saying they were going to fire them for being on the line, and they were taking pictures and all that. But they couldn't fire us. So the women would go."

"Believe me," Berta added, laughing, "they would love to have fired us if they could!"

And so, in the face of a considerable army, the women of Clifton and Morenci began rolling their groggy children out of bed at 4:00 A.M. and making their way in the predawn light to the top of the hill. Most of them now groan remembering the difficulty of organizing their households around this strange new schedule—Phelps Dodge's "state-of-emergency" twelve-hour shift change—but they also agree that the all-women pickets were "kind of fun." It had never been their habit to go anywhere but the grocery store without their husbands—socializing spots like the bar were traditionally off limits to women alone or in groups—so the female camaraderie on the line was a heady discovery.

The Women's Auxiliary received notice that it was technically barred from the lines along with the strikers, because of its legal affiliation with the unions. Undaunted, the women organized under a new title, "Citizens for Justice," and refused to stay home. Carrying hand-painted signs housewives, waitresses, mothers, and daughters came out to the roadside to make the most public stand of their lives.

"We had to try and keep the number *down* to ninety-nine," says Shirley Randall. "All women. We knew we couldn't just quit. We asked the men not to go, so they couldn't say we were doing anything wrong. The men were more rowdy—the rock throwers."

This last point is debatable; Cleo Robledo said the opposite. "You better believe the women turned out. And oh, they were brave! The scabs, the DPS, all of them hate facing the women worse than they hate facing the men. Even if there were just five, seven women up there in that little island, they'd call out the DPS. Oh, yes. 'Get them up here, we can't stand these women!' They were afraid of the women because I think we're much more . . . verbal."

Their "verbs" were sharply curtailed, though, by the presence of armed guards. "When we were on the line," Diane said, "you really had to maintain. You couldn't be rowdy—you knew they were watching. I remember one time we were on the line and I looked up and said, 'They have snipers on the hill!' Everyone turned and, sure enough, they were all up there, right above the mine. There's a little shack up there. Always before we had just seen the Guard and the DPS when they were right there near us. When I saw the snipers up there, with their guns ready, I felt like, man, we don't have a chance; don't do anything. I felt they would shoot us, I honestly did—that they wouldn't hesitate.

"They said we were dangerous. But none of us, even when the guys were there, not one of us was *ever* armed. Sometimes bats, or chains. But bats and chains against machine guns? We couldn't even defend ourselves. No way." Still, Diane said, the all-women pickets were as rowdy as they could be, under the circumstances. "We kept getting court injunctions put on us for this or for that, so we couldn't flip anybody off, no bad words or whatever. Finally they had us to where all we could do was just wave."

This was hard to take. "To stand there and smile and wave at the scabs!" Berta said. "When we were so angry!"

They stayed on the line in spite of the accumulation of both legal and physical barriers, which included immense piles of sand that had appeared at the main gate early in the strike, entirely smothering the roadsides where the picket lines had been in the past. "When they put those piles of sand up there," Berta said, "we moved the picket to the Federal Market. This was when the National Guard was still here. The next day they had signs up saying it was private property and that you couldn't park there unless you were going to buy something. So everybody would park and go buy a piece of bubble gum or something before coming back out to the line." Even-

tually they won a court order that allowed them to stand on top of the "berms," or sandpiles, by the main gate. . . .

If calling in the troops was meant to intimidate strikers and their supporters, it ultimately had the opposite effect. Townspeople who were initially neutral grew infuriated by the display of force and placed their hearts and their feet behind the strikers' side of the line. It was soon impossible to find a person in Clifton who had not been drawn into the strike. "At the beginning," Cleo Robledo explained, "we didn't know exactly what was going on, so we just sat back and watched things. Then it really hit us. Then we got involved." . . .

The combination of psychological and strong-arm tactics did not pass unnoticed by the rest of the corporate world. Myron Magnet noted in *Fortune* magazine (August 22, 1983): "Phelps Dodge is set on breaking this strike. Tough tactics like these haven't been seen since the 30's. . . . Companies whose contracts have yet to expire could well be emboldened by Phelps Dodge's example." On July 1, after the company announced its intentions to bring workers through the picket lines, Phelps Dodge stock rose a quarter, to $28^1/_2$; by the end of the month it was up to $29^1/_2$.

Pat Scanlon said that the Monday morning the Morenci mine was shut down was a psychological turning point: "Once that occurred, then that hardened the attitudes of people on the management side. We said, 'By God, we're going to show these thugs that they can't do that to us.' So we proceeded to hire replacements. Not withstanding the outlawry and abuse they took, there were plenty of people willing to come to work. We gave each one of them a certificate, if you will, saying we would not lay him off to make room for a returning striker; he was a permanent replacement as that term is defined by the law. It just happened that during that period the Supreme Court had decided that an employer's agreement to do that is an enforceable contract. If the employer then violates the agreement and does lay him off, then the laid off replacement has a personal right of action against the employer. So what we were doing was burning our bridges."

I asked Mr. Scanlon, to make sure I understood, if he meant that as far as this strike was concerned, Phelps Dodge had burned its bridges after forty-two days. He replied, "That's about right."

The stakes were high on all sides. Angel Rodriguez, president of USWA Local 616 in Clifton, said that P.D. was seeking to terminate every agreement they'd had for the last forty years. "Contract language, working conditions, medical and insurance, things that have taken many strikes to win," he told *Village Voice* reporter Joe Conason. "We couldn't give those things away—they weren't ours to give. Our fathers and grandfathers won those things."

Liz Hernandez-Wheeler, head of the Tucson Union Support Committee, explained: "The labor movement is going to suffer considerably if this strike is lost. It will establish a precedent for many companies in this state, and in the country, to engage in this type of union-busting tactics. We're already seeing it."

As the "union-busting tactics" grew more overt, defense of their civil liberties became as much of an issue to the strikers as their contract. "I definitely think there's more than a strike happening," said Fina Roman. "The blatant violation of civil and human rights that is running rampant here is an indication that more than the strike needs to be defended. More than the strike needs the attention of the people who can bring solutions to this community.

"For just innumerable years Clifton was a safe community; people knew everyone else; everyone looked after everyone else's children. There was just a family atmosphere throughout the community. Now that no longer is true. Unfortunately it isn't always those who have crossed the picket line, but the law enforcement agencies, who are causing the problems. They are forever questioning people who they meet walking down the street. We're used to walking everywhere—it's a small community, and people enjoy walking. Now we're questioned when we are found walking. This is strange to us. I think an investigation has to be undertaken to find the reasons for our rights being violated. There is a right-to-work law in Arizona, but that doesn't mean that we must forfeit all other rights."

What they were being asked to forfeit had no apparent limits. Strikers in Clifton were ques-

tioned not only for walking but for standing, driving, and speaking. They were issued traffic tickets for driving too slowly, and arrested for carrying tire-changing tools in their cars. Their homes were watched at night by armed officers. Ray Isner told the press, "We've had countless individuals arrested in their homes. The show of force is excessive. Women have been arrested in front of their children. As many as a dozen DPS officers have encircled homes."

Most residents of Clifton can't say exactly how long the National Guard occupation lasted, because the effects stayed with them long after the olive-drab convoy pulled out. Diane McCormick's assessment was typical: "They were here forever. I guess it must have been about two weeks."

Also, many people didn't make a clear distinction between the National Guard and the DPS, since all were outsiders and the sense of invasion was the same. The so-called "siege" by the National Guard lasted approximately ten days. "But really," said Jean Lopez many months later, "we've been under siege since then. They pulled the Guards out, but the DPS have been here all along. The storm troopers—you can see them up there on the picket line any day. I knew it was going to be a long strike, but I never expected anything like this. I don't think anybody did."

In Ajo, too, strikers felt their town could never return to normal. They no longer knew what to expect from a future that had always seemed exceedingly predictable. Personal rights they'd spent a lifetime taking for granted had vanished along with their paychecks. But still they were sure the strike would be resolved. Like most red-blooded Americans, they had utter faith in the notion that justice would prevail. "I know the unions are going to win," said Janie Ramon, "and that P.D. is not going to get away with what they're doing to us. I realize it's going to take a while. But to me it's worth it." . . .

We Go with Our Heads Up

A little bit of success is a powerful thing. For the first time in their lives, the women of Clifton began to see themselves as a force to be reckoned with. Before they knew it, they were keeping the whole town running. But it didn't happen overnight. "You have to remember," Jessie Tellez explained, "how people around here feel about women. Oh, we have responsibility, all right. When you're bringing up your children, anything that goes wrong in the house, the husband blames the wife for that. In the beginning I was very submissive, while I was raising my children. My son who lives in California says, 'When I see on TV that lady that comes out with the Kool-Aid, that reminds me so much of you.'

"But I guess I have always been strong-minded, and things bothered me. When people started going to the picket line there were ten Anglo women to one Hispanic. I started asking around, and the Mexican-American women told me their husbands didn't allow them to go. Their husbands thought it was a disgrace for women to be on the picket line."

Jessie said the turning point was when picketers began getting arrested without just cause. "That made people very angry, and they wanted to stand up. When the man was arrested, the wife would show up the next day. And seeing more women show up, other women got encouraged.

"It was the same with the auxiliary. Many of the ladies, their husbands wouldn't allow them to go to the meetings at first. Then they would let them go, but the men would drop them off and pick them up. I used to ask them, 'Don't you know how to drive?' and they'd say, 'Well, yes.' And I'd say, 'Do you have to go and drop your husband off if he has a meeting?' 'Well, no,' they'd say. I didn't want to cause problems at home, but then I could see that they were so frustrated."

At first, a number of men who dropped off their wives at auxiliary meetings actually sat outside the hall and waited during the meetings—to protect the women, they said, in case of a scab attack. The women tolerated this heavy-handed chaperoning but increasingly resented it. When the "guards" eventually dwindled to just one man who persisted in coming to meetings with his wife, they asked him to knock it off. "He just couldn't let her out of his sight, is what it was," one of the members said. After that, he stayed home. So did his wife.

Most others cut the apron strings. "Now the women have gotten the car," Jessie said. "They come by themselves, and they stay as long as they want, and after the meeting they gather and have coffee or something, and they go home when they feel like it. That doesn't mean our husbands like it, but this is a right we take for ourselves. I told them, 'Don't you feel great?' "

They did. Around this time, some of the auxiliary women created an uproar by going to the bar "alone"—meaning in a group, without husbands. The gesture itself was substantially more intoxicating than the beer. . . .

Undaunted by threats, the Morenci Miners Women's Auxiliary organized a support system to meet the basic needs of the striking families, who comprised virtually the whole town of Clifton and much of Morenci. The most urgent project was a food bank. Berta Chavez, whose five children made her plainly aware of the need, was one of the food bank's founding mothers.

"In the beginning of the strike," she said, "I just didn't have anything to feed the kids. Talk about learning not to take things for granted! So I went to some of the other ladies in the auxiliary, and they were really nice. They gave me a bag of macaroni and cheese, beans, and rice. I was so happy.

"We realized this was something a lot of people needed, so I started getting food from everywhere I could, and donations, and we threw it all in together down at the back of the Steelworkers' Hall. We were asking all the merchants. Some were generous, some didn't want to get involved, and I got some donations that were anonymous. I tried to get food from the federal government too, but then you have to give it to everybody, and I was just working for the strikers. Finally, we raised enough money and got a little bit of food and started helping people out. It was real nice."

The unions, which had more resources than the auxiliary and at this point a far greater infrastructure, helped to acquire donations to the food bank. Through their connections with a federally funded agency, they enabled the auxiliary to distribute free turkeys for Thanksgiving. Shirley Randall said she felt humiliated when she had to line up for free food at Thanksgiving. "I don't even like to go to yard sales—I'm afraid of what Mrs. Jones is going to think. I stood in that line, though. Otherwise we wouldn't have had a turkey."

Reservations faded fast when it dawned on Shirley and everyone else that Mrs. Jones had hungry kids of her own to think about. These were extraordinary times, and they would have to rely on one another as they never had before. Shirley headed up a day-care cooperative in which women took turns watching the kids while others held picket duty or did organizing. When Jessie Tellez's roof began to leak, she decided she would just have to think of a skill she and her husband could exchange with another striker who could fix it. Barter became central to their lives, and in some way—however direct or convoluted—every essential need was met. . . .

[But] not every need was met smoothly. They had shortages in some areas and a surplus in others—mainly clothing, which was donated literally by the ton from outside communities. "We've had to stack them in the church, everywhere," Anna said. "We even ended up taking clothes down to Mexico. You don't want to discourage a charitable act, you know, but . . . If only we could eat them!"

Members of the auxiliary wrote letters to national teachers' unions and associations to solicit money for their children's schoolbooks. They also sent mailings to international unions and to every women's auxiliary they could think of. In answer to their letters and their prayers, support groups for the copper strikers sprang up all over the country.

Resourcefulness was the one precious commodity the women had in abundance. When tension grew in the high school—where strikers' kids had to wear someone else's last-year's clothes, and everybody knew it—Berta hit on the idea of forming a break-dancing group called the Small Town Breakers. It was a stroke of genius that defused the bomb of adolescent anger and channeled it into an all-absorbing project. They had car washes to raise money for uniforms, and Berta found places for the group to perform. She was characteristically optimistic. "Now that people have seen what they can do, I think they'll get more involved with the kids. After the mayor saw them dance he called and asked if I could use a couple thousand dollars for the kids to have breaker of the month or some-

thing like that. This is getting us places. I tell the kids, next time, maybe Hollywood."

Far from being overwhelmed, Berta and Jessie and their friends enjoyed organizing their town. They looked forward to their "Wednesday night out" for the auxiliary meeting. "I can't wait to get a babysitter and go," Trudy Morgan said. "I haven't missed a meeting since I don't know when."

The enthusiasm grew on them. At one time the auxiliary meetings were as efficient as possible, but now they spilled over into prolonged, friendly potlucks. The women looked for reasons to meet more often than once a week. When the union organized a stress workshop and brought in a therapist from out of town, only women attended. "Wouldn't you know it," commented Jessie Tellez. "But when she found out about our meetings, the therapist said, 'You're giving each other therapy and you don't even know it. You ought to meet twice a week.'" It was the only way they were going to last, and they knew it. . . .

Women at first saw their auxiliary work as an extension of their years as housewives, but by the time they were telling their husbands to iron their own shirts, it had become something else—among other things, a blessed escape from domestic labor. For the duration of the strike and after, contradictions persisted around the question of whether the auxiliary work ran with, or against, the grain of traditional female roles. Plainly, it involved a new level of economic consciousness for many women.

For Berta Chavez, for instance. "You know," she said, "two years ago we would *never* have thought we could be doing these things. Running things this way. I'd probably still be charging at that stupid store. I used to go into the P.D. store every day, look around, and charge. It's so easy. All this time, all the money we were making we were giving straight back to them. Now I see how they get you coming and going. I never go in there at all. It's hard to believe we were so dumb. Now we're doing everything for ourselves—how did we wise up so fast?"

It's a good question. Berta felt that the hardships of the strike forced her and her friends to look beyond the superficial concerns that can preoccupy life in a small town (any town, for that matter) and see what mattered when push came to shove—things like friendship, family, and community. Berta had never read Karl Marx or the doctrine of "from each according to his capabilities," but she had a clear notion of what it means to give what you can, accept what you need, and be part of a community that cares for all its members. It was an expansive notion for a group who, as one of them put it, had always thought of themselves as "just a bunch of little old measly housewives." . . .

Epilogue

It's impossible to point to a single day on the calendar and declare, "This is when the copper strike ended." By 1987, the National Labor Relations Board had ruled in favor of Phelps Dodge, to no one's great surprise, and the unions had been decertified. The strikers had no more ammunition with which to fight by then, but neither did Phelps Dodge have much reason to celebrate. The company's mining and smelting interest in Arizona—once the youthful, healthy giant among the state's industries—was an ailing skeleton. In order to concentrate its resources on new solvent extraction technology and the purchase of a large mine in western New Mexico, Phelps Dodge had sold a part interest of the Morenci operation to the Sumitomo Company of Japan and had more or less turned its back on the rest of its Arizona mines. The Ajo plant was closed, and the town of Ajo may as well have rolled up its sidewalks. The countdown had begun for closing down operations in Douglas within the year. Although there was plenty of other commerce in that small town, and life would go on, there was a pall over the downtown. The grand old Gadsden Hotel with its marble columns and tiffany glass—built in 1927, when the copper boom still promised the world to Arizona—had never felt emptier: a ghost of good fortune that time forgot. Dust accumulates quickly in the desert.

Morenci and Ajo also had the feel of ghost towns in the making. Chase Creek, once the heart and soul of Clifton, now had a catatonic, staring look from all the boarded-over windows and empty storefronts. The whole town looked weary. Most of the retirees had stayed on in Clifton, and

some of the younger families kept up the difficult life of divided households, with one spouse driving to a job in some faraway city. . . .

The union holdout had progressed like the most dreaded kind of disease: slow, painful, and terminal.

Even so, for some of the families in Ajo, Clifton, and Morenci, the strike had an odd sort of happy ending. In 1987 and 1988, the unions and their advocates won several important legal victories.

First of all, nobody went to prison. Of all the strikers and supporters who were arrested and charged with felonies, only one—Viviano Gonzalez—was ever convicted. He had been charged with resisting arrest when a police officer stopped him from taking cigarettes to his father, who was jailed in Ajo. (The officer, who outweighed Viviano by some hundred pounds, said the defendant was beating him up.) On appeal, Viviano was acquitted. Thus, in spite of all the allegations against the "lawless mob" in Ajo, Clifton, and Morenci, no striker or strike supporter was found to have broken any law. In fact, most were never even prosecuted.

Antonio Bustamante, a Tucson attorney who defended many of those arrested in Clifton at the first Women's Auxiliary rally, believes the state never intended to prosecute them. "This was just a classic case of the use of excessive force to break a strike," he said. "Phelps Dodge didn't even have to pay for it; the taxpayers of Arizona did. The county attorney in Clifton was perfectly willing to use the law in this underhanded way. In the end, the charges against the strikers amounted to nothing, and he knew it."

The U.S. Constitution guarantees a fair and speedy trial to those accused of a crime; one by one, time limits for processing the cases were simply allowed to lapse. For example, many of Bustamante's clients were arrested on May 5, 1984; in November 1985, a judge dismissed the charges because the state had taken no further action beyond the initial arrests. The case against Beverly Cole—who threw a paper cup on the ground at a picket line and ended up with charges of littering, felony fraud, and forgery—was technically still pending more than three years later, only because she had not yet gotten around to filing for a dismissal. No action was ever taken to bring her to trial.

In retrospect, Bustamante felt it was unfortunate that many people had accepted plea bargains. Dozens were arrested and charged with felonies at the June 30 rally, for example, but the state offered to reduce the charges against any who would plead guilty to misdemeanors instead. Because they were working with such limited finances by that time, the weary unions thought it wise to avoid going to court. But some of those who were arrested, like Berta Chavez, with her charge of "assault with deadly fingernails," refused the plea bargains and demanded their day in court. They never got it.

"When anybody persisted, the county attorney dropped them like flies," Bustamante said. "The state never took one case to trial. They didn't *dare* take those cases before a jury.

"Obviously, the state knew that these charges were ridiculous. The point is that they didn't care about prosecuting these people; they only wanted to intimidate them. This is a way of controlling a population—it's so easy, so convenient. Just slap them with some charge or other, set a huge bail, and make them sit in jail. Or harass them to the extent that with any move they make they'll accumulate more charges against themselves. Eventually they have to leave town in order to breathe. It's very effective. It doesn't even matter that later the charges will never hold up in court—the damage is already done."

The strategy had been fairly effective. The frequent arrests and excessive bonds drained union and personal resources down to the bitter copper of their last pennies. Some people who were perceived to be leaders of the strike were forced into silence, or forced out of town.

Perhaps the most important effect of all was that the legal offensive helped to turn away public sympathy. Newspapers were crowded for days at a time with accounts of arrests, police actions, and felony charges against the strikers. It is a cultural peculiarity of the United States that we believe our citizens don't run into trouble with the law unless they have done something wrong. [Former] Attorney General Edwin Meese said it himself, in 1987: innocent people don't get arrested. At a time when the strikers sorely depended on popu-lar support, the public perception of the strike was skillfully manipulated in the direction of a guilty verdict.

"This was just a textbook example," Bustamante said, "of how the legal and law enforcement systems in this country can be used to break a strike."

Eventually the strikers struck back. Not only had they done nothing wrong, they said, but they themselves had been wronged, and they intended to prove it. The unions launched three separate civil rights suits, each on behalf of many plaintiffs, against the government and Phelps Dodge.

The first suit was filed against Phelps Dodge, Pima County, and Sheriff Clarence Dupnik, on behalf of six labor unions and eleven strikers arrested in Ajo on charges of rioting and other felonies and misdemeanors during August 1983. Among the plaintiffs was Soila Bom, the first person jailed during the strike, who had been arrested for calling someone "scab" over the telephone. Another was Natalie Muñoz, who was arrested in her home, in front of her daughter, and dragged away in her nightgown. (The charge was "rock throwing," and she was acquitted.) A third plaintiff was the striker who was arrested and jailed for not carrying his driver's license.

The suit claimed that Phelps Dodge and Pima County consciously and in concert set out to get the strikers off the streets by overcharging them and setting inordinately high bail bonds—fifteen thousand dollars per person, in most cases, for individuals who were well known by everyone in the community. (One, for example, was a member of the volunteer fire department.) The case also charged that Pima County selectively prosecuted strikers while allowing nonstrikers to commit such acts as cutting a striker's throat (he survived, with a nasty scar) and breaking another striker's jaw with the butt of a rifle. In the former case, there were no charges; in the latter, the attacker was released on his own recognizance and paid no damages to the striker.

"In all, thirty-four incidents were used at the trial showing this discriminatory pattern of law enforcement," said union attorney Michael McCrory. "What we wanted to show was that strikers were arrested no matter how slight the infraction, and scabs were not, no matter how great."

Another interesting piece of history emerged during the trial: the plaintiffs alleged, and documented from several sources, that Pima County had made a list of some thirty strike supporters they wished to charge—*two weeks before their alleged crimes were committed.* McCrory says the arrest warrants and amounts of the bail were prepared and signed by the justice of the peace of Ajo, Helen Gilmartin, and put into a vault. He is convinced this was done at the urging of Phelps Dodge, on the assumption that a good old-fashioned police roundup would do wonders to get things settled down in this little town. If the allegation was true, it wouldn't have been the first time; Phelps Dodge had used precisely the same tactic during the great Bisbee strike of 1917.

After a five-week trial, a jury announced on April 21, 1987, that it was ruling in favor of every one of the plaintiffs. They had been held on excessive bonds, arrested without cause, or discriminated against when authorities ignored similar offenses committed by workers who crossed the picket lines.

The charges against Phelps Dodge were dropped, because the jury felt the evidence of company conspiracy with law enforcement was insufficient (this decision was being appealed). But Pima County and Sheriff Clarence Dupnik were held responsible for the injuries to the strikers and their rights. Soila Bom had been arrested without probable cause, the jury said, and it awarded her $30,500 compensatory and punitive damages. In all, the jury awarded over $200,000 to the plaintiffs and striking unions whose constitutional rights had been violated.

The other two civil rights suits on behalf of the strikers were similarly resolved. In the second, twenty plaintiffs from Clifton and Morenci charged the Clifton police force, Greenlee County Sheriff Bob Gomez, and the Department of Public Safety with discriminatory law enforcement. The case was settled out of court in 1988, with the DPS agreeing to pay approximately $70,000 damages. The plaintiffs also charged that Phelps Dodge had conspired with law enforce-

ment, but once again it was decided, this time by a judge, that there was insufficient evidence.

The third civil rights case resulted from the rally of June 30, 1984, and was filed specifically against the DPS for its actions on that day. Fourteen of the twenty plaintiffs settled out of court, literally on the eve of the trial, for a total of $180,000. Among these plaintiffs were Ricardo and Angelita Delgado, the elderly couple who had fled into Alice Miller's liquor store and been tear-gassed.

Six plaintiffs did not settle and went to trial before U.S. district judge Charles Hardy. Four of these plaintiffs received judgments that the DPS had falsely arrested them, and each was awarded damages ranging from ten to seventeen thousand dollars. The plaintiffs' attorneys also showed during this trial that police reports had been falsified throughout the strike.

None of the strikers received damages for being wrongfully tear-gassed. The judge said the tear-gassing was an affront to human dignity but that the police were justified in doing it, nevertheless. Thus, Ray Aguilar, whose only charge was that he had been wrongfully tear-gassed, and Alice Miller, the liquor store owner who was gassed and arrested two days before her son's birth, received nothing. A DPS officer testified that he spoke to Alice after she ran out of her gas-filled store (albeit in a confused state) and that he arrested her for refusing to leave the scene of a riot. The judge ruled she had not been falsely arrested but later said he wished to reconsider. Six months later he reversed his position on the "justifiable gassing," saying that DPS Lieutenant Terrence DeBoer should have given those in the liquor store a chance to leave before ordering the use of tear gas. He awarded fifteen thousand dollars damages to Miller and a thousand dollars to Ray Aguilar and two others.

McCrory said he believed that all his Clifton clients might have been awarded much more—possibly an amount in the millions—if they had gone before juries, as the Ajo plaintiffs did. But they were not disappointed by the monetary awards, he said, because their motivations for pursuing the civil rights suits were less financial than ethical. Soila Bom confirmed this sentiment, saying that her main concern was proving to others what the strikers had known all along—that they did nothing wrong and were treated unfairly. The money was just icing on the cake. . . .

In January 1989, the Ninth U.S. Circuit Court of Appeals reinstated the union's suit claiming conspiracy between Phelps Dodge and local law enforcement, citing a meeting at which a P.D. representative allegedly told the Pima County sheriff that he hoped bail would be set high and declared that he "wanted those people off the streets." As of this writing, the suit still awaits trial.

McCrory said his clients felt relieved and vindicated by their victories in court but that the long legal battle had done little to revive their beleaguered faith in "the system," especially because most were never allowed a hearing before a jury. He feels the legal system abandoned the strikers from the beginning—from the moment they were first deemed "undesirables"—and that it's not surprising that they've been left feeling bitter.

"They wanted a chance to go before a jury, and let that jury fairly decide. They would have been better off if they could have abandoned all the legal processes and lawyers' games and been allowed just to stand up and tell their story."

World Views of Pro-Life and Pro-Choice Activists

Kristin Luker

. . . When pro-life and pro-choice activists think about abortion, abortion itself is merely "the tip of the iceberg." Different beliefs about the roles of the sexes, about the meaning of parenthood, and about human nature are all called into play when the issue is abortion. Abortion, therefore, gives us a rare opportunity to examine closely a set of values that are almost never directly discussed. Because these values apply to spheres of life that are very private (sex) or very diffuse (morality), most people never look at the patterns they form. For this reason the abortion debate has become something that illuminates our deepest, and sometimes our dearest, beliefs.

At the same time, precisely because these values are so rarely discussed overtly, when they are called into question, as they are by the abortion debate, individuals feel that an entire world view is under assault. An interesting characteristic of a world view, however, is that the values located within it are so deep and so dear to us that we find it hard to imagine that we even have a "world view"—to us it is just reality—or that anyone else could not share it. By definition, those areas covered by a "world view" are those parts of life we take for granted, never imagine questioning, and cannot envision decent, moral people not sharing. . . .

In the course of our interviews, it became apparent that each side of the abortion debate has an internally coherent and mutually shared view of the world that is tacit, never fully articulated, and, most importantly, completely at odds with the world view held by their opponents. . . . To be sure, not every single one of those interrelated values that I have called a "world view" character- ized each and every pro-life or pro-choice person

interviewed. It is well within the realm of possi- bility that an activist might find some individual areas where he or she would feel more akin to the values expressed by their opponents than by those on their own side. But taken as a whole, there was enough consistency in the way people on each side talked about the world to warrant the conclusion that each side has its own particular "world view," that these world views tend to be isolated from competing world views, and that forced to choose, most activists would find far more in common with the world view of their side than that of their opponents.

Pro-Life Views of the World

To begin with, pro-life activists believe that men and women are intrinsically different, and this is both a cause and a product of the fact that they have different roles in life: . . .

> [Men and women] were created differently and we're meant to complement each other, and when you get away from our [proper] roles as such, you start obscuring them. That's another part of the confusion that's going on now, people don't know where they stand, they don't know how to act, they don't know where they're coming from, so your psychiatrists' couches are filled with lost souls, with lost people that for a long time now have been gradually led into confusion and don't even know it.
>
> I believe that there's a natural mother's instinct. And I'm kind of chauvinist this way, but I don't believe men and women are equal. I believe men and women are very dif-

ferent, and beautifully different, and that they're complementary in their nature to one another.

Pro-life activists agree that men and women, as a result of these intrinsic differences, have different roles to play: men are best suited to the public world of work, and women are best suited to rear children, manage homes, and love and care for husbands. Most pro-life activists believe that motherhood—the raising of children and families—is the most fulfilling role that women can have. To be sure, they live in a country where over half of all women work, and they do acknowledge that some women are employed. But when they say (as almost all of them do) that women who work should get equal pay for equal work, they do not mean that women should work. On the contrary, they subscribe quite strongly to the traditional belief that women should be wives and mothers first. Mothering, in their view, is so demanding that it is a full-time job, and any woman who cannot commit herself fully to it should avoid it entirely. . . .

For a woman to shift gears from her emotional role in the home to a competitive role in the office is not only difficult, they argue, but damaging to both men and women, and to their children.

These views on the different nature of men and women and the roles appropriate to each combine to make abortion look wrong three times over. First, it is intrinsically wrong because it takes a human life and what makes women special is their ability to nourish life. Second, it is wrong because *by giving women control over their fertility*, it breaks up an intricate set of social relationships between men and women that has traditionally surrounded (and in the ideal case protected) women and children. Third and finally, abortion is wrong because it fosters and supports a world view that deemphasizes (and therefore *downgrades*) the traditional roles of men and women. Because these roles have been satisfying ones for pro-life people and because they believe this emotional and social division of labor is both "appropriate and natural," the act of abortion is wrong because it plays havoc with this arrangement of the world. For example, because abortion formally diminishes male decision-making power, it also diminishes male responsibility. Thus, far from liberating women, pro-life people argue, abortion oppresses them.

One of the problems [of abortion], I think, is the further degradation of women in society. I know that feminists would disagree with me on this and I consider myself a feminist, so it's difficult for me to relate to other feminists on this issue. I think having abortion as an alternative—as a way out, I guess—makes it easier for men to exploit women than ever before. I think they are less inclined probably to take responsibility for their actions or to anticipate the consequences of their actions as long as abortion is available. And I think it makes it harder for women who do not choose to engage in premarital sex to say no, or to be accepted in society, because there's always this consideration that there's something wrong with them.

. . . Because pro-life people see the world as inherently divided both emotionally and socially into a male sphere and a female sphere, they see the loss of the female sphere as a very deep one indeed. They see tenderness, morality, caring, emotionality, and self-sacrifice as the exclusive province of women; and if women cease to be traditional women, who will do the caring, who will offer the tenderness? . . .

In this view, everyone loses when traditional roles are lost. Men lose the nurturing that women offer, the nurturing that gently encourages them to give up their potentially destructive and aggressive urges. Women lose the protection and cherishing that men offer. And children lose full-time loving by at least one parent, as well as clear models for their own futures.

These different views about the intrinsic nature of men and women also shape pro-life views about sex. The nineteenth century introduced new terms to describe the two faces of sexual activity, distinguishing between "procreative love," whose goal is reproduction, and "amative love," whose goal is sensual pleasure and mutual enjoyment. . . .

For the pro-life people we talked with, the relative worth of procreative sex and amative sex was clear. In part this is because many of them, being Catholic, accept a natural law doctrine of sex, which holds that a body part is destined to be used for its physiological function. As one man put it: "You're not just given arms and legs for no purpose. . . . There must be some cause [for sex] and you begin to think, well, it must be for procreation ultimately, and certainly procreation in addition to fostering a loving relationship with your spouse."

In terms of this view, the meaning of sexual experiences is distorted whenever procreation is not intended. Contraception, premarital sex, and infidelity are wrong not only because of their social consequences but also because they strip sexual experience of its meaning. . . .

Because many pro-life people see sex as literally sacred, they are disturbed by values that seem to secularize and profane it. The whole constellation of values that supports amative (or "recreational") sex is seen by them as doing just that. Values that define sexuality as a wholesome physical activity, as healthy as volleyball but somewhat more fun, call into question everything that pro-life people believe in. Sex is sacred because in their world view it has the capacity to be something transcendent— to bring into existence another human life. To routinely eradicate that capacity through premarital sex (in which very few people seek to bring a new life into existence) or through contraception or abortion is to turn the world upside down. . . .

Pro-life values on the issue of abortion . . . also draw more directly on notions of motherhood (and fatherhood) that are not shared by pro-choice people. This might seem obvious from the fact that pro-life people often account for their own activism by referring to the notion that babies are being murdered in their mothers' wombs. But pro-life feelings about the nature of parenthood draw on other more subtle beliefs as well.

Pro-life people believe that one becomes a parent by *being* a parent; parenthood is for them a "natural" rather than a social role. One is a parent by virtue of having a child, and the values implied by the in-vogue term *parenting* (as in *parenting classes*) are alien to them. The financial and educational preparations for parenthood that pro-choice people see as necessary are seen by pro-life people as a serious distortion of values. Pro-life people fear that when one focuses on job achievement, home owning, and getting money in the bank *before* one has children, children will be seen as barriers to these things. As one pro-life woman put it:

> There has been a very strong attitude that the child represents an obstacle to achievement. Not just that the child is something desirable that you add further down the line . . . but that the child is an obstacle to a lifestyle that will include the yacht and weekend skiing. . . . A great many couples are opting not to have any children at all because of the portrayal of the child as an obstacle, especially to a woman's career and a two-salary family.

. . . Pro-life people tacitly assume that the way to upgrade [parenthood] is to make it an *inclusive* category, that all married people should be (or be willing to be) parents. In particular, women who choose to be in the public world of work should eschew the role of wife and mother, or, if they marry, should be prepared to put the public world of work second to their role as wife and mother. If a man or woman is to be sexually active, they feel, he or she should be married. And if married, one should be prepared to welcome a child whenever it arrives, however inopportune it may seem at the time. In their view, to try to balance a number of competing commitments—especially when parenthood gets shuffled into second or fourth place—is both morally wrong and personally threatening.

Pro-life people also feel very strongly that there is an anti-child sentiment abroad in our society and that this is expressed in the strong cultural norm that families should have only two children. . . .

Since one out of every five pro-life activists in this study had six or more children, it is easy to see how these values can seem threatening. In the course of our interviews, a surprising number of activists said they did not feel discriminated against because of their pro-life activities, including their opposition to abortion, but that they did feel socially stigmatized because they had large families. As one woman with several children said: "[My husband,] being a scientist, gets a lot [of questions]. You know, having a large family, it's just for the poor uneducated person, but if you have a doctor's degree and you have a large family, what's wrong with you?" The pro-choice argument that parents must plan their families in order to give their children the best emotional and financial resources therefore sounds like an attack on people with large families. "[People think] children can't possibly make it and be successful if they come from a large family . . . because you can't give them all the time and energy that they need. Well, first of all, I'm here [at home], I'm not out working, which adds to the amount of time that I can give."

. . . Because pro-life people believe that the purpose of sexuality is to have children, they also believe that one should not plan the exact number and timing of children too carefully, for it is both wrong and foolish to make detailed life plans that depend upon exact control of fertility. Because children will influence life plans more than life plans will influence the number of children, it is also wrong to value one's planned accomplishments—primarily the acquisition of the things money can buy—over the intangible benefits that children can bring. Thus, reasoning backwards, pro-life people object to every step of the pro-choice logic. If one values material things too highly, one will be tempted to try to make detailed plans for acquiring them. If one tries to plan too thoroughly, one will be tempted to use highly effective contraception, which removes the potential of childbearing from a marriage. Once the potential for children is eliminated, the sexual act is distorted (and for religious people, morally wrong), and husbands and wives lose an important bond between them. Finally, when marriage partners who have accepted the logic of these previous steps find that contraception has failed, they are ready and willing to resort to abortion in order to achieve their goals.

This is not to say that pro-life people do not approve of planning. They do. But because of their world view (and their religious faith) they see human planning as having very concrete limits. To them it is a matter of priorities: if individuals want fame, money, and worldly success, then they have every right to pursue them. But if they are sexually active (and married, as they should be if they are sexually active), they have an obligation to

subordinate other parts of life to the responsibilities they have taken on by virtue of that activity. . . .

Thus, abortion offends the deepest moral convictions of pro-life people in several ways. To begin with, it breaks a divine law. The Commandment says "Thou shalt not kill." The embryo is human (it is not a member of another species) and alive (it is not dead). Thus, according to the reasoning by syllogism they learned in childhood religion classes, the embryo is a "human life," and taking it clearly breaks one of the Commandments.

Moreover, the logic used by pro-choice advocates (and the Supreme Court) to justify abortion affronts the moral reasoning of pro-life people. For them, either the embryo is a human life or it is not; the concept of an intermediate category—a *potential* human life—seems simply inadmissible. Further, the argument that individuals should arrive at a *personal* decision about the moral status of this intermediate category is as strange to most of them as arguing that individual soldiers in wartime should act according to their own judgment of the wisdom of the army's battle plan. . . .

. . . Pro-life people, like the pro-choice people we will examine shortly, have a consistent, coherent view of the world, notwithstanding the fact that like anyone else, they cannot always bring their behavior in line with their highest ideals. The very coherence of their world view, however, makes clear that abortion, and all it represents, is profoundly unsettling to them. By the same token, the values that pro-life people bring to bear on the abortion issue are deeply threatening to those people active in the pro-choice movement.

Pro-Choice Views of the World

On almost all the dimensions just considered, the values and beliefs of pro-choice diametrically oppose those of pro-life people, as does the logic whereby they arrive at their values. For example, whereas pro-life people believe that men and women are inherently different and therefore have different "natural" roles in life, pro-choice people believe that men and women are substantially equal, by which they mean substantially similar. As a result, they see women's reproductive and family roles not as a "natural" niche but as potential barriers to full equality. The organization of society, they argue, means that motherhood, so long as it is involuntary, is potentially always a low-status, unrewarding role to which women can be banished at any time. Thus, from their point of view, control over reproduction is essential for women to be able to live up to their full human potential. Here is how one woman put it:

> I just feel that one of the main reasons women have been in a secondary position culturally is because of the natural way things happen. Women would bear children because they had no way to prevent it, except by having no sexual involvement. And that was not practical down through the years, so without knowing what to do to prevent it, women would continually have children. And then if they were the ones bearing the child, nursing the child, it just made sense [for them to be] the ones to rear the child. I think that was the natural order. When we advanced and found that we could control our reproduction, we could choose the size of our families or whether we wanted families. But that changed the whole role of women in our society. Or it opened it up to change the role. It allowed us to be more than just the bearers of children, the homemakers. That's not to say that we shouldn't continue in that role. It's a good role, but it's not the *only* role for women.

Pro-choice people agree that women (and men) find children and families a satisfying part of life, but they also think it is foolhardy for women to believe that this is the only life role they will ever have. They argue, in essence, that pro-life women who do not work outside the home are only "one man away from disaster." A death, a divorce, a desertion, or a disability can push a woman with no career skills or experience perilously close to the edge of penury—as shown by the ever-increasing numbers of "displaced homemakers"—widows and divorcees left with virtually no financial or employment resources.

At the same time, pro-choice people value what I have called "amative" sex, that is, sex whose primary purpose is not reproduction. The idea that sexual activity is valuable and indeed sacred because of its inherent reproductive capacity strikes many pro-choice people as absurd. From their point of view, if the purpose of sex were limited to reproduction, no rational Creator would have arranged things so that an individual can have hundreds or even thousands of acts of intercourse in a lifetime, with millions of sex cells—egg and sperm always at the ready. More to the point, they argue that belief in the basically procreative nature of sex leads to an oppressive degree of *social regulation of sexual behavior, particularly the behavior of women,* who must be protected (in their viewpoint, repressed) because free expression of sexual wishes will get them "in trouble" and lead the species into overpopulation. . . .

Significantly, many of the pro-choice activists described themselves as having grown up in families with traditional, "sex-negative" values that focused on the dangers of uncontrolled sexual feelings. They now see themselves as seeking a set of "sex-positive" values, for themselves and for the society as a whole, that emphasize the pleasure, beauty, and joy of sex rather than the dangers. When pro-choice people speak of being raised under "sex-negative" values, they mean that sex was not openly talked about, that it was certainly not portrayed as something to be enjoyed for its own sake, and that budding childish sexuality—masturbation and adolescent flirting—was often treated harshly. Premarital sexuality leading to pregnancy was a "fate worse than death." . . .

Pro-choice people believe that sexual activity is good as an end in itself. For much of a lifetime at least, its main purpose is not to produce children (or to remind them of that possibility) but to afford pleasure, human contact, and, perhaps most important, intimacy. Whereas for pro-life people sex is *inherently* transcendent—because a new life may be created at any time—for pro-choice people, it is *potentially* transcendent, and its spiritual meaning is a goal to be pursued rather than a fact to be faced. Despite the claims of some pro-life people, pro-choice people *do* believe that sex can be sacred, but it is a different kind of sacredness that they have in mind. For them, sex is sacred when it is mystical, when it dissolves the boundaries between self and other, when it brings one closer to one's partner, and when it gives one a sense of the infinite. Transcendent sex, for them, grows out of feelings experienced in the present rather than beliefs about what may happen in the future. It can be achieved only when people feel secure, when they feel trusting, and when they feel love for themselves and for the other. . . .

These general attitudes about the nature and meaning of sex influence pro-choice views on contraception. To be sure, the significance of contraception in itself is not a very salient issue for most pro-choice people. They see using contraceptives as something like taking good care of one's teeth—a matter of sensible routine, a good health habit. (Indeed, they find pro-life objections to contraception mysterious and dismiss them as "medieval" or "religious.") They do have some pragmatic concerns about contraceptive methods—how unpleasant or how safe they are—but contraception in the abstract has no moral connotations for them. Since the primary moral value they see in sexuality is its potential for creating intimacy with the self and another, a good contraceptive (and a moral one, to stretch the term) is one that is safe, undistracting, and not unpleasant to use. And since they *do* use contraception to postpone childbearing for long periods of time, their ideal contraceptive is easy to use, *highly effective,* and not a risk to their health. . . .

Pro-choice people do have one clearly moral concern about sexuality, however: most of them oppose the use of abortion, instead of traditional methods of contraception, as a routine method of birth control. In part, their opposition is pragmatic; repeated abortions have their own set of health risks. But physical risks are not the whole story. Here is what a pro-choice minister said:

Last time at my class in human sexuality, a young woman brought this up [the morality of abortion as birth control], and I was grateful to her because I seldom bring it up myself because it's a spiritual issue. There's a spiritual force within a woman when she's pregnant, and people of great spiritual sensitivity have to deal with the reality of that potential life. A lot of people don't think there's this kind of subtlety, and when they do I'm very support-

ive of them. Yes, there's a spiritual issue involved. I take the idea of ending the life of the fetus very, very gravely. . . . [That] doesn't in any way diminish my conviction that a woman has the right to do it, but I become distressed when people regard pregnancy lightly and ignore the spiritual significance of a pregnancy.

As this comment suggests, opposition to abortion as a routine form of birth control is based on a complex and subtle moral reasoning. For most pro-choice people, the personhood of the embryo does not exist at conception, but it does develop at some later time. The pro-choice view of personhood is thus a *gradualist* one. An embryo may not be a full person until it is viable (capable of sustaining its own life if born prematurely), but it has the rights of a potential person at all times, and those rights increase in moral weight as the pregnancy continues. . . .

. . . A great many pro-choice activists in this study, particularly those active in helping women have abortions, also find multiple abortions morally troubling. Some of them even volunteered the fact that they felt like personal failures when a woman came back to them for a second, third, or higher-order abortion. At first glance, this would appear to be illogical: if it is morally acceptable for a woman to end one pregnancy with an abortion, why is it wrong for her to end subsequent pregnancies by abortion? For pro-choice people, the answer is simple. . . . The first abortion presumably represents the lesser of several evils, where the abortion of an embryo is seen as less morally wrong than bringing a child one cannot effectively parent into the world. But since most women are given contraceptive services after an abortion, every abortion after the first represents a case where a woman had the option of avoiding pregnancy and did not. Except in extraordinary cases, pro-choice people see this bringing of an embryo into existence when it could have been avoided as morally wrong.

It is in the context of the relative rights of babies and embryos that pro-choice values about parenting—about the kind of life the baby-to-be might be reasonably expected to have—play such an important role. Pro-choice people have very clear standards about what parenting entails: it means giving a child the best set of emotional, psychological, social, and financial resources that one can arrange as a preparation for future life. Pro-choice people believe that it is the duty of a parent to prepare the child for the future, and good parents are seen as arranging life (and childbearing) so that this can be done most effectively.

These values about what constitutes a good parent therefore support and shape pro-choice attitudes toward children and the timing of their arrival. Since children demand financial sacrifices, for example, couples should not have them until they have acquired the financial position to give their children the best. Otherwise, under pressure, parents will come to resent a child, and this will limit their ability to be caring, attentive, and nurturing to their children. As a corollary, pro-choice people want children who feel loved, who have self-esteem, and who "feel good about themselves"; they believe that parents should postpone childbearing until they have the proper emotional resources needed to do the intense one-to-one psychological caring that good parenting requires. (It is these two factors that they have in mind when they make the statement, which pro-life people find unfathomable, that they are not "ready" for childbearing.) . . .

Since pro-choice activists think that in the long run abortion will enhance the quality of parenting by making it optional, they see themselves as being on the side of children when they advocate abortion. In contrast to pro-life people, who believe that parenthood will be enhanced by making it *inclusive,* that is, making it a mandatory part of the package of being a sexually active person, pro-choice people feel that the way to improve the quality of parenthood is to make it more *exclusive.* Here is what a minister had to say:

[My attitude on abortion] stems out of, I think, the same basic concern about the right [of children] to share the good life and all these things; children, once born, have rights that we consistently deny them. I remember giving a talk [in which I said] that I thought one of my roles was to be an advocate for the fetus, and for the fetus's right not to be born.

I think the right-to-lifers thought I was great until that point. . . . I think if I had my druthers I'd probably advocate the need for licensing pregnancies.

In part, this attitude stems from the value placed on planning. A planned child is a wanted child, and a child who is wanted starts out on a much better basis than one who is not. . . .

Connected to this value is an acceptance of teen-aged sex. Pro-choice people are concerned about teen-aged *parenthood* because young people and the unwed are in no position to become good parents, but they have no basic objection to sexual activity among young people *if they are "responsible,"* that is, if they do not take the risk of becoming parents. Because pro-choice people view the goal of sex as being the creation of intimacy, caring, and trust, they also believe that people need to practice those skills before making a long-term commitment to someone. They may practice them with a number of people or with the person they intend to marry. In either case, premarital sex is not only likely to occur but desirable. Because pro-choice people see premarital sex as reasonable and because their values give them no intrinsic reason to be against it, any concerns they may have about premarital and teen-aged sex are almost exclusively pragmatic. In some respects, pro-choice people agree with the pro-life conclusion: teenagers are not ready to be parents. But whereas pro-life people see the answer as chastity, pro-choice people are skeptical. In part because of the experiences of their own lives, they do not believe that individuals choose not to have sex merely because someone tells them that they shouldn't. Taboos, from their point of view, merely inhibit planning for sex, not sex itself. This point was made by a pro-choice woman who has spent much of her professional life counseling teenagers. She said it is unreasonable to tell young people they aren't supposed to have sex at all and then ask them to be responsible about it:

If driving were fraught with all the moral and ethical dilemmas [posed by sexual experience]. would you stand up in the motor vehicle department, hold your head up high and say, "Look world, I'm being responsible, I'm taking out a license"? Hell no, you'd do it the way all of us did it—we took the car out before we were licensed, just a little bit at a time. And that's what we're doing with sex.

. . . Pro-choice people emphasize that abortion is an *individual, private* choice. As one activist said:

> Well, of course you can't deny that abortion is ending something that's alive, but we take the position that the decision to bear a child, to raise a child, is a private decision—an ethical private decision—and the state has no [legitimate] interest in regulating it. Now if this is a matter of conscience, and if your beliefs are contrary to abortion, then of course you can decide not to have an abortion, even if it means some other sacrifice.

This comment illustrates three key features of pro-choice moral logic. First, there is a distinction between an embryo and a child, which all pro-choice people take for granted. Second, there is the idea that the embryo, though not a baby or a full human being, is nonetheless "alive" and therefore has some implicit moral rights. Finally, there is a pluralist bias: if a person has a different moral view of abortion, she should follow her own conscience, "even if it means some other sacrifice." Morality thus consists of weighing a number of competing situations and rights and trying to reconcile them under general moral principles rather than specific moral rules. This view is not confined to laypeople in the pro-choice movement; it is embraced by men and women of the clergy as well. One minister said: "Throughout [an earlier] period, my theological thinking [was still] an amorphous thing, but I felt okay. The bottom line on it was that if there be a God, then God could hardly object to people asking questions. And I looked at life, as I guess I still do to some extent, as a kind of laboratory where you test things and what's okay [you keep] and what isn't you junk it." . . .

World Views

All these different issues that divide pro-life and pro-choice activists from one another—their views on men and women, sexuality, contracep-

tion, and morality—in turn reflect the fact that the two sides have two very different orientations to the world and that these orientations in turn revolve around two very different moral centers. The pro-life world view, notwithstanding the occasional atheist or agnostic attracted to it, is at the core one that centers around God: pro-life activists are on the whole deeply committed to their religious faith and deeply involved with it. A number of important consequences follow.

Because most pro-life people have a deep faith in God, they also believe in the rightness of His plan for the world. They are therefore skeptical about the ability of individual humans to understand, much less control, events that unfold according to a divine, rather than human, blueprint. From their point of view, human attempts at control are simply arrogance, an unwillingness to admit that larger forces than human will determine human fate. One woman made the point clearly: "God is the Creator of life, and I think all sexual activity should be open to that [creation]. That does not mean that you have to have a certain number of children or anything, but it should be open to Him and His will. The contraceptive mentality denies his will, 'It's my will, not your will.' And here again, the selfishness comes in."

. . . While individuals can and should control their lives, pro-life people believe they should do so with a humility that understands that a force greater than themselves exists and, furthermore, that unpredicted things can be valuable. A woman who lost two children early in life to a rare genetic defect makes the point: "I didn't plan my son, my third child, and only because I was rather frightened that I might have a problem with another child. But I was certainly delighted when I became pregnant and had him. That's what I mean, I guess I feel that you can't plan everything in life. Some of the nicest things that have happened to me have certainly been the unplanned." Another woman went further: "I think people are foolish to worry about things in the future. The future takes care of itself." . . .

For pro-life people, once the belief in a Supreme Being (and by definition a common sense of culture) is lost, a set of consequences emerge that not only creates abortion per se but creates a climate where phenomena such as abortion can flourish. For example, once one no longer believes in an afterlife, then one becomes more this-worldly. As a consequence, one becomes more interested in material goods and develops a world view that evaluates things (and, more importantly, people) in terms of what Marxists would call their "use value." Further, people come to live in the "here-and-now" rather than thinking of this life—and in particular the pain and disappointments of this life—as spiritual training for the next life. When the belief in God (and in an afterlife) are lost, pro-life people feel that human life becomes selfish, unbearably painful, and meaningless.

. . . One of the harshest criticisms pro-life people make about pro-choice people, therefore, which encapsulates their feeling that pro-choice people are too focused on a short-term pragmatic view of the present world rather than on the long-term view of a transcendent world, is that pro-choice people are "utilitarian."

In part, pro-life people are right: the pro-choice world view is not centered around a Divine Being, but rather around a belief in the highest abilities of human beings. For them, reason—the human capacity to use intelligence, rather than faith, to understand and alter the environment—is at the core of their world; for many of them, therefore, religious or spiritual beliefs are restricted only to those areas over which humans have not yet established either knowledge or control: the origin of the universe, the meaning of life, etc. As one pro-choice activist, speaking of her own spiritual beliefs, noted: "What should I call it? Destiny? A Supreme Being? I don't know. I don't worship anything, I don't go anyplace and do anything about it, it's just an awareness that there's a whole area that might be arranging something for me, that I am not arranging myself—though every day I do more about arranging things myself."

Whatever religious values pro-choice people have are subordinated to a belief that individuals live in the here and now and must therefore make decisions in the present about the present. Few pro-choice people expressed clear beliefs in an afterlife so that their time frame includes only the worldly dimension of life. Thus, the entire articulation of their world view focuses them once again on human—rather than divine—capacities and, in particular, on the capacity for reason.

There are important implications to the fact that reason is the centerpiece of the pro-choice universe. First, they are, as their opponents claim, "utilitarian." . . . Utilitarianism is consonant with many of the pro-choice side's vaguely Protestant beliefs and, more to the point, with their value of rationality and its extensions: control, planning, and fairness. Second, as this heritage implies, they are interventionists. From their point of view, the fact of being the only animal gifted with intellect means that humans should use that intellect to solve the problems of human existence. What the pro-life people see as a humility in the face of a God whose ways are unknowable to mere humans, pro-choice people see as a fatalistic reliance upon a Creator whom humans wishfully endow with magical powers. These same values lead pro-choice people to be skeptical of the claim that certain areas are, or should be, sacrosanct, beyond the reach of human intervention. *Sacred* to them is too close to *sacred cow*, and religion can merge imperceptibly into dogma, where the church could persecute Galileo because science was too threatening both to an old way of thinking of things and an established power structure. Truth, for pro-choice people, must always take precedence over faith.

Because of their faith in the human ability to discover truth, pro-choice people are on the whole optimistic about "human nature." While in their more despairing moments they can agree with the pro-life diagnosis of malaise in contemporary American life . . . they emphatically disagree upon the solution. Rather than advocate what they see as a retreat from the present, an attempt to re-create idealized images of the past, they would argue that "the Lord helps those who help themselves" and that people should rally to the task of applying human ingenuity to the problems that surround us. . . .

Thus, in similar ways, both pro-life and pro-choice world views founder on the same rock, that of assuming that others do (or must or should) share the same values. Pro-life people assume that all good people should follow God's teachings, and moreover they assume that most good-minded people would agree in the main as to what

God's teachings actually are. (This conveniently overlooks such things as wars of religion, which are usually caused by differences of opinion on just such matters.) Pro-choice people, in their turn, because they value reason, assume that most reasonable people will come to similar solutions when confronted with similar problems. The paradox of utilitarianism, that one person's good may be another person's evil, as in the case of the pro-life belief that a too-effective contraceptive is a bad thing, is not something they can easily envisage, much less confront.

What neither of these points of view fully appreciates is that neither religion nor reason is static, self-evident, or "out there." Reasonable people who are located in very different parts of the social world find themselves differentially exposed to diverse realities, and this differential exposure leads each of them to come up with different—but often equally reasonable—constructions of the world. Similarly, even deeply devout religious people, because they too are located in different parts of the social world and, furthermore, come from different religious and cultural traditions, can disagree about what God's will is in any particular situation. When combined with the fact that attitudes toward abortion rest on these deep, rarely examined notions about the world, it is unambiguously clear why the abortion debate is so heated and why the chances for rational discussion, reasoned arguments, and mutual accommodation are so slim.

THINKING ABOUT THE READINGS

Holding the Line

- According to Kingsolver, why were these women so willing to sacrifice everything they had for the sake of the strike? Could they have conceivably done otherwise? From a conflict perspective, how did the media serve the mining company's interests in the way it portrayed the strikers? Do you think the women would have been as influential had this been a strike in a large urban city instead of a small, isolated, homogeneous, and close-knit community?

World Views of Pro-Life and Pro-Choice Activists

- Describe the world views of pro-life and pro-choice activists. How do they differ? How are they similar? How closely do these ideologies reflect your preconceived notions about both groups? Consider your own stand on the controversial issue of abortion. How closely do your views coincide with those of the activists (on your side) who Luker studied? How might a clear understanding of each other's world views (instead of the more common superficial stereotyping) affect the outcome of the national abortion debate?